Federalism and Economic Reform

This collection focuses on the ways in which federalism has affected and been affected by economic reform, especially global integration. The editors and contributors focus in particular on the political economy of institutional and economic change – how the division of authority between national and subnational governments shapes debates over policy changes, as well as how the changing economic environment creates incentives to modify the basic agreements among levels of government. Each chapter contains a historical overview and an in-depth account of division of authority, lines of accountability, and legislative, bureaucratic, and other arenas in which the levels of government interact for a particular country. The analyses are based on reform (or nonreform) episodes for each country, with most coming from recent history, but some spanning the century. As a collection, the country studies span a range of developing and industrial countries with varying political systems and divisions of jurisdiction between national and subnational governments. The editors offer a concluding chapter with lessons for further analysis.

Jessica S. Wallack is Assistant Professor of Political Economy at the Graduate School of International Relations and Pacific Studies, University of California, San Diego. Her research explores the politics and logistics of economic policymaking and implementation. She has published articles in journals such as the *Journal of International Economics*, the *Latin American Journal of Economic Development*, the *World Bank Economic Review*, and *De Economist*. Professor Wallack has served as a consultant to the World Bank, the Inter-American Development Bank, and the Asian Development Bank. She received her doctorate from the Stanford University Graduate School of Business.

T. N. Srinivasan is Samuel C. Park Jr. Professor of Economics at Yale University. He has previously taught at the Indian Statistical Institute, Delhi, and at numerous American universities. In addition to numerous articles and papers in various economics and policy journals, he has authored or edited twenty-one books, most recently *Frontiers in Applied General Equilibrium Modeling* (Cambridge University Press, 2005), coedited with Timothy J. Kehoe and John Whalley. He is a Fellow of the American Academy of Arts and Sciences and the Econometric Society, a member of the American Philosophical Society, and a Foreign A~~~~~~ National Academy of Sciences. He was name~ the American Economic Association in 2003. ests include international trade, developmen and microeconomic theory.

Federalism and Economic Reform

International Perspectives

Edited by

JESSICA S. WALLACK
University of California, San Diego

T. N. SRINIVASAN
Yale University

CAMBRIDGE
UNIVERSITY PRESS

CAMBRIDGE UNIVERSITY PRESS
Cambridge, New York, Melbourne, Madrid, Cape Town, Singapore, São Paulo

Cambridge University Press
40 West 20th Street, New York, NY 10011-4211, USA

www.cambridge.org
Information on this title: www.cambridge.org/9780521855808

First published 2006

Printed in the United States of America

A catalog record for this publication is available from the British Library.

Library of Congress Cataloging in Publication Data

Federalism and economic reform : international perspectives / edited by Jessica S. Wallack,
T. N. Srinivasan.
p. cm.
Includes bibliographical references and index.
ISBN-13: 978-0-521-85580-8 (hardback : alk. paper)
ISBN-10: 0-521-85580-2 (hardback : alk. paper)
1. Economic policy – Case studies. 2. Political planning – Case studies. 3. Federal
government – Case studies. 4. Intergovernmental fiscal relations – Case studies.
I. Srinivasan, T. N., 1933- II. Wallack, Jessica Seddon. III. Title.
HD87.F43   2006
338.9 – dc22   2005017040

ISBN-13 978-0-521-85580-8 hardback
ISBN-10 0-521-85580-2 hardback

Contents

List of Contributors

José Roberto Afonso Economist, Consultant to Nacional Congress, and former head of Office of Fiscal and Employment Affairs at Banco Nacional de Desenvolvimento Economico e Social (BNDES), Brazil

Tamar Asadurian Ph.D. Candidate, Department of Politics, New York University

Roy Bahl Dean and Professor of Economics, Andrew Young School of Policy Studies, Georgia State University

Richard M. Bird Director, International Tax Program, Professor of Economics, Joseph L. Rotman School of Management, University of Toronto, and Petro-Canada Fellow, C. D. Howe Institute

Alberto Diaz-Cayeros Associate Professor of Political Science, Stanford University

José Antonio González Director General de Seguros y Valores, Secretaría de Hacienda y Crédito Público, Mexico

John R. Madden Professor of Economics and Deputy Director, Centre of Policy Studies, Monash University, Australia

Jorge Martinez-Vasquez Professor of Economics and Director of International Studies Program, Andrew Young School of Policy Studies, Georgia State University

Emmanuel Nnadozie Senior Economic Affairs Officer, United Nations Economic Commission for Africa

Fernando Rezende Professor, Brazilian School of Public Administration, Getulio Vargas Foundation, and Special Advisor to the Ministry for Development, Industry and Trade

Fernando Rojas Economist, World Bank

Nirvikar Singh Professor of Economics and Director of Santa Cruz Center for International Economics, University of California, Santa Cruz

T. N. Srinivasan Samuel C. Park Jr. Professor of Economics and Chair of the South Asian Studies Council, Yale University, Senior Research Fellow, Stanford Center for International Development

Mariano Tommasi Professor of Economics and Chairman of Department of Economics, Universidad de San Andres

François Vaillancourt Professor of Economics and Fellow, CRDE, Université de Montréal

Jessica S. Wallack Assistant Professor of Political Economy, Graduate School of International Relations and Pacific Studies, University of California, San Diego

Leonard Wantchekon Associate Professor of Politics, Economics, and Africana Studies, New York University

Acknowledgments

This book has benefited greatly from advice and support of others.

We are grateful for financial support from the Stanford Center for International Development (SCID), the Koret Foundation, the Bechtel Initiative, the Lynne and Harry Bradley Foundation, and the William and Flora Hewlett Foundation. Nick Hope, Deputy Director, and Anne Krueger, former Director, of SCID provided valuable guidance in the initial stages of the project as well as continued encouragement and comments on the papers. We could not have organized the conferences and discussion sessions without the assistance of Helen McMahon, Nichelle Sevier, Yo-Ling Ma, and other staff members in the SCID office.

We are also indebted to a long list of scholars for their comments on various drafts of the country chapters and overview framework. Shankar Acharya, Suman Bery, Frank DesRosiers, Francine Frankel, Steve Haber, Al Harberger, Anjini Kochar, David Laitin, Santiago Levy, Ron McKinnon, Charles McLure, Rakesh Mohan, Guillermo Mondino, Steven O'Connell, Govinda Rao, N. K. Singh, Teresa Ter-Minassian, and Barry Weingast provided both authors and editors with valuable suggestions for improvement. We are also grateful for comments from Scott Parris and several anonymous referees on an earlier draft of this manuscript.

ONE

Analyzing Federalism

Stylized Models and the Political Economy Reality

Jessica S. Wallack and T. N. Srinivasan

I. INTRODUCTION

How does federalism affect policymaking? How do the details of the division of policy authority as well as expenditure and revenue powers across levels of government affect prospects for efficient and responsive governance? How does the economic, social, and political context – especially the recent wave of globalization and domestic economic liberalization – affect the workings of any given federal arrangements?

These questions have given rise to a large and varied positive literature on the actual workings of federalism as well as a significant normative literature full of suggestions for how federations should allocate fiscal and other decision-making authority across several levels of government. The literature ranges from stylized models of the costs and benefits of different ways of allocating fiscal authority among social planners in closed economies to detailed research on the nuances of interactions among levels of government in particular countries, time periods, and policy areas.

On one end of the spectrum of research on federalism, national and subnational governments are assumed to act as benevolent social planners who are omniscient and omnipotent, with national planners capable of addressing any externalities from subnational social planners' actions that spill over from one region to another. Social planners at all levels are assumed to have all the relevant information and capacity for enforcement of their decisions. Opportunistic behavior is assumed to be nonexistent. Evaluating fiscal federalism in a closed-economy setting is another common simplification used to keep models tractable and implications for federal design and function clear.

1

On the other end of the spectrum, political economy analyses incorporate policymakers with diverse abilities and less than public-minded motivations, economic settings that include both international and domestic factors, and other historical and social details. This part of the literature also considers various constraints on the central governments' ability to carry out policies. A smaller subset of the analyses of federalism delves into the dynamics of federalism, analyzing the politics of assigning responsibilities to various levels of government and the factors behind evolving federal structures. The constantly changing de jure and de facto arrangements for central–subnational government interaction present perhaps the most complex challenge for analyzing federalism.

The lessons from across the research spectrum are sometimes conflicting. Policy recommendations that make sense in theory may have demonstrable negative consequences in practice, in part because theory may abstract from consequential aspects of reality. Some federal arrangements we see in countries around the world may make no sense from a public economics perspective. The most stylized models that deliver the broadest implications for assigning taxation and expenditure powers have little explicit advice about how to design federal institutions to withstand bargaining among levels of government, corrupt politicians, and political pressures from interest groups. In-depth country studies, however, offer narrower, context-specific "best practices" and the causal links between federalism and political or economic outcomes may be difficult to verify. Our understanding of how and why federations evolve over time remains limited.

This book jumps into the fray with a collection of case studies of the evolution and interaction of federalism, economic reforms, and globalization in Argentina, Australia, Brazil, Canada, China, India, Mexico, and Nigeria. The countries vary widely in level of economic development and socio-political characteristics, but all share the common challenge of governance with several distinct levels of government.

Each case study focuses on several key questions. First, how have federal institutions evolved over time? What are the forces behind changes in fiscal arrangements, power sharing among levels of government, and political as well as economic institutions? Second, how does the changing economic environment, especially globalization as exemplified by greater openness to international capital and trade flows, affect federalism? What new strains, if any, does globalization place on federal governments and how have the countries we study responded? Third, what kinds of institutional and political arrangements are associated with greater macroeconomic stability and more flexibility to carry out economic reforms? What specific features of the federations we study make these countries vulnerable to shocks, overborrowing, and other well-known dangers of federalism? How does the division of policymaking power across levels of government affect the prospects for economic reforms such as privatization and opening to the international economy? Integration with world capital and goods markets raises new policy challenges such as financial sector reform and regulatory reform for all countries; division of power across levels of governments may affect nations' ability to respond.

The authors use analytical narratives to explore these questions.[1] Much of the analysis of the politics of federalism and the interaction among the institutions, policymakers, and economic environment is based on game-theoretic reasoning, but the presentation is narrative. The various chapters include detailed descriptions of the evolution of federal institutions over the past century, the current economic and political circumstances, and other aspects of the country contexts. The format borrows analytical clarity from formal theory, but without being bound to the same stark stylized representation of federalism.

This introductory chapter provides context for the country case studies by discussing the range of the literature on fiscal federalism from models of "economic federalism" to the more complicated politico-economic analysis of federalism.[2] A concluding chapter highlights the findings that emerge from the country studies.

II. OVERVIEW OF COUNTRIES

The countries studied represent a varied cross section of six developing and two industrialized federal nations (Table 1.1). Incomes per capita varied from over US$25,000 Purchasing Power Parity (PPP) in Australia and Canada to US$758 (PPP) in Nigeria in 2002. The range of levels of development allows us to see federalism interacting with a variety of economic environments. Canada and Australia provide examples of federalism against a context of relatively efficiently functioning democracies and markets, whereas, in other countries, the workings of federal

---

[1] See Bates et al. (1998) for a methodological overview and examples of analytical narratives.

[2] The term *economic federalism*, as well as the terms *cooperative federalism* and *majority-rule federalism* used in the next sections, is drawn from Inman and Rubinfeld (1997).

Table 1.1. *Economic Overview*

Country	GDP per Capita (PPP, Constant International $), 2002	Annual Growth (per Capita GDP), 1991–2002	Population (millions), 2002	Trade Openness (% GDP), 2002	Annual % Growth Trade/GDP, 1991–2002	FDI (% GDP), 2002	Annual % Growth FDI/GDP, 1991–2002
Argentina	9,633	1.43	36.48	40.49	10.57	0.77	17.48
Australia	25,032	2.17	19.66	41.76	1.94	4.06	30.12
Brazil	6,878	1.22	174.49	29.41	6.21	3.66	36.10
Canada	26,114	1.60	31.36	82.46[i]	4.38	2.87	22.61
China	4,054	8.77	1280.40	54.77	5.35	3.89	20.15
India	2,365	3.52	1048.64	30.82	5.92	0.59	42.42
Mexico	7,947	1.22	100.82	56.38	4.20	2.29	15.36
Nigeria	758	–0.61	132.79	81.26	1.78	2.94	10.25

[i] This figure is for 2001.

Source: World Development Indicators (2004).

states interact with the challenges of nation-building and economic development.

Brazil and Argentina, two much-studied Latin American federations, were included as examples of countries in which authoritarian regimes have historically alternated with democratic ones. The countries also have a common history of macroeconomic instability, including episodes of hyperinflation and significant subnational overborrowing. Brazil has taken significant steps to limit these vulnerabilities, whereas Argentine economic reforms have stalled with the 2001 crisis. With Mexico's increased integration of its economy with those of the United States and Canada after the adoption of NAFTA over the past decade and the current challenge of second-generation reforms and increasing economic disparities across states, its economic circumstances resemble those of Brazil and Argentina, but the political context of transition from one-party to multiparty rule provides some contrast.

The world's two most-populous nations, China and India, one a thriving multiparty democracy, the other an authoritarian one-party state, are included. Both are actively pursuing economic reform and greater international integration as well as facing the challenge of eradicating poverty. China's federalism is also distinct from others in the study in that most of the decentralization has been in the economic rather than the political realm.

Nigeria, the poorest country in the sample, is resource-rich but has significant economic challenges to overcome in addition to consolidating a relatively new and unstable democracy.

Cross-border flows of goods, services, and capital as well as international migration are increasingly important facets of the economic environment for all countries. Table 1.1 summarizes several indicators of global integration for the countries studied in this book. Trade flows (imports and exports) as a percentage of GDP range from a low of 29% in Brazil to a high of 81% (driven mostly by oil exports) in Nigeria, with others closer to the high end.[3] India's growth in the trade to GDP ratio over the 1990s is the highest, at 5.9% per year, but growth in other countries has not been significantly lower. The large developing countries – Brazil and China – are among the highest recipients of foreign direct investment

[3] It is important to note that these numbers are not necessarily indicators of policy orientation. Whereas India's low level of integration is likely related to its high tariff and nontariff barriers, Nigeria's apparent "openness" reflects the dominance of oil. The trade to GDP numbers may also be misleading: GDP measures value added; trade is gross value. The ratio will thus be inflated for countries that import intermediate goods and then reexport.

relative to GDP, but higher income Canada is also among the top. Foreign direct investment as a percentage of GDP is growing fast as well, particularly in India.

All of the countries except China have at least one tier of elected subnational governments with a structure that parallels the central government.[4] Most of the elected subnational governments have no formal accountability to the central government. India is an exception, as its states have centrally appointed governors alongside their elected legislatures and executive chief ministers. The state governors are nominally appointed by the president, but that are effectively agents of the more powerful central government and its head, the prime minister.[5] Although the legislatures are elected by the citizens and propose governments of their choosing that are accountable to the legislatures, the central government is constitutionally empowered (Article 356) to suspend elected state governments or temporarily replace them by central rule.[6]

Nigeria's transition to democracy is the most recent. The 1999 Constitution provides for an executive, judicial, and bicameral legislative branch at the national level and state level, the third-tier local government areas have an elected chairman and council of leaders.

China's structure stands out among the countries in this study as being economically decentralized but politically centralized. It is clearly not a federal country in the political sense. The cession of control over local economies and reduction of controls on local government-owned enterprises has in some ways substituted for political decentralization to elected subnational leaders. The arrangement is generally regarded as economically beneficial in that provinces' economic powers offset the threat of central government expropriation and provide a stable environment for investment, but its political effects are unclear.[7]

The political units at the first tier of subnational governments, however, are still quite large in several countries we study. The smallest Indian state has a population of 60,000 and many are in the tens of millions. The

---

[4] With the exception of a few elected leaders at the fourth (township) tier of government or below, subnational leaders are appointed by the levels above them.

[5] The Indian president and state governors are not quite the analogues of constitutional heads of state, nor are they heads of government. The Constitution endows them with the power to force candidates for prime ministership (or chief ministership at the state level) to prove that they have support of a majority of members of the Parliament or state legislature. Indian state governments have an unusual dual accountability.

[6] This power was used relatively frequently in the past, but it has been exercised less recently.

[7] China is the model for Weingast's (1995) account of "market preserving federalism."

largest, the state of Uttar Pradesh, has a population of over 166 million. Argentina's provinces range from 115,000 to over 14 million people.

Smaller political units have varying degrees of independence. Canada, Australia, and India have lower tiers of governments that are under the states/provinces' control. Elected local governments (called districts, *taluqs*, and *panchayats* in order from largest to smallest substate jurisdictions) are under the Indian state governments' control and state-level finance commissions determine how to allocate funds to lower levels of government. The constitutional status of India's panchayats was recently clarified, giving them a greater role in decision making while reiterating that they are under state governments' control, in 1993. Canada and Australia's municipalities are also subject to provincial control but have no constitutional status. China's five tiers of government are similarly hierarchical. Each level of government determines tax-sharing agreements, grant distributions, and expenditure responsibilities for the level immediately below. The first tier governments delegate local functions such as waste disposal and maintenance of local infrastructure to these levels of government.

The Nigerian and Brazilian local governments are more directly connected to the central government. The Nigerian National Assembly prescribes the states' allocation of transfers to this third tier and the Brazilian central government transfers resources directly to the municipal governments. This third tier of government is constitutionally recognized and largely independent of the second tier.

Ethno-linguistic and socioeconomic heterogeneity varies across countries as well, from the ethnically divided Nigerian states and multilingual, multicultural India to the relatively more ethnically homogeneous, but economically diverse China. This diversity within nations has had varying effects on the federal states: interstate and center-state politics are heavily influenced by ethno-linguistic differences in Canada and Nigeria, but economic differences appear to dominate in relationships among states in socioeconomically heterogeneous Brazil. Competition for shares in national revenues and negotiation over the terms and extent of redistribution comprise a major part of politics in all of the countries.

The more ethnically diverse states have shown some tendency to subdivide over time, producing smaller, more ethnically homogenous units, but this is not a widespread phenomenon. Indian states were formed after independence so that the language spoken by a majority of its population would be the same. There have been a few new states created since then; most recently three new states were created in the late 1990s.

However, violent separatist movements, notably in Kashmir and also in the northeast, continue to be active. The Nigerian federation has changed the most: There were originally three regions in 1946 and there are thirty-six currently.

III. ECONOMIC FEDERALISM

Inman and Rubinfeld (1997) summarize economic federalism as

preferring the most decentralized structure of government capable of internalizing all economic externalities, subject to the constitutional constraint that the central government policies be decided by an elected or appointed 'central planner'. (p. 45)

The analyses of federalism in this subsection of the literature abstract away from policymakers' career objectives, possible corruption, and ideologies as well as the question of how the federal system interacts with the economic and social environment around it. The advantage of such an approach is that it produces straightforward, general conclusions and policy prescriptions. The ideas discussed in this section continue to shape the international policy community's views on the benefits of greater decentralization.

The economic federalism literature proposes several advantages of dividing taxation and expenditure authority across levels of government. Local governments are assumed to have an information advantage in identifying local needs. Decentralization also allows for more variety in the provision of public goods so that local preferences can be satisfied.[8] Mobility ensures efficient matching of citizens with jurisdictions that provide the public goods they prefer.[9] Local governments are also potential laboratories for policy experiments.

Economies of scale, agglomeration, and externalities could offset these benefits of decentralization to varying extents. Some public goods may have economies of scale that cannot be obtained in smaller subnational jurisdictions. Agglomeration economies favor concentration of economic activities in metropolitan cities, so that tax bases might be concentrated in one jurisdiction while revenues for services are needed in another area, perhaps where some of those who work in the city live. Local policies can have spillovers for other jurisdictions – environmental regulations in one town can affect pollution in another town, for example.

---

[8] Oates (1972, 1994).
[9] Tiebout (1956), Bewley (1981).

The same mobility that ensures matching of citizens with jurisdictions also limits the potential for redistribution by subnational policies. Progressive taxation and generous welfare benefits are likely to drive the well-off away and attract the poor, eroding the scope for redistribution.[10] The most stylized analyses thus generally recommend that the central government carry out most redistributive policies.[11] As the country case studies will show, this kind of centralized redistribution may no longer be as ideal when central governments redistribute to ensure longer tenure in office or other non-welfare-related goals.

Gordon's (1983) derivation of optimal tax rates for a federation provides another example of the kinds of policy recommendations that this subsection of the literature offers. The paper works out the central and subnational taxes a benevolent social planner would set, solving six equations that balance a variety of welfare goals.

The solutions to these complex calculations are unlikely, however, to be the taxes that any kind of politicians would choose.[12] The approach ignores policymakers' potentially opportunistic motivations as well as strategic interactions among levels of government. The general policy prescription is to have as much central control over tax rates and bases as possible, since subnational governments will overlook the many externalities that their taxation decisions create.[13] Competition for businesses and citizens may lead subnational governments to set inefficiently lower business and income taxes, for example. Subnational governments' efforts to exclude socially beneficial but locally unpopular activities (such as dumps or nuclear-waste processing) can lead to excessive taxation in other cases. Lower level governments' quest to tax less mobile bases is also likely to lead to regressive taxation since the poor tend to be among the least mobile.[14]

These clear prescriptions, however, are based on strong and possibly unrealistic assumptions. The assumption that central and local governments are able and benevolent social planners who do not interact strategically with each other, though unrealistic, plays a crucial role in the

[10] Gramlich (1985).

[11] Central control over redistribution is complicated, however, by the difficulty of separating redistribution from provision of public services. See Musgrave (1997) for a discussion of the implications of ongoing devolution for redistribution.

[12] Inman and Rubinfeld (1996).

[13] Only the special case of a Tiebout (1956) economy – in which states compete for residents and uses a residential head tax to pay for public goods – achieves efficiency within a decentralized tax setting.

[14] Oates and Schwab (1986), Inman and Rubinfeld (1997), Wildasin (1989).

cost–benefit analysis for decentralization, for example. The economic federalism framework also focuses on closed economies, in contrast to the reality of international integration.

Economic federalism analyses also offer few insights into how federal structures are chosen and change over time. The literature provides principles for allocating rights to taxation and expenditure responsibilities, but it does not examine whether these are associated with a unique and stable political equilibrium. Tiebout's (1956) assertion that people will "vote with their feet" to sort themselves into separate jurisdictions with responsive subnational leaders is one of the few theories in the conventional analysis that proposes a mechanism (albeit one whose convergence to a unique and stable equilibrium is not assured without additional assumptions) for how federalism moves toward distributing resources efficiently. Nevertheless, it is only a theory of an equilibrium in which people and subnational governments are optimally matched and does not speak to the constant revisions to the federal bargain between the states and central government.

IV. POLITICAL FEDERALISM

Political federalism adds an additional layer of complication by dropping the assumption that central governments are omniscient social planners. Policymakers are primarily politicians in this framework, motivated by prospects of reelection, the "perks" of office (which could include private returns from its corrupt use), lobbyist contributions, and other factors in addition to (or instead of) general social welfare. Administrators at all levels may or may not have the capacity and power to enforce the policies they deem desirable. Policymakers may or may not have complete information for determining which policies are desirable.

The literature on political federalism also assumes that levels of government interact strategically, so that the central government is no longer autonomously able to alter subnational policies. Central governments must bargain with subnational governments to gain support from all or at least some minimum fraction of them. The change in assumptions has significant consequences for the optimal federal institutions and has additional explanatory power for the outcomes we observe in decentralized countries.

The increasing prevalence of political considerations in the analysis of federalism over the past decades was inspired in part by the growing public choice literature as well as the reality that the assumptions underlying the early work on federalism did not match the reality of governments in many countries. Subnational governments have had little incentive to act as social planners who maximize local welfare. Nigeria's subnational governments, for example, have only recently been elected and were previously appointed by the central government. Although the number of countries with locally elected mayors in Latin America has increased from three to seventeen over the past two decades, the administrative capacity of these lower levels of government is still questioned. Citizens in large subnational regions may not have much tighter control over their subnational representatives than they do over central government representatives. Subnational governments do not have as much autonomy to respond to their constituents' demands, as the division of responsibilities is not as clean as envisioned, for example, in Oates (1972). The countries studied here often have a poor match between local governments' mandates and the resources available to them.

IV.1. Political Policymakers

Policymakers motivated by prospects for reelection or the perks of office cannot be expected, necessarily, to use government budgets like social planners seeking the maximum welfare for their country or region. They can be expected to use information strategically, complicating the potential for social-planner-like governance even if the incentives were present. Politicians may also be corrupt.

The reality of politicians as policymakers raises several new challenges for the design of federal institutions. First, expenditure, taxation, and grant assignments must somehow create incentives for lower level governments to spend efficiently and responsibly. Subnational governments may overspend on capital when capital transfers are easier to obtain than funding for current expenditures or vice versa, for example. Their regional policies can distort national efforts to allocate funds toward priority projects or groups.

Politicians need to be motivated to expend effort and will not simply pursue the socially optimal action. Subnational governments, for example, need to be rewarded for increasing tax effort. Zhuravskaya (2000) shows that weak fiscal incentives for Russian cities to increase their own revenues lead these subnational governments to overregulate and restrict business. The fiscal arrangements prevent the subnational governments from retaining the increased revenues that would result from providing a good business climate.

The common pool problem in which subnational politicians overspend from the pot of national resources (including both taxes and captive savings in the financial system) is also pervasive. The economic federalism prescription of central government dominance in taxation provides little fiscal restraint since costs of expenditure are distributed nationally. Subnational governments' overexpenditure can contribute significantly to the country's overall debt burden.[15] Subnational incentives to overborrow are especially pronounced when all local governments can borrow at the same interest rate rather than facing differential costs of capital that reflect their particular level of indebtedness. Subnational control over regional banks can also drain the national financial sector, as the central government may face the choice of bailing out regional banks or suffering more widespread financial repercussions that spill over subnational borders.

Second, federal arrangements must provide incentives for the revelation of information or at least minimize costs of auditing and oversight. Subnational governments may conceal information from the central government to gain more resources to spend on attracting votes in elections or rewarding key supporters, making it more difficult for the central government to behave as a social planner even if it wanted to. They might overestimate the costs of providing primary education, for example, to attract more funds from the central government.[16] The vast literature on agency theory suggests a variety of ways that the central government (the principle) can design directives to motivate the subnational government (the agent) to perform, but these are often second-best solutions relative to a world in which omniscient and benevolent social planners operated at both levels of government.

Moving away from social planners changes the cost–benefit analysis for federalism. In tax assignment, for example, the benefits of centralized taxation for reducing externalities and welfare-decreasing tax competition, for example, have to be weighed against the benefits of decentralized taxation for making subnational governments internalize the costs of their expenditures. The political federalism literature also focuses on different potential costs of decentralized taxation than the economic federalism literature. Whereas in the economic federalism literature one worries about taxes being too low owing to a race to the bottom to compete for mobile factors, in the political federalism literature one also worries about

---

[15] Stein (1997), Ter-Minassian (1997).
[16] Cornes and Silva (2003), for example, show that the central government may have to offer information rents to lower level governments to achieve some distributional goals.

taxes being too high when politicians at each level of government act as revenue-maximizing "Leviathans." Optimal tax structures balance these two pressures, instead of centralizing most power to set tax rates.[17]

Federalism also complicates governments' efforts to mitigate income shocks when politicians opportunistically seek to increase their level of government's disposable revenues.[18] There is a tradeoff between risk sharing (coinsurance) and fiscal indiscipline. Central government commitments to reimburse states for expenditures after decisions have been made provide full insurance, but they may also exacerbate the common pool problem since states will anticipate paying only a fraction of the resources that they spend. Lump-sum ex ante transfers made before spending decisions prevent the common-pool problem but do not insulate states as well from shocks to income. The less room there is for subnational spending decisions (the more centralized the country), the less chance there will be for a common-pool problem to emerge and the more insurance can be provided without causing fiscal indiscipline.[19]

The politics of federalism, however, suggest that competition across jurisdictions may have more benefits than implied by the economic federalism literature. Economic federalism praised competition in public goods provision, whereas the political federalism literature envisions competition in governance quality. Gordon and Wilson (2003), for example, look at the case where competition is over "waste." Residents control regional tax rates; officials determine how the money is spent. The residents' ability to move to other jurisdictions provides discipline on the composition of expenditures that would not be present if all expenditure decisions were centralized. The overall level of spending in a federation might be higher or lower than in a unitary state (depending on how much spending on public goods there is when waste is decreased) but the composition will always be better in a federation.

IV.2. Constraints on Central Government Autonomy

The political federalism literature models constraints on central government autonomy in various ways. "Cooperative federalism," like economic federalism, is a normative theory of federalism. Restricting the central

---

[17] Brennan and Buchanan (1997, 1980), Keen and Kotsogiannis (2003).

[18] This may be either to claim credit for popular projects to ensure reelection, or to siphon off resources for personal enrichment.

[19] Sanguinetti and Tommasi (2004) model this tradeoff.

government's policies to only those that would be accepted by all subnational units ensures that any changes made are Pareto-improving, but it could rule out those that require transfers among units; nor does it match any political system functioning today. It does not assume an omnipotent, benevolent central planner, however, and shifts more of the burden of obtaining economies of scale and offsetting externalities to the state governments. The framework assumes that states will bargain among themselves or in a national legislature to compensate each other for externalities or divide output from shared utilities and other large-scale public works.[20]

Prescriptions for the division of responsibilities across national and subnational governments vary between the economic and cooperative federalism literatures. Welfare benefits, for example, would be seen as the province of the central government in an economic federalism analysis since state-level differences would lead the poor to migrate to high-benefit areas that would eventually become bankrupt. Cooperative federalism analyses, in contrast, might argue that subnational governments can be in charge of welfare benefits without loss of efficiency – they would simply make an arrangement in which some areas would compensate others proportionally to the number of émigrés that were covered.

Inman and Rubinfeld (1997) point out several reasons to be skeptical of cooperative federalism's policy prescriptions. Even in the case where property rights over revenue or resources do exist, bargaining is unlikely to be successful where states have irreconcilable ideas of fairness or imperfect information about each other or the problem that is being addressed. Costs of bargaining could be substantial when many states are involved in the bargain.[21]

The transactions costs are likely to be too high for cooperation among subnational governments to be widespread.[22] Most federal countries (including those studied in this volume) do not have formal institutional infrastructure for enforcing contracts among subnational governments and supporting discussion of contentious issues among regional

---

[20] Wittman (1989), Ellickson (1979).

[21] Inman and Rubinfeld (1997) review the empirical evidence on state cooperation and find that the overall record "has not been impressive" (p. 49). They argue that although economic federalism calls for too much centralization, cooperative federalism may call for too little centralization.

[22] Dixit (1998, 2003) lists numerous aspects of economic policy and modern institutions that he argues can only be rationalized as efforts to overcome transactions costs in policy-making and planning.

governments without involving central government oversight. Political parties may support coalition-building between subnational governments, but these will shift as policymakers in power change.

"Majority-rule federalism," however, starts with an assumption that the central government can only implement policies approved by a majority of the subnational governments and derives an optimal division of responsibilities across levels of government in this case. Tullock (1969), for example, weighs the economic benefits of central provision of services against inefficiencies arising from central government political bargaining. The cost–benefit analysis for decentralization versus centralization depends on the efficiency of the legislature, which in turn depends on its size, organization, and distribution of agenda-setting powers among other factors.[23]

Subsequent work has built on the democratic federalism framework to incorporate more detailed specification of the structure of subnational representation in national governments, the role of party allegiances in constraining national decisions, undemocratic governments, and other features of political systems around the world.

Acknowledging constraints on central government autonomy, like the assumption of self-interested and possibly inept policymakers, changes conclusions about the costs and benefits of decentralization. It also suggests a new set of criteria for evaluating federalism: (i) How can federal arrangements constrain self-interest? (ii) How can federal arrangements create incentives for cooperation among and across government tiers?

First, central governments' dependence on subnational cooperation can lead to competition among states (generally thought of as a benefit of decentralization) to be welfare-decreasing. Cai and Treisman (2004) point out that interjurisdictional competition to attract capital and labor can reduce welfare if subnational politicians compete by shielding investors and others from central government taxation and regulation. Competition is thus likely to be state-eroding when the central government's enforcement capacity depends on state cooperation.

Second, subnational governments can check national governments' ability to carry out policy changes, a degree of restraint that can have both positive and negative consequences. Weingast (1995) brings out the positive aspects with his theory of market-preserving federalism. When

---

[23] The literature on legislative organization and efficiency of policymaking is large and varied. See Weingast, Shepsle, and Johnson (1981), Krehbiel (1992), and Weingast and Marshall (1988) among others.

federalism rewards subnational governments for success and punishes them for predation, it can solve the same commitment problem as separation of powers or democracy: It ensures that a state powerful enough to govern will not be able to use this power to prey upon the private sector.[24]

Other authors point out that federalism automatically creates more veto players that have to sign off on any economic reforms.[25] Subnational governments are likely to desire fiscal adjustment and other macroeconomic reforms less than the national government – since the macroeconomic costs of overspending and overborrowing are dispersed across other regions – and so act as brakes on economic reforms. Financial sector reform can be particularly contentious when subnational governments rely on regional banks for deficit financing. Many areas of economic reform, such as privatization, require both central and subnational government action so that central government policy initiatives can only achieve limited results. Subnational governments have less incentive to initiate such macroeconomic policy changes, as they are less likely than national governments to be held accountable for a country's macroeconomic instability. Subnational governments may also demand extensive subsidies in exchange for continued support for the federation, making it difficult to reduce overall government size.[26]

Third, the widely noted negative macroeconomic effects of federalism stem in large part from central governments' inability to restrict opportunistic subnational government behavior.[27] The central government may not be able to commit credibly to bail out indebted subnational governments or recapitalize failing regional banks, for example, if subnational governors influence voting in the national legislature. It cannot coordinate subnational regulation or enforce conditions for transfers if it cannot in some way monitor and punish subnational policymakers. It will face difficulties implementing economic reforms if all policies must be approved by a legislature of politicians loyal only to their state-level constituencies. Empirical studies of macroeconomic performance in federations generally support the warnings.[28]

The political federalism literature's more realistic portrayal of policymakers and of intergovernmental relations raises as many questions as it

---

[24] See also Montinola, Qian, and Weingast (1995) for a discussion of market preserving federalism in the Chinese context.

[25] Wibbels (2000), Rodden and Wibbels (2002), Tsebelis (2002).

[26] Treisman (1999).

[27] See Prud'homme (1995) for a comprehensive warning about the negative macroeconomic consequences of federalism.

[28] Wibbels (2000), World Bank (1997), Rodden, Eskeland, and Litvack (2002).

answers, however. Some aspects of politics and political institutions have received more attention than others, for example. Much of the work has focused on democracies, with less attention to the workings of federalism in dictatorships or countries without locally elected officials. Politicians tend to be the focus of analysis more than bureaucrats. The effects of corruption on federalism have also gotten less attention than the impact of federalism on corruption.[29]

The addition of more realistic assumptions does not always lead to clear policy suggestions about how to achieve federalism. Some of the work covering less developed countries, for example, does not assume functioning, accountable, or political structures at all levels of government but focuses on arguing that administrative capability and political accountability somehow be improved before or during decentralization without mapping out a path.[30]

V. POLITICO-ECONOMIC FEDERALISM

The most complex subset of analyses of federalism, which we call politico-economic federalism, incorporates federal institutions' economic environments and their political context. The work in this genre, much of it written over the past decade, considers the interaction of federal institutions with the economic context of international integration and economic reforms. Part of this interaction involves the dynamics of federalism – how institutions evolve over time as policymakers respond to political and economic pressures.

The politico-economic end of the spectrum may best describe the reality of how sharing taxation and expenditure power among levels of government affects and is influenced by its context, but this descriptive power comes at the cost of generality of lessons for the design of federalism. This book and other efforts to untangle the interactions between federalism and its economic and political context leave many open questions.

V.1. Federalism in a Global Context

Integration with the international economy affects the cost–benefit analysis for federalism. One set of benefits of decentralization comes from

[29] Bardhan and Mookherjee (2000)'s analysis of the relative susceptibility of local and central governments to capture is one analytical paper that explicitly studies corruption at central and local levels; the work of Fisman and Gatti (2002) and Treisman (2000) has a more empirical emphasis.

[30] Bahl and Linn (1994), Fiszbein (1997).

the fact that it carves out variety within a country, so that people have a place to move to that matches their preferences for taxation, public goods, and so on. With international labor mobility, however, this kind of sorting could take place across countries so that the internal degree of decentralization need no longer be welfare-enhancing. Integration with the international economy can also increase costs of decentralization if subnational governments are allowed to borrow on the reputation of the central government. International interest rates are less elastic with respect to subnational borrowing than domestic interest rates would be, providing less of a curb on government indebtedness.

Policy prescriptions also change when we consider federations embedded in the international economy. Janeba and Wilson (2003)'s model of the effect of decentralization on international tax competition, for example, provides very different policy implications than those of economic federalism. Whereas economic federalism advocates centralization of taxation to avoid the externalities associated with subnational tax competition, Janeba and Wilson show that decentralized choice of tax rates can be welfare-enhancing. Their model has regional and central governments choose a tax rate to finance the provision of public goods for which they are responsible and maximize residents' welfare. The subnational governments' ability to choose tax rates has two externalities: the horizontal externality, in which lowering tax rates attracts capital from other jurisdictions, and the vertical externality, in which lowering the subnational tax rate attracts more capital into a country.[31] The central government can manipulate the relative size of the two externalities by changing the division of expenditure responsibilities that must be paid for. The authors show that there is a degree of decentralization of expenditure responsibilities (and hence necessity for tax collection) chosen independently by each country that is welfare-enhancing for both nations.

Incorporating international integration raises a new set of questions to be analyzed and challenges for the design of federalism. This book addresses some of them.

First, assuming open capital and goods markets as well as some degree of international labor mobility changes the constraints on both national and subnational policies. In an economy closed to capital flows, for example, subnational borrowing is naturally limited by the consequences of its

---

[31] The allocation of capital across countries is determined by the relative size of the sum of central and subnational tax rates. All subnational units choose the same tax rate in equilibrium.

borrowing on interest rates, but its borrowing has little effect on interest rates in an open economy with no power on the world capital markets. Subnational governments can continue incurring liabilities unless investors' caution or national government controls force them to internalize the costs of their borrowing too much.

What creates and maintains hard budget constraints in an internationally integrated setting?[32] An integrated capital market, an aspect of "globalization," raises the premium on having hard budget constraints at all levels of government. Foreign-currency-denominated debt at variable interest rates has far more potential to be destabilizing than domestic obligations as it exposes countries to exchange-rate risk and interest-rate shocks as the result of contagion, market sentiment, or business cycles in other countries. Integration in capital markets also increases the resource pool for financing deficits at all levels of government. Subnational governments with captive state-owned banks, access to subsidized credit from the national government, or expectations of bailouts in case of default will have an incentive to overborrow in any case, but spillover effects of this overborrowing, including higher interest rates, will gradually contain borrowing in an economy closed to external capital flows. These checks on indebtedness will not be present in economies open to external capital, unless the national government can make a credible commitment not to bail out subnational governments and investors come to view further lending as highly risky. Furthermore, national-level spillovers from subnational borrowing on international markets – frequently an increase in volatile short-term foreign debt that can (and often is) withdrawn quickly – lead to crisis and sudden lack of access to credit rather than a gradual increase in costs of capital to equilibrate supply and demand.

Integration in global capital markets, however, increases the strength of market discipline that can be brought to bear. Market-based limits, where the subnational governments' borrowing is only restricted by lenders' perceptions, can only work where there are relatively informed lenders who are not subject to political pressures to renew loans.

International private investors, unlike central governments with subnational constituents or state-owned banks with managers appointed by subnational governments, are unlikely to continue lending beyond sustainable levels unless they have some expectation that the central government

---

[32] See Rodden and Eskeland (2003) for detailed case-study-based responses to this question.

will bail out subnational debtors.[33] As in the previous sections on equity concerns and competition for resources, globalization can create powerful incentives for good policies if harnessed by domestic institutions.

Second, the institutions governing the interaction between national and subnational governments take on new significance when all levels of government have the potential to interact with the international market. The assignment of expenditure and revenue jurisdictions, for example, determine the tools with which subnational governments can compete for resources in the international economy. How can these powers be allocated to avoid distortions such as a "race to the bottom" when subnational governments compete by offering tax and regulatory concessions that are ultimately subsidized by the country as a whole?

Third, the considerably larger resource flows in the international economy relative to the pool that the national government can allocate itself means that controlling market forces to reach particular distributional goals is nearly impossible. Potential spillovers from foreign investment outweigh the effects of direct transfers, thus limiting the extent of redistribution through fiscal policy. However, the distributional impact of opening to foreign trade and investment on market prices for factors could be not only quantitatively more significant but also more egalitarian than politically determined domestic transfers. What kinds of policies ensure that inequality does not increase and/or that overall poverty declines? We would expect policies that enable effective market participation rather than shield individuals or corporations from market forces to have more noticeable effects.

V.2. Dynamics of Federalism

"What kinds of political arrangements are likely to lead to policy choices approximating the ideals set forth in the economic federalism literature?" is a driving question for the politico-economic subset of the literature. Inman and Rubinfeld (1996)'s theoretical paper, for example, shows that universalistic legislatures are not likely to choose optimal tax structures since policy will be driven by the wishes of state representatives. More

---

[33] Public lending and foreign aid, in contrast, can weaken incentives for macroeconomic discipline if debt cancellation, relief, and rescheduling decisions are made on the basis of political or diplomatic factors or if loan conditionalities (such as those attached to World Bank or International Monetary Fund loans) are selectively enforced. Increasing integration with global capital markets, however, has reduced the weight of concessional loans in many countries' debt.

hierarchical legislatures, stronger nationally elected politicians (such as the executive), and constitutional restrictions on the kinds of taxes that subnational governments can have will lead to more efficient outcomes. Dixit and Londregan (1998) carry out a similarly motivated positive analysis of grant regimes. They argue that grant mechanisms are determined by a game played at many levels of reelection-seeking government. The key insight is that the central government has to take into account that the local governments will further redistribute funds in the way that serves local electoral needs best. Central governments will distribute funds differently than in a unitary state where they could just reach directly to voters. The same question could be asked in many other areas.

Theory provides some clues, but we are still learning empirically how federations change over time. When can we expect federal states to be moving toward efficient equilibrium? What are the consequences of these different kinds of contracts for a country's ability to respond to changing economic and political environments, including greater integration? What determines whether federations have centripetal or centrifugal tendencies?

We would expect federal (and nonfederal) states to get stuck in inefficient arrangements, for example, when possibilities of beneficial exchange across time and issues in the political arena are somehow limited, perhaps by politicians' short time horizons, political instability, or mistrust generated by underlying ethnic or socioeconomic heterogeneity. Federal bargains will be more difficult to change when provisions are written into constitutions or otherwise require supermajorities or unanimity for revisions.

The federal bargains in the countries studied in this book are clearly incomplete contracts, originally derived from self-interested bargaining and modified along the way by negotiations among politicians in all tiers of government. These arrangements display different degrees of stability: The formal division of policy jurisdictions is in some cases enforced by outside parties (such as the courts or constitutions), in other cases self-enforcing (even if not collectively optimal), and in a few circumstances not enforced at all.

VI. MOTIVATIONS FOR THIS STUDY

The basic insights of the economic federalism literature on the advantages and disadvantages of sharing responsibilities across levels of government continue to form the backbone for much policy advice, but the political and politico-economic literatures list numerous and important caveats for evaluating decentralization.

Making sense of these caveats and assessing their applicability to a particular country setting can be difficult, however. Much of the empirical work in this area consists of single-country studies or cross-country regressions that do not delve into the mechanisms underlying the correlations found. There is a tendency to use a dichotomous federalism – nonfederalism divide rather than look at the factors that determine variation in performance among federal systems.[34]

We hope that the studies contained in this volume are able to contribute some raw empirical material that improves our understanding of federalism's interaction with economic and political conditions around the world.

Bibliography

Bahl, R., and J. Linn (1994). "Fiscal Decentralization and Intergovernmental Transfers in Less Developed Countries," Publius: The Journal of Federalism 24 (Winter).

Bardhan, P., and D. Mookherjee (2000). "Capture and Governance at Local and National Levels," AEA Papers and Proceedings 90(2): 135–139.

Bates, R., A. Greif, M. Levi, J.-L. Rosenthal, and B. Weingast (1998). *Analytic Narratives*. Princeton: Princeton University Press.

Bewley, T. (1981). "Acritique of Tiebout's Theory of Local Public Expenditures," Econometrica 49: 713–40.

Brennan, G., and J. Buchanan (1977). "Towards a Tax Constitution for Leviathan," Journal of Public Economics 8: 255–273.

Brennan, G., and J. Buchanan (1980). *The Power to Tax: Analytical Foundations of a Fiscal Constitution*. Cambridge, UK: Cambridge University Press.

Cai, H., and D. Treisman (2004). "State Corroding Federalism," Journal of Public Economics 88: 819–843.

Cornes, R., and E. Silva (2003). "Public Good Mix in a Federation with Incomplete Information," Journal of Public Economic Theory 5(2): 381–397.

Dixit, A. (1998). *The Making of Economic Policy: A Transactions Cost Politics Perspective*. Cambridge, MA: MIT Press.

Dixit, A. (2003). "Some Lessons from Transaction Cost Politics for Less-Developed Countries," Economics and Politics 15(2): 107–133.

Dixit, A., and J. Londregan (1998). "Fiscal Federalism and Redistributive Politics," Journal of Public Economics 68: 153–180.

Ellickson, R. (1979). "Public Property Rights: Vicarious Intergovernmental Rights and Liabilities as a Technique for Correcting Intergovernmental

---

[34] Rodden and Wibbels (2002) is one of the few papers to focus on the institutional correlates of macroeconomic performance variation among federations. The paper's results, based on cross-country regressions, demonstrate the need for in-depth research on the mechanics of the relationship between federalism and macroeconomic peformance.

Spillovers," in Daniel Rubinfeld, ed., *Essays on the Law and Economics of Local Governments*. Washington, DC: Urban Institute.

Fisman, R., and R. Gatti (2002). "Decentralization and Corruption: Evidence Across Countries," Journal of Public Economics 83: 325–345.

Fiszbein, A. (1997). "Emergence of Local Capacity: Lessons from Colombia," World Development 25(7): 1029–43.

Gordon, R. (1983). "An Optimal Taxation Approach to Fiscal Federalism," Quarterly Journal of Economics 95: 567–586.

Gordon, R., and J. Wilson (2003). "Expenditure Competition," Journal of Public Economic Theory 5(2): 399–417.

Gramlich, E. M. (1985). "Reforming U.S. Fiscal Arrangements," in J. M. Quigley and Daniel Rubinfeld, eds. *American Domestic Priorities*. Berkeley: University of California Press.

Inman, R., and D. Rubinfeld (1996). "Designing Tax Policies in Federalist Economies: An Overview," Journal of Public Economics 60: 307–34.

Inman, R., and D. Rubinfeld (1997). "Rethinking Federalism" Journal of Economic Perspectives 11(4): 43–64.

Janeba, E., and J. Wilson (2003). "Decentralization and International Tax Competition," CESInfo Working Paper 854.

Keen, M., and C. Kotsogiannis (2003). "Leviathan and Capital Tax Competition in Federations," Journal of Public Economic Theory 5(2): 177–199.

Krehbiel, K. (1992). *Information and Legislative Organization*. Ann Arbor: University of Michigan Press.

Montinola, G., Y. Qian, and B. Weingast (1995). "Federalism, Chinese Style: The Political Basis for Economic Success in China," World Politics 48: 50–81.

Musgrave, R. (1997). "Devolution, Grants, and Fiscal Competition," Journal of Economic Perspectives 11(4): 65–72.

Oates, W. (1972). *Fiscal Federalism*. New York: Harcourt, Brace, Jovanovich.

Oates, W. (1994). "Federalism and Government Finance," in J. Quigley and E. Smolensky, eds., *Modern Public Finance*. Cambridge, MA: Harvard University Press.

Oates, W., and R. Schwab (1986). "Economic Competition among Jurisdictions: Efficiency Enhancing or Distortion-Inducing?," Journal of Public Economics 35: 333–54.

Prud'homme, R. (1995). "The Dangers of Decentralization," World Bank Research Observer 10(3).

Rodden, J., G. Eskeland, and J. Litvack (2003). *Fiscal Decentralization and the Challenge of Hard Budget Constraints*. Cambridge, MA: MIT Press.

Rodden, J., and E. Wibbels (2002). "Beyond the Fiction of Federalism: Macroeconomic Management in Multitiered Systems," World Politics 54(July): 494–531.

Sanguinetti, P., and M. Tommasi (2004). "Intergovernmental Transfers and Fiscal Behavior: Insurance versus Aggregate Discipline," Journal of International Economics 62: 149–170.

Stein, E. (1997). "Fiscal Decentralization and Government Size in Latin America," background paper for the Economic and Social Progress Report 1997. Washington, DC: Inter-American Development Bank.

Ter-Minassian, T., ed. (1997). *Fiscal Federalism in Theory and Practice*. Washington, DC: International Monetary Fund.

Tiebout, C. (1956). "A Pure Theory of Local Expenditures," Journal of Political Economy 64: 416–24.

Treisman, D. (1999). "Political Decentralization and Economic Reform: A Game-Theoretic Analysis," American Journal of Political Science, 43(2): 488–517.

Treisman, D. (2000). "The Causes of Corruption: A Cross-National Study," Journal of Public Economics 76(3): 399–457.

Tsebelis, G. (2002). *Veto Players: How Political Institutions Work*. Princeton: Princeton University Press.

Tullock, G. (1969). "Federalism: Problems of Scale," Public Choice 6: 19–29.

Weingast, B. (1995). "The Economic Role of Political Institutions: Market-Preserving Federalism and Economic Development," The Journal of Law, Economics, and Organization 11(1): 1–31.

Weingast, B., and W. Marshall (1988). "The Industrial Organization of Congress," Journal of Political Economy 89: 642–64.

Weingast, B., K. Shepsle, and C. Johnson (1981). "The Political Economy of Benefits and Costs: A Neoclassical Approach to Distributive Politics," Journal of Political Economy 1981 89: 642–64.

Wibbels, E. (2000). "Federalism and the Politics of Macroeconomic Policy and Performance," American Journal of Political Science 44(4): 687–702.

Wildasin, D. (1989). "Interjurisdictional Capital Mobility: Fiscal Externality and a Corrective Subsidy," Journal of Urban Economics 25: 193–212.

Wittman, D. (1989). "Why Democracies Produce Efficient Results," Journal of Political Economy 1989 97: 1396–1424.

World Bank (1997). World Development Report 1997: The State in a Changing World. Washington, DC: World Bank.

Zhuravskaya, E. (2000). "Incentives to Provide Local Public Goods: Fiscal Federalism, Russian Style," Journal of Public Economics 76: 337–368.

TWO

Federalism in Argentina and the Reforms of the 1990s

Mariano Tommasi*

Federalism in general, and fiscal federalism in particular, are crucial axes of Argentina's history, of Argentina's current situation, and of Argentina's possible futures. This paper provides a tour of the recent history of fiscal federalism in Argentina and an overview of its current configuration and main problems.

Federalism is ingrained in the Argentine political system in several ways that are crucial for national policy. Provincial governors are important players in the national game, as they are often party bosses wielding substantial leverage over national politicians via electoral mechanisms and party practices. Provinces are also heavily dependent on central monies for their finances, leading to a particular intertwining of national and subnational politics and policies. This federal connection is, in turn, intertwined with some more general characteristics of the workings of the Argentine policymaking process, which is characterized by the inability to establish and enforce efficient intertemporal agreements. This inability maps into policies that are either too volatile (responding to political opportunism) or too rigid, as a protection against that opportunism. These policy characteristics are particularly salient in the federal fiscal domain.

* I received valuable comments from Antonio Federico, Richard Bird, Al Harberger, Guillermo Mondino, Nirvikar Singh, François Vaillancourt, an anonymous referee, and participants at the Center for Research on Economic Development and Policy Reform (Stanford University) Project on Federalism in a Global Environment. I am greatful for the excellent research assistance of Emmanuel Abuelafia, the very valuable input from Valeria Palanza and Juan Sanguinetti, and especially the very helpful comments of the editors, Jessica Seddon Wallack and T. N. Srinivasan.

After a brief description of some general characteristics of Argentina and of its fiscal federalism in Section I, Section II focuses on the relationship between federalism and the market-oriented reform process of the 1990s. The 1989 economic crisis provided the incentives that led to the initiation of the reforms, triggering a series of delegation patterns conducive to the adoption of the reform agenda. The political and institutional processes of implementing these reforms left a heavy imprint on the outcomes. Though many features associated with a state-led model were dismantled, some "illiberal enclaves" were left in the provincial economies and intergovernmental arrangements as subnational interest groups exerted their influence at the national level.

Section III, the core of the paper, explores the most salient "institutional" moments in which the federal fiscal system has been modified throughout the 1990s. The analysis shows a mixed picture of some (partial) efficiency-enhancing reforms, the (partial) accommodation to changing circumstances, and a basic inability to establish the intertemporal agreements that would be necessary for the deep reform of the system. This section also explores some of the connections between federalism and the Argentine implosion of 2001–2002 and illustrates the interaction of federal and provincial policymaking in the education sector.[1]

I. BASIC FACTS ABOUT ARGENTINA AND ITS FISCAL FEDERALISM

I.1. Some Basic Facts about Argentina

I.1.a. History. The Argentine nation was born out of the union of various colonial regions with differing economic and social characteristics.[2] In 1810 the city council of Buenos Aires deposed the last Spanish viceroy, marking the beginning of the independence movement. In 1816, delegates from different parts of the country convened in Tucumán to sanction the

---

[1] The analysis of education sector reforms is developed in more detail in the 2002 Working Paper version (Stanford Center for International Development Working Paper 147, Section). Even though some of the postulated benefits of decentralization might be at work, the implementation of reforms and the quality of policymaking and delivery in the social sectors has been tainted by several of the characteristics of fiscal and political federalism in Argentina highlighted throughout the paper.

[2] In spite of being a former Spanish viceroyalty, fiscal and military technologies at the time of independence were such that what later became Argentina was a collection of political units (now provinces) with deep local roots. Hence, Argentina is, in the words of Stepan (1999), more of a "coming together" federation than of a "holding together" one. See also Escudé (1988).

declaration of independence of the United Provinces of the Rio de la Plata. The first four decades after independence were characterized by violent struggles over the constitution of a national government. That process led to the Constitution of 1853, establishing a constitutional federal republic, which was substantially modified in 1860 before the province of Buenos Aires endorsed it. The provinces were given precedence over the nation and were granted autonomy in the administration of their territories. A specific set of federal government functions was established, the provinces were granted residual powers over any matters not specified to be federal functions, and the internal economic union was promulgated with the elimination of internal customs controls. Despite some later modifications (including the recent reform of 1994), the essential federalist structure of the 1853–1860 Constitution remains in force today.[3]

By the beginning of the twentieth century, Argentina was one of the most developed countries in the world.[4] However, after the Great Depression, as a result of a combination of democratic breakdown and poor economic policies, Argentina entered a path of economic decline that, except for brief spells (most notably the early and mid-1990s), continues to the present. The reliance on state-centered and inward-looking growth strategies resulted in massive public sector deficits, accelerating inflation, and economic stagnation. Although industrial promotion programs were initially popular among the growing pool of urban workers, they ultimately led to an onerous taxation of agriculture, Argentina's prime source of wealth, and contributed to major reallocation of resources. The debt crisis of the early 1980s led the government to resort to money creation to meet financial responsibilities. To avoid a growing inflation tax, Argentines withdrew their resources from the financial system, saving and investing abroad at record levels. Economic stagnation ensued. By the end of the 1980s, labor productivity had fallen, social services and basic infrastructure had deteriorated, and poverty had become a serious and growing problem. When the Menem administration took office in July 1989, Argentina was gripped by recession and monthly inflation of up to 200%. During the 1990s the country underwent a market-oriented transformation that created the expectation of renewed prosperity. Sadly,

---

[3] The national Constitution was sanctioned in 1853 and reformed in 1860, 1866, 1898, 1949, 1956, 1957, 1972, and 1994. Argentina had a very interrupted democratic history since 1930. Military dictatorships ruled the country in the periods 1930–1932, 1943–1946, 1955–1958, 1962–1963, 1966–1973, and 1976–1983.

[4] In the 1890s, Argentina was the sixth richest country in the world in per capita terms; in the 1920s it remained among the top ten, ahead of both Germany and Italy.

after a decade under the illusion that things had started to change, the country has recently regressed to its historical downward trend.

I.1.b. Political Institutions. Argentina is a federal republic, with a presidential form of government and a bicameral legislature. The members of the Chamber of Deputies (currently 257) are elected from twenty-four multimember districts, the twenty-three provinces and the federal capital, for four-year terms. The deputies are elected from closed party lists using the D'Hondt divisor form of proportional representation. One-half of the Chamber is renewed every two years, with every district renewing one-half of its legislators. The twenty-four jurisdictions send to the national congress a number of deputies in proportion to their populations. The Argentine system tends to strongly overrepresent the smaller provinces, since even the smallest-population provinces have a minimum of five deputies. Until the 1994 Constitutional reform, all the districts were represented by two senators, elected indirectly for nine-year terms by the provincial legislatures, using the plurality formula. The new Constitution introduced a third minority-party senator for each province, as well as the direct election of senators, which went fully into effect in 2001.

This malapportionment has its roots in recent political history.[5] Whereas the original Constitution allocated seats in the Chamber of Deputies proportionally to district population, the 1976–1983 military government introduced amendments that bolstered representation of the peripheral region in that body. These amendments added three additional deputies to each province beyond those allotted on the base of population, and they established that no province would be represented by less than five deputies.

This was not the first time that the outgoing military tinkered with political institutions to favor those provinces it believed would be closer to them in the future.[6] In 1972, the 1966–1973 dictatorship promulgated a law that furthered malapportionment in the Chamber of Deputies. The outgoing military government also promulgated the 1973 *Coparticipación* law that increased the degree of redistribution toward some backward provinces. Malapportionment has also been fostered by the strategy of Peronist and military governments of converting national territories into provinces and also as a means of increasing congressional and subnational

---

[5] Stepan (1999) utilizes three indicators of malapportionment across twelve modern federal democracies, and in all the indicators Argentina is the worst case.

[6] This in itself is a reflection of the relevance of subnational politics in Argentina.

political power for themselves. Currently, 88% of Argentines live in the fifteen original districts (dating from the time of national consolidation in the mid-nineteenth century), whereas only 12% live in the nine provinces of more recent creation.

I.1.c. Provinces: General and Political Characteristics. Electoral rules and party statutes and practices make provincial governors (as regional party leaders) individually and collectively very powerful actors in national politics.[7] Subnational and local governments also have ample constitutional independence in expenditure powers.[8] As I will describe in more detail later, this feature interacts with a large degree of federal fiscal imbalance that makes provinces very dependent on "common-pool" funds and creates incentives for exchanging votes in national congress for money to the provinces.

I.1.d. Provinces: Economic and Demographic Characteristics. The provinces have diverse geographic and demographic characteristics (see Table 2.1). The province of Buenos Aires is by far the largest, with almost 14 million people. There are about three jurisdictions with around 3 million people each (Córdoba, Santa Fe, and the City of Buenos Aires). Mendoza has 1.6 million inhabitants, and seven provinces have populations in the 0.8–1.3 million range. Another twelve jurisdictions have populations that range from 200,000 to 620,000. Finally, there is Tierra del Fuego, at the tip of the continent with about 100,000 inhabitants. The level of economic development varies substantially as well. The high-population provinces are at the top of the scale, whereas other provinces are blessed with particularly strong natural resource bases (prime land in the humid pampas or the oil riches of the south). There is a concentration of lesser developed provinces in the north, though migration has led to significant pockets of poverty even in the more developed regions. The

---

[7] See Jones et al. (2002 and 2004) and Spiller and Tommasi (2003).

[8] Each province has a lower level of government, consisting of municipalities, which have their own elected mayor and legislative body; they differ substantially in size and importance. Each province has autonomy to organize its territory into local municipal jurisdictions, according to its provincial constitution and supplementary provincial laws. There are approximately 2,150 municipalities and towns in Argentina. The legal autonomy, expenditure responsibilities, and financing arrangements of local government vary across provinces. Municipal governments are responsible for about 7–8% of total public expenditures in Argentina. In most cases their activities are restricted to traditional urban functions of local street maintenance, street lighting, municipal parks, and solid waste disposal.

Table 2.1. *Basic Characteristics of the Argentine Provinces*

Province	Population (thousands) (2001 census)	GDP per Capita (estimated 1999)	% of Population in Poverty[i]	Population in Poverty (thousands)	Geographic Area (sq. km)	Vertical Fiscal Imbalance (% national resources/ total resources)
C.A.B.A.	2,729	15,634	8	221	200	8
Buenos Aires	13,756	8,325	17	2,352	307,571	47
Catamarca	331	4,887	28	93	102,602	87
Cordoba	3,053	6,132	15	461	165,321	57
Corrientes	927	5,569	31	291	88,199	81
Chaco	979	5,967	40	387	99,633	84
Chubut	408	6,303	22	89	224,686	58
Entre Rios	1,152	6,447	21	237	78,781	71
Formosa	489	4,520	39	191	72,066	95
Jujuy	609	3,812	36	216	53,219	81
La Pampa	299	7,633	14	40	143,440	63
La Rioja	288	5,836	27	78	89,680	90
Mendoza	1,574	6,511	18	277	148,827	54
Misiones	961	4,721	34	323	29,801	81
Neuquén	472	6,464	21	101	94,078	32
Rio Negro	549	6,083	23	127	203,013	67
Salta	1,065	3,836	37	395	155,488	76
San Juan	617	6,341	20	122	89,651	83
San Luis	367	6,367	2	9	76,748	68
Santa Cruz	197	6,278	15	29	243,943	49
Santa Fe	2,976	7,061	18	524	133,007	58
Sgo. del Estero	796	4,269	38	304	136,651	85
Tucumán	1,332	4,925	28	369	21,571	75
T. del Fuego	100	7,682	22	22	22,524	61
Total	**36,027**	**7,722**	**20**	**7,169,381**	**2,780,440**	**56**

[i] Povertyis measured as having "basic needs unsatisfied," or Necesidades Basicas Insatisfechas (NBI) in Argentine government statistics.

Sources: Instituto Nacional de Estadisticas y Censos (INDEC) (2001), World Bank (2002), also author calculations.

rich province of Buenos Aires, for example, has about one-third of the poor in Argentina.

I.2. Fiscal Federalism

I.2.a. Revenue. Although the Argentine Constitution establishes substantial room for subnational taxation, in practice provinces have delegated to the national government large amounts of revenue-raising

Table 2.2. *Revenues for Year 2000 (Percentage of Total)*

	Federal	Provincial	Municipal	Total
	Level of Government			
Income tax (personal and corporate) & capital gains tax	19%			19%
Social security contributions	21%			21%
Good, services, and transaction taxes	38%	10%	0.1%	47%
Wealth tax	2%	4%	0.3%	6%
Trade taxes	3%			3%
Other	1%	3%		5%
Total	**83%**	**17%**	**0.4%**	**100%**

responsibility (income, sales, excise, and fuel taxes), leading to the situation depicted in Table 2.2.[9]

I.2.b. Spending. The resulting revenue concentration contrasts with a spending decentralization process whereby the responsibility for key social functions resides in provincial hands. The only activities that are the exclusive domain of the national authorities are those associated with defense and foreign affairs. The national government shares responsibility with the provinces for economic and social infrastructure, whereas the latter have exclusive competence in primary and secondary education and local (municipal) organization and services. The Constitution defines a broad area of public services for which both national and provincial authorities can participate in legislation and public service provision, though the tendency in the past two decades has been for the national government to decentralize the direct operation to the provinces. Thus the provinces are currently in charge of most of the social expenditures (including basic education, health services, poverty programs, and housing) as well as economic infrastructure.

The national government, however, maintains some regulatory power in many of these areas and directly manages many programs within these sectors, such as social security, income support to the poor, and

---

[9] Such delegation is the outcome of a process that has its high point around the 1930s crisis, when the reduction in foreign-trade tax revenues forced a substitution toward other tax sources. This evolution is analyzed in Iaryczower, Saiegh, and Tommasi (1999).

Table 2.3. *Expenditure Assignments of Federal (F), Provincial (P), and Municipal (M) Governments*

Expenditure	Delivery of Service	Financing	Regulatory Powers
Defense	F	F	F
Environmental policy	F, P, M	F, P, M	F, P, M
Education			
Primary	P, M	P, M	F, P, M
Secondary	P	P	F, P, M
University	F	F	F
Foreign affairs	F	F	F
Health	F, P, M	F, P, M	F, P
Health insurance	F, P	F, P, M	F, P
Immigration policy	F	F	F
International trade	F	F	F
Interstate trade regulation	F	F	F
Justice	F, P, M	F, P, M	F, P, M
Monetary policy	F	F	F
Public safety			
Prisons	F, P	F, P	F, P
Police	F, P	F, P	F, P
Roads	F, P, M	F, P, M	F, P
Social housing	P	F, P	
Social welfare	F, P	F, P	F, P
Transport			
Sea	F	F	F
Rail (passengers)	P	F	F, P
Air	P	. . .	F, P
Unemployment insurance	F	F	F

complementary educational programs subsidizing the poorest schools.[10] Table 2.3 shows the assignment of responsibilities.

As we can see in Table 2.4, subnational governments are responsible for almost 50% of the total consolidated public sector expenditures.[11]

[10] The complexities of national – provincial interactions are illustrated in the paper by Tommasi (2002) with the case study of education decentralization.

[11] The overall extent of involvement of government in the production of goods and services diminished abruptly in the 1990s after various economic reforms (described in more detail in Section II), especially through a reduction at the national level. Government spending in this area dropped from 4.27% of GDP (22% of total spending of the national government) in 1990 to 0.56% (3%) in 2000. The largest component of this drop is in the energy and fuel sector. In contrast, the share of economic activities in provincial government spending has been relatively constant, at about 1% of GDP (10% of total provincial public spending).

Table 2.4. *Expenditure by Level of Government for Year 2000 (Percentages)*

	National Government	Provincial Governments	Municipalities
Total expenditure	**52**	**40**	**8**
Administration	39	46	15
Services	31	52	17
Debt service	84	15	1
Social expenditure	51	41	7
Education	20	78	3
Health	50	44	6
Water	15	85	0
Housing	1	99	0
Social assistance	25	53	23
Pensions	80	20	0
Employment	91	9	0
Other services	65	12	23

Source: Ministry of the Economy.

I.2.c. Transfer System. A high degree of vertical fiscal imbalance results from this expenditure decentralization and tax centralization. In 2000, for example, 56% of total resources received by the provinces came from the common pool of national taxes, whereas only 44% was financed directly by provincial revenues. The last column in Table 2.1 shows the percentage of total revenues coming from central sources, by province.[12] Not only is the vertical fiscal imbalance quite large in general, but it is also quite asymmetric among provinces. Fifteen of the twenty-four provinces finance less than 30% of their spending with their own resources.

Argentina addresses this large vertical fiscal imbalance through a complex system of intergovernmental transfers. The most important component of this system is the tax-sharing agreement (TSA, called *Coparticipación*), which is the process by which part of the taxes collected by the central government are reallocated to the provinces. Over time, the system has tended to redistribute in favor of the least-developed and low-population-density provinces.[13] Even though in a general sense the pattern of redistribution goes "in the right direction," it is very far from being objective and transparent.

---

[12] This vertical imbalance is the result of tax assignment, of the incentives resulting from tax assignment and from the overall federal fiscal game, and of the tax-raising efforts that provincial and national authorities exercise given those incentives.

[13] These provinces are overrepresented in Congress.

The last *Coparticipación* law, sanctioned in 1988, established a set of taxes to be shared: The federal government would retain 42% of the revenue from these taxes, 57% would be distributed among the provinces, and the remaining 1% would be set aside "to finance unforeseen crises in the provinces." The law also set the percentages of "secondary" distribution (i.e., the share of that 57% going to each of the provinces). Several other laws regulating the distribution of specific taxes to finance predetermined activities have supplemented the basic *Coparticipación* law. Several important changes were introduced through "fiscal pacts" in the 1990s that will be explained in more detail later in the chapter. These various reforms introduced new types of transfers besides *Coparticipación*. Additionally, a variety of special channels link some fractions of specific taxes to specific, often economically unrelated, spending purposes. Figure 2.1 depicts Argentina's so-called federal fiscal labyrinth.

The 1994 constitutional reform stipulated that a new tax-revenue-sharing agreement had to be decided and put in place by January 1, 1997. The constitutional mandate remains unfulfilled. In the 1999 and 2000 fiscal pacts, the (then new) national government promised to the provinces some fixed-sum transfers and some minimum revenue guarantees, assuming the role of residual claimant. These clauses were violated by the national government during the 2001 crisis, and the grievances over those obligations were a compounding factor in the political stalemate that led to the demise of President De la Rúa and to Argentina defaulting on its debt in late December 2001.

I.2.d. Borrowing.[14] Within Argentina's federal structure all levels of government are generally permitted to borrow both domestically and abroad. During the 1980s both levels of government borrowed extensively, reflecting the weak fiscal management of the period. In addition, both accumulated sizable arrears on payments of wages and pensions, to suppliers and for debt service. The federal government tried to consolidate those arrears during the 1990s; the clearance operation totaled 9% of 1995 GDP.

In many provinces, the provincial Constitution imposes some restrictions on the borrowing ability of the government and in some jurisdictions it requires an extraordinary legislative majority to approve new debt.

---

[14] Note that this description of the system is based on its workings before the catastrophe of late 2001. Argentina has since entered a political and economic "twilight zone," and it is very hard to predict what monetary, financial, and fiscal system Argentina will have at the end of this process. Several of the statements in the text might no longer be true by then.

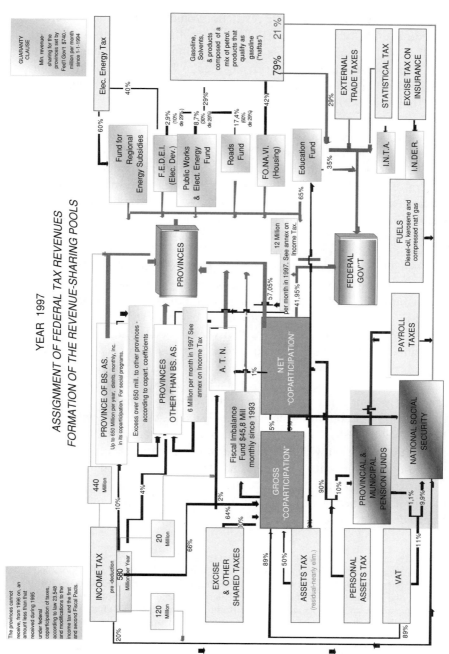

Figure 2.1. Federal fiscal labyrinth. *Source:* Argentine Ministry of Interior.

Some Constitutions also impose restrictions on the level of indebtedness and on the use of debt. Nevertheless, often these restrictions are not fulfilled, and in many provinces they are too loose to be binding (Braun and Tommasi, 2002). It is not surprising then to find that borrowing limits have little effect on the fiscal behavior of provinces (Jones, Sanguinetti, and Tommasi, 1999).[15]

Most provincial state banks were legally dependent on the provincial executive power until recently. They were considered to be akin to the central bank of each province: They provided funds to the provincial governments upon demand and, in turn, received rediscounts from the Central Bank.[16] Given their portfolios of bad assets (resulting to a significant extent from lending to provincial governments) provincial banks were among the prime candidates for restructuring and consolidation, a process that was accelerated after the 1995 Mexican crises induced a run against most provincial financial institutions. Nowadays only eight provincial banks remain in the hands of the provincial public sectors.

There are no ex ante limitations on the ability of provinces to borrow from commercial banks. The main steps taken throughout the 1990s consisted in the elimination of the provincial banks as sources of credit in several provinces. The 1991 convertibility law ended the ability of provincial banks to rely on the central government as a lender of last resort. The central bank can no longer discount any loans from provincial banks.[17]

Provincial bonds and some provincial loans are subject to ex ante federal government controls. Bonds have to be reviewed and registered by the Ministry of Economy, which reportedly exercises this role with a light touch (Webb, 1999). There have even been some bonds issued on the international market without prior review by the Ministry of Economy.

The borrowing control mechanisms center on the arrangements that the provinces make to collateralize their debt. Usually this is done with a pledge of *Coparticipación* as collateral. These are generally handled by the Banco de la Nación, a semiautonomous federal agency that, among other

---

[15] The Argentine case is not unique. It seems that the effectiveness of rules for subnational indebtedness is also quite limited in the Colombian case, in spite of what looks like a fairly sophisticated "traffic light" system. Echevarría, Rentería, and Steiner (2000) show that seventeen out of twenty-seven departments and thirteen out of twenty-six municipalities are actually in the red. See Braun and Tommasi (2002) for an argument against the reliance on "rules" when there is not an adequate governance structure for their enforcement.

[16] For example, those rediscounts amounted to over 2% of annual provincial spending during 1983–1990.

[17] Nevertheless, the central government still found ways to help the Bank of the Province of Buenos Aires in 2001, as is discussed later in the chapter.

functions, handles the distribution of *Coparticipación* to the provinces.[18] Provinces with a weak credit position have to give irrevocable instructions for the Banco de la Nación to deduct the debt-service payments up-front from their *Coparticipación*. Provinces with a stronger credit rating are able to satisfy their creditors with the less onerous pledge that the creditor can collect from the Banco de la Nación only if there is a default in payment. The percentage of tax revenues withheld for this purpose in 2000 runs from 2% in Buenos Aires and La Pampa, to 85% in Tucumán, 92% in Jujuy, and 97% in Rio Negro. The average went from 27% in 1997 to 32% in 2000.[19]

During 2001 and 2002, there was a large increase in the issuance of provincial bonds, quasi-money, to pay wages and other inputs. The stock surpassed US$5 billion. This operation was started by several provinces, most notably Buenos Aires, and it was followed by a national government attempt to coordinate the process, leading to a "federal" provincial bond (LECOP) of national circulation. In 2003 the national government started a "Monetary Unification Program" with the aim of consolidating these issues. By 2004 most provinces have adhered to this program.

II. MARKET-ORIENTED REFORMS OF THE 1990s: THE FEDERAL CONNECTION[20]

In the 1990s Argentina lived through a process of sweeping transformation in some economic institutions and policies, an experience that has been regarded in the literature (at least until recently) as a salient case of radical and "unconstrained" reform. A closer scrutiny of the process and its outcomes demonstrates that the building and maintenance of the political support for the reforms determined the pace, depth, and characteristics of the "new policies and institutions." The idiosyncrasies of Argentina's political institutions and political configurations, including prominently the federal dimension, conditioned the coalition-building strategy and hence the outcomes.

---

[18] There were times at which the central government would delay payment of shared taxes (especially during inflationary times). Several complaints and struggles eventually led to this more automatic system.

[19] In 2003 an executive decree attempted to consolidate provincial debt and to cap percentages of *Coparticipación* withheld at 15%.

[20] This section is based partly on Bambaci, Saront, and Tommasi (2002) and references there is, especially Gibson and Calvo (1997, 2000), who introduce the terminology of "peripheral" and "metropolitan" components of the Peronist coalition.

The 1989 economic crisis provided incentives as well as an opportunity for President Menem to initiate reforms. Even in the context of a favorable partisan composition of key institutions such as Congress, with high concentration of political power, there were limits set to the reforms, however, by the coalition that combined economic interest groups with the provincial base of electoral support of the Peronist Party. These limits were translated into concessions on the design and sequencing of reforms. Though many features associated with a state-led model were dismantled, some "illiberal enclaves" were left in the labor market, in the health market, and in the provincial economies and intergovernmental arrangements.

II.1. Reforms

The (then) unprecedented economic and social crisis of the late 1980s led to the transfer of office from President Alfonsín to President Menem being moved forward by six months. Upon taking office in July 1989, the new administration passed through Congress far-reaching legislation delegating reformist powers to the executive, sidestepping the need for congressional intervention. The State Reform Law allowed the Executive to privatize most state-owned enterprises. Early privatizations and a deepening of trade liberalization were the most notable outcomes of the first stage of reform. Stabilization during this period failed, however, resulting in renewed inflationary episodes in 1990 and the resignation of two Ministers of the Economy. The Convertibility Plan of 1991 marks the beginning of a second stage during which most of the structural reforms were enacted: monetary policy (Convertibility Law and Central Bank independence),[21] fiscal reform (simplification of the tax system and strengthening of the tax-collection agency), liberalization of domestic and external markets, and strengthening of the privatization program. Table 2.5 provides a summary of the main reform measures.

II.2. The Politics of Reform

The case of Argentina attracted a lot of attention, among other things because the reforming government was based on a populist party, traditionally associated with state-centered and inward-looking economic

---

[21] It is a (sad) paradox of Argentine policymaking that the architect of these measures, Domingo Cavallo, was the same Minister of the Economy who, ten years later (in 2001), was to start dismantling both convertibility and Central Bank independence.

Table 2.5. *Calendar of the Main Policy Reforms, Mid-1989 to 1998*

Year	Monetary and Financial Policy	Fiscal Policy	Trade Policy	Privatization	Deregulation
1989	• Elimination of currency restrictions on transactions • Bonds' reprogramming	• Suspension of industrial promotion subsidies • Increase in public utility prices • State companies audit; mechanisms for their privatizationm • VAT generalized and rate reduced (15% to 13.5%) • Reduction in income tax rates	• Raise in export duties and reduction in import tariffs • Suspension of cash payment of exports' refunds		
1990	Bonex Plan	• Integrated budget for state companies • Reduction in the number of areas of central administration • Increase corporate asset tax and VAT (to 15.6%), extension of VAT's base • Derogation of taxes on capital and net worth	• Increase in export duties and reduction of import tariffs • Mercosur talks	• Telephones • Airlines • Petrochemicals • Air, oil, and roads concessions	
1991	• Convertibility Law	• State debt law • VAT increased to 16% and later to 18%; introduction of personal assets tax	• Elimination of most export duties • Reduction in import duties (0%, 11%, and 22%)	• Telephone companies' stock sale • Association deals and concessions for fuel extraction	• State entities dissolution • Cargo transport

(continued)

Table 2.5. (*continued*)

Year	Monetary and Financial Policy	Fiscal Policy	Trade Policy	Privatization	Deregulation
1992	• Central Bank Charter • Financial Regulation Law • Authorizations to constitute reserve requirements in dollars	• Nation/provinces agreement: transfer of services • Extended Facilities Agreement with IMF • Extension of VAT's base; increase in income tax rate • Nation/provinces agreement: minimum monthly income from nation warranted • Regularization of debt to pensioners	• Temporary imports' regime • Mercosur's Constitution Treaty • Imports' statistics tax increase • Export refunds increased • Advance in Mercosur preferential system	• Railway concession • Gas transport and distribution • Water supply • Electricity supply • Iron and steel companies	• Mining • Pharmaceutical products • Car transport • Ports law
1993	• Brady Plan • Prohibition of deposits for less than 30 days • Mutual Funds Law • Securitization rules	• Sanction of retirement system reform • Nation/provinces agreement: tax structure coordination • Income tax modification	• Agreement for the Common External Tariff in Mercosur; tax-free zones regime	• YPF (energy company) • Hydroelectric and thermal stations • Electricity transmission • Railway and subway concessions	

1994	• Financial Institutions Law modification: equal treatment for domestic and foreign capital	• Reduction in employer contributions • Social security system started operating	• Definition of Common External Tariff in Mercosur	• Power stations • Electricity distribution • Gas transport and distribution stock sale
1995	• Central Bank Charter modified • Fiduciary Funds Law • Deposits insurance	• Increase in VAT rate: 21%; extension of base of income tax and personal assets tax • Partial and transitory elimination of the reduction in employer contributions	• Common External Tariff in force • Raise in import tariffs • Reduction in export refunds	• Power stations • Bahia Blanca Petrochemical
1996	• Modification of the Financial Institutions Law: legal framework applicable to the assets and liabilities of liquidated financial institutions	• Employer contributions reduction • Raise in fuel taxes; extension of income tax base • Modification of family allowances regime	• Modification of maximum refunds extra- and intrazone. • Suspension of refunds to the production of capital goods	• Provincial banks
1997/ 1998	• Increase in liquidity requirement • Mercosur: rule for the operation of banks of one country in the market of another	• Increase in income tax rates • Tax reform: reduction in social security taxes; reduction in VAT rate (21% to 10.5%) for basic food products; VAT's base expansion to exempt products; raise in internal tax rate • Labor law reform	• Increase in external tariffs, derogation of statistics tax	• Post office • Airports • Transfer mechanism of nuclear stations • Congressional approval to sell Banco Hipotecario Nacional

Source: Heymann (2000).

41

policies. The crisis led the president to embark on actions leading to economic stabilization.[22]

The electoral results throughout Menem's presidency were favorable to the party in government and were reflected in the resulting distribution of institutional power. Between 1989 and 1999, the Peronist party was entitled to the plurality of seats in both Chambers of Congress, as well as to a large fraction of the provincial administrations (Table 2.6). This partisan distribution, the delegation of legislative faculties to the Executive, and the Executive's control over the Supreme Court as well as the use of certain resources of doubtful constitutionality enabled the Executive to concentrate political power.

In addition, Menem frequently used decrees of "necessity and urgency" and line-item vetoes in his bargaining with Congress. The favorable partisan composition at key institutional nodes was furthered by a law that increased the number of members of the Supreme Court from five to nine. Through this device Menem was allowed to appoint (with agreement of the Senate) four judges. When one of the previous judges resigned in protest, Menem was granted the opportunity for a fifth appointment.[23] This power composition implied that several of the pivotal political negotiations were with actors within the party, most notably, union leaders and provincial powers.

Contrary to some superficial readings of the political economy of reforms in Argentina, the economic reform process was not carried out by an executive power in isolation of social, political, and institutional actors. Rather, reforms were the product of a series of transactions between the Executive and some key actors (mostly within the governing coalition) at every step of the process.

II.3. The Federal Connection and the Purchase of Provincial Support

The institutional overrepresentation of peripheral provinces, together with the "subnational drag" on legislators' incentives, meant that no national winning electoral or legislative coalition could be put together without the support of the regional power brokers in the periphery.

As noted at the beginning of the chapter, legislators tend to act as provincial agents rather than experienced national policymakers. They

---

[22] In Bambaci, Saront, and Tommasi (2002) we explore the decision-making process leading to push for this reform package.

[23] For a longer historical analysis of political interference with the Supreme Court and its effects, see Iaryczower, Spiller, and Tommasi (2002).

Table 2.6. *Electoral Results and Partisan Composition during Menem's Government*

a. Electoral Results, 1989–1997

Political Party	1989[ii] (%)	1991[i] (%)	1993[i] (%)	1994[iii] (%)	1995[ii] (%)	1997[i] (%)
Peronist Party (PJ) and Allies	47	40	43	39	50	36
UCR and Allies	33	29	30	20	17	7
Center and Provincial Parties	12	16	18	12	1	9
Left and Center-Left Parties (including Frepaso up to 97)	7	10	3	17	31	6
Alianza (UCR + Frepaso)	–	–	–	–	–	36
Others	2	4	6	12	2	6

b. Partisan Composition of the Chamber of Deputies, 1987–1999

Political Party	Deputy Periods					
	1987–89 (%)	1989–91 (%)	1991–93 (%)	1993–95 (%)	1995–97 (%)	1997–99 (%)
Peronist Party (PJ)	43	50	50	50	52	47
Unión Cívica Radical	46	37	33	33	27	26
Center-Right Provincial Parties	6	7	9	9	8	11
Other Parties	5	6	5	8	12	16

c. Partisan Composition of the Senate, 1986–1998

Political Party	Senate Periods			
	1986–89 (%)	1989–92 (%)	1992–95 (%)	1995–98 (%)
Peronist Party (PJ)	47	54	62	56
Unión Cívica Radical	39	30	23	29
Center-Right Provincial Parties	15	16	15	14
Frepaso	–	–	–	1

d. Partisan Composition of Provincial Governorships, 1987–1999

Political Party	Gubernatorial Periods		
	1987–91 (%)	1991–95 (%)	1995–99 (%)
Peronist Party (PJ)	77	61	61
Union Civica Radical	9	17	22
Provincial Parties	14	22	17

[i] Legislative elections.
[ii] Legislative and presidential elections.
[iii] Elections for Constitutional Assembly.

tend to respond to the interests of provincial party bosses, especially provincial governors.[24] This strength of provincial governors has been reinforced by the fact that, as indicated in Table 2.6, the national executive has had contingents of its own party of about 50% throughout the period, increasing the marginal value of the block of votes under any given provincial party leadership.

Small "peripheral" provinces have had special importance. The general importance of small provinces results from their overrepresentation in the national Congress. These provinces have an institutional representation that far exceeds their population (and their economic importance). In the period of market-oriented reforms, the peripheral regions held 83% of Senate seats and 52% of Chamber of Deputies seats. Party politics do not seem to temper this influence: Peripheral provinces have always been a central part of the Peronist coalition as well.[25]

Independent provincial parties have also played an important role in lending presidents the support needed to pass legislation in Congress, as shown in Palanza and Sin (1997). In particular, during the Menem reform years the Peronist Party (PJ) had the majority of seats in the Senate, but not in the Lower Chamber. (The president chose to present his bills through the Senate.) Despite the general agreement attained with the main opposition party, *Unión Cívica Radical* (UCR) – which guaranteed the PJ would always have the required quorum in Congress – Menem faced several obstacles when he tried to pass his reform projects. The way out of the gridlock was to buy provincial party support. Palanza and Sin (1996) have documented the denial of support made by provincial party legislators during the first rounds of negotiation, and how their positions changed to be aligned with the PJ when voting.[26]

In sum, the peripheral coalition played an important role in bolstering the political capabilities of the reformist Menem administration. The need to buy this provincial support affected the reform process in several ways. The burden of the costs of reform was shouldered predominantly by the metropolitan constituency. The reforms were timed in a fashion that did imply earlier and heavier hits on the central provinces, as well as differential benefits in favor of peripheral provinces.

---

[24] The lists of congressional candidates that are presented to the voters are made up at the provincial level, using a variety of mechanisms, most of them driven by the local political elite. De Luca, Jones, and Tula (2002) and Jones et al. (2004) provide the details.

[25] See Sawers (1996, pp. 199) and references therein.

[26] Examples of legislation that was sanctioned by the aid provided by provincial parties are, among others, law 23809 (Privatization of Altos Hornos Zapla), law 23871 (Fiscal Reform), law 23897 (Payment of Oil Royalties), and law 24154 (Transformation of YPF SA, the later privatized oil company).

All provinces benefited from improved tax collection owing to low inflation and from overall gains in tax bases, but there was a redistributive component favoring the provinces that are net recipients in the common pool of *Coparticipación*. The main impact on provincial tax revenues in the reform process came from the increase in tax revenues resulting from the Olivera-Tanzi effect from the substantial drop in inflation, from tax reforms increasing and generalizing the value added tax (VAT) and from the consumption boom in the early years after convertibility.[27] A very simple simulation of these effects (treating private sector and public sector as a unit) shows that the central provinces of Buenos Aires, Córdoba, and Santa Fe (and the capital city of Buenos Aires) were net losers, the province of Mendoza was almost indifferent, and all the other provinces were net winners.[28]

Similarly, the estimated 37% reduction in public employment (both in the central administration and in privatized public enterprises) was concentrated in the metropolitan region. We do not have the exact figures of the territorial distribution of the reduction of national public employment, but even under the assumption that the reduction was uniform across the territory, 74% would have taken place in the metropolitan region (Buenos Aires, Córdoba, Mendoza, Santa Fe, and the city of Buenos Aires), and 26% in the periphery. It is likely that the actual distribution of layoffs was even more concentrated in the center.[29]

Focusing on the evolution of unemployment, Table 2.7 indicates that the increase in unemployment was concentrated in the metropolitan provinces.

Additionally, peripheral provinces were given some specific "handouts," of which the most salient were (i) the subsistence and increase of "industrial promotion schemes"; (ii) the 1992 Fund for Regional Imbalances; (iii) the asymmetric reduction of labor taxes; and (iv) the distribution of *Aportes del Tesoro Nacional* (ATNs or National Treasury Contributions).

---

[27] The latter effect is common to all exchange-rate-based stabilizations, in this case reinforced by the reappearance (after many years) of credit. See, for instance, Rebelo and Vegh (1995).

[28] The simulation (available upon request from the author) computes the net gain from change in VAT revenues received by the province minus change in VAT collection in the province, adding different estimates for the Olivera-Tanzi gain. (It implicitly treats money taken from citizens of province *j* and that given to the government of province *j* as equivalent.)

[29] Even beyond labor shedding, other reform measures such as deregulation were also concentrated on national rather than subnational regulations. (See the description of the degree of fulfillment of fiscal pacts in the next section.)

Table 2.7. *Unemployment*

Region	Unemployment Rate 1989	1993	Change
Metropolitan	7.6%	10%	**2.4%**
Periphery	9.4%	9%	**−0.3%**

"Industrial promotion" is a very distortive and controversial system of tax exemptions for some industries in a number of peripheral provinces, dating originally from 1956. The main beneficiaries are the provinces of Catamarca, San Luis, San Juan, La Rioja, and Tierra del Fuego. The exemptions are decided in each year's national budget. The system has survived in spite of the fact that every year there is a heated discussion over its continuation. President Menem extended the range of sectors benefited by the regime.

In the negotiation of the 1992 Fiscal Pact (see the next section), a fund to cover regional disequilibria ("Fund for Regional Imbalances") was created, distributing money with criteria different from the *Coparticipación* law. Its distribution is reflected in Table 2.8.

The Fiscal Pact of 1993 (see the next section) included reductions in the (national) employer payroll taxes, which would be reduced anywhere from 0% to 80%, depending on region and sector of production. This

Table 2.8. *Distribution of Funds from the 1992 "Fondo de Desequilibrios Regionales"*[i]

	$US Millions	% Total		$US Millions	% Total
Buenos Aires	0	0	Mendoza	26	5
Capital Federal	0	0	Misiones	26	5
Catamarca	26	5	Neuquen	30	6
Córdoba	6	1	Rio Negro	30	6
Corrientes	0	0	Salta	30	6
Chaco	0	0	San Juan	26	5
Chubut	36	7	San Luis	26	5
Entre Rios	23	4	Santa Cruz	36	7
Formosa	26	5	**Santa Fe**	6	1
Jujuy	26	5	Santiago del Estero	26	5
La Pampa	30	6	Tierra del Fuego	36	7
La Rioja	26	5	Tucumán	26	5

[i] Metropolitan provinces in bold letters.

Table 2.9. *Distribution of Employer Payroll Tax Rates after 1995 Modification*[i]

Province	Rate (%)	Province	Rate (%)
Capital Federal	**27**	La Rioja	18
Buenos Aires	**26**	Tucumán	18
Córdoba	**23**	Corrientes	16
La Pampa	22	Chubut	15
Santa Fe	**22**	Jujuy	15
Entre Rios	21	Misiones	15
Mendoza	21	Salta	15
Neuquen	20	Tierra del Fuego	15
Río Negro	20	Chaco	14
San Luis	20	Formosa	14
San Juan	19	Santa Cruz	14
Catamarca	18	Santiago del Estero	14

[i] Metropolitan provinces in bold letters.

Source: Ministry of Labor.

complex and distortive system was simplified in March 1995, unifying tax rates across sectors but maintaining a provincial differentiation based on, amazingly, the "distance from the Capital City." The resulting rates are presented in Table 2.9.

Finally, the discretionary transfer par excellence in the Argentine federal fiscal system are the ATNs, a fund of 1% of *Coparticipación* revenues that is distributed by the Ministry of the Interior "to cover temporary fiscal imbalances in the provinces." Traditionally, it has been distributed in the most political of manners, independently of the fiscal situation of the province. In 1994, for instance, 20% of ATN money went to the small province of La Rioja, followed by 2.4% to San Luis and 2.3% to Santiago del Estero.

III. THE FEDERAL FISCAL SYSTEM AND ITS EVOLUTION IN THE 1990s

The federal fiscal system in Argentina has been under attack for many years by scholars, analysts, international organizations, participants (governors as well as national and provincial finance ministers), and the public. The analysis in this section shows a mixed picture of some (partial) efficiency-enhancing reforms, the (partial) accommodation to changing circumstances, and a basic inability to strike the intertemporal agreements that would be necessary for the deep reform of the system.

III.1. Major Deficiencies of the Federal Fiscal System[30]

(a) *High deficits, increasing indebtedness, and procyclical finances of provincial governments.* Provincial deficits have contributed to the fiscal vulnerability of the convertibility regime.

(b) *Bailouts.* In several instances, and through several different channels, the federal government undertook rescue operations to finance some provinces (Nicolini et al., 2000).

(c) *Poor provincial tax collection and poor national tax collection.* Low provincial and federal tax compliance relate to the lack of incentives of provincial authorities to raise local taxes or to assist in the enforcement of national taxes.[31]

(d) *Distortionary national taxation.* Selective tax sharing creates a national bias toward the nonshared taxes, which end up being inefficiently high. In the past, these taxes included trade taxes and the inflation tax. After the reforms of the 1990s, this applies to payroll taxes and more recently to a tax on financial transactions.[32]

(e) *Very distortionary provincial taxation.* More than 50% of the provinces own revenues comes from the "gross receipts" business turnover tax, a multistage sales tax that accumulates tax burden across the stages of production. The tax can lead to large differences in effective rates across different types of final goods and producers of the same good (depending upon the individual producer's ability to vertically integrate.)

(f) *Inefficiencies in the fiscal mix and difficulties for national fiscal adjustment.* Under conditions of fiscal stress, the national government is forced to adjust too much on the (national) spending side, given that any effort on the tax side automatically "loses" 50% into funds to the provinces, which tend to spend it.

---

[30] This listing is taken from a consensus developed over a couple of years at a Forum on Fiscal Institutions convened by Fundación Gobierno y Sociedad (CEDI, Iaryczower and Tommasi, 1999). A more detailed diagnostic is provided in Tommasi, Saiegh, and Sanguinetti (2001).

[31] See, for instance, Gómez Sabaini and Gaggero (1997).

[32] Trade taxes and the inflation tax reappeared at the center of the political scene with the fall of convertibility. Some provincial tax-sharing proposals after the abandonment of convertibility included clauses that requested some form of sharing of the inflation tax.

(g) *Inefficiencies in the provision of local public goods.* The federal system does not provide stable financing for critical goods provided by the provinces such as education.

(h) *Insufficient capital spending by provinces.* Capital spending is increasingly financed by earmarked transfers from the center.

III.2. Explaining Persistent Inefficiencies

An overly simplified version of the economists' political economy analysis would state that reforms take place when reforming heroes prevail over the dark forces of political constraints.[33] Under such a view, lack of reform would be explained on the basis of the veto power of those actors who benefit from the inefficient status quo. Even though useful for some purposes, such a view of the policy process has serious limitations.

First, there are very few reforming heroes around; most actors are self-interested, both in the economy as well as in the polity. The proclaimed "heroes" (Harberger, 1993) are people who try to advance their careers; whether they act as heroes or not will depend on the incentives that the political and professional environment provides to them. Second, the policy process is more continuous than the episodic notion implicit in the reform epic. Third, and most importantly, if the desired reforms are truly welfare enhancing, the key question is why the political system does not provide for the necessary political transactions that will allow the implementation of welfare-improving measures accompanied by compensation to those who stand to lose from the reforms.

I argue in the following that the key deficiency of Argentina's institutional environment is that it does not allow for the agreement and enforcement of the political trades necessary to effect efficiency-enhancing reforms. We use a "transaction cost politics" approach to analyze the failure to reform several deficiencies of fiscal federalism in Argentina as well as several other features of the evolution of the federal fiscal system.[34] *I argue that the inefficiencies of the system are the outcome of noncooperative play in a federal fiscal game.*

The federal fiscal system regulates intergovernmental relations in the face of varying economic and political shocks. An ideal system would have the flexibility to adjust to changing circumstances – such as technological changes (or fashions) that call for a reallocation of the assignment of

---

[33] See Tommasi and Velasco (1996).

[34] This concept originates in the work of North (1990) and Dixit (1996). The use here is closer to the treatment in Spiller and Tommasi (2003) and (2004).

fiscal responsibilities, or shocks from the international financial markets that call for fiscal adjustment. Unfortunately, the Argentine federal fiscal system has leaned toward rigidity as both national and subnational governments try to protect themselves from the possible opportunism of the other actors. Implementation of the more important aspects of reform agreements has failed because of time consistency problems and because of the lack of adequate enforcement. Rigidities such as minimum revenue guarantees were gradually introduced in intergovernmental negotiations, as a way of ensuring weak property rights in a weak institutional environment.[35] In the end, the rigidities derived from the inadequate institutional environment led to a situation in which markets and social events moved much faster than the capacity of the Argentine political system to respond, leading to the tremendous crisis that Argentina suffered during 2001–2002.

The features identified in Section III.1 are the outcome of noncooperative play in the federal fiscal game and of the rigidities that the players impose on the system to protect themselves from the opportunistic (noncooperative) actions of each other.[36] Subnational governments, for example, often take a lax fiscal stance in expectation of a bailout if crisis comes. This opportunistic behavior by subnational governments is often matched by opportunism on the part of the federal government, whose generosity at bailout time depends on the political alignment of the subnational government in question, or on the exchange of bailouts for favorable votes in the national Congress. The distortions to the tax system can also be seen as a consequence of noncooperative behavior – in this case avoidance of sharing taxes.

To answer the question of *why noncooperative play occurs*, one needs to look into the general determinants of cooperation in these types of games – such as payoffs, time horizons, intertemporal commitment ability, etc. – and to map those abstract elements into the observable characteristics of Argentina's *fiscal* and *political* federal institutions.[37]

---

[35] In Tommasi, Saiegh, and Sanguinetti (2001) we explain in more detail each of the deficiencies described in Section III.1 as the outcome of a non-cooperative equilibrium in the intertemporal game.

[36] We can interpret the evolution and performance of the federal fiscal system as the outcome of a noncooperative game involving national and subnational authorities. As a first approximation I will treat that game as orthogonal to the agency problem between the citizens and their political representatives, as if the latter were perfect agents. That is, of course, not true, and I will raise a flag whenever that interaction needs to be made explicit.

[37] A listing of the determinants of the degree of cooperation and more detailed mapping to Argentine institutions can be found in Spiller and Tommasi (2003) and Tommasi,

Inherited features of the federal *fiscal* system turn out to be important determinants of the incentives to cooperate in further stages of the federal fiscal game. For instance, the large degree of vertical fiscal imbalance and large dependence on central funds are obstacles to developing subnational governments' incentives to raise local taxes as well as to the enforcement of agreements leading to tax decentralization.[38]

Key *political* variables are those that impinge upon the qualities of the arenas of intergovernmental decision making in fostering cooperation: One comprises the channels for direct intergovernmental relations (such as the Premiers' Conference in Australia); the other is the structure of subnational representation in the federal government. The exact incentives of subnational and "purely national" actors and the exact rules of the game they play will depend on the details of political institutions for selecting players and regulating their interaction. The Argentine central government is a political arena with particular electoral rules in which the representation of subnational interests interacts with some "purely national" interests. The purely national actors have some more encompassing interests owing to the broader electoral base of the president; they also have some opportunistic political interest in receiving the credit for certain actions, such as distributing welfare programs, while avoiding the blame for things such as raising taxes or cutting teachers' wages.[39]

III.3. The Institutional Environment of the Argentine Federal Game

The environment for intergovernmental transactions in Argentina has not contributed to cooperation over time. Given Argentina's political and economic instability since the 1930s (with periods of military interruptions and high inflation), political actors have tended to adopt myopic perspectives, attempting to attain short-term fiscal benefits, and building awkward mechanisms to protect themselves from each other's opportunism.

Saiegh, and Sanguinetti (2001). Fiscal and other economic features of the country play a role similar to the one played by market characteristics (elasticity, observability of price discounts, etc.) in oligopoly games in determining the possibility of enforcing cooperation. See, for instance, Green and Porter (1984).

[38] Notice that there is a two-way intertemporal interaction between cooperation in intergovernmental relations and features of the federal fiscal system.

[39] This is one of the points where our discussion departs from the assumption of orthogonality between problems of intergovernmental cooperation and principal-agent problems between citizens and politicians.

This historical legacy (analyzed in Iaryczower et al., 1999) has deeply affected the revenue-sharing system. Changes in some actors' bargaining power have been reflected in shifts in the system of transfers. For instance, during military governments, retention at the national level increased. Often the military, on its way out of power, has redistributed funds toward the provinces, with biases toward some regions that it expected to be more politically akin to the military, thus limiting incoming national governments' resources. Also, with the return to democracy, the newly elected governors were able to command a larger share of revenues out of the national government.[40] The degree of vertical fiscal imbalance increased over time, while the incentives for provincial taxation decreased with frequent national bailouts.

There have been reinforcing interactions between the federal fiscal domain and the overall incapacity of the Argentine polity to implement efficient intertemporal exchanges. The most salient characteristics of Argentine politics affecting federal fiscal agreements were the lack of national policy incentives of national legislators, the disproportionate power of governors in national politics, the financial dependence of provinces from the center, the Executive's capacity to unravel legislative agreements, and the weakly institutionalized arenas for executive federalism. The combination of all those institutional features led to low-quality intergovernmental interactions.

Electoral incentives and practices (described in Section II and in Jones et al., 2002, 2004) make national legislators politically dependent on provincial party bosses, who often coincide with governors. That connection, and the provincial dependence on national monies, form the roots of a peculiar crisscrossing of federal monies for provincial votes that creates many distortions in national policies and in provincial incentives. The relatively weak role of Congress is also the product of the Executive's ability to undo legislative agreements – partly as a result of constitutional capacities given to the president and partly for lack of adequate enforcement technologies such as an independent Court or a professional bureaucracy (Spiller and Tommasi, 2003, 2004). This underinstitutionalization of policymaking arenas prevents the achievement of stable, efficient agreements and encourages the mutual imposition of rigidities. We will see several examples of this in the evolution of the federal fiscal system described in the remainder of Section III.

---

[40] Often these modifications were accompanied by elements of interprovincial redistribution, depending on coalitional politics and vote-buying at the time.

III.4. The Evolution of the Federal Fiscal System: Background

The federal fiscal system, particularly the tax-sharing agreement, has a long and complicated history in Argentina.[41] When democracy returned to the country in 1983, after many years of military interruptions, the system had already acquired some of its distinguishing features: A large fraction of spending was in the hands of the provinces (around 25%),[42] a large fraction of that spending was financed out of federal government monies (67%), and the fraction of central government support was very heterogeneous across provinces. Successive changes made the tax-sharing system more redistributive and at the same time more convoluted.

With the democratization process initiated in December 1983, the newly elected governors sought a new tax-sharing (*Coparticipación*) regime. Negotiations began in 1984, but a new accord could not be reached, and the previous regime dating from 1973 expired. Consequently, 1985 was characterized by the absence of a legal regime for sharing tax revenues between the federal and provincial levels. All transfers to the provinces were channeled under the discretionary mechanism of ATNs. In practice, each province negotiated *bilateral* agreements with the federal government (Schwartz and Liuksila, 1997).

During 1987, the provinces and the federal government sought the enactment of a more explicit norm, which was achieved in the 1988 law 23.548. The law increased the provinces' share of tax revenue to a historical peak and tended to validate the share that each province had obtained in the 1985–1987 period through a coefficient that constituted a "magic number."[43] Although the law established this *Coparticipación* regime for

---

[41] A more extensive view of the system is provided in Iaryczower, Saiegh, and Tommasi (1999) and Eaton (2001).

[42] The fraction was much higher than that if we focus on the more discretionary spending, after subtracting interest payments and pensions.

[43] The details of the negotiation of the 1988 law are provided in Saiegh and Tommasi (1998). The political context was the defeat at the midterm congressional elections of the governing Radical administration in the hands of Peronism. The national government was under International Monetary Fund (IMF) pressure to pass a tax reform to improve the fiscal situation, and the powerful Peronist governors (and their legislators) were able to exchange the passage of tax reform for a tax-sharing agreement that was more favorable to the provinces and that included an important sacrifice of resources by the province of Buenos Aires, then in Radical hands. This last element constituted the background for a later special fund "*Fondo del Conurbano Bonaerense*" obtained by the province, which was the basis for the development of a clientelistic network (often utilized for political mobilization) by Eduardo Duhalde, who was vice president during 1989–1991, governor of Buenos Aires from 1991 to 1999, and President of Argentina during 2002–2003. Fondo del Conurbano consisted of a 10% deviation of the income tax (with a maximum of

1988 only, it was extended for many years. The main features of the 23.548 law prevailed until 1992.

Analyzed in the following are the main episodes of what might constitute "the reform of fiscal federalism in Argentina," the so-called Fiscal Pacts of 1992 and 1993, the Constitution of 1994, and the Fiscal Pacts of 1999 and 2000.

III.5. The Fiscal Pacts of 1992 and 1993

Two of the most salient moments in the recent history of fiscal federalism in Argentina were the so-called Fiscal Pacts of 1992 and 1993. For brevity, and given their closeness in time, I will treat them jointly. To begin with, it is important to clarify several important contextual factors around the time of the pacts.

III.5.a. Background. The main background of the pacts, and of some related measures, was the success of the core of Menem's economic policies in the early 1990s.[44] In terms of their impact on intergovernmental relations, the main effect of the "market-oriented reforms" was to shift the net fiscal position of the national and provincial governments in a way that increased provincial total revenues, relatively decreased national total revenues, and increased national spending responsibilities.[45]

The increase in provincial total revenues came mostly from an increase in shared taxes and a "sympathetic" increase in provincial tax revenues.[46] The increase in shared taxes was due to a reverse Olivera–Tanzi effect after stabilization and to changes in the structure of taxes. The new structure of taxes was characterized by a large increase in VAT (owing to increased rates and base) and income taxes and by a decrease in trade

---

$650 million per year) to the Province of Buenos Aires for financing social programs in the poor suburbs surrounding the federal capital.

[44] The transfer of some Education and Health responsibilities to the provinces, discussed in Box 2.1, is an example of the related measures.

[45] These factors tend to be ignored in some papers, which, in interpreting the evolution of fiscal federalism in the 1990s, speak of a process of "fiscal recentralization," ignoring these environmental changes that did require some shift of resources toward the center. Those papers, which include those by Faletti (2001), Haggard and Webb (2001), O'Neill (2001), Remmer and Wibbels (2000), and Eaton (2001), present some interesting political theorizing, but without due attention to these "economic" factors.

[46] This is because the main provincial tax is the sales turnover tax, which, in spite of being very inefficient, benefits substantially from economic growth and from low inflation.

Table 2.10. *National Tax Revenues*[i]

	Social Security	External Trade	VAT	Fuel and Internal	Income Tax	Other Taxes	Total Legislated Taxes	Inflation Tax
1988	10,901	3,651	6,333	7,898	3,093	7,083	38,962	11,758
1989	8,574	5,836	4,574	6,268	2,343	809	35,718	26,421
1990	9,308	4,537	5,796	5,130	1,380	6,077	32,231	13,052
1991	12,114	1,750	8,805	6,062	1,444	6,997	37,175	2,536
1992	9,926	2,219	15,376	5,268	2,892	4,083	39,768	
1993	11,203	2,537	17,000	4,352	4,389	2,540	42,086	
1994	11,558	2,735	17,432	4,231	5,846	2,133	43,934	

[i] In millions of year-2000 pesos.

taxes owing to economic liberalization.[47] The drop in relative national revenues was due to this decrease in its exclusive trade taxes, as well as to the loss of seigniorage from reduced inflation. Table 2.10 gives a sense of the quantitative significance of these changes.[48]

Inflation was reduced from 4,923% in 1989 to 3.9% in 1994. This was accompanied by a reduction in inflation tax revenues from 26.421 billion pesos (74% of national government revenues from legislated taxes) in 1989 to 2.536 billion pesos (7%) in 1991, to zero from 1992 onward.

On the side of spending responsibilities, other than the transfer of some education and health services (Box 2.1), the main change was induced by pension reform. Pension reform consisted of a series of measures, all of which increased the short-term fiscal burden of the national government. The main component of the reform was giving workers the option of staying in the public pay-as-you-go system or moving to one of private accounts. Given the nature of the transition, most senior workers stayed in

[47] During Argentina's Import Substitution Industrialization (ISI) times, special tax treatments were the name of the (political) game (Eaton, 1997). Over the years these efforts resulted in narrow tax bases, differentiated rate structures, and significant tax evasion. By the late 1980s virtually all investment activity was subsidized through the tax system. One of the main components of Menem's reform effort (briefly summarized in Table 2.5) was a tax reform that attempted to broaden the tax base, flatten tax rates, and improve tax collection. The national executive played a skillful strategy of sequencing tax reform and renegotiation of tax sharing in such a way that it first obtained approval of tax base broadening, then gradually increased rates, and only then renegotiated tax sharing.

[48] The table does not capture the reinforcing composition effect from the fact that Olivera-Tanzi used to affect shared taxes but not trade taxes. Furthermore, during inflation periods, there was gaming not only from taxpayers but also from the national government, further delaying the transfer of (depreciating) shared taxes.

the public system, whereas the younger workers moved to the private one, increasing the short-term fiscal burden of servicing pension obligations. It was originally estimated that the burden would be of the order of 2% of GDP and that it would dwindle in about ten years. This factor was a crucial component of the negotiations of the Fiscal Pacts.[49]

In terms of the political and legal background of the pacts, during 1992 the distribution of federal taxes between the federal government and the provinces was affected by a series of laws and decrees aimed at providing funds to increase social security payments. The provinces reached the point of initiating legal action in the Supreme Court. Indeed, a clause in the first Fiscal Pact stated that those provinces that had initiated legal action against the national government (in reference to those decrees) had to cancel the processes underway.

III.5.b. Objectives. As already stated, the Fiscal Pacts of 1992 and 1993 were not simple exercises in "reforming the federal fiscal system" in the "heroic" approach to reform. They were a manifestation of rather complex political exchanges that included some efficiency-enhancing reforms (some achieved and some not), some attempts at solving economic urgencies of the moment, other attempts to adjust some allocations to changing circumstances, and some clever (and opportunistic) political maneuvering.

Among the "worthy" objectives pursued by the federal government we might include the following: an attempt to push for fiscal retrenchment at the provincial level, an attempt to push for the reform of some very inefficient provincial taxes,[50] and privatization of some provincial public utilities as well as public provincial banks. As far as outcomes, the provincial level did not follow the fiscal retrenchment of the central government. Whereas national spending as a percentage of GDP decreased from 21.2% in 1989 to 17.5% in 1992 and 16.4% in 1993, provincial spending went from 9.1% to 11.5% and 12.5%.[51] Also, although Minister Cavallo had been

---

[49] Another contextual factor that deserves mention was the fact that the federal government had rescheduled its external debt and was deepening its first-generation reforms through further privatization.

[50] The federal government was seeking from provinces to substitute the turnover tax by a consumption tax, to eliminate the highly distortionary provincial stamp tax, and to eliminate provincial labor, financial, and energy taxes. Minister Cavallo was very adamant in achieving the elimination of the "very inefficient" provincial tax on financial transactions.

[51] Unfortunately, the federal government was not totally consistent with its own retrenchment effort later in the game, especially in the events surrounding the reelection efforts of President Menem.

very adamant in achieving the elimination of the "very inefficient" provincial tax on financial transactions, in his 2001 reincarcanation be reinstated the same tax on financial transactions in the context of economic emergency as an exclusive national(!) tax. The caretaker government of 2002–2003 so extensively debated with the provinces over the distribution of that "emergency" inefficient tax that, as often the case with emergency measures in Argentina, it became a more durable feature of the fiscal landscape.

III.5.c. Content and Political Exchanges. The 1992 Pact, the so-called Federal Pact was signed in August 1992. It diverted 15% of *Coparticipación* funds to help pay for reform of the national social security system. In return, the government established a guaranteed floor on *Coparticipación* payments.[52]

To reach this pact, the president used other transfers as well as the reform itself to put together a coalition that spanned both houses. The coalition included Buenos Aires province for its weight in the Chamber of Deputies and the low-population provinces for their weight in the Senate. A new special fund, *Fondo del Conurbano*, helped secure the support of legislators from Buenos Aires. For the small provinces, the new arrangement promised *Coparticipación* revenues, plus discretionary transfers that, in a few cases, were very high (related to the explanation in Section II.

In the second fiscal pact, in exchange for the "worthy" requests previously listed, the federal government agreed to increase minimum coparticipated transfers, postpone, and possibly forego, certain provincial debt obligations, and take over responsibility for funding provincial social security systems. In the context of this fiscal pact, the federal government had the obligation to accept the transfer of provincial social security systems and to harmonize contributions and pensions with the newly approved national social security system. Additionally, the federal government would support the privatization of public enterprises and reduce

---

[52] The Minister of Economics' initial objective was to agree on a fixed monthly transfer of $720 million – equal to what the provinces had received in December of 1992 plus an additional $100 million pesos. The extra 100 million was to cover the newly decentralized education expenditures. Whatever money remained after the transfers was to be used to finance the pension system. Though provincial governors rejected this initial proposal, the final agreement was somewhere in between and the main items of Cavallo's proposal were maintained, (i.e., a fixed monthly amount and the possibility to use part of the resources collected to fund the pension system). The 1993 Fiscal Pact raised the minimum monthly floor to $740 million.

Table 2.11. *1992 Fiscal Pact*

Agreement	Degree of Fulfillment
a. 15% of the total coparticipation (prior to all distribution) was assigned to finance the Pensions System and the DGI.	Total
b. The federal government guaranteed a monthly transfer of 725 million pesos to the provinces.	Total
c. A monthly fund of 43.8 million pesos ("Fondo de Desequilibrios Regionales") was established to finance regional imbalances. This fund was distributed among provinces without regard of the secondary distribution stated in Law 23.548.	Total
d. The federal government would automatically transfer resources from the National Housing Fund (FONAVI), Federal Electricity Development Fund (FEDEI), and the Federal Roads Fund (Fondo Vial Federal).[i]	Total
e. Provinces would ask their legislatures to sanction balanced budgets.	Nil
f. Both the federal government and the provinces committed themselves not to increase their expenditures more than 10% above the 1992 current expenditure.	Only five provinces have fulfilled this

[i] These funds were supported by a law and had their own distributional pattern, different from that of to *Coparticipación* law.

the role of provincial banks through privatization of management and ownership.

III.5.d. The Pacts and Their Fulfillment. Tables 2.11 and 2.12 reflect the main components of the pacts and the degree to which they have been fulfilled.

Table 2.12 shows that the degree of fulfillment is very uneven across provinces and across reforms, with some key reforms (such as the replacement of the turnover tax) failing altogether. The following description by Schwartz and Liuksila (1997, pp. 408–412) is particularly telling:

Tax reform was clearly the centerpiece of the second fiscal pact. Provinces adhering to the pact committed themselves to eliminating stamp taxes on checking accounts, taxes on the transfer of fuel, gas and electricity and, most important, phasing out the provincial turnover tax....

Initially, the provinces were slow to join this second pact, largely because of the revenue implications of the tax reforms, particularly the initial stipulation to

Table 2.12. *Degree of Fulfillment of Fiscal Pacts*

The legend for the shading in the table is:

- Total fulfillment
- Partial
- no fulfillment
- municipal
- no

Issues	C.F.	B.A.	Cat.	Cord.	Corr	Cha.	Chu.	E.R.	For.	Juj.	L.P.	L.R.	Men.	Mis.	Neu.	R.N.	Sal.	S.J.	S.L.	S.C.	S.F.	S.E.	Tuc.
1.Tax on contratcs																							
1.1. Short term reduction																							
1.2. Medium term reduction																							
2. Specific taxes																							
2.1. Tax on oil																							
2.2. Tax on gas																							
2.3. Tax on electrical energy																							
2.4. Tax on sanitary services																							
3. Tax on bank accounts and payroll																							
3.1. Bank accounts																							
3.2. Payroll taxes																							
4. Turnover Tax																							
4.1. Primary production																							
4.2. Financial services																							
4.3. Insurance services																							
4.4. Foreign currency transactions																							
4.5. Industry																							
4.6. Utilities																							
4.7. Construction																							
4.8. Tourism																							
4.9. Research and development																							
5. Real estate taxes																							
5.1. Valuation																							
5.2. Tax rates																							
6. Tax agencies																							
7. Consumption tax																							
8. Tax on cars																							
8.1. Valuation																							
8.2. Tax rate																							
9. Privatization's and concessions																							
9.1. Energy firms																							
9.2. Sanitary and water utilities																							
9.3 Provincial Banks																							
Transfer of Provincial Pension System																							

Note: The province of Buenos Aires privatized the water company during 1999.

Source: Based on information from the Secretaria de Programación Económica, Ministry of the Economy, Government of Argentina. ("Secretary of Economic Planning and Statistics, Ministry of the Economy.")

abolish the provincial turnover tax before June 1995. While the provinces were
free to replace the turnover tax with other taxes, many have not yet done so....

Overall, there is no easy short-term alternative for replacing the provincial
turnover tax....

Other alternatives for improving provincial revenue would be beneficial in the
long run, but would not yield short-term results.... Similarly, improving real state
taxation would require substantial initial efforts, including, for example, improving property mapping and property registries; providing better and more consistent application of valuation techniques; improving the exchange of information
between local tax offices, property registries, ...

The announcement in December 1993 that federal payroll taxes levied on
employers would be reduced, depending on region and sector, in those provinces
participating in the second pact, increased pressure on provincial governments
to join. By May 1994, all but one provincial legislature had ratified the second
fiscal pact, and most had taken at least some initial steps toward implementation.
Also the provinces were given a minimum revenue guarantee and some other
guaranteed fixed payments that provided a floor of federal transfers equivalent
to about 4.5% of GDP annually.

The second fiscal pact clearly shows the "horse-trading" that is involved in
implementing structural reforms of the system of fiscal federalism.... but came at
the expense of making payroll taxes an explicit instrument of regional and sectoral
policies, and contributed to the growing social security deficit.

This example illustrates the inability to make intertemporal trades that
have the nature of investments (i.e., upfront costs and a later stream of
benefits that could be appropriated). It shows that the extant governance
structure of federalism in Argentina cannot support such trades.

All in all, the pacts of 1992 and 1993 left a mixed landscape including
some successes such as the privatization of some provincial banks and
some failures such as the nonreform of provincial tax systems. Clearly, the
basic incentives and fundamental governance of the underlying federal
fiscal game were not altered. That is reflected in the later reform attempts,
such as the one in the 1994 Constitution, to which we now turn.

III.6. Reform of the Tax-Sharing Regime
in the Constitution of 1994

When President Menem was ending his first term, his interest in
reelection – in those days not permitted by the Constitution – moved him
to promote the reform of the Constitution. He made an agreement with
former president Alfonsín, known as "*Pacto de Olivos.*" They expected
Congress to agree upon their proposal without further changes. However,
when the agreement was made public, several provincial leaders saw the
opportunity to get some aspects of the federal fiscal regime engraved in

the Constitution. They made their support in Congress conditional on the inclusion of this subject among those to be reformed. Given Menem's political ambitions, provincial leaders were in a position to negotiate some fiscal benefits. As already explained the late 1980s and 1990s were years in which several changes were introduced into the federal fiscal regime. Provincial leaders were well aware of the uncertainties they faced, and they saw the opportunity to negotiate a constitutional agreement that would protect them against future acts of opportunism from the federal government.

The final constitutional text with regards to federal fiscal arrangements was the outcome of complex negotiations between the federal government (the president and national ministers) and the provinces (provincial governors and provincial party leaders in general). The alliances among these actors varied throughout the process, changing according to the issues at stake and the positions adopted by their districts in these issues.

The provinces initially tried to get actual sharing coefficients to get written into the Constitution, but the national executive was able to convince them to replace that with procedural mechanisms with regards to the future sharing agreement. The provinces were able to establish a procedure that would in principle protect them from the federal government's unilateral influence.[53] The negotiations at the constitutional convention as well as the final text are very clear illustrations of *transaction cost politics* at work. We present now an annotated summary of the final text (National Constitution, 1994, Article 75, 2nd paragraph)

(a) *A "Ley Convenio" based on understandings between the Nation and the provinces will establish systems of Coparticipación in taxes.*

A Ley Convenio is a special procedure that requires that any law, after being enacted by Congress, must be authorized by each provincial legislature before acquiring validity. This clause results from actors' distrust of each other, originated in past failures to honor agreements or open attempts to violate them. Because of their belief that if anything were left unchecked someone's interest might be endangered, they agreed on a procedure that requires several instances of approval. The conditions put forth to accept the agreement are so demanding that it would be rare to see such an agreement come to life, as illustrated by the failure to produce a law by the time of this writing.

---

[53] At a more disaggregated level, one could also say that the procedures decided on benefited the small provinces more than large (rich) provinces such as Buenos Aires.

(b) *The automatic delivery of funds is guaranteed.*

Comments not necessary.

(c) *All taxes collected by the national government (other than foreign trade taxes) should be shared.*

This is to avoid the opportunistic creation of nonshared taxes.

(d) *The distribution between the Nation and the rest of the districts – and among these districts – shall be carried out in direct conformity with the capacities, services, and functions performed by the jurisdiction, in compliance with objective distribution criteria. This distribution must be based on principles of equity and solidarity, prioritizing the achievement of similar levels of development, living standards, and equal opportunities throughout the national territory.*

This looks like a protection imposed by provinces to guarantee certain levels of resources, given the differences with the federal government and among themselves in terms of capacities, services, and functions performed by each jurisdiction. Provinces tried to protect themselves from arbitrary changes in the percentages they were entitled to receive from tax collection, a fear clearly resulting from the lack of criteria backing those percentages.

(e) *The Ley Convenio is to be originated in the Senate and shall be enacted with the absolute majority of all the members of each House.*

This procedure should be interpreted as a warranty to provinces in general that actors such as Buenos Aires (owing to its numerical superiority in the House) or the federal government (an actor with sufficient resources to buy support) would not be able to get away with a reform of the federal fiscal regime that was not supported by most of the provinces. The selection of the Senate as the chamber where the bill should originate avoids the relative numerical advantage of some provinces in the House. The requirement of absolute majority of all members in each chamber also imposes protection against opportunism.

(f) *It may not be unilaterally amended or regulated, and must be approved by the provinces.*

The explicit mention of unilateral actions is a clear demonstration of the general concerns of the provinces, precisely in the direction emphasized in our framework. The ability of the national executive to undertake unilateral actions has been behind the inability to enforce the political transactions necessary to build a more efficient system.

(g) *No transfer of jurisdiction, services, or functions can be done without the corresponding reallocation of funds approved by a law from Congress and by the relevant province or the City of Buenos Aires, as required in each case.*

This clause intends to protect the provinces against opportunistic actions by the national government. Their caution is a response to previous experiences with decentralization of public services, in which the national government did not always transfer adequate funding alongside responsibilities. (See Box 2.1 for the case of education decentralization.)

(h) *A Federal Fiscal Entity ("organism") shall be in charge of controlling the implementation and execution of this article, in accordance to what the above-mentioned law shall establish. The representation of all provinces and of the City of Buenos Aires in the composition of this institution is guaranteed.*

The requirement that a federal fiscal institution be created to control the implementation of decisions is a clear sign that the federal government – the "default" actor in charge of the implementation – is not a beneficiary of the provinces' trust. Along with all the other mechanisms set forth to ensure that they would not be tricked into loses when designing the regime, provinces thought that whatever was decided could be misinterpreted – or bluntly ignored – by the federal government during the ongoing implementation phase. To prevent such a course of events, the implementation is to be supervised by an organism in which all of the districts will be represented. This is a clear illustration of the importance of governance in a context of incomplete contracting.[54]

All the highlighted points reflect very clearly the transaction-cost-politics nature of the problem. The very constitutional status of the issue is a reflection of its importance and of the fear of opportunism by some actors. Furthermore, all the important clauses represent the actors' attempt at protecting themselves (by procedural means, by forbidding certain actions, or by adding veto gates) against opportunistic behavior.

---

[54] We have developed proposals of reform of fiscal federalism in Argentina that, from this incomplete contracting perspective, put most of the weight on the adequate design of this federal fiscal institution. See Iaryczower, Sanguinetti, and Tommasi (2000). For a more general discussion of intergovernmental arrangements from an incomplete contracting perspective, see Saiegh and Tommasi (2000).

Box 2.1. *Federalism and Social Sector Reform in Argentina:*
The Case of Education Decentralization

Over the past couple of decades, decentralization of social services has become one of the new tenets of the "Washington-sponsored" reform agenda faced by developing countries. Argentina has not been immune to these new winds. Out of a mix of conviction, foreign pressure, political opportunism, and shortsighted fiscal moves, Argentina has decentralized a large part of its social policy during the 1990s. Even though some of the postulated benefits of decentralization might be at work, the implementation of reforms, especially the quality of policymaking and delivery in the social sectors, has been tainted by several of the characteristics of fiscal and political federalism in Argentina highlighted throughout this paper.

Education decentralization was in large part driven by fiscal-federal opportunism of the central government, reflecting of the Argentine federal system's inability to adjust in efficient ways. Ideally, reforms such as decentralization should be carried out in response to technological or democratic advantages of decentralized provision, and money should follow function (and not vice versa). The Argentine polity is a far cry from that model.[i]

From the beginning of the twentieth century, the provision of education had been mostly in the hands of the national government. Between 1956 and 1976 there were unsuccessful and partial attempts at transferring national public schools to the provinces (as the Constitution originally stipulated). In 1978, mostly for fiscal considerations, the military government appealed to the Constitution and to "true federalism" to decentralize public schools, unloading 6,564 establishments and 897,400 pupils onto the provinces. Provinces objected to the abruptness of the procedure and to the lack of accompanying funds.

The same argument of "real federalism" was the basis for a new adjustment of public accounts in 1992. In December 1991 the Menem administration passed a law that decentralized the management and finance of secondary education from the federal to the provincial levels.[ii] In 1993 a "Federal Education Law" was sanctioned. These laws altered the traditional role of the central government from provider of schooling services to "helmsman" in education policies.

This process was largely contested by the provinces. Many interpreted decentralization not as an opportunity for greater local autonomy but as an attempt by the federal government to abandon its financial responsibilities in the education sector. The transfer of the responsibility for schooling from the national to the provincial levels, although publicly espoused by local governments as a reaffirmation of federalist principles, was privately rejected by some out of a concern for federal fiscal and political abandonment.[iii]

The bargaining process over education decentralization started, then, in the 1992 national budget law submitted to Congress in 1991. From there the negotiations went intergovernmental with a very active role of governors and of the national Ministry of the Economy. The national and provincial education ministries only entered center stage later on, in the discussion over the implementation of the federal education law that complemented the decentralization law.

Even though there have been recommendations of the Federal Education Council stressing the pedagogical advantages of decentralization, the true motor in the actual process was the pressure from the National Finance Ministry (from their Finance Minister Cavallo).[iv] The transfer of educational services in the 1990s took place without any actual transfer of additional resources to the provinces (following the experience of 1978).

The Ministry of the Economy insisted that the decentralization should be financed out of the large increase in shared revenues that followed the implementation of the convertibility plan. Based on the evidence presented by the ministry (including projections of future revenues) and on circumstantial political pressure, governors agreed that the transfer would, in principle, be financed with those "extra" *Coparticipación* resources as long as the national government would guarantee that it would cover the cost of services transferred in case those revenues were to fall below the monthly average of April–December 1991.

The mechanism finally used to "finance the transfer" was to define a "retained" amount of US$711.2 million (corresponding to the estimate of the cost of the transfer) subtracted from the secondary *Coparticipación* and distributed to the recipient provinces as a function of the estimated cost of the services transferred (essentially payroll costs). This was, in fact, a redistribution of secondary *Coparticipación* toward the provinces with more teachers. The law also established that if the increase in shared revenues with respect to a 1991 baseline was (in the aggregate of provinces) less than the cost of services transferred, the national government would guarantee the larger amount.

After a brief debate in Congress, a law transferring educational services was sanctioned in December 1991. Law 24.049 constituted the beginning of a series of (bilateral) negotiations between the national government and the provincial governments that would conclude two years later, in

December 1993, with the signing of the last agreement of transference between the national government and the governor of the Province of Buenos Aires, Eduardo Duhalde. (The first agreement was signed with President's Menem province of La Rioja.) Thirteen provinces signed before November 1992 (within a year of the sanction of the law), and eleven signed later. The province of Buenos Aires was the last one to sign, probably because of the importance of the transfer – since 33% of all the transferred schools corresponded to the province of Buenos Aires. The province was able to negotiate additional funds of almost 91 million pesos. More generally, the provinces that signed later were those that achieved the grant of funds for the improvement of public buildings.

It is still too early to pass any definitive judgment on the overall impact of education decentralization. Even though some methodologically sound studies (Galiani and Schargrodsky, 2002) seem to find evidence that decentralization improved the performance of public school students in test scores, almost none of the theoretical arguments on the virtues of decentralizing a public service like education seems to have any real bite in the actual decentralization of education in Argentina. Most of those arguments depend on channels by which "government is brought closer to the people" and do not seem to apply to the size of Argentine provinces that are more a historical accident of military and fiscal technologies two centuries ago than "optimal school districts."

With regard to the impact of education decentralization on the achievement of equity objectives, decentralization might have increased the traditional asymmetries in the quality of public education across provinces. In poor and isolated localities, the lack of technical and financial resources has maintained the dependence on the central government. Provincial governments are circumscribed to instituting the curricular plans handed down from the national Ministry or implementing compensatory programs that are federally funded. Fiscal difficulties in several provinces led to violent demonstrations, which even caused the central government to intervene in one province to restore order. In more developed localities, provincial governments have taken education decentralization as an opportunity to detach themselves from the central government's sphere of control.

In spite of the "decentralization of education" several actors continue to operate nationally. A telling example occurred in 1999, when teachers' unions, with strong support from other sectors of society, staged a permanent camp in front of the national Congress, demanding increases in teachers' wages (which are, de jure, a provincial responsibility).

Interestingly, some preliminary survey work indicates that citizens are not very well aware of who is responsible for what. Furthermore, de facto citizens might be right in assigning final responsibility to the national government, once one takes into consideration the overall workings of the federal fiscal system. In that specific example, the national government did validate those beliefs by establishing a special tax on cars(!) to subsidize those wage increases.

What actually happened in the decentralization of education in Argentina – "use the excess *Coparticipación* revenues from improved taxation, and I guarantee you a floor" – would have been roughly consistent with the idealized decentralization "transaction" only under very specific circumstances. That would have been a "fair" deal only insofar as we assume that the spending needs in all other dimensions of provincial public finances will be constant, or there is an agreement that an important shift in composition is desired.[v]

The "revenue guarantee" also appears to have been a shortsighted arrangement. It was never a binding constraint, as shared revenues were always above the estimated cost of the transfer owing to good economic performance in the late 1990s. At the level of individual provinces "the extra funds," however, do not appear sufficient to cover the cost of the transferred services even in years prior to the later crisis, especially if we take into account the increase in coverage and in the potential population. The total cost of the decentralized services, plus the cost of implementing other aspects of the later Federal Education Law, is several orders of magnitude above the original "guaranteed" estimates. Nonetheless, sitting governors might have been more interested in the short-term funding they obtained through the negotiated agreements than in the medium- to long-term sustainability of the exercise.

In general, the overall experiment shows the crisscrossing patterns of national and provincial politics that have been emphasized in this chapter. One feedback of education reform onto fiscal federalism is provided by the fact that, after decentralization, the budgetary flexibility of provincial governments has been reduced, as schooling expenses now require a large fraction of provincial budgets. This has implications for possible paths of future fiscal adjustment.

---

[i] In terms of federal spending in education, the decentralization process led to a net spending reduction of US$400 million. This corresponded (roughly) to a reduction of US$800 million in basic education and an increase of US$400 million in other items, especially university education. Funding for the politicized and ineffective national public universities is a hot ticket in budget politics, since the parties, especially UCR, use the universities as a

temporary employment agency for their activists and as a platform for political co-optation.

ii It is interesting to notice that, *in an appendix to that law*, hospitals and other
social services were also transferred. This process implied the transfer of 1,905
schools with 112,000 teachers and 14,200 nonacademic employees, servicing
around a million students, as well as 20 health clinics with 9,200 employees
and 22 family/childhood institutes employing 1,700 agents. (The bundling of
the two sectors in one law reflects an underlying fiscal drive over sectoral
considerations.)

iii Hanson (1996) reports that "the transfer of the secondary schools was a surprise
move. The first notification that the attempt would be made came when the
national budget was produced and distributed. The budget had deleted its
historic financial support for secondary education. The outcry was so intense
that the central government was almost obliged to delay the transfer while it
developed a justification, held public debate and passed a law."

iv For instance, one distinguished independent deputy, Federico Clerici, declared
that "the main force behind this transfer has been the compromise to reduce
federal government spending by $1200 millions." Deputy Dumon from the
opposition UCR stated: "We treated, within the *Congreso Pedagógico*, the
issue of decentralization as a social concern, but we were confronted with big
news: the decentralization we were instrumenting was not that of *Congreso
Pedagógico*, but the one we had promised to the IMF in the 1990 letter of
intent" (Repetto et al., 2001). There is additional evidence confirming the
suggestion that the genesis of the actual process of education decentralization
was related to memos exchanged between the executive and the IMF, hardly
an institution specializing in education (Nores, 1999).

v It is worth noting that since the city of Buenos Aires at the time was receiving a
fixed sum of *Coparticipación* taxes, this implied that the city, which became "independent" in 1995, received additional functions without additional funding.

These procedures, while giving some assurances to the parties involved,
have at the same time decreased the likelihood that any effective change
could occur.

III.7. The Saga Continued: No Law, More Pacts, and the Crisis of 2001–2002

The Constitution required that the "Ley Convenio" establishing the new
tax-sharing agreement be sanctioned by the end of 1996. That constitutional mandate was not fulfilled then, and it has not been fulfilled yet.
There have always been one or several projects on the table, but none
has mustered enough support (not even within the Executive) to get serious political attention. Argentina has been signing agreements with the
IMF throughout the period, promising "to pass a *Coparticipación* law"

but systematically failing to do so. Beyond some autistic tendencies in the IMF and in the Argentine national bureaucracy,[55] this reflects on some deeper issues. The complex procedural constraints imposed by the Constitution do not facilitate the passage of a new law, and this adds to the "transaction-cost-politics" intrinsic complexity of the problem of passage of a "definitive" regime. Furthermore, the usual agenda-setter in these things is the national executive, and it is not obvious that it is in its best interest to move to a regime that, if well done, would limit some of its own unilateral moves.[56]

Ex post, it is obvious that the fiscal path of Argentina was a far cry from what would have been necessary to avoid the terrible crisis of 2001–2002. Both a more relaxed fiscal stance in the second Menem administration and the dynamics of provincial finances put the country on a risky path that, when coupled several negative shocks and the wild fluctuations in international market conditions and sentiment, precipitated the crisis. From 1993 to 1998, when the Argentine economy was generally performing well and the Argentine government was receiving substantial nonrecurring revenues from privatization and enjoyed other temporary fiscal benefits, the public sector debt over GDP nevertheless rose by 12 percentage points. This clearly was not an adequately disciplined or sustainable fiscal policy.[57]

Table 2.13 summarizes the behavior of provincial, national, and consolidated finances from 1993 to 2001. It is clear that, especially at the provincial level, there was high growth of spending during the good years after the Tequila shock and that the adjustment to the difficult times starting in 1999 was far too delayed.[58] From 1996 to 1999, primary expenditure increased almost 20% at the provincial level and 14% at the national level.

---

[55] The former relates to incentive problems typical of large-scale international bureaucracies and their modes of operation, which in general do not lead to adequate investments in understanding the deeper political determinants of the countries' policies and practices. The latter is due to some features of the Argentine bureaucracy, which are endogenous to the workings of political institutions in Argentina (including the federal fiscal and political mess), these are explored in more detail in Spiller, and Tommasi (2003) and Bambaci, Spiller, and Tommasi (2004).

[56] Here we are emphasizing the short-term self-interest of the political actors running the Executive at a given point in time.

[57] This is not the place for a complete analysis of all the determinants of the Argentine crisis. For our current purposes, it suffices to say that a tighter fiscal position throughout the good years of the second half of the 1990s would have been very desirable. [For a more detailed analysis of the initiation, dynamics, and downfall of convertibility, see Galiani et al. (2003).]

[58] Of course, in a normal country in normal times, you would not want fiscal retrenchment in a recession. Yet Argentina is not a normal country in normal times, but a country suffering from (well-deserved!) deep credibility problems, forcing the need for contractionary fiscal moves after having lost the opportunity of fiscal savings during the good times.

Table 2.13. *Fiscal Figures for 1993–2001*[i]

a. Provincial Governments

	1993	1994	1995	1996	1997	1998	1999	2000
Fiscal Deficit	2,072	2,359	3,527	1,840	1,377	2,470	4,633	3,230
Deficit/Total Expenditure	8%	8%	12%	6%	4%	7%	13%	9%
Debt Services	472	571	721	1,004	1,052	1,190	1,431	1,856
Debt Services/Total Revenues	2%	2%	3%	3%	3%	4%	4%	6%
Total Revenues	25,507	27,371	26,694	29,081	32,617	33,111	32,235	32,150
Change in Total Revenues		7%	–2%	9%	12%	2%	–3%	0%
Primary Expenditure	26,793	28,990	29,222	29,269	31,678	33,871	34,933	33,503
Change in Primary Expenditure		8%	1%	0%	8%	7%	3%	–4%
Total Expenditure	27,265	29,561	29,942	30,273	32,730	35,061	36,365	35,359
Change in Total Expenditure		8%	1%	1%	8%	7%	4%	–3%

b. National Government

	1993	1994	1995	1996	1997	1998	1999	2000	2001
Fiscal Deficit	–2,207	1,019	2,544	5,889	4,582	4,170	7,348	6,936	8,170
Deficit/Total Expenditure	–5%	2%	5%	11%	8%	7%	12%	11%	14%
Debt Services	2,914	3,150	4,084	4,608	5,745	6,660	8,224	9,656	9,630
Debt Services/Total Revenues	6%	6%	8%	10%	10%	12%	14%	17%	19%
Total Revenues	50,727	51,078	50,294	47,669	55,377	56,726	58,455	56,571	51,319
Change in Total Revenues		1%	–2%	–5%	16%	2%	3%	–3%	–9%
Primary Expenditure	45,082	48,214	47,583	48,325	53,908	54,139	55,000	53,706	49,799
Change in Primary Expenditure		7%	–1%	2%	12%	0%	2%	–2%	–7%
Total Expenditure	47,996	51,364	51,667	52,933	59,653	60,800	63,224	63,362	59,429
Change in Total Expenditure		7%	1%	2%	13%	2%	4%	0.2%	–6%

c. Consolidated (1993–2001)

	1993	1994	1995	1996	1997	1998	1999	2000	2001
Fiscal Deficit	−135	3,378	6,071	7,729	5,959	6,640	11,981	10,166	11,777
Deficit/Total Expenditure	0%	5%	10%	13%	8%	9%	16%	14%	18%
Debt Services	3,386	3,721	4,805	5,612	6,797	7,850	9,655	11,512	13,560
Debt Services/Total Revenues	6%	6%	8%	9%	10%	11%	13%	17%	21%
Total Revenues	62,517	63,677	62,479	60,864	70,319	71,504	72,846	70,680	66,274
Change in Total Revenues		2%	−2%	−3%	16%	2%	2%	−3%	−6%
Primary Expenditure	58,158	62,432	62,296	61,708	67,911	69,677	72,089	69,168	64,431
Change in Primary Expenditure		7%	0%	−1%	10%	3%	3%	−4%	−7%
Total Expenditure	61,544	66,153	67,100	67,320	74,708	77,528	81,745	80,680	77,991
Change in Total Expenditure		7%	1%	0%	11%	4%	5%	−1%	−3%

[i] In millions of year–2000 pesos.

Source: Ministry of Economy.

The less than perfect fiscal discipline by national and provincial authorities is the consequence of the same old political game being played, in
spite of the fact that some of its explicit channels had been closed by
the convertibility regime and by some further measures. The closing of
some channels of financial irresponsibility led to an overly enthusiastic
assessment of Argentina's overall fiscal sustainability by international
organizations such as the World Bank and the International Monetary
Fund, both of which were fairly bullish about accomplishments such as
the privatization of several provincial banks and by the approval of a
Fiscal Responsibility Law in 1999.[59]

The perverse behavior of public finances was in large measure linked
to the 1999 presidential campaign. Early in the game, President Menem
attempted a blatant move to run for a third term, a move that led to
a relaxation of the national fiscal stance to gain support in spite of its
obvious lack of constitutionality. Even worse than that, the other con-
tender for the Peronist candidacy was the governor of Buenos Aires,
Eduardo Duhalde. First in fighting Menem's reelection bid, and then in
fighting the interparty presidential competition as the Peronist candidate,
Duhalde made generous use of the largest budget in the country, that of
the Province of Buenos Aires. Given the importance of the province, and
the federal fiscal linkages emphasized in this chapter, those actions had
dire consequences for Argentina.

Buenos Aires accounts for 30% of GDP, 30% of total provincial spending, 31% of personnel expenditure, and 23% of total provincial debt by
2000. By the third quarter of 2001 (shortly before the Argentine implosion), Buenos Aires' deficit represented 57% of the consolidated provincial deficit. Its deficit had a markedly different behavior from 1991 to 1997,
when it was less than 8% of total spending, than since 1998, in which
it represents more than 13% of provincial spending. (See Figure 2.2.)
Total spending in Buenos Aires grew 30% between 1995 and 2001, much
higher than the 10% increase in the other provinces and the 15% increase
in national spending (Figure 2.3). This led to fiscal disequilibria of 19%
in 1999, 18% in 2000, and 20% in 2001 and to an increase in its debt stock
of 69% in the 1997–1999 period. Provincial public employment rose from
320,000 in 1995 to 405,000 in 1999, with the largest increase (17%) occurring from 1998 to 1999. Personnel expenditures rose 49% in the 1996–1999
period.

In spite of all these efforts, Duhalde lost the 1999 presidential election
to Fernando De la Rúa, the candidate of an alliance of the traditional UCR

---

[59] See Braun and Tommasi (2002) for a more detailed critique of some of those assessments.

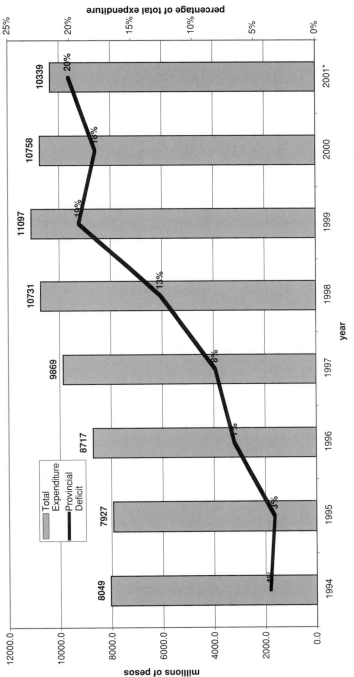

Figure 2.2. Province of Buenos Aires: total spending and fiscal deficit 1994–2001.

73

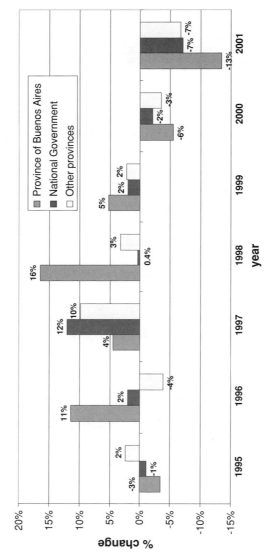

Figure 2.3. Change in primary spending 1995–2001 for province of Buenos Aires, national government, and other provinces.

74

with Frepaso (a recent federation of center-left parties). Duhalde was replaced in the province by the Peronist candidate Carlos Ruckauf, who did not do much to improve the fiscal situation.[60] The impending default of the province was one of the main concerns of the National Ministry of the Economy throughout 2001. In a sense, there was a perverse political war of attrition to see who (the radical national authorities or the Peronist provincial authorities) was blamed for the imminent financial disaster.

In April 2001, the province of Buenos Aires and the federal government signed a bilateral agreement to improve the provincial fiscal situation. The agreement established a nominal deficit ceiling, a primary spending cut, and the federal government's commitment to provide financial support. The former, in the finest Argentine tradition, was not fulfilled by the province, but the latter was used in November 2001 when the Central Bank gave a US$65 million rediscount to the Provincial Bank of Buenos Aires (one of the surviving dinosaurs) to avoid the provincial default. The *Banco Provincial* also received a Central Bank waiver on the liquidity requirements on public deposits, as well as some additional tinkering with bank regulation to make its asset portfolio look better. (These changes happened after the convenient removal of the previous Central Bank president and his replacement by somebody more "understanding.")

All of this, other than reflecting on the weakness of Argentine institutions, is also a perverse "Buenos Aires" revenge for the redistribution away from the province in the previous decades. Unfortunately, instead of a more rational limitation on redistribution within the system, we have these perverse dynamic interactions between the fiscal realm and the political realm. The late 1990s saw the two bigger fiscal players of the country involved in a spending binge, in hopes that the other political player would be the one to foot the bill.

Another connection between the Argentine disaster and fiscal federalism can be traced to the effects of the 1999 and 2000 fiscal pacts, signed, respectively, just after the presidential election and before the incoming administration took office.

The turn of the century found Argentina trying to overcome the harsh recession that began in the middle of 1998, mainly as a result of the

---

[60] Ruckauf, who was vice president during Menem's second term, was "promoted" from Governor of Buenos Aires to Foreign Minister in the Duhalde national government that eventually followed (on January 1, 2002) the anticipated resignation of De la Rúa. It seems that Ruckauf was moved out of the province of Buenos Aires so that the very likely impending financial disaster (or alternatively the very high political cost of the huge adjustment necessary) did not explode in his (loyal) hands.

Brazilian and Russian crises, intensified by the Brazilian devaluation. As soon as the results of the presidential election were known, the future Economics Minister (José Luis Machinea) announced that the budget projected for 2000 needed serious changes, mainly because the rate of growth for the coming year would be lower than that declared by the Menem administration. This was a difficult task since opposition (Peronist) governors, who controlled a large chunk of the congressional vote, denied their support. To carry out budgetary changes that would permit the country to comply with the deficit limits allowed by previous agreements with the IMF (and reflected in the 1999 "Fiscal Convertibility Law"), the incoming administration decided to bargain for a new fiscal pact.[61] This agreement was attained in December 1999, four days before the De la Rúa administration came into office.

The central government committed to transfer a fixed amount to the provinces, independently of the revenues collected. The new administration envisioned that through an increase in income and sale taxes (*"impuestazo"*), the additional amounts needed to neutralize the fiscal deficit would be collected. The central government also committed to implement a plan of financial assistance and financial reform (FFDP) to allow the provinces to afford their 2000 needs.[62] The provinces committed "to pass Solvency and Fiscal Responsibility laws" and to fulfill the terms of the FFDP if they chose to adhere to that. The degree of fulfillment is summarized in Table 2.14.

After taking office, the De la Rúa administration was characterized by a rather quick political deterioration, including the resignation of the (Frepaso) Vice President Carlos Alvarez. In that context, the government needed an additional fiscal pact to pass a consistent budget for 2001. The bargaining dynamics were similar to what we have studied so far in this chapter: an executive under foreign pressure for "consistency," opportunism by some provinces, some topical issues included alongside quasi-structural reforms, some efficiency-enhancing paragraphs here and there (on budgeting practices and fiscal transparency), and so on. Governors complained loudly about the lack of fulfillment of the previous pact, or

---

[61] This was not the first time in Argentine history that the national government is, under IMF pressure, forced to sign an agreement with the provinces that leads to further costs down the road. For some previous episodes (in particular, the 1988 Tax-Sharing Law), see Saiegh and Tommasi (1998). This reinforces a point that I have been making in this and related papers (see, for instance, Braun and Tommasi, 2002): International organizations should understand better the political economies of the countries in which they operate.

[62] The latter was called *Fondo Fiduciario para el Desarrollo Provincial* (FFDP), with the usual political euphemism of using the word "development" for what are mostly financial adjustment programs.

Table 2.14. *1999 Fiscal Pact*

Agreement	Degree of Fulfillment/Accomplishment
a. The federal government fixed a monthly transfer of 1,350 million pesos to the provinces.	Total until the 2001 disaster
b. Both the federal and the provincial governments commit to sanction the new *Coparticipacion* law (required by the 1994 Constitution) during year 2000.	Nil
c. The provincial governments commit to pass both Solvency and Fiscal Responsibility Laws in their provinces along the lines of the Federal Fiscal Responsibility Law.	Fourteen provinces had passed this kind of law; many of those provincial laws have not been fulfilled afterward[i]
d. Implementation of the FFDP program.	Mixed
e. Tax harmonization in all levels of government[ii]	Nil
f. The federal government commits to finance provincial pension system deficits gradually if the province allows a federal audit.	There was some assistance to the provinces of Córdoba and Santa Fé

[i] The federal FRL was not fulfilled either. See the details in Braun and Tommasi (2002).
[ii] Interestingly,this later pacts call for the fulfillment of clauses of the 1992 and 1993 pacts that are as yet unfulfilled. This reflects on the inability of the system to enforce agreements.

rather some provinces complained about other provinces not fulfilling it. They committed (once again!) to pass a *Coparticipación* law. Provincial governments gained some more room to administer the few remaining national social programs (of limited use to solve the deep social problems of the country, but of high political leverage given the clientelistic use of targeting). Table 2.15 shows the main compromises and their fulfillment.

The most important clause in practice was the establishment of a fixed amount to be transferred to the provinces. The following depiction (of both pacts), from González, Rosenblath, and Webb (2002), is useful:

One major component of the Federal Agreement was that during the year 2000, the provinces would receive a fixed amount in automatic transfers. This provided the provinces with predictability in income, but the amount was also designed to allow the federal government to keep a larger share of incremental revenues expected both from an economic recovery and an increase in federal tax pressure. The calculation of the monthly fixed amount of US$1.350 billion during 2000 was roughly based on the average of the previous two years.

The Agreement also established that during 2001 the provinces would begin to receive an average of the three most recent years' legal amounts (i.e., an

Table 2.15. *2000 Fiscal Pact*

Agreement	Degree of Fulfillment
a. The federal government fixed a monthly transfer of 1,364 million pesos to the provinces for 2001 and 2002 and guaranteed a monthly transfer of 1,400 million pesos for 2003, 1,440 million for 2004, and 1,480 million for 2005	The later bargaining over this point was a compounding factor in the 2001 disaster
b. The provinces and the federal government commit not to increase primary spending	Both levels of government increased primary expenditure the first semester of 2001
c. The provinces pledged to sanction pluriannual budgets	Solvency and Fiscal Responsibility Laws establish this budget procedure Mostly unfulfilled
d. Transparency and wide diffusion of the fiscal and financial accounts	Partial fulfillment (nil in some provinces)
e. Implementation of the Fiscal and Social National Identification System	Partial fulfillment
f. Federal Agreement on Tax harmonization within 120 days	Nil
g. Budget increase for social and employment programs for 2001[i]	Was assigned in the budget but was underexecuted
h. Federal Agreement on Modernization of the State (within 120 days)	Nil
i. All governments commit to sanction a new Coparticipación law in 2001	Nil

[i] Half of this increase has to be distributed among provinces proportionally, and 50% according to 23.548 *Coparticipación* law proportions.

average of what the provinces would have received under existing fixed percentages established in the general *Coparticipación* and tax-sharing laws). In this way, the idea of moving towards a moving average of recent years' percentage shares was put in place. However, in addition, the provinces were offered a minimum guarantee for 2001 that was set at a level 1 percent higher than the fixed amounts of 2000. . . .

[D]ebt-restructuring deals were offered to smaller provinces, and the federal government promised that they would facilitate larger provinces' debt restructuring via private banks and the multilateral development banks. Plus, they would finance part of provincial employee pension systems' deficits if reforms were made to make the systems consistent with the national system. (Many smaller provinces had already passed their pension systems to the federal government; however, this feature was attractive to the larger provinces that still have their pension systems.)

One year later, this agreement was followed by a more comprehensive *Compromiso Federal por El Crecimiento y la Disciplina Fiscal*, signed in November 2000 by all provincial Governors, except the Governor of Santa Cruz, a small province in the south. This agreement included a number of clauses for provincial reforms in the area of state modernization, budgeting and the transparency of fiscal accounts. In terms of stabilizing transfers, this new agreement established a timetable for switching permanently to the moving average concept. However, as described below, there would still be guaranteed minimum amounts over transition period.

For 2001 and 2002, the provinces would receive a fixed monthly amount equal to US$1.364 billion. This figure was the guaranteed minimum for 2001 that had been stated in the previous 1999 *Compromiso* (where the actual amount was to be an average of three most recent years). Now it would be *both* a floor and ceiling for *both* 2001 and 2002. The amount itself implies an increase of US$14 million, or about 1 percent, over the amount received during 2000.

From 2003–2005, the provinces would start to receive a moving average of the three most recent years shared revenue amounts. In other words, it would be an average of what they would have received according to the old laws during the three most recent years. In case this moving average were to coincide with recessionary or low growth years, a guaranteed minimum amount is set: US$1.4 billion per month in 2003, US$1.44 billion in 2004 and US$1.480 billion in 2005. These minimum amounts represent approximately 2.6 to 2.8 percent increase per year in nominal terms.

Note that it is not clear what the federal government would do with the expected savings from the lower transfers. A fiscal stabilization fund that would lock up the savings so that they could be used later during recessions is not explicitly established by this *Compromiso*, although there is general language stating that this fund would be established in due course. Depending upon what growth rates one assumes, over the five year period, the provinces would lose anywhere from US$1.5 to US$7 billion in transfers that they would have otherwise received.

Any major recessions over the period would have implied that the provinces could break even or come out ahead. As it turned out, the floor did not strongly favor the provinces during the first half of 2001. In addition, the federal government created a new financial transactions tax with the revenues proceeding exclusively to the federal treasury. However, during the second half of the year, the fixed transfers would have implied significantly more resources than otherwise would have been the case. For 2001, as a whole, the provinces were to receive about $2.8 billion (about 1.1 percent of GDP) in transfers beyond what they would have received without the guarantee. This contributed to substantial fiscal, political and social stress during the latter part of the year. Ultimately, the federal government was not able to transfer the full guarantee and arrears accumulated.

The bickering over the lack of fulfillment of this clause was an important fact in the political dynamics leading to the demise of the De la Rúa government and the ensuing Argentine default. The procrastination in provincial governments signing a new agreement was a key factor in demolishing Argentine credibility in the eyes of international markets (The Economist, 2001).[63]

---

[63] Additional details of these dynamics, including the evolution of provincial government bonds, are provided in Section III.9 of the working paper version (Tommasi, 2002).

In December of 2001, President De la Rúa was ousted from government because of the incapacity of his administration to govern. This, in turn, had to do with idiosyncratic limitations and shortsightedness of the president and his entourage, with the fragility of the coalition that took him to power, and with the fierce opposition of Peronist provincial governors. The street riots and manifestations that marked the departure of De la Rúa were in part spontaneous mobilizations of the middle classes after their bank savings were expropriated but also largely a result of the mobilization of violent protests by the Peronist machinery of the province of Buenos Aires. After three presidents in a week, finally an agreement was reached in Congress to place the boss of that machinery, Eduardo Duhalde, in the presidential seat. At that point, it became patently clear that the real power in Argentina resides in provincial governors.[64] Their struggles for the economic crumbs of Argentina and for the presidential succession also marked the limits for the caretaker government of Duhalde (2002–2003).

In the presidential election of 2003, power was disputed among three Peronist governors and two more ideological center-right and center-left candidates. The Peronist governor of Santa Cruz, Nestor Kirchner, became the president. His government has been a (reasonably successful so far) attempt to build a governing coalition with several other provincial governors, plus some additional urban and ideological center-left electoral constituencies. As has been the case for the past several years, proposals for a new *Coparticipación* law (under IMF pressure) have always been on the table, but not sanctioned, and fiscal pacts have been signed in 2002, 2003, and 2004. In 2004 there was also a new "Fiscal Responsibility law," which was passed only after the right amount of "pork" was delivered to the mischievous governor of that day (the governor of Córdoba, Peronist José Luis de la Sota). We have no reason to believe that conditions are now any better for the instrumentation of a more fundamental and effective reform of the federal fiscal system.

IV. CONCLUSION

This chapter as well as many others in this book make abundantly clear that real-world fiscal federalism is more a story of self-interested

---

[64] Perhaps one positive aspect of the crisis was that some relevant actors such as the IMF finally understood the underlying political game and started dealing directly with the provinces in an attempt to build some more sustainable form of fiscal compromise.

politicians involved in a multiarena contest for political benefits than an exercise on optimal public finance design. This means that intergovernmental relations should be taken into account in their broader political interpretation when discussing "technical" issues such as tax reform or expenditure decentralization.

This chapter provides several examples in which naïve technical readings of what are fundamental political economy issues can lead to error. We find such a problem in the discussion of education decentralization, in the multiple technical recipes to resolve the problems of Argentine fiscal federalism, and in the optimism about some "fiscal rules" in Argentina.

Fiscal federalism in Argentina is profoundly intertwined with the national political system, through the political and fiscal interdependence among the national and subnational spheres. Many of the deficiencies of national economic policymaking have a "subnational drag." Fundamental reforms that could improve national and subnational policymaking would require complementary changes in federal fiscal arrangements and in the national electoral system. But, as highlighted repeatedly in this chapter, none of those reforms seems very likely at the time of this writing, partly because of the transactional complexity of their possible implementation and partly because some of these reforms go against the interests of the current power brokers.

Even if we recognize those difficulties, we should not ignore the fact that all interventions are political interventions and that there is no real escape for economists (and international organizations) interested in improving economic welfare from a truly political economy.

Bibliography

Bambaci, J., T. Saront, and M. Tommasi (2002). "The Political Economy of Economic Reforms in Argentina," Journal of Policy Reform 5(2): 75–88.

Bambaci, J., P. Spiller, and M. Tommasi (2004). "The Bureaucracy," Chapter 9 in P. Spiller and M. Tommasi, eds., *The Institutional Foundations of Public Policy: A Transactions Theory and an Application to Argentina.* Cambridge, UK: Cambridge University Press, forthcoming.

Braun, M., and M. Tommasi (2002). "Fiscal Rules for Subnational Governments: Some Organizing Principles and Latin American Experiences," Paper presented at the IMF/World Bank Conference on Fiscal Rules, Oaxaca, Mexico, February.

CEDI (1999). "Consensos Básicos sobre Relaciones Fiscales Federales y Coparticipación" (notes of a Forum on Fiscal Institutions taken by M. Iaryczower and M. Tommasi). Cuaderno de Opinión 4, Center of Studies for Institutional Development, Fundación Gobierno y Sociedad. Constitution of Argentina.

De Luca, M., M. P. Jones, and M. I. Tula (2002). "Back Rooms or Ballot Boxes? Candidate Nomination in Argentina," Comparative Political Studies 35: 413–36.

Dixit, A. (1996). *The Making of Economic Policy: A Transaction-Cost Politics Perspective*. Cambridge, MA: MIT Press.

Eaton, K. (1997). The Politics of Tax Reform: Economic Policymaking in Developing Presidential Democracies. Ph.D. Thesis, Yale University.

Eaton, K. (2001). "Decentralization, Democratization, and Liberalization: The History of Revenue Sharing in Argentina 1934–1999," Journal of Latin American Studies 33(1): 1–28.

Echavarría J., C. Renteria, and R. Steiner (2000). "Decentralization and Bailouts in Colombia." Mimeo, Inter-American Development Bank.

Escudé, C. (1988). "Argentine Territorial Nationalism," Journal of Latin American Studies 20(I): 139–165.

Faletti, T. (2001). "Federalismo y Decentralización Educativa en la Argentina. Consecuencias (no queridas) de la descentralización del gasto en un país federal," in E. Calvo and J. M. Abal Medina, eds., El federalismo electoral argentino: sobrerrepresentación, reforma política y gobierno dividido en la Argentina. Buenos Aires: INAP/EUDEBA.

Galiani, S., and E. Schargrodsky (2002). "Evaluating the Impact of School Decentralization on Educational Quality," Economia: Journal of the Latin America and the Caribbean Economic Association 2(2) Spring: 275–314.

Galiani, S., D. Heymann, and M. Tommasi (2003). "Great Expectations and Hard Times: The Argentine Convertibility Plan," Economia: Journal of the Latin American and Caribbean Economic Association 2(2) Spring: 109–160.

Gibson, E., and E. Calvo (1997). "Electoral Coalitions and Market Reforms: Evidence from Argentina." Mimeo, Northwestern University.

Gibson, E., and E. Calvo (2000). "Federalism and Low-Maintenance Constituencies: Territorial Dimensions of Economic Reform in Argentina," Studies in Comparative International Development Fall, 35(3): 32–55.

Gómez Sabaini, J. C., and J. Gaggero (1997). "Lineamientos para una Reforma del Sistema Tributario Argentino," Cuadernos de Economía 31, Ministerio de Economía de la Provincia de Buenos Aires.

González C., D. Rosenblatt, and S. Webb (2002). "Stabilizing Intergovernmental Transfers in Latin America: A Complement to National/Subnational Fiscal Rules?," paper prepared for the IMF/World Bank Conference Rules-Based Fiscal Policy in Emerging Market Economies, Oaxaca, Mexico, February 14–16.

Green, E., and R. Porter (1984). "Non-cooperative Collusion under Imperfect Price Information," Econometrica 54: 975–994.

Haggard, S., and S. Webb (2001). "Transfers and Incentives: Intergovernmental Fiscal Relations in Latin American Federations." Mimeo.

Hanson, M. (1996). "Educational Change under Autocratic Governments: The Case of Argentina," Comparative Education 32(3): 303–317.

Harberger, A. (1993). "Secrets of Success: A Handful of Heroes," American Economic Review 83(May): 343–350.

Heymann, D. (2000). "Políticas de reforma y comportamiento macroeconómico," in D. Heymann and B. Kosacoff, eds., *La Argentina de los Noventa: Desempeño económico en un contexto de reformas*. Buenos Aires: Eudeba.

Iaryczower, M., S. Saiegh, and M. Tommasi (1999). "Coming Together: The Industrial Organization of Federalism," Working Paper 30, Centro de Estudios para el Desarrollo Institucional, Fundación Gobierno y Sociedad, Argentina.

Iaryczower, M., J. Sanguinetti, and M. Tommasi (2000). "Una propuesta de reforma al federalismo fiscal argentino," Documento de Opinión 8, Centro de Estudios para el Desarrollo Institucional, Fundación Gobierno y Sociedad, Argentina.

Iaryczower, M., P. Spiller, and M. Tommasi (2002). "Judicial Decision Making in Unstable Environments, Argentina 1935–1998," American Journal of Political Science 46(4): 699–716.

Instituto Nacional de Estadisticas y Censos (INDEC). (2001). "Census Data." Avai-lable at http://www.indec.mecon.ar/Censo 2001.

Jones, M., S. Saiegh, P. Spiller, and M. Tommasi (2002). "Amateur Legislators – Professional Politicians: The Consequences of Party-Centered Electoral Rules in a Federal System," American Journal of Political Science 46: 656–669.

Jones, M., S. Saiegh, P. Spiller, and M. Tommasi (2004). "Congress and Career Paths of Argentine Politicians," Chapter 6 in P. Spiller and M. Tommasi, eds., *The Institutional Foundations of Public Policy: A Transactions Theory and an Application to Argentina*. Cambridge, UK: Cambridge University Press, forthcoming.

Jones, M., P. Sanguinetti, and M. Tommasi (1999). "Politics, Institutions, and Public Sector Spending in the Argentine Provinces," in J. Poterba and J. von Hagen, eds., *Fiscal Institutions and Fiscal Performance*. Chicago: University of Chicago Press.

Nicolini, J. P., J. Posadas, J. Sanguinetti, P. Sanguinetti, and M. Tommasi (2000). "Decentralization, Fiscal Discipline in Subnational Governments, and the Bailout Problem: The Case of Argentina." Mimeo, Inter-American Development ment Bank.

Nores, M. (1999). "The Argentine Decentralization Reform. An Implementation Analysis." Mimeo, School of Education, Harvard University.

North, D. (1990). "A Transaction Cost Theory of Politics," Journal of Theoretical Politics 2(4): 355–367.

O'Neill, K. (2001). "Return to Center? Fiscal Decentralization and Recentralization in Comparative Perspective," paper prepared for the 2001 Meeting of the Latin American Studies Association, Washington, September.

Palanza, V., and G. Sin (1996). "Estudios de caso: ley 23.696 (reforma del Estado), ley 23.697 (emergencia económica)." Typescript: Universidad del Salvador, Buenos Aires.

Palanza, V., and G. Sin (1997). "Partidos provinciales y gobierno nacional en el Congreso, 1983–1995," Boletín de la Sociedad Argentina de Análisis Político 3(5): 46–94.

Rebelo, S., and C. Vegh (1995). "Real Effects of Exchange-Rate Based Stabilizations: An Analysis of Competing Theories," in B. Bernanke and J. Rotemberg, eds., *NBER Macroeconomics Annual 1995*. Cambridge, MA: MIT Press.

Repetto F., K. Ansolabehere, G. Dufour, C. Lupica, F. Potenza, H. Rodríguez Larreta (2001). "Transferencia Educativa Hacia las Provincias en la Década del 90: Un Estudio Comparado," Working Paper 57, Centro de Estudios para el Desarrollo Institucional, Fundación Gobierno y Sociedad, Argentina.

Remmer, K., and E. Wibbels (2000). "The Political Economy of Decentralization in Latin America," APSA-CP American Political Science Association Comparative Politics Section Newsletter 11 (Winter): 28–31.

Saiegh, S., and M. Tommasi (1998). "Argentina's Federal Fiscal Institutions: A Case Study in the Transaction-Cost Theory of Politics," paper prepared for the Conference "Modernization and Institutional Development in Argentina," United Nations Development Program, Buenos Aires, May.

Saiegh, S., and M. Tommasi (2000). "An Incomplete Contracts Approach to Intergovernmental Transfer Systems in Latin America," in S. Burki and G. Perry, eds., *Decentralization and Accountability of the Public Sector. Annual World Bank Conference on Development Economics in Latin America and the Caribbean 1999.*

Sawers, L. (1996). *The Other Argentina: The Interior and National Development.* Boulder: Westview Press.

Schwartz, G., and C. Liuksila (1997). "Argentina," in T. Ter-Minassian, ed., *Fiscal Federalism in Theory and in Practice.* Washington: International Monetary Fund.

Spiller, P., and M. Tommasi (2003). "The Institutional Foundations of Public Policy: A Transactions Approach with Application to Argentina," Journal of Law, Economics, and Organization 19(2): 281–306.

Spiller, P., and M. Tommasi (2004). *The Institutional Foundations of Public Policy: A Transactions Theory and an Application to Argentina.* Cambridge, UK: Cambridge University Press, forthcoming.

Stepan, A. (1999). "Towards a New Comparative Analysis of Democracy and Federalism: Demos Constraining and Demos Enabling Federations." Mimeo, All Souls College, Oxford University.

The Economist (2001). "Argentina's Economy. At Last, a Deal," The Americas, November 17, p. 36.

Tommasi, M. (2002). "Federalism in Argentina and the Reforms of the 1990s" Working Paper 147, Center for Research on Economic Development and Policy Reform, Stanford University.

Tommasi, M., S. Saiegh, and P. Sanguinetti (2001). "Fiscal Federalism in Argentina: Policies, Politics and Institutional Reform," Economia: Journal of the Latin America and the Caribbean Economic Association 1(2): 157–211.

Tommasi, M., and A. Velasco (1996). "Where Are We in the Political Economy of Reform?," Journal of Policy Reform 1: 187–238.

Webb, S. (1999). "Argentina: Hardening the Provincial Budget Constraints." Mimeo, LCSPR, World Bank.

World Bank (2002). "Reforma de Politicas e Instituciones a favor de la Eficiencia y la Equidad del Gasto Publico," Informe 25991–AR. Washington D.C.: World Bank.

THREE

Australia

Central Fiscal Dominance, Collaborative Federalism, and Economic Reform*

John R. Madden

I. INTRODUCTION

The Australian federation, as it has evolved over the past century, has a number of distinguishing characteristics. A high degree of separation of taxes with federal government control over major tax bases has led to a very high level of vertical fiscal imbalance. Much of the dynamics of center–state relations occurs against the backdrop of fiscal dominance by the federal government. Borrowing by all levels of government is subject to a process of Loan Council endorsement. With regard to redistribution, Australia employs the most elaborate system of horizontal fiscal equalization of any federation.

During the 1980s a worsening external debt position helped focus attention on structural weaknesses in the Australian economy. Efforts to rectify these weaknesses and increase public and private sector efficiency have led Australia to undergo a wide range of economic reforms, including some changes to federal institutions and arrangements, over the past two decades. There have been changes to the borrowing rules for national and subnational governments, a new tax-sharing arrangement, and reviews of intergovernmental administrative bodies. A significant

* The financial support of CREDPR is acknowledged. I am grateful to Jessica Seddon Wallack and T. N. Srinivasan for their helpful comments and suggestions on successive drafts of this chapter. I am also grateful for comments from Nick Hope and Govinda Rao, the discussants for this paper at the Workshop on Federalism in a Global Environment held at Stanford University on June 6–7, 2002, from other participants at the workshop, and from James Giesecke, Mark Picton, and an anonymous referee. The usual caveats apply.

increase in collaborative federalism over the past decade has facilitated major reforms to Australia's internal markets.[1]

Over the past decade the Australian federal system has delivered substantial reform of the nation's internal markets, which has allowed Australia to increase its competitiveness and take advantage of greater global integration. Whereas most Organization for Economic Cooperation and Development (OECD) countries experienced a slowing of GDP per capita growth in the 1990s compared with the previous decade, Australia's experience was the reverse of this. Much of the acceleration in the Australian per capita growth rate in the past decade resulted from an improved productivity growth (Parham et al., 2000). Reduction of import barriers and reforms that improved domestic competition appeared to be important factors in overcoming the structural weaknesses in the economy and allowing Australia to catch up with best-practice productivity in other industrial countries.

The substantial increase in collaborative federalism that started the 1990s had, however, a wider agenda than internal market reforms. Federal–state government financial arrangements were a key item. Attempts by the states to achieve a greater degree of fiscal independence that would return real autonomy over their expenditure assignment have been unsuccessful, but they appeared to play a role in the dynamics of economic reform. The prospect of federal financial reforms operated as one of the incentives to the states to participate in federal–state collaborative economic reforms. From July 2000 the states began receiving all revenue from the federal government's new goods and services tax (GST). This in their eyes was perhaps a more desirable outcome than an expansion of their own taxing powers.

The economic reform process has not met the universal approval of the Australian population or its media. The term *economic rationalism* has entered popular parlance in Australia in a pejorative way (see Coleman and Hagger, 2001). Although such opposition has not stopped the reform process nor limited all governments' reaffirmation of their commitment to continued reform, the timing of many reforms, particularly the politically harder ones, has been pushed back a number of years. Opposition to reforms has caused a substantial backlash in many of the more rural

---

[1] The term *collaborative federalism* is adopted from Painter (1998), who presents considerable evidence of a major increase in intergovernmental cooperation during the 1990s and argues that this has made a significant change in the nature of Australian federalism. Painter (pp. 122–124) carefully distinguishes between collaboration and arm's–length cooperation.

electorates. Rural and regional Australia have not fared as well as Australia's capital cities in obtaining the benefits of globalization and reforms. Economic reforms aimed at lowering cross-subsidization of communication services and the like have resulted in considerable political pressure for putting a moratorium on reforms that hurt what is colloquially known as "the bush." Notions of common citizenship rights to a certain level of government services are widely held throughout the Australian community and such concepts underlie the country's horizontal fiscal equalization (HFE) system.[2] However, there has been constant debate between the more populous and the smaller states about the benefits of what is the most detailed fiscal equalization system of any federation. HFE is designed simply to allow states an equal capacity in service provision and has had little impact on the regional divide between winners and losers in the growth stakes.

Before analyzing the reforms of the 1990s and ongoing reforms, we look at some of the major political and economic features that make up the landscape of Australian fiscal federalism.

II. AUSTRALIAN POLITICAL STRUCTURE

II.1. The Federation

Australia comprises six states and two territories. (See Figure 3.1 for a map showing state and territory boundaries.) The states are the original colonies that formed the Commonwealth of Australia by adopting a federal constitution in 1901. The two territories were administered by the federal government for much of the twentieth century, but in recent decades they have been self-governing and are now treated for virtually all intents and purposes like states.[3] Unless otherwise noted, the term "states" will be used to cover both states and territories. The federal government is usually referred to as the Commonwealth Government and this is the terminology that is used in the remainder of this chapter.

---

[2] Garnaut (2002, p. 235) considers Australians to have an unusual focus on "horizontal" equity, which he defines as "similar treatment of people in similar positions in the society."

[3] The Northern Territory and Australian Capital Territory were granted self-government in 1978 and 1988, respectively. The Commonwealth still administers a number of small offshore territories. However, the territories may not be on quite the same footing as the states, as instanced by the Commonwealth in 1997 rendering invalid a Northern Territory 1995 law allowing euthanasia.

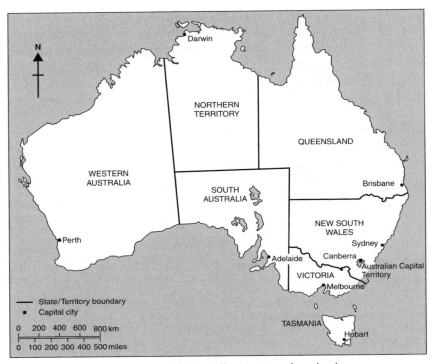

Figure 3.1. Map of Australian states and territories.

II.2. The Constitution

The Constitution gives a small number of powers exclusively to the Commonwealth Government, notably the minting of money and (of particular relevance) the imposition of customs and excise duties. The Commonwealth also shares many powers with the states, particularly in areas of interstate and international activities. The main areas of federal powers of this type are defense, foreign affairs, taxation, trade, communication, banking, insurance, social welfare, quarantine, and industrial disputes that extend over state borders. Although these powers are nominally held concurrently with the states, most of these areas have been vacated by the states, and where a state law is inconsistent with Commonwealth law, the Constitution determines that the latter prevails. The states have sole (residual) powers, in general, over law and order, education, health, social and community services, natural resources, rail and road transport, urban and industrial development, public utilities, and ports. However, the Constitution's provision that the Commonwealth Parliament can "grant financial assistance to any State on such terms and conditions as the

Parliament thinks fit"gives the federal government the capacity to influence state policy and administration in these areas.[4]

Other sections of the Constitution relevant to this chapter

- give the Commonwealth government exclusive power over customs
  and excise (Section 90) and
- prescribe that all trade within Australia should be absolutely free (Section 92).

There are approximately 650 local government units in Australia. This
third tier of government is not formally recognized by the Australian
Constitution and was established by state government legislation. State
governments delegate to local governments such functions as local public works, waste disposal, town planning, recreation, local transport, and
certain health and welfare services.

II.3. Mechanisms for Revising Center–State Relations

Although center–state relations have changed markedly since federation,
hardly any of this change has been via constitutional amendments. Changing the Constitution requires a referendum in which an amendment is
supported by an overall majority and a majority in four of the six states
(Section 128). Some forty-four proposed changes put to referenda have
only resulted in eight amendments, and those adopted were of a largely
uncontentious kind. However, decisions by the High Court, Australia's
highest court (which can review the constitutionality of Commonwealth
and state legislation), have led to significant changes via interpretation
of particular sections of the Constitution.[5] For instance, the Court's ruling that the Commonwealth could override state governments through
its external affairs powers when the Commonwealth had an international
agreement on a matter has extended the Commonwealth's role into areas
that had been previously seen as being exclusively within the purview of
the states.[6] A series of High Court decisions have severely narrowed the
state governments' tax base.

Over time the Commonwealth has also been able to strengthen its position in many areas, limiting the real autonomy of the states by exercising

---

[4] See the Australian Constitution, Section 96.

[5] The High Court is analogous to the United States Supreme Court, but it is inclined to
make much more literal interpretations of the Constitution than its U.S. counterpart.

[6] In 1983 the High Court ruled in favor of Commonwealth legislation that prevented the
Tasmanian government from constructing a hydro electric dam largely on the basis of
Australia's international environmental obligations.

Box 3.1. *Intergovernmental Interactions*

THE INSTITUTIONS OF INTERGOVERNMENTAL RELATIONS

The key institutional bodies are the following:

- *Council of Australian Governments*: This meeting of the Prime Minister, Premiers (states), and Chief Ministers (territories) has now super-
  seded Special Premiers' Conferences.
- *Ministerial Council for Commonwealth–State Financial Relations or
  Treasurers' Conference*: This annual meeting is held to discusses grant
  allocations to the states (which until recently this was done at the
  annual Premiers' Conferences).
- *Loan Council*: This council considers government borrowings and has
  the same membership as Treasurers' Conference (see Section IV.3 for
  details).
- (Special-purpose) Ministerial Councils: These act include ministers at
  Commonwealth and state level of a particular portfolio.

There are also supporting committees of officials, working parties, and
joint boards and commissions.

THE BUREAUCRACIES

The Commonwealth and state governments each have their separate
bureaucracies, which operate as completely separate entities. These
bureaucracies primarily interact through the various bureaucratic committees just mentioned. In addition there are of course innumerable informal relations among officials from the various governments.

STATE–STATE INTERACTIONS

Prior to many of the meetings of ministers or officials outlined here, the
state members of the particular bodies meet, without the Commonwealth
members, to discuss the agenda, issues, and presumably tactics.

There are also interjurisdictional agencies that administer joint
projects that might involve substantial externalities. A prime example
is the Murray–Darling Basin Ministerial Council, which has members
from the Commonwealth and each of the states through which this river
system flows. The Council makes decisions about sustainable water allocations and the environment of the river basin.

POLITICAL IMBALANCE

The smaller states are overrepresented in the Senate. Each of the original states has twelve member Senate electorates with senators being elected on the basis of proportional representation. The territories have two senators each. There is no state imbalance in the House of Representatives, where the government of the day is determined. The electorate consists of 150 single-member seats with representatives chosen by preferential voting. The two most populous states have just below 60% of the population and seats.

Voting in the Senate virtually never occurs on state lines, although state issues undoubtedly play an important role in internal party policy formation. All major parties are federally structured, with state branches being responsible in the main for senate nominations.

its rights to make grants conditional as well as by its domination of the Loan Council, the body controlling government borrowing.

Important changes to Commonwealth–state relations have also come through changes to the various bodies through which the processes of intergovernmental relations operate (Painter, 1998). Australia has a long tradition of establishing intergovernmental bodies through which the executive arms of the various governments can confer, bargain, and make collaborative decisions on policies and programs. Warhurst (1987, p. 261) notes a hierarchy of cooperative intergovernmental arrangements, from formal ministerial council meetings, down through "formal and informal agreements, policies, and programs," to day-to-day contacts. Wettenhall (1985) lists intergovernmental agencies established during different decades, starting with the River Murray Commission in 1914. According to Painter (1998, p. 92), "the number and scope of all types of intergovernmental arrangements has accelerated in recent years."[7]

The evolution of the Premiers' Conference is particularly interesting. In the early years of federation, Premiers' Conferences occurred only periodically and covered a wide range of topics. Over time they developed into an annual meeting that mainly involved the Commonwealth announcing the size of its various grants to the states. Additional Premiers' Conferences were still held from time to time to discuss various issues. As

---

[7] Painter (1998) discusses, in detail, changes to many facets of intergovernmental relations in the 1990s that made Australian federalism "fundamentally" more collaborative. However, in this chapter, my concern is more with the major reform decisions that gave Australia a stronger federal economy.

Table 3.1. *Basic Features of Australian States and Territories, 2002–2003*

	Area (thousands of km²)	Population (millions)[i]	GDP (A$ billion)[ii]	Average GDP Growth Rate (%) 1992–93 to 2002–03[iii]	Average GDP per Head Growth Rate (%) 1992–93 to 2002–03[iii]	Per Capita Disposable Income[iv] (A$)
New South Wales	800.6	6.682	265.3	3.6	2.5	26,189
Victoria	227.4	4.911	192.6	4.0	2.8	25,492
Queensland	1,730.7	3.801	128.9	4.6	2.7	21,647
South Australia	983.5	1.526	48.8	2.8	2.4	22,394
Western Australia	2,529.9	1.950	83.5	3.5	1.9	24,045
Tasmania	68.4	0.477	12.7	1.5	1.5	20,171
Northern Territory	1,349.1	0.199	9.0	3.5	1.9	26,078
Australian Capital Territory	2.4	0.323	15.0	3.1	2.5	36,831
Australia[v]	7,692.0	19.873	756.2	3.8	2.5	24,677

i At end of financial year.

ii A$ indicates Australian dollars.

iii Average annual compound growth rate (chain volume measures) from 1992–1993 to 2002–2003.

iv Gross household disposable income per head of mean population.

v Slight differences from first three column totals are due to inclusion of Commonwealth-administered territories in figures for Australia as a whole.

Source: Australian Bureau of Statistics publications: *Year Book Australia 2001* (Cat. No. 1301.1), *Australian Demographic Statistics, March Quarter 2004* (3101.0), *Australian Economic Indicators October 2004* (1350.0), *State Accounts 2002–03* (5220.0).

we shall see, in the 1990s such Special Premiers' Conferences, and subsequent meetings of the Council of Australian Governments (COAG),
became an important component in the growth of a more collaborative
federalism in Australia.

III. ECONOMIC BACKGROUND

The basic features of the economies of Australia's eight states and territories are shown in Table 3.1. Although there are differences across the
states, the variations in economic structure and standards of living among
the states are not particularly large. Over the past decade the export-
oriented states of Queensland, Western Australia, and the Northern Territory have grown slightly faster than the two most populous states, New
South Wales and Victoria (which together make up around 60% of the
economy). The two smallest states (not including the territories), South
Australia and Tasmania, have grown at much lower rates than the rest
of the economy, and both have somewhat more elevated unemployment
rates.

A graph of Australia's GDP growth rate over the past two decades is
shown in Figure 3.2. As can be seen the nation enjoyed a healthy growth
rate of around 4% in a typical year of the 1990s.[8] This partly reflects the
effects of productivity-increasing economic reforms put in place during
the decade. It was the experience of the 1980s that formed a catalyst
for those reforms. One of the most important of these experiences was
the worsening current account deficit, which, following a marked deterioration in the three years prior to 1985–1986, led to Treasurer Paul
Keating's warning that corrective action needed to be taken to avoid an
external debt crisis. Keating identified the cause of the deficit as the fall in
prices for Australian export commodities, but he stated that overcoming
this required fundamental structural adjustment.[9] The primary macroeconomic instrument used by the government to tackle the external deficit
problem was increases in interest rates to dampen strong growth in GDP
and consequentially reduce imports. A tight fiscal policy was also introduced, of which severe cuts in grants to the states was a main component.

---

[8] The poor growth rate in 2000–2001 probably reflects a distortion resulting from the timing
of investment activity associated with the introduction of the goods and services tax.

[9] In a popular radio interview Keating put the case dramatically, saying, "if this government
cannot get the adjustment . . . then Australia is basically done for. We will just end up being
a third-rate economy . . . a banana republic" (quoted in Bell and Head, 1994, p. 13). This
rhetoric was successful in awakening the Australian public to the problem and preparing
the ground for the government's policy reaction, although probably at some political cost.

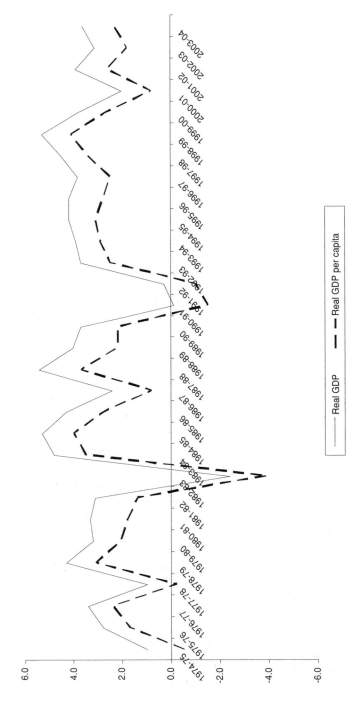

Figure 3.2. *Growth in Australian real GDP (percentage change on preceding year). Source:* Australian Bureau of Statistics, *Australian National Accounts: National Income, Expenditure and Product* (Cat. No. 5206.0), Table 3. Key National Aggregates: Annual (Electronic product – time series)

Whether Australia's current account deficit presented a problem that warranted the drastic interest rate policy imposed by the government is debatable, particularly as the majority of Australia's external debt was private. Pitchford (1989, 1990) and Sjaastad (1989) present persuasive arguments that no satisfactory case had been made that the Australian current account deficit was excessive. Whether there was any sort of external account crisis and the degree of efficacy of the government's monetary policy in overcoming it are debatable, but the "crisis" did appear to galvanize governments and business toward the idea that microeconomic reforms (trade liberalization and internal market reforms) were needed as a long-term solution.[10] This matter is examined further in Sections VI.1 and VIII.

IV. STRUCTURE OF FISCAL FEDERALISM

IV.1. Vertical Fiscal Imbalance

Australia exhibits a very high degree of vertical fiscal imbalance (VFI) in comparison to similarly long-established federations.[11] This high degree of VFI is due basically to subnational governments being shut out from the major sources of government revenue in modern economies, namely, personal and company income tax and all forms of sales taxes. The states' exclusion from the latter taxes results from the High Court's interpretation of the (federally exclusive) excise tax as including any taxes that might directly affect the production or sale of goods.[12] The Commonwealth's total control over income taxes dates back to 1942, when the Uniform Income Tax Act was introduced as a temporary wartime measure. In Section VII.2 we discuss why the states, despite having the legal right to reimpose state income taxes, have never found themselves able to do so successfully.

Australia's level of VFI has been very high for over half a century. There was some lowering of the level in the mid-1990s, but Grewal (1995)

---

[10] The term *microeconomic reform* is very commonly used in Australia "to refer to changes in government policy directed at improving the efficiency of use and allocation of Australia's resources" (Productivity Commission, 1998, p. 1).

[11] The Review of Commonwealth–State Funding (2001) indicated that Australia's VFI was considerably greater than those for Germany, Canada, and the United States. According to the Review, states' reliance on federal grants was 37% for Australia, but only 25% for Germany, 16% for Canada, and 9% for the United States.

[12] For a detailed review of the many High Court rulings that involved unusually wide interpretations of excise, as opposed to the economist's definition of excise as a production tax, see Saunders (1997).

argues that this came at the cost of the states making a greater tax effort in the area of inefficient taxes.[13] In 1997 the High Court banned the states' business franchise fees on tobacco, alcohol, and petroleum products, ruling that they were effectively excise taxes.[14] This adverse decision eliminated over 15% of the states' own-source revenue. The Commonwealth instigated a rescue package, increasing its own tax on the affected products (the Safety Net Surcharge) and handing the revenue back to the states. There were, however, various complications owing to significant interstate differences in franchise tax rates, and it was clearly a stopgap measure (James, 1997). The problem was solved in July 2000 when a Goods and Services Tax (GST) was introduced in Australia.[15] Under an intergovernmental agreement all GST revenue collected by the Commonwealth government would be provided to the states, which would no longer receive the general-purpose-revenue assistance they previously received from the Commonwealth. In terms of the federal government's tax mix, the GST mainly replaced the wholesale sales tax and a portion of personal income taxes. However, under the agreement the states acquiesced to the discontinuance of the Safety Net Surcharge and to a requirement that they cease to impose several of their existing (more inefficient) taxes.[16]

Revenue sharing of taxes collected by the national government is often considered to be a way of reducing the level of VFI (Groenewegen, 1990). However, it is unclear whether the GST arrangements have lowered Australian VFI in any meaningful sense. Although the Commonwealth has argued recently that the GST should be regarded as a state tax that is merely collected by the Commonwealth, the Australian Bureau of Statistics (ABS) treats the GST as a Commonwealth tax.[17] The GST revenue-sharing arrangements do not have constitutional force, unlike

---

[13] Mathews and Grewal (1997) standardize conventional measures of VFI to remove the effects of discretionary policy changes. The standardized measure shows a much-reduced improvement in the 1990s and a higher imbalance than in the early 1970s.

[14] New South Wales sought to defend a challenge to the tobacco franchise fee by reopening the definition of excise duty. Painter (1998) argues that the state did so in an attempt to establish a more certain revenue base.

[15] Prior to this Australia, unlike most developed countries, did not impose any form of value-added tax.

[16] The states were required to cease accommodation taxes, financial institutions duty, and stamp duty on marketable securities, and to adjust their gambling taxes to take into account the GST. It was also agreed to review in 2005 whether a range of other state government stamp duties should be retained and to cease state debit taxes at that date.

[17] It is worth noting that following the High Court's 1997 decision the ABS continued to treat business franchise taxes as state taxes, since in that case the Commonwealth was undoubtedly collecting these taxes on the states' behalf.

the case of Germany's revenue-sharing arrangements. It is worth noting in this respect that from 1976 to 1985, a fixed share of Australian income taxes (or of all federal taxes after 1981) was earmarked as the states' share, but this was abandoned in 1985–1986 as a fiscal contraction saw the Commonwealth sharply cut its grants to the states. Sharman (2001) speculates that this might also happen eventually in the case of the assignment of revenue from the GST to the states. Using the ABS definition, in 2002–2003 the Commonwealth still collected 72% of total general government revenues even though its own-purpose outlays represent only 51% of general government outlays. In contrast, state and local governments raised only 24% of total revenues. (See Tables 3.2 and 3.3 for government finance statistics that show the basic features of expenditure and revenue assignments.) These figures differ very little from historical measures of VFI over an extended period.

IV.2. Grants

Table 3.4 shows Commonwealth payments to state and local governments by major grant category for the year 1997–1998 (the final year that the states were permitted to collect business franchise taxes on their own behalf), 2000–2001 (the first year of operation of the GST), and 2002–2003. There was a substantial increase in the size of Commonwealth payments between 1997–1998 and 2000–2001, largely explained by the Commonwealth replacing revenue from the now discontinued state franchise (and certain other) taxes with GST revenue.

Although the Commonwealth agreed to distribute to the states all GST revenue from the year the tax was introduced (2000–2001), for each state this would have amounted in that year to less than the revenue forgone from the previous grants scheme (including the abolished state government taxes and certain expenditures agreed to by the state government).[18] The Commonwealth guaranteed under the intergovernmental agreement that no state's budgetary position would suffer as a result of the introduction of the GST. To meet this obligation the Commonwealth is paying state governments additional grants, or Budget Balancing Assistance (BBA), to cover the difference between GST revenue and a guaranteed minimum amount, computed as the revenue forgone.

---

[18] The state governments agreed to fund a First Home Owners Scheme and to compensate the Commonwealth for the cost of administering the GST.

Table 3.2. *Share of Each Jurisdiction in General Government Outlays, 2002–2003*[i]

	Share (%)				Total Expenditure: All Governments (A$ billion)[iii]
	Commonwealth Government	State	Local	Multijurisdictional[ii]	
Social security and welfare	90	9	1	–[iv]	77.376
Health	43	56	1	–	47.597
Education	2	71	0	27	41.004
General public services	59	23	17	1	16.406
Public debt transactions	64	34	2	–	15.821
Transport and communications	12	62	27	–	15.438
Defence	100	0	0	–	13.307
Public order & safety	14	82	3	–	13.095
Housing and community amenities	7	47	46	–	9.228
Other economic affairs	53	37	9	–	7.085
Recreation and culture	28	39	33	–	7.281
Agriculture, forestry and fishing	39	61	1	–	4.138
Fuel and energy	78	21	~0	–	4.298
Mining, manufacturing and construction	70	20	10	–	2.156
Other	~0	70	30	–	0.888
TOTAL	51	39	6	4	275.120

[i] Excludes transactions among other sectors within general government.

[ii] This category basically consists of public universities.

[iii] A$ indicates Australian dollars.

[iv] – indicates zero.

Source: Australian Bureau of Statistics, *Government Finance Statistics* 2002–03 (Cat. No. 5512.0). Shares for total row are based on unpublished ABS data. Shares for expenditure by purpose are estimates by the author. An underlying assumption for all estimates is that transactions between levels of government are generally grants to lower levels of government.

Table 3.3. *Own-Source Revenues by Government, 2002–2003[i], in A$ billion[ii]*

	Commonwealth Government	State Governments	Local Governments	Multi-jurisdictional[iii]
Income taxes	131.278	–[iv]	–	–
Payroll taxes	3.085	10.157	–	–
Taxes on property[v]	0.013	14.166	7.201	–
Goods and services taxes	31.257	–	–	–
Excise & levies	21.468	0.003	–	–
Taxes on international trade	5.573	–	–	–
Taxes on gambling	–	3.843	–	–
Taxes on insurance	–	3.132	–	–
Motor vehicle taxes	–	4.693	–	–
Other taxes	1.639	0.328	–	–
Sales of goods and services	3.805	10.491	6.148	5.692
Dividend income	3.958	3.263	0.040	0.050
Other revenue	4.113	8.806	2.892	0.853
TOTAL	206.189	58.882	16.281	6.595

[i] Figures are for general government revenue exclusive of current grants and subsidies.
[ii] A$ indicates Australian dollars.
[iii] This category basically consists of public universities.
[iv] – indicates zero.
[v] Includes taxes on financial and capital transactions.
Source: Australian Bureau of Statistics, *Taxation Revenue* 2002–03 (Cat. No. 5506.0) and *Government Finance Statistics* 2002–03 (Cat. No. 5512.0).

In 2000–2001, Commonwealth grants – comprising GST revenue, the BBA, and specific-purpose payments (SPP) – made up about half of total state general government revenue. Revenues from GST and BBA are distributed among the states on the basis of Commonwealth Grants Commission (CGC) recommendations, to equalize fiscal capacities, in the same manner as was the case for the general purpose grants that the GST replaced. Australia's system of horizontal equalization and reform possibilities are discussed in Section IV.4.

The SPPs (or tied grants) for both recurrent and capital purposes amount to around 40% of total Commonwealth grants to the states. Although SPPs have a long history in Australia, it was not until the 1970s that there was a rapid growth in these types of grants.[19] The

[19] See Section V for a discussion of the reasons behind the rapid growth in SPPs in the 1970s.

Table 3.4. *Total Commonwealth Payments to State and Local Governments*
as a Percentage of GDP

	1997–1998	2000–2001	2002–2003
General purpose payments	2.8	–[i]	–
GST revenue provision to the states	–	3.6	4.0
Budget balancing assistance	–	0.4	0.1
National competition policy payments	∼0	0.1	0.1
Special revenue assistance	0.1	∼0	–
Specific purpose payments "to" the states	2.0	2.1	2.1
Specific purpose payments "through" the states	0.6	0.7	0.7
Specific purpose payments direct to local government	∼0	0.1	0.1
Total Commonwealth payments to the states	5.6	7.0	7.2

[i] – indicates zero.

Source: First column of figures derived from 1997–1998 budget outcome figures in Commonwealth Treasurer *Budget Paper No. 3* (1998–1999). Next two columns derived from Commonwealth Treasurer *Final Budget Outcome* (2000–2001) and (2002–2003). GDP figures (at current prices) used in the calculations are from *Australian Economic Indicators* (Cat. No. 1350.0), various issues.

Commonwealth promised that SPPs would not be reduced as part of the GST reform process. The CGC does not make recommendations regarding the distribution of SPPs, but it does adjust its recommendations on the distribution of general purpose grants to offset much of the interstate differences in the allocation of SPPs. Thus, as Garnaut and FitzGerald (2002b, p. 291) attest, "the CGC effectively controls the allocation of all Commonwealth payments across the states." The bulk of SPPs cover current and capital expenditure in education, hospitals, roads, and housing. Certain SPPs merely pass through the state governments, notably to higher education and local governments. Most SPPs are not subject to any rigorous matching requirements, but they do involve intricate intergovernmental arrangements. Section VII.2 describes how desires to reform SPP conditions have been an integral part of the collaborative federalism reform push of the 1990s.

IV.3. Public Sector Borrowing

The Loan Council, a unique feature of Australian federalism, has supervised borrowings of three tiers of government for over seventy years. It commenced operations on a voluntary basis in 1927 to coordinate terms and conditions of loans by Commonwealth and state governments who were competing for funds in a thin domestic capital market – the former to refinance World War I debt and the latter to finance soldier settlement and infrastructure development (James, 1992).[20] In 1927 the Council was formalized by the Financial Agreement, later ratified in a 1928 constitutional amendment. The Council until recent times comprised the heads of governments of the Commonwealth and each of the states or their nominees. The Commonwealth had two votes, plus a casting vote. Although it was possible that the Commonwealth could be outvoted, in practice it could also dominate the Loan Council because of its near monopoly over major revenue sources.[21] From the time of the inflationary economic boom of the early 1950s the Commonwealth began using the Council as an instrument of macroeconomic management (James 1992). A number of commentators have noted that this allowed the Commonwealth not only to influence the economy but also to circumscribe the fiscal independence of the states (Saunders, 1990).

Gramlich (1984) notes that the more stringent the Loan Council restrictions were, the more creative the states were in devising ways of circumventing the Council. Initially this took the form of employing statutory authorities, not covered by the Financial Agreement, to undertake borrowing on behalf of general government. In 1936 a voluntary "Gentlemen's Agreement" was negotiated to bring such borrowing under Loan Council supervision. From the 1970s the states found new methods to circumvent the Council through the exploitation of unconventional financing arrangements, such as leveraged leaseback schemes (which also involved some tax avoidance) and "security deposits" (Gramlich, 1984).[22] In the four years prior to 1983–1984 the share of state and local authority borrowings approved by the Loan Council plunged from 95% to 25% (James, 1992). With the effectiveness of the Loan Council compromised, the Gentlemen's Agreement was abandoned in 1984 in favor of a system of global limits over total borrowing.

---

[20] Mathews (1984) notes that the "existence of the Loan Council itself helped to blunt overseas criticism and improve the credit standing of Australian governments."

[21] The states did outvote the Commonwealth in 1951, but they could not raise the funds to reach the higher borrowing limit.

[22] Attempts to circumvent the Loan Council have not been exclusively a state activity. An attempt in 1975 by senior federal government ministers to evade the Loan Council ultimately led to a constitutional crisis and the dismissal by the Governor-General of the Whitlam government (Mathews and Grewal, 1997, pp. 63–65).

Under the new arrangements states were free to determine the terms and conditions of their borrowing. The states had begun to set up central borrowing authorities, and in 1991–1992 a ceiling of 22% of overseas debt in state borrowing was lifted. Pressure to further relax controls was still present, particularly given deregulation of the private financial sector in the mid-1980s. In particular, government business enterprises (GBEs) were seen to be at a disadvantage relative to private sector firms owing to Loan Council borrowing constraints. As we shall see, governments were in the process of placing their GBEs on a commercial basis and this led in 1991 to exemptions from control under the global limits for GBEs operating in competitive markets. New procedures were agreed to in December 1992; these would switch the focus from global limits to the relating of borrowing allocations to governments' deficit (surplus) adjusted for a number of other transactions that have the characteristics of borrowings (Australian Loan Council, 1993).[23]

Improved reporting requirements to provide accurate, transparent, and meaningful information that facilitates financial market scrutiny of public sector finances are a key part of current requirements. Each government nominates a Loan Council Allocation (LCA) for approval by their fellow Loan Council members, but the LCAs are not binding in a legal sense. With the reforms of the early 1990s, the Loan Council had moved "from an approach based on rigid compliance to one based on the establishment of a credible and transparent framework for the allocation of net borrowings" (Australian Loan Council, 1993).

In virtually deregulating government borrowings the Loan Council stated they wished to provide the basis for the states to assume "greater freedom and responsibility in determining their financing requirements." However, to ensure that borrowings were consistent with the states' fiscal and debt positions as well as the nation's overall macroeconomic strategy, the Loan Council implemented a joint Commonwealth/State budget forecasting exercise. Until 1998 the LCAs nominated by the states were considered in the light of the *National Fiscal Outlook*, which contains nationally agreed debt targets.[24] Since then each government's own forecasts have been used to set their own targets. Governments are now

---

[23] For this exercise the budget result that is estimated combines underlying general government and the public trading enterprise sector. Public financial enterprises are excluded.

[24] In considering the appropriateness of LCA nominations the Council also considers such matters as public sector risk exposure to infrastructure projects with private sector involvement.

required to present three years of forward estimates, plus actual outcomes, within a uniform presentation framework.

Although the traditional functions of the Loan Council might well be redundant (Painter, 1998, p. 105), the Loan Council would appear to be playing as an important a role as ever in ensuring budgetary responsibility by state governments. The motivations for the introduction of the new borrowing arrangements, circumvention of the Loan Council rules, and GBE–private sector capital market distortions bear testimony to the difficulties of instituting hard budget constraints on subnational governments. There is evidence that the new approach does put pressure to bear on state governments to exercise fiscal responsibility. Credit ratings of state governments by international agencies are given considerable media attention and voters seem to be very attuned to the dangers of fiscal mismanagement.[25] These factors are no doubt partly an outcome of some adverse experiences of the 1980s, discussed in Section VI.1. It can be seen that the market and political pressures reinforce each other.

However, although the state governments have enjoyed credit rating upgrades in recent years, with the majority now having a Standard and Poor's AAA rating,[26] it is not clear whether this is all due to the new Loan Council approach. By the time the new arrangements were legislated in 1994,[27] most state governments had already determined a path for moving their annual budgets into surplus. As Australia began to emerge from recession in 1991–1992 the aggregate level of state general government deficits peaked and by 1995–1996 the states had in aggregate achieved an annual surplus. The eight state governments' combined accounts were in deficit in only one of the following five years. It remains unclear, however, how well the Australian arrangements might perform in producing workable hard-budget constraints in a situation where decentralized governments were not committed to sound financial management.

The arrangements do not prevent the Commonwealth from ever bailing a state out of financial trouble.[28] However, the strict reporting rules,

---

[25] Australian state politicians are quick to point out the interest savings involved when the credit rating of their state is upgraded.

[26] This rating is for the state nonfinancial public sector.

[27] The new arrangements were agreed to by Commonwealth, state, and territory governments in the Financial Agreement Act of 1994.

[28] Credit rating agencies would no doubt be aware that the Commonwealth Government does at times assist states that find themselves in financial difficulties. In 1990, the State Bank (of Victoria) collapsed and was rescued by the Commonwealth Bank, which acquired it at the behest of the federal government. This occurred shortly before the partial privatization of the Commonwealth Bank commenced.

budget forecasting process, and a narrow tolerance rule for departures from LCAs should mean that a dangerous state government debt problem is highly unlikely to develop in the future without warning.[29] If financial market discipline fails, the Commonwealth should be able to use its fiscal dominance to head off any such emerging problem. A precedent for strong Commonwealth action occurred during the global limits arrangements, when the Commonwealth threatened Queensland with a reduction in its general revenue grants if that state exceeded its borrowing limits (Senate Select Committee, 1993). In the new GST environment, the Commonwealth retains actual control over the aggregate level of SPPs, which it should be able to use as a general lever on the states as a whole if current Loan Council arrangements ever broke down.[30] It also might threaten changes to an individual state's share of total grants as a specific lever on that state.

IV.4. Horizontal Fiscal Equalization

Australia has for many years employed a system of interstate transfers aimed at removing regional disparities associated with fiscal imbalance. The CGC was established in 1933 to recommend special grants for states suffering disabilities arising from federation. For many years these grants involved only a few claimant states. However, in 1982 Commonwealth grant procedures began to be used to distribute all general-purpose grants to the states. Grewal (1999) considers that Australia "has adopted arguably the most elaborate and comprehensive approach" to HFE of any federation. The CGC assesses state per capita shares of the revenue pool on the basis of *both* revenue-raising capacities and the unit costs of providing public services in each of the states.

The Commonwealth Grants Commission (CGC) (1999) describes the principle of fiscal equalization it employs as that where

[s]tate governments should receive funding from the Commonwealth such that, if each made the same effort to raise revenue from its own sources and operated

---

[29] If a government becomes aware that its borrowing is likely to exceed its LCA by more than 3% it must report this to the Loan Council, with an explanation that may be made public. Tolerance limits have been exceeded by governments at various times, but not to an extent that has caused concern.

[30] Although the Commonwealth stated its intention not to reduce the level of SPPs, this is unlikely to constrain it in dealing with any future state government(s)' intransigence over borrowing levels.

at the same level of efficiency, each would have the capacity to provide services at the same standard.

Intergovernmental grants that compensate states for disabilities have been a feature of the Australian federation for much of its history, but they have been the target of a continued campaign for their elimination by the two largest states (New South Wales and Victoria) over the past dozen or so years. These states have been long-term donor states, in the sense that they receive less than their population share of total Commonwealth funding to the states. Together with Western Australia, which recently joined the category of donor state after a long history as a claimant state, New South Wales and Victoria commissioned an independent inquiry on whether the current system [of allocation] is effective in relation to[31]

(i) efficient allocation of resources across Australia to enhance national employment and economic growth;
(ii) achievement of equitable outcomes for all Australians; and
(iii) simplicity and transparency.

There are substantial reasons for considering the CGC approach to be ineffective in all three areas.[32] There is a long literature on the question of HFE. Proponents of equalization point to the work of Buchanan (1950), Boadway and Flatters (1982), and others as providing a sound theoretical foundation for HFE. In a report to the New South Wales Treasury, Swan and Garvey (1995) consider the nine main arguments in support of HFE and find each unconvincing. Even if there were some merit in these arguments, none of them, Swan and Garvey point out, form the basis for the methods employed by the CGC. For instance, the CGC makes much of the fact that its method protects the autonomy of the states by not requiring them to provide the same standard of public services as the other states; it merely provides them the capacity to do so. Buchanan's 1950 paper argues for equalization, however, on the basis that equals in different states should be treated equally. Even if the CGC designed its formula to enable this, fiscal autonomy means that such equal treatment still may not occur.

There has been some debate in Australia about the efficiency effects of the HFE system. Petchey (1995) argues that equalization can correct for inefficient migration that is motivated by the desire to capture rents that

---

[31] See Garnaut and Fitzgerald (2002a).

[32] This certainly is the finding of the Review produced by the states' independent inquiry, which was released at the end of August 2002.

only accrue to persons who locate in a particular region.[33] Dixon, Madden, and Peter (1993), in contrast, find that HFE results in inefficiencies arising from overmigration to regions that are less efficient in the production of public services, but they also demonstrate that this sort of inefficiency is necessarily relatively small. These and other authors have normally taken it as given that the CGC's redistribution formula is policy neutral (in the sense that a state cannot influence the amount of its grant by adopting a particular policy stance) as the Commission claims. However, Swan and Garvey (1995) demonstrate that the formula, because it uses population rather than revenue and expenditure weightings to compute standard expenditure and revenue efforts, causes claimant states to specialize in areas of expenditure and revenue raising in which they are inefficient. Swan and Garvey estimate the annual dead-weight cost of this inefficiency (conservatively, they say) at A\$13 to \$54 million.

A more serious inefficiency arising from HFE emanates from the well-known flypaper effect. Dixon et al. (2002) find that the ratio of the quantity of discretionary state government goods to the quantity of private goods and leisure increases with the per capita level of Commonwealth grants to a state. Given that states with larger grants normally find it more expensive to produce government goods (i.e., an expenditure disability) one would expect, if anything, a negative relationship (i.e., a reduction in quantity purchased as the price rose). Under the assumption that households have a similar preference pattern for public goods across states, the positive relationship that was found would appear to be evidence of a flypaper effect. That is, state governments that receive large grants value discretionary state government expenditure more than their citizens do.[34] Dixon et al. develop an ingenious small general equilibrium model that captures the main elements of a federal system. It includes, *inter alia*, state governments that choose their quantity of discretionary state government goods and their tax rate to maximize a combination of private goods, leisure, and discretionary public goods for the state. The numerical values for the (Cobb–Douglas) function's exponents differ from those of the corresponding utility function for households. Dixon et al. find that a change from HFE to equal per capita grants increases economic welfare

---

[33] Thus, if in a two-region world mineral royalties were distributed to all residents of a region, this would encourage overmigration to the mineral-rich region in the sense that the marginal product of labor would differ between regions.

[34] The distinction between discretionary and nondiscretionary state government expenditure would appear to be an attempt to distinguish between expenditure in areas where there are unavoidable state disabilities and areas where the level of expenditure is a matter of policy choice.

by about A\$169 million per annum. Most of this gain is due to a reduction in the flypaper effect as labor relocates to states where the government's preferences for public goods are more in line with their preferences.[35]

In addition to the inefficiencies captured by this modeling exercise, the elaborate HFE process in Australia generates a degree of waste simply through the cost of its administration. Revenue disabilities (positive or negative) are separately assessed by the CGC for nineteen categories of revenue items. Computations of expenditure disabilities are based on separate assessments for forty-one expenditure categories and are computed for a range of factors, such as the physical environment, dispersion, urbanization, diseconomies of scale, and population characteristics.[36] Assessment of each category involves detailed information from the states on policy and other factors that affect revenue and expenditure. Often the required data are not available or incomplete, and the CGC must use its judgment. Despite the acknowledged professionalism of the CGC, the complexity of the process (including adjustments to allow for interstate differences in SPP receipts) leaves it open to question. The process also involves lobbying costs as states seek to influence the outcome by attempting to convince the CGC to alter the categories to which various items are assigned.[37]

Although the CGC is only an advisory body, its recommendations are generally accepted by government. The CGC is highly respected for its independence and impartiality. The Commission is a frequent promoter of the HFE method that it employs, seeing it as delivering interstate equity while still allowing diversity of behavior (see, for instance, Commonwealth Grants Commission, 1995, and Rye and Searle, 1997). The late Russell Mathews, a member of the CGC for almost twenty years, described HFE as the linchpin of the Australian federation in one of his numerous articles on the subject (Mathews, 1994).

CGC commissioners are appointed by the Commonwealth Minister for Finance and Administration, following consultation with the states,

---

[35] Dixon et al. (2002) also find that the effects of diminishing marginal returns from labor tax reductions (and increasing marginal congestion costs) in a positively affected state means that the welfare benefits from a reallocation of funds toward a donor state or away from a subsidized state initially rise and then fall. The interstate differences in the slopes of these benefit curves gives rise to an optimal allocation of grants (in pure economic efficiency terms) that differs from equal per capita grants.

[36] In the past the number of categories were even larger – thirty-one in the case of revenue and seventy in the case of expenditure (Grewal, 1999).

[37] Grewal (1999) provides an example of one state's grant significantly increasing as the result of out-patient expenditure being switched from Community Health Services to Hospital Services.

but with no requirement for any particular state composition of the Chairperson and three members. However, the HFE formula does result in a consistent pattern of redistribution of general purpose funding from the two most populous states of New South Wales and Victoria to Queensland, South Australia, Tasmania, the Australian Capital Territory, the Northern Territory, and, until recently, Western Australia.

The CGC process has for many years been seen as one that forms a unifying role in the federation. It forms a convenient way for the Commonwealth to transfer a potentially divisive issue to a body outside of the political arena, thus avoiding the risks and probable odium of deciding matters of redistribution by a simpler formula or some other method open to political lobbying. The degree to which Australia's fiscal equalization system might be an outcome of its electoral system does not appear to have been a subject for research, or even speculation. As in the United States, all states (but not the territories) have equal representation in the Senate. Whereas senators generally vote along party lines and virtually never along state lines, interstate issues are likely to play a role in determining policy positions within each of the main federally structured political parties. Senators from the claimant states do form a majority, though this leverage does not seem to be used to influence policy. Also, the amount redistributed away from the donor states (which comprise around 70% of the Australian population) is not large in per capita terms, though for the smaller claimant states the per capita amount received is relatively large. Significantly, in an attempt in early 2001 to have the HFE system changed, New South Wales and Victoria sought to restrict HFE payments so that they would be received only by the three states with the largest disabilities, namely South Australia, Tasmanian, and the Northern Territory, effectively trying to isolate politically Queensland and the Australian Capital Territory.[38] The move has been unsuccessful so far, and whether the nature of the HFE system might be partially politically determined remains an open question.

V. THREE PERIODS OF "NEW" FEDERALISM

Over the past three decades there have been three major periods of "new federalism" reforms. The first reform program, advanced by Gough Whitlam (Labor Prime Minister, 1972–1975) stemmed from the Australian Labor Party's view of federalism as standing in the way of

---

[38] Both Queensland and the Australian Capital Territory enjoy strong fiscal positions (New South Wales Treasurer, 2001).

implementing its social policy agenda (Galligan and Mardiste, 1992). Its members felt that the best way of introducing their policies was to use the Commonwealth's existing powers under the Constitution, particularly those powers relating to traditional grants. The Commonwealth would be the initiator of policy in areas of traditional state responsibility by the introduction of a new raft of SPPs. The share of SPPs in total Commonwealth grants more than doubled in the three years of the Whitlam government. The legacy of this significant change in the composition of Commonwealth grants continues to have a profound effect on Australia's fiscal federalism system up to the present time.

The second "new federalism" reforms of the Fraser government (1976–1983) were largely a reaction to the previous government's federalism policies. Fraser's Liberal government reaffirmed its allegiance to federalism, which the Australian Liberal Party had always supported as promoting democracy and accountability by dividing power (Roberts, 2001). The Fraser federal government instituted new financial arrangements with the states with the expressed aim of increasing state independence in terms of both expenditure and revenue. SPPs were reduced, as various Whitlam programs, particularly urban and regional development, were wound back. As noted earlier, revenue sharing was introduced by the Fraser government by designating fixed portions of personal income tax for each of the three tiers of government in place of general purpose payments. Enabling legislation passed in 1978 by the Commonwealth gave the states power to adjust the income tax rate for their residents. The Commonwealth would collect the surcharge (or administer the rebate) and adjust the state's tax entitlement as appropriate. The reasons why no state instituted a surcharge or rebate in the period until the *Income Tax (Arrangements with the States) Act* was repealed in 1989 are discussed in Section VII.2.

The third "new federalism" reform period did not commence until the 1990s. By that time the Hawke Labor government had been in office seven years and had undertaken reforms in a wide range of other areas.[39] Hawke proposed a series of Special Premiers' Conferences to undertake a major cooperative review of intergovernmental relations in Australia. On the agenda was a microeconomic reform program to improve Australia's international competitiveness, a plan for greater coordination in public service delivery to remove duplication and overlap, an

---

[39] The third reform period started with the Hawke Labor government (1983–1991) and continued during the Keating Labor government (1991–1996). The Howard Liberal government (1996 to 2005) continued the reform program.

effort to harmonize industrial relations and environmental issues, and a review of Commonwealth–state government financial arrangements.

The new federalism of Hawke differed from previous federal reform programs, as it did not involve an unequivocal unilateral action by the federal government. At the first Special Premiers' Conference in October 1990, the state premiers clearly showed their willingness to engage in the process and the conference put in place an agenda for reform. It is commonly held, however, that the states' priorities differed from those of the Commonwealth (see, for instance, Fletcher and Walsh, 1992). The federal government's primary motivation was to enable it to advance its microeconomic reform program in a drive to improve the efficiency of the Australian economy and its international competitiveness (Painter, 1998).

However, much of the reform program involved areas within states' jurisdictions so that their cooperation was essential. The states also had begun to develop a microeconomic reform program of their own, particularly in the area of GBEs, and linking their program with that of the Commonwealth had the advantage of achieving these reforms while possibly avoiding some of the political cost. Painter (1998) argues, however, that the states saw the posibility of changing fiscal federalism arrangements to acquire greater control over revenue sources and over expenditure in their constitutionally assigned areas such as education, health, housing, and transport. In these areas their objectives largely ran counter to those of the Commonwealth.

Painter considers that the extensive growth in collaborative federalism the intergovernmental review initiated is reshaping Australia's federal system in a fundamental way. Although center–state friction is still prevalent, he argues that intergovernmental committees at ministerial and official levels have for a decade worked toward policy and administrative solutions aimed at national approaches, removing interstate regulatory incompatibilities and interstate barriers. It could be argued that the signing of just a few intergovernmental agreements instigated the most important reforms that the process delivered to the Australian economy.

VI. COLLABORATIVE FEDERALISM

VI.1. "Crises" and Reform

The external balance "crisis" helped set the climate of ideas that convinced the federal government that there were structural deficiencies in the Australian economy (Gerritsen, 1992). From the time of taking office in 1983, the Labor government had shown a strong pragmatic tendency that made it amenable to economic advice and it introduced a number of major deregulatory reforms early in its first term. A strong campaign for trade liberalization by the Industries Assistance Commission (IAC) and other advisers to government began to take effect. In a May 1988 Economic Statement, major phased tariff cuts were announced.[40] A continuation of this program in a 1991 Industry Policy Statement meant that most nominal tariff rates were phased down to 5% by 1996. It is difficult to ascertain the degree to which a macroeconomic crisis spurred a reform climate, but there were clear long-run motivations in the government's trade policy. Thus Corden (1997, p. 117) hypothesizes that the Labor government was pursuing tariff reduction policies because it had come to believe that this "would raise national efficiency or productivity, and thus also make both higher real wages and improved welfare provision possible."

Having put in place reforms to make Australia more open to external competition (by financial market deregulation, floating the dollar, and lowering import barriers), the federal government began to turn its attention to internal barriers to trade. In 1989 the IAC was renamed the Industry Commission and its brief was extended to encompass the broad scope of microeconomic reform.[41]

A number of forces were also acting in the 1980s to increase the state governments' proclivity toward microeconomic reform by the end of the decade. One of the major forces was the Commonwealth Government's external debt reduction policy. During the latter half of the 1980s the federal government's fiscal contraction fell heavily on grants to the states (Mathews and Grewal, 1997, pp. 537–538). This was compounded by the negative impact of the 1991–1992 recession on the states' narrow tax base.[42] The revenue decreases intensified the states' concern with VFI and made them amenable to any reforms that might include changes to this area within the package.

---

[40] Nominal tariff rates above 15% would be reduced to that figure, whereas those between 15% and 10% would be reduced to the lower figure. However, the two most inefficient industries – 1. motor vehicles and 2. textiles, clothing, and footwear – were exempted and have faced much slower reductions in the levels of assistance they receive.

[41] Prior to this the IAC inquired primarily into the effects of protection against imports.

[42] Most states were for some time shielded from the federal cuts by increases in own-source revenues from those taxes that had booming asset prices and property values in their base. However, this position was rapidly reversed with the 1991–1992 recession.

However, the Australian state governments were also responsible for the financial difficulties into which they fell in the second half of the 1980s. This too proved to be a stimulus for reform. Several state governments' problems arose from state development corporations (such as the Victorian Development Corporation) providing venture capital to risky undertakings that failed and state banks (in Victoria and South Australia) collapsing in the wake of injudicious lending practices. In Victoria, the state government assured depositors of the safety of a financially troubled building society (Pyramid), despite the government seeming to have information to the contrary (Norman, 1995, p. 39). Having effectively provided a guarantee, the Victorian government had to sustain substantial costs in paying out depositors. Similar imprudent actions in Victoria and other states compounded the deficit problems of those states.

The first state to begin to make reforms to cope with the problem was New South Wales, which implemented a range of financial management measures and expenditure restrictions.[43] It began an extensive program of reforming its GBEs, which were severely overstaffed and heavily subsidized. Other states followed suit, reforming their GBEs, with the main purpose of repairing their financial position.[44] During the early 1990s all state governments that had experienced financial problems began to take action to reduce their burgeoning debt. The Hawke initiative to reform intergovernmental relations was seen by the states as an opportunity to improve fiscal arrangements with the Commonwealth, which they saw as a major cause of their financial problems (Painter, 1998).

VI.2. The Collaborative Federalism Reform Process

In this section we look principally at a process of reform that occurred in the first half of the 1990s. In particular we look at the process that resulted in national competition policy. This policy, as it was implemented, required collaborative behavior by governments, and it was one of the driving forces behind a change to the federal system itself, namely, through a significant increase in collaborative federalism structures and behavior.

To put the reforms to intergovernmental relations, and their major successful outcome – competition policy – in perspective, a brief overview of the different reform periods of the last two decades should be helpful.

---

[43] Not all states experienced a financial crisis. Queensland, a traditionally low taxing and spending state, and the Australian Capital territory were exceptions.

[44] Painter (1995) notes that it was only by taking large dividends from its GBEs that the New South Wales government managed to balance its budget.

The period from 1983 to 1988 was concerned mainly with external and financial market reforms. The Australian dollar was floated in 1983, financial markets were deregulated between 1984 and 1986, and a program of trade liberalization commenced in 1988. The reform periods are, as might be expected, not absolutely discrete, with further tariff-reduction plans being introduced in 1991 and phased in over subsequent years. Although Australia now has very low trade barriers, removal of the remnants of protection (particularly in regards to motor vehicles and clothing, textiles, and footwear) is still being slowly implemented.

Toward the end of this reform period, a second reform period – this time of internal markets – commenced. The two-airline policy was abandoned in 1987, with new entrants permitted from 1990. The Commonwealth and state governments began to reform their GBEs in the late 1980s. This second reform period was soon overtaken by the collaborative-federalism reform period. The broad reform areas that were agreed on at the October 1990 Special Premiers' Conference (see Section V) formed the basis of the agenda for a series of meetings, both at heads of government level and for working parties of officials. Early action was exhibited with the establishment of national commissions for both road and rail transport and a national electricity grid management committee. By July 1991 there was also an in-principle agreement that there should be mutual recognition by the states of each other's regulations on goods and occupations. Parallel with these nationwide cooperative reforms, individual governments continued their own reform programs, particularly in relation to the infrastructure industries.[45]

While these reforms were advancing, however, the path to the comprehensive national competition policy agreement and to the other cooperative reforms of Hawke's new federalism was not smooth. It is instructive to examine a little of the history of the process leading to the intergovernmental agreement on national competition policy.

Indeed the collaborative federalism process was almost derailed later in 1991 when it became a central issue in a Labor Party leadership battle. Paul Keating, who was soon to become prime minister, criticized the collaborative process through which, he said, the Commonwealth could lose control of important macroeconomic instruments. The federal government subsequently rejected a state income tax proposal by the state premiers, who in turn withdrew from the next scheduled Special Premiers' Conference.

---

[45] This period also saw the reforms to the Loan Council that resulted in the current system.

Box 3.2. *Mutual Recognition*

Mutual recognition, which was agreed to in 1992 and implemented the following year, was designed to remove state regulatory barriers that prevented goods, services, and labor from moving freely between Australian states. Under mutual recognition, goods that met regulatory requirements in the state of origin could be sold in another state, regardless of any conflicting regulations in the destination state. Similarly, members of a regulated occupation in one state could enter an equivalent occupation in another state without satisfying any additional requirements (Office of Regulatory Review, 1997).

But the reform process was remarkably resilient. The premiers held their own meeting and agreed on a scheme for introducing mutual recognition that involved referring power to the Commonwealth to enact uniform legislation. Among other matters that were resolved at this meeting was an in-principle agreement for a national competition policy. Nor did that more centralist Paul Keating, upon assuming the prime ministership, stop the momentum that collaborative federalism had built up. The need for state government involvement in ongoing microeconomic reform was an important element in the process continuing.

In 1992 it was agreed that the Council of Australian Governments would be established, following a proposal by the state premiers for a permanent forum. COAG, which replaced the Special Premiers' Conferences, would meet at least once a year; the regular Premiers' Conference on financial grants would also continue. A more generous position by the Commonwealth Government on general-revenue funding to the states also helped the process along.

However, a considerable amount of federal–state conflict also continued. Proposed "anti-union" industrial relations reforms by Victoria's Liberal government were overridden by the federal Labor government using its external affairs power. In this atmosphere, the states refused to take part in a review of competition policy (Painter, 1998). The Commonwealth went ahead and established an independent review of national competition policy to be conducted by a committee headed by Professor Fred Hilmer. The Committee's report (Hilmer et al., 1993) outlined an array of competition reforms that were to form the basis of the bulk of the collaborative-federalism competition-policy reforms.

It was not clear to the Hilmer Committee that the reforms had to involve intergovernmental collaboration. Although the Committee declared that it supported the adoption of a cooperative model, this view was "tempered by the need to provide streamlined decision-making..." (Hilmer et al., 1993, p. xxxvi). The Committee felt that the Commonwealth could largely implement the reforms unilaterally if need be and, in any event, its preferred implementation method was by the states referring some of its powers to the Commonwealth. However, it was not certain that the unilateral approach was constitutional. The type of collaborative approach eventually adopted was probably the most politically feasible approach.

Microeconomic reform was very much on the agenda in the second half of 1993 and an intergovernmental working group was established to determine new initiatives. All governments publicly affirmed the need for microeconomic reform. However, some states had reservations surrounding the creation of national markets.[46] Painter (1998, p. 48) argues that there has been a long history of smaller states attempting to protect their markets from interstate imports. The states also saw the intergovernmental considerations on competition policy as an opportunity to obtain a better financial deal from the Commonwealth. The states argued that the new microeconomic reform initiatives advanced by the Commonwealth would cost them revenue, whereas reforms previously engaged in by the states were designed to improve their budgetary position. The states made their agreement to competition policy conditional on Commonwealth compensation for consequent loss of revenue and on progress in reducing the level of tied grants.

An impasse developed over this issue at the April 1994 COAG meeting (Painter, 1998, p. 52). It was overcome, however, by the meeting agreeing that "all governments should share the benefit" and that the relative impacts on Commonwealth and state revenues would be assessed by the Industry Commission (COAG 1994). The Commission's report provided computable general equilibrium model results that showed large GDP gains from implementing what it termed "Hilmer and related reforms."[47]

---

[46] For example, the South Australian government were unwilling to pass over the control of its transmission system to a national electricity grid or to allow free interstate trade in gas through a pipeline network (Painter, 1998, p. 47).

[47] The Commission estimated that the reforms would increase Australian GDP by 5.5%. This was a smaller projected increase than estimated by most previous studies, although larger than the 3.4% estimate by Madden (1995) in a report commissioned by the Business Council of Australia, a major advocate of the reforms. Quiggin (1996, 1997) challenged

It also estimated that the reforms would increase state and local government revenues by 4.5%, compared with a 6.0% increase for the Commonwealth (Industry Commission, 1995, p. 83).

The national competition policy reforms (Box 3.3) were agreed to at a COAG meeting in April 1995. As is dealt with in more detail in the next section, the agreement essentially involved a commitment by the Commonwealth and state governments to carry out a comprehensive program of reforms over a number of years in their particular jurisdiction. The agreement outlined the different areas to be reformed (or reviewed) under the overall national competition policy framework. Although many of the detailed reforms were left to the states to initiate, it was agreed that there would be a series of competition policy payments to the states, conditional on the states meeting the timetable for reform. The states also gained a "permanent" arrangement under which the real per capita value of the annual general purpose grants they received would be maintained (Painter, 1998).

This period marked the high point of the collaborative federalism process in Australia. The most important items on the reform program put in place have to a very significant degree been carried through. Given that it was arguably "the most comprehensive program of economic reform in the country's history" (Samuel, 1999), it is perhaps not surprising that other large-scale reform initiatives should make little progress while the competition policy program was being worked through. Some progress has been made in removal of certain areas of overlap and duplication in SPPs, although the states' call for more general untying of grants has not been answered. In late 1995 political reasons caused the states to drop their demands for a state income tax option and focus their attention on seeking a tax-sharing arrangement (Painter, 1998).[48]

The years from 1996, following the election of a federal Liberal government in March of that year, could be viewed as a consolidation of the reform period. The national competition policy program, under whose umbrella the bulk of microeconomic reform now fell, was implemented over the following years (although not on schedule). The Howard

---

the Commission's computations as being very much an overestimate. Whiteman (1999) provides a good rejoinder to some of Quiggin's major criticisms.

[48] Painter points out that the federal Labor government was seeking to exploit the prospect of a state income tax in the upcoming election. Most state governments at this time were Liberal and thus were concerned with the damage their calls for new tax arrangements might mean for their federal party's electoral prospects.

Box 3.3. *National Competition Policy*

The national competition policy comprised intergovernmental agreements that set up template Commonwealth legislation that the states would apply to their jurisdictions. These agreements essentially extended Australia's competitive conduct (or antitrust) rules to all areas of the economy as well as set out principles for overseeing the pricing policies of GBEs, thereby ensuring competitive neutrality between GBEs and private-sector competitors,[i] structural reform of government monopolies, reviews of anticompetitive legislation, the formation of rules that allowed business to gain third-party access to the services of essential infrastructure, and the application of competition principles to local government.

The commencement of the national competition policy reform program in 1995 affected a wide range of activities. The reviews of anticompetitive legislation included those of state and Commonwealth statutory marketing arrangements (which involve quantitative restrictions on a wide range of agricultural products), state government building regulations and approval processes, and state-government-approved private monopolies in the taxi and newsagents industries. Reviews were expected to increase the extent of competitive tendering to provide general government services for both the Commonwealth and the states. State government legislation to extend competitive conduct rules to unincorporated enterprises would remove monopolies and restrictions within the legal and medical professions, in dentistry, and in optometry and pharmacy.

Reform of state government GBEs in public utilities and ground and water transport and Commonwealth GBEs in communications and air transport is of particular importance for competitiveness. For instance, the states were to establish an interstate electricity network to allow free trade in bulk electricity, to ensure cost-reflective electricity pricing, and to introduce competitive neutrality in GBEs' financing structure. In rail, states were to remove statutory monopolies, continue corporatization, separately fund community service obligations, and institute competitive neutrality in pricing. Port authorities were to be corporatized, regulatory and commercial activities were to be separated, and berthing and other facilities were to be contracted out or privatized. Instances of planned Commonwealth reforms were the removal of Australia Post's monopoly in letter delivery, the ending of the legislated duopoly in telecommunications, and the achievement of a commercial return on nonregulatory services to aviation.

---

[i] Competitive neutrality prevents GBEs from obtaining a competitive advantage over private businesses, merely by dint of the former's public ownership. This means that the GBEs should face the same tax regime, regulations, and other incentives as private businesses.

government was a strong supporter of microeconomic reform, although its determination to generate a surplus federal budget led to a retreat from the guarantee to the states on the level of general purpose funding. The economic reform process turned toward tax and labor market reform. During recent years the collaborative reform process has shifted into the background with annual COAG meetings focusing on the more detailed reforms. COAG has issued communiqués on over fifty subjects, but the communiqués on competition policy and microeconomic reform issues clearly involve its most sweeping reforms. COAG agreements range from gun control (1996) to a new corporations agreement (2002). Probably the most important COAG reform outside competition policy has been on water resources policy, which is an important area for Australia. The pressure to lower the degree of VFI has been reduced as state governments have moved to sound financial positions after a decade of tight expenditure control. State governments have been successful in their demand for part of the revenues from a growth tax; currently all revenue from the GST is assigned to the states.

VII. VERTICAL FISCAL IMBALANCE REFORM BIDS

VII.1. VFI – A Problem?

Since the Commonwealth gained control of all income taxation sixty years ago, VFI has been an area of public disagreement between the states and the Commonwealth. How committed the states have been to their call for the reduction of VFI is a question considered in section VII.2. The states' main concern has been the pressure that VFI has placed on their revenue and, ever since SPPs became a major source of funding, on having to meet conditions relating to tied grants. It may be argued that VFI has remained because all levels of government have something to gain from it. It provides a way for the Commonwealth to institute policies in areas constitutionally assigned to the states, and it allows state politicians to take credit for expenditure on many SPP-supported projects while avoiding the responsibility of fully funding the project.

There is a considerable literature in Australia on the problems associated with the nation's high level of VFI (e.g., James, 1992; Grewal, 1995; Mathews and Grewal, 1997; Painter, 1998; Walsh, 1991, 1993, 1996b). The cited works criticism of VFI includes the following:

- Centralized control of revenue has caused a centralization of decision making that acts against the responsiveness to regional diversity that is at the heart of federalism.
- The intergovernmental grants system causes a "blurring" of responsibility and insufficient accountability to taxpayers for expenditure decisions.
- Fiscal illusions are created as governments and voters fail to consider more than the own-revenue costs of state government expenditure.
- The pattern of public expenditure is distorted toward items that receive tied grant funding.[49]
- States are forced to rely on a narrow range of inefficient taxes.
- There is less scope for beneficial tax competition (of the sort that lowers excess burdens and compliance costs).
- State taxes are perceived to act on business,[50] even if this is not their incidence, leading voters to underestimate the tax cost of public expenditure.

The case against VFI is by no means incontrovertible. Brennan and Pincus (1998) call into question whether a conventionally measured flypaper effect necessarily means state government expenditure is out of line with voter preferences. They note that even if states could levy the full range of taxes, the marginal burden from a state tax is likely to be higher than for a federal tax. VFI thus might be evidence of a tax system designed to minimize excess burden. Thus, when a federal tax is levied on behalf of the states at an appropriate rate, observing that a state spends all of its grant, rather than the proportion a state would spend out of an increase in private income, need not be indicative of any problem. Brennan and Pincus also question the degree of fiscal illusion. They note that state voters are also federal voters and find it difficult to see why

---

[49] This is a form of the "flypaper effect." However, in this chapter we use a wider interpretation of the flypaper effect. Under this latter definition, a flypaper effect is indicated by an increase in the ratio of state government to private consumption with an increase in grant income.

[50] See Walsh (1993).

a system of grants that led to waste in every state would continue to be supported by federal taxpayers.[51]

There is, however, some empirical evidence of a flypaper effect operating in Australia. Dollery and Worthington (1999) find that, in Tasmania, local authorities with a higher than average dependency on grants also have higher than average public expenditure. However, they note that this might just be capturing the disability factors already allowed for by the Local Government Grants Commission. The analysis by Dixon et al. (2002), discussed in Section IV.4, avoids that problem, allowing for the disability factors by examining the relationship between quantities of public goods and grants. Dixon et al. find, at least for their database year and under the assumption of uniform household preferences across states, what appears to be a clear flypaper effect.[52] For their simulations they take the state with the smallest per capita grant, Victoria (which receives Commonwealth grants of 8% below the average), to have government preferences that reflect household preferences for every state. This is a good working assumption that would have no bearing on the analysis of HFE. However, if one traced the grant–expenditure relationship back toward the vertical axis, we would find that a hypothetical state that received hardly any Commonwealth grants would have even lower household preferences for government goods than that of the Victorian government.[53] The average state received a Commonwealth per capita grant (including SPPs) of well over two thousand dollars in 2000–2001. However, the most highly subsidized state (outside of the Northern Territory, which receives three times the average), Tasmania, receives close to 30% above the average. The size of the average Commonwealth grant, and a reasonably strong estimated relationship between the public

---

[51] On average, Australian voters would not gain from a system that encouraged waste and presumably would not be in favor of the federal taxation required to support it. A federal political party that made this connection and offered to reduce transfers would presumably gain electoral support.

[52] The authors assume that there is no clear pattern of household preferences that coincidentally saw citizens of subsidised states preferring a higher ratio of public to private goods. If there was a high correlation between the level of grants per capita and poorer states, such a pattern of household preferences might be expected (since poorer states, even though they might not have particularly high government expenditure per capita, could have a high public to private goods ratio simply because their household consumption is low). But in Australia the level of grants per capita is basically unrelated to a state or territory's income.

[53] One cannot trace the relationship right back to the vertical axis, as the relationship is specified in log-linear form (i.e., between the state government goods (Cobb–Douglas) exponent and the log of Commonwealth per capita grants).

to private goods ratio and the size of the per capita grant, suggests a replacement of the Commonwealth grants with own-source taxes *might* involve a very substantial reduction in a state governments' preference for public consumption.

The welfare effects of such a hypothetical reduction in VFI are uncertain. Presumably there would be little loss in administrative efficiency if the Commonwealth still were the collection agency for most taxes. However, with state governments setting the rates, there could be a less efficient tax mix. Also, horizontal as well as vertical tax competition could distort overall tax rates. The forgoing claim that horizontal tax competition lowers excess burdens might be invalid, for this sort of tax competition might produce quite the reverse effect on balance, particularly for taxes on mobile factors of production. It is difficult to assess whether lowering VFI might lead to an increase or decrease in the current practice of providing (often nontransparent) tax concessions on businesses (Industry Commission, 1996a).

However, given the apparent distortion in government expenditure levels associated with VFI, it would appear, on the face of it, that the gains from moving closer to vertical balance are likely to outweigh the costs.[54] This result is even more likely if the claim by Walsh (1996a) is correct. He considers that wasteful competition to attract new business development has almost certainly been "induced by Australia's degree of imbalance in fiscal powers and by the associated lack of breadth and flexibility in the sources of revenues available to the states." However, although it would seem desirable for Australia to reduce its level of VFI, accomplishing this has proved to be no easy task. In the next subsection we look at the main effort of state governments to reduce VFI by attempting to reenter Australia's major tax field, income taxes.

VII.2. State Income Tax

There have been four occasions when serious consideration has been given to income taxes once again being imposed at the state level (Sharman, 1993). The first occurred in the early 1950s when certain states challenged the legitimacy of the uniform tax legislation in the High Court. Although the High Court did determine that the states had the right to impose their own income tax, the challenge essentially failed because it

---

[54] However, further work is necessary before one could have confidence in such a conclusion.

was determined that the Commonwealth could "use its power to attach conditions to grants to block the States from re-entering the income tax field" (Garnaut and FitzGerald, 2002b, p. 290). This made it extremely difficult for the states to make a unilateral decision to recommence collecting income tax. The advent of more generous financial grants from the Commonwealth appears to have been sufficient to end the state governments' moves to reenter the income tax field.[55]

The Commonwealth Government's 1978 legislation to allow the states to charge (pay) an income tax surcharge (rebate) was essentially the Fraser government's own initiative. The states' agenda had moved on. The rapid growth in SPPs in health, education, and urban development during the proceeding Whitlam government had shifted the states' concerns to the size and composition of Commonwealth grants (Grewal, 1995). In 1975, the premiers requested that grants to the states be made on the principle of compensating the states for not having access to income tax revenue. The introduction by the Fraser government of a tax-sharing scheme in 1976 (see Section V) may be considered a sort of response to the premiers' demand (Grewal, 1995, p. 22). However, the 1978 Act allowing a state income tax surcharge (rebate) did not attract any state government interest in taking up the opportunity thus provided. This might partly be explained by the states being in a relatively good financial position at the time, despite reductions in SPPs and general-purpose capital funds. Sharman (1993, p. 228) maintains that the states were concerned that the surcharge scheme "might help the Commonwealth escape from some of the odium for a high level of personal income taxes, and aid its attempts to wind back its financial commitments to the states." Proponents of a state income tax argue that the surcharge scheme could have been instituted in a way that would have induced the states to take advantage of it but that the Commonwealth failed to give the states any tax room (Walsh, 1993). By this they mean that the Commonwealth's practice of maintaining its standard income tax rates means that states wishing to get direct access to income tax revenue through a surcharge would have to increase the marginal tax rates on its residents. Mathews and Grewal (1997) and Sharman (1993) argue that the only way to have made the system work would have been for the Commonwealth to reduce its income tax rate

---

[55] In 1970 a linkage drawn by the Commonwealth between VFI and being able to employ a satisfactory system of horizontal fiscal equalization caused the smaller states to lose enthusiasm for a state tax. Then in 1971, the Commonwealth, having raised the bulk of the payroll tax, effectively transferred the collection of that tax type to the states (Sharman, 1993).

and, at the same time, to reduce its aggregate grants to the states by the amount of the revenue forgone. This would have allowed the state to impose a surcharge that avoided any increase in tax rates on its residents, not lose any revenue, and have greater financial control because part of its revenue came via its own surcharge, rather than a grant from the Commonwealth.

The question of the distribution of tax powers arose again in the mid-1980s, when the Hawke government proposed options for a wide-ranging reform of the Australian tax system. Ultimately, these reforms had to wait another fifteen years for the advent of the GST, but the prospect of such reforms, *inter alia*, led the states to form a working party on the income tax issue. However, the Commonwealth showed their opposition to the prospect of a state income tax by repealing the Act that contained the surcharge/rebate provisions in 1989. As discussed in Section VI.2, the Commonwealth continued with this opposition into the 1990s despite the advent of the collaborative federalism period.

The main reason provided by the Commonwealth in repealing the income tax surcharge/rebate legislation was that it posed a danger to macroeconomic policy. However, this view was beginning to be seriously challenged at the beginning of the 1990s (Walsh, 1991; Madden, 1993). The report of the Working Party on Tax Powers (1991) concluded that a reduction in the level of VFI would not significantly damage the Commonwealth's capabilities in macroeconomic management or income distribution. The Working Party's viewpoint was of some importance as treasury officers from the Commonwealth as well as the states were members. Walsh (1993) considers this to be the first serious attempt by the states to regain an income tax capacity. Previous attempts he claims (Walsh, 1993, p. 1) were no more "than an ambit claim designed ultimately to secure more generous grants." Certainly the states pursued the matter with vigor during the early years of the intergovernmental reform process. Sharman (1993, p. 232) argues that the states now saw "a state income surcharge as a logical extension of their arguments for greater state autonomy coupled with the possibility of greater financial security than the present system had given them." However, the latter can be satisfied by an arrangement for sharing revenue that, as previously noted, the states successfully pursued after 1995. Although it is quite possible that some state premiers saw a state income tax as ensuring a more efficient federalism, it would seem that weakening the Commonwealth's fiscal dominance was a more likely goal. Nevertheless, the states' motivation in pursuing the matter, particularly because they now have access to 100%

of GST revenue, appears to have largely vanished for the foreseeable future.

VII.3. Overlap and Duplication

In considering what direction federal fiscal relations should move, Garnaut and FitzGerald (2002b) assume that the degree of VFI will continue to remain around its current level. These authors (who also authored the review of Commonwealth–state funding referred to in Section IV.4) direct their attention to the problems of HFE and the SPPs. With regard to the SPP arrangements, they note the considerable costs of managing a system that requires "continuous negotiation over conditions and guidelines, boundaries, administration, performance, reporting and accountabilities" (p. 294). Commonwealth and state officials engage in endless games to assert control, and although Commonwealth conditions do place restrictions on the states, Garnaut and FitzGerald note that "The States utilize the fungibility of money to retain a high degree of de facto control." This process carries clear costs of complex and confusing organizational arrangements. Many critics have pointed to the associated blurring of accountability.

There appears to have been little analysis of Australian SPPs in terms of conventional public expenditure theory, such as accounting for interstate spillovers from state government expenditure. The Commonwealth does appeal to the goal of ensuring that national objectives are met. Their expressed aim in the use of SPPs is to support their own policy objectives through the grant system rather than taking over responsibility for traditional state government functions. The states, however, appear to distrust these motives, as they perceive that the Commonwealth tends to focus on those projects that carry the least financial risk for it.[56]

The states have for many years made the case that the best way to avoid duplication and overlap is for the Commonwealth to abandon control of all areas already adequately covered by state legislation (Painter, 1998). This is now less likely than ever to occur. The GST intergovernmental arrangements (whereby after a transitional period the level of states' aggregate general-purpose current funding will be determined by the level of total GST receipts) creates a severe restriction, in a political sense at least, on the possibility of SPPs being reduced in favor of untied funding.

---

[56] This perception has been related via personal communications with state Treasury officials.

An intergovernmental working group was established to develop some best-practice principles on SPP and other matters that could be approved by the state governments. These include simpler accounting and reporting arrangements, less legalistic agreements, clearly defined objectives and processes, and a degree of flexibility in how state governments might decide delivery arrangements (Tasmanian Treasury, 2001). Although elements of these principles are now being referred to in the negotiation of new SPP agreements, the Commonwealth has yet to agree to the principles because of its objection to an input–output focus that the states consider to be a key principle. The states wish to claim any productivity improvements as being available to a state government for other projects. Opening up such a clear channel for fungibility of funds is unlikely to get Commonwealth Government approval.

Garnaut and FitzGerald (2002b) state that there is "wide support" for the consolidation of the plethora of SPPs. They advocate that a small number of sectoral programs could be monitored by assessing performance against agreed objectives with Commonwealth officials ceasing to be involved in the management of programs. It might take some time for governments to agree, but some progress in eliminating a degree of the problems associated with SPPs appears to be occurring.

VIII. CONDITIONS FOR SUCCESSFUL REFORMS

In Section V, some of the ingredients that led to the collaborative-federalism competition-policy reforms were discussed. In particular it was noted that the external balance and budgetary crises helped set the climate for economic reform, the former for Commonwealth reforms and the latter for state government reforms. In this section we consider this matter in more detail as well as other factors that contributed to microeconomic reforms in general and the collaborative-federalism reforms in particular.

There has been some limited consideration given in the literature to the timing of Australia proceeding down the microeconomic reform path. Gerritsen (1992) maintains that the contraction of Australian manufacturing that had been occurring since the 1970s despite high levels of protection had disheartened private interests who were the beneficiaries of the market distortions. This allowed various advisers, who had been making the public interest case for many years, to gain ascendancy. Gregory (1992) put forward a similar argument on the waning of support for protection, as it became clear that certain industries "would need ever-increasing levels of assistance if they were to maintain their market shares."

Gregory also argued that the poor performance of the Australian economy in the 1970s and 1980s had increased the demand for microeconomic reform in general. Dollery (1994) refined Gregory's argument by contending that when net rents to demanders and suppliers of regulation fell sufficiently, reform would occur.[57] Thus, following Peltzman (1989), he shows that Australian deregulation can be explained within the theory of regulation. Dollery and Wallis (2000) contend that the arguments of Rodrik (1996) can be used to explain how distributional uncertainty has led to infrequency of reforms in Australia, plus some recent "reform fatigue," and that the Australian conditions (particularly the 1986 "crisis") allowed agents for change to persuade a majority of citizens to accept reform (as was the case in New Zealand; see Wallis, 1997).

It is important to put the Australian balance-of-payments "crisis" in context. It certainly was not a dire crisis that needed urgent action.[58] Indeed, as previously discussed, there were strong reasons for not considering it as a crisis at all. However, the matter did have a major impact on policymaking at the time and it marked the start of a long period of economic reform. Australia had already commenced on a reform path prior to the "crisis," in the early to mid-1980s. There had been a long campaign for Australia to lower its protective barriers against imports from the time the Vernon Committee illustrated the cost of Australian protection in 1965. Important steps were taken in 1973 with the replacement of the Tariff Board by the Industries Assistance Commission (who were to take into account the economy-wide impacts of assisting a particular industry) and a 25% tariff reduction. At the end of the 1970s and the beginning of the 1980s there was a strong move toward free-market ideas in Australia as was the case internationally. The then Liberal government considered a number of microeconomic reforms, but little was accomplished before they were replaced by the Hawke Labor government. The new government was anxious to be seen as good economic managers, as the previous Labor government of eight years before had been considered incompetent in that area. Although a balance-of-trade crisis need not lead to economic reforms aimed at long-run targets, in this case the

---

[57] Dollery's argument relies upon unchanged costs of lobbying in a given industry – as explained by Dollery (1996) in a rejoinder to Quiggin (1995).

[58] Corden (1997, p. 120) notes the difference with developing countries' crises, commenting that Australia was able to "embark on more gradual reforms."

Hawke government saw rational economic policies of the sort advised by the Treasury as the path to success. The sudden success of the advocates of trade liberalization in 1988 (see Section VI.1) is indicative of the Hawke government's approach.

The structure of the Australian public service also appears to have played an important role in the promotion of rational economic ideas. During the 1970s the public service began to recruit numerous economists who carried with them the arguments for deregulation that had emerged in the international literature. Leading Australian economists, such as Max Corden and Bob Gregory, had a direct influence on the IAC staff. Key government departments, particularly the Commonwealth Treasury, and the research bureaus (which were less subject to ministerial direction), began to release public documents advocating reforms. It was particularly important that a body such as the IAC (and its successors, the Industry Commission and the Productivity Commission) issued independent reports.[59] This meant that rational economic analysis reached the public arena with some official status, even when it did not meet the approval of the government of the day. The Commission thus played an important educative role in making the cost of economic distortions transparent and in helping to establish an intellectual climate conducive to reform.

A further factor in the success of the reforms during the Hawke–Keating Labor governments was government and opposition support for many of the reforms, at least in terms of their broad thrust. It is frequently observed that nonconservative governments are often very successful in achieving economic reforms. It may be, as Corden (1997) speculates, that Labor governments, once they are convinced that economic-efficiency reforms will improve the welfare of their supporters, take the same preparedness to be radical in the pursuit of these reforms that they had previously demonstrated in their pursuit of social reforms (and, in a former time, interventionist policies).

The national competition policy agreed to by the 1995 COAG meeting did not involve the immediate implementation of any actual reform;

---

[59] The change of name to Industry Commission in 1990 signified a broadening of the Commission's role from one concerned mainly with inquiring into industries competing with imports to examining the resource allocation effects of government policies for industries throughout the economy. In 1996 the Industry Commission, the Bureau of Industry Economics, and the Economic Planning Advisory Commission were merged to form the Productivity Commission. The new Commission allowed a further extension of its predecessor's role, while maintaining "the principles of independence, transparency and an economy-wide view" (Industry Commission, 1996b, p. xix).

rather, it was an agreed reform program that would be implemented over a number of years. Part of that program involved legislation, part involved executive action, and part involved the carrying out of reviews that might lead to unspecified actions within a broad set of principles. Although the Hilmer report covered a very wide scope of economic reforms, the report included mostly general principles with only brief references to examples of particular industry sectors or classes of persons that might be affected. The mounting of concerted opposition to such a document would not have been an easy task. Dissenting voices were heard in the media in the early part of 1995, leading up to the Council of Australian Governments' decision to agree to the national competition policy. However, on the other side there were some very united lobbyists who provided concerted backing for the policy. A major supporter was the Business Council of Australia. Together with the National Farmers Federation and other peak industry groups the Council staged a forum titled, "Making Hilmer Happen" a few weeks before the COAG decision. Among the constituencies of these industry groups were some potential losers from the reforms. However, major employer bodies had been pushing for microeconomic reform for some years as a way of increasing the international competitive position of their membership in general.

The general public appeared uncertain about what the reforms entailed, but there also seemed to be widespread awareness that the reforms were expected to boost household income by a considerable amount. The average Australian household, it was estimated, would enjoy an boost in annual real consumption of A\$1,500 within five to ten years (Industry Commission, 1995). Economic modeling simulations also indicated that the benefits of the reforms would be widespread, with increases in average real household income in each state (Madden, 1995). Sophisticated economic analysis was an important aid to those groups who were pressing for the reforms. The Industry Commission (1995) provided a very detailed economic modeling study of the estimated effect of each reform. It may be argued that the results they produced represented the outer envelope of likely benefits, but it was difficult for reform opponents to dispute the potential for large benefits to flow from the reforms.[60]

In the immediate lead-up to the 1995 COAG meeting the state governments appeared to pose the only imminent danger to the smooth passage

---

[60] The only substantial academic criticisms of the Industry Commission's estimate were those by Quiggin (1996, 1997), as noted in Section V.2. However, these criticisms were mainly published after the 1995 COAG agreement.

of the competition policy agreement. The states had good reasons for supporting most of the reform program, but they also had concerns about how certain reforms might act on their revenues. Here the modeling work of the Industry Commission played a crucial role. The IAC demonstrated that the reforms would have a major positive effect on state government budgets (see Section VI.2). The benefits to Commonwealth government revenues were estimated to be even greater. The matter was resolved by the inclusion in the national competition policy agreement of a commitment for the Commonwealth to transfer over time around A$12.5 billion (1994–1995 prices) to the states. Of this amount A$4.2 billion was explicitly labeled as competition policy payments that were conditional on the states complying over the following years with the national competition policy timetable.

The characteristics of the political leaders involved were of particular importance in commencing the collaborative federalism arrangements at the beginning of the 1990s. Hawke had considerable abilities, experience, and interest in consensus politics. All but one of the state governments belonged to the same political party as the federal government. The leader of the one Liberal state government was strongly committed to reform. The federal opposition supported the proposed intergovernmental reforms and potential losers from the reforms were not identifiable as a group that could effectively oppose reform. Although factors such as political alignment and particular government leaders (in particular, the replacement of Hawke by Keating) changed, the underlying motivations for reform were sufficient to maintain the momentum of the collaborative-federalism process once started, at least in terms of microeconomic reform.

The overall success of the national competition policy and mutual recognition appears to lie largely in the common central and state government desire for the reforms. Whereas many of the major national competition reforms have been delivered, a significant number of perhaps more minor reforms in the competition policy agenda have been delayed or diluted. In these instances there have been unified special interest groups who have been able to effectively exploit that part of the competition policy agreement that allows restrictions on competition to continue if removal of the restrictions is not justified by the public interest. Although the public interest does include the efficient allocation of resources, under the agreement it also covers factors such as equity, ecology, safety, and regional development. In some instances, state anticompetitive regulation review boards contain "balanced" numbers of interested parties, which mitigates clearly disinterested judgments. In general, however, the reviews have worked well and have often brought the anticipated deregulation.

The limited extent of reforms affecting VFI appears to arise from strong central government opposition and from the objectives of the states not being clearly attached to removing the alleged distortions inherent in VFI, but rather in obtaining increased (untied) funding. Sharman (1993, p. 233) also notes that the SPP process has become deeply entrenched in government processes. Human capital is tied up in the current process and bureaucratic empires that have been built up to administer the SPPs represent a hidden opponent of change.

IX. REFORM OUTCOMES

National competition policy has been in place now for the best part of a decade and many of the listed reforms have been undertaken. Extensive reviews of Commonwealth and state government progress in their implementation of the competition policy program are conducted by an independent advisory body, the National Competition Council (NCC). Five tranches of payments to the states in recognition of their reforms have been made. There have been instances where part of a payment to certain states has been delayed until a particular reform has been carried out, but these have not been the rule. Very occasionally small amounts of competition policy payments have been permanently withheld.

The national competition policy program is, however, far behind schedule. The original agreement had set a completion date of December 2000 for the core of the reform program. Although significant reforms have occurred, particularly in the areas of GBEs, the reform timetable has now been extended to 2005 and beyond. Nevertheless, the policy can be judged an overall success. Implementation of any large-scale project often takes longer than expected and national competition policy has proved to be no different. Although it has been the more politically tractable reforms that have been implemented the fastest, it is in these reform areas where many of the biggest impacts on economic welfare were expected to arise.

The NCC's reports assess far too wide a range of reforms to summarize here. However, there are some notable instances of major reforms that have occurred: National markets in electricity and gas, for example, are largely in place and a generic access regime has been introduced. GBEs are progressively adopting competitive neutrality and paying for community service obligations from funding received directly from the government's budget for that purpose. Markets in which GBEs operate are increasingly being made more contestable. Numerous GBEs have been corporatized and many have been privatized.

The NCC can note the exact progress of each of the reforms in each jurisdiction, but reporting on the economic welfare consequences of the reforms instituted so far is rather more difficult. To do this properly would require redoing the economic modeling simulations for each of the reforms instituted. These simulations mainly involved industry productivity shocks, the size of which were estimated by comparisons with international benchmarks using data envelopment analysis and similar estimation techniques. The task now would be to assess how much of the productivity gaps between Australia and best-practice partners had been reduced over the period since particular reforms were implemented.[61] Data availability and consistency problems are likely to make this a very difficult task to do properly. Giesecke and Madden (2003) have developed an alternative method of conducting historical simulations with a dynamic computable general equilibrium model to uncover the change in productivity growth rates resulting from a set of reforms. However, to date, this method has been applied only for a very limited number of reforms. Currently, the Productivity Commission is making an initial attempt at an ex post check of the Industry Commission's (1995) welfare-gains estimates. However, the problem of separating the portion of productivity and price effects resulting from national competition policy from that resulting from technological and other changes is likely to make this a very difficult task.

To date, the Productivity Commission (1998) and Samuel (1999 and 2000) have been able to provide lists of estimated price reductions in areas where there have been reforms. For instance, Samuel (2000) observes that national average electricity prices have fallen by 23% to 30%, and in New South Wales and Victoria there have been even greater price reductions for electricity of up to 60%. He notes that since 1995, Western Australian gas prices have halved and rail freights for the Perth–Melbourne route have fallen by 40%. Such price reductions are indicative of substantial productivity improvements over the period, and no doubt much of this is due to national competition policy reforms, although some proportion

---

[61] This would require making the assumption that any change in the gap was due to the competition policy reform. This is not a particularly satisfactory assumption, but it is certainly no worse than the assumption made by the Industry Commission (1995) when it assumed that the entire productivity gap with world best practice would be eliminated by national competition policy.

will be due to other causes. Also, it is difficult to assess what the benefits would have been if the national competition policy agreement had not been reached and each government had simply proceeded with its own microeconomic reform program. However, the substantial price reductions must mean that state governments have allowed some of the productivity gains to be expressed in terms of lower prices for their GBE output, rather than the states just aiming to improve their own budgetary position as might have occurred without national competition policy.

Gains also seem to have flowed from the first of the major collaborative-federalism reforms, mutual recognition. The Office of Regulatory Review (1997) judged that there had been an increase in the level of interstate mobility of goods and occupations. For instance, a significant percentage of those registering for regulated occupations in various states are doing so under the mutual recognition provisions.

X. CONCLUDING REMARKS

Reforms to Australian federalism over the past dozen years have brought some undoubted benefits by way of the delivery of a program of microeconomic reform and of more workable constraints on government borrowings. However, most of the distinguishing features of Australian federalism – a very high vertical fiscal imbalance, fiscal domination by the Commonwealth, and an over elaborate system of horizontal fiscal equalization – remain very much the same. How does this leave the Australian economy in terms of its ability to handle economic shocks and to be competitive in a globally integrated world?

Certainly the Australian economy has been performing well. In a speech on Australia's economic development, the Head of the Australian Treasury, Henry (2001), displayed a decade average GDP per capita growth chart for Australia and the OECD as a whole over the four decades to the 1990s. Australia's GDP growth rate per capita was 3.2% in the 1960s and 1.7%, 1.5%, and 2.4% for the following decades. The corresponding figures for the OECD were 4.0%, 2.3%, 2.1%, and 1.6%, respectively. Not only did the 1990s represent Australia's best result since the 1960s, it also was the only one of the four decades in which Australia outperformed the OECD average.

Many commentators have attributed Australia's good performance to its microeconomic reform program. Over the last six years of the 1990s Australia enjoyed an average productivity growth rate of 2.4%, which exceeded that of all OECD countries except Norway (Samuel, 2000).

Despite the microeconomic reform program requiring continued and concerted action by nine governments, the Australian federal system has delivered the essential reforms and can be reasonably expected to complete at least reviews of the remaining reforms on the original national competition policy program over the next few years. Apparently, reform-induced productivity improvements represent one of the upsides of the increase in collaborative federalism over the past dozen years.

The Australian federal system appears to work reasonably well with regard to macroeconomic policy. The new Loan Council arrangements that rely on market discipline appear to have played their part in reducing state government deficits. Although the current downturn in international share markets is causing problems for state superannuation funds, at the moment states have sufficient budgeted surpluses to absorb this. Madden (1993) did demonstrate that the present narrow range of state government taxes could lead to fiscal-policy reactions by the states that might partly frustrate short-run contractionary fiscal policy targeting the current account deficit. This might have been of relevance in the 1980s when the Commonwealth decreased grants to the states for this purpose. Walsh (1996b, p. 10) saw the current Loan Council arrangements as providing a way in which the Commonwealth and the states might formally cooperate in forming national fiscal policy, but this does not seem an immediate prospect, particularly following the discontinuation of the *National Fiscal Outlook*. Under current macroeconomic settings, the federal system does not seem to be putting any major constraints on Commonwealth policy.

One area not covered in this chapter relates to labor market policy. Here the federal system might be putting some constraints on policy. Currently, Australia has a federal industrial relations system plus five state systems. The missing state is Victoria, which in 1997 referred its industrial relations power to the Commonwealth. The present system does bring with it some costs as employers in each state, except Victoria, must deal with two industrial relations systems. These costs have declined as Australia has substantially moved away from centralized wage fixing to bargaining at the enterprise level. At this stage, moves by other states to refer their industrial relations power to the Commonwealth do not appear imminent. However, in 1999, the Commonwealth canvassed the idea of using its corporations power to extend its industrial relations power over the states (Wooden, 2000).[62]

---

[62] Under the Constitution, the Commonwealth can only legislate on conciliation and arbitration when an industrial dispute crosses over state borders.

The period of microeconomic reform appears to have coincided with one of growing regional disparities in Australia. From the mid-1980s to the mid-1990s employment declined in twelve of fifty-five regions throughout Australia (Productivity Commission, 1999). All of the regions with declining employment were in rural or remote areas. Contributing to this result were declining terms of trade in agriculture and mining, labor-saving productivity improvements, and reductions in government spending. There are some increasing regional income disparities and some evidence exists that more rural areas have to face regional adjustment problems. Lloyd et al. (2000) showed that, from 1991 to 1996, average real household income growth rates varied widely across regions, both within and among states. Although certain rural areas had good growth rates, and the South Australian and Tasmanian capitals suffered real per capita income declines, in general capital cities fared better than other areas. Interregional disparities in economic performance appear to have continued into the period after the national competition policy was first implemented and the question of the degree to which the policy contributed to these disparities became one of political importance.

The Howard government, when it took office in 1996, phased out the regional development initiatives of the previous government. Australia has an extensive system of social safety nets and the new government maintained that these should be adequate to deal with structural adjustment in regional Australia. However, there clearly was a policy vacuum with respect to the regions and the latter part of the 1990s saw a strong regional backlash against national competition policy reforms in particular. A number of state governments lost office in the wake of regional objections to government economic reforms. This has resulted in slower progress in the implementation of competition policy and Australia is now showing some signs of "reform fatigue." Governments are now beginning to introduce actual compensation for reforms, for instance, in the case of dairy deregulation, so that certain reforms can proceed.

The Australian wage system is not conducive to smooth regional adjustment. Groenewold (1997) estimates that in the long run interstate migration does tend to eliminate differences in state unemployment rates. However, Australia has not yet completely lost all vestiges of its historic wage-fixing system, and this has meant that in the short run regional wages are unable to adjust quickly enough to dampen negative (or positive) affects on regional unemployment. Nonetheless, as Australia moves ever closer to collective bargaining at the enterprise level, rather than national and state arbitrated awards, regional adjustment problems are likely to decrease.[63] Furthermore, Giesecke and Madden (2003) show that microeconomic reforms can actually ease regional adjustment problems when productivity improvements lead to sufficient price reductions.

A question of interest is the role that fiscal equalization might have in affecting the extent of regional disparities. The degree to which HFE acts to reduce interstate disparities among household incomes did not figure in the Australian debate on fiscal equalization for many years (Grewal, 1999). The HFE process in Australia is aimed purely at offsetting fiscal disabilities. It is often thought that, since three of the recipient states (Tasmania, South Australia, and Queensland) have had below-average gross state product per capita for many years, HFE involves a progressive redistribution. However, the major recipient state, the Northern Territory, has a per capita gross state product considerably above the average. Harding et al. (2002) find that HFE does not reduce Australian income inequality as measured by the Gini coefficient. Nor is HFE likely to play any significant role in ameliorating the effects of economic shocks in the short term. The CGC recommendations are the outcome of a relatively slow process and HFE operates at a different geographical level than that at which the main structural adjustment pressures are felt.

As we have seen, VFI is likely to have reduced the efficiency of the Australian economy, particularly given the use of HFE to distribute general purpose grants and the cumbersome system for administering SPPs. A replacement of the present overly complex system of fiscal equalization and a complete streamlining of SPPs would seem obvious ways of increasing economic efficiency.[64] However, except for HFE, there has been no quantitative assessment of the costs of VFI, and how important it is for Australia to reduce the level of imbalance is currently uncertain.

The collaborative-federalism process itself may well have brought with it a further cost in terms of a reduction in the states' autonomy. To the extent that there has been an associated reduction in competitive

---

[63] Currently, only around 20 percent of Australian workers are still covered by awards. They receive annual wage increases (Safety Net Awards) via the Australian Industrial Relations Commission. However, Harding and Harding (2004) estimate that almost a third of workers not covered by Safety Net Awards still have their wages influenced by Safety Net Award increases.

[64] There are reasons why some degree of redistribution among state governments should perhaps continue. For example, there could be a national security justification for high grants to the Northern Territory (Dixon et al., 2002). The advantages of formula-based redistribution computed by an independent CGC has long been recognized. However, the CGC method should be greatly simplified, with a gradual reduction in the degree of redistribution.

federalism, this may not be entirely a bad thing. Forsyth (1995, p. 71) contends that "the pattern of competition in Australia has given competitive federalism a bad name." The Industry Commission (1996b) raises concerns that most state budgetary assistance to industry is selective, discretionary, and nontransparent. This is perhaps the next area where a program of collaborative reforms should be introduced.

Collaborative federalism may have in some ways strengthened the Commonwealth's fiscal dominance, but it may also have brought a form of horizontal intergovernmental competition that appears to be of clear benefit to economic efficiency. State governments now compete to provide a more efficient economic environment than other states by instituting reforms that also attract competition policy incentive payments. The Commonwealth Treasury prepares competitive indices for each state, thus establishing another public performance indicator that encourages state governments to compete against each other for electoral reasons. One of the most important forms of quasi-competition is in terms of financial management, where states acknowledge credit ratings from international agencies as important in attracting international capital to their state. Despite some quite important flaws in Australia's fiscal federal system as outlined in this chapter, the collaborative-federalism competition reforms of the 1990s have added to Australia's productivity growth and therefore have promoted its competitive standing in the global environment.

Whether collaborative federalism is likely to continue to be a catalyst for significant reform is not as clear. Collaborative structures are only useful in those areas where a consensus exists, or where incentives can be provided by winners to compensate losers. National competition policy and other reform programs that are widely supported will benefit from the collaborative process. But, as Painter (1998) notes, the process did not remove VFI because there was no common ground on the matter. However, with such fundamentals of Australian fiscal federalism unchanged, the incentives for collaboration may weaken once the economic threats that led to the collaborative reform process have dissipated.[65] Without more far-reaching reforms of the ongoing problems of Australia's federal system, the discord between Commonwealth and the states, which Painter (1998, p. 186) claims has persisted through the collaborative process, is likely to surface again.

The seeds of such discord may well lie in the arrangement to distribute all GST revenues to the states and territories. As noted in Section VII.2

---

[65] I thank the referee for this point.

this has eased the states' concern over VFI. However, figures recently released by the Commonwealth Treasurer indicate that GST revenue has grown much faster than expected and the states will therefore receive a windfall gain. In an apparent attempt to reclaim some of these funds, the Commonwealth Government has indicated that it will not continue competition policy incentive payments beyond 2005–2006. Rather, these funds will be diverted to finance the new National Water Initiative that was agreed to at the June 2004 COAG. The states had been lobbying for the existing competition payments to be built into their base funding and for new competition payments to be negotiated for further collaborative economic reforms. It is unclear whether these latest developments will result in the states lessening their participation in the reform process. In 2003 the states walked out of a COAG meeting to register their dissatisfaction over the Commonwealth's position on public hospital funding. But the Commonwealth fiscal dominance meant that the premiers soon agreed to the Commonwealth's A$42 billion funding offer. It is likely that the states could find themselves in a similar position on future reform policies. In these circumstances, what commenced as collaborative structures might reinforce the ongoing centralist tendencies within the Australian federation.

Bibliography

Australian Loan Council (1993). Future Arrangements for Loan Council Monitoring and Reporting. Canberra.

Bell, S., and B. Head (1994). "Australia's Political Economy," in S. Bell and B. Head, eds., *State, Economy and Public Policy in Australia*, pp. 1–24. Melbourne: Oxford University Press.

Brennan, G., and J. J. Pincus (1998). "Is Vertical Fiscal Imbalance so Inefficient? or the Flypaper Effect Is Not an Anomaly?," University of Adelaide Working Paper 98–6, Adelaide.

Boadway, R., and F. Flatters (1982). "Efficiency and Equalization Payments in a Federal System of Government: A Synthesis and Extension of Recent Results," Journal of Economics 15(4): 613–633.

Buchanan, J. M. (1950). "Federalism and Fiscal Equity," The American Economic Review 40(4): 583–599.

Coleman, W., and A. J. Hagger (2001). *Exasperating Calculators: The Rage over Economic Rationalism and the Campaign Against Australian Economists*. Sydney: Macleay Press.

Commonwealth Grants Commission (1995). *Equality in Diversity: History of the Commonwealth Grants Commission*, 2nd Edition. Canberra: Australian Government Publishing Service.

Commonwealth Grants Commission (1999). State Finances – Report on General Revenue Grant Relativities 1999, Canberra.

Corden, W. M. (1997). *The Road to Reform: Essays on Australian Economic Policy*. Melbourne: Addison-Wesley.

Council of Australian Governors (COAG). (1994). "COAG Commuinique, 19 April 1994." available at http://www.coag.gov.au/meetings/190894.index. htm.ncp

Dixon, P. B., J. R. Madden, and M. Peter (1993). "Simulations of the Economic Effects of Changing the Distribution of General Revenue Assistance among the Australian States," Economic Record 69(207): 367–381.

Dixon, P. B., M. R. Picton, and M. T. Rimmer (2002). "Efficiency Effects of Inter-Government Financial Transfers in Australia," Australian Economic Review 35(3): 304–315.

Dollery, B. E. (1994). "The Timing of Microeconomic Reform in Australia," Economic Papers 13(3): 84–90.

Dollery, B. E. (1996). "Similar Triangles and the Theory of Regulation: A Rejoiner to Quiggin," Economic Papers 15(1): 94–96.

Dollery, B. E., and J. Wallis (2000). "A Note on the Timing of Microeconomic Reform in Australia," Economic Analysis and Policy 30(1): 63–73.

Dollery, B. E., and A. C. Worthington (1999). "Fiscal Illusion at the Local Level: An Empirical Test Using Australian Municipal Data," Economic Record 75(228): 37–48.

Fletcher, C., and C. Walsh (1992). "Comparative and International Administration. Reform of Intergovernmental Relations in Australia: The Politics of Federalism and the Non-Politics of Managerialism." Public Administration 70 (Winter): 561–616.

Forsyth, P. J. (1995). "Microeconomic Reform in a Federal System: Constraints and Incentives," in P. Carroll and M. Painter, eds., *Microeconomic Reform and Federalism*. Canberra: Federalism Research Centre, Australian National University.

Galligan, B., and D. Mardiste (1992). "Labor's Reconciliation with Federalism," Australian Journal of Political Science 27: 71–86.

Garnaut, R. (2002). "Equity and Australian Development: Lessons from the First Century," Australian Economic Review 35(3): 227–243.

Garnaut, R., and V. FitzGerald (2002a). A Review of the Allocation of Commonwealth Grants to the States and Territories: Final Report. Review of Commonwealth-State Funding, Melbourne.

Garnaut, R., and V. FitzGerald (2002b). "Issues in Commonwealth-State Funding," Australian Economic Review 35(3): 290–300.

Gerritsen, R. (1992). "The Politics of Microeconomic Reform: A Bear's-Eye View," in P. J. Forsyth, ed., *Microeconomic Reform in Australia*, pp. 24–41. Sydney: Allen & Unwin.

Giesecke, J. A., and J. R. Madden (2003). "Regional Labor Market Adjustment to Competition Policy Reforms: A Dynamic CGE Framework for Assessment," Australian Journal of Labor Economics 6(3): 409–433.

Gramlich, E. M. (1984). "'A Fair Go': Fiscal Federalism Arrangements," in Caves, R., and L. Krause, eds., *The Australian Economy: A View from the North*, Washington, D.C.: Brookings Institution: 231–274.

Gregory, R. G. (1992). "An Overview of Microeconomic Reform," in P. J. Forsyth, ed., *Microeconomic Reform in Australia*, pp. 305–313. Sydney: Allen & Unwin.

Grewal, B. S. (1995). "Vertical Fiscal Imbalance in Australia: A Problem for Tax Structure, not for Revenue Sharing," CSES Working Paper No. 2, Centre for Strategic Economic Studies, Victoria University, Melbourne.

Grewal, B. S. (1999). "Federalism and Fiscal Equalization: Should India Follow the Australian Path?," in I. Copland and J. Rickard, eds., *Federalism: Comparative Perspectives from India and Australia*. New Dehli: Manohar.

Groenewegen, P. (1990). *Public Finance in Australia*, 3rd Edition. Sydney: Prentice Hall.

Groenewold, N. (1997). "Does Migration Equalise Regional Unemployment Rates? Evidence from Australia," Papers in Regional Science 76(1): 1–20.

Harding, A., N. Warren, G. Beer, B. Phillips, and K. Osei (2002). "The Distributional Impact of Selected Commonwealth Outlays and Taxes and Alternative Grant Allocation Mechanisms," Australian Economic Review 35(3): 325–334.

Harding, D., and G. Harding (2004). "Minimum Wages in Australia: An Analysis of the Impact on Small and Medium Sized Businesses," A Report to the Department of Employment and Work place Relations, Canberra: Commonwealth of Australia.

Henry, K. (2001). "Australia's Economic Development," Address to the Committee for the Economic Development of Australia, 40th Anniversary Annual General Meeting, Sydney, 19 November, 2001.

Hilmer, F. G., M. R. Rayner, and G. Q. Taperell (1993). National Competition Policy: Report by the Independent Committee. Canberra: AGPS.

Industry Commission (1995). The Growth and Revenue Implications of Hilmer and Related Reforms, Report to the Council of Australian Governments, Canberra, March.

Industry Commission (1996a). State, Territory and Local Government Assistance to Industry, Report 55. Canberra: AGPS.

Industry Commission (1996b). Annual Report 1995–96. Canberra: AGPS.

James, D. W. (1992). *Intergovernmental Financial Relations in Australia*. Sydney: Australian Tax Research Foundation.

James, D. (1997). "Federalism up in Smoke? The High Court Decision on State Tobacco Tax," Current Issues Brief 1 1997–98. Canberra: Department of the Parliamentary Library.

Lloyd, R., A. Harding, and O. Hellwig (2000). "Regional Divide? A Study of Incomes in Regional Australia," NATSEM Discussion Paper 51, National Centre for Social and Economic Modeling, University of Canberra.

Madden, J. R. (1993). "The Economics of Vertical Fiscal Imbalance," Australian Tax Forum 10(1): 75–90.

Madden, J. R. (1995). "Implementing the Hilmer Reforms: The Effects on the National and State Economies," Business Council Bulletin, Competition Policy Supplement, 14–19.

Mathews, R. (1984). The Australian Loan Council: Co-ordination of Public Debt Policies in a Federation. Reprint Series 62, Centre for Research on Federal Financial Relations, The Australian National University, Canberra.

Mathews, R. (1994). Fiscal Equalization – Political, Social and Economic Linchpin of Federation. The Inaugural Russell Mathews Lecture on Federal Financial Relations for the Federalism Research Centre, The Australian National University, Canberra, 11 May 1994.

Mathews, R., and B. Grewal (1997). *The Public Sector in Jeopardy: Australian Fiscal Federalism from Whitlam to Keating*. Melbourne: Centre for Strategic Economic Studies, Victoria University.

New South Wales Treasurer (2001). Budget Paper No. 2, 2001–02 Budget Statement, Sydney, 2001.

Norman, N. R. (1995). *Refocusing Fiscal Reform*. Melbourne: Business Council of Australia.

Office of Regulatory Review (1997). *Impact of Mutual Recognition in Australia*, Canberra: AGPS.

Painter, M. (1995). "Microeconomic Reform and the Public Sector," in M. Laffin and M. Painter, eds., *Reform and Reversal: Lessons from the Coalition Government in New South Wales 1988–1995*, pp. 91–109. Melbourne: Macmillan.

Painter, M. (1998). *Collaborative Federalism: Economic Reform in Australia in the 1990s*. Cambridge, UK: Cambridge University Press.

Parham, D., P. Barnes, P. Roberts, and S. Kennett (2000). Distribution of the Economic Gains of the 1990s, Productivity Commission Staff Research Paper, AusInfo, Canberra.

Peltzman, S. (1989). "The Economic Theory of Regulation After a Decade of Deregulation," Brookings Papers on Economic Activity. Microeconomics, 48–58.

Petchey, J. (1995). "Resource Rents, Cost Differences and Fiscal Equalization," Economic Record 71: 343–353.

Pitchford, J. D. (1989). "Does Australia Really Have a Current Account Problem?," Economic Papers 8(4): 25–32.

Pitchford, J. D. (1990). *Australia's Foreign Debt: Myths and Realities*. Sydney: Allen & Unwin.

Productivity Commission (1998). Microeconomic Reform by Australian Governments 1997–98, Annual Report Series 1997–98. Melbourne: AusInfo.

Productivity Commission (1999). Impact of Competition Policy Reforms on Rural and Regional Australia, Report 8. Canberra: AusInfo.

Quiggin, J. (1995). "Similar Triangles and the Theory of Regulation," Economic Papers 14(3): 86–88.

Quiggin, J. (1996). *Great Expectations: Microeconomic Reform and Australia*. Sydney: Allen & Unwin.

Quiggin, J. (1997). "Estimating the Benefits of Hilmer and Related Reforms," Australian Economic Review 30(3): 256–272.

Review of Commonwealth-State Funding (2001). Background Paper to a Review of the Allocation of Commonwealth Grants to the States and Territories, Melbourne.

Roberts, W. (2001). "Liberalism: The Nineteenth Century Legacy," in J. R. Nethercote, ed., *Liberalism and the Australian Federation*. Sydney: Federation Press.

Rodrik, D. (1996). "Understanding Economic Policy Reform," Journal of Economic Literature 34(1): 9–41.

Rye, C. R., and B. Searle (1997). "The Fiscal Transfer System in Australia," in E. Ahmad, ed., *Financing Decentralized Expenditures. An International Comparison of Grants.* Cheltenham, UK: Edward Elgar.

Samuel, G. (1999). "Progress on National Competition Policy," presentation by the President of the National Competition Council to the Committee for Economic Development of Australia, Sydney, 21 July.

Samuel, G. (2000). "National Competition Policy – A Five-year Stocktake," paper presented to CEDA Meeting, Melbourne, 7 July.

Saunders, C. A. (1990). "Government Borrowing in Australia," The Journal of Federalism 20: 35–52.

Saunders, C. A. (1997). "The High Court, Section 90 and the Australian Federation," in N. A. Warren, ed., *Reshaping Fiscal Federalism in Australia*, Australian Tax Research Foundation Conference Series No. 20, Sydney: ATRF, 21–39.

Senate Select Committee on the Functions, Powers and Operation of the Australian Loan Council (1993). Third Report Canberra: Parliament of the Commonwealth of Australia.

Sharman, C. (1993). "Changing Federal Finance: The Politics of the Reintroduction of State Income Taxes," in D. J. Collins, ed., *Vertical Fiscal Imbalance and the Allocation of Taxing Powers*, Australian Tax Research Foundation Conference Series No. 13, 221–237.

Sharman, C. (2001). "Federalism and the Liberal Party," in J. R. Nethercote, ed., *Liberalism and the Australian Federation*. Sydney: Federation Press.

Sjaastad, L. J. (1989). "The Deficit: A Crisis of Minor Proportions," Economic Papers 8(4): 19–24.

Swan, P. L., and G. T. Garvey (1995). The Equity and Efficiency Implications of Fiscal Equalization, unpublished report, Sydney.

Tasmanian Treasury (2001). Newsletter of the Department of Treasury and Finance 2(4), October, Hobart.

Wallis, J. (1997). "Conspiracy and the Policy Process: A Case Study of the New Zealand Experiment," Journal of Public Policy 17(1): 1–30.

Walsh, C. (1991). "Reform of Commonwealth-State Relations: 'No Representation Without Taxation,'" Federalism Research Centre Discussion Paper No. 2, Australian National University, Canberra.

Walsh, C. (1993). "Vertical Fiscal Imbalance: The Issues," in D. J. Collins, ed., *Vertical Fiscal Imbalance and the Allocation of Taxing Powers*, Australian Tax Research Foundation Conference Series No. 13, 31–53.

Walsh, C. (1996a). "Refoccusing Commonwealth-State Financial Relations," Business Council Bulletin 126 (January): 30–37.

Walsh, C. (1996b). "The Challenges of Globalization: Lessons from the Australian Experience," South Australian Centre for Economic Studies Discussion Paper 96.3, University of Adelaide, Adelaide.

Warhurst, J. (1987). "Managing Intergovernmental Relations," in H. Bakvis and W. M. Chandler, eds., *Federalism and the Role of the State*. Toronto: University of Toronto Press.

Wettenhall, R. (1985). "Intergovernmental Agencies: Lubricating a Federal System," Current Affairs Bulletin 61(11): 28–35.

Whiteman, J. (1999). "The Potential Benefits of Hilmer and Related Reforms: Electricity Supply," Australian Economic Review 32(1): 17–30.

Wooden, M. (2000). *The Transformation of Australian Industrial Relations.* Sydney: Federation Press.

Working Party on Tax Powers (1991). Taxation and the Fiscal Imbalance between Levels of Australian Government: Responsibility, Accountability and Efficiency, 4 October, Commonwealth and State Treasuries.

FOUR

The Brazilian Federation

*Facts, Challenges, and Perspectives**

Fernando Rezende and José Roberto Afonso

I. INTRODUCTION

Following decades of protectionism and a powerful interventionist state, the Brazilian economy suddenly exposed itself to external competition and went through a rapid process of privatization. The institutional reforms implemented in the 1990s helped stabilize the economy and create a friendlier environment for attracting investments and fostering growth. In spite of the still-looming uncertainties regarding the prospects for reconciling sustainable development and macroeconomic stability, the results achieved in the past decade are on balance positive.

The federal regime affected and was affected by the process of moving from a closed, state-controlled economy to an open, privately run market. Indeed, the greater the degree of subnational governments' interests in proposed reforms, the more difficult it became to implement the reforms. In some cases, subnational governments had to be lured into accepting changes that reduced state and local autonomy. The power of state and local governments in the National Parliament created the necessity for bargaining over compensation for reduced autonomy or financial losses even in cases where subnational governments did not have direct policy oversight.

* The chapter reflects the authors' opinions and not necessarily those of their affiliations. The statistical base was organized by economist Erika Amorim Araujo. The text utilizes information available at the end of December 2001, particularly data available at the site Banco Federativo (http://www.federativo.bndes.gov.br). The chapter benefited from comments made by T. N. Srinivasan and Jessica Seddon Wallack, as well as by participants in the seminar held in Stanford in June 2002, to whom the authors wish to express their gratitude.

Of the reforms that topped the agenda for modernizing the Brazilian economy during the 1990s, three deserve special attention: privatization, public employment, and social security and taxation. Given the central role of healthy public finances in the strategy for macroeconomic stability, these reforms were the object of intense debate and much disagreement. Of these, privatization has been the only successful reform so far. Some advances were made in reducing future claims on the national budget, but the tax reform has not yet succeeded in alleviating the excessive burden on the competitiveness of the Brazilian economy.

This chapter will explore these three reforms, providing some facts, showing what was accomplished, and indicating the main reasons for the failures to implement deeper changes and succeed in the negotiations. The analysis focuses on the challenges the Brazilian Federation faces in the wake of institutional reforms that may affect the balance of power in the federation and reduce state and local government autonomy.

With this in mind, the chapter is organized as follows. To set the stage for looking into the future, Section II provides a brief historical account of the main facts behind the decision to adopt a federal regime in the 1889 Constitution. The main goal of this historical recompilation is to stress the fact that fierce resistance to a strong central government and some important secession attempts marked the seven decades that preceded this decision. The reasons behind these movements – loose economic ties among the Brazilian regions and significant external economic relations of Brazilian states – may return again, echoing the past.

Section III summarizes recent developments that shaped the way the Brazilian Federation looks today. Two important events had decisive influences: the transition from authoritarian rule to democracy, following the demise of the military regime in 1985, and the policies adopted in the 1990s to put an end to an era of high inflation, focused on eliminating the public deficit and enforcing fiscal discipline. Whereas the 1988 Constitution pushed for greater decentralization and subnational autonomy, the anti-inflationary drive required hard budget constraints that impinged upon federal autonomy. It is difficult to reconcile macroeconomic needs with subnational autonomy in the Brazilian context.

The issues involved in appraising the measures adopted to adjust the fiscal accounts to meet the targets set in the macroeconomic stabilization plan are the subject of the Section IV. This section highlights the difficulties faced in implementing reforms aimed at cutting public spending and social security benefits as well as enforcing fiscal discipline at all levels of government in the Brazilian Federation. The so-called Fiscal Responsibility Law, approved in 2000, shows good prospects for the near future, but it is still too early to make a reliable appraisal of its ability to sustain fiscal discipline, given the resistance to altering well-entrenched habits of budgetary profligacy.

Section V describes the privatization program, its successes, and some implications. In less than a decade most of the formerly state-owned enterprises were sold in public auctions, generating substantial resources that helped avoid any rapid increase in the public debt and contributed to Brazil's ability to save tax money previously used to cover subsidies for more important social needs. In addition, the privatization program contributed to increases in productivity that reinforced competitiveness of the Brazilian manufacturing sector in domestic and international markets.

The last of the three reforms dealt with in this chapter – taxation – is the subject of Section VI. In spite of taxation being recognized as the most important reform of the past decade, it has been impossible, so far, to reach an agreement as to the new model for assigning tax powers in the Federation. Intergovernmental and regional conflicts have played a large part in this impasse. This section stresses the point that these conflicts may increase in the nearby future, owing to the possibility of greater regional domestic inequalities following the economic integration of the Americas, in the absence of a new approach to regional development policies.

Whereas macroeconomic pressures for healthy public finances motivated the privatization program and imposition of hard budget constraints, pressure groups and intergovernmental conflicts blocked the passage of more ambitious proposals for cuts in public spending and moving ahead to implement a tax reform needed to improve competitiveness and bring about a more balanced federal regime. Further pressures arising from the calendar of regional economic integration may give new impetus to the institutional reforms that are still needed for integration of the Brazilian Federation in the global economy.

II. HISTORY

Contrary to conventional wisdom, the decision to adopt a federal regime in Brazil was not merely an imitation of the North American model. The integrity of the Brazilian territory has long been threatened by attempts at secession. During colonial times, relationships among the Brazilian states were practically nonexistent, not only because of distance and lack of means of communication, but also because of the absence of economic motives for interchange. Trade in Brazilian raw material was a monopoly of the Portuguese crown, which maintained bilateral relations with the more important Brazilian states.

Important separatist movements followed the declaration of independence from Portugal. Nourished by the ex-metropolis and supported by the Portuguese military garrisons in their territories, the former provinces of Pernambuco, Bahia, and Pará refused to acknowledge the authority of the new Emperor. Loyal troops forced the rebels to surrender after eleven months of cruel battles to maintain the integrity of the territory conquered during the colonial period. The monarchic project, conceived by José Bonifácio, also helped to maintain national unity.

Of the insurrections of the time, the longer and bloodiest of all occurred in the province of Rio Grande do Sul. The "Farrapos War" went on for a decade (1835–1845), being resolved only after much effort of the imperial army, which suffered heavy material and human losses. The leaders of this movement proclaimed the creation of the "Estado Rio Grandense" as an independent and sovereign state willing to form part of a union, through a federation, to other Brazilian states that came to adopt the same ideals and the same regime.[1]

Since independence, conflict between demands for greater provincial autonomy and pressures for centralization has been at the roots of insurrections against the imperial power. In a time where economic relations among the states were almost nonexistent, the eruption of these conflicts was no surprise, as there was no coincidence of interests. Furthermore, the separatist drive was fueled by a spurious correlation between liberalism and decentralization, which was attributed to pure conservatism intentions to reinforce power at the central level.

It was no surprise, then, that the birth of the republic was seen as a victory of the liberal spirit, whose main manifestation was the rally for the abolition of slavery. The Republican Constitution of 1891 wholly enshrined the ideas of decentralization and federal autonomy, initiating a cycle with alternating periods of decentralization and centralization of power. This cycle is still a peculiar feature of the Brazilian Federation (Box 4.1).

The unity of the country was no longer a matter of concern at the beginning of the nineteenth century. Other conflicts (such as *Canudos, Revolta dos Marinheiros*) that emerged in the First Republic (1889–1930) were due more to social conditions or political divergences than to secession attempts. From this point on, revolts have had more to do with centralization or decentralization, backed by regional interests. The issue still dominates the debate on the nature of Brazilian federalism.

---

[1] See Gonzaga Duque (1998, p. 168).

Box 4.1. *The Moving Pendulum – Centralization and Decentralization Cycles in the Brazilian Federation*[i]

1891–1930: In the first four republican decades the Brazilian Federation was highly decentralized. A weak federal government was accompanied by strong independent states, with power to regulate and tax domestic and foreign trade. Subnational governments were also responsible for most of the state's activities in the provision of public goods.

1930–1945: Vargas's dictatorship led to an increasing concentration of powers in federal hands to put into place a more integrated domestic market and set the basis for industrialization. Regulation of domestic and foreign trade moved to federal hands and nationwide taxes were created. The influence of the states' oligarchies on national policies was curtailed, even though state governments kept autonomy to apply their own taxes and even to create additional ones.

1946–1964: Democratization following the end of World War II moved the pendulum back toward decentralization. Subnational autonomy was seen as necessary to support greater social responsibilities and a stable democracy. However, concentration of manufacturing production in the Southeast aggravated regional disparities and increased political rivalries. Fiscal incentives for investments in the Northeast were granted, in an attempt to reverse the trend toward regional concentration of economic activity.

1964–1968: The advent of the military regime after the 1964 coup shifted the pendulum back to centralization. To that end, the tax reform of the mid-1960s played a key role. Taxation powers of the federal government were reinforced, allowing for an increase in overall tax burden to finance infrastructure modernization and accelerate the pace of development. As in the previous centralization round, states were not deprived of their autonomy to tax. Indeed, they were assigned the power to apply a broad basis value added tax in substitution for the existing turnover tax. At the same time, a revenue-sharing mechanism was instituted to enhance revenues of those who had a narrow tax base.

1968–1980: Democratization led again to a new move toward decentralization. Federal autonomy benefited from a decision to give the states the sole privilege to tax oil, telecommunication, and electric energy, thus enlarging their tax base. Furthermore, a significant increase in federal revenues shared with states and local governments benefited less developed states and small municipalities. The power of local governments was ratified as municipalities acquired the status of members of the Federation.

1980–2005: Opposing forces are at play. Macroeconomic demands for fiscal adjustment and policy coordination led to an increase in the federal government's share in total tax collections and greater control over subnational debts. On the opposite side, calls for efficiency and accountability in public policies fueled the decentralization drive in public spending. Pressures from globalization and regional integration make it difficult to find a way to reconcile these two trends.

---

[i] *Source:* Serra and Afonso (1999), Afonso (1994, 1996), Affonso (1995), Varsano (1996), Oliveira (1995), Rodriguez (1995), Silva and Costa (1995), and Camargo (1993). For additional information see Goldsmith (1986) on the Brazilian economic history, Fausto (1995) on Brazilian history, and Camargo (1993), Carvalho (1993), and Love (1993) on the centralization–decentralization issue.

Huge regional inequalities were and continue to be at the root of the problem. Not by chance, the turning points of these cycles were associated with changes in the socioeconomic environment that weakened the forces that supported the status quo. Growing concerns in some of the poorer regions – mainly the South and the Northeast – over the increasing dominance of the Southeast – mainly São Paulo and Minas Gerais – in economic and political affairs, following the abolition of slavery and rise in industrialization, were a key factor in the early twentieth century. The areas with weaker economies saw a strong federal government as the sole way to make their interests prevail in the design of development policies. The prosperous regions, of course, demanded less of a role for the central government and more state autonomy.

Over time, regional and social problems remained intertwined. The decentralization that followed the inauguration of the republic increased the power of local oligarchies and fed growing discontent with living conditions of the population, giving room to the 1922 rebellion and the onset of the authoritarian period installed in 1930. The social reforms promoted during the Vargas era were a landmark in Brazilian social policy history. Nevertheless, the duration of Vargas's dictatorship (from 1930 to 1945) gave way to the rebirth of liberal ideas that led to the ousting of Vargas fifteen years after his arrival on the national scene. Social discontent mounted in the two decades that followed, feeding leftist groups that menaced the regime and leading to the military coup of 1964. This marked the start of a new round of centralization. Twenty years later the democratic government that took power in 1985 aimed to improve social conditions. It has had modest results, however, as social inequalities remained impervious to changing political conditions.

III. RECENT DEVELOPMENTS

The centrifugal forces that led to the present characteristics of the Brazilian Federation were in place well before the 1988 Constitution. The military rulers devised a gradual and controlled transition to democracy in the mid-1970s. Poorer regions and local groups were granted an increase in political power to counteract the dominance of opposition parties in the industrialized areas and more important urban agglomerations. At the same time, an aggressive program of public investments in infrastructure in backward regions followed by an increase in federal transfers to less-developed states provided economic substance to fulfill the aim of maintaining central government control over the process of political liberalization.

The political reform enacted in 1977 increased the number of representatives of poorer states in the National Parliament, postponed direct elections for governors to 1982, decreed that two out of three state representatives in the Senate would be nominated by an electoral college, and reduced the quorum for passing constitutional amendments in the National Parliament to a simple majority. Other conditions were established to assure control of the military over the Electoral College that would preside over the presidential election to be held in 1985. Control of the central government over national politics was thus assured.[2]

On the economic front, the regional policy contemplated in the national development plan contained investments in infrastructure and social programs oriented toward the less-developed North, Northeast, and Center-West regions. Together, these programs included investments aimed at improving conditions for economic growth in these regions totaling US\$ 2.2 billion for 1975–1979. These investments contributed to bringing per capita income of less developed regions close

---

[2] The main goal of the 1977 political reform was to curb the advance of the opposition to the military regime, since its previous success in municipal elections increased the fears of further advances in the elections for state governors scheduled for 1978.

to the national average, thus reducing internal disparities until the mid-1980s.

The steady increase in the percentage of federal tax revenues transferred to states and municipalities followed by special provisions to benefit the poorest North and Northeast regions comprised another important component of the economic measures adopted in this period.[3]

During the long transition period to democratic rule, the demands for decentralization led to further increases in the transfer of federally collected tax revenues to states and local governments. The percentage of the two main federal taxes shared with states and municipalities through special funds – the *Fundo de Participação dos Estados* (FPE – State Participation Fund) and the *Fundo de Participação dos Municípios* (FPM – Municipal Participation Fund) – went up again in 1984 and in 1985 before reaching the level attained in the 1988 Constitution.[4]

Imbalanced political representation has its roots in the arrival of the republic and increased after World War II, but reached its climax with the 1988 Constitution. Along with political decentralization, the 1988 Constitution ushered in important shifts in regional representation in the central government. As of 1988, poor and sparsely populated states were entitled to a minimum of eight representatives in the Chamber of Deputies, whereas the bigger ones face a ceiling of seventy representatives. These conditions led to an overrepresentation of the North and an underrepresentation of the Southeast. The former has 14.5% of the seats for 8% of the population, whereas the latter has 32.2% of the seats for 43% of the population. In extreme cases, the number of votes required to elect a representative to the lower house in the more-developed states is sixteen times higher than the same figure for less developed, sparsely populated ones.

As commonly found in other federations, states' representation in the Senate is equal: Each state has three seats regardless of its size or economic importance. In this case, disequilibria result from a great number of states in less developed regions. With 43.3% of the Brazilian population, the North, Northeast, and Center-West regions command 74% of

---

[3] Ten percent of the amount transferred to the states in 1976 and 1977 and 20% in 1978 were diverted to a special account to be distributed exclusively to Northern and Northeastern states. These same states were also freed from the obligation to allocate part of these funds in investments.

[4] These funds were created in the 1967 Constitution to share the proceeds of federal taxes with states and municipalities. To distinguish them from other transfers of federal resources to subnational governments, they are sometimes referred to as Constitutional Funds.

Box 4.2. *Revenue Sharing in the Brazilian Federation*[i]

The revenue-sharing system has two main components. The first, sometimes referred to as Constitutional Funds, consists of funds set up in the Constitution and assumes the characteristics of a classical revenue-sharing mechanism. The other includes arrangements for providing federal resources to finance specific social policies carried out at the state and local levels.

1964–1967: A tax reform enacted by the military regime established the basis of the present revenue-sharing system. Twenty percent of the proceeds of the main federal taxes (on manufacturing production and income) was earmarked in equal parts to the FPE and the FPM and distributed on a formula basis.

1968: The percentages of federal taxes shared with states and municipalities were halved, and a Special Fund formed with 2% of the same taxes was created to provide for greater federal control over the use of fiscal resources. The subnational governments' fiscal autonomy was reduced to a minimum and remained so until the beginning of the gradual transition to democracy.

1975–1983: Constitutional amendments enacted in 1975 and 1980 led to a progressive increase in the share of state and local governments in federal collection of income and manufacturing taxes. As a result, states and municipalities recovered the losses imposed in 1968. The percentage of these two taxes forming the FPE and the FPM reached 10.5% each in 1983.

1984–1988: Acceleration in transition to democratic rule increased the subnational governments' pressure for a larger share in tax revenues. FPE and FPM rose again in 1984 and 1985, reaching 14% and 16% of federal taxes, respectively. At the same time, measures were adopted to curb federal attempts to reduce state and local government's participation in tax receipts.

1988: With the new Constitution the percentage of federal taxes forming FPE and FPM rose again for five consecutive years, reaching 21.5% and 22.5%, respectively, in 1993. An additional 10% of the manufacturing tax formed a separate fund to compensate the states for not taxing the exports of manufactured goods. On top of that, 3% of the Federal Income Tax Withholding (IR) and the Federal Excise Tax (IPI) was earmarked to a regional development fund to finance investments in the North, Northeast, and Center-West regions.

[i] *Source:* Varsano et al. (1988). See Tables A.3 and A.4 for details on the impact of changes in revenue-sharing mechanisms on the distribution of tax revenues in the federation.

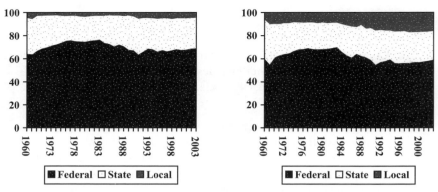

Figure 4.1. Tax collection and disposable tax revenue in Brazil for 1960 and 1972–2003. *Source:* Varsano et al. (1998) Tables A.3 and Araujo (2001) A.4.

the votes in the Senate. Given the special powers of the Brazilian Senate (e.g., all legal propositions and constitutional amendments approved in the lower house have to be submitted to the Senate, whose approval is required to put them into effect), this disproportional representation in the upper house adds to the imbalance in political representation in the Chamber of Deputies. These characteristics led Stepan (1997) to name Brazil as the main example of what he terms "a demo constraining federation."

It is worth noting, though, that in cases of huge internal regional inequalities, a disproportional representation may be justified because it puts issues of regional inequalities on the national agenda. Souza (1999), for example, makes this point by arguing that in situations like those found in Brazil, a demo constraining condition may be useful as it spotlights the need to pay attention to regional disparities.

Over time, changes in revenue-sharing mechanisms in the Brazilian Federation were closely associated with the political cycle, with centralization of political power being accompanied by an increase in state and local governments' shares in federal revenues (Box 4.2).

Fiscal decentralization reached its peak in the mid-1990s, when the effect of changes introduced by the 1988 Constitution was fully achieved. The state and local government share of disposable tax revenues went up to 44% from the 30% observed ten years before. As shown in Figure 4.1 the municipalities were the main beneficiaries of the decisions adopted in 1988, having increased their share in the fiscal pie to 17% in 2003.

Box 4.3. *Social Security in the 1988 Constitution*[i]

In a reaction to the emphasis attributed to economic problems during the military regime, the 1988 Constitution increased the role of the state in social areas, with special attention to pension systems of private workers and public servants. The main changes introduced in the general regime were an increase in coverage, a five-year reduction in retirement age for rural workers, and a rise in benefits granted to them. The ensuing boom in rural pensions reached its peak in 1994.

All public servants, at the federal, state, and municipal levels, had job stability and were granted the right to receive for life a pension equal to the wage of fellow workers who remained active. Coupled with provisions for early retirements (after completing thirty-five years in the service for men and thirty years for women), these rules helped to increase the number of retired public servants in the 1990s. Fear of losing some of the benefits under changes included in various proposals to reform the social security system also contributed to an increase in applications for retirement.

The financial impact of these measures was significant. Resources needed to cover for pension payments rose to 51.4% of federal personnel expenses, up from 44% in 1995.

In addition to increasing social security benefits, the 1988 Constitution granted every disabled person and every elderly, poor person the right to receive from the federal government a benefit equal to the minimum wage for life, established universal access to the public health system, regardless of previous affiliation to a pension fund, and instituted a social budget to be financed with earmarked contributions.

Resources allocated to social expenditures in 1999 amounted to 16% of the GDP (about US$ 82 billion), of which 60% went to social security benefits. Other important components of the social expenditures are health, education, and unemployment insurance.

[i] *Source:* Amadeo et al. (2000), Giambiagi and Além (2000), and Najberg and Ikeda (1999).

In spite of its decentralization drive, the 1988 Constitution left the seeds for a quick reversal. It increased the responsibility of the federal government in securing social rights of Brazilian citizens (Box 4.3) and opened room for the creation of earmarked contributions to finance free universal access to public services.

In practice, the new Constitution installed a dual fiscal regime combining the traditional assignment of tax powers in the federation and mechanisms for revenue sharing with a new, more loosely controlled, dimension of fiscal relations specifically related to the financing of social policies. Insofar as more than half the revenues collected through the most important federal taxes (income taxes and a value added tax collected at the manufactured level) were to be transferred to states and municipalities, the outcome was easy to predict. Federal tax authorities came to rely more on earmarked contributions not shared with subnational governments (hereafter named "social contributions") to meet their social responsibilities, which not only interrupted the revenue decentralization trend observed since the mid-1970s but also led to an undesirable deterioration in the quality of the Brazilian tax system.

The deterioration of economic conditions following the opening of the Brazilian market to external competition did not allow state and local governments to fully exercise the autonomy supposedly granted by political and fiscal decentralization. On one hand, a low average rate of economic growth did not permit gains from an increase in their competence to tax. Transfers from above failed to materialize as expected. On the other hand, growing needs for achieving fiscal discipline to avoid macroeconomic problems meant greater restrictions on spending. One important instrument for the exercise of political power at state and local level – the budget – was severely affected.

Budget constraints at the state level meant lesser financial ability for these governments to cope with demands from their constituencies regarding provision of urban and social services. During the 1990s, state finances moved along a path that reflected unstable macroeconomic conditions, with a growing share of budgetary revenues being used to cover personnel expenses, social security benefits, and interest on the public debt. Local governments were pressed to raise fiscal efforts to meet their constituencies' demands for an increase in social spending given the retreat of federal agencies. In spite of a constitutional call for decentralization of responsibilities in social services, a strong movement in this direction was constrained by lack of financial means.

In fact, the constitutional provision for decentralizing public spending in social programs was affected by the centralization of revenues earmarked for that purpose. Social contributions (with the exception of contributions to pension systems) remained the sole competence of the federal government, which controlled decisions over collection and utilization of these resources. Even though empirical studies show that

Table 4.1. *National Revenues from Taxes and Social Contributions, 1988 and 2003*

	1988	2003
	(% GDP)	
National Tax Burden	22.4	35.8
Federal Tax Revenues[i]	15.8	24.7
Social Contributions	1.1	7.4
Cofins[ii]	0.8	3.8
PIS/Pasep[iii]	0.3	1.1
CPMF[iv]		1.5
CSLL[v]		1.0

[i] Total tax collections adjusted to account for transfers to states and municipalities.
[ii] Turnover tax earmarked for social programs.
[iii] Tax earmarked for unemployment benefits.
[iv] Tax on financial transactions.
[v] Tax on net profits.

Source: Araujo (2001), with new data for 2003.

state and municipalities have increased the amount of money applied in traditional social services activities – mainly education and health – the bulk of the financial resources needed to improve the quality of human life come from social contributions collected by the federal government. Aside from the traditional payroll tax that supports pension benefits, the money collected from these contributions rose to 7.4% of the GDP in 2000, up from the modest figure of 1.1% of the GDP in 1988 (Table 4.1).

Even though a significant portion of revenues for social contributions are handed back to subnational governments through ad hoc negotiations (*convênios*) they are targeted to specific areas, mainly basic health care, primary education, and aid to poor families, meaning that their autonomy is affected. States also do not have any guarantee as to the availability of these funds over time. The funds are subjected to annual revisions and to changing political relations that do not provide a solid ground for a sustainable decentralization of state responsibilities in social policies. Between 1996 and 2000 the amount of money transferred to state and municipalities to help finance local provision of social services doubled, reaching US$7 billion. About two thirds of this total went to basic health services, whose financing is now facing changes aimed at reducing instability in the resources available.

The 1988 Constitution also conferred the status of members of the Federation upon municipalities, so that these share the same rights and duties of the states. The three-tier Federation inscribed in the Constitution reflects the long tradition of municipal autonomy in Brazil and led to less control of the states over its municipalities. Political reasons as well as efficiency arguments based on the idea that bypassing the states would speed the process of providing municipalities with the resources needed to better attend the needs of the local community contributed to the move toward increased transfers of federal money to local governments. This trend was to the detriment of the role of member states in the Brazilian Federation.

Monetary stabilization achieved in 1994 brought further difficulties to the management of fiscal and local politics. During the preceding high-inflation era, postponing spending and freezing wages of public employees easily adjusted the fiscal accounts, while revenues were fully indexed to inflation. The efficacy of this practice disappeared with a stable currency, increasing the pressure on state and local government politicians to adjust their spending. They faced more severe constraints in adjusting their budgets while trying to meet their constituencies' expectations. The problem assumed an important dimension when the new authorities who took power in 1995, following the adoption of the 1994 stabilization plan, inherited problems derived from their predecessors' lax spending.[5] As shown in Table 4.2, 2002 figures for subnational governments' consumption and wage payments were far above the 1988 level.

Growing financial difficulties faced in 1995 were met by obtaining advances on future tax revenues using private bank loans with high interest rates and by delaying consumption and wage payments. These practices led to renewed pressures to reschedule debts with the federal government, including those already included in previous renegotiations (see Box 4.6).

The deterioration of state and local governments' fiscal accounts in the second half of the 1990s was mainly a result of exogenous factors. High interest rates were an important ingredient of monetary stabilization strategy, increasing the burden of interest payments on state and municipal budgets. Because high interest rates implied a less dynamic economy, own revenues and federal transfers could not cover the additional commitments of public money, thus increasing the subnational deficit.

Whereas the federal government could reshape its fiscal situation by increasing the tax burden through social contributions, state and local

---

[5] By the end of 1994, state and local governments granted generous wage increases to public employees, believing that revenue increases in the first months of the Real Plan would continue and ignoring the disappearance of the inflation tax.

Table 4.2. *Selected Public Expenditure Items, 1988–2002*

	Federal		Subnational[i]		Total	
	1988	2002	1988	2002	1988	2002
			(% GDP)			
Intermediate Consumption	2.6	2.0	2.1	4.8	4.7	6.8
Personnel	3.2	3.0	4.7	7.1	7.9	10.1
Gross Fixed Capital Formation	1.1	0.4	2.1	1.8	3.2	2.2
TOTAL	6.9	5.4	8.9	13.7	15.8	19.1
% Nonfinancial Expenditures[ii]						
Intermediate Consumption[iii]	55	30	45	70	100	100
Personnel	41	30	59	70	100	100
Gross Fixed Capital Formation	34	18	66	82	100	100
TOTAL	44	28	56	72	100	100

[i] States and municipalities.
[ii] Excludes all expenses related to the management of the public debt.
[iii] Purchase of goods and services.
Source: IBGE.

officials did not have this option. The primary deficits of the subnational governments were offset by a surplus in federal accounts from 1995 to 1998, however, avoiding an overall deficit.

IV. FISCAL FEDERALISM, ECONOMIC CRISIS, AND MACROECONOMIC STABILIZATION

The main fiscal adjustments needed to support macroeconomic policies during the second half of the nineties were the following:

(a) an important increase in revenues collected at the federal level through social contributions not shared with states and municipalities, which were responsible for the sharp increase in the tax burden ratio;

(b) a curb on public investments, with important negative consequences for the quality of infrastructure and basic public services;

(c) more stringent conditions applied to the expansion of public debt at state and local levels, following the renegotiations conducted in 1997–1998; and

(d) implementation of an important privatization program, which freed the government to keep subsidizing inefficient state-owned enterprises.

The political difficulties of pushing ahead the reforms necessary for making progress in cutting administrative expenses and social security benefits did not open room for trimming budgetary costs. Even with some reduction in the first two categories, cuts in investments were necessary. These also affected the competitiveness of Brazilian exports and the nation's ability to avoid rising deficits in foreign trade.[6] Measures to help reduce the imbalance in public sector pension systems were approved in renewed efforts to reform the social security system, but these changes will not have a significant immediate effect on federal finances (see Box 4.4).

The ability of less-developed regions to close the interregional gap in GDP became more limited as privatization of basic infrastructure went along with a virtual disappearing of savings at the federal level. The continued disparities fed further resentments within the Federation.[7]

Federal arrangements influenced the reforms even as the reforms affected them. The power of the states in national politics limited the central government's options with respect to fiscal adjustment. There is not much room for reallocating expenses in the federal budget once all of the conditions attached to utilization of the resources administered by the central government, especially transfers to subnational governments, are considered. Less than 5% is left to cover the maintenance of basic services and minor investments. Thus, in spite of the freeze in wages for public servants in place since 1995 and measures taken to reduce the annual rate of increase in pension payments, federal budget investments remained virtually nonexistent. Tax increases had to pay for interest on the public debt and cover the target set for the primary surplus.

Some of the measures taken for fiscal adjustment were a serious blow to competitiveness. The lack of investment in infrastructure is one aspect, but the reintroduction of turnover taxes in the Brazilian tax system is perceived by all to be the worst problem affecting Brazilian producers in the world market.[8] A broad enquiry put out recently by the Brazilian Confederation of Industrial Associations (Confederação Nacional da Industria – CNI) revealed the tax system to be the main factor that constrains businesses' export performance as well as their ability to keep their shares in domestic markets. Inefficient taxes – the traditional turnover taxes plus

---

[6] Despite constitutional amendments to reduce some privileges of public employees and cut the structural deficit of public pension schemes, state and local governments' payroll costs in 2000 remained at the 1996 level.

[7] The inability of the federal budget to support infrastructure investment in less-developed regions, through direct investment or subsidies, may reduce their chances of closing the gap in regional GDP.

[8] Turnover taxes had been abolished in the 1967 tax reform.

Box 4.4. *Public Employment and Social Security Reform*[i]

PUBLIC EMPLOYMENT

Constitutional Amendment 19 prohibited accumulation of jobs, modified rules for acquiring tenure, and suppressed the sole regime for admission, giving way for applying more flexible norms in hiring new entrants in the public service sector.

Law 9.962/2000 allowed for the adoption of the rules applied to private workers for new public employees.

SOCIAL SECURITY

Constitutional Amendment 20 changed various norms applied to the concession of social security benefits:

- Eligibility for retirement after thirty-five years of working life (thirty years for women) would depend on proof of actual contribution to the social security system.
- The possibility for early retirement was eliminated, thus extending working life of the labor force (by five years).
- Procedures for calculating the value of benefits became a matter of ordinary law (and thus became easier to alter than before).
- Special advantages granted to university professors and airline employees, among other professional categories were discontinued.
- The minimum age for retirement in public services was set at sixty for men and fifty-five for women.
- More rigorous criteria were established for exempting philanthropic institutions from social security contributions.
- New entrants in public service were exempted from privileges granted to current public employees.
- The contribution of public entities to supplementary pension plans would not be allowed to surpass employees' contribution.

Law 9.876/99 changed criteria for establishing pension values upon retirement with the goal of achieving actuarial equilibrium in the medium and long run.

Constitutional Amendment 41 focused mainly on measures to reduce the unbalance in the public sector pension system. The main changes were the following:

- Pensions of retired public servants became liable to a 11% tax, the same tax ratio applied to salaries of government employees.

- New entrants in the public service would not earn their last salary upon retirement and lost the previous pension–salary parity granted by the 1988 Constitution.
- The minimum age for retirement rose to fifty-five for women and sixty for men from the previous levels of forty-eight and fifty-three, respectively, and allowances for earlier retirement were cut off.

---

[i] *Source:* Ministério do Planejamento (1999) and Najberg and Ikeda (1999).

the new tax on financial transactions – accounted for one-fourth of federal tax collections in 2001 and represented an additional burden on the order of 11% of the value added in sectors with a more extended production chain.[9]

The revival of turnover taxes in Brazil did not have any parallel in the world. A relatively recent study by a consulting firm shows that Brazil was preeminent among a few countries that still apply this kind of tax. (Arthur Andersen, 1999) Of the twenty-eight countries included in this study (ten from the OECD, eight from Asia, and nine others from Latin America) turnover taxes were applied in six countries only, with the following rates: Brazil at 3.65%, Argentina, Bolivia, and the Philippines at 3%, Venezuela at 1.5%, and Colombia at 1%. At the time of the report, only Brazil (0.38% rate) and Colombia (0.2%) applied a tax on financial transactions, though Argentina has since added a transactions task. These data show how far the Brazilian tax system was from the practices adopted by its main competitors in the world market.[10]

Mounting pressures from private business leaders led the government to change the tax legislation to take into account the deleterious impact of turnover taxes on the economy. The Pis/Cofins contributions adopted the value-added-type mechanisms of debts and credits to assess tax liabilities to reduce the cascading effect on business, albeit in an imperfect manner.[11] Imports were also subjected to these contributions so as to avoid

---

[9] Varsano et al. (2001) showed that the effective total tax burden ratio from these taxes varies from 0.74% of the value added (noncommercial services) to 10.8% (steel production).

[10] Reintroduction of turnover taxes had to do with the need to raise resources to cover social obligations of the federal government following an increase in subnational governments' share in federal income and value added taxes decreed by the 1988 Constitution. More recently, however, these taxes were used to generate the primary surpluses in the fiscal accounts set in the monetary stabilization program.

[11] Revenue considerations led to a cautionary approach. Small businesses as well as most service activities were kept aside from the debt and credit mechanism, provoking distortions. In addition, claims of an overshooting in setting the new tax rates led to

Box 4.5. *Criteria for Distributing the Municipal Revenue Fund*

Criteria applied to the distribution of federal revenues shared with local governments through a special fund (the FPM) establishes the following:

- The states' capital cities receive 10% of the FPM.
- All other municipalities receive 86.4%.
- The remaining 3.6% comprises an additional quota for municipalities with more than 156,216 inhabitants.

The individual quota of states' capital cities is directly related to their population and inversely related to the states' per capita income.

The individual quota of noncapital cities is set by indices derived from a formula that favors the less populated municipalities. The index varies from 0.6 for those with less than 10,188 inhabitants to 4.0 for municipalities with more than 156,216 inhabitants. In between, sixteen population brackets form a distribution of individual indices that grow at decreasing rates, thus allowing for smaller per capita transfers as population increases.

unfair competition in the domestic market. Tradable goods sectors benefited from the changes, though the new rules increased the burden on services.

The overreliance of states and local governments on federal transfers also had important implications for the attainment of macroeconomic equilibrium. In spite of a constitutional mandate to revise the formula adopted to distribute federal transfers among its beneficiaries, this revision never occurred. Some attempts to introduce new variables to correct unbalances in the revenue-sharing mechanism were soon abandoned since the conflicts of interest appeared nearly impossible to resolve.

A practical solution was adopted in 1992: The share for each state and municipality of federal funds was established through negotiations based on the actual figures of the previous year, remaining fixed since then. As expected, the more-developed states and the bigger municipalities lost some ground in the process (Box 4.5).

As the amount transferred increased, the unbalance already in place gained further impetus. Budgets per capita in small municipalities were as much as three times higher than corresponding figures for densely

considerable criticism with regard to the prospect of further increases in the overall tax burden.

populated urban areas and big metropolitan cities. The same applies to the states, albeit on a minor scale: Less developed, sparsely populated states show per capita budgets 1.5 times higher than those of more-developed states.[12]

The overdose of transfers brought additional distortions to the Federation, among them a financial incentive for fragmentation at the local level that led to the creation of 1,465 new municipalities in the past decade. There has been a 30% increase in the number of municipalities over the past sixteen years. As the rules set out in the 1988 Constitution allowed for political separation of former *distritos* based only on a public referendum carried out in the region demanding secession, the outcome was easily predicted. Newly founded municipalities profited from partition, leaving the other part of the old municipality impoverished.

Another important negative consequence was the loss of interest of local taxpayers in local politics. As most of their budgets come from transfers, accountability at the local level was severely affected. With the exception of capital state cities and some other important urban areas, own revenues represent less than 20% of the municipal current revenues, meaning that Tiebout's classical approach to competitiveness at the local level has limited application to the Brazilian case.[13] A similar argument could be made with respect to the states, as in twelve out of twenty-seven states own revenues account for less than 50% of their respective budgets.[14]

The way fiscal decentralization evolved in the Brazilian Federation provoked a growing mismatch between revenues and responsibilities. On the one hand, socioeconomic dynamics led to increasing concentration

---

[12] Data for the year 2000 from the National Treasury Secretariat (Finance Ministry of Brazil) show that the smaller Brazilian municipality (Bora, SP) had per capita revenue of US$1,390, of which two-thirds came from the FPM. In the same year the municipality of Sao Paulo (with more than ten million people) presented a per capita budget of only US$407, with the FPM representing less than 1% of its revenue. At the state level, Amapa, in the Brazilian Amazon, having less than half a million inhabitants showed per capita revenues of US$912, with more than 70% of it coming from transfers, whereas the state of Sao Paulo (with thirty-seven million inhabitants) presented a per capita budget of US$624 (with less than 0.3% from transfers).

[13] In spite of the disincentive to local fiscal effort built into the revenue-sharing system, a significant improvement in tax collections at the municipal level was observed in Brazil recently, with practically all municipalities showing some effort to make use of the local tax basis. As discussed later, competition on the expenditures side was also constrained by dependence on federal money earmarked to social programs.

[14] Eleven of those showing this condition belong to the North and Northeast regions. The other is the Federal District.

of modern economic activities and population in medium-size cities and large urban centers in more developed industrial areas of the country. On the other, the criteria for distributing fiscal and financial resources ran in the opposite direction, with money flowing in greater proportion to less dynamic and sparsely populated rural regions. Thus, whereas a high proportion of public money had been diverted to administrative and low priority expenses, demands for urban and basic social services in metropolitan areas and urban agglomerations could not be properly attended to.

As mentioned before, a side mechanism for intergovernmental cooperation in financing decentralization of responsibilities grew in line with the increase in federal government collection of contributions earmarked for public provision of social services. The ensuing increase in dependence of member states and large municipalities on federal money to attend to basic demands of their constituency narrowed the possibilities for people and business to profit from competition among jurisdictions in the allocation of expenses. Federally established rules led to a greater standardization of public spending at the same time that the conditions for accessing loans granted by federal-owned financial institutions also reduced the autonomy of state and local governments.

The increase in transfers submitted to ad hoc negotiations also brought negative political implications. Because access to resources suffer from volatile political alliances, the quality of services provided may deteriorate for reasons that are beyond administrative capabilities of local administrators. Additionally, since there is no possibility of having reliable projections of financial flows in the nearby future, the process of decentralization has been proceeding on tenuous ground.[15]

Instead of moving in the direction of consolidating the decentralization achieved in 1988, the latest developments moved back toward centralization, with further interference of the federal government in shaping decisions to be implemented at the subnational level.

The impact of economic openness further contributed to this outcome. The Brazilian manufacturing industry, exposed to external competition after centuries of isolation, lost ground in domestic markets and could not participate in the more dynamic sectors of the international market. As a result, the national trade accounts deteriorated, going from US$15 billion

---

[15] The necessity of annual ad hoc negotiations is the main factor behind the uncertainties concerning the availability of resources at the state and local governments to finance social policies with money supplied by the federal budget.

Table 4.3. *State-Owned Banks – Present Situation*

Privatized	9
Under Federal Control	6
Liquidated	10
Non-Bank Financial Agencies	16
In States' Hands	7

Source: Planning Minister.

surpluses in the last years of the 1980s to a deficit of US$7 billion in 1997. Because of a sharp decrease in imports, following some slowing in the rate of economic activity, the external deficit turned into a surplus again in the vicinity of US$2 billion in 2001.[16]

External vulnerability also increased the difficulty of facing the financial crisis of the 1990s without sacrificing federal autonomy. Tight monetary and fiscal policies were accompanied by stringent norms to govern the actions of state and local governments. Besides the reforms already mentioned, renegotiation of the states' debts to the federal government, financial sector reform, and privatization of state-owned banks to cut one of the lines of states' debt financing were important components of the measures adopted to adjust state and local government finances.

The fragility of the state-owned banks came to the fore in the aftermath of monetary stabilization, giving the federal government the opportunity to intervene. A special program was created to force state governors to hand over control of these institutions in exchange for federal assistance in clearing their financial situations before privatization or liquidation. As a result, only eight financial institutions remain in state government hands. The others have been privatized or are in the process of being liquidated or transformed into nonbanking organizations. Table 4.3 summarizes the present situation.

Under rules set out by Law 9.496/97, the federal government signed debt renegotiation agreements with twenty-four states amounting to

---

[16] The balance in trade accounts remained positive – averaging a US$10 billion surplus – during the first half of the 1990s, beginning to show growing deficits in 1995, until reaching a high of US$7 billion in 1997. Smaller improvements were observed in the last years of the past decade till the reduction in economic activity helped to move to the positive side again in 2001. The deficit rose in the first years of the monetary stabilization plan (Plano Real) owing to a decision to use the exchange rate to support the transition to a stable currency. After devaluation, in December 1998, results in the trade accounts began to improve.

Box 4.6. *Calendar of State Debt Renegotiations, 1989–1999* [i]

1989: After the collapse of the stabilization plan launched in 1986, Law 7976 authorized a federal-owned bank (Banco do Brasil) to refinance state debts for twenty years. Because the refinancing was limited to debts with the National Treasury, this operation did little to solve the states' financial problems that continued to deteriorate under the impact of high interest rates and accelerating inflation.

1991: Law 8388 established new conditions for refinancing debts not included in the 1999 renegotiations: Twenty years for repayment under a 6% interest rate and monthly installments limited to 11% of revenues in the first year and 15% thereafter. As the conditions were not accepted, this proposal did not materialize.

1993: Along the lines set by Law 8.388/91, Law 8.727/93 allowed for the refinancing of outstanding debts with federal financial institutions, including payments overdue since 1991. Limits for repayment were lowered to 9% of revenues in the first year and 11% thereafter. Even though the new conditions allowed for the regularization of debt payments, they did not cover the entire problem, since debts with private banks and bonds were not included.

1995: After the 1995 stabilization plan (Plano Real), the federal government changed its approach to the renegotiations of state debts and introduced new measures to control indebtedness. From then on, refinancing was associated with public sector reforms, including privatization and conditions for meeting targets set for adjusting the fiscal accounts. New agreements would have to be submitted to the state legislature.

1996: Provisional Measure 1.560, giving the federal government power to renegotiate all kinds of debts, introduced new rules. Negotiations should be carried on an individual basis, depending on measures adopted by the states. The final aim was to bring the total financial liabilities of the states to levels below their net revenues.

1997–1998: Law 9.496/97 established criteria to be adopted in the renegotiations, setting targets for the total debt, primary surplus, wage costs, tax collections, and privatization. Twenty-four out of twenty-seven states signed agreements with the federal government under the rules of this law.

---

[i] *Source:* Lopreato (2000) and Rigolon and Giambiagi (1999).

US$82 billion (equivalent to 10.5% of the GDP) on rather favorable conditions: thirty years for repayment and a fixed interest rate between 6% and 7.5%. In addition, repayment should not surpass 15% of current revenues (and could be as low as 11%). Under these agreements, states cannot issue new bonds until their total liabilities become smaller than yearly revenues. Furthermore, they lose the special benefits if they do not comply with their obligations, and the federal government becomes entitled to sequester their shares in federal revenues, making it useless any attempt to evade the constraints built into these agreements.[17] For the first time in recent history, renegotiations of states' debts included provisions that cannot be seen as part of a classical bailout.

International financial crises brought further difficulties to the Brazilian economy and the federation. The same medicine applied to counteract the impact of the Asian and Russian crises – tight monetary and fiscal policies – added to the difficulties of states and municipalities in responding to demands from their populations. With the economy going at low speed, tax revenues did not provide enough room to improve public policies. Discontent mounted, to the despair of local officials who intended to make use of a constitutional amendment that allowed for reelection at all levels. The election results allayed fears that reelection at the municipal level would give no opportunity for opponents to win: Only 40% of the mayors were reelected in the year 2000 municipal elections.

To avoid the risk of repeating past experiences of successive renegotiations of states' debts, which could jeopardize the attainment of fiscal targets set in the federal government's agreement with the IMF, further restrictions on states' indebtedness followed the 1997–1998 renegotiations. Senate Resolution 78/98 prohibited new loans of any kind to states that had a primary deficit in the twelve-month period prior to application, reduced indebtedness margins, and mandated a gradual reduction in the debt/revenue ratios. Contracts signed with the states also prohibited the issue of new debt in case of failure to meet the trajectory set for reducing the debt/revenue ratio as well as any new debt that would alter that trajectory.[18]

---

[17] The efficacy of these rules was provided by a notorious case. After attempting to default in 1999, the governor of the state of Minas Gerais was forced to back away from his intent as the debt was paid with funds retained by the federal government under the provisions of the agreement.

[18] The main sources of states' debt financing included the states' banks (before privatization), federal financial institutions, and private banks, the latter being used mainly

Table 4.4. *State and Local Government Spending – Selected Functions from 1996 and 2003*

	States[i]		Municipalities[ii]		Total	
	1996	2003	1996	2003	1996	2003
			(% GDP)			
Public Safety	0.8	1.3	N.D.	0.1	0.8	1.3
Housing and Urban Services	0.2	0.1	1.0	1.0	1.1	1.1
Transportation	0.7	0.5	0.7	0.3	1.3	0.8
Health and Sanitation	0.8	1.5	1.1	2.0	1.9	3.5
Education and Culture	2.2	2.6	1.4	2.2	3.6	4.8
Social Security and Aid	2.0	1.3	0.5	0.6	2.5	2.0
Total	**6.7**	**7.3**	**4.6**	**6.2**	**11.3**	**13.5**

[i] *Source:* National Treasury Secretariat (Brazilian Finance Ministry) – "Execcução Orçamentária dos Estados 1995–2003."

[ii] *Source:* National Treasury Secretariat (Finance Ministry of Brazil) – "Finanças do Brasil" (1996) and "Perfil e Evolução das Finanças Municipais" (2003).

On the supply side, controls created by the National Monetary Council and the Central Bank imposed ceilings on financial institutions' exposure to loans granted to states, municipalities, and institutions under their control.

The tough restrictions on managing fiscal resources at the subnational level brought important results from a macroeconomic perspective. Consolidated state and local government fiscal accounts reached a primary surplus of 0.92% of the GDP in 2003, from a deficit of 0.7% in 1997. From the viewpoint of the urban public services, though, the price was high.

As shown in Table 4.4, subnational governments' spending on public safety, transportation, housing, and urban services remained at 3.2% of the GDP in 2003 (the same figure for 1996), even though urbanization kept growing. The same did not occur with spending on social services (education, health, and sanitation), which went up to 8.3% of the GDP in 2003, from the 5.5% level registered in 1996 owing to federal money provided for increasing decentralization of social services.

More recently, Congress has passed important new legislation, setting tough conditions to be observed in managing government accounts to sustain fiscal responsibility in the Federation. The so-called Fiscal Responsibility Law (LRF) approved in May 2000 intends to enforce fiscal discipline

for short-term loans. Federal government guarantees were also demanded for accessing resources provided by multilateral organizations.

at the federal, state, and local governments, establishing objective and clear rules to be observed in administering revenues and expenditure policies, the public debt, and government assets. Transparency is emphasized as a condition for social control of the actions of governments to make taxpayers conscious of the use public administrators make of resources extracted from taxation. Among the noteworthy norms set by the LRF, are the following:

(a) Limits for personnel spending: Remuneration of public employees shall not exceed 60% of net current revenues.
(b) Indebtedness limits: The federal Senate might approve revision of present limits to be proposed by the president of the republic.
(c) Yearly fiscal targets: Budgetary planning must look ahead, setting fiscal targets for three future consecutive years.
(d) Provision for recurrent expenditures: Public authorities cannot take actions that create future expenses lasting for more than two years without pointing to a source of financing or a compensating cut in other expenses.
(e) Special provision for electoral years: The law prohibits outgoing governors and mayors in their last year in office from obtaining advances on tax revenues through short-term loans, or from giving wage increases and contracting new public servants.

Failure to fulfill obligations imposed by the LRF leads to several administrative penalties, to which personal incriminations, included in an additional "Law of Crimes of Responsibility" ("*Lei de Crimes de Responsabilidade*"), may be added. More serious misbehaviors may be punished with the loss of the mandate, being barred from having a job in the public service, fines, and imprisonment. It is worth emphasizing that all levels of government, including the central government, have to abide by the conditions established in the LRF.

Four years after its implementation, the LRF has demonstrated its importance for the good performance of the Brazilian public sector accounts. A sizable part of the good results achieved in recent years with respect to the fulfillment of the fiscal adjustment targets set for the primary surplus in the consolidated accounts of the federation (which grew to 4.25% of the GDP in 2003 from the 3.1% level for 1999) can be attributed to the fiscal austerity imposed at the subnational level. The evidence is impressive. Since 1988 (the last year of negative results) the total state and local government primary surplus has grown, steadily reaching 0.92% of the GDP in 2003. It is worth noting that this fiscal effort practically matches the effort of the federal government, in spite of the fact that the latter has a larger and diversified tax basis. In 2003, states and municipalities as a whole generated a primary surplus that amounted to 11% of their net revenues, nearly matching the federal government's performance.

The economic crisis of the 1990s and the measures adopted by the federal government to achieve macroeconomic stabilization under new conditions of exposure to economic openness and free movement of capital forced important changes that caused a partial reversal of subnational autonomy. Even though these measures have been successful in attending to the immediate goal of sustaining monetary stabilization, they brought low levels of GDP growth, lack of investment in basic infrastructure, and deterioration in the quality of urban and social services. In part, these undesirable outcomes could have been averted had the government allowed the exchange rate to float earlier as demanded by some. As an increase in external vulnerability followed the appreciation of the real, recourse to tighter monetary and fiscal policies made it difficult to reconcile stabilization and growth objectives.

Up to now, administrative measures and imposition of tight budgetary constraints substituted for political institutions as a means to attend to macroeconomic objectives. In the process, the Federation was not prepared to face the challenges posed by globalization. Political institutions remained feeble, commanded by clientelism and old habits, and several proposals for a thorough political reform did not find any room to prosper.

Nevertheless, some positive signs of subnational budgetary discipline can be found, several in cases that belie the conventional belief that budgetary discipline at the subnational level cannot occur without a strong federal hand to guide the actions of mayors and governors. Two states in the poor Northeast region, Ceará and Bahia, governed by distinct political groups for more than twelve years, have shown very important positive results in managing public money, meriting the approval of their respective populations.

More recently, the state of São Paulo, which in addition to being the richest state in the Brazilian Federation had been well known for bad behavior in budgetary policy, also made important strides in the direction of maintaining a sound fiscal situation.

Renegotiations of state debts also helped to improve the situation everywhere. Between 1997 (when renegotiations started) and 2000, the aggregate outstanding debt of the Brazilian states dropped by an average of 25%. As a result, the aggregate debt/revenue ratio fell to 1.91 in 2000 from the 2.86 figure reached in 1997. Owing to indexation of the renegotiated debts and a low growth rate, more recent data show an increase in the ratio of states' debts to the GDP, which cannot be ascribed to fiscal misbehavior.[19]

Aside from the need to sustain a sound macroeconomic environment, the main challenges the Brazilian Federation currently faces are to resume economic growth and reduce social and regional inequalities. To that end, the present rules governing intergovernmental relations do not make a positive contribution. A more cooperative federalism is needed.

V. PRIVATIZATION, REGIONALISM, AND INTERGOVERNMENTAL CONFLICTS

Brazil began to abandon its long-standing tradition of having a strong interventionist government early in the 1990s. Shortly after its inauguration, in January 1990, the Collor de Mello administration launched an ambitious privatization program aimed at achieving fast results. However, despite some facilities being granted to private investors (e.g., treasury liabilities sold in the market with huge discounts were accepted at face value in public auctions), the initial goal of attaining US$17 billion in revenues from privatization in the first two years of the program turned out to be very unrealistic. Legal battles and the political crisis that led to the impeachment of Collor de Mello in September 1992 were the main factors behind the slow pace of the program in its infancy.

During the first phase of privatization, from 1990 to 1994, thirty-three public enterprises were turned over to private hands, providing the federal Treasury with resources in the vicinity of US$12 billion (US$8.6 billion from proceeds of sales and US$3.4 billion from transfer of debts to the new owners). By the end of 1994, the federal government no longer participated in steel and fertilizer production and had already given up most of its involvement in petrochemicals. Privatization of state monopolies was not even considered, however (Pinheiro, 1999; Pinheiro and Giambiagi, 2000; BNDES, 2001).

---

[19] As a percentage of the GDP, states' debts grew almost four percentage points between 2000 and 2003, when they reached 17.9%. The main explanation for this result is the difference between the higher growth in wholesale price index, used to adjust debts, compared with the dismal performance of the economy in this period.

The Cardoso administration, which took power in 1995, put the abolition of state monopolies high on his agenda for reforms. A set of constitutional amendments was presented to Congress in the first months following the beginning of Cardoso's first term in office, with the federal government pushing Congress to approve the passage of these amendments.[20] At the same time, state governments also began to implement their own privatization programs.

At the federal level, privatization was an important component of the monetary stabilization program conducted under the Plano Real. Political support from the population for policies that would end the era of high inflation helped the government to get approval from Congress to pass the constitutional amendments needed to abolish state monopolies in telecom, mining, electricity, and gas. At the state level, privatization began to be seen as an important source of resources to finance investments and cancel past debts.

Important institutional changes also helped to motivate privatization. The National Council for Privatization (CND) was created to allow for a better coordination of decisions concerning the sale of state monopolies, which also benefited from a new legislation for the provision of public utilities by private business. The special status the 1988 Brazilian Constitution provided to domestic investors in the fields of mining and electricity was also abolished, contributing to faster privatization of these sectors.

Between 1995 and 2001 (up to July) thirty-four federal and thirty-nine state-owned enterprises got into private hands, totaling sales of US$91.1 billion, including the assumption of debts by private investors. The privatization program proceeded at a high speed. In less than a decade, the state moved out of important activities that had been under its absolute control for nearly half a century. Private business currently controls railways and telecom, the most important Brazilian ports, more than half the distribution and a significant part of electricity generation, and a small share in water supply and sanitation (Box 4.7).

From the viewpoint of more immediate goals, the privatization program was a success. Public auctions raised considerable interest of both foreign and domestic investors, with selling prices much higher than the

---

[20] To be approved, a constitutional amendment has to be supported by three-fifths of the votes in two successive rounds, in the Chamber of Deputies and in the Senate. Moreover, it has to return to the form if the Senate modifies the text approved by the Deputies.

Box 4.7. *Privatization Program – Second Phase*[i]

1995–1996: Beginning in 1995, the Cardoso administration gave great priority to privatization, which become an important component of the structural reforms. The National Council for Privatization was created and sale of government enterprises not protected by monopolies was completed. In this new phase, public utilities were put high on the privatization agenda, and improvement in the quality of services provided by new owners was stated as an important objective for privatizing. The adherence of state governments to the privatization mood was also an important characteristic of this period, as the federal government gave support to the sale of state-owned enterprises. Total sales of federal and state-owned enterprises added up to US$8.1 billion in this period.

1997: The sale of a big government controlled mining company (the Vale do Rio Doce Company) for US$6.9 billion was the high mark of the year. This was followed by concessions to private business to explore mobile phone services in three important areas of the Brazilian territory, made possible by the approval of a new legislation for telecom, which added more than US$4.7 billion in revenues. The first sale of a government-owned financial institution and important advances at the state level also took place in 1997. Privatization of state-controlled electricity enterprises amounted to US$15.1 billion, whereas state-owned financial firms also began to be privatized.

1998: Sales of telecom companies stood out as the more important privatization of the year. Total transactions amounted to US$18.9 billion, 64% above the minimum price set for sale. Some advances were also made in the privatization of federally administered ports. State governments also showed good results in the fields of electricity and banks, to which the sale of a state-owned Telecom Company was an important addition. In financial terms, 1998 reached a high of US$37.5 billion in proceeds from privatization, of which US$10.8 billion referred to state governments.

1999: Results were modest. Performance of the states was much better than the federal one. Total proceeds reached US$3.9 billion, of which only US$554 million originated from sales of federal assets. Electricity and gas sectors were the leaders.

2000: The decision to sell government shares in excess of the amount required to keep federal government control of the big oil company

(Petrobras) helped to push up the results of the year. Proceeds from privatization reached US$7.7 billion, not including US$3.3 billion generated by the states through the sale of electricity and financial services companies.

2001 (up to July): Further concessions for exploration of mobile phone services were the main achievements, with revenues on the order of US$2.6 billion.

[i] *Source:* BNDES (2001).

minimum set by consultants hired to appraise the net worth of the state enterprises sold in the second phase of the privatization process. Since 1991, 136 privatizations took place in Brazil (97 conducted by the federal government and 39 by the states). The importance and characteristics of the program are revealed in the details presented in Table 4.5, Figure 4.2, and Figure 4.3.

The share of the public sector in total investment, a common measure of the degree of state intervention in the economy, shows the extent of the privatization program in reducing state control. This ratio fell by one-third between the beginning and the end of the 1990s, dropping to 7% in 1999 from a high of 25% in 1991. Spending by public enterprises on

Table 4.5. *Privatization Program, 1991–2002*

Sector	US$ Billions	% Total
Telecommunications	33.4	31.8
Electricity	32.2	30.6
Mining	8.8	8.3
Steel	8.2	7.8
Financial Institutions	6.4	6.0
Oil	4.8	4.6
Petrochemicals	3.7	3.5
Transportation	2.3	2.2
Gas	2.1	2.0
Sanitation	0.7	0.7
Ports	0.4	0.4
Others	2.3	2.2
1991–1994	11.9	11.3
1995–2002	93.4	88.7
Total	**105.3**	**100.0%**

Source: BNDES.

US$ billion

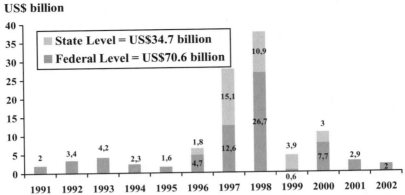

Figure 4.2. Evolution of the privatization program, 1991–2002. *Source:* BNDES.

personnel also dropped to less than half the level attained in the early 1990s. (Table 4.6)

Foreign capital played an important role in the privatization process. Foreign investors acquired about half of the shares offered in public auctions. On the whole, foreign capital accounted for 36% of revenues generated under the National Privatization Program, 49% of revenues from privatization of state government enterprises, and 60% of the proceeds from telecom. Portuguese, Spaniards, and North Americans, in this

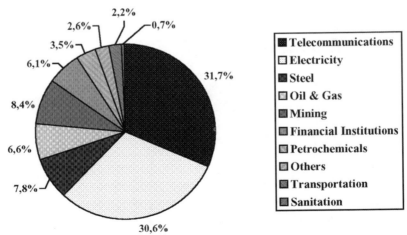

Figure 4.3. Sectoral composition of privatizations, 1991–2002 (US$105.3 billion). *Source:* BNDES.

Table 4.6. *Share of Public Enterprises in Gross Domestic Capital Formation (GDCF) and in Total Public Sector Personnel Costs*

Year	Total		Federal Public Enterprises		States Public Enterprise	
	GDCF	Personnel	GDCF	Personnel	GDCF	Personnel
1991	24.2	19.7	16.9	12.4	7.3	7.3
1999	7.0	8.2	3.4	4.9	3.6	3.3

Source: IBGE – Federal Statistics Bureau.

order, led the group of foreigners involved with the Brazilian privatization program.

Recent research (Ferreira, 2000; Novaes, 2000; Pinheiro, 1999; Pinheiro and Giambiagi, 2000) generally shows that privatization carried out during the above-mentioned period brought significant benefits for the country, namely, the following:

(a) modernization of enterprises helped by foreign investment;
(b) greater access to services for the population;
(c) reduction of the fiscal burden of subsidizing deficits of state enterprises;
(d) financing external debt through Foreign Direct Investment (FDI), which also helped to control the expansion of the public debt; and
(e) a substantial increase in industrial productivity.

As mentioned before, the slowing down of the privatization drive from 1999 onward, which coincided with the inauguration of a new term for the Cardoso administration, reflected a situation in which more difficult negotiations were required. External shocks provoked by the Asian and Russian crises also helped to reinforce the views of those who oppose privatization on ideological and equity grounds. The maxi-devaluation of the real in 1999 altered perspectives for the Brazilian economy and required a reappraisal of the privatization program. A weakened government, a feeble performance of the GDP, and an increase in risk perception brought down asset values, making it difficult to proceed at the same pace as before. The case of state-owned banks was an exception since their privatization was a condition for the states to renegotiate their debts with the federal government.

The targets set for privatizing the electricity industry were missed by a wide margin. Some progress was made in the distribution component of this industry, because state governments, who owned this part of the business, were hard-pressed to find ways to raise cash to ameliorate their financial troubles. The bulk of the generation, however, is still in public hands. The deterioration of the international scenario, with limited prospects for attracting foreign resources, led to further delays.

A poor regulatory framework contributed to increased public opposition to the advance of the energy privatization program. Regulatory rules are established by federal law and conducted by federally created agencies, but the relations of federal regulatory bodies and their state counterparts are not clearly set. The ensuing energy crisis, caused by a dry 2001 summer season in a context of paralyzed public investments and unclear definitions regarding guarantees for return on private investments, led to supply shortages and consumption rationing, calling for a time to reappraise the energy privatization program.[21]

At the state level there are different regulatory arrangements. Some states opted for having specific purpose agencies, whereas others chose to create a single agency for overseeing the variety of activities handed to private business in their jurisdiction. The power of state and local governments in areas such as transportation and water supply and sanitation adds further difficulties for the advance of privatization in these sectors.

The privatization program has been, so far, described as a case of success based on the resources invested, modernization of the areas under private administration, and access to services, as well as contribution of proceeds from sales of public assets to reduce expansion of the public debt. Nevertheless, the setback provoked by the 2001 energy crisis cast some dark clouds over some aspects of privatization. Contrary to what was done in the case of telecommunication, where public enterprises were allowed to invest to improve asset values before being auctioned, energy firms were not allowed to do so since the government expected to move quickly toward privatization. Given this ban on public investment and the limited private investment as foreign investors waited for judicial claims to be overruled by courts, a shortage in energy supply will ensue, provoking additional delay in the privatization schedule.

One negative side effect of privatizing basic infrastructure was its impact on prospects for development in backward regions. In the past public enterprises played an important role as a vehicle for better exploring the growth potential of backward and frontier regions, by helping to

---

[21] The telecommunications sector provides a contrast. Regulation preceded privatization, thus helping to transfer the control to private hands.

build and modernize the infrastructure required for attracting modern business activities. As decisions to invest migrate to private hands, and because the federal government lacks capacity to invest or to provide subsidies, the potential for an increase in regional inequalities cannot be ignored. These factors may be behind the states' recent turn to more aggressive approaches to attracting private investments.[22]

It should be noted that monetary stabilization achieved in the mid-1990s, together with consolidation of democracy and the advance of privatization, led to the resumption of large inflows of direct foreign investment, reversing the downward trend observed in the beginning of the decade. On average, FDI in the 1996–2000 period was ten times higher than the level attained in previous years. A significant part of it referred to acquisitions of publicly owned assets in public auctions, but some important new ventures were also made, mainly in automotive and agribusiness sectors.

For the first time in recent Brazilian history, the inflow of foreign direct investments occurred in a context of a liberalized financial market and aimed not only at the domestic but also the regional market (Mercosur). This new round of foreign investment started a fierce competition among the Brazilian states to attract the best projects.

The so-called fiscal war had its roots in a vacuum created by the absence of a federally sponsored regional policy to counteract the tendency to concentrate modern economic activities in the already more industrialized state of São Paulo. Without strong actions to promote economic growth in less developed regions, the tendency toward a reduction in the GDP gap among the five main regions that had been going on since the end of the 1970s, came to a halt in the mid-1980s. Regional disparities have remained unaltered since then. Incipient movement in the opposite direction threatens a new wave of increasing regional inequalities, which may bring political instability in its wake.[23]

---

[22] Government control over investments in basic infrastructure – (transportation, energy, and telecommunications) as well as in basic manufacturing inputs (steel) was an important instrument for promoting regional development as decisions to invest could take into consideration national goals of reducing regional disparities. After privatization, infrastructure investments in backward regions will have to rely on access to public funds, which are in short supply.

[23] In a country with a high degree of internal labor mobility, as is the case of Brazil, one could expect that migration would lead to a reduction in per capita GDP disparities over time. This does not mean, however, that it will achieve a better balanced federation. To that end, specific actions to raise development prospects for states in less developed regions are needed to avoid regional antagonisms.

The main tool of the new competition for investments among the Brazilian states is the granting of tax benefits supported by generous financial concessions. Brazilian states have been conceding even greater advantages to foreign and local investors to house the location of new manufacturing plants. This process has provoked strong criticism, based mainly on the argument that public money is being diverted to benefit foreign capital to the detriment of actual and future population demands. The mixed origin–destination principle applied to the state value added tax also favors escalation of the fiscal war since most of its financial costs are supported by the more industrialized state of São Paulo.[24]

A renewed attempt to put an end to the fiscal war by adopting a uniform national legislation and the destination principle for the states' Tax on the Circulation of Goods, Interstate and Intercity Transportation and Communication Services, Even When the Operation Is Initiated Abroad (ICMS – *Imposto sobre Operações Relativas à Circulação de Mercadorias e sobre Serviços de Transporte Interestadual e Intermunicipal e de Comunicação, ainda que as Operações se Iniciem no Exterior*) is blocked in the Brazilian Parliament at the time of writing. Despite the Parliament having agreed in principle to a proposition to change the Constitution to that end, further considerations with respect to financial compensation from the federal government and maintenance of benefits already granted to investors brought the negotiations to a halt.

It should be noted, though, that other elements also played a role in investors' decisions concerning the location of their industrial plants. Political stability and good governance, for instance, were behind some decisions by those in traditional manufacturing industries to abandon their plants established in the southern corner of the country and move their investments to the Northeast and opt for the states of Bahia and Ceará as their point of destination.

The new wave of investments in the automotive industry witnessed the location of the new plants in the southern states of Paraná, Rio de Janeiro, Minas Gerais, and Rio Grande do Sul, not very far from the main industrial center of São Paulo. Automakers chose cities well known

---

[24] Every good produced in other states and sold in São Paulo carries a nominal fiscal credit that reduces tax collections in São Paulo. It should be noted that credit is given even though there is a full rebate of the tax collected at the origin. (For details of the nature of the fiscal war see Box 4.8.)

Box 4.8. *The Fiscal War*[i]

The so-called fiscal war occurred in the wake of a virtual abandonment of past regional policies by the federal government after the negative impact of the macroeconomic crisis on federal finances. Being left alone, state governments opted for making increased use of fiscal benefits to attract private investments and promote industrial development.

The main weapon in this particular war was the mixed origin–destination principle applied to the state value added tax, which interacted poorly with the complexity of production. When production occurs in a less developed region and the good is consumed in a more developed one, two-thirds of the tax is collected at origin and one-third at destination, These proportions are reversed when goods are produced in developed states to be sold in less developed ones.

To attract new investments, producer states grant rebates of the tax due at origin. Moreover, when production is sold in the main consumption centers, investors can claim credit for the tax supposedly collected at the origin. Thus, the immediate financial burden of these benefits is really supported by the state where the good is consumed.

A new wave of domestic and foreign private investments, formed in the beginning of the 1990s, gave impetus to this war. Fears of losing ground in the dispute for these investments, given better externalities found in the main industrial centers, led less developed states to offer greater advantages.

Once started, the fiscal war tends to escalate, as investors test alternate locations in search for even better concessions as competitors in other states demand equal advantages to sustain a level playing field. Conflicts in the federation mount as threats to change location tend to equalize conditions everywhere.

In the end, fiscal benefits may backfire. As everybody engages in the war, benefits tend to converge, thus losing their efficacy as a tool for attracting investments. At that stage, decisions to invest turn back to basics: good infrastructure and social conditions. As the fiscal incentives reduce financial ability of less developed states to improve these conditions, they are prone to lose the war. Regional disparities may increase in the absence of a federal-sponsored regional policy.

[i] *Source:* Prado and Cavalcanti (1999, 2000) and Varsano (1997).

for the quality of their environment and of their labor force. The only case of a car maker deciding to move northward, to the state of Bahia, followed the rejection of standing agreements (made by the previous state administration) by new political leaders in the State of Rio Grande do Sul.

With few tools available to the Federation, competition was concentrated in two main policy areas. The first entailed fiscal and financial benefits to attract investments. The other tactic involved political support to have access to federal sources of financing. In the end, this kind of competition may lead to a negative sum game. To attract investments, state and municipalities forwent future budgetary revenues, which reduced their capabilities to respond to actual pressing needs as well as future pressues that will result from an increase in urbanization. By reducing their own resources in the future, municipalities become more dependent on access to federal resources, losing autonomy with respect to policies that create a favorable environment for business. Benefits achieved in the short run may thus be transformed with significant costs in the medium and long run, adding more instability in federal relations.

Competition among member states within a federation is regarded by some as beneficial from the viewpoint of efficiency. On this account, if state and local governments use public resources to create a better economic and social environment for people and business, competition over who receives approval will enhance economic efficiency and social satisfaction. Of course, this implies that authorities at the subnational level have autonomy to make decisions concerning the allocation of their resources, whether their own revenues or transfers. As mentioned before this condition is not fully found in the Brazilian Federation, meaning that in our case the competition in place is more likely to provoke economic distortions and social injustice.

VI. TAX REFORM AND REGIONAL INTEGRATION

There is a broad consensus on the inadequacy of the Brazilian tax system. It hinders competition in domestic and foreign markets, impinges on economic efficiency, puts additional burden on investments, induces tax evasion, and submits taxpayers to a cumbersome legislation. Nevertheless, no attempts to reform the tax system in the past fifteen years have succeeded.

Given its importance for the purpose of federal autonomy and the success of regional integration, tax reform has been on the agenda for the past fourteen years. No proposal has yet found a way to accommodate the conflicts of interest involved in any attempt to make profound structural changes in the tax system. Whereas private business emphasizes the urgency of a tax reform to establish a level playing field for competition with foreigners, states and municipalities fear that any change in the present regime will impinge on their autonomy to raise revenues and dispose of the resources collected in their jurisdictions, as well as leaving no room for policies aimed at reducing regional disparities.

There are reasons to argue that integrating into the global economy and into regional economic blocs could lead to greater internal disparities in Brazil while creating conditions for weakening the degree of national cohesion by allowing for more intense external economic relations and closer ties with foreign neighbors.

The Amazon provides a good example of the case in point. Already, the economy of the Brazilian Amazon is well connected with the exterior. Economic relations of the Amazon with the northern hemisphere tend to proceed at a faster pace given the potential for exporting products derived from its natural resources (minerals, forestry, and grains, as well as the well-known biological richness) to markets eager to consume natural products. Prospects for the output of the Free Zone of Manaus to reach the markets of Caribbean and Andean countries have also improved as investments in infrastructure facilitate commerce within the Amazon Basin and the Caribbean.

The poor Northeast region also faces new possibilities for cutting dependence from inputs and capital goods originated in the South. A sizable portion of traditional manufacturing industries is already moving to the Northeast to benefit from low production costs and proximity to external markets. In the global economy, industrialization of the Brazilian Northeast is not necessarily dependent on events in the South since it gains access to machinery and other inputs from abroad that are often better, in terms of quality and prices, than those domestically produced.

In the southern part of the country, Mercosur raises positive expectations, but other regions see economic integration in the Southern Cone as posing concrete danger for the national goal of a less uneven regional development in Brazil. Within-Mercosur trade has already multiplied several times since its inception, to the benefit of southern Brazilian states.

A recent study on the domestic regional impact of integration, under three distinct scenarios – Free Trade Area of the Americas (FTAA), free trade with the European Economic Community (EEC), and free trade with all Brazilian commercial partners (Tironi, 2001) – shows that each possibility might lead to concentration of economic activity in the already more developed areas of the Brazilian territory.

In the global economy, governments' ability to deal with domestic regional inequalities depends even more on cooperation. Traditional location factors – a low-paid labor force, availability of raw material, proximity of consumer markets, and low degree of labor organization – lose force at a time when facilities to move goods and services at long distances, increase in e-commerce, and the abandonment of antagonism among labor and capital render those factors obsolete. The obsolescence of traditional location factors also makes fiscal incentives less effective. Regional policy should be supportive of efforts to create a friendly economic environment, not focused on the concession of subsidies or tax holidays. This entails a joint federal and state effort to create a modern infrastructure, raise the quality of human resources, and invest in building capacity to generate and apply scientific knowledge to economic and social aims. To that end we need not only to reform the tax system but also to rebuild the foundations of the fiscal federalism model set up in the mid-1960s.

One of the points of dispute in the debate over tax reform is an incorrect association between harmonization and unification. State governments have correctly opposed renewed attempts from above to give up their competence to institute the value added tax that they have administered since 1965. The strong fear of facing the need to change the backbone of the fiscal federalism structure put in place thirty-five years ago is another reason for failure. Without having the courage to redesign the revenue-sharing mechanisms enshrined in the Constitution, the possibility of solving conflicts of interest are very low.

It is not necessary to unify, but it is to harmonize. Harmonization requires a common consumption tax basis but not uniform tax rates. Thus, a uniform consumption VAT shared by the federal and the states governments will have to be considered. This proposal poses new challenges for assuring fiscal balance in federal regimes with high regional inequalities, since it calls for a simultaneous revision in fiscal equalization mechanisms.

Sharing a tax is not the same as sharing its proceeds. In the latter, the fiscal system is wholly centralized and revenues of the central government tax are divided according to a specific formula. When the tax is shared, both central and state governments are entitled to explore the same tax basis under a common legislation. Autonomy to set the rules of taxation is jointly put in the hands of the National Parliament, but each partner keeps the ability to set rates, collect the tax, and dispose of its share.[25]

A common tax basis and national legislation would form a powerful incentive for intergovernmental cooperation in the field of tax administration, bringing benefits for taxpayers and administrators. On the taxpayer's side, a uniform rule for appraising fiscal obligations means lower compliance costs and alleviates the need to apply to distinct jurisdictions to resolve conflicts. On the side of the tax administrators, unification of tax registers and joint audits improve efficiency, reduce tax evasion, and minimize administrative costs.

With a harmonized consumption tax, competition for attracting economic activities through fiscal benefits will impact only the revenues of those who make these concessions, removing the main reason for a "fiscal war." Governments would have to rely more on improvements of basic infrastructure, urban services, and social programs to attract investment and promote development.

Sharing a broad-based consumption tax would also ensure a close association with income and consumption level in each member of the Federation. Compensatory transfers may thus be reduced to levels required to maintain a minimum standard of services everywhere in the country, allowing for a greater role of local governments in the provision of urban and social services.

Opportunities for applying the benefit principle of taxation also increase with the possibility of exercising greater autonomy at the local level. Big cities play an important role in the global economy while facing increasing difficulties in matching revenue and expenditure needs. Local taxes on property and on retail sales do not create economic distortions and may thus be better used. Charges imposed on the beneficiaries of public services provided at the municipal level could also be important to improve local public finances.

Stability in the tax system is another important advantage of sharing a tax. When a broad-based tax is shared in a federation, frequent changes in legislation are less likely to occur, as proposals will require enough support to overcome reactions of those who may not be in accord with the intended modification. It is worth noting that stability of fiscal rules becomes even more important as globalization and regional integration proceed, given its importance for attracting investments and for decisions to increase productive capacity.

---

[25] Of course, there are limits to rate differentials owing to mobility of the tax base.

However, emphasis on microeconomics put aside considerations of equity in taxation. Progressivity in income taxation is affected by increasing mobility of capital and high-paying jobs. Applying selective taxes on consumption is also constrained by competition in domestic and international markets. Equity may thus be better achieved by means of conceding priority to public programs designed to equalize opportunities for social mobility in the use of public resources.

The total tax burden is also subject to international constraints and to macroeconomic standards of a sound fiscal policy. Efficiency in public spending is the only way to maintain an adequate level of public services without surpassing the implicit limits on taxation.

In Brazil, and probably in other federations, antagonisms among the states have gained new impetus. These tensions are also manifested through the increasing resentment of taxpayers in richer states of the high tax burdens required to sustain generous fiscal incentives and transfers that often benefit the well-off living in poorer regions of the country.

The prevalence of these tensions in Brazil precludes an immediate move toward cooperative federalism. On the contrary, the search for individual gains, including by means of improving external economic relations, at the expense of a more intense interchange with other regions of the country, may appear more profitable from the viewpoint of each particular state in the Federation. The likelihood of a national economic disintegration along with the deepening of the international integration should not be overlooked.

VII. CONCLUSION

Brazil has been engaged in an effort to push institutional reforms to better integrate into the global economy since the early 1990s. The agenda for reforms was broad and included privatization of public enterprises, abolishment of state monopolies, reform of financial sector, modernization of the public administration, reform of social security, and modernization of the tax system. Their utmost priorities were the achievement and sustainability of macroeconomic stabilization. Many of these changes have important implications from the viewpoint of the federal regime that did not receive consideration.

In the process of emphasizing a stable currency, both economic development and federal autonomy were negatively affected. As mentioned, states were forced to privatize state banks as part of a deal to renegotiate their debts with the federal government. Meanwhile, tougher conditions were put in place to block the access of states and municipalities to credit, including private and multilateral loans. With their ability to collect taxes undermined by a sluggish rate of growth and the spread of informal activities, Brazilian states became more dependent on federal money to finance even basic social spending. As the national effort was focused on keeping the targets set for the primary surplus, public services deteriorated. This was to the detriment of the poor, who relied and continue to rely on these services to meet their basic needs.

The agenda for reforms missed one important aspect for better dealing with federal issues, namely, evolving a new regional policy. In the context of a closed economy and a strong interventionist state, which prevailed up to the 1980s, regional policy relied on federal fiscal benefits for private investments in less developed regions and in heavy public investments financed by the federal budget or conducted by public enterprises, mainly in basic infrastructure. Both disappeared as a result of the fiscal crisis and the privatization program, leading the states to compete for private investment. Many did so by granting generous fiscal rebates without due consideration of future impacts on their budgets.

In spite of the need for a new regional policy, this issue has not yet been raised to a priority on the federal government agenda. Without concerted actions to create favorable conditions for decentralizing production and income, antagonism within the Federation will surely increase, creating political instability and making it harder to move quickly toward the full implementation of the agenda for reforms.

Proposals for changing the tax system, though high on the reform agenda, failed for not paying due attention to factors that point to further regional unbalance. The emphasis on worldwide competitiveness and the centrifugal forces that develop in the wake of the advance of regional integration call for the insertion of the domestic regional issue in the process of design of a new tax system to remove the obstacles imposed to the advance of the tax reform.

To achieve the twin goals of competitiveness and regional equilibrium, tax reform must face controversial issues involved in the federal arrangements established in the middle of the 1960s and carried on through the 1988 Constitution. In this revision, a proper balance between competition and cooperation in the Federation should be accomplished. Autonomy to set tax rates and freedom to dispose of revenues enable member states to compete for attracting private investments through fiscal prudence and quality of the public services provided. However, a fair competition does not preclude the need for cooperation. Intergovernmental cooperation to reduce internal gaps in infrastructure, human resources, and technological capabilities are needed to avoid an increase in regional disparities and consequent antagonisms.

Bibliography

Affonso, R. B. A. A Federação no Brasil: Impasses e Perspectivas, in Affonso, R. B. A., and Silva, P. L. B., orgs., *A Federação em Perspectiva: Ensaios Selecionados*. São Paulo: Fundap, 1995.

Affonso, R. B. A. and Silva, P. L. B., orgs., *Desigualdades Regionais e Desenvolvimento*. São Paulo: Fundap/Unesp, 1995 (Série Federalismo no Brasil).

Afonso, J. R. Descentralização Fiscal na América Latina: Estudo de Caso do Brasil. Santiago: Cepal, 1994 (Série Política Fiscal, 61).

Afonso, J. R. Descentralizar e Depois Estabilizar: A Complexa Experiência Brasileira. Revista do BNDES. Rio de Janeiro, 3 (5): 31–62, jun. 1996.

Amadeo, E., Levy, J. V. F., Siguelmann, D., Melo Filho, P. G. M., Silva Filho, G. A., and Fausto, S. Orçamento Social da União. Brasília: Secretaria de Política Econômica, dez. 2000 (mimeo).

Araujo, E. A. Carga Tributária – Evolução Histórica: Uma Tendência Crescente. Rio de Janeiro: BNDES, jul. 2001 (Informe-se, 29).

Arthur Andersen. Pesquisa sobre Tributação, 1999 (mimeo).

Banco Nacional de Desenvolvimento Econômico e Social (BNDES). Privatização no Brasil: 1991/2001. Rio de Janeiro: BNDES, 2001 (mimeo).

Camargo, A. La Federación Sometida. Nacionalismo Desarrollista y Instabilidad Democrática, in Carmagnani, M., org., *Federalismos Latinoamericanos: México, Brasil, Argentina*. México City: Fondo de Cultura Económica, 1993.

Carvalho, J. M. Federalismo y Centralización en el Imperio Brasileño: Historia y Argumento, in Carmagnani, M., org., *Federalismos Latinoamericanos: México, Brasil, Argentina*. México City: Fondo de Cultura Económica, 1993.

Fausto, B. *História do Brasil*. São Paulo: Edusp, 1995.

Ferreira, C. K. L. Privatização do Sector Elétrico no Brasil, in Pinheiro, A. C., and Fukasaku, K., orgs., *A Privatização no Brasil*. Rio de Janeiro: BNDES, 2000.

Giambiagi, F., and Alem, C. *Finanças Públicas: Teoria e Prática no Brasil*. 2nd edition. Rio de Janeiro: Ed. Campus, 2000.

Goldsmith, R. *Brasil 1850–1984: Desenvolvimento Financeiro sob um Século de Inflação*. São Paulo: Harper & Row, 1986.

Gonzaga D. *História das Revoluções Brasileiras*. São Paulo: Unesp, 1998.

Instituto Brasileiro de Geografia e Estatística (IBGE). Síntese dos Indicadores Sociais 2000. Rio de Janeiro: IBGE, 2001.

Lopreato, F. L. C. O Endividamento dos Governos Estaduais nos Anos 90. São Paulo: Instituto de Economia da Unicamp, mar. 2000 (Texto para Discussão, 94).

Love, J. L. Federalismo y Regionalismo en Brasil, in Carmagnani, M., org., *Federalismos Latinoamericanos: México, Brasil, Argentina*. México City: Fondo de Cultura Económica, 1993.

Ministério do Planejamento, Orçamento e Gestão. Estudo dos Eixos Nacionais de Integração e Desenvolvimento. Brasília: Ministério do Planejamento, Orçamento e Gestão, 1999 (mimeo).

Najberg, S., and Ikeda, M. Previdência no Brasil: Desafios e Limites, in Giambiagi, F., and Moreira, M. M., orgs., *A Economia Brasileira nos Anos 90*. Rio de Janeiro: BNDES, 1999.

Novaes, A. Privatização do Setor de Telecomunicações no Brasil, in Pinheiro, A. C., and Fukasaku, K., orgs., *A Privatização no Brasil*. Rio de Janeiro: BNDES, 2000.

Oliveira, F. A Crise da Federação: Da Oligarquia à Globalização, in Affonso, R. B. A., and Silva, P. L. B., orgs., *A Federação em Perspectiva: Ensaios Selecionados*. São Paulo: Fundap, 1995.

Pinheiro, A. C., and Giambiagi, F. Os Antecedentes Macroeconômicos e a Estrutura Institucional da Privatização no Brasil, in Pinheiro, A. C., and Fukasaku, K., orgs., *A Privatização no Brasil*. Rio de Janeiro: BNDES, 2000.

Pinheiro, A. C. Privatização no Brasil: Por Quê? Até Onde? Até Quando?, in Giambiagi, F., and Moreira, M. M., orgs., *A Economia Brasileira nos Anos 90*. Rio de Janeiro: BNDES, 1999.

Prado, S., and Cavalcanti, C. E. G., orgs., *Guerra Fiscal no Brasil*. São Paulo: Fundap, 2000 (Série Federalismo no Brasil).

———, *Aspectos da Guerra Fiscal no Brasil*. São Paulo: Fundap, 1999 (Série Estudos de Economia do Setor Público, 5: 6–16).

Rigolon, F., and Giambiagi, F. A. Renegociação das Dívidas Estaduais e o Regime Fiscal dos Estados, in Giambiagi, F., and Moreira, M. M., orgs., *A Economia Brasileira nos Anos 90*. Rio de Janeiro: BNDES, 1999.

Rodriguez, V. Federalismo e Interesses Regionais, in Affonso, R. B. A., and Silva, P. L. B., orgs., *A Federação em Perspectiva: Ensaios Selecionados*. São Paulo: Fundap, 1995.

Secretaria do Tesouro Nacional (STN). (2003). "Perfil e Evoluçâo das Finanças Municipais." Brasília: STN.

Secretaria do Tesouro Nacional (STN). Finanças do Brasil. Brasília: STN (various years).

Serra, J. and Afonso, J. R. Federalismo Fiscal À Brasileira: Algumas Reflexões. Revista do BNDES, Rio de Janeiro, 6(12): 3–30, dez. 1999.

Silva, P. L. B., and Costa, V. L. C. Descentralização e Crise da Federação, in Affonso, R. B. A., and Silva, P. L. B., orgs., *A Federação em Perspectiva: Ensaios Selecionados*. São Paulo: Fundap, 1995.

Souza, C. Redemocratização, Federalismo e Gasto Social no Brasil: Tendências Recentes. XXIV Encontro Anual da Associação Nacional de Pós-Graduação em Ciências Sociais (ANPOCS), Rio de Janeiro, 1999.

Stepan, A. Toward a New Comparative Analysis of Democracy and Federalism: Demos Constraining and Demos Enabling Federations. Coréia do Sul, 1997 (mimeo).

Tironi, L. F., org., *Aspectos Estratégicos da Política Comercial Brasileira*. Brasília: Ipea, 2001.

Varsano, R., Pereira, T. R., Araujo, E. A., Silva, N. L. C., and Ikeda, M. Substituindo o PIS e a Cofins – e Por Que Não a CPMF? – por uma Contribuição Social Não-cumulativa. Brasília: Ipea, out. 2001 (Texto para Discussão, 832).

———, Afonso, J. R., Araujo, E. A., Pessoa, E. P., Ramundo, J. C. M., and Silva, N. L. C. Uma Análise da carga Tributária do Brasil. Brasília: Ipea, ago. 1998 (Texto para Discussão, 583).

Varsano, R. A Guerra Fiscal do ICMS: Quem Ganha e Quem Perde. Brasília: Ipea, jul. 1997 (Texto para Discussão, 500).

Varsano, R. A Evolução do Sistema Tributário Brasileiro ao Longo do Século: Anotações e Reflexões para Futuras Reformas. Brasília: Ipea, jan. 1996 (Texto para Discussão, 405).

FIVE

Changing with the Times

Success, Failure, and Inertia in Canadian Federal Arrangements, 1945–2002*

Richard M. Bird and François Vaillancourt

Canada is one of the oldest and, from most perspectives, one of the most successful federal countries in the world. But success has not come easily. Over the 135 years of its existence, Canada has changed in many ways. As the decades rolled by, its territory expanded greatly, the number of provinces (and territories) included in the union grew, its degree of political independence from Britain increased, and, from 1976 to 1985 and from 1994 to 2003, a political party whose explicit objective is separation of one of its provinces gained control of a major province while at the same time Canada's degree of economic dependence on the United States rose to new levels. These and other major changes in the nature of both the country and its environment have required equally major changes in the institutions of Canadian federalism. The union continues to endure, but not without a good deal of effort and not without continuing pressures and strains.

We examine three aspects of Canada's federal arrangements over the past half century. The marked change that has taken place in the sharing of the personal income tax between the federal and the provincial governments is a success story: Successful changes were gradually made over time to accommodate new economic and political circumstances. The

* This is the fourth and final draft of the chapter prepared for the Federalism Project, Stanford University. We thank Sandrine Bourdeau-Primeau, Isabelle Gauthier, Stephen Laurent, and Linda Lee for their research assistance; Jessica Seddon Wallack and T. N. Srinivasan for comments on the first version of the chapter; Frank Desrosiers and Ron McKinnon and the conference participants for their comments at the conference; and an anonymous reviewer for a final set of comments.

unsuccessful attempt to amend the Constitution Act of 1982 to satisfy the demands of Québec, the majority francophone province in Canada, was a failure in spite of great political effort. Finally, an example of a desirable, oft-discussed reform that has not happened is the creation of a national securities commission to replace the existing provincial commissions. We conclude the chapter with a few general observations.[1]

I. CANADA: A BRIEF INTRODUCTION[2]

Canada was created in 1867 by the union of three British colonies: Nova Scotia, New Brunswick, and Canada. The former colony of Canada was divided into two provinces: Ontario (the former Upper Canada) and Québec (Lower Canada). Three other British colonies soon joined the new country: Manitoba (the Red River colony) in 1870, British Columbia in 1871, and Prince Edward Island in 1873. In 1905, two new provinces, Saskatchewan and Alberta, were created out of federal lands.[3] Finally, Newfoundland (now officially Newfoundland and Labrador), which since 1933 had also been British colony following a short-lived period of independence, joined Canada in 1949.[4] Figure 5.1 gives a current map of Canada.

I.1. Constitutional Setting

Although there is some debate on this point among historians, it seems fair to state that the drafters of the Canadian Constitution (the British North America Act or BNA Act) intended to create a strong central government, largely in reaction to the recent Civil War in the United States and

---

[1] Although it may not need saying, we should perhaps emphasize that this selective account of a few aspects of Canadian federalism necessarily leaves out much more than it includes both in content and especially in terms of references. Articles could be, and have been, written about most sentences in this chapter, and books about most paragraphs. We have tried to strike a balance between accuracy and comprehensibility to those not initiated in the mysteries of Canadian federalism. We may not always have succeeded.

[2] For further discussion of many of the points noted in this section, see Bird and Vaillancourt (2001).

[3] The area of a number of other provinces, notably Ontario and Québec, was also expanded considerably by the inclusion in their jurisdiction of former federal lands in 1912.

[4] In addition to these ten provinces, as shown on the map, there are also three sparsely populated northern territories: Yukon, Northwest Territories, and, since April 1, 1999, Nunavut (the eastern part of the previous, larger Northwest Territories), although they are not further discussed here.

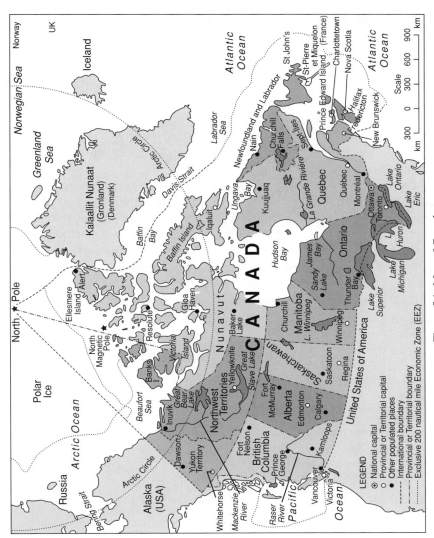

Figure 5.1. Map of Canada.

the perceived threat to Canada arising from that war.[5] The new government of Canada was, for example, given sole possession of the key revenue source at that time – customs duties – and made responsible for economic development (banking, railways, tariffs, etc.), whereas the new provinces were left to handle such local matters as education, health, and social services, none of which were deemed very important in the nineteenth century. To further reinforce central power, the federal government was also permitted, in certain circumstances, to disallow provincial legislation and to declare certain "local works" of national interest; an example of this was uranium mining during World War II.[6]

The preeminence of the federal government remained essentially unchallenged until the end of World War I. During the 1920s and 1930s, however, matters began to change when a series of decisions by the Judicial Committee of the Privy Council in London (which remained Canada's final court of appeal until 1949) reserved the field of transfers to individuals (workers compensation, welfare, unemployment insurance, and old age pensions) for the provinces. As a result of these decisions, explicit constitutional amendments were required to allow for the creation of federal programs of unemployment insurance (in 1940) and old age pensions (in 1951).[7] These amendments were made with the assent of all provinces. Despite this judicially imposed restraint, however, the federal government clearly remained dominant and fairly assertive in its relations with the provinces through both the depression of the 1930s and the succeeding war years.[8]

Indeed, as we discuss in the next section, World War II raised centralization, in fiscal terms, to a new height. In the ensuing decades, the federal government used its new fiscal power to intervene decisively in such constitutionally provincial fields as welfare, health (which in fact was mainly privately provided until 1957), and postsecondary education. Using what is called its "spending power" (Box 5.1) the federal government offered

---

[5] This threat may be inferred from both American political rhetoric and, more concretely, incursions into the province of Canada by Union veterans in upstate New York – the "Fenian raids" (so called because most of those involved were violently anti-British Irish immigrants).

[6] The disallowance power was last used in the 1930s with respect to some financial laws introduced by Alberta's Social Credit government.

[7] Curiously, no amendment seemed needed for the introduction of federal family allowances in 1944 (during World War II).

[8] For example, as just noted, some provincial legislation was disallowed in the 1930s, and the federal government's writ clearly dominated provincial financing in the depression years (Bird and Tassonyi, 2001).

Box 5.1. *The Federal "Spending Power"*

The federal "spending power" refers to the power of the federal government to pay money to people or institutions for purposes with respect to which the federal Parliament does not have the power to legislate. The precise nature and extent of this "power" is not set out constitutionally, nor has it been determined judicially, or for that matter in any other way, in Canada. Nonetheless, discussion about the existence of and meaning of the spending power has played an important role in the evolution of Canadian federalism. In effect, this is the language often used in Canada to discuss the virtually universal problem of overlapping jurisdictions in federal states.

Although the federal government used grants in the early part of the twentieth century in the area of roads (Turgeon and Vaillancourt, 2002) and old age pensions (50/50 sharing of costs with provinces of pensions for citizens aged seventy and over), it is fair to say that this power became a contentious issue after World War II when it was used in the areas of postsecondary education, health, and welfare. From 1951 to 1967 the federal government introduced the following transfer programs:

- 1951: grants to universities and then to provinces for postsecondary education. These grants were made on a per capita basis (increasing progressively from C$0.50 in 1951 to C$5 in 1966) and were paid directly to universities until 1967. They were replaced by cost-sharing (50/50) and a per capita grant.
- 1957: transfers to provinces for hospital insurance. These transfers covered 25% of provincial admissible costs and 25% of the national average cost.
- 1966: merging of programs financing payments to certain specific groups of individuals into a single program called the Canada Assistance Plan (CAP). This program covered 50% of the admissible costs of provincial welfare programs.
- 1967: transfers to provinces for medical insurance (Medicare, covering fees of physicians). This program paid to each province 50% of the national average cost.

In 1977, the postsecondary transfer and the two health transfers changed from conditional grants (with a list of acceptable spending items) to block grants [called Established Programs Financing (EPF) and paid both in cash and through tax points ceded to the provinces]. EPF payments were tied to population and GDP growth and some general conditions in the area of health were specified in 1984.

In 1995, CAP was merged with EPF and the resulting block grant, called the Canada Health and Social Transfer, is distributed according to provincial population. (See Box 5.2 for further discussion.)

major financial inducements to the provinces to modify their behavior in these and other areas that were constitutionally within subnational jurisdictions.

Canadians may often argue about the constitution, as we discuss in a later section, but there is never any question about which constitution is under discussion, since there is only one constitution in Canada. There are no provincial constitutions. Moreover, since municipal governments have no constitutional status in the BNA Act, they are entirely the creatures of provincial law and hence completely subject to provincial whims and wishes. Provinces thus can at will modify the number, boundaries, and powers of their local governments, and they have frequently done so.[9]

The constitution contains a list of exclusive federal powers, a list of exclusive provincial powers, and a list of concurrent powers (agriculture and immigration with federal paramountcy, and pensions with provincial paramountcy). Federal powers include defense, foreign affairs, money and banking, transportation, and communications. Provincial powers include education (subject to linguistic and religious safeguards for minorities), health, municipal and local affairs, police, and so on. There are no explicit provisions for reviewing the federal–provincial division of powers nor is there any official body responsible for suggesting initiatives in this area. There is no constitutional provision for interprovincial interaction, though provinces purchase some educational services from one another and make other contractual arrangements (for example, for police training and a common land registry system in the Maritime provinces). In addition to the constitution, various agreements in areas such as immigration help define the roles and responsibilities of the provincial and federal governments, but such agreements play only a minor role. Of greater relevance are the legal documents linked to federal transfers (laws, regulations, etc.) and judicial decisions of the Supreme Court in areas such

---

[9] For further discussion, see Tindal and Tindal (2000). Actually, there are two major forms of local government in Canada, municipalities and school boards, and in some provinces, for historic reasons, some school boards do have constitutional protection on the basis of religion (Catholic/Protestant) or language (French/English).

as telecommunications (cable television was deemed to be a federal and not a provincial jurisdiction in the 1960s) and environmental issues, which have, according to more recent judgments, been determined to be both a federal and a provincial responsibility. Such judgments are important because the list of powers drafted in 1867 does not always deal clearly with more recent developments and concerns.

I.2. Political Setting

Canada is a monarchy with the Queen (of Canada and the United Kingdom), the formal head of state, being represented by a governor general, who is appointed on the advice of the Prime Minister and who has a purely ceremonial role. Parliament has two chambers, the House of Commons and the Senate. Although the older eastern provinces have a disproportionate share of Senate seats relative to their population, this does not matter much since the appointed Senate is ineffectual.[10] Members are elected to the House of Commons in British parliamentary fashion, that is, by a plurality of votes in a single-round election in a territorially based constituency. The combination of a 1915 requirement that no province can have a number of members less than its number of senators and a 1985 requirement that no province can suffer an absolute drop in its number of members in the House means that some provinces have smaller constituencies than others. To adjust for population increases in some provinces, the number of members of parliament has to be increased – from 301 to 308 following the 2001 census, for example.

Canada has generally been controlled by a government with a majority (usually Liberal since 1945) in the House of Commons. Majority governments have similarly also governed in the unicameral systems of

---

[10] The Senate is formally appointed by the governor general, which means it is really appointed by the prime minister. Since members serve until age seventy-five, it is quite possible that at any point in time the majority of senators were appointed by a different party than that currently in power. However, although in constitutional terms the Senate has almost the same powers as the House of Commons, it has not vetoed a bill from the Commons since 1939. The Senate consists of twenty-four members from the Maritime provinces (ten each from Nova Scotia and New Brunswick and four from Prince Edward Island), twenty-four from Québec, twenty-four from Ontario, twenty-four from the western provinces (six each), six from Newfoundland, and one from each of the three territories. Some of the western provinces have long argued for a "Triple E" senate – equal membership from every province, elected, and "effective" – and, as we shall see, at one stage this demand reached the constitutional negotiation stage, although it got nowhere in the end.

the provinces for most of the time. Coalitions, formal or implicit, among parties thus play a role in policy decisions only very rarely. The most important recent case occurred in the second Trudeau government in 1972, when the (left-leaning) New Democratic Party (NDP) supported (in an informal coalition) the Liberal minority in exchange for a more nationalistic energy policy, which included the creation of a new state petroleum company, Petro Canada.[11] Provincial parties, despite often bearing the same name as federal parties (e.g., Liberal, New Democratic Party, and Progressive Conservative), are not formally linked to the federal party or for that matter to the provincial party of the same name in other provinces. Governments controlled by these parties can and often have taken opposite policy stands to their federal counterparts, even though their membership may be partially shared, thus resulting in informal links. Interest groups too cross provincial lines and again link federal and provincial politics. Nonetheless, party discipline is notably strong in Canada at both the federal and provincial levels. Members rarely defy party leaders and almost never formally change parties. When they do, they are seldom reelected, since electoral finances are tightly controlled by the central party offices – federal or provincial, as the case may be. Finally, very few politicians in Canada have successfully crossed from the provincial to the federal sphere. The highest political goal of a successful provincial premier is usually to win another majority; it is not to leap to the federal level.

A final important political fact is that, except for three short periods totaling about two years, since 1968 the federal Prime Minister has been a bilingual Québec member of parliament (MP). Nonetheless, by far the most important source of political tension in Canada in recent decades has clearly arisen from the presence of a francophone majority in Québec (see Table 5.1). To understand recent events one must know that most Québec francophones – like most anglophone Canadians – are unilingual. Not surprisingly, francophones (individuals with French as their mother tongue) are significantly less mobile than anglophones (individuals with English their mother tongue) within Canada. Moreover, a majority of Québec's francophones voted for "sovereignty-association" in 1995. We discuss in a later section of the chapter the various attempts that have been made to recognize this reality more fully than at present in some constitutional form, and why they have, to date, failed.

---

[11] The National Energy Policy of this era contributed considerably to the dissatisfaction with federal policies felt in the western provinces, particularly Alberta – a dissatisfaction mirrored to this day in the inability of the federal Liberals to develop a firm political base in the West.

Table 5.1. Key Demographic, Economic, and Geographic Features of Canada's Provinces and Territories,[i] 2003

	Canada	NFD	PEI	NS	NB	QUÉ	ONT	MAN	SASK	ALTA	BC	YU	NWT	NU
Area (km²)	9,984,670	405,212	5,660	55,284	72,908	1,542,056	1,076,395	647,797	651,036	661,848	944,735	482,443	1,346,106	2,093,190
Population (thousands)	31,630	520	138	936	751	7487	12,238	1163	995	3154	4147	31	42	29
Population Density (thousands/km²)	3.2	1.3	24.4	16.9	10.3	4.9	11.4	1.8	1.5	4.8	4.4	0.1	0.0	0.0
% Population Anglophone[ii]	59.3	98.4	93.9	93	64.7	8	71.6	75.8	85.7	81.8	74.1	87.1	78.1	27.6
% Population Francophone[ii]	22.7	0.4	4.3	3.8	32.9	81.2	4.4	4.1	1.9	2	1.5	3.1	2.6	1.5
GDP (millions of dollars)	1,214,601	18,015	3,883	28,813	22,358	254,263	493,416	38,078	36,778	170,631	142,418	1,310	3,332	916
GDP per Capita	38,400	34,644	28,138	30,783	29,771	33,961	40,318	32,741	36,963	54,100	34,342	42,258	79,333	31,586
% Area	100	4.1	0.1	0.6	0.7	15.4	10.8	6.5	6.5	6.6	9.5	4.8	13.5	21.0
% Population	100	1.6	0.4	3.0	2.4	23.7	38.7	3.7	3.1	10.0	13.1	0.1	0.1	0.1
% GDP	100	1.5	0.3	2.4	1.8	20.9	40.6	3.1	3.0	14.0	11.7	0.1	0.3	0.1

[i] NFD, Newfoundland; PEI, Prince Edward Island; NS, Nova Scotia; QUÉ, Québec; ONT, Ontario; MAN, Manitoba; SASK, Saskatchewan; ALTA, Alberta, BC, British Columbia.
[ii] 2001 figures.

Sources: Authors using Statistics Canada data (Cansim II 384 0013) Census 2001, Statistics Canada. "Mother Tongue, 2001, Counts for Both Sexes for Canada, Provinces and Territories." Area is from http://www.statcan.ca/english/Pgdb/phys01.htm.

Finally, as a rule in Canada each government administers its own policies, although there are a few interesting exceptions. One exception is with respect to taxes, where the federal Canadian Customs and Revenue Agency (CCRA, formerly Revenue Canada) collects provincial personal income tax for all provinces except Québec as well as a joint federal–provincial VAT called the Harmonized Sales Tax (HST) for three provinces (Newfoundland, New Brunswick, and Nova Scotia). However, in Québec the provincial Ministère du Revenu du Québec (MRQ) administers the federal sales tax (the Goods and Services Tax, GST).[12] The federal Royal Canadian Mounted Police (RCMP) provides provincial police services to eight provinces (Québec and Ontario have their own provincial police services) and also to about 200 municipalities within those eight provinces under cost recovery contracts.[13] Such contract policing accounted for over half of RCMP employees and for 57% of its budget in 2000–2001.[14] Provinces and the federal government collaborate through various working groups of federal and provincial civil servants and through informal regular contacts between their civil services.

I.3. Economic Setting

Canada is the second largest country in the world, with an area of 10 million square kilometers. This immense and varied territory may roughly be divided into five regions: the Atlantic coastal area (which in turn is divided into four small provinces), the central heartland along the St. Lawrence River and the upper Great Lakes (divided between the huge central provinces of Québec and Ontario), the great plains (beginning in the province of Manitoba and extending through Saskatchewan to Alberta), the mountain region ending on the coast of British Columbia, and, finally, the great northern expanse, extending from the northern sectors of most provinces (except the three small Maritime provinces) into the treeless reaches of the three sparsely populated northern territories. Despite this vast territory, however, most Canadians live within a few hundred kilometers of the U.S. border and have important cultural commonalities (such as television-viewing habits in English Canada) and economic ties with the United States (e.g., 85% of Canadian exports go

---

[12] See Bird and Gendron (1998) for a full discussion of sales taxation in Canada.

[13] In the case of British Columbia, the contract is with the province to provide services to specific municipalities. Elsewhere, the RCMP contract directly with local governments. Similar contract policing arrangements exist with a number of aboriginal bands and with a few airports.

[14] See http://www.rcmp-grc.gc.ca/dpr/performance01e.pdf.

to the United States). Most also live in urban areas, increasingly in such major metropolitan areas as Montréal, Toronto, and Vancouver.

Table 5.1 summarizes some key demographic, economic, and geographic features of the different provinces.[15] As shown in the table, there are important disparities both in size, with the GDP share of the largest province (Ontario) being over 100 times larger than the smallest (Prince Edward Island), and in incomes, with GDP per capita in the richest province (Alberta) being almost twice as high as GDP per capita in the poorest province (Prince Edward Island).[16]

Two major events have influenced Canada's economy over the past decade. Most importantly, in 1989 Canada signed a Canada–USA Free Trade Agreement (CUFTA) that was expanded in 1993 to include Mexico and became the North America Free Trade Agreement (NAFTA). From 1989 to 2000, exports as a share of GDP went from 26% to 46%, with exports to the United States rising particularly dramatically, from 19% to 38% of GDP. This change was accompanied by a major restructuring of the manufacturing sector, particularly in Ontario, from a branch plant economy to what is now essentially an integrated part of the American economy. Initially, this restructuring was very difficult to accomplish, not least because it took place in the depth of a serious recession in 1990–1991. Subsequently, however, the increased integration with the United States undoubtedly boosted Canada's recovery and led to relatively good growth performance later in the decade.

More recently, however, the events of September 11, 2001, the consequent border closing, and the new U.S. concern for border security in general have put great pressure on Canada to respond in a way that meets U.S. security concerns while serving Canada's overwhelming economic interest in swift and secure access to American markets (Dobson, 2002). Another recent policy concern, again arising from Canada's increasing economic integration with the United States, was the steady depreciation of the Canadian dollar over the decade, from 87 cents US in 1991 to little more than 60 cents in 2002. But this was followed by a quick reappreciation with the value in the 75–80 cents range by mid-2004. Some linked this decline to concerns about the slow growth of real income and productivity and argued that the logical course is for Canada to "dollarize," that is, to adopt the U.S. dollar as its currency. In an ongoing debate reminiscent in

---

[15] The data in Tables 5.1–5.4 are for calendar 2003 (population and GDP) or fiscal year 2003–2004 (revenues and expenditures).

[16] The reader should be cautious in using data for the three territories, which owing to their small economies are quite variable from one year to the next and may reflect unique situations in a given year.

many ways of those in the European Union about the euro, others see little gain from having to forgo flexibility in monetary policy. In these and other ways, the long-standing Canadian obsession with relations with the United States has been considerably strengthened by the free-trade agreements.

The second important event over the past decade has been more narrowly Canadian. From 1974 onward the federal government ran an annual budgetary deficit that by 1995 had reached 5% of GDP, with accumulated gross debt reaching a level of 120% of GDP. Such a situation was unsustainable. In the first half of the 1990s, however, the combination of strong economic growth driven in good part by exports to the United States and much tighter federal fiscal policy than in any other OECD country, including both increases in taxes and cuts in spending (including cuts in transfers to provinces), turned things around. Since 1997, the federal government has been in a budgetary surplus position and has been paying down debt.[17] Although most provinces also eliminated or reduced their deficits by 2000, they did so with more difficulty, in part owing to the nature of their expenditures and in part because of the federal transfer cuts. Indeed in 2003–2004, most provinces were again in a deficit position (see Table 5.3). This divergent recent experience has led some to reopen the question of the appropriateness of the current assignment of revenues and expenditures in Canada.[18]

I.4. Fiscal Setting

Provinces in Canada are constitutionally able to tax anything they want to tax (except international and interprovincial trade), setting their own rates, using their own definition of tax bases, and collecting taxes themselves. In fact, they raise most of their considerable resources from the same sources as the federal government – taxes on income and sales. Of course, as Tables 5.2–5.4 show, there are wide variations in provincial taxation, both in terms of structure and importance in provincial revenues. Not all provinces levy payroll taxes and Alberta alone does not levy a sales tax. The dependence of provinces on federal transfers varies widely: Newfoundland, for example, receives five times the transfers that Alberta does. Money may not lie at the heart of Canada's federal problems, but

---

[17] The latest surplus for 2003–2004 is of the order of C$9 billion.

[18] This was done, most notably, by Québec's Séguin Commission (2002), although it should be noted that others have supported this argument (Mintz and Smart, 2002).

Table 5.2. *Main Features of Provincial Taxes in Canada, 2003*

Province	Personal Income Tax[i] (Federal and Provincial)		Corporate Income Tax[ii] (Manufacturing)		Sales Taxes[iii]		Payroll Tax[v]	Capital Taxes[vi]
	$10,000	$200,000	Provincial	Total	Rate	Type[iv]		
Newfoundland	26.57	48.64	5	27.12	8	HST	2	–
Prince Edward Island	25.80	47.37	7.50	29.62	10	Prov.	–	–
Nova Scotia	16.00	47.34	16	38.12	8	HST	–	0.25/0.50
New Brunswick	16.00	46.84	13	35.12	8	HST	–	0.30
Québec	13.36	48.22	8.93	31.02	7.50	GST+	4.26	0.60
Ontario	16.00	46.41	11	33.12	8	Prov.	1.95	0.30
Manitoba	27.90	46.40	16	38.12	7	Prov.	2.15	0.30/0.50
Saskatchewan	27.00	44.00	10	32.12	6	Prov.	–	0.60
Alberta	16.00	39.00	13/12.50	35.12/34.62	0	–	–	–
British Columbia	22.05	43.70	13.50	35.62	7.50	Prov.	–	–

i PIT rates are for a single taxpayer with assessed income of either $10,000 or $200,000. See Table 5.5 for the provincial PIT rates.
ii Source: *Finances of the Nation*, 2003, Canadian Tax Foundation, Tables 4.2 and 4.3.
iii Source: *Finances of the Nation*, 2003, Canadian Tax Foundation, p. 5.6.
iv HST, harmonized sales tax; GST+, base similar to GST: Prov., provincial.
v Source: *Finances of the Nation*, 2003, Canadian Tax Foundation, Table 4.6.
vi Capital taxes are general/Bank rates.

Source: Finances of the Nation, 2003, Canadian Tax Foundation, Table 4.6.
Source: Finances of the Nation, 2003, Canadian Tax Foundation, Table 3.12.

Table 5.3. *Canadian Provincial and Territorial Governments, Revenues and Expenditures, 2003*

	Canada	NFD	PEI	NS	NB	QUÉ	ONT	MAN	SASK	ALTA	BC	YU	NWT	NU
Total Revenues	247470	4761	1129	7531	6236	66702	81154	9681	8533	28402	30999	667	969	1024
% Revenues from Own Sources	82.61	62.19	64.48	69.83	67.96	83.71	85.73	71.99	82.61	88.31	86.49	19.79	1.24	9.86
% Transfers	17.4	37.8	35.5	30.2	32.0	16.3	14.3	28.0	17.4	11.7	13.5	80.2	98.8	90.1
Personal Income Taxes % of Own Sources	25.5	24.8	22.7	26.9	22.5	31.2	26.9	25.4	17.7	18.6	18.6	26.5	716.7	28.7
Corporate Income Taxes % of Own Sources	5.6	4.8	4.1	5.1	2.6	5.0	7.3	4.5	4.4	7.2	3.1	6.1	0.0	4.0
General Sales Taxes % of Own Sources	14.9	21.1	23.5	18.7	18.8	13.9	20.5	16.3	12.1	0.0	14.7	0.0	0.0	0.0
Fuel Taxes % of Own Sources	3.7	4.6	5.1	4.7	5.5	3.1	4.2	3.3	5.0	2.4	4.1	5.3	150.0	3.0
Property Taxes % of Own Sources	1.6	0.0	6.7	0.0	7.2	0.0	0.0	3.1	0.0	4.6	5.9	1.5	91.7	3.0
Payroll Taxes % of Own Sources	4.2	3.0	0.0	0.0	0.0	8.1	5.4	3.9	0.0	0.0	0.0	0.0	0.0	0.0

Other Taxes % of Own Sources	44.3	41.7	37.9	44.5	43.3	38.8	35.6	43.5	60.8	67.2	53.6	60.6	0.0	61.4
Total Revenues % of GDP	25.8	39.3	37.7	33.6	33.9	32.7	20.5	31.2	28.3	24.3	26.1	61.8	29.1	140.1
Own Revenues % of GDP	21.3	24.5	24.3	23.5	23.0	27.4	17.5	22.5	23.4	21.4	22.6	12.2	0.4	13.8
Total Spending (millions of Canadian dollars)	257987	5129	1223	7350	6346	69429	88097	9958	8872	25453	33500	685	1189	1073
Deficit/Surplus (millions of Canadian dollars)	−10517	−368	−94	181	−110	−2727	−6943	−277	−339	2949	−2 501	−18	−220	−49

Sources: Authors using Statistics Canada data (Cansim II 385 0001).
GDP: Department of Finance Canada, Fiscal Reference Tables 2003, various tables.

Table 5.4. *Provincial Personal Income Tax Rates, Canada, 2003*[i]

Newfoundland and Labrador	10.57% on the first C$29,590 of taxable income + 16.16% on the next $29,589 + 18.02% on the amount over C$59,180
Prince Edward Island	9.80% on the first $30,754 of taxable income + 13.80% on the next $30,754 + 16.70% on the amount over $61,509
Nova Scotia	9.77% on the first $29,590 of taxable income + 14.95% on the next $29,589 + 16.67% on the amount over $59,180
New Brunswick	9.68% on the first $32,183 of taxable income + 14.82% on the next $32,184 + 16.52% on the next $40,279 + 17.84% on the amount over $104,648
Québec	16% on the first $27,095 of taxable income + 20% on the next $27,099 + 24% on the amount over $54,195
Ontario	6.05% on the first $32,435 of taxable income + 9.15% on the next $32,435 + 11.16% on the amount over $64,871
Manitoba	10.90% on the first $30,544 of taxable income + 14.90% on the next $29,455 + 17.40% on the amount over $65,000
Saskatchewan	11% on the first $35,000 of taxable income + 13% on the next $64,999 + 15% on the amount over $100,000
Alberta	10% of taxable income
British Columbia	6.05% on the first $31,653 of taxable income + 9.15% on the next $31,654 + 11.70% on the next $9,376 + 15.70% on the next $15,574 +16.70% on the amount over $88,260
Yukon	7.04% on the first $32,183 of taxable income + 9.68% on the next $32,184 + 11.44% on the next $40,279 + 12.76% on the amount over $104,648
Northwest Territories	7.20% on the first $32,183 of taxable income + 9.90% on the next $32,184 + 11.70% on the next $40,279 + 13.05% on the amount over $104,648
Nunavut	4% on the first $32,183 of taxable income + 7% on the next $32,184 + 9% on the next $40,279 + 11.50% on the amount over $104,648

[i] Federal tax rates for 2003 are 16% on the first C$32,183 of taxable income; 22% on the next C$32,184 of taxable income; 26% on the next C$40,279 of taxable income; and 29% of taxable income over C$104,648.

Source: Finances of the Nation. 2003. Canadian Tax Foundation. Table 3.9.

it has certainly been a critical factor in how they have been resolved, as we discuss in the next section with respect to sharing the income tax.

Table 5.5 presents expenditures by level of government. Provinces are the main players in the health and education fields, whereas the federal

Table 5.5. *Spending by Type for Each Level of Government and by Level for Each Type, Canada, 2003*

	General Services	Protection of Persons & Property	Transportation & Communication	Health	Social Services	Education	Transfers to Other Governments	Debt Charges	Other	Total (millions of dollars)
% Type for Each Level										
All governments	3.4	8.0	4.3	19.3	26.1	14.8	–	10.8	13.1	463431
Federal	3.73	10.61	1.14	3.06	37.90	2.42	14.64	12.05	14.45	50027
Provincial	1.6	3.5	3.8	33.4	16.9	22.7	0.5	9.0	8.5	257987
Municipal	8.9	16.1	16.1	2.0	5.3	14.5	–	5.7	33.2	51395
% Level for Each Type										
Federal	46.1	56.2	11.2	6.7	61.8	7.0	95.9	47.5	46.8	50027
Provincial	26.5	24.2	48.7	96.2	36.1	85.4	4.1	46.6	36.1	257987
Local	28.7	22.3	41.3	1.1	2.2	10.9	–	5.8	28.0	51395

Source: Authors using Statistics Canada data (Cansim II 385 0001).

government is the main provider of general services, protection services, and social services (old age and unemployment programs).

There are three major types of federal–provincial transfers in Canada: equalization (about C$10 billion), the Canada Health and Social Transfer, or CHST (about $20 billion),[19] and program-specific transfers (about $5 billion) for official language, housing, legal aid, etc., with various criteria used to allocate funds. Box 5.2 briefly describes the first two programs.[20] In addition, of course, a certain amount of interprovincial redistribution occurs in federal programs such as unemployment insurance or child benefits. Unemployment premiums are the same across provinces and industries, whereas unemployment rates vary significantly across provinces, resulting in transfers among provinces (Vaillancourt and Rault, 2003). The progressivity of the income tax system and the income tested nature of child benefits also result in implicit transfers among provinces.

Finally, provinces have free access to both national and international capital markets for borrowing purposes, with the sole constraint being their credit rating. This has resulted in provinces adopting financial discipline overall, although some excesses may occur from time to time.[21] Over the past twenty years, most federal government enterprises (crown corporations) have been privatized, although Canada Post remains federally owned as does the Canadian Broadcasting Corporation/Société Radio Canada. In addition, the federal government still owns 18% of Petro Canada, an integrated oil company set up, as noted earlier, in the early 1970s, as well as Atomic Energy of Canada, a manufacturer of nuclear reactors. Public enterprises remain important at the provincial level. The provinces own lotteries, liquor stores (except Alberta), and (again except for Alberta), electricity providers, although privatization is under consideration in some provinces. The decision to privatize provincial enterprises is solely a provincial one with no federal input. Public enterprises remain most important in Québec, which has a number of important crown corporations and also owns large stakes in many Québec businesses through the Caisse de Dépôt et Placement, which invests the assets

---

[19] The CHST is now divided as of April 1, 2004 into the Canada Health Transfer (CHT) and the Canada Social Transfer (CST).

[20] Perry (1997) provides a detailed discussion and history. See Vaillancourt (2000a) for more information on small transfers.

[21] For detailed discussion of subnational borrowing in Canada, see Bird and Tassonyi (2001).

Box 5.2. *Major Federal–Provincial Transfer Programs*

EQUALIZATION

This program, introduced in 1957 and constitutionally protected in 1982, takes into account the tax capacity of provinces, compares it to a five-province (Québec, Ontario, Manitoba, Saskatchewan, and British Columbia) standard for each of a given set of taxes, calculates for each tax the surplus/deficit amount using the average provincial tax rate (collections/base), sums the deficits net of surplus, and thus obtains equalization per capita, which, multiplied by the population, yields the annual equalization payment, which cannot be negative. The formula is as follows:

equalization province $J(>0)$

$$= \left[\sum_{i=1}^{N} \left[\left(\begin{matrix} \text{per capita} \\ \text{tax base } i \\ \text{standard} \end{matrix} - \begin{matrix} \text{per capita} \\ \text{tax base } i \\ \text{province } J \end{matrix} \right) \times \begin{matrix} \text{average} \\ \text{tax} \\ \text{rate } i \end{matrix} \right] \right] \times \begin{matrix} \text{population} \\ \text{province } J \end{matrix},$$

where N has varied over time from 3 (1957) to 33 (1997) and includes all major taxes (personal, corporate, sales, fuel, alcohol, tobacco, payroll, etc.) used by the provinces. Equalization payments are from federal general revenues with no province-to-province transfers. Transfers have the purpose of raising the revenues of recipient provinces and are not linked to specific spending. Ceilings and floors apply in some years (see Boadway and Hobson, 1998, for more details). Some commentators allege that this system leads to those provinces receiving equalization either setting tax rates too high without regard to their impact on their tax base or not encouraging economic activity as much as possible since increases in the associated tax base reduces equalization payments almost one for one. Unsurprisingly, the existence of this effect is vigorously denied by provincial officials.

CANADA HEALTH AND SOCIAL TRANSFER

This program had its beginnings in several open-ended conditional grants (see Box 5.1) but took its current form only in 1999. It provides for an equal per capita grant to each province: The federal government sets the

per capita amount of the grant. The amount of the block grant is paid as
follows:

per capita grant = per capita value of + remainder as cash
equal across   personal income tax   grant.
provinces   room transferred in
                     1977 (13.5% of tax
                     field)

Since the cash grant varies inversely with the value of transferred tax
room and the value of a 1% point of transferred tax room varies with
provincial income, poor provinces receive more of the CHST in cash
and rich provinces less. Hence, Newfoundland receives about 55% of its
CHST transfer in cash and Ontario about 45%. Québec receives only
40% of this transfer in cash because in 1965 it received an extra 16.5%
of personal income tax room (see Section II). This transfer is nominally
related to expenditures on postsecondary education, health, and social
services but in practice is not in any way earmarked or otherwise linked
to spending in those areas. The same calculations will be used for the
CHT and CST.

of both the pension plans of civil servants and the Québec social security
plan.[22]

II. THE PIT AND THE PENDULUM: THE RISING ROLE
OF PROVINCIAL TAXES

In 1933, the first year for which we have official data, the federal government accounted for 42% of all own government revenues, provincial
governments for 18%, and local governments for 40%. By 2000, these
percentage shares had become 44%, 45% and 11%, respectively. These
numbers may suggest that the key change was in the relative importance of the different subnational governments, rather than in the role of
the federal government. At the end of World War II, however, the federal
government was in fact collecting 82% of all revenues.[23] In this section
we tell the tangled tale of how, over the next few decades, the size of the

[22] The Québec Pension Plan (QPP) is an earnings-related plan financed by an earmarked
payroll tax. It is identical to the Canada Pension Plan (CPP), a federal–provincial scheme
operated by the federal government, except in terms of its investment policy. For detailed
discussion, see Vaillancourt (2000b).
[23] The long-term swings in revenue shares are discussed in Bird (1970a, 1979).

Table 5.6. *Standard Abatement Rates for Canada and Québec, 1947–2003 (Selected Years)*

	Canada			
	PIT (%)	CIT (%)	Succession (%)	Québec PIT (%)
1947	5	5	50	5
1954	10	7	50	10
1958	13	9[i]	50	13
1960	13	9	50	13
1964	16	9	50	19
1965	21	9	75	44
1966	24	9	75	47
1967	28	10	75	52
1972	30.0	10	ii	54.0
1977–[iii]	39.0	10	ii	55.5

[i] An additional 1% abatement is available as of that year until 1967 in lieu of federal per capita grants to universities Only Québec takes it up.
[ii] Federal estate and gift taxes were repealed in 1972.
[iii] Since 1977, the abatements rates have remained unchanged.

Sources: Moore et al. (1966), Perry (1989), Smith (1998), Commission sur le déséquilibre fiscal (Séguin Commission, 2002).

federal share returned to its predepression level, with particular emphasis on the story of the income tax. The story is not a simple one to follow, but some help may be provided by Tables 5.6–5.8.

II.1. The Swings of the Pendulum

The depression had taken its toll on provincial finances in Canada by the mid-1930s, with the western (now oil-rich but then poor) province of Alberta being driven to the brink of bankruptcy. In response to this and other crises in provincial (and local) finance, in 1937 the federal government established the Royal Commission of Dominion–Provincial Relations (commonly called the Rowell–Sirois Commission). When this Commission reported in 1940, after the beginning of World War II, it recommended that, to avoid such crises in the future, not only should responsibilities, taxing powers, and debt be centralized but in addition a system of equalizing grants, designed to respond to provincial fiscal needs, should be established. Although the opposition of British Columbia, Alberta, and Ontario – the three provinces that would not have qualified for these grants – meant nothing was done at the time, all provincial premiers agreed to cooperate with the federal government throughout

Table 5.7. *Personal Income Tax Revenues in Canada, 1947–2002*

	Total PIT (millions of dollars)	Federal % of PIT	% Federal in Québec	% Federal ROC[ii]	Total PIT % GDP	Federal PIT % GDP	Provincial PIT % GDP
1947[i]	660	100.0	100.0	100.0	5.4	5.4	0.0
1952	1 225	100.0	100.0	100.0	5.5	5.5	0.0
1954	1 309	98.1	iii	100.0	5.6	5.5	0.1
1957	1 676	97.6	iiii	100.0	5.6	5.4	0.1
1962	2 378	84.9	83.5	87.0	6.2	5.3	0.9
1967	5 112	71.4	55.9	75.8	7.3	5.2	2.1
1972	11 385	69.3	50.7	75.8	10.3	7.2	3.2
1977	23 656	60.4	40.6	69.0	10.7	6.5	4.2
1982	43 932	58.6	38.1	66.8	11.6	6.8	4.8
1987	70 333	59.3	41.4	66.0	12.6	7.5	5.1
1992	101 226	58.7	43.0	64.1	14.5	8.5	6.0
1997	120 956	60.6	47.8	64.5	13.8	8.4	5.4
1998	129 089	61.3	47.5	65.4	14.3	8.8	5.5
2000	143 514	62.4	48.4	65.4	13.6	8.5	5.1
2002	138 906	61.8	50.8	66.2	12.7	7.9	4.9

[i] Figures for year ending December 31.
[ii] Rest of Canada: B.C., Alberta, Saskatchewan, Manitoba, Ontario, N.B., N.S., P.E.I., and, after 1949, Newfoundland.
[iii] Data not available.
Sources: 1947–67: Statistique Canada CS11-516F (1983), "Statistiques Historiques du Canada," Tables H53, H76.
1972–82: Statistics Canada: 13–213 S, "Provincial Economic Accounts – Historical Issue. 1961–1986," Table 9.
1987–98: Statistics Canada, CANSIM labels D26728 and D26731.
2000: Department of Finance Financial Reference Tables 32 and 35 and Commission sur le Déséquilibre Fiscal.
2002: Department of Finance Canada, Fiscal Reference Tables 2003. Table 32. 35, and 38.
Canada Revenue Agency, Interim Statistics 2004 Edition, Interim Basic Table 5.5: All Returns by Province and Territory.
Department of Finance Quebec, 2004–4005 Budget, Table 2.19.
GDP: 1947–62: "Statistiques Historiques du Canada"; 1967–98: CANSIM label D23257; 2002: Statistics Canada, CANSIM II 384 0013.

the war. Under the Wartime Tax Agreements (the "tax rental" agreements), the provinces surrendered ("rented") all rights to impose income taxes to the federal government in exchange for fixed annual payments.[24] These agreements – though seen by some as a scheme of blackmailing the

[24] Succession duties (inheritance taxes) were also included in these arrangements. The disappearance of these taxes as a result of interprovincial tax competition in Canada following their abolition at the federal level is discussed in Bird (1978).

Table 5.8. *Corporate Income Tax Revenues in Canada, 1947–2002*

	Total CIT (millions of dollars)	Federal % of CIT	Total CIT % GDP	Federal CIT % GDP	Provincial CIT % GDP
1947	653	90.50	5.40	4.90	0.50
1952	1 342	95.20	6.10	5.80	0.30
1954	1 116	95.60	4.80	4.60	0.20
1957	1 51	85.80	5.00	4.30	0.70
1962	1 693	76.70	4.40	3.40	1.00
1967	2 417	75.30	3.50	2.60	0.90
1972	3 92	74.00	3.60	2.60	0.90
1977	7 238	70.90	3.30	2.30	1.00
1982	11 755	78.40	3.10	2.40	0.70
1987	16 99	69.80	3.00	2.10	0.90
1992	14 517	68.80	2.10	1.40	0.60
1997	31 46	62.90	3.60	2.30	1.30
1998	29 068	63.40	3.20	2.00	1.20
2000	46 035	65.90	4.40	2.90	1.50
2001	37 837	65.00	3.50	2.30	1.20
2002	40 350	63.80	3.70	2.40	1.30

Sources: See Table 5.7.

provinces into accepting fiscal centralization (Granatstein, 1975, p. 173) – are seen by others to have been a reasonable compromise, given the times.[25]

Following the expiration of the wartime agreements in 1946, the next forty-five years of federal–provincial fiscal history can be divided into six periods.

II.1.a. 1947–1957. Unable to reach a postwar federal–provincial consensus, the federal government simply offered to continue the tax rental agreements with any province that was interested. The idea was both to ensure stable annual revenue for the agreeing provinces and to achieve an efficient and uniform national tax system. In the end, seven (of the then nine) provinces signed tax rental agreements for 1947 to 1952.[26] In exchange, these provinces were to receive the most beneficial combination of per capita payments, Wartime Tax Agreement payments, and statutory subsidies. Newfoundland also signed up when it joined Canada in 1949.

[25] For example, Smith (1998, p. 35) compares the Canadian solution of "temporary centralization" to the much more definitive centralization that took place in Australia under similar circumstances.

[26] The fiscal year in Canada runs from April 1 to March 31.

The two largest provinces, Ontario and Québec, did not enter into the new tax rental agreements. Instead, both provinces chose to impose their own corporate income tax (CIT), initially at a rate of 8.5%, which was higher than the 7% credit for provincial CIT that had been offered by the federal government against its own CIT for nonsigning provinces.[27] Neither province chose to impose a personal income tax (PIT), however, even though the federal government offered a similar 5% credit for such a tax against its own PIT.

The eight signing provinces renewed the agreements for 1952–1957. In addition, Ontario also joined the agreements in late 1952, on the condition that it could levy succession duties at the expense of an equivalent reduction in the rental payments it was to receive. Québec, however, fearful of Ottawa's centralizing tendencies, not only remained outside the agreements but also proceeded in 1954 to establish its own provincial PIT, calculated initially as a tax on tax (at 15% of federal rates). This move led the federal government to make some adjustment in how it treated provincial taxes. The previous credits for provincial taxes were changed to "abatements," and these abatements were increased for the PIT from 5% to 10% in an attempt to accommodate the new Québec PIT.[28]

II.1.b. 1957–1967. The next set of federal–provincial arrangements, taking effect in 1957, saw some more substantial changes, including the establishment of the first formal equalization system. The most important points of the 1957–1962 tax arrangements were as follows:

- Provinces were to receive payments (on a derivation basis for agreeing provinces) or abatements (for nonagreeing provinces) equal to 10% of federal PIT, 9% of CIT, and 50% of federal succession duties. The PIT share was increased to 13% in late 1957 by a minority federal government.
- Equalization payments were introduced to bring each province's (whether agreeing or not) per capita yield of the three "standard" taxes (PIT, CIT, and succession duties) up to the level of the two provinces

[27] We do not attempt here to tell the tale of further developments in the CIT, some of which were related to the huge increases in oil prices in the 1970s and consequently had major regional implications. For a recent review of provincial CITs and other business taxes, see Bird and McKenzie (2001).

[28] An "abatement" may be claimed whether or not any provincial tax is paid, whereas a credit can be claimed only against tax paid (Burns, 1980, p. 111). In effect, an abatement is thus similar to the refundable tax credits that have subsequently become a feature of Canada's PIT (see Bird, Perry, and Wilson, 1998).

with the highest per capita yield. In other words, equalization was provided independent of the tax arrangements.

- Finally, federal stabilization payments were to be made (instead of "guaranteed minimum payments"), and annual "rental" payments were made equal to the yield of each standard tax in any province that rented any one or more of them.

II.1.c. 1962–1967. In 1962, the system still essentially in place came into being, with federal collection of provincial PITs in all provinces except Québec and of CIT in seven provinces. Two features of the new agreement are of particular interest. First, the federal government would collect provincial PIT and/or CIT at no cost provided that the base was identical to the federal base. Second, federal "withdrawals" would recognize the provinces' need for "tax room." Specifically, federal PIT was reduced by sixteen percentage points in 1962 and then by one additional percentage point in each of the next four years until the reduction (abatement) reached twenty percentage points in 1966.

The introduction of these new tax collection agreements made the provincial part of income taxation clearly identifiable for the first time in the postwar period. Canadians outside of Québec now had to fill out additional lines for the "provincial" PIT as part of their federal PIT tax form. Although the provinces were free to determine their own rates, they had to use the federal levels of exemptions and deductions and the rate structure set by Ottawa if they wanted Revenue Canada to collect their income tax. Only Québec was free to set its own exemptions and rates.[29]

Another important change during this period was that "opting-out" (also referred to as "contracting-out") was introduced. What this meant was that provinces that wished to do so would have a reduced federal PIT in lieu of transfers, provided they agreed to maintain the same programs as those financed by transfers. Additional equalized PIT abatements were made available to any province in lieu of conditional grants for shared costs programs for hospital insurance (up to a fourteen percentage point reduction in federal PIT rates) and various welfare and health programs (six points). But only Québec proceeded to "opt-out" for all these programs, with the result that the federal income tax imposed in that province has for many years been lower than that imposed in the "rest of Canada" (ROC). Opting-out does not increase or decrease the revenues of Québec since transfers are reduced by an equivalent amount. It does, however,

---

[29] Lachance and Vaillancourt (2001) describe how the Québec PIT has evolved over time.

allow Québec to reflect its own preferences in tax matters over a greater share of personal income than other provinces. Differences in the tax treatment of children (greater tax benefits in Québec) and of those with high incomes (more progressivity in Québec) are the result. The provincial government can also introduce tax preferences for investments in Québec without having to negotiate with the federal government for the right to do so. Conversely, federal preferences in tax matters have less room to influence individual choices in Québec than in the ROC. Québec's choice of this option reflected the long-standing greater desire for autonomy in that province than in other provinces.

II.1.d. 1972–1977. Following the report of a federal Royal Commission on Taxation in 1967 (the Carter Commission), major reforms were made to the federal income tax in 1971, including a new and broader definition of taxable income, which now included capital gains, and lower marginal rates for middle- and high-income taxpayers. In the 1972 fiscal arrangements, the abatement system was abandoned, and the federal government simply lowered its tax rates to make room for higher provincial taxes.[30] In effect, all provinces were now free to set their tax rates as they saw fit with no implicit norm (the abatement level) set by the federal government. However, provinces still had to calculate taxes as a percentage of the federal tax – thus using not only the same base but also the same progressive rate schedule – if they wanted the federal government to collect their PITs.

II.1.e. 1977–1999. During the 1960s, health services had mainly become publicly funded (comprising 70–75% of total health spending) in Canada, with the federal government covering half the costs incurred by provincial health systems through two open-ended conditional grants. By the mid-1970s, the federal government was very unhappy with the high and unpredictable growth of its share of health costs, which had been driven up both by inflation and by the spending decisions of provinces financed by "50 cent dollars." It therefore decided to replace the previous conditional grants financing health care (and also one for postsecondary education) by a system of block grants called Established Program Financing (EPF), which was to be escalated by a moving average of GDP growth. Initially, the provinces were not all that unhappy with this change: Some provinces,

---

[30] A "revenue guarantee" was provided to offset the effects of the 1971 federal PIT changes on provincial revenues.

such as Ontario, had themselves become increasingly discontented with the constant bickering over which costs qualified for cost-sharing. In addition, as part of the realignment of federal and provincial fiscal responsibilities associated with this change, the federal government once again withdrew to some extent from the PIT field to provide more tax room for the provinces to raise their own PITs as they saw fit.

II.1.f. 2000 and Beyond. In 1999, when the federal government replaced Revenue Canada by the CCRA, it agreed to collect provincial PITs at any rates imposed by the provinces so long as they used federal taxable income as a base. The previous "tax-on-tax" approach was thus replaced by a "tax-on-income" approach, allowing provinces for the first time to determine the progressivity of their own PIT rather than accepting that set by the federal tax schedule.[31] Alberta immediately took advantage of this opportunity by introducing a 10% flat tax. Some other provinces have varied slightly the degree of progressivity of their tax rates. Table 5.5 shows the provincial PIT rates for 2001.

II.2. What Happened and Why

Table 5.6 shows the evolution of the tax shares of provincial and federal level of governments in Canada from 1947 to 1977. The impact of the 1972 reform and also the subsequent withdrawal by the federal government are clearly evident, as is the special treatment of Québec. Indeed, the two largest increases (in percentage terms) of provincial tax share are both clearly related to Québec – the doubling of the abatement in 1954 and the opting-out arrangements of 1965. Tables 5.7 and 5.8 show the consequences in terms of revenues of these arrangements. Unsurprisingly, provincial PIT is much more important in Québec than in the ROC.

The most interesting question in the context of the present chapter is the following: How did so major a change in who gets the revenue of the single most important tax in Canada take place with so little fuss? According to our reading of the evidence, four reasons may be suggested.

First, no constitutional revisions were required since, as already indicated, the federal government and the provinces have the power to set their own tax rates and bases. Once agreement was reached between

---

[31] Actually, imposing a flat rate on an amount determined by applying a progressive rate accentuates the original progressivity. The "tax-on-base" approach had been proposed by the western provinces several years earlier.

the governments, only simple legal changes were required. Given the strong party parliamentary system at both federal and provincial levels, agreed changes were implemented with no serious opposition or discussion. Indeed, to an astonishing extent, the entire process occurred without much public awareness or discussion. Canadians may have to complete additional items on the tax form for their provincial PIT but for the most part they seem singularly unaware of its existence.[32] As the discussion in this section indicates, Canada's "executive federalism" or "federal–provincial diplomacy" as it has been called (Simeon, 1972) appears to function best when not in the public eye.

Nonetheless, as discussed further in Section IV, invisibility alone need not lead to a solution. Other factors played a part. In the case of federal and provincial tax shares, precedent was important. Since the provinces (and their dependent municipalities) had earlier played a much larger role in the tax field, to some extent the postwar developments could be seen as a return to normality, despite the pressure in the early postwar years to maintain a more important stabilization role for the central government. The shift back to greater direct provincial responsibility for taxation was also reinforced by the perceived need for greater fiscal discipline in cost-shared programs.[33] With history and economics on its side, and politics not strongly against it, a major shift in taxation proved feasible.

Leadership was also key in pushing the changes through. Nothing happens in politics unless someone makes it happen. In this case, one province, Québec, was willing to take the leadership role in the fight, thus providing an umbrella under which others could subsequently shelter to the extent they chose to do so. Why it did so is open to interpretation. The following factors probably all came into play:

1. The Union Nationale, a Québec-only conservative party, had been in power from 1936 to 1940, when it lost to the provincial Liberals, who won in part on the strength of a promise by the federal Liberals that there would be no compulsory military service.[34] This promise was not kept, however. The draft was introduced in 1944 and the Union Nationale was reelected the same year and

---

[32] This may be about to change with the new "freer" and hence more distinct "tax-on-income" provincial PITs.

[33] The last such cost-shared program, for social services, was replaced in 1996 by a new block grant called the Canada Health and Social Transfer (see Box 5.2), into which the previous EPF transfer was folded.

[34] The issue of conscription had bitterly divided Québec and the ROC during World War I, and it was equally divisive during World War II.

then again in 1948, 1952, and 1956, always under the same leader, Maurice Duplessis. It was thus a strongly nationalist government – one that had proposed a law protecting the French language as early as 1938 – that introduced the provincial PIT in 1954.

2. There was a consensus among the elites in Québec, as evidenced by the work of the Tremblay Commission, which began its work in 1953 and reported in 1956, that the federal government had been acting in a centralizing fashion and thus that the Québec government should fight back.[35]

3. The relatively low additional tax (5%) burden initially proposed and the geographic immobility of the francophone population meant that little, if any, loss of welfare or tax base resulted from this choice. Thus there was little economic cost to a politically well-received measure.

When one player in the game is strongly for something, and most other players have little or nothing to lose by going along, it is not too surprising that a positive sum outcome seems to have emerged.[36] The other provinces would gain from increased control over revenues and the federal government would gain because as a quid pro quo it got more control over its expenditures.

Finally, contrary to the constitutional struggle discussed in the next section, Canadians turned out to be willing to accept a substantial degree of nonuniformity in fiscal matters. Canadians living in Québec pay lower (16.5% less) federal PIT than Canadians living in other provinces owing to the opting-out arrangements of 1965, as modified in 1977. However, the province receives lower federal cash transfer payments (CHST) since the higher provincial PIT replaces dollar for dollar the federal transfers that would have been funded by federal PIT. Provincial politicians sometimes grumble about the lower cash transfers, but the differential federal tax rates seem to bother no one – although perhaps in part because almost no one outside of Québec seems to know they exist.

---

[35] Old ideas never die. Indeed, sometimes they do not even fade away. In March 2002, the Séguin Commission reported on fiscal disequilibrium in Québec and Canada. Its recommendation that the federal government replace its transfers to Québec by the ceding of tax room was endorsed by all three major provincial parties and by almost all commentators. Broad support for reduced federal taxation in Québec thus continues to be evident.

[36] Critical to this outcome was the underpinning provided by the equalization system, which essentially ensured that no province could lose in an expanding economy in which everyone's fiscal health was improving.

II.3. Does It Matter?

We have told a complicated story in this section of how, over time, the federal (provincial) share of personal income taxes decreased (rose) steadily in the postwar period, with a quite distinct system emerging in the province of Québec. We have also offered some reasons why this happened in terms of the underlying political structure and pressures operating during this period. It all, we suggest, seems appropriate in the Canadian context. However, if one looks at the situation as it is has developed in Canada in terms of the canonical model of tax assignment, Canada's present confused and confusing sharing of revenue bases is less obviously sensible; indeed, it would seem conducive to reduced accountability, reduced economic efficiency, probably reduced redistributive equity, and likely increased administrative costs.[37] Of course, all these negatives, if they are such, might be judged to be offset by gains from restoring and maintaining the basic political equilibrium. Still, these aspects of the rise of provincial PITs perhaps deserve brief attention.

Consider first the cost issue. Clearly, the existence of separate Québec and federal PITs administered by different agencies implies increased compliance and administrative costs.[38] However, the unified administration of the federal and provincial PITs in the ROC means that, at least until now, there have been few if any costs as a result of the developments discussed here. Matters are a bit less clear-cut with respect to the other points mentioned. Traditionally, for example, it is argued that PIT should be a central tax in part because of its redistributive role. But this presumes that the only appropriate domain for redistribution is the nation as a whole, which is certainly arguable in a federal context. Similarly, although accountability would probably be greater if taxpayers had to grapple directly with a provincial tax office, the clearly distinguished provincial PIT rates probably make it clear enough who is doing what to whom. Finally, even with respect to efficiency, it is by no means obvious why different rates imposed on the same base in different parts of a country in which different provinces can and do provide different packages of public services is less efficient than a more uniform system: Indeed, the contrary argument seems clearer in a federal context. In short, political institutions in this instance appear to have worked to produce a broadly

---

[37] One of us has argued elsewhere that the canonical model itself makes little sense (Bird, 2000), but this is beyond the scope of the present discussion.

[38] For a discussion of these costs, and estimates of the costs if Ontario adopted its own PIT, see Ontario Economic Council (1983) and Erard and Vaillancourt (1993).

acceptable result, and there seems to have been no obvious downside to the Canadian success story with respect to the development of strong provincial income taxes.

III. QUÉBEC AND CONSTITUTIONAL REFORM: THE ROAD TO NOWHERE

Like all good stories, the tale of Canada's recent constitutional travails has three parts: 1. the buildup – a promising prelude; 2. what was supposed to be the main event, the repatriation of the Constitution; and 3. the failure to secure agreement on the new Constitution, increasingly frantic efforts to redeem matters, and yet another failure and, it seems, a renewed resolution not to try again.

III.1. The Prelude: 1960–1980

In the previous section, we discussed the central role played by Québec in bringing about a reduction of the federal government share of income taxes. This role is perhaps best understood in the context of the modernizing forces, emerging after the war and particularly strong from 1960 onward, which marked the beginning of "la Révolution Tranquille." This "Quiet Revolution" was a period of rapid social and political change in the province of Québec from 1960 to 1966 (Durocher, 1996). Although significant industrialization, urbanization, and rapid economic growth had taken place within the province throughout the first half of the twentieth century, the Union Nationale party that had governed Québec since 1944 seemed increasingly anachronistic as it held to a very conservative ideology and relentlessly advocated traditional, rural, Catholic values. Under the new Liberal government of Jean Lesage elected in 1960, the goal became instead *le rattrapage* – catching up to the social, political, and economic developments that had taken place elsewhere in North America (McRoberts, 1988).

An important element in the resulting change was the rapid expansion of the Québec state to assume functions previously fulfilled by the Catholic Church in the areas of education, health, and welfare. With the establishment of the provincial ministry of education in 1964, and subsequent reforms in secondary and postsecondary education, for example, Québec's provincial government assumed full authority over all educational institutions in Québec and for the first time took full control of curricular matters. The state now played a critical role in educating and training the youth of Québec for the new economy it was simultaneously attempting to build.[39]

The other major focus of the Lesage government was the economy, with particular attention to correcting the underrepresentation of francophones in the upper levels of the Québec economy (Vaillancourt, 1996). The province's economic development had long been dominated by English-Canadian and American interests. The new government thus took as an important goal to become "maîtres chez nous" (masters in our own house – the house very clearly being Québec, not Canada). Both through public enterprises, notably Hydro-Québec, and through increased governmental support for French-Canadian-owned businesses, the government attempted to strengthen the francophone presence in the Québec economy and to create new opportunities for French-Canadians in positions traditionally held by anglophones. Whatever its economic merits, the resulting increased role of the state in the province's affairs clearly helped to create a new national pride and confidence among francophones in Québec.

The political modernization of Québec also marked the beginning of a long series of confrontations with the federal government. Only the Québec government, Lesage's Liberals argued, could assume the new responsibilities that Québec's social and economic development demanded. Consequently, the provincial government needed not only to oversee all areas currently in its jurisdiction but also to assume some of the responsibilities held by the federal government. This, it was argued, required constitutional amendments to provide certainty for the new arrangements. Québec's new strategy in federal–provincial relations challenged the established procedures of Canadian federalism. In 1964, the initial disagreements between Ottawa and Québec over participation in federal–provincial shared-cost programs were settled by a symmetrical opting-out offer exercised asymmetrically, as previously discussed. With Québec's new "special status" within Confederation, however, the constitutional situation became increasingly complex and began to play a more important role in Canadian politics.

Two attempts were made to alter the formula for amending the constitution in the period from 1960 (when Québec began to be the dominant

---

[39] Unsurprisingly, the new government also largely welcomed the concurrent expansion of the provincial role in health and welfare matters, funded initially in large part by federal transfers.

factor in Canadian politics) to 1976 (when the first separatist government was elected). The old amendment formula in place since 1867 had
required an act of the British Parliament, enacted at the request of the federal government. The first attempt to alter this formula was the so-called
Fulton–Favreau formula for constitutional amendment. This proposal had
three critical elements:

1. No changes could be made in the federal–provincial division of
   powers without the consent of all the provinces. Each province
   thus had a veto on amendments.
2. However, powers could be delegated by the provinces to Ottawa
   and vice versa with the approval of the federal government and at
   least four of the provinces.
3. For most other constitutional amendments the "7/50 rule" would
   be required: consent of the federal parliament plus the legislatures
   of seven of the provinces representing at least 50% of the Canadian
   population.

Initially in 1964 all ten provincial premiers unanimously agreed to
accept the Fulton–Favreau formula and promised to pass the enabling
legislation. Subsequently, however, criticism in Québec became so strong
that Premier Lesage was convinced by 1966 that Québec had to reject
the formula (Russell, 1993). Later in 1966 a revamped Union Nationale
Party defeated the Liberals in the provincial election. The new Premier
of Québec, Daniel Johnson, who had called the Fulton–Favreau formula
a straitjacket, demanded constitutional changes that would be explicitly
based on a "deux nations" (two nations) concept of Canada.[40] Having
been elected with the slogan "Égalité ou indépendance" (Equality or
independence), the Union Nationale argued that the only alternative to
restructuring Canada (based on the somewhat vague concept of "associate states") was for Québec to separate.

The second attempt to change amendment procedures was the Victoria
Charter, based on an agreement in principle between the federal and
provincial governments in 1971. This document contained sixty-one articles dealing with a wide variety of issues: fundamental democratic rights,

---

[40] Like the "distinct society" later, "deux nations" turned out to be one of those symbolic
phrases that, so to speak, suffered a lot in translation, being generally understood in
Québec to be a simple statement of the obvious francophone reality of Québec and in
the ROC to be a denial of Canadian nationhood.

language rights, provincial participation in the appointment of Supreme Court justices,[41] the commitment of both levels of government to reduce regional disparities and inequities, and a new federal–provincial division of powers in the area of social policy (particularly programs affecting the family, youth, and occupational training) (Meisel and Rocher, 1999). Under the Victoria Charter, most constitutional amendments would require approval by the following:

1. the House of Commons (the Senate would only be able to suspend an amendment);
2. all provinces that have or had in the past 25% of Canada's population (i.e., Ontario and Québec);
3. two of the four Atlantic provinces; and
4. two of the four western provinces with at least 50% of the western population.

The Québec government, though once more back in Liberal hands, soon rejected the Charter, however, on the grounds that it offered Québec insufficient autonomy in the implementation of social policy.

The election of the sovereignty-oriented Parti-Québécois (PQ) government in 1976 increased the sense of urgency about the need for major constitutional change. A provincial[42] referendum on "sovereignty-association" (the meaning of which has never been entirely clear, which was presumably in part its intent) was held in May 1980. René Lévesque, the PQ premier and leader of the Yes side, emphasized the immense costs to Québec of federalism and the feasibility of independence, whereas the No side, led by Québec Liberal leader Claude Ryan and federal Prime Minister Pierre Trudeau, promised "renewed federalism" if Quebecois rejected the sovereignty option. On May 20, 1980, 60% of Quebecois voted against the proposal for sovereignty.

Two major attempts at amending the constitution had thus failed because the Québec government judged that it did not do well enough in the negotiations. Meanwhile, that government's own attempt to obtain a larger political mandate for more drastic change had also failed. Matters seemed to be at a dead end – though not for long.

---

[41] The Constitution requires that three of the nine judges come from Québec, in part because there is a different (civil) law system in that province. The question is, who chooses these judges? We shall return to this matter later.

[42] The referendum was provincial in that it was held only in Québec, was administered by the Québec election commission, and had funding rules and so on set provincially.

III.2. The Eventual Amendment

Indeed, as it turned out an important result of the failure of the PQ referendum was yet another attempt to repatriate the constitution. Unlike the earlier attempts, however, this one succeeded – or did it?

The first moves were not promising. Shortly after the referendum, a First Ministers' conference[43] – the mechanism used to consult the provinces in all attempts to repatriate the constitution – ended in failure in September 1980. Prime Minister Trudeau soon announced, however, that the federal government would nonetheless proceed unilaterally with repatriation, as well as with the introduction of a Charter of Rights and Freedoms and an amending formula. The amending formula would include the system of regional vetoes that had been proposed in the Victoria Charter (which, it will be recalled, contained vetoes for both Ontario and Québec). There was an important difference, however, in that the federal government was to be allowed to obtain the consent of the provinces by a referendum vote, thus bypassing the provincial governments by appealing directly to the population.

All provinces except Ontario and New Brunswick initially objected to the federal proposals. Manitoba, Québec, and Newfoundland asked their courts of appeal whether provincial consent was a constitutional requirement for a request to the British Parliament to change the constitution in the ways contemplated by the federal government. The courts in Manitoba and Québec said provincial consent was not a requirement; Newfoundland's court took the opposite view (Russell, 1993). Finally, in September 1981, the Supreme Court ruled that although the federal government's request to the British Parliament did not legally require provincial consent, unilateral action went against Canada's constitutional conventions. Ottawa, said the Court, should obtain a "substantial degree" of provincial consent. The federal government respected the Court's decision and returned to negotiations in November 1981.

The counterproposal made by the eight objecting provinces stressed Senate reform, financial compensation for a province's withdrawal from any federal programs, and an amending formula based on the "7/50 rule" that had been used in the Fulton–Favreau proposal of the 1960s. Importantly, since this amending formula treated all provinces equally, Québec,

---

[43] These conferences have no constitutional or legal status but have emerged as an ad hoc mechanism for resolving (or at least discussing) federal–provincial issues. They have no set frequency and are convened by the federal Prime Minister. Provincial leaders meet in an annual premiers' conference.

Box 5.3. *Changes in the 1982 Constitution*

- Canada's constitution can now be amended with the approval of the Canadian Parliament and a minimum of seven provinces representing 50% of the population. Amendments concerning the monarchy, Canadian Parliament, the Supreme Court of Canada, and the amending formula itself require unanimous provincial consent. Amendments to the constitution no longer require the consent of the British Parliament.
- The Canadian Charter of Rights and Freedoms was added. Importantly, however, the "notwithstanding" clause of the Charter permits Parliament or any provincial legislature to enact legislation, even if it is in violation of the Charter, for a renewable five-year period.
- The principle of fiscal equalization was constitutionally recognized. That is, the federal government should make transfers that ensure all provinces have sufficient revenues to provide reasonably comparable levels of public services at reasonably comparable levels of taxation.
- The rights of Canada's aboriginal peoples were constitutionally recognized for the first time.
- Provinces were given joint power to regulate interprovincial trade in natural resources and to levy indirect taxes on natural resources. (This provision related mainly to concerns of certain western provinces.)

by supporting it, in effect was abandoning the right to veto that it would have had under the federal proposal. Late on the third night of the federal–provincial conference, however, seven of the eight dissident provincial premiers (and thus nine provinces representing a "substantial degree") came to an agreement with the federal government. One province did not agree: Québec.

Despite this lack of agreement, the federal government proceeded. On April 17, 1982, in a ceremony in Ottawa, Queen Elizabeth II officially proclaimed the 1982 Constitution Act. Canada's "new" constitution consisted of most of the original 1867 British North America Act as well as several important changes agreed to by the federal government and nine of the provinces, as shown in Box 5.3.

However, many crucial constitutional issues remained unresolved. Neither the division of powers nor the reform of federal institutions had been addressed in the constitution; the increasing restive aboriginal population had not been satisfied;[44] and, most immediately important, Québec had once again been isolated. Indeed, the province was now subject to a constitution to which it had not agreed. Moreover, the new restrictions soon began to bite where they hurt most – with respect to language.

Specifically, the introduction of the Canadian Charter of Rights and Freedoms led to some changes in the language laws that had been enacted in Québec to ensure the dominance of the French language in the province. The 1977 *Charter of the French Language* (Bill 101) restricted access to English schools to children who had either a parent or an older sibling who had received their elementary education in English in the Province of Québec (known as the "Québec clause"). In 1984, the Supreme Court of Canada ruled that this Québec clause was incompatible with the "Canada clause" of the Charter of Rights, which protects minority language educational rights for any citizen of Canada whose first language learned is either English or French. The provincial law was subsequently modified so that children who had a parent educated in English anywhere in Canada – not just Québec – had access to an English school in Québec.

Québec was thus not happy: It had lost its implied veto and its language law had been weakened. However, from the perspective of the federal government, repatriation was a success in the sense that two main federal goals – a Canadian amending formula and a Charter of Rights – had been attained. Provincial governments in the ROC were also fairly satisfied. From their perspective, that the arrangement discomforted a separatist government in Québec was not a big problem.

III.3. A Never-Ending Story?

But the story was hardly over. The constitution may have been amended, but the issue of constitutional reform had by no means been put to rest. In the 1984 federal electoral campaign, Brian Mulroney, the new leader of the federal Conservatives – like Pierre Trudeau, a bilingual native of Québec – promised that, if elected, he would reach an honorable constitutional agreement with Québec. He was elected, and constitutional discussions between first ministers were renewed in 1985.

---

[44] As Bird and Vaillancourt (2001) discuss, although there are less than a million aboriginal people in Canada (most importantly in relative terms in the western provinces of Manitoba and Saskatchewan), they are heavily dependent on federal support for their health, education, and subsistence. Nonetheless, as most recently seen in British Columbia, aboriginal issues are increasingly important on the provincial policy agenda also.

The government of Québec, now the provincial Liberals, presented five conditions that, if all parties accepted them, would, they said, allow Québec to sign the Constitution of Canada. The five conditions were the following:

1. constitutional recognition of Québec as a "distinct society" (see Box 5.4);
2. an enhancement of Québec's role in the field of immigration;[45]
3. Québec's direct involvement in the selection of the three Québec judges on the Supreme Court of Canada;
4. Québec's ability to opt out of federal programs in areas of exclusive provincial jurisdiction and, importantly, be entitled to fiscal compensation;[46] and
5. a Québec veto on constitutional amendments affecting provincial interest.

After extensive discussion, in April 1987 the first ministers drafted the so-called Meech Lake Accord, under which the powers sought by Québec in its last four conditions would be extended to all provinces. In the field of immigration, a jurisdiction constitutionally shared by both Ottawa and the provinces, the Meech Lake Accord gave each province the right to negotiate a new agreement with the federal government concerning the selection of new immigrants.[47] With respect to the Supreme Court of Canada, all provinces would now be able formally to nominate individuals to sit as judges. In the matter of federal-spending programs, any province could opt out of new federal shared-cost programs in areas of exclusive provincial jurisdiction and still be entitled to compensation, provided that the provincial program complied with the national objectives. Finally, all provinces would receive greater veto powers. In addition, the Accord also specified that a federal–provincial first ministers' conference would be held annually to discuss the issues of Senate reform and fisheries.

---

[45] This issue relates to language: Most immigrants to Canada, usually allophones (mother tongue that is neither English or French) choose to move to English-speaking areas (especially Toronto and Vancouver) to be able to educate their children in English.

[46] Of course, this is a revisitation of the "opting-out" discussed in Section II.

[47] As of March 2000, six provinces had signed immigration agreements with the federal government even though the Meech Lake Accord was not ratified. These agreements can be classified as limited (New Brunswick and Newfoundland), expanded (Manitoba, Saskatchewan, and British Columbia), and, in a class of its own, the long-standing Québec agreement (Vander Ploeg, 2000).

Box 5.4. *Recognition of Québec as a "Distinct Society"*

Although one of Québec's most repeated wishes is to be recognized as "distinct," it is interesting to note how distinct it already is both through the exercise of powers available to all provinces and special constitutional provisions and negotiated federal–provincial arrangements.

EXERCISE OF PROVINCIAL POWERS

The timeline proceeds as follows:

1954 – A provincial personal income tax collected by the province is introduced.

1965 – A separate social security scheme for Québec (QPP) with funds administered by the Caisse de Dépôt is created; these funds are used in part to promote ownership of Québec's economy by francophones.

1977 – French is declared the official language of Québec; international immigrants are required to send children to French language schools; signage requirements and language-of-work requirements are imposed.

1979–1983 – Various savings incentives for Québec firms are created (e.g., investments through tax deductions, credits administered through the provincial PIT, etc.).

CONSTITUTIONAL PROVISIONS AND NEGOTIATED ARRANGEMENTS

1867 – Québec imposes civil laws system, in contrast to common law system used eleswhere in Canada.

1867 – One-third of Supreme Court must be from Québec.

1965 – Provinces are allowed to opt out from federal transfer programs with compensating tax room.

1977 – All provinces offered a special role in selecting immigrants, in accordance with constitutional provision that immigrantion in a joint federal–provincial field. Québec took particular advantage of the offer to exercise choice.

1992 – Collection of federal GST begins in Québec.

1998–2000 – Québec receives federal funds for National Child Benefit/ Early Childhood Development programs without subscribing to any agreement.

2004 – Québec receives additional federal funds for health with asymmetric reporting conditions.

To be adopted the Meech Lake Accord had to be ratified by Parliament and by the legislatures of all the provinces. Once the resolution was supported by one legislature, the other legislatures had three years to ratify it. Québec's National Assembly was the first to pass the resolution of approval on June 23, 1987. Ratification by the remaining nine provincial legislatures therefore had to occur before June 23, 1990. Despite considerable criticism of the Accord's "Distinct Society" clause throughout the ROC, by the fall of 1988 only two small provinces, New Brunswick and Manitoba, had not ratified the agreement. In April 1990, however, with the deadline less than three months away, the new Liberal government in Newfoundland rescinded its support for the Meech Lake Accord. Still more negotiations followed, leading eventually to New Brunswick ratifying the accord. But the two other provinces did not.

Despite its near success,[48] the failure of the Accord was interpreted by many Quebeckers as an outright rejection of their aspirations and hopes by English Canada. The immediate result was a sharp rise in the polling support for sovereignty, reaching a high of 60% at one point. The political picture nationally was also altered by the rejection of Meech Lake. A number of members of the Conservative and Liberal parties left to create the Bloc Québécois – a federal party somewhat paradoxically committed to Québec independence. This party, supported by Québec nationalists, actually won enough seats in the 1993 federal election to form Canada's official opposition party in Parliament until the election of 1997.[49]

Prior to this, however, from the failure of Meech in June 1990 to the spring of 1992, yet another series of extensive public consultations as well as negotiations among first ministers were held. The end product of this process was the Charlottetown Accord, which was much more complex than Meech Lake. It is summarized in Box 5.5.

In October 1992, for the first time in Canadian history, a national referendum was held to decide whether Canada's constitution should be renewed based on the Charlottetown Accord.[50] The participation rate

---

[48] To illustrate how close matters were, Manitoba's legislature failed to approve because of the filibustering of one aboriginal member, who objected to the lack of any move with respect to aboriginal matters. It has been alleged that Newfoundland's objections were rooted in the strong views of its then premier, a close ally of former Prime Minister Trudeau, who was definitely not a supporter of the Accord.

[49] It did so in large part because of the virtual disappearance of the federal Conservative Party, which lost Québec on this issue and the rest of Canada on fiscal and trade issues.

[50] The referendum was organized by the Québec government in Québec and by the federal government outside Québec; it was neither required nor binding constitutionally.

Box 5.5. *The Charlottetown Accord*

The as Accord covered five areas:

Unity and diversity: This section included the Canada clause, expressing Canadian values and recognizing Québec as a distinct society; it states a commitment to preserving a balanced social (protecting universal health care, adequate services, and high-quality education) and economic union (following economic policy objectives that had been outlined by the federal government in a September 1991 proposal).[i]

Political institutions: This section included a traditional western demand, particularly by Alberta, for a triple-E (equal, elected, and effective) Senate that would include six senators from each province and one from each territory, with guaranteed aboriginal representation; the Supreme Court of Canada, with its composition and its appointment process would be constitutionally entrenched; and Québec would be guaranteed 25% of the seats in the House of Commons.

Roles and responsibilities: This section included the right for a province to opt out of a federal shared-cost program in an area of exclusive provincial jurisdiction and still be entitled to financial compensation provided that the program is compatible with the national objectives; provincial rights to negotiate agreements with the federal government concerning immigration; and exclusive provincial jurisdiction over cultural matters (not including the Canadian Broadcasting Corporation or the National Film Board).

First peoples: This section explicitly recognized that aboriginal peoples have an inherent right to self-government (but went into no details).

Amending formula: A greater number of issues would require unanimous provincial consent.

---

[i] As discussed in the next section, Canada has never been a full economic union.

---

was 75%, higher than the usual participation rate in elections. The Charlottetown Accord was rejected by 54% of those who voted. Interestingly, the rejection rate was only a bit higher (55%) in Québec than in the ROC. In the end, the Accord received majorities in only four provinces (New Brunswick, Newfoundland, Prince Edward Island, and Ontario) and one territory (Northwest Territories).

The constitutional quest that had begun in the 1960s, resulted in the repatriation of 1982, and given rise to the devastation of many hectares of forests for the printing of proposals and counterproposals seemed at last to have come to an end in Canada as a whole with this referendum. But Québec had by no means given up. The defeat of the federal Conservative government in 1993 was soon followed by a victory by the PQ in the 1994 Québec provincial elections. The new provincial government soon held a second Québec referendum on "sovereignty-association" – still a term difficult to interpret – in October 1995. As in 1980, the sovereignty option was again defeated. This time, however, it received 49.4% of the vote and a solid majority of the francophone vote. The unity of Canada was clearly still in question.

This very close result motivated the premiers of the other provinces to return to the constitutional debate. Without the presence of the federal government, a meeting of provincial leaders was held in Calgary in 1997 to find a proposal that might bring Québec to agree to the Constitution. In September 1997, despite Québec Premier Lucien Bouchard's refusal to attend the meetings, the other nine premiers submitted the Calgary Declaration for the approval of the federal government and the provincial legislatures. In essence, this Declaration recognized Québec's unique character within the Canadian Confederation while restating the equality of all the provinces. All nine provinces quickly ratified it. Québec, however, rejected the proposal, criticizing it for its lack of concreteness with respect to provincial powers.

In response to a request by the federal government, in August 1998 the Supreme Court of Canada declared that Québec, under both constitutional and international law, does not have the right to unilaterally decide its independence. One result was that in June 2000 the federal parliament adopted the so-called Clarity Act, intended to remove any ambiguity from future referendums on sovereignty by insisting both that the question be clear[51] and that there be a clear majority before negotiations of any kind take place between the federal government and the province seeking sovereignty. The Act makes the House of Commons responsible for determining whether a referendum question is clear, that is, whether the question "would result in a clear expression of the will of the population of a province on whether the province should cease to be part of Canada and become an independent state." The Act also gives the

---

[51] A common joke was that "sovereignty-association" meant an independent Québec within a strong and united Canada!

House of Commons the right to decide how much of a majority would constitute a clear will to secede.

III.4. How Did We Get Here from There?

What may come next in the constitutional saga of Canada remains to be seen. Is this the end? Or will there be still more chapters in this long and involved story? We cannot, of course, answer these questions. We note, however, that in the September 2004 agreement on a ten-year plan for financing health care,[52] a specific aspect was that Quebec would be treated asymmetrically in terms of reporting requirements;[53] such a treatment was also available to other provinces but not sought by them and it is an agreed upon asymmetry, not a constitutionally recognized one. Instead, we shall consider briefly why the most recent attempts to incorporate Québec's desires into the constitution and thus make the province a willing partner in Canada have failed. No doubt, every Canadian has his or her own opinion on these complex matters, but we suspect many would agree that several factors were critical to this failure.

One clearly critical issue turned on the recognition of Québec as a "distinct society." The issue is both semantic and factual. "Distinct" does not have the same connotation of superiority in French that it tends to do in English. Thus, what was meant more as equivalent to "different" in French appeared generally to be understood as meaning "special treatment" in English Canada. The resulting confusion was not helped when the federal government argued that this status meant nothing in fact, whereas the Québec government stated the contrary. Symbolism is important in politics, and when two parties disagree on both the meaning and the significance of an important symbol, it does not bode well for negotiations. This issue was exacerbated in the Meech debate when in December 1988 the Québec government used the "notwithstanding" clause of the new constitution to override a Supreme Court ruling that Québec's French-only sign law violated the Charter of Rights. (Interestingly, although Québec had not agreed to the new constitution, it was nonetheless governed by it.) Québec's use of provincial powers to exempt itself from Canada's Charter of Rights clearly intensified opposition in the ROC to the "distinct

---

[52] "A Ten-Year Plan to Strengthen Health Care," available online at http://www.pm.gc.ca/eng/news.asp?id=260.

[53] Asymmetrical Federals that Respect's Quebec's Jurisdiction, available online at http://www.pm.gc.ca/grfx/docs/QuebecENG.pdf.

society" clause and to the Meech Lake Accord in general. To put this in other terms, the Charter's emphasis on individual rights – its major selling point in the ROC – clearly conflicted with the constitutional provisions supporting the collective rights that were of most interest to many in francophone Québec.

A second important factor in the defeat of both the Meech Lake and the Charlottetown Accords was the opposition of leading figures in the federal Liberal party, in particular former federal Prime Minister Pierre Trudeau. We noted earlier that one reason for the relative success of the fiscal path to changing federal–provincial relations was the existence of a "champion" – often the Québec provincial government. One reason for the failure of the constitutional path to change has been, so to speak, a standoff between champions. It may be difficult for non-Canadians to understand the extent to which much of the convoluted constitutional discussion of recent years in Canada seems to reflect deeply held conflicting beliefs within what may be called the "political elite" of Québec. Throughout much of the postwar period, the federal government has not only been elected in large part owing to its support from Québec voters but has also been led by Quebeckers. One might think that federal and provincial governments that were both elected (in part at least) by the same people, that were often of the same political party, and that were often led also by people from the same province and linguistic group would have been able to strike a deal. It was not to be. It may take a very different leadership at both provincial and especially federal levels before any final accommodation is ever reached with Québec.

Finally, and in notable contrast to the fiscal case discussed earlier, many of the more recent constitutional discussions were largely held in public. Most unusually for Canada, members of the public were consulted and encouraged to take part in the process. They did, and they may perhaps be considered to have rendered a verdict of "a plague on all their houses." Some have deplored the secretive and quasidictatorial way in which majority governments can legislate in the Westminster parliamentary system, at least as it works in Canada. The reluctance of foxes to give up their right to guard henhouses is well known. Nonetheless, it may well be that matters such as constitutional revision, which are complex, highly symbolic, and intrinsically remote from daily life, simply cannot be resolved through simple Yes/No votes. If, as recent experience suggests, Canadians do not trust their legislatures but cannot decide themselves what to do, the prospect of any definitive constitutional revision seems limited. We shall return to this point in the final section of this chapter.

IV. AN SEC FOR CANADA: AN IDEA WITHOUT A CHAMPION?

As mentioned in Section II.2, invisibility alone is not enough for success, as our final example – the case for a national securities regulator – illustrates. The Canadian constitution explicitly assigns banking to the federal government. Thus banks have a federal charter and are supervised by a federal agency. Other financial institutions such as trusts and insurance companies, however, can either have a federal or provincial charter and may thus choose to be supervised by one or the other level of government (except in matters of consumer protection and market conducts where provincial supervision applies). Still other financial institutions, such as credit unions and brokerage firms (stockbrokers), are subject to provincial supervision as are stock exchanges.[54] Provincial powers in the area of financial institutions flow implicitly from their constitutional powers over property and civil rights and "all matters of a merely local or private nature." The resulting fragmentation of the securities industry (in contrast to the United States' single Securities and Exchange commission) has been decried for decades. Nonetheless, no sustained attempt has been made to change matters, despite the concerns many have expressed about the effects of globalization – or, better, "contintentalization" – of Canadian capital markets. Since 1996, however, some important changes toward a national securities commission like the SEC have nonetheless taken place.

IV.1. The Issue Arises

The first in-depth discussion of a national securities commission for Canada appears to have been in the 1966 report of the Royal Commission on Banking and Finance (Porter Commission).[55] This report noted that there was wide interest among brokers, dealers, and corporation lawyers in more uniform legislation across Canada. Further, it noted that some progress had recently been made in this direction. Alberta, British Columbia, and Saskatchewan, for example, had modeled their Acts on the Ontario Act (although in no case had the Ontario Act been adopted

---

[54] In the mid 1980s, banks were first allowed to own brokerage firms and within a few years most large stockbrokers were owned by banks. An accord (the Hockin–Kwinter Accord, after the names of the ministers who signed it) was reached in 1987 between the federal and Ontario governments that these brokerage firms would be subsidiaries of banks regulated by the provinces.

[55] The first mention of this issue we have found is in 1935 in the report of the Royal Commission on Price Spreads.

without at least several minor changes). Moreover, the Québec Act too was much like the Ontario Act, although it provided the commissioners with greater powers. Still, the fact remained that a securities issuer seeking national distribution for a new issue in Canada was faced with registering under ten securities acts that are dissimilar in varying degrees, as well as with the requirements of the relevant companies' legislation. Even where the legislation was similar, the discretionary powers allowed the different provincial commissions, and the varying adequacy with which they were staffed, could result in important differences in administrative practices. This situation, said the Porter Report (Poter Commission, 1966, p. 346), "increases the legal difficulties of bringing a new issue to market and leaves the issuer and underwriter open to the risk of delay caused by the failure to meet the requirements of a single jurisdiction."

Consequently, the Commission suggested that the federal government should encourage the development of uniform standards of security legislation and legislation in Canada, noting that a federal agency might, in addition to establishing uniform standards, attract portfolio investment from abroad as well as expanded capital from domestic sources. While noting that the principal arguments against a federal regulator were that it might become too bureaucratic and costly and that most security regulation problems were only of local or regional significance and best dealt with at the provincial level, the Porter Report concluded by noting that the industry itself agreed that a single federal agency "would be preferable to ten provincial agencies, and there is no inherent reason for believing that a federal agency would lead to costly delays" (p. 349).

The ball of a national security regulator – like the (SEC) in the United States – thus appeared to have been placed squarely into play. In 1968, the federal department of Consumer and Corporate Affairs (no longer in existence) proposed setting up this agency but nothing happened. Banwell (1969, pp. 21–22) noted that "there is a necessity for national administration and regulation, and such a scheme appears most readily attainable though co-operation between the governments. Such a scheme also appears to carry the best opportunity for effective control over the industry and its activity." In 1973, a study was commissioned (and published in 1979): It proposed setting up a federal commission with primacy in interprovincial and international securities matters (Anisman and Hogg, 1979). Again, nothing was done.

The issue was again raised in study for the Royal Commission on the Economic Union and Development Prospects for Canada (the McDonald Commission) by Courchene (1986). Courchene began his analysis of securities legislation by stating that "one prerequisite for achieving market efficiency is to ensure that the market is truly national in scope" (p. 154) but noted that the federal presence in regulating Canadian securities markets was virtually nonexistent compared to other federations such as the United States. However, as he went on to say, "because of the dominance of the TSE [Toronto Stock Exchange] and the OSC [Ontario Securities Commission], securities legislation tended to be more national in scope than would be expected from a decentralized regulatory process" (p. 156). Nonetheless, he argued, many analysts believed that an overarching federal role in the securities area was needed because of "the increasing inter-provincial and international nature of the securities business, the spread of computerization which may eventually replace the trading floors of the stock exchanges with a Canada-wide automated trading system, and the inherent difficulty of applying provincial regulatory measures beyond provincial boundaries" (p. 157). In conclusion, Courchene quoted Anisman and Hogg (1979), approvingly, as follows: "The limitations on provincial jurisdiction not only cast doubt on the ability of the provincial commissions to enforce their own acts in connection with inter-provincial and international transactions but also on the ability of the provinces, even acting cooperatively, to enact a scheme that will satisfactory regulate the entire securities market." Nonetheless, in the end the possibility of national securities regulation was not even mentioned in the main body of the McDonald Report.

In 1991, the federal department of Finance examined the issue once more. This time, it was mentioned in the federal throne speech (a statement of policy intent by the government for the next parliamentary session). Opposition was soon heard from the western provinces and from the Investment Dealers Association of Canada (IDA). Following on this exchange, Tse (1994, p. 428), picking up a theme touched on earlier by both the Porter Commission (1966) and Courchene (1986), noted that Ontario and all western provinces "have gone to the extent of enacting uniform securities legislation and a further group of Uniform Act Policies." In contrast to Banwell (1969), however, who thought that what was needed was essentially more interprovincial cooperation, Tse (1994) went on to argue that the existence of such legislation actually proves the need for a federal body because, despite the cooperative efforts of the provinces, significant gaps remained in the regulatory structure. In his view, a federal securities commission was needed for the protection of market players, the efficient allocation of resources, the efficient raising of capital, and the effective prosecution of securities offences. Nonetheless, Tse (1994,

p. 430) concluded that on constitutional grounds there remained a clear need for "some provincial securities regulation" and that "[t]o the extent that securities are property and fall within the enumerated head of property and civil rights in the province, the general rule must be that securities are more properly a provincial concern."

IV.2. It Becomes a Policy Issue . . . For a While

In 1996, for the second time, official notice was taken of this question. Building on a 1993 Atlantic Premiers meeting, during which the issue was raised, work on a possible Memorandum of Understanding (MOU) was carried out in 1994. The draft MOU proposed that an autonomous Canadian Securities Commission be delegated regulatory powers from both the federal and provincial governments. This laid the foundation for the February 1996 throne speech to state explicitly that "the [federal] government is prepared to work with interested provinces towards the development of a Canadian Securities Commission." To some extent, this proposal seems to have reflected the explicit support for this idea that had been expressed a few months earlier by two of the most prominent industry groups – the IDA, which had changed its position since 1991, and the Canadian Bankers Association (CBA). Speaking at a conference in Toronto, the President of IDA noted that a Canadian Securities Commission would be "the most logical, efficient and sensible approach" if the country was starting from scratch, a suggestion that was seconded by the CBA. Efficiency and a better match between markets and regulators were cited as reasons for adopting a national body. Recognizing constitutional and political realities, however, it was noted that the federal government need not necessarily run a national commission: It might instead be a national body run by the provinces.

Mention of this proposal in the throne speech elicited a mixed reaction from the provinces. The Ontario Securities Commission supported it, the Québec Securities Commission opposed it, and the Alberta and British Columbia commissions had reservations and expressed fear that a national securities commission might be a threat to stock markets in western Canada. One explanation for these diverse reactions might be that, although provincial Securities commissions are a source of revenue for the respective provinces, Ontario probably would have come out a winner. The other three provinces had developed separate financial markets for junior stocks (francophone firms in Québec in all sectors; mainly mining and petroleum stocks in the West) with less stringent regulations for stock issuers than in Ontario. Local brokers who fear regulation (and competition) from outside dominated these markets. Centralizing securities regulation would likely, it was argued, lead to a decline in capital markets outside Toronto and hence be detrimental to small businesses raising funds on local capital markets.

In the event, the idea of a possible Canadian securities commission was not even examined by the MacKay Task Force on the Future of the Canadian Financial Services Sector, which reported in 1998. The apparent federal initiative of 1996 thus seemed to be dead, at least in official circles. In early 2002, however, the issue rose from the dead, when a symposium on this topic was organized in Toronto and a review of the Ontario Securities Act "recommend(ed) that the provinces, territories and federal government work towards the creation of a single securities regulator with responsibility for the capital markets across Canada" (Ontario Securities Commission, 2002). Submissions to the committee preparing this review had emphasized the importance of regulatory costs and the need for a single voice for Canada on the international scene.[56] Repeating their earlier roles, however – the people had changed but the institutional interests had not – the president of the TSE argued for a single national regulator, while Québec's securities commission again said no.

The federal Minister of Finance gave new life to this idea by asking Mr. MacKay to examine the issue in October 2002. He reported in November 2002, calling for the creation of a Wise Person's Committee.[57] This was done by the aforementioned minister in March 2003 with said committee reporting in December 2003.[58]

The following recommendations are taken from the Executive Summary, with emphasis put on the federalism aspects:

- The federal government enacts a new Canadian Securities Act that provides a comprehensive scheme of capital markets regulation for Canada.

---

[56] Estimates from the British Financial Service Agencies show costs for 2000 of C$493 million for Canada, C$497 million for the United Kingdom and C$235 million for Australia, with employees numbering 3,780 in Canada, 2,765 in the United Kingdom and 2,113 in Australia (Ontario Securities Commission, 2002).

[57] "Minister of Finance Receives Report on Canadian Securities Regulation," available online at http://www.fin.gc.ca/news02/02-094e.html.

[58] Their report "It's Time: Report of the Wise Persons' Committee to Review the Structure of Securities Regulation in Canada," is at http://www.wise-averties.ca/reports/html/E_Final/index.html.

- Amendments to the legislation would not be implemented if a majority of the provinces representing a majority of the population of Canada objected.
- The Canadian Securities Act is administered by a single Canadian Securities Commission consisting of nine full-time, regionally representative commissioners.
- The Commission includes two commissioners from each of Ontario and Quebec, one commissioner from each of British Columbia and Alberta, and two commissioners from the remaining provinces and territories. There would be no regional restriction on the ninth commissioner.
- A Securities Policy Ministerial Committee consisting of the ministers responsible for securities regulation in each province and the federal Minister of Finance is established to provide a forum for policy and administrative input.
- The Commission is responsive to the needs of Canada's capital markets, makes the best use of existing expertise, and has excellent on-the-ground service delivery where

  - the Commission's head office, located in the National Capital Region, is responsible for policy development, the coordination of regional and district office activity, and dealings with other Canadian financial sector regulators and international matters;
  - strong, functionally empowered regional offices in Vancouver, Calgary, Winnipeg, Toronto, Montreal, and Halifax review prospectuses and registration applications, grant exemptions, conduct compliance reviews, and investigations and initiate enforcement proceedings, as well as contribute to policy development;
  - and where necessary, there will be additional district offices to ensure effective and consistent issuer and investor treatment across Canada.

These recommendations were justified mainly by arguing that the structure of the capital market in Canada is a national one, not a provincial one, and that Canada is the exception in the world among industrialized countries in not having a national securties exchange, making the interface with the international regulatory environment more difficult. Reactions to these recommendations were similar to those observed in the past: The Ontario Securities Commission[59] endorsed them while other

---

[59] "Reforming Securities Regulation in Canada," available online at http://www.osc.gov. on.ca/About/Speeches?sp_20040420_db-ciri.jsp.

provinces (in particular Alberta, British Columbia, and Québec), re-grouped under the label "Provincial–Territorial Securities Initiative" did not, putting forward in September 2004 the following:[60]

- a "passport system" for securities regulation, resulting in a single window of access to capital markets in participating provinces and territories, to be established by August 2005, and
- highly harmonized, streamlined, and simplified securities laws to be implemented by the end of 2006.

Interested parties such as the IDA argue for reform since in their words, "Canada cannot afford to maintain a balkanized structure in a globalized world" and believe that the federal solution is more likely to work than the provincial one of Uniform Securities Laws (USL) and a passport system.[61]

In view of the extensive rationalization of Canadian stock exchanges that has taken place in the past few years, largely in response to global pressures, the lack of discussion of this issue is hard to understand. The Vancouver and Alberta exchanges, where junior stocks were traded, merged into the Canadian Venture Exchange (CDNX) (with the smaller Winnipeg exchange joining CDNX in March 2000). The TSE thus became the sole Canadian exchange for senior stocks, giving up derivative trading to the Montréal stock exchange in exchange for its delisting of these stocks. A small market for junior stocks was also kept in Montréal. In 2001 these junior stocks were moved to the CDNX, which was then taken over in the fall of 2001 by the TSE. Regulation may not have been rationalized (let alone nationalized) but securities trading, it seems, has moved a long way in this direction.

Why has the idea of creating a national securities commission never gotten off the ground in Canada? The reason was hardly public opposition: The public probably never even noticed that the issue existed. Perhaps the most obvious explanation is that the issue had no real champion. Provincial regulators seem to have collaborated sufficiently closely to avoid any kind of a race to the bottom in terms of standards. Collaboration was undoubtedly facilitated by their small number, and by the way in which the market was almost explicitly carved up among the different

---

[60] "Securities Reforms: Provinces and Territories Agree to Implement Passport System," available http://www.securitiescanada.org/.

[61] "Regulatory Reform: In the Home Stretch," Report by Investment Dealers Association of Canada. Available at: http://www.ida.ca/Files/Media/RecSpeech/2004RegulatoryReform_en.pdf.

exchanges. In any case, the combination of provincial resistance, particularly from Québec but also from the western provinces, and the lack of federal enthusiasm meant the idea never really appeared on the political horizon.

The most recent proposal is bolstered by legal opinions that state that the federal government does have the right to intervene in this area, something that was doubted in the past, and by the fact that it is a national regulatory rather than a federal one that is called for, as evidenced by its governance structure. However, it remains to be seen if the minority federal government elected in June 2004 will want to expand political capital to impose such a structure on a majority of reluctant provinces.

In addition, despite the recent flurry of interest, perhaps the economic gains from a more "national" approach to regulation are less than they might have been in the past. Interlisting of shares of Canadian firms in the United States is increasing. From 1980 to 1998, the number of interlisted firms increased from 82 to 244, and the volume of trading of these shares in the United States increased from 23% in 1991 to 31% in 1995 (Beaulieu and Bellemare, 2000). This increased degree of integration with the United States (which subjects many larger Canadian firms to SEC rules) combined with the national scope of Canada's few banks and the increasing mergers between financial institutions may mean that national securities regulation is an issue whose day may already have passed.

In any case, it should be understood that Canada is not, and never has been, a full internal common market. There has been a long tradition of accepting that provinces not only may have their own economic policies but can and do sometimes implement them in ways that reduce national economic efficiency.[62] Partly in response to the pressures arising from NAFTA and other international agreements, however, some attempt was made to address some of these issues through an "Internal Agreement on Trade" (IAT) that was signed by the provinces and territories on July 1, 1995. The aim of this agreement was to reduce existing barriers, to prevent the creation of new ones, and to harmonize standards. The agreement is based on six general rules: nondiscrimination, right of entry and exit, the absence of obstacles, legitimate objectives, reconciliation, and transparency.

---

[62] For an early detailed analysis of the many ways in which Canada is not a common market, see Trebilcock et al. (1983). Most of the contributors to this volume, like most Canadian economists, deplored this fact, but the point is that a certain degree of politically motivated fragmentation of labor, capital, and product markets is, and long has been, a fact of Canadian life.

This all sounds good, at least if one thinks that "market-preserving" federalism requires nationwide application of rules affecting commerce. However, both the importance and impact of the IAT are debatable. In reality, few goods and services were ever subject to interprovincial trade barriers, and the proportion of the labor force in occupations subject to restrictions is small. Perhaps the most notable change resulting from IAT has been the use of open tendering with no "place of business" clause by provincial governments in 1995. This provision was extended to the important municipal, academic, schools, and hospitals sector, in 1999, although with British Columbia and Yukon not agreeing. Despite such progress, very little has changed with respect to procurement by public enterprises, or energy, or the processing of natural resources, or transportation, to list the other main sectors affected to some extent by provincial attempts to protect local interests.[63]

A small illustration of how things work in Canada may help explain the perhaps surprising lack of concern about such obviously inefficient provincial policies. Since 1998, the provinces have been attempting to reach agreement on a uniform rule with respect to the coloring of margarine. Québec, which has a relatively large dairy industry, requires that margarine must not be colored to look like butter. Other provinces do not. Thus, margarine producers in Canada usually produce two shades of yellow margarine to meet market demand and the PQ restrictions. The titanic struggle on this issue continues and may well do so for years to come. A country that can live with different shades of yellow margarine, as well as with many other provincially differentiated economic policies, has had little difficulty in living with different provincial securities regulations.

With respect to capital markets more specifically, there has been an emergence of various Labor Sponsored Venture Capital Funds (LSVCF), which grant PIT credits for investments by individuals in funds that will invest within the borders of their provinces to help save or create employment, with as usual, Québec leading the way. Such funds are clearly a new source of fragmentation of the Canadian capital market (Vaillancourt, 1997), which is the last thing needed, it might be argued, in the face of the increasing absorption of that market within the American market. Nonetheless, there seems to be no evidence that variability across provinces in access to financial instruments such as rights offerings (Mohindra, 2002) matters in any measurable way, and such measures have not given rise to any serious policy debate.

---

[63] See Trebilcock and Schwanen (1995) for detailed discussion of the IAT.

Regulatory federalism in Canada, as illustrated here by the case of securities regulation, thus does not easily fit the Weingast (1995) conception of "market-preserving federalism." The "competitive" subnational governments envisaged in that framework may have a substantial regulatory role, but they are assumed to exercise that role within a common market enforced by the federal government to ensure nationwide free markets and full mobility of factors, goods, and services. In many fields, as the case we have discussed here illustrates, Canada's federal government either cannot exercise such a role or has chosen not to do so. Provincial regulators may attempt to coordinate to some extent, but in the end, as noted here, they may often be tempted to use their powers at least to some extent for competitive purposes. Nonetheless, from the perspective of what may be labeled "nation-preserving" federalism, even such a less than perfect common market may perhaps be considered to be "efficient" in a broader sense, or so it might be argued.[64]

V. ARE THERE ANY LESSONS?

We have discussed three very different cases in this chapter. Although it is not easy to generalize from such disparate instances, nonetheless a few key points do seem to emerge.

First, Québec matters a lot. It has long been a commonplace in Canadian political thought that Canada is as it is largely because of the existence of a large, linguistically distinct province. Certainly, our examples support this conclusion. Québec's interest obviously drove the constitutional debate, although it hardly got what it wanted in this instance. Québec pushed for more tax room and obtained it in the early 1960s. More recently, it has opposed a national securities commission and has helped to block it. At the present time, there is a debate in Canada on the funding of health services. All provinces are arguing that the federal government is not providing enough money to the provinces. Some are requesting changes in transfers, and some are requesting more tax room. Unsurprisingly, Québec is in the latter camp. In true Canadian style, to further its argument, it created a Commission on Fiscal Disequilibrium (the Séguin Commission), which reported in early 2002, and, in the recent Québec style, there has also been some discussion of a provincial referendum on tax-sharing but this has been set aside as of September 2002. Will Québec once more lead the way in changing the fiscal balance between

---

[64] For an early argument along these lines, see Bird (1986, pp. 212–214).

the federal and provincial governments? Other provinces may of course also take the lead from time to time, as, for example, Saskatchewan did in the development of the health system, Ontario in the long debates leading to the old-age pension reforms of the early 1950s, and, perhaps, Alberta with its new flat tax. For the past forty years, however, not only has Québec been the most distinct province but also generally the one with the most clearly articulated, cross-party-supported, and strongly presented interest. It may not always get its way, but it generally knows what its way is, which is more than can be said for most of the other provinces, or, often, for the federal government.

A second key factor is the relative financial and political strength of the federal government and the provinces. In the 1960s, for example, although it clearly dominated fiscally, the federal government was a minority government faced by majority governments in Québec. Currently, both are relatively fiscally strong and both have majority governments. Some years ago Bird et al. (1979) suggested that the reduction in federal fiscal surpluses after the mid-1970s would severely reduce federal ability to "buy off" dissidents with increased transfers. It did, and this may have been one factor behind some of the developments discussed earlier in this chapter. The return to fiscal solvency at the federal level at the end of the 1990s, however, has led to renewed federal attempts to, as it were, plant the flag in areas long jealously guarded by the Québec government, such as postsecondary education. It is true that the federal government conceded significant extra financial resources to the provinces in September 2000 when it faced an election and both big provinces, Ontario and Québec, united in asking for more transfers. Nonetheless, buoyed by its surplus revenues, it may soon provoke another conflict by creating some tax-related concessions for health or in some other way flex its fiscal muscles again. Changing fiscal and political strengths at the different levels of government thus obviously also play a critical role in determining future outcomes.

Finally, an important additional factor is the nature of the change required. Tax sharing and transfers could be modified simply by changing laws; this would be an easy and relatively quiet task for a majority government in Canada. However, recognition of Québec as a distinct society required a constitutional amendment and extensive public discussion. Following the close-run 1995 referendum, the House of Commons adopted a resolution affirming the distinct character of Québec and indicating that it intended to be guided by this in its legislation. Subsequently, in February 1996, a federal law was adopted giving the regions, including

Québec, a veto to be exercised by the federal government on constitutional changes. Finally, in the 1996 throne speech, it was stated that a majority of provinces had to agree before new federal–provincial cost-shared programs could be implemented and that nonagreeing provinces would receive financial compensation for implementing similar programs. Québec's constitutional demands thus seem to have largely been met in a sense. Until now, however, none of these provisions has been used, and of course none of them have constitutional status (and are thus more easily reversible).[65]

In the end, as is so often the case with political institutions, political outcomes may reflect not so much the details of the institutions within which different political actors act as the degree of trust they have in the motives and reliability of other relevant actors. If, as in the case of sales tax reform in the early 1990s, for example, all governments have broadly similar interests and basically trust each other's technical competence, a good working agreement can often be reached without the need for much formal legislation, let alone constitutional affirmation (Bird and Gendron, 1998). If external circumstances dominate [e.g., international capital markets and basically fiscal responsible electorates in the case of public borrowing (Bird and Tassonyi, 2001)] the precise degree and kind of regulation may not be critical. However, when an issue such as "distinct society" is raised to the status of a political icon, with high and conflicting symbolism attached to it by both sides, agreement at any level may prove impossible to reach, at least so long as the practical issues of what to do in the face of real problems are discussed in these terms.

The long-term answer for Canada, if there is one, may thus be to put aside the search for unreachable and untenable long-term solutions and to continue in the future, as in the past, to deal with problems as they come up rather than attempting to determine in advance exactly who should deal with what in what way. "Muddling through" may not only describe how Canadian federalism has to date dealt with changing times: It may also, as Lindblom, Simon, and many others have argued,[66] describe the best way in which fallible people – let alone fallible politicians – have

---

[65] Some of the recent discussion of these issues has taken place in the framework of what is called the "Social Union" agreement signed by the federal government and all provinces but Québec in February 1999. So far this agreement has not amounted to much in reality, and there is considerable debate about its future, or lack of it (see, for example, Richards, 2002, and Dufour, 2002).

[66] See, for example, Lindblom (1968), Popper (1957), Simon (1956), and, more recently, Breton (1996), as well as Bird (1970b) for an application of this approach to tax policymaking in Canada.

yet developed to cope with the complex reality of managing a multiethnic federal country in a globalizing world. Ad hoc dispute resolution or incremental accommodation to changing circumstances may be less intellectually attractive than more holistic approaches, but it seems more likely to yield satisfactory results in Canada. The existing system has, over time, proved surprisingly flexible, so "if it ain't broke, don't fix it."

Informal "executive federalism" has on the whole worked well in the past and may continue to be the best way in the future to cope with the situation, even in the face of the new pressures emanating from below the border. When life is complex, interests divergent, and the policy environment uncertain and changing, pragmatic resolutions of specific problems such as those discussed in the fiscal and regulatory fields may, we suggest, continue to work better for Canada and Canadians than attempts to revise constitutions or reach more principled resolutions of grand issues.[67] Such at least seems to us to be the main lesson emerging from the experiences discussed in this chapter.

Bibliography

Anisman P., and P. W. Hogg (1979). "Constitutional Aspects of Federal Securities Legislation," in *Proposals for a Securities Market Law for Canada, Background Papers*, vol. 3, pp. 135–200. Ottawa: Minister of Supply and Services.

Banwell, P. T. (1969). "Proposals for a National Securities Commission," *Queen's Intramural Law Journal* 1(3): 3–35.

Beaulieu, M. C., and G. Bellemare (2000). "Canadian Stock Market and North American Integration" Isuma 1(1). Available online at http://www.isuma.net/vo/n01/beaulieu/beaulieu-e.shtml

Bird, R. M. (1970a). *The Growth of Government Spending in Canada*. Toronto: Canadian Tax Foundation.

Bird, R. M. (1970b). "The Tax Kaleidoscope: Perspectives on Tax Reform in Canada," Canadian Tax Journal 18: 444–478.

Bird, R. M.(1978). "Canada's Vanishing Death Taxes," Osgoode Hall Law Journal 16: 133–145.

Bird, R. M. (1979). *Financing Canadian Government: A Quantitative Overview* Toronto: Canadian Tax Foundation.

Bird, R. M. (1986). *Federal Finance in Comparative Perspective*. Toronto: Canadian Tax Foundation.

Bird, R. M. (2000). "Rethinking Subnational Taxes: A New Look at Tax Assignment," Tax Notes International 20 (19): 2069–96.

---

[67] This, however, allows the sovereignist option to retain some legitimacy as its proponents can argue that there is unfinished constitutional business. Although this option seems unlikely to carry the day in the near term, one should recall that it was pronounced dead in the mid-1980s, only to almost win in 1995. "Muddling through" is not a riskless approach.

Bird, R. M., and P.-P. Gendron (1998). "Dual VATs and Cross-Border Trade: Two Problems, One Solution?," International Tax and Public Finance 5 (3): 429–442.

Bird, R. M., and K. J. McKenzie (2001). Taxing Business: A Provincial Affair? Commentary No. 154. Toronto: C.D. Howe Institute.

Bird, R. M., and A. Tassonyi (2001). "Constraints on Provincial and Municipal Borrowing in Canada: Markets, Rules, and Norms," Canadian Public Administration, 44 (1): 84–109.

Bird, R. M., and F. Vaillancourt (2001). "Fiscal Arrangements for Maintaining an Effective State in Canada" Environment and Planning C: Government and Policy 19(2): 163–187.

Bird, R. M., D. B. Perry, and T. A. Wilson (1998). "Canada," in K. Messere, ed., *Tax Systems in Industrialized Countries* pp. 39–92. London: Oxford University Press.

Boadway, R., and P. Hobson (1998). *Equalization: Its Contribution to Canada's Economic and Fiscal Progress* Kingston: John Deustch Institute.

Breton, A. (1996). *Competitive Governments.* Cambridge, UK: Cambridge University Press.

Burns, R. M. (1980). *The Acceptable Mean: The Tax Rental Agreements, 1941–62.* Toronto: Canadian Tax Foundation.

Canadian Tax Foundation (1999). *Finances of the Nation 1999.* Toronto: Canadian Tax Foundation.

Courchene, T. J. (1986). *Economic Management and the Division of Powers.* Toronto: University of Toronto Press for Royal Commission on the Economic Union and Development Prospects for Canada (McDonald Comission).

Dufour, C. (2002). Restoring the Federal Principle: The Place of Québec in the Canadian Social Union, Policy Matters, vol. 3, no. 1, IRPP.

Durocher, R. (1996). "Quiet Revolution," in *Canadian Encyclopedia Plus.* Toronto: McClelland and Stewart. CD-Rom

Erard, B., and F. Vaillancourt (1993). "The Compliance Costs of a Separate Personal Income Tax system for Ontario: Simulations for 1991," in A. Maslove, ed., *Taxation in a Subnational Jurisdiction*, pp. 137–170. Toronto: University from Toronto Press (Fair Tax Commission).

Granatstein, J. L. (1975). *Canada's War: The Politics of the Mackenzie King Government, 1939–1945.* Toronto: Oxford University Press.

Lachance, R., and F. Vaillancourt (2001). "Québec's Tax on Income: Evolution, Status and Evaluation," in Douglas Brown, ed., *Tax Competition and the Fiscal Union: Balancing Competition and Harmonization in Canada*, pp. 39–47. Kingston: Institute of Intergovernmental Relations.

Lindblom, C. E. (1968). *The Policy-Making Process.* Englewood Cliffs, NJ: Prentice-Hall.

McRoberts, K. (1988). *Québec: Social Change and Political Crisis*, 3rd edition. Toronto: McClelland and Stewart.

Meisel, J., and G. Rocher (1999). *Si je me souviens bien/ As I recall: Regards sur l'histoire.* Montreal: L'Institut de Recherche en Politiques Publiques.

Mintz, J., and M. Smart (2002). "Why Québec's Tax-Point Transfers Are a Good Idea," The National Post, March 25.

Mohindra, N. (2002). *Securities Market Regulations in Canada.* Vancouver: Fraser Institute Critical Issues Bulletin.

Moore, A. M., J. H. Perry, and D. I. Beach (1966). *The Financing of Canadian Federation: The First Hundred Years.* Toronto: Canadian Tax Foundation.

Ontario Economic Council (1983). *A Separate Personal Income Tax for Ontario.* Toronto: Ontario Economic Council.

Ontario Securities Commission LLP (2002). Five Year Review Committee Draft Report Reviewing the Securities Act.

Perry, D. B. (1977). *Financing the Canadian Federation, 1867–1995: Setting the Stage for Change.* Toronto: Canadian Tax Foundation.

Perry, J. H. (1989). *A Fiscal History of Canada – The Postwar Years.* Toronto: Canadian Tax Foundation.

Popper, K. (1957). *The Poverty of Historicism.* London: Routledge & Kegan Paul.

Porter Commission (1966). Report of the Royal Commission on Banking and Finance (Ottawa).

Richards, J. (2002). The Paradox of the Social Union Framework Agreement, Backgrounder No. 59. Toronto: C.D. Howe Research Institute.

Russell, P. H. (1993). *Constitutional Odyssey: Can Canadians Become a Sovereign People?* Toronto: University of Toronto Press.

Séguin Commission (2002). Commission on Fiscal Imbalance, A New Division of Canada's Financial Resources (Québec).

Simeon, R. (1978). *Federal-Provincial Diplomacy.* Toronto: University of Toronto Press.

Simon, H. (1956). *Administrative Behavior,* 2nd edition. New York: The Free Press.

Smith, E. H. (1998). *Federal-Provincial Tax Sharing and Centralized Tax Collection in Canada,* Special Studies in Taxation and Public Finance No. 1. Toronto: Canadian Tax Foundation.

Tindal, C. R., and Tindal, S. N. (2000). *Local Government in Canada,* 5th edition. Scarborough, ON: Nelson Thomson Learning.

Trebilcock, M., and D. Schwanen, eds. (1995). *Getting There: An Assessment of the Agreement on Internal Trade.* Toronto: C.D. Howe Institute.

Trebilcock, M., J. Pritchard, J. Whalley, and T. Courchene (1983). *Federalism and the Canadian Economic Union.* Toronto: University of Toronto Press.

Tse, D. (1994). "Establishing a Federal Securities Commission," Saskatchewan Law Review 58 (1): 427–440.

Turgeon, M., and F. Vaillancourt (2002). "The Provision of Highways in Canada and the Federal Government," Publius 32(1): 161–180.

Vaillancourt, F. (1996). "Language and Socioeconomic Status in Québec: Measurement, Findings, Determinants and Policy Costs," International Journal of the Sociology of Language, Special Issue on Economic Approaches to Language and Language Planning, 121: 69–92.

Vaillancourt, F. (1997). "Labour Sponsored Venture Capital Funds in Canada: Institutional Aspects Tax Expenditures and Employment Creation", in P. Halpern, ed., *Financing Growth in Canada,* pp. 571–592. Calgary: University of Calgary Press (Industry Canada).

Vaillancourt, F. (2000a). "Federal-Provincial Small Transfer Programs in Canada, 1957–1998: Importance, Composition and Evaluation," in H. Lazar, ed., *Canada: The State of the Federation 1999/2000,* pp. 189–212. Kingston: IIGR, Queen's University.

Vaillancourt, F. (2000b). "The Québec Pension Plan," in P. Boothe, ed., *A Separate Pension Plan for Alberta*, pp. 23–40 Western Studies in Economic Policy No. 5. Edmonton: Institute for Public Economics, University of Alberta Press.

Vaillancourt, F., and S. Rault (2003). "The Regional Dimension of Federal Intergovernmental and Interpersonal Transfers in Canada, 1981–2001," Regional and Federal Studies 13(4): 130–152.

Vander Ploeg, C. (2000). Canadian Intergovernmental Agreements on Immigration, Background Paper 2, A National Conference on Canadian Immigration, Canada West Foundation.

Weingast B. (1995). "The Economic Role of Political Institutions: Market-Preserving Federalism," Journal of Law, Economics, and Organization 11: 1–31.

SIX

Fiscal Federalism and Economic Reform in China

Roy Bahl and Jorge Martinez-Vazquez[1]

I. INTRODUCTION

Because of history, size, and economic potential China is a force to reckon with. It is a nation of 9.6 million square kilometers populated by 1.26 billion people with a varied geography: Traveling from west to east (Figure 6.1) one starts with the vast dry areas, moves to the mountains, valleys, and higher altitudes of the center, and ends up in the more temperate coastal regions, which have more rain, lower altitudes, and better communication and transportation systems. A main theme of this chapter is that, in great part owing to geography, but also owing to overt government policies, wealth and economic well-being tend to increase monotonically from west to east. That reality significantly conditions the past, present, and future of fiscal federalism in China.

A standard grouping of China's provinces is used in Table 6.1 to describe the economic geography. The Northern Region includes the large and rich cities of Beijing and Tianjin. These two cities, together with Shanghai in the Eastern Region and Chongqing in the Southwest Region, are granted provincial status, much as is the case for Moscow and St. Petersburg in Russia. The Northern Region also contains the relatively poor province of Inner Mongolia. The Northeast Region, also known as Manchuria, contains several relatively rich provinces with a long tradition of manufacturing dating back to Japan's occupation of this area in the first part of the twentieth century. The Eastern Region includes the

[1] We would like to thank T. N. Srinivasan, Baoyun Qiao, Jessica Wallack, and an anonymous referee for helpful comments. We acknowledge the able assistance provided by Li Zhang and Wenbin Xiao.

Table 6.1. *Key Features of People's Republic of China in 2002*[i]

	Area		Population		Population Density (persons per km²)	GDP		GDP per Capita (yuan/person)
	(1,000 km²)	(%)	(10,000 persons)	(%)		(100 million RMB)	(%)	
China	**9600**	**100**	**128453**	**100**	**134**	**118021**	**100**	**7468**
Northern Region	**1573**	**16.4**	**14838**	**11.6**	**94**	**15138**	**15.8**	**10202**
1. Beijing	17	0.2	1423	1.1	837	3213	3.3	22577
2. Tianjin	11	0.1	1007	0.8	915	2051	2.1	20369
3. Hebei	188	2.0	6735	5.2	358	6123	6.4	9091
4. Shanxi	156	1.6	3294	2.6	211	2018	2.1	6125
5. Inner Mongolia	1201	12.5	2379	1.9	20	1734	1.8	7290
North eastern Region	**802**	**8.3**	**10715**	**8.3**	**134**	**11587**	**12.1**	**10813**
6. Liaoning	146	1.5	4203	3.3	288	5458	5.7	12986
7. Jilin	187	1.9	2699	2.1	144	2246	2.3	8322
8. Heilongjiang	469	4.9	3813	3.0	81	3882	4.0	10181
Eastern Region	**791**	**8.2**	**36761**	**28.6**	**465**	**45090**	**47.0**	**12266**
9. Shanghai	6	0.1	1625	1.3	2708	5409	5.6	33285
10. Jiangsu	103	1.1	7381	5.7	717	10632	11.1	14404
11. Zhejiang	102	1.1	4647	3.6	456	7796	8.1	16776
12. Anhui	139	1.5	6338	4.9	456	3569	3.7	5631
13. Fujian	121	1.3	3466	2.7	286	4682	4.9	13508
14. Jiangxi	166	1.7	4222	3.3	254	2450	2.6	5804
15. Shandong	153	1.6	9082	7.1	594	10552	11.0	11619

	1028	10.7	35714	27.8	347	30315	31.6	8488
Central South Region								
16. Henan	168	1.7	9613	7.5	572	6169	6.4	6417
17. Hubei	188	2.0	5988	4.7	319	4976	5.2	8309
18. Hunan	210	2.2	6629	5.2	316	4341	4.5	6548
19. Guangdong	192	2.0	7859	6.1	409	11770	12.3	14976
20. Guangxi	236	2.5	4822	3.8	204	2455	2.6	5092
21. Hainan	34	0.4	803	0.6	236	604	0.6	7523
South western Region	**1259**	**24.4**	**20217**	**15.7**	**161**	**10425**	**10.9**	**5157**
22. Chongqing	82	0.9	3107	2.4	379	1971	2.1	6345
23. Sichuan	485	5.1	8673	6.8	179	4875	5.1	5621
24. Guizhou	176	1.8	3837	3.0	218	1185	1.2	3088
25. Yunnan	395	4.1	4333	3.4	110	2232	2.3	5152
26. Tibet	120	12.5	267	0.2	22	161	0.2	6046
North western Region	**3024**	**31.5**	**9273**	**7.2**	**31**	**5466**	**5.7**	**5895**
27. Shannxi	206	2.1	3674	2.9	178	2036	2.1	5542
28. Gansu	450	4.7	2593	2.0	58	1161	1.2	4479
29. Qinghai	702	7.3	529	0.4	8	341	0.4	6448
30. Ningxia	66	0.7	572	0.4	87	329	0.3	5757
31. Xinjiang	1600	16.7	1905	1.5	12	1598	1.7	8390
Maximum	**1600**	**16.7**	**9613**	**7.5**	**2708**	**11770**	**12.3**	**33285**
Minimum	**6**	**0.1**	**267**	**0.2**	**8**	**161**	**0.2**	**3088**

i *Source:* Population and GDP are based on the data from China's Yearbook 2003. Areas are from each province's or municipality's official Web site.

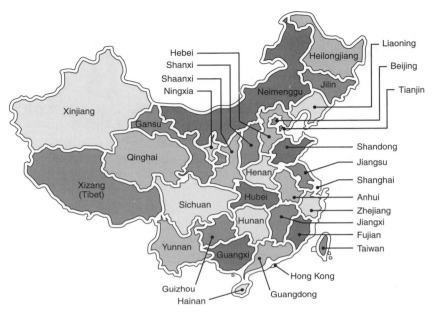

Figure 6.1. Provinces of China. *Source:* ACASIAN, Lex Berman.

richest enclave in the country, the city of Shanghai, and the coastal or close-in provinces stretching from Shandong to Fujian. Most of these provinces have been recipients of foreign direct investment flows since the "openness" policy began in 1978. They also enjoy relatively high levels of per capita income. The Central South Region includes the fertile interior agricultural provinces between China's two great rivers, the Yellow River and the Yangtze River, except for Shandong province, which is part of the Eastern Region. The Central South Region also includes the coastal province of Guandong (geographically next to Hong Kong), which accounted for more than 10% of China's GDP in the year 2000. The Southwest Region provinces have a humid climate but a mountainous terrain. The Northwest Region is geographically more isolated, with an arid climate, and is inhabited heavily by ethnic minorities. These last two regions, in the west, contain many of China's poorest provinces.

The objectives of this chapter are to examine the role of fiscal federalism in the economic growth, modernization, and globalization of China's economy since the pro-market reforms started in 1979 and to examine how other economic policies and the forces of globalization have shaped and conditioned fiscal federalism in China.

This chapter is divided into three main parts. In the first, we describe the institutional arrangements for fiscal federalism in China. Second, we study the process of economic reform and the main trends that have framed and conditioned fiscal federalism in China. We pay special attention to the process of foreign direct investment and its impact on regional development and on economic and fiscal disparities across China. The final section examines the fiscal reform challenges that have resulted from a history of economic reforms. Throughout this chapter, we continue to return to two central points. First, fiscal federalism issues in China are inextricably linked to tax policy and tax administration issues.[2] Second, fiscal federalism in China is significantly conditioned by other government economic policies regarding demographic issues, the financial sector, and foreign investment and globalization trends. The way forward for an improved system of intergovernmental fiscal relations in China will no doubt require active tax policy reform and upgraded tax administration, but it must also reach for policy reform outside the fiscal domain. For example, the reforms of migration policy, the pension systems, and even of the banking system will have considerable impacts on the shape of fiscal federalism in China.

II. CHINA'S FISCAL AND POLITICAL ARRANGEMENTS

On the surface, China's governance appears to be very decentralized. Local governments in China are organized in a hierarchical way with each level of government reporting to the next highest level (see Figure 6.2). About 70% of government budgetary expenditures are made at the subnational government level. This is a very high share by international standards. Moreover, the structure of governance gives the feel of a decentralized system. There are approximately 47,000 local government units, which would seem to indicate a desire to get government relatively close to the people. And though China is a unitary state, it has some of the features of a fiscal federalism: It has a hierarchical central, provincial, and local structure of government, and its provinces are given considerable latitude in forming the intergovernmental system that finances and regulates their local governments. In particular, they may share revenues among local governments within the province as they choose.

In reality, however, China's governance is much less decentralized than the large subnational government expenditure share would indicate.

---

[2] See Bahl (1999).

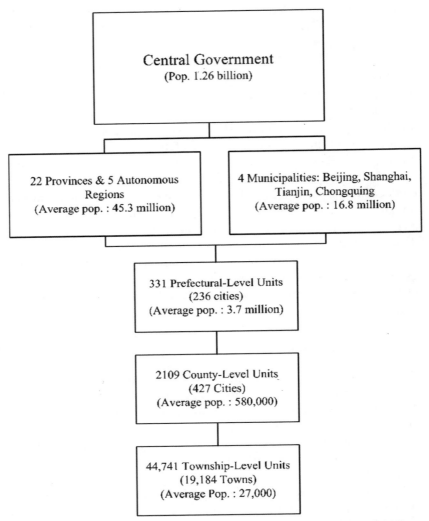

Figure 6.2. Structure of government in China. *Source:* World Bank (2002).

There is a significant command and control element in the intergovernmental fiscal system that includes several binding expenditure laws and numerous expenditure mandates. Subnational governments have very little by way of formal revenue-raising powers. They are financed primarily by shares of central taxes and grants. The political structure of its governance and intergovernmental fiscal system may inhibit China's ability to capture the potential efficiency gains from fiscal decentralization.

The subnational governments have reacted against this centralization by creating a kind of "backdoor federalism" (Bahl, 1999). They have been entrepreneurial in negotiating contracts with their enterprises, levying informal charges and maintaining significant off-budget accounts, indirectly borrowing from state banks to cover deficits, and erecting trade barriers to maximize local revenues. In part, this led the government to adopt a major intergovernmental fiscal reform in 1994 to recentralize the fiscal system. Although some recentralization has occurred, some of the incentives for fiscal entrepreneurship by subnational governments are still in place.

The present system of fiscal decentralization in China is probably not sustainable in the long run, assuming that the goal is to give subnational governments an incentive to improve local public services and to promote economic growth. Moreover, as discussed in the following, there are significant regional fiscal disparities that sooner or later will have to be addressed. Part of the way forward for China will almost certainly include a significant revision of the intergovernmental fiscal system.

II.1. Political Representation and Accountability

Local governments in China are organized in a hierarchical way with each level of government reporting to the next highest level (see Figure 6.2). The thirty-one provincial-level governments vary greatly in size and level of economic development. For example, Shandong and Sichuan provinces have populations that are approaching 100 million, whereas Tibet has a population of less than 3 million (Table 6.1). GDP per capita is over 30 thousand yuan in Shanghai province but less than 3 thousand yuan in Guizhou province. The subnational governments have very different jobs to do in meeting expenditure needs, and they have very different financial capabilities.

The structure of government described in Figure 6.2 is quite decentralized, but relatively little power is directly invested in local voters. Arguably the biggest difference between China and the decentralized systems in the West is the absence of popular political representation. Theory and practice tell us that provincial and local councils must be popularly elected, and the chief local officers must be locally appointed, for the efficiency gains from decentralization to occur (Bahl and Linn, 1992). Local officials must be accountable to those who elect them and the local population must have the right to vote out those who do not satisfy their wishes. Without popular elections, the general population has no direct way of revealing its preferences for more or less or different public services. China's federalism, termed "market preserving" by some analysts (Qian and Weingast, 1997) has practically never included political decentralization.[3] The Communist Party has not been separated from the state and there is no secure system of property rights. The provincial governors and chief local officers are still appointed, thus their accountability is upward to the level of government and the political body that appointed them.

Some would argue that this is not negative, at least in terms of economic growth. With the opening of the Chinese economy, and with the new flexibility given by fiscal decentralization, local officials had more of the wherewithal to pursue economic development for their regions. The central government encouraged this economic growth emphasis and rewarded those who were successful with it. Some have attributed China's better economic performance than Russia's to China's resolve toward economic growth and to its continued political centralization (Blanchard and Shleifer, 2000). The Chinese version of federalism that empowered centrally appointed local officials, rewarded their successes, and encouraged them to compete with one another appears to have been a successful alternative to political decentralization. The reward system favored those who could show greater economic progress, and although in some cases protectionism and fiscal abuses resulted, in other cases the provincial leadership displayed their comparative advantages. All of this, and the backing away from "entitlement" subsidies to state-owned enterprises (SOEs), led to what one might call a market-preserving approach. Coupled with the other economic policies just described, however, this entrepreneurial freedom appears to have led to growing disparities in the fiscal health of subnational governments. Political decentralization also has the advantage of making local officials more accountable and responsive to the needs and preferences of their constituencies. China's decentralization experience has been criticized precisely for the lack of concern of local officials for local needs and services and their concentration on fulfilling the wishes of the central authorities, focusing exclusively on rapid economic growth.

---

[3] In recent years, a democratic experiment has been running in a number of provinces at the township or lower levels. Zhang et al. (2002) have investigated through village surveys conducted over several years the relative performance of these local governments with elected officials compared to that of appointed cadres. Interestingly, they find that elected officials are perceived as taxing constituents less and providing them with higher levels of public services.

Table 6.2. *Distribution of Revenues and*
Expenditures of Subnational Governments

	Percentage Share	Percentage Change Since 1994–1995
Province	28.2	1.8
Prefecture	30.2	−1.1
County[i]	41.5	−0.6

[i] Includes townships.
Source: World Bank (2002).

II.2. Expenditure Assignment

For most functions of government, the assignment of expenditures in China more or less follows along the lines of that made in other countries. The center provides services with national benefits, provinces provide those services with regional benefits, and local governments provide services with limited spillover effects. In 1999 the central government accounted for about 36% of spending and is dominant in the areas of defense, debt service, and geological prospecting. Technological upgrading, research and development, and industry expenditures appeared to be concurrent functions. The local governments were dominant in the social service sectors (health, education, and welfare) and in agricultural development. Local governments accounted for about half of all capital construction expenditures. This is essentially the pattern of responsibility one would expect to find in any country.

Where the statistics for China look a little different is in the distribution of expenditures among the three levels of subnational government. The data in Table 6.2 show that a heavy expenditure delivery burden is placed on the lowest levels of local government (counties and townships).

There are three important problems with this pattern of expenditure assignment. First, the exact assignment of expenditures is murky. There is no law that spells out exactly which level of subnational government is responsible for which functions. In effect, it is left to the provincial government to decide which of the local governments will be responsible for which functions. As a result, there can be overlap in the delivery of services, and expenditure decisions may be driven as much by politics as by efficiency considerations (Hu, 1995; Lou, 1997). The high incidence of concurrent expenditure assignments creates problems because even if it is clear which level of government can regulate expenditures and which level is responsible for implementation, there remains considerable murkiness as to which level is actually responsible for financing these expenditures or how these financing responsibilities are divided. This has allowed upper level governments to push down funding responsibilities, which in many cases has meant an (inefficient) underprovision of public services.

Second, and probably most important, there are problems with misassignment; that is, certain expenditure functions are matched with the "wrong" level of local government. Responsibility for much of the social safety net lies with the subnational governments. China stands practically alone in the world in assigning responsibility for unemployment compensation, health insurance, and pensions to prefecture (city) and county governments. These welfare expenditures are financed on a pay-as-you-go basis from enterprise payroll taxes, general revenues, and special central subsidies. The level of expenditures required to meet expenditure needs in these areas has been beyond the reach of some local governments. The result has been a growing problem with pension arrears that has required central government financial intervention.

An assignment issue also arises with respect to health and education services, which are the responsibility of the lowest level county and township governments. These local governments in many cases have neither the financial nor the administrative capacity to handle the social service functions.

Third, there is no balance between the assignment of expenditure responsibilities and the revenues available to finance these expenditures. In the prereform period of the 1980s, central transfers supported a "basic" level of expenditures for each province. As the financing scheme shifted toward contracts and then tax sharing on a derivation basis, the link between expenditure needs and revenues became weaker. In fact, under the present tax-sharing system, the money flows to those provinces where the economy is strongest.

The distribution of central resources among provinces almost certainly is not equalizing. Within provinces there also may be an exacerbation of the mismatch between expenditure needs and revenues made available. The provincial governments allocate revenues among their constituent units, and, as in the case of the central government, some recentralization occurred after the 1994 reform. As may be seen in Table 6.2, the share of provincial governments in revenues and expenditures grew by 1.8% since the 1994 reform. The share of the lowest level governments, where the social service responsibilities are greatest, has actually declined. This pattern follows the spirit of the 1994 reform that revised the revenue side of the intergovernmental fiscal system but did not address expenditure assignment. In fact, China has done relatively little, since its economic and fiscal reforms began, to change expenditure responsibilities among levels of government.

The economic reforms that widened the fiscal capacity disparities among Chinese provinces combined with expenditure misassignments to worsen fiscal balance in the intergovernmental system. At least these data suggest that the weaker provincial governments were more prone to push their deficits down to the local level. This no doubt has led to increasingly deficient social service levels, more pressure to find "informal" sources of local revenue, and likely an increased propensity for migration.

II.3. Expenditure Management and Budget Autonomy

In theory, subnational governments in China have budget autonomy in that they may approve their own budgets. In practice, their autonomy may be more limited because several national budget laws prescribe minimum expenditure growth rates for some functions, and numerous unfunded expenditure mandates are imposed on lower level governments. The most important of these is the mandated labor cost for civil servants. It is also important to note in this regard that subnational governments cannot determine the aggregate level of their formal budgets because they have no autonomy in revenue raising. However, as we discuss further in the following, subnational governments face soft budget constraints. In addition, the lack of timely information and reporting to the center leaves subnational governments a considerable degree of freedom on actual patterns of spending, including over tied (special-purpose) grants. All these factors provide greater (informal) budget autonomy.

Although there may be a hard budget constraint on local governments in that they cannot formally run budget deficits, it is also the case that the local budgets are far from being hard expenditure plans. Budgets in China are organized on a top-down basis (the center informs the province of the budget constraint, the province informs the prefecture, etc.) and the process typically begins late in the fiscal year. Moreover, there is uncertainty about the revenues available to the local governments, since conditional grants are distributed on an ad hoc basis and provinces have not held to stable revenue-sharing systems. Consequently, the budgets of local governments are not firm expenditure plans. Under such a scheme, one should expect budget deficits.

In fact, the subnational governments do run deficits (Bahl, 1999; Wong, Heady, and Woo, 1995). If a deficit does occur, the higher level government must decide if it will be partly or fully covered by a deficit or "year-end" grant. The four rounds of pay increases for civil servants since 1999, along with associated increases in pension and unemployment benefits, clearly contributed to problems of fiscal imbalance and brought many local governments to the brink of insolvency, especially at the county and township levels. The growing number of bailouts to local governments is a clear indication that current expenditure assignments are both unsustainable and increasingly blurred. Other methods of financing the deficit include using extrabudgetary funds and borrowing from government or from the industrial bank. The soft budget constraint is also encouraged by policy loans from the banking system to the SOEs, which may partly finance social service expenditures and may become a contingent liability of the subnational governments.

The problem is especially complicated because about half of all expenditures made by subnational governments are off-budget. Subnational governments have levied a variety of off-budget fees, charges, and informal taxes since the early 1990s, and they have spent these funds to augment their expenditure programs. In some cases the impact of extrabudgetary funds is considerable. The World Bank (2002) reports that personnel expenditures for education in Hunan province were equivalent to 125% of total budgetary expenditures for education, and the comparable figure for health expenditure was 220%. The appeal to local governments of extrabudgetary accounts is easily seen: Extrabudgetary taxes are not shared with higher level governments and extrabudgetary expenditures are not subject to the same regulation and controls as are budgetary expenditures. Although many of the fees and quasitaxes used as extrabudgetary financing have been criticized as chaotic and excessive, many have been levied with the blessing of the central government and in some cases under the supervision of upper level governments (Wong, 1998). One interpretation of this is that the center recognized the need for more local autonomy and more local resources but was not yet ready to take the step of providing formal local revenue-raising autonomy. A backdoor federalism was seen as a good substitute in the 1990s. However, off-budget revenues and expenditures can have the additional cost of being more distortionary than their budget counterparts. Moreover, such informal taxes and charges introduce an element of uncertainty into the tax system that may discourage local investment.

II.4. Revenue Assignment

Revenue assignment in China has taken the form followed by most transition countries. Some central government taxes are assigned fully or in part to the provincial governments. The province may in turn assign revenues to their lower level governments, subject to very few restrictions. In fact, there is a wide variation in the practice among the Chinese provinces. The remaining amount of revenues for subnational governments is provided by grants and subsidies. Subnational governments have no independent taxing powers and no powers to set tax rates.[4] The revenue system is very centralized.

Revenue assignment to the subnational governments is no simple matter. Excise duties and taxes on international trade are held exclusively for the central government. All other taxes in the system are shared with provincial governments at rates ranging from 0% to 100%. Sharing is always on a basis of origin of collections. The result of this system, as practiced in China, is that the overall share of total collections going to the subnational governments is about 44%.

Economic policies have favored the development of the coastal provinces, as discussed in the following, and the shared tax system of financing the provinces has reinforced this favoritism. Moreover, the growing political strength that strong economic growth has given to the coastal provinces makes it less likely that this counterequalizing feature of fiscal federalism will be abandoned.

There are some misassignments on this list of shared taxes. The most notable relate to origin-based revenue sharing of VAT and the enterprise income tax, which may not be the proper taxes to share with subnational governments on a derivation basis. The individual income tax holds more promise as a proper revenue source for subnational governments in a system of fiscal federalism.

VAT. The VAT is particularly inappropriate as a shared tax on a derivation basis. Tracking and policing the origin of collections is no easy administrative matter. VAT payments can be credited to provinces other than those where the value added takes place, causing the "wrong" province to receive the revenue. Given the challenges of VAT administration and the importance of this revenue source to the central government, one might question the wisdom of allocating tax administration effort to verify that the interprovincial allocations are being correctly made. Moreover, to assign VAT on a basis of origin of collections is to invite provinces to institute protectionist measures. Examples of protection policies abound. Henan and Anhui provinces ban imports of tobacco from Guizhou. Many local businesses are prohibited from opening branches outside their home

---

[4] The lone exceptions are that local governments may set the rate of the land use tax within a prescribed range and may chose whether or not to levy the entertainment tax.

region.[5] There is nothing in China that approximates an interstate commerce clause that would require free trade among provinces.

ENTERPRISE INCOME TAX. The enterprise income tax is a poor choice for provincial government finance. It is fraught with problems that have plagued its use as a subnational tax in many countries. As the Chinese economy develops and enterprises begin to operate in many provinces, as comparative advantage tells us they will, the problem of allocating profits among the provinces will appear. The United States has learned well the great problems that come with trying to allocate the net income of companies across state boundaries (Fisher, 1996; McLure, 1998). Other problems with a subnational government enterprise income tax are worrisome: The tax base (profits) is cyclically unstable, and provincial and local government revenues can be significantly affected by changes in central government tax or industrial policy. Moreover, the combination of a monopoly state banking system, regional banks, and derivation sharing of 100% of enterprise profit taxes invites a moral hazard problem.

The enterprise income tax is a mainstay of the Chinese finance system, and this is not likely to change, even with the next round of reform. But, in the long run, it cannot be the primary source of income for local governments. Local industrial policy and enterprise income taxation are too closely intertwined, the profitability outlook for SOEs is guarded, and the tax administration is not yet up to the task of extensive coverage beyond the state sector.

INDIVIDUAL INCOME TAX. The individual income tax is a much better choice for subnational government finances. It meets the "correspondence test" in that the burden is mostly borne in the provincial/local area. There also are administrative efficiencies. The provincial and local governments and their tax administrations are most familiar with the economic situation of the local enterprises that withhold the tax, and collection rates are likely to be enhanced by local administration. The Chinese system does assign administrative responsibility to the provincial governments, but it does not give them any power to determine the tax rate or tax base. At the time of the 1994 reform, all revenues from this tax were retained by the provincial governments. In theory, this would give a maximum incentive for local collection effort.

The central government appears to take a different view of the efficacy of the individual income tax as a local revenue source and has begun to

---

[5] This contrasts markedly with the concept of China's "market-preserving federalism," as discussed, for example, in Qian and Weingast (1996).

recapture revenues from this tax. The sharing of the individual income tax was amended to provide the central government with a higher tax share, with implementation beginning in January 2002. The main justification for this reform is to provide the central government with additional revenues so as to increase the pool or funds for the equalization transfer system. The plans are for the central government to allocate all incremental revenues resulting from this reform to local governments, mainly those in the central and western provinces, and middle-western regions, via the equalization grant system (Zhang and Martinez-Vazquez, 2002). The central government share will be 50% in 2002 and 60% in 2003. This is a small but important step toward undoing some of the fiscal advantage the government policy has given to the now "rich" provinces.

TAX ADMINISTRATION. Prior to the 1994 reform, there was a unified central tax administration system. This is not unusual for the former socialist economies. Taxes were assessed and collected locally and passed up to the center under the rules of an origin-based tax-sharing system. Most taxes were collected directly from enterprises and the system had the significant advantage that locally based officials had a good familiarity with the tax base. There also was an incentive for efficient collections in that the province was able to keep a share of all taxes collected. In theory, all local tax administrations would follow the same set of assessment and collection rules, and a uniform tax system would result.

However, the approximately 600,000 local tax administration officials were not closely supervised by the central government, and so a divided loyalty grew. These officials were close to the leadership of their local governments, and to local enterprises, but technically reported to the central government. To the extent they acted more in concert with the local government they were able to honor negotiated tax arrangements (tax contracts) between local governments and local enterprises and to enforce the central tax system with varying degrees of enthusiasm.

The result was that the tax system was not administered in the same way in all provinces, and tax administration became a significant part of tax policy. The 1994 reform addressed this problem, in part, by assigning income taxes to subnational governments, along with the responsibility for income tax administration (but not the authority to set the tax rate or tax base). The VAT and its administration became a strictly central government affair and locally based, and central government staff would be more closely supervised to address the divided-loyalty problem.

III. ECONOMIC REFORM AND FISCAL FEDERALISM

III.1. Recent Reforms and Growth

With the economic liberalization reforms starting in 1978, which provided for special economic zones in a few coastal provinces, China's government left behind any pretension of an egalitarian distribution of income (Yao and Zhu, 1998). This was a major political decision inspired by Deng Xiaoping's belief that some of China's regions would need to grow faster in the early years of reform to benefit the rest of the country at some future time. The essence of the reform was to progressively disengage from an economy driven by the state plan in favor of an allocation of resources driven by market forces.[6]

There has been considerable discussion about whether or not the gradualist strategy for reform adopted by China's government provided the country an advantage over the "shock therapies" adopted by Russia and several Eastern European countries.[7] Causation not withstanding, there is general agreement that China's rate of economic growth during its period of liberalization has been extraordinary. The data in Table 6.3 show the rate of growth in output per capita for the provinces, the regions, and for China as a whole for selected years since 1975. Although there are variations, with better and worse performers, these data show that economic growth has been widespread. Between 1980 and 1999, real income per capita in China increased more than fivefold. Provinces that benefited early from the inflow of foreign direct investment (FDI) grew the fastest. For example, from 1980 to 1999, output per capita in Jiangsu province increased nearly sixteenfold and in Guandong province almost thirteenfold.

Several fundamental institutional reforms were behind this rather spectacular rate of economic growth.[8] In the agricultural sector, the reforms known as the "production responsibility system" and later the "household contract responsibility system" led to significant income growth in the rural areas. After rural income growth slowed in the mid-1980s, China's government turned to the development of township and village enterprises (TVEs) to increase incomes in rural areas and to absorb

---

[6] According to Wong (1998), by the mid-1990s, the share of GDP produced in the state sector had fallen to less than 20% and SOEs accounted for less than 45% of gross industrial output.

[7] See, for example Naughton (1996), Bouin (1998), and Martinez-Vazquez and Wong (2003).

[8] See Yao and Zhu (1998).

Table 6.3. *Growth Rates of Gross Regional Product (GRP) per Capita in Selected Years*

Province or Region	1975	1980	1985	1990	1995	1999
Beijing	11.85	10.90	6.09	3.71	11.81	7.28
Tianjing	2.69	8.48	9.35	3.67	14.06	3.85
Hebei	9.38	1.94	11.25	1.02	13.03	8.41
Shanxi	6.14	0.78	5.41	3.34	9.95	−3.42
Inner Mongolia	9.22	1.16	19.72	3.22	7.98	6.99
Northern Region	**8.09**	**4.55**	**10.04**	**2.27**	**11.78**	**6.21**
Liaoning	7.37	11.28	12.86	1.03	6.39	6.13
Jilin	11.17	5.40	7.38	1.17	4.61	5.91
Heilongjiang	5.23	8.22	8.42	4.27	8.74	5.63
North eastern Region	**7.21**	**9.19**	**10.33**	**1.98**	**6.67**	**6.02**
Shanghai	3.82	7.04	12.29	4.57	13.87	−2.32
Jiangsu	4.80	4.08	17.67	1.48	14.66	9.65
Zhejiang	−4.87	15.06	21.50	3.74	15.94	9.32
Anhui	1.57	1.10	14.85	0.09	13.11	6.63
Fujian	0.55	17.90	16.42	6.37	13.71	6.75
Jiangxi	6.89	2.84	13.44	2.28	16.92	6.79
Shandong	27.44	11.89	11.40	7.58	13.70	9.59
Eastern Region	**6.51**	**7.87**	**15.01**	**3.53**	**14.33**	**8.29**
Henan	4.54	13.88	11.91	3.94	13.88	7.22
Hubei	9.95	5.22	14.82	3.17	13.55	7.70
Hunan	8.33	4.08	10.83	8.39	9.35	4.62
Guangdong	9.09	14.64	19.05	8.00	13.33	7.14
Guangxi	4.46	8.10	9.06	4.68	10.18	6.84
Central South Region	**7.53**	**9.61**	**14.03**	**6.15**	**12.77**	**7.17**
Sichuan + Chongqing	12.72	7.98	14.44	4.09	7.67	4.91
Guizhou	7.68	2.71	6.45	3.28	5.97	6.83
Yunnan	2.78	7.22	11.51	5.35	9.78	5.99
Southwestern Region	**9.63**	**7.07**	**12.63**	**4.22**	**7.94**	**5.33**
Shannxi	3.57	6.36	15.13	2.21	8.01	7.69
Gansu	14.76	7.74	11.69	6.20	7.21	7.34
Qinghai	5.27	25.20	2.99	7.48	6.43	6.67
Ningxia	2.08	6.39	14.89	1.23	7.19	7.41
Xinjiang	13.11	5.15	13.38	15.54	7.12	5.44
Northwestern Region	**8.49**	**7.67**	**12.97**	**6.22**	**7.47**	**7.03**
China	**7.40**	**7.83**	**13.07**	**4.03**	**11.79**	**7.28**
Mean	**7.28**	**7.92**	**12.30**	**4.32**	**10.56**	**6.15**
Maximum	**27.44**	**25.20**	**21.50**	**15.54**	**16.92**	**9.65**
Minimum	**−4.87**	**0.78**	**2.99**	**0.09**	**4.61**	**−3.42**
Coefficient of Variation	**0.79**	**0.70**	**0.36**	**0.71**	**0.33**	**0.46**

Source: www.ccer.org.cn.

unemployed or excess farmers. In the urban areas, the major institutional changes that led to economic growth included the reform in the governance of SOEs, allowing profit sharing and retention of profits, and also the introduction of different forms of ownership. Under this system, both private ownership and FDI were allowed in China, and the latter became a powerful engine of economic growth.

The general economic reforms were accompanied by several fiscal reforms. After some experimentation during 1978–1983, the Chinese government introduced the first comprehensive reform of the fiscal system in 1984, which became known as the "Fiscal Responsibility System" (FRS). This was a contracting system involving fixed periods of time, in which generally local governments were allowed to retain part of the tax revenues collected after the remittance of a fixed sum to the central government. The system appeared to be incentive compatible because local governments could keep more revenues if they collected more tax. However, the FRS led over time to several important problems for the central government. Local governments found ways to contribute fewer fiscal resources to the central government by, for example, giving local enterprises tax exemptions at the expense of central government revenues or hiding resources from the central government in extrabudgetary funds. These problems led to the decrease of the central government share in total budgetary revenues and also to a lower share of total budgetary revenue in GDP. Realizing the shortcomings of the contracting system, the central government adopted the "Tax Sharing System" (TSS) in 1994. The 1994 reform was prompted by the central government's loss of control over the fiscal system. It was unable to generate adequate revenues for its programs, it could not enforce uniformity in the application of its tax laws, and its fiscal initiatives were being thwarted by negotiation and off-budget practices of the subnational governments. There were five commonly cited concerns that were to be addressed by the reform:

1. The revenue share of GNP was declining, in the face of significant budgetary needs. The tax/GNP share fell from 23% in 1985 to 11% in 1994.
2. The central government claim on total national revenues was falling relative to that of subnational governments. Central government budgetary expenditures were 65% of those of subnational governments in 1985, but only 43% by 1994.
3. The central government was losing its ability to steer subnational government fiscal policy, and the subnational governments were becoming increasingly aggressive about making their own policies.

These policies were usually informal, but they were effective. For example, local governments influenced the local tax administration cadre in the way in which they collected and assessed taxes, they negotiated tax contracts with local enterprises, and they used extrabudgetary taxes and expenditures.

4. The tax system, supposedly based on national law, was becoming less uniform as subnational governments made use of these discretionary powers. The amount of taxes paid by an enterprise might be more a function of the deals it made with the local government than of the national tax law. The system was becoming less transparent and more of a "backdoor" approach to fiscal federalism.

5. The tax structure was in need of adoption of modern practices to move it toward less complexity, to provide proper incentives for enterprise management decisions, and to continue to move its focus away from a regulatory function.

The 1994 TSS was quite comprehensive in that it covered tax policy, tax administration, and intergovernmental fiscal relations. However, it did not address any significant issue related to expenditure assignment. The reform program was more or less true to the goals of addressing the problem issues that have been raised here.

The *tax policy* reforms were more addressed at modernization of the tax structure. The following were its major elements: (i) The number of taxes in the system was reduced from thirty-two to eighteen, thereby reducing the complexity of the system. (ii) The top marginal income tax rate for enterprises was reduced from 55% to 33% and surtaxes were eliminated; the tax rate schedule was unified to subject all enterprises (regardless of ownership) to the same regime; the deduction of loan principal repayment was disallowed; and an accelerated depreciation schedule was adopted. (iii) The practice of allowing local governments to negotiate tax contracts with individual enterprises was disallowed. (iv) The indirect tax system (with three main taxes and 250 rates) was simplified. The VAT was expanded, a credit invoice system of determining VAT liability was adopted, and specific excises on certain consumption goods were adopted.

The *tax administration* before 1994 was characterized as having "divided loyalties." Technically, tax officials were employees of the central government, but there was relatively little central supervision. Ties to local governments and to local enterprises were much closer. It was alleged that local tax administrations influenced the pattern of tax collections so much that they were making tax policy. The 1994 reform created separate tax administrations at the central and local levels. It established a local tax bureau, under the direct supervision of the local governments, with responsibility for, among others, the administration of income taxes. The central government tax administration would be responsible for the VAT and for all taxes on centrally owned enterprises.

The 1994 reform of the *intergovernmental fiscal system* was meant to reduce the degree to which the subnational governments had discretion to negotiate outcomes, and it was meant to claw back a greater revenue share for the central government. If successful, it would increase the transparency of the system. The main elements of the reform were as follows: (i) Income tax revenues were fully assigned to the subnational governments. This would reduce the incentive to avoid tax sharing through negotiated deals with the enterprises. (ii) The VAT remained a central government tax but with an agreement that 25% of revenues would be shared on a formula basis. This would make revenue sharing more "top down" than "bottom up." (iii) Local governments lost much of their backdoor autonomy (extrabudgetary revenues, tax administration influence, and enterprise contracting) in favor of a more transparent and defined program.

The two main goals of the 1994 reform – increasing the share of government revenues in GDP and the share of central government revenue in the total budgetary revenues – were reached after several years.

The potential for future economic growth in China has been constrained by the inefficient allocation of resources in the economy owing to low labor and capital mobility.[9] The low mobility of economic inputs is to a large extent determined by government economic policies introduced under planned socialism: In the case of labor, strict migration control was imposed under the household registration system (or *Hukou*), and in the case of capital the key role is still played by the state banking system and the allocation of funds on nonmarket criteria. A quite different form of constraint on economic growth, it has been argued, may be the lack of democratic institutions in the country. Further economic growth and macroeconomic stability in the future will require first, addressing the migration problem, and second, addressing the modernization of the financial system and most critically the reform of the banking system. Rising unemployment and the long-term viability of pension funds are other issues in the current population dynamics that should be of concern to

---

[9] This means that China's growth performance could have been even better than it has been and that in the future, greater labor and capital mobility should contribute to sustained economic growth.

government authorities. Although we discuss migration issues, the issues of unemployment and pension funds will not be discussed here.[10]

Economic globalization has been one of the strongest engines of economic growth in China with the country absorbing a big proportion of worldwide FDI funds. However, the impact of FDI on employment, income, and growth has been uneven across the country in part because of explicit central government policies (e.g., restricting FDI to only some areas) and in part because of basic economic geography and comparative advantages of the coastal regions. Thus one possible disadvantage of the FDI boom in China has been the exacerbation of economic disparities among different regions of the country and possibly between the urban and rural dwellers within each region. The recent entry of China into the World Trade Organization (WTO) may reinforce these past patterns via lower protection of domestic agricultural products and other sources of income in the interior provinces.

We turn now to current problems in the labor and capital markets. In particular, we review options to address the migration problem, especially in the context of the twin threats of rising unemployment and the viability of pension funds. Next, we review some of the implications of the weakness of the banking system and the alternative reforms that have been proposed. We then examine what evidence there is that the lack of democratic institutions has hindered or may be hindering economic growth in the country. Last, we study the phenomenal growth of FDI, its determinants and sources, and its impact on economic disparities.

III.2. Population and Migration Trends: The Floating Labor Phenomenon

The fiscal profile of subnational governments can be significantly affected by population and migration patterns. Population growth increases the

---

[10] Unemployment problems do not directly relate to fiscal federalism. However, in China the long-term viability of pension funds is at the heart of fiscal decentralization reform. This is because, as discussed in the following, the pension system in China is mostly a local government expenditure responsibility. This atypical assignment of responsibilities dates back to the self-reliance policies favored by Chairman Mao. Throughout the country different pension systems have been reporting liabilities growing much faster than contributions. Because these are "pay-as-you-go" systems, the existing population dynamics augur more serious problems in the future. According to *The Economist* (2002), the ratio of workers to pensioners was expected to fall from 10 to 1 in 1995 to 2 to 1 in 2050. In fact the central government budget has been making contributions to many local pension systems over the past decade to keep them afloat. This issue is further discussed later with possible reforms to expenditure assignments.

demand for basic services and strains the current infrastructure. Similar effects can result from sudden bursts of immigration. Rapid increases in population can overwhelm any system of local public services. Even those local jurisdictions losing population may be subject to fiscal distress if the migration implies a loss in revenue bases without much change in expenditure needs, as is the case when the active population migrates, leaving behind retirees and school-aged children. Of course, migration from poorer to richer areas is an important instrument for reducing economic disparities among regions through employment and wage rate convergence and through the remittances of migrants to their home region.

Traditionally, Chinese people have been restricted in their freedom to move inside their country. The *Hukou* system of household registration in effect largely confined people to the place of their births.[11] Currently, the household registration system still makes it illegal for rural households to migrate to urban areas and for residents in poor provinces to migrate to richer provinces without special permits.[12] The household registration system is defended these days as a way to prevent urban chaos.

It is likely that the rural reforms of the late 1970s and early 1980s weakened the ability of government to control migration and labor mobility. However, during the 1980s and 1990s the official rate of migration remained quite low. For example, the officially recorded number of people who moved from one county to another between 1985 and 1990 amounted to 0.24% of the rural population in 1990 aged five or older. This is not surprising since after the successful rural reforms in the early 1980s, the government encouraged only local migration. The *Hukou* system was never removed. But despite its illegality, there appears to be migration in China. The numbers are not official but China's so-called floating population has been estimated to be as large as 100 million

---

[11] Under the household registration system, or *Hukou*, readopted by the People's Republic of China from long-standing Chinese traditions, households were designated as rural or urban. The designation, which went beyond mobility issues, was openly unfair toward rural households. In effect, *Hukou* meant that only designated urban households were allowed to reside in cities and towns employed by state enterprises and with access to subsidized foods and other benefits. See Dayal-Gulati and Husain (2002). In 1958 the "Regulation on the Registration of Households" required that all households register in their place of residence and that they should gain official permission for any changes in residence.

[12] Being illegal within China means being excluded from regular public benefits, including children's education and health services, pension benefits, or the ability to own a house.

workers.[13] As in the case of "illegal" fees in China, there is some recognition and even support for migration at the provincial level.[14]

The low level of rural to urban migration over the past two decades has meant that the mean value of the provincial urbanization ratio increased only from 23% in 1979 to 29% in 1999. However, provinces with considerable amounts of FDI and rapid economic growth, such as Jiangsu and Guandong, experienced faster increases in their urban population ratio. Therefore, at least in some provinces there must have been sizable rural to urban migration. However, rural to urban migration was relatively small for the country as a whole. The level of interprovincial migration is even more difficult to gauge indirectly from population figures.[15] From what is known and despite the fast economic growth in China during these two decades, the level of migration appears to have been low.[16] The government policy of controlling population movements has been effective, at least until recently. The low migration has had important economic consequences. An important consequence from the viewpoint of fiscal federalism is that the reduction in economic differences or the convergence of incomes across and within provinces has been slower than it otherwise would have been (Kanbur and Zhang, 1999; and Demurger et al., 2002). But migration is an area in a state of rapid flux in China. The latest accounts are that the grip of the *Hukou* system is loosening and there is a larger than previously thought and rapidly growing "floating" population that is not constrained by the *Hukou*. A recent article in the New York Times,[17] states the official count of migrant workers at 114 million (not including family members), and quotes government experts predicting the number will rise to 300 million by 2020, and eventually to 500 million. Migration is a theme to which we return.

---

[13] Officially reported figures are smaller. China's State Statistical Bureau (1998) conducted a 1% survey of the population in 1995 and estimated that there were 53.5 million floating migrants that year, of which 17.8 million were interprovincial migrants.

[14] Some provinces are managing and coordinating labor flows among themselves. Montinola et al. (1995) describe the Guandong efforts to coordinate its immigration with the provinces where the migrant workers originate, mostly in the nearby provinces of Hunan, Guangxi, and Sichuan.

[15] For example, migration movements do not seem to get captured in official statistics since the provinces' relative shares in the total population for China have not changed much over the years.

[16] The combination of low migration and fast economic growth is not unique to China. For example, in India, GDP grew at an average rate of 6% during 1980–2000, but rural–urban migration (except for large metropolitan areas) has been modest.

[17] Jim Yardley, "In a Tidal Wave China's Masses Pour from Farm to City," New York Times [Late Edition (east coast)], September 12, 2004, p. 6.

III.3. Lack of Capital Mobility

The significant lack of capital mobility has had a direct impact on the differential economic development of the provinces and thus on fiscal federalism. Testing for capital mobility is no straightforward matter, but generally, the greater the capital mobility, the lower the correlation we should expect between savings and investments in particular jurisdictions.[18] Despite the fact that savings and investment data are notoriously noisy, Zhao (1998) tested this proposition for China and found a high correlation between saving and investment rates at the province level. His results strongly suggest a low level of capital mobility across provinces.

Dayal-Gulati and Husain (2002) argue that, to some extent, the lack of mobility has been engineered by central government tax policies. The profit retention system that was in place in the early 1980s discouraged capital mobility because retained profits were part of local government revenues, and thus, local governments discouraged enterprise transfers to other locations. The changes in tax policy in the late 1980s and 1990s that featured the contract responsibility system (fixed profit remittances by enterprises), coupled with the revenue-sharing arrangements of that period, led to increased interregional capital mobility. The trend was for subnational governments to offer fiscal incentives (often tax incentives and holidays) to attract investment. Capital mobility was driven by tax differentials rather than by differences in resource endowments and cost advantages. Current features of the tax system and revenue assignments among different levels of government also encourage protectionism by provincial and local governments, another factor that decreases capital mobility.[19]

The state control over bank loans, achieved through the monopoly state bank system, has played an even more decisive role in discouraging capital mobility. The state banks have continued to favor large SOEs in their lending programs. Historically, fewer SOEs have located in the western and central provinces than in the eastern and coastal provinces of China (Demurger et al., 2002; Dayal-Gulati and Husain, 2002).

Capital formation (gross investment in fixed assets) has varied significantly across provinces. For example, capital formation reached in 2002 more than Renminbi (RMB) 323 billion yuan in Guandong province and only RMB 6.6 billion yuan in Tibet. Because of the importance of FDI,

---

[18] See Feldstein and Horioka's (1980) analysis of international capital mobility.
[19] The issues of local protectionism and tax policy are discussed further later in the chapter.

the coastal provinces became very quickly the largest absorbers of capital. In 2000, four coastal provinces alone (Jiangsu, Zhejiang, Shandong, and Guandong) accounted for one-third of capital formation in China (Table 6.4). Several of these provinces were the ones experiencing the fastest increase in capital formation over the past twenty years. The relative importance of Jiangsu and Guandong provinces in annual capital formation almost doubled from 1979 to 2000. In contrast, the relative contribution to capital formation of the Manchurian rust-belt provinces of Liaoning, Jilin, and Heilongjiang was cut in half from 1979 and 2000.

III.4. The Fragility of the Financial System[20]

The financial system in China has been traditionally dominated by the banking sector and, in turn, the banking system has been dominated by the state-owned banks (SBs). There is wide consensus of opinion that China's banking system faces difficult challenges. Estimates of nonperforming loans reach as high as 50% of all assets, with thin capitalization and close to negligible levels of loan loss provisions. Some estimates put the cost to the government of recapitalizing the banking system at around half of current GDP.[21]

CAUSES. The main cause for the problems in the banking sector in China is the quasifiscal role that banks were forced to play (by the central authorities) for so many years (Hofman, 1998).[22] The People's Bank of China and the state banking system were asked to perform "policy lending," for capital investments and social expenditures of SOEs.[23] Another

---

[20] For a review of the issues and a historical perspective see Baizhu et al. (2000).

[21] See OECD (2002) and *The Economist* (2002). However, China has been able to navigate the 1977–1979 global financial crisis much better than its Asian neighbors. The main reason is that the Chinese yuan is not convertible on the capital account and that FDI represents most of the capital inflow in China. Consequently, China has had little exposure to private debt denominated in foreign currency (Naughton, 2000).

[22] As is shown in the following, government revenues fell continuously as percentage of GNP from the beginning of the market-oriented reforms in 1978. Despite this rapid drop in revenues, budget deficits did not rise to unsustainable levels. Part of the explanation is that budget expenditures also declined significantly and that a considerable share of the slack in funding needs was taken up by extrabudgetary expenditures and off-budget accounts (also discussed later). However, as Hofman (1998) argues convincingly, another part of the answer is that budget and extrabudget funds were supplemented during much of the period by quasifiscal activities of the central bank and the banking system.

[23] After gaining independence from the Ministry of Finance in 1978, the central bank or People's Bank of China saw a transfer of its commercial lending activities to the Industrial and Commercial Bank of China (ICBC). This new state-owned bank (SB) was designated

Table 6.4. Percentages of Capital Formation by Province (Shares in National Total)

Province	1980	1985	1990	1994	1995	1996	1997	1998	1999	2000	2001
Coastal											
Beijing	4.64	3.86	4.34	4.10	4.37	3.92	3.90	3.95	3.90	3.92	4.12
Tianjin	3.34	2.70	2.13	2.00	2.04	1.95	2.02	2.04	1.89	1.84	1.90
Hebei	5.19	4.54	4.29	4.48	4.88	5.31	5.97	5.85	5.99	5.58	5.23
Liaoning	7.49	5.83	6.37	5.61	4.59	3.91	3.87	3.73	3.67	3.83	3.82
Shanghai	6.35	4.86	5.50	7.09	8.31	8.72	8.03	6.96	6.18	5.65	5.37
Jiangsu	4.85	7.87	8.63	8.41	8.72	8.71	8.94	8.99	9.13	9.05	8.89
Zhejiang	4.65	4.19	4.53	6.36	7.05	7.23	6.88	6.55	6.28	6.85	7.47
Fujian	2.56	2.28	2.80	3.40	3.54	3.53	3.65	3.72	3.61	3.36	3.05
Shandong	9.78	7.97	8.13	7.00	6.86	6.96	7.28	7.29	7.40	7.68	7.56
Guangdong	5.35	7.57	9.24	13.52	12.08	10.40	9.33	9.46	10.08	9.76	9.52
Guangxi	1.75	1.73	1.66	2.42	2.20	2.13	1.95	2.03	2.06	1.99	1.97
Hainan	0.48	0.63	0.86	1.39	1.03	0.83	0.68	0.65	0.63	0.58	0.56
Subtotal	**56.43**	**54.05**	**58.50**	**65.77**	**65.66**	**63.59**	**62.51**	**61.21**	**60.82**	**60.08**	**59.45**
Inland											
Shanxi	3.94	3.76	2.99	1.84	1.53	1.49	1.62	1.89	1.92	1.89	1.91
Inner Mongolia	n.a.	2.15	1.72	1.59	1.42	1.23	1.29	1.24	1.28	1.30	1.34
Jilin	2.92	2.55	2.27	1.91	1.77	1.76	1.48	1.49	1.66	1.77	1.83
Heilongjiang	5.38	4.59	3.95	2.56	2.53	2.54	2.72	2.84	2.62	2.59	2.64

Anhui	2.42	3.31	2.98	2.52	2.76	2.74	2.79	2.58	2.58	2.62	2.59
Jiangxi	2.63	1.81	1.71	1.50	1.47	1.59	1.56	1.61	1.64	1.66	1.78
Henan	n.a.	5.21	4.99	3.97	4.18	4.48	4.73	4.44	4.41	4.46	4.38
Hubei	4.96	4.22	3.50	3.75	4.29	4.40	4.40	4.36	4.34	4.29	4.18
Hunan	4.50	3.43	3.01	2.66	2.72	3.03	2.84	3.01	3.14	3.22	3.26
Chongqing[i]	–	–	–	–	–	1.43	1.51	1.77	1.87	1.98	2.16
Sichuan	4.47	4.50	3.94	3.62	3.52	3.59	3.85	4.20	4.06	4.24	4.24
Guizhou	1.95	1.36	1.25	0.89	0.90	0.93	1.00	1.08	1.11	1.22	1.44
Yunnan	2.92	1.90	1.84	2.03	1.98	2.00	2.19	2.38	2.39	2.11	1.98
Tibet	0.25	0.31	0.18	0.13	0.19	0.14	0.14	0.15	0.19	0.20	0.23
Shannxi	3.88	2.38	2.51	1.79	1.68	1.66	1.72	1.93	2.06	2.25	2.29
Gansu	1.77	1.39	1.44	1.00	1.01	0.96	1.07	1.17	1.28	1.33	1.36
Qinghai	1.03	0.70	0.54	0.29	0.29	0.35	0.40	0.41	0.43	0.47	0.54
Ningxia	0.56	0.56	0.53	0.39	0.36	0.35	0.36	0.39	0.43	0.49	0.53
Xinjiang	n.a.	1.82	2.15	1.80	1.73	1.73	1.81	1.84	1.78	1.84	1.90
Subtotal	**43.57**	**45.95**	**41.50**	**34.23**	**34.34**	**36.41**	**37.49**	**38.79**	**39.18**	**39.92**	**40.55**

[i] Data are not available prior to 1996.

Source: www.ccer.org.cn.

275

cause for the poor performance of SBs is that, because they have operated with a soft budget constraint, they have shown a marked tendency to undertake risky and even speculative investments, possibly contributing to stock market and real estate speculation (Woo, 1998).

CONSEQUENCES. The continued practice of administrative lending (as opposed to market lending) by the monopoly state banking system has meant that most of the funds are claimed by the larger state enterprises (SOEs). One view on the implications of these policies is that since fewer of those are located in the western provinces, these lending practices have exacerbated regional economic disparities (Demurger et al. 2002). What might make things even more unfair for the interior and western provinces is that if the banking system were rescued by the central government all of China, including the poorer western provinces that never benefited much from SOBs' loans, would somehow bear the costs. A different view on the implications of these policies is that administered lending has been used by the government to offset the perceived imbalances in market-based lending and cannot be assumed to be concentrated in the richer provinces. Significantly, globalization, in particular competition from imports, has likely contributed to the losses of SOEs and hence to the bad shape of SOBs.

III.5. Foreign Direct Investment and Regional Economic Growth

FAST GROWTH OF FDI. The single most important factor behind the different rates of economic development in China's provinces has been the phenomenal flow of FDI over the past two decades and its concentration in a few provinces. The US$0.88 billion of FDI that China was receiving in 1985 grew to US$41.1 billion in 2000.[24] Besides the obvious huge economic

---

as the bank for residents and firms in urban areas. Other SBs include the Bank of China, designated the international exchange and remittance bank, the People's Construction Bank, designated to handle large infrastructure projects, and the Agricultural Bank of China (ABC), designated to provide financial services to the rural sector. In 1981 two new SOBs were created: China's Investment Bank and the Bank of Communications. Interest rates have remained centrally controlled and at the same time SBs have been asked under government orders to lend to "strategic" industries and unprofitable SOEs in what have become known as "policy loans" (Woo, 1998). In 1995, the government transferred all "policy loan" obligations to three SBs: the State Development Bank of China, the ABC, and the Export–Import Bank of China.

[24] Total FDI in China exceeds the amounts reported in Table 6.5. There we only report the FDI that is allocable to one of China's provinces. FDI in China takes four different

potential, there are several other reasons for the fast growth of FDI in China. One reason is that China has had and continues to have significant restrictions on its equity market. This has left little room for foreign investors other than direct investment in assets (Feng and Zhang, 2000).[25] A second reason has been the very unique process of "roundtripping" of Chinese capital, whereby Chinese firms divert their profits offshore only to have the same profits brought back to China as "foreign direct investment," which than qualifies for whatever tax preferences are offered by central and local authorities.[26] According to Wong (1998), round tripping accounted for as much as 25% of FDI in China in the mid-1990s.[27]

GEOGRAPHIC CONCENTRATION OF FDI. From the start, with the opening economic policies of 1978, FDI has clustered in the coastal provinces of the country. In 2000, about 87% of the FDI flow in China was going to the twelve coastal provinces and less than 13% to the other eighteen inland provinces (Table 6.5).[28] This distribution pattern has become only slightly more favorable to the inland provinces over the past decade. What are the causes of this concentration? Initially, it was government policy. At the start of the Open Door Policy, the government in reality only opened some coastal areas in the provinces of Guandong and Fujian, designated as "special economic zones." In the mid-1980s the special treatment for Guandong and Fujian was extended to many other coastal areas. By the early 1990s the same privileges were extended throughout China, including most central and western provinces. The literally thousands of special economic zones, each offering customized preferential tax treatment, became a drain to tax collections. With the fiscal reforms of 1994, many special economic zones were closed down and subnational governments' ability to provide tax privileges was withdrawn.

In reality, the high concentration of FDI continues to survive. Notice that six provinces (Guandong, Fujian, Jiangsu, and the cities of Shanghai, Tianjin, and Beijing) received over two-thirds of FDI in 1998, the most

forms: equity joint ventures, contractual joint ventures, wholly owned foreign firms, and joint exploration (for offshore oil). See, for example, Kaiser et al. (1996) for a dissection of FDI flows.

[25] The financial crises that affected a number of countries in Southeast Asia in the late 1990s appears to have strengthened the resolution of the Chinese government to continue to closely regulate capital markets and control short-term capital flows.

[26] This contrasts sharply with the experience of other countries in transition from socialism. For example, in Russia, it has been estimated that more than US$50 billion are diverted abroad every year, but hardly ever has this capital come back.

[27] See also Broadman (1995).

[28] In 2000, the twelve coastal provinces represented 61% of GDP.

Table 6.5. *Shares of FDI for Coastal and Inland Provinces*

Province	1985	1990	1991	1992	1993	1994	1995	1996	1997	1998	1999	2000	2001	2002
Coastal Provinces														
Beijing	n.a.[i]	8.57	5.65	2.97	2.52	4.23	3.76	3.64	3.44	4.51	5.53	5.98	3.54	3.29
Tianjin	4.99	2.57	2.17	1.97	2.05	2.98	4.08	4.71	5.43	5.50	6.27	6.23	6.45	3.01
Hebei	0.44	1.22	1.76	1.52	1.35	1.53	2.09	2.90	3.24	3.58	3.58	2.49	1.52	1.49
Liaoning	1.78	7.69	7.24	3.73	4.64	4.17	3.77	3.92	4.79	4.81	5.11	6.21	6.24	6.50
Shanghai	7.07	5.48	4.05	10.69	8.76	9.47	8.72	11.07	10.40	7.94	7.55	7.69	8.80	8.14
Jiangsu	1.35	4.37	5.38	11.92	11.35	12.24	12.82	11.90	12.53	14.52	15.86	15.63	14.27	19.42
Zhejiang	1.85	1.50	2.11	2.50	3.90	3.35	3.37	3.57	3.25	2.88	3.80	3.92	4.43	5.86
Fujian	13.34	8.98	14.88	12.03	10.84	10.88	10.83	9.57	9.08	8.76	0.00	0.00	7.85	7.32
Shandong	0.63	4.67	4.14	8.27	6.97	7.43	6.99	6.08	5.41	4.85	6.12	7.23	7.25	9.02
Guangdong	58.33	45.19	42.08	30.17	28.34	27.54	27.31	27.27	25.33	26.24	30.24	29.77	25.99	21.60
Guangxi	1.42	0.94	0.89	1.53	3.30	2.39	1.80	1.56	1.90	1.93	1.58	1.28	0.77	0.80
Hainan	2.37	3.11	4.06	3.84	3.96	2.56	2.83	1.85	1.54	1.57	1.20	1.05	0.94	0.98
Subtotal	**93.57**	**94.28**	**94.42**	**91.14**	**87.96**	**88.79**	**88.38**	**88.05**	**86.33**	**87.09**	**86.83**	**87.48**	**88.04**	**87.43**
Inland Provinces														
Shanxi	0.05	0.11	0.10	0.46	0.27	0.09	0.17	0.32	0.58	0.53	0.97	0.55	0.47	0.40
Inner Mongolia	n.a.	n.a.	n.a.	n.a.	n.a.	n.a.	n.a.	0.13	0.18	0.12	0.23	0.27	0.37	0.34
Jilin	0.29	0.52	0.42	0.56	0.90	0.93	1.07	1.06	0.87	0.89	0.75	0.82	0.68	0.47
Heilongjiang	0.26	0.78	0.44	0.87	0.86	1.00	1.20	1.29	1.59	1.15	2.03	2.02	1.73	0.68

Anhui	0.18	0.30	0.22	0.42	0.97	1.08	1.29	1.19	0.94	0.70	0.90	0.77	0.67	0.73
Jiangxi	0.59	0.19	0.45	0.82	0.79	0.77	0.77	0.71	1.03	1.02	0.79	0.55	0.79	2.06
Henan	0.64	0.32	0.88	0.91	1.29	1.25	1.29	1.23	1.40	1.35	1.23	1.31	0.72	0.77
Hubei	0.00	0.90	1.07	1.73	2.02	1.76	1.67	1.62	1.71	2.01	2.27	2.30	2.42	2.72
Hunan	1.99	0.35	0.53	1.09	1.64	0.95	1.31	1.65	1.98	1.79	1.62	1.66	1.62	1.72
Chongqing	n.a.	n.a.	n.a.	n.a.	n.a.	n.a.	n.a.	0.51	0.83	1.01	0.59	0.59	0.51	0.37
Sichuan	n.a.	0.32	0.38	0.71	1.41	1.51	0.76	0.53	0.54	1.10	1.12	1.06	1.17	1.06
Guizhou	0.17	0.14	0.17	0.17	0.16	0.19	0.15	0.07	0.11	0.10	0.10	0.06	0.06	0.07
Yunnan	0.18	0.08	0.07	0.20	0.37	0.60	0.60	0.42	0.36	0.32	0.38	0.31	0.13	0.21
Shannxi	1.56	1.30	0.73	0.39	0.89	0.70	0.87	0.77	1.36	0.66	n.a.	n.a.	0.00	0.69
Gansu	0.33	0.15	0.02	0.40	0.21	0.08	0.17	0.21	0.09	0.08	0.10	0.15	0.15	0.12
Qinghai	n.a.	n.a.	n.a.	0.01	0.03	0.01	0.02	0.01	0.03	0.02	n.a.	n.a.	0.40	0.09
Ningxia	0.03	0.03	0.02	0.03	0.04	0.14	0.09	0.07	0.03	0.01	0.02	0.03	0.03	0.04
Xinjiang	0.18	0.22	0.09	0.09	0.20	0.14	0.18	0.16	0.05	0.05	0.06	0.05	0.04	0.04
Subtotal	**6.43**	**5.72**	**5.58**	**8.86**	**12.04**	**11.21**	**11.62**	**11.95**	**13.67**	**12.91**	**13.17**	**12.52**	**11.96**	**12.57**

[i] n.a., not available.

Source: http://chinadataonline.org.

recent year with complete data. One province alone, Guandong, received over one-fourth of all FDI in 1998, though this is down from a 58% share in 1985 (Table 6.5).

SOURCES AND CAUSES OF FDI. One peculiarity of the FDI process in China is that it has come disproportionately from overseas Chinese, particularly those residing in Hong Kong. The second source of FDI has been Taiwan, followed at a distance by Japan and other industrialized nations.[29] Part of the advantage for Hong Kong is related to the "round-tripping" phenomenon previously discussed. However, also proximity and ethnic and cultural factors explain the concentration of FDI from Hong Kong in Guangdong and FDI from Taiwan in Fujian. Japanese investment has tended to concentrate in Manchurian provinces. Investment from other countries has been spread over large cities in search of domestic markets. The coastal provinces also have geographical advantages. For example, Guandong province benefited from its proximity to Hong Kong. Zhang (1994) argues that the success of Guangdong province in attracting FDI from Hong Kong is to a large extent due to administrative decentralization and local initiative.[30]

DETERMINANTS OF THE GEOGRAPHIC DISTRIBUTION OF FDI. A number of studies have researched the determinants of the geographical distribution of FDI. What they have found is that several factors tend to attract FDI: the availability of infrastructure including transport and communications, openness of the provincial economy, size of market, coastal location, and unemployment rate. Other factors seem to discourage FDI, notably higher wage levels and higher illiteracy rates.[31] However, the nature of FDI in China likely changed from the 1980s to the 1990s (Naughton, 1996). During the 1980s (and early 1990s) Hong Kong investments in Guandong province and Taiwan investments in Fujian province represented almost half of all FDI and all output was expected to be exported. Starting in 1992, China began to offer foreign investors access to domestic markets. Therefore, the determinants of FDI in the two periods may differ substantially. In fact, Sun, Tong, and Yu (2002) find that the importance of the determinants of FDI do change in the two periods. An interesting finding

---

[29] Whereas FDI from Hong Kong and Taiwan has been largely concentrated in labor-intensive manufacturing, U.S. and European FDI has concentrated on capital- and technology-intensive industries (Sun and Tipton, 1998).

[30] For example, local governments in Guangdong province were allowed to authorize limited amounts of FDI.

[31] See, for example, Wei et al. (1999), Feng and Zhang (2000), and Dayal-Gulati and Husain (2002).

by Sun et al. (2002) is that the cumulative FDI relative to the cumulative domestic investment has a negative impact on FDI flows. They basically do not explain this result, but one may wonder whether some form of protectionism is at work.

IMPACT OF FDI ON FISCAL FEDERALISM. From the perspective of this chapter on fiscal federalism, the most important aspect of the FDI phenomenon in China is the impact it has had on the differential rates of economic growth and therefore regional disparities in fiscal capacity.[32] The impact of FDI on regional growth in China has been quite thoroughly studied, but always the problem is separating the independent effect of FDI from all other factors that affect growth.[33] It is fair to state that there is a lack of consensus in the literature. Some studies (Lee, 1995; Jin, Qian, and Weingast, 1999; Wei and Wu, 2001) conclude that, as a result of the market-oriented reforms started in 1978, the regional distribution of income was not very much affected or actually was improved. In contrast, Dayal-Gulati and Husain (2002) find that the convergence of per capita income across all provinces to the same steady-state level does not hold over the past two decades. However, they find conditional convergence, that is, convergence of provincial per capita incomes to their steady states, and that provincial disparities appear to be primarily influenced by the relative importance of FDI in the provinces. Similar conditional convergence is found by Chen and Fleischer (1996), Jian, Sachs, and Warner (1996), Kanbur and Zhang (1999), Shi (2001), and Demurger et al. (2002). Sun and Chai (1998) also find similar results at the national level and, in addition, they find (from a study of the Guandong province) that FDI also played a critical role in exacerbating intraprovincial economic inequality.[34]

---

[32] Of course, the impact of FDI on economic growth goes beyond investment itself since it is accompanied by the transfer of technology, managerial skills, and other forms of human capital that help the recipient provinces grow faster. The focus on provincial GDP growth and FDI may not be entirely justified given that provinces in China are quite large and that FDI tends to be concentrated even within provinces. The lack of more disaggregated regional data prevents more targeted analysis.

[33] For other studies that examine the impact of FDI see OECD (2002). There is disagreement in the literature on whether fiscal federalism itself has contributed to economic growth in China. See, for example, Zhang and Zou (1998) and Qiao et al. (2002).

[34] A much larger literature is reviewed in Naughton (2000), who notes the sometimes contradictory and even paradoxical results, but the weight of the evidence is that since 1990 there has been a trend toward increased divergence. Some of the differences in results seem to be explainable by whether the price deflators used are province specific. In the latter case, much of the convergence results disappear.

But the differences in provincial growth in China should be seen in the broader context of interregional redistribution going back to the planned economy. Provinces have had access to different levels of resources through industrial investment policies and official pricing policies that have favored urban, as opposed to rural, areas and eastern or coastal provinces, as opposed to inland provinces (Yao and Zhu, 1998; and Naughton, 2000). Coastal provinces also have had the natural advantage of location. Demurger et al. (2002) decomposed provincial growth into geography effects and policy effects for 1996–1999. They find both geography and policy effects to be powerful, with policy effects more so. They recommend reducing disparities to extend the "preferential" deregulation policies to the interior provinces.[35]

In summary, the phenomenal flow of FDI over the past two decades into China, in combination with its concentration in a few particular areas of the country, has led to considerable growth in the country but its geographical distribution has been and remains uneven. This has important implications for the design of a workable fiscal federalism.

III.6. Further Globalization of China's Economy

World Trade Organization membership in 2002 created high expectations for deeper economic reforms in China. The most significant impact on the economy will be in those sectors that China's government had protected from foreign investment, including agriculture, financial services, and telecommunications. In the case of agriculture, for example, the losses in employment, it is feared, will add to the overall threat of rising unemployment in the country. The conversion process may also affect income distribution within China, but it is not clear what the final outcome will be. For example, Zhai and Li (2000) simulate the impact of WTO accession on income disparities in China. They conclude that, given the dominant role played by agricultural trade liberalization and despite the gains in efficiency, rural households will be the main losers and that rural–urban economic disparities could increase. In contrast, Wei and Wu (2002) find that the impact of globalization will be to reduce rural–urban income inequalities and that, although inequality in the distribution of income within urban areas will rise, in rural areas it will decline. Whatever the

---

[35] Other factors may be at work. For example, rising returns to education in the past decade may be an additional contributor to the rise in income inequality in China given the higher levels of education in the eastern or coastal provinces (Zhang and Zhao, 2002).

final impact of WTO membership may be on the sectoral and regional distribution of employment and income, there is little doubt but that it will make the local economies more exposed to international trends. As the provinces trade more with the rest of the world, it will weaken the links between the center and local governments. This again will have important implications for the design and management of the system of intergovernmental fiscal relations in China.

III.7. The Political Role of Fiscal Federalism

In 1978, China's government made the momentous decision to abandon rigid communist ideology in favor of a more pragmatic market-oriented socialism and at the same time to open the country's economy to the world. If economic growth is the test, the decision was a good one. However, a puzzle for many is how China has been able to grow so fast over the past two decades in the absence of democracy, and in many ways also in the absence of the rule of law and private property rights.[36] Different explanations have been offered, but a common element in all of them is the role played by fiscal federalism. In the view of Montinola et al. (1995) "federalism, Chinese style" has provided incentives for production and competition while creating a protection for the reform, including credible limits on the central government's ability for economic extraction, fiscal claw back, or any other form of appropriation of resources. Fiscal federalism and its associated jurisdictional competition also placed limits on patronage and political spoils by the central authorities and altered center–local relations in a way that will be difficult to reverse. Similar views are held by Qian and Weingast (1996), who see China's fiscal decentralization reforms in the 1980s as "market-preserving federalism." The reforms empowered local governments with responsibility over their own economies and hardened local budget constraints.[37] The reforms also contributed to create, but still did not produce, a common market with free mobility of goods and factors across subnational jurisdictions.

---

[36] Li and Lian (1999), however, point out that there has been rapid growth under authoritarian regimes before, including Meiji Japan, the German Second Reich, the Asian Tigers, and Franco's Spain.

[37] Empowering local governments with responsibility over their own economies has meant that local officials have become entrepreneurs and local governments have become owners of industry. This is completely at odds with the role of government in a market economy.

Li and Lian (1999), however, explain China's success as due to "market-preserving authoritarianism." The formula for growth in China, in their view, has been the combination and balance between economic decentralization and budget autonomy with political control and coordination from the center. Three conditions have made the system work, according to Li and Lian (1999). First, political leaders perceive it is in their interest to promote market activities for China to catch up economically. Second, their policies were made more credible by imposing self-constraints and by distributing some authority and resources to a large number of decision makers, including those in lower level governments. Third, the center is able to use incentive schemes, coordination, and enforcement devices to balance autonomy and controls.

There are two additional political effects of fiscal federalism that have been less emphasized in the literature. First, the rapid economic development of the coastal provinces compared with the rest of the country created a political asymmetry with first class and underclass provinces. The wealthier coastal provinces have been much more effective in the past two decades in protecting their interests, as witnessed, for example, by the introduction of a hold harmless provision in the 1994 revenue-sharing reforms. Second, the asymmetry with first class and underclass provinces has led to the political weakening of the center vis-à-vis the provinces, in particular those in the coastal regions. Globalization, through foreign direct investment and exports, has probably also contributed to the weakening of the center compared with the wealthier provinces in the east. For example, in the revenue-sharing reforms of 1994, the wealthier provinces managed to extract from Beijing a tax rebate transfer, which in effect protected them from losing significant revenues, and left the equalization grant system without significantly more funds to compensate the poorer inland provinces.[38]

III.8. Recapitulation: The Policy Environment for Fiscal Federalism

Multiple factors have been at work in the widening of economic disparities across China's provinces. The natural cost advantage provided by geographical location to the coastal provinces has been reinforced by

---

[38] Wang (1997) discusses how the center, to get acceptance of the 1994 reform, had to bribe Guandong and other rich coastal provinces, since these provinces were capable of blocking institutional change.

three sets of central government policies. First, the central government opened up the economy by providing special fiscal status and additional economic resources to very few provinces. What followed were high levels of FDI and quite different rates of economic growth and levels of economic development within China. It is not clear how further globalization of the Chinese economy will affect these disparities. Second, this situation has been exacerbated by population policies that have severely limited migration out of the poorer provinces in the central and western parts of the country. Third, access to capital funds by these poorer provinces in the center and west has continued to be limited by the bureaucratic decisions of the monopoly state banking system that still favors state enterprises and projects in the coastal provinces. Meanwhile, the costs of rescuing an insolvent banking system will be spread to all parts of the country. The general outcome has been an unbalanced distribution of political power and wealth in favor of the coastal provinces. A second outcome has been the political weakening of the center vis-à-vis the wealthier coastal regions and therefore further limitations for Beijing to implement fiscal federalism policies.

IV. REFORMS AND FEDERALISM

We now turn to the question of reform. Specifically, we ask how China's institutions for fiscal federalism might be adjusted to either reinforce economic policy or to compensate for the disparities that have arisen as a result of the economic reform.

IV.1. Intergovernmental Transfers

The Chinese system of intergovernmental transfers to provinces has been evolving over the past two decades, but it has retained its basic approach of origin-based shared taxes. There is little distinction in China between revenue assignment and intergovernmental transfers. One would not be too far off the mark by characterizing the system as one that attempts to define a vertical share in central taxes for the provinces, supplemented by grants and subsidies for myriad purposes and with considerable redundancy. The result appears to have been a limited degree of equalization among provinces and a complex system of transfers by any standards.[39]

---

[39] See Zhang and Martinez-Vazquez (2002).

Shared taxes are allocated on a derivation basis (i.e., by point of collection). The company income tax and the individual income tax until recently have been fully retained by the collecting provincial governments, and they were assessed and collected locally. However, the subnational governments had no power to set the tax rate or define the tax base. It is common in China to refer this as a "local tax" but in fact this is incorrect. In effect, the provincial government is a collection agent for a central tax, and it may retain all, or a designated percentage, of the collections. Beginning in January 2001, all income tax revenues above a base figure were shared 50–50 between the central and local governments. In 2003, the central government's share rose to 60% versus 40% for local governments.[40]

The value added tax is also shared with the provincial governments, though the formula is more complicated. At the time of the major intergovernmental reform in 1994, a base amount of revenue sharing was identified as the difference between the amounts received from all transfers in 1993, less the sum of proposed "local taxes" and 25% of VAT collections. This held all provinces at the same level as the previous year, and it protected the subsidized position of the "deficit" provinces. An additional 30% of the increment in national VAT and consumption tax collections was added to this amount to provide revenue growth. The VAT is collected by the national tax administration service.

The other form of intergovernmental transfers consists of a series of equalization and conditional grants. The structure of these grants has changed over time but now accounts for approximately 50% of all transfers. The conditional grants include capital grants and cost reimbursement grants, the latter of which are to assist subnational governments to cover some pension and unemployment compensation costs. The most notable features of equalization grants are the general complexity of the distribution formula, and until quite recently, their low level of funding. This latter feature is noticeable because of the large fiscal disparities in revenue capacity and expenditure needs across China's provinces. The recentralization of a share of personal income tax revenues (up to 60%) in recent times has been motivated by the central government as a way to increase the funds available for equalization purposes.

VERTICAL SHARES. Throughout the 1980s and the early 1990s, the rate of revenue mobilization in GNP fell in China. By the time of the landmark

---

[40] These additional central government revenues have been earmarked for equalization transfers to the central and western regions of the country.

1994 reform, it had dropped to less than 12% of GNP. Successive reforms in the intergovernmental transfer system had favored the provincial governments, so that their share had been increasing. Prior to the 1994 reform, the central share of total revenues had fallen to 22%. This left the central government with too little revenue to aggressively pursue national infrastructure needs, social service improvements, or interprovince equalization.

In fact, the vertical share of local governments may have been even greater. It has been estimated that the extrabudgetary revenues raised by local governments were half as the size of budgetary revenues. Although the 1994 reform closed off some of the avenues and incentives for raising extrabudgetary revenues, the amounts remain quite significant.

The 1994 reform was meant to increase overall tax effort and to rebalance the system in favor of the center. The enterprise income tax base was broadened, and the VAT was modernized by introducing a credit-invoice system and by extending the coverage to all production sectors and to some services. The enterprise contracting system was eliminated. The new intergovernmental transfer system eliminated the provincial contracting system, passed the income taxes fully to the subnational governments, and made the VAT a (shared) central tax.

Another important part of the 1994 reform was to create a separate local tax administration service with responsibility for administering the "local taxes." This provided an incentive for subnational governments to increase the rate of revenue mobilization and, together with full retention of income tax collections, removed a reason for pursuing revenue options that were off-budget.

Revenue mobilization in China has increased significantly and had reached a level equivalent to 15% of GNP by the end of the decade. Although this is not a high level of taxation by international standards, it is well above the 1994 level. There was also a shifting of the balance back to the central government in terms of revenues available. The central share increased from 22% in the prereform period to about 56% by 2000. However, as noted in the following, part of the negotiations that led to this fiscal recentralization was a rebate on indirect taxes that would benefit the higher income provinces, a hold harmless provision for the formerly subsidized provinces, and a commitment to funding an equalization grant.

FISCAL DISPARITIES AND EQUALIZATION. There are significant disparities in per capita incomes and per capita expenditures across the thirty-one provinces. As may be seen in Table 6.1, the per capita income in the highest income province is on the order of ten times that in the lowest.

Per capita subnational government revenues were on the order of eighteen times higher in 2000 and per capita subnational government expenditures were on the order of ten times higher also in 2000 (Table 6.6). As Table 6.6 shows that, on average, per capita revenues and expenditures have been substantially higher in the coastal provinces than in the inland provinces for the past two decades.

The intergovernmental transfer system does have some equalizing elements, but it is not designed explicitly as a system that will reduce disparities in unmet expenditure needs or fiscal capacity. Some of its components are equalizing and some are counterequalizing. It is difficult to use a priori reasoning to reach a conclusion about the degree of horizontal inequity inherent in this system. The sharing of income taxes is likely to be quite counterequalizing, as is the portion of revenue sharing that is based on increments in the value added and consumption taxes. This is because these are all shared taxes based on origin of collection and will favor provinces with a stronger economic base. The "base amount" of revenue sharing built into the distribution formula reflects the subsidy that was paid to deficit provinces in the pre-1994 reform period. Therefore, some equalizing component was built-in, but this effect has become less important in the formula as the weight of the incremental VAT sharing and income taxation has become greater since 1994.

It is not clear if the grant system is equalizing, but it does contain factors that suggest that it might be. The component of the grant system that reflects cost reimbursement for social insurance expenditures could be allocated to redress expenditure needs, and therefore it might be an equalizing component. The World Bank (2002) reports that about 60% of transfers net of tax rebates went for social security expenditures, safety net expenditures, and transfers to offset the costs of increased civil service wage increases. Most of these funds were distributed to provincial governments in the inland regions. Though we have no up-to-date empirical estimates of the equalization impacts of these grants, a study of the distribution of earmarked grants in the 1990s showed a positive correlation between earmarked grants received and the level of income of the province (Bahl, 1999, Chapter 4). However, the conditional grants are allocated in an ad hoc way, and there is no way to make an a priori judgment about whether they are allocated more heavily to places with deficient infrastructure and basic services. Nonetheless, from the data reported in Table 6.6 we can infer that the overall fiscal system is equalizing. The range between the maximum and minimum values in per capita revenues is considerably larger than that for per capita expenditures, for

Table 6.6. *Provincial per Capita Fiscal Outcomes (RMB Yuan)*

	Revenues		Expenditures	
	1979	2002	1979	2002
Coastal Provinces				
Beijing	532	3753	224	4416
Tianjin	509	1706	206	2634
Hebei	69	449	67	856
Liaoning	254	951	101	1644
Shanghai	1525	4363	239	5307
Jiangsu	101	872	54	1165
Zhejiang	68	1220	47	1614
Fujian	51	787	64	1147
Shandong	79	672	44	948
Guangdong	67	1529	55	1935
Guangxi	35	387	59	871
Hainan	25	576	34	1149
Average	**146**	**1064**	**70**	**1494**
Inland Provinces				
Shanxi	83	458	85	1015
Inner Mongolia	25	474	114	1654
Jilin	58	487	82	1344
Heilongjiang	171	608	89	1395
Anhui	44	316	42	721
Jiangxi	36	333	55	809
Henan	47	309	42	655
Hubei	68	407	61	854
Hunan	55	349	48	804
Chongqing	n.a.[i]	406	n.a.	984
Sichuan	n.a.	337	n.a.	809
Guizhou	24	282	49	825
Yunnan	36	477	68	1216
Tibet	−12	274	274	5163
Shannxi	60	409	70	1102
Gansu	97	294	75	1057
Qinghai	62	399	183	2244
Ningxia	84	463	173	2003
Xinjiang	44	611	135	1896
Average	**52**	**385**	**57**	**988**
All China	**92**	**668**	**63**	**1198**
Mean	**148**	**805**	**98**	**1620**
Minimum	**−12**	**274**	**34**	**655**
Maximum	**1525**	**4363**	**274**	**5307**
Coefficient of Variation	**1.98**	**1.17**	**0.69**	**0.75**

[i] n.a., not available.

Source: http://chinadataonline.org.

all selected years since 1979. Also, the coefficient of variation for the distribution of per capita expenditures is significantly lower than the coefficient of variation for the distribution of per capita revenues. Somehow, the fiscal system manages to reduce the disparities implied by revenues. However, the data reported in Table 6.1 also show that the degree of equalization achieved is not high since substantial disparities in expenditure per capita remain.[41]

There is also a significant disparity within regions, in the level of income and expenditure needs, and there is evidence that the fiscal systems within some regions are not equalizing. Bahl's (1999) empirical work on Jiangsu and Sichuan for the first year after the 1994 reform showed that both provinces were characterized by significant disparities among local governments in income and expenditure levels. Both provinces reduced expenditure disparities somewhat using intergovernmental transfers and shared taxes. However, even after this degree of equalization, large fiscal disparities remained.

IV.2. Interdependence of the Tax System and Fiscal Federalism

A distinguishing feature of the Chinese fiscal system is that tax policy, tax administration, and intergovernmental fiscal relations are not separable. The major form of intergovernmental transfer is shared central government taxes; hence tax policy changes affect the flow of resources to subnational governments; the performance of the tax system depends crucially on the efficiency of the tax administration system; and tax administration is carried out by both the central and the subnational governments. The main point here is that central government tax policy choices, and changes in tax administration procedures, are key policy decisions affecting the intergovernmental fiscal system. If one is to understand the strengths and weaknesses of the Chinese system of fiscal federalism, one must understand the strengths and weaknesses of all three of its legs.

China's tax system has been evolving over the past two decades. Government policymakers have paid more attention to reform of the tax and transfer system than they have to expenditure assignment. At present, the primary revenue producers in the system are consumption taxes (notably

---

[41] A more complete measure of equalization goes beyond disparities in expenditures per capita and should incorporate differences in expenditure needs and also differences in fiscal capacity to finance those needs. China's current equalization grants still measure needs and capacity deficiently.

the value added tax), the enterprise income tax, and to a lesser extent the individual income tax.

Taxes account for about 15% of GDP. This is not a high share by international standards. An international comparison suggests that a country at China's level of per capita income, and with China's degree of foreign trade openness and population characteristics should raise about 17% of GDP more in taxes (Appendix A). Although there is room for increased taxation, one could not say that China's level of taxation is either inordinately low or high.[42] The revenue performance of the tax system has been erratic in the past decade. Revenues fell from 19% to 11% of GDP in the early 1990s but have now risen back to 15%.

Whether or not the level of taxation is a major concern, there are structural problems with the tax system that may compromise China's competitive position. However, any of these changes is likely to affect the fiscal disparities among provinces and their comparative advantage in attracting investment.

VALUE ADDED TAX. China moved a step closer to a modern tax system with the reforms of the VAT it enacted in 1994. The base of the tax was broadened and a credit-invoice system was implemented. A more productive VAT means a faster growing base for subnational governments. The VAT is more friendly to the export sector than are other forms of indirect tax, and it is a productive revenue generator. The stronger the provincial economy is, the greater will be the revenue benefits.

There remain two important structural changes to consider for the value added tax. One is to bring the services sector more fully into the tax net thereby increasing revenues in provinces with large taxable service sectors. The other needed change is to fully allow credit for taxes paid on capital inputs. The Chinese government frequently invokes its concern with overinvestment as a justification for tax structure choices. There are better ways to deal with overinvestment than disallowing the VAT credit on capital inputs; e.g., make the general tax regime neutral with respect to the investment decision, and adopt a more realistic approach to rationing credit for capital investments. Allowing credit for capital inputs would produce a revenue loss for the central government and especially for the producing provinces. Whether this would be offset by increased economic activity in investment-friendly provinces, and in those that produce

---

[42] However, note that we have understated the level of Chinese taxes by some (unknown) amounts by not including the extrabudgetary revenues of local governments.

intermediate goods, is an open question. Almost certainly, however, there would be differential impacts across the provinces.

ENTERPRISE INCOME TAX. The enterprise income tax is in need of reform (Bahl, 1999). The tax code still treats domestic enterprises differently from foreign-owned enterprises and joint ventures. The latter are taxed at significantly lower rates. Such distortions may channel funds away from domestic investment. Moreover, the differentially lower rate may not be necessary to attract foreign investment, because of the availability of tax credits in the home country and the relatively high rates of return in China. A full unification of the tax structure on foreign and domestic enterprises is a reasonable reform measure.

A more difficult question relates to capital cost deductions. Although depreciation rates were accelerated with the 1994 reform in China, they still do not match up well to capital consumption rates allowed in other countries. In addition, all interest expenses are not deductible. The net result of these provisions is that true profits are overstated and capital investment is discouraged. The enterprise income tax should be based on proper depreciation rates and full deductibility of interest costs.

If these two reforms were undertaken, it would have revenue implications for the "local" tax base of provinces. Adopting parity in rates for foreign and domestic firms would in the short run increase the revenues of provinces that have heavier foreign investment. A more realistic schedule for capital consumption allowances would lower enterprise income tax revenues in all provinces, but less so in provinces where industry is more profitable.

INDIVIDUAL INCOME TAX. The individual income tax meets the tests for a provincial revenue source in a fiscal federalism. However, in China, it is used as an intergovernmental transfer of the shared tax type and there is no rate-setting autonomy at the provincial level. The central government could go in two directions with the individual income tax. It could restructure the tax to move toward a local government-financing device, providing additional autonomy, or it could increase the productivity of this tax and then claw back the revenues to use for equalization purposes. As of 2003, it is following the latter path.

In this latter scenario, the reforms that are being discussed in China at present will lead to a more productive income tax and possibly a larger revenue pool for equalization purposes. These reforms include increasing the threshold for payment of the tax, simplification for reducing evasion, and improving the efficiency of assessment and collection. There is some possibility that the reform of the individual income tax, unlike the reform of the VAT or enterprise income tax, could be disparity reducing.

LOCAL GOVERNMENT TAXES. China does not give its local governments any taxing powers. Nor is there popular local election or complete population mobility. However, a program of informal subnational government taxation did emerge in the form of extrabudgetary revenue raising. Local government used a backdoor approach to capture some of the efficiency gains that one might expect in a fiscal federalism. The 1994 reform limited the use of these extrabudgetary taxes. The absence of broad-based provincial and local government taxes probably results in smaller regional disparities in resources available.

One autonomous local government tax that is used in China is the property tax. This is the standard for local government taxation in most countries around the world. A charge for the use of property, based on some notion of value, would seem an appropriate way to finance public services, especially in urban areas. At present, China does not have a property tax based directly on land or building values. However, there are at least six different local government taxes that are related to the use of land or the transfer of land use. These generate only small amounts of revenue, but they do have the feature of giving the local governments some autonomy in setting tax rates. The more urbanized provinces would gain most from an expanded property tax.

V. CONCLUSION

The most important conclusion of this chapter is that China's road to fiscal federalism reform has been and continues to be strongly conditioned not only by tax policy and tax administration reform but also by a wide range of economic policies. In most countries, these considerations are thought to be well outside of the relevant policy framework for reviewing the impacts of fiscal federalism. These interdependencies between fiscal federalism and other aspects of economic reform set China's experience with fiscal federalism decidedly apart from the experience of most other countries. We have seen that there are in particular three sets of policies that have constrained the ability of the fiscal federalism system to operate efficiently and fairly. These policies in different ways have raised the demands on the system of fiscal federalism to moderate some of the results of the economic reforms (e.g., to produce a more equal distribution of public goods and services throughout the national territory).

First, demographic policies, in particular the restrictions to internal migration through the residence registration system or *Hukou*, have put additional fiscal pressures on poorer local governments in the central and western provinces where it appears that a good share of the population would have migrated to the richer local jurisdictions in the coastal provinces if they were given the chance. The additional burdens take the form of higher expenditure needs from the unemployed, higher incidence of poverty, and otherwise higher demand for basic services such as education and health and so on. The other side of the coin is that expenditure needs are easier to meet and the overall fiscal health of jurisdictions in the richer coastal provinces is improved under current migration policies. In fact, the current arrangements allow the coastal provinces to benefit from illegal migrant labor without bearing the costs of social services, pensions, and so on. However, the redesign and reform of the intergovernmental system will need to take into account the higher costs of industrial restructuring in the northeast and in some coastal provinces.

Second, China's financial system, through the role of the monopoly state banking system, has traditionally channeled more funds to the richer coastal provinces where there has always been a higher concentration of SOEs. The poor quality of many of these loans has driven the SOBs to the verge of default. The inevitable rescue of the SOBs will not only draw resources from all parts of China, including those that never benefited much from the administered loan policies, but, given its size with respect to GDP, also noticeably reduce the pool of central government funds available for equalization. The result will be that the poorer jurisdictions in the center and western provinces will suffer.

Third, globalization forces and industrial development policies adopted by China's central government also have disproportionately helped the coastal provinces vis-à-vis those in the center and western regions of the country. The momentous policy decision to open China to the world and allow FDI in 1979 benefited just a few "special economic zones" in the east coast at first and then a larger number of areas still in the coastal provinces. By the time FDI was allowed in the rest of the country, in the poorer provinces of the center and the west, the central government had disallowed, and rightly so, the wide use of tax incentives and holidays to attract investment. Thus with their geographic disadvantage (and no tax advantages to offset it) as well as other disadvantages such as poor infrastructure and public services, jurisdictions in the center and western areas of the country have not yet been able to benefit from globalization forces. The fear is that China's accession to the WTO will impose significant losses to rural agricultural areas in the already poorer areas of the country. Meanwhile, the lack of horizontal integration of the Chinese economy contributed to small positive spillovers from the richer to the poorer provinces, thus validating the first part of Deng Xiaoping's famous phrase pronounced in 1978 after his fact-finding trip to the southeastern provinces: "Let part of us be richer first."[43]

Given the remarkably uneven development of the different regions in China, one would have expected a system of fiscal federalism that aggressively tried to compensate for the existing fiscal disparities. And yet, as we have seen, it has been only very recently that fiscal decentralization reform has started to address this serious problem. It is as if China's central government over the past two decades has been operating under the belief that there is a policy tradeoff between economic growth and regional fiscal equalization and as if it has chosen unequivocally to stand on the side of economic growth.[44]

The policy choices actually may have to do more with political economy issues than with the preferences of a benevolent planner-dictator. The lopsided coastal-heavy regional development of China has contributed to an asymmetric distribution of political power in the country. With the fast development of the coastal provinces, their voices in Beijing have become much more notable and influential than those in the rest of the country. In addition, this asymmetric process of development eventually has transferred political power from Beijing to some of the provincial capitals. The negotiations that protected the revenue shares of the richer provinces from fiscal recentralization in 1994 are evidence of this power. The continued modernization of the tax system, to better capture the benefits of a market economy, will be driven by these same voices. However, the recent tax reforms with the recentralization of a share of personal income tax revenues for redistribution to the interior provinces signals that Beijing still has the last say on key fiscal issues.

Besides the lack of adequate equalization effort, China's fiscal federalism is afflicted by several other problems, which in some ways tend to aggravate the situation of the poorer subnational governments. In particular, the assignment of expenditure responsibilities for most social welfare issues, including pension systems, to subnational governments may be

---

[43] The post-1979 policies and the general acceptance of growing regional inequalities contrast with the heavily redistributive policies favored in earlier times by Chairman Mao, which pushed for the development of the interior, poorer areas of China.

[44] See Qiao et al. (2002).

hurting poorer regions disproportionately.[45] The centralization of some of those expenditure responsibilities would increase efficiency in the delivery of services and would also be equalizing. Other necessary reforms in the fiscal federalism system, such as providing a noticeable degree of tax autonomy to subnational governments, are likely to further increase fiscal disparities. An alternative strategy would be to substitute locally raised revenues for transfers in the richer provinces. This points once more to the critical importance in the future of redesigning and strengthening the grant system, in particular that for issuing equalization grants.

Reforming revenue assignments in China will still require simultaneous reform efforts in tax policy and tax administration. Besides increasing revenue mobilization and improving vertical balances, these reforms still need to reduce distortions in the allocation of resources and to improve equity in the distribution of tax burdens. This reform agenda should include the further development of the personal income tax and property taxes at the local level. The centralization of VAT revenues could help finance the centralization of expenditure responsibilities in social welfare. Thus the reform agenda may have both decentralizing and centralizing measures. However, the message of this chapter is that the chances for success and failure of possible reform in the system of fiscal federalism need to be considered in the contexts of reform in the tax system and the wider environment of population, financial sector, and other central government policies. Righting these other policies can be as effective as, or even more effective than, fiscal policy in increasing the well-being of those in the poorer regions of China.

There is also a need for deep reforms in expenditure assignments. First, the assignment of responsibilities needs to be clarified in the law, especially for "concurrent" services area at the provincial and local levels, and unfunded expenditure mandates need to be dramatically reduced. Second, responsibility for much of the social safety should be reassigned at the province and central levels, relieving subprovincial governments of their current responsibilities in unemployment compensation, health insurance, and pensions. Health and education services, now the responsibility of the lowest level county and township governments, should be reassigned to higher level governments in those cases where local

---

[45] However, in terms of pensions, the regional score card is not entirely clear. In particular, the poorer western provinces generally have young populations, whereas the richer coastal provinces (and the northeast) tend to have aging populations with high dependency ratios.

governments have neither the financial nor the administrative capacity to handle these social service functions.

Bibliography

Bahl, R. (2001). *Fiscal Policy in China*, Ann Adcbor: The 1990 Institute and University of Michigan Press.

Bahl, R., and J. Linn (1992). *Urban Public Finance in Developing Countries*. New York: Oxford University Press.

Blanchard, O., and A. Shleifer (2000). "Federalism with and without Political Centralization: China versus Russia," NBER Working Paper 7616, March.

Bouin, O. (1998). "Financial Discipline and State Enterprise Reform in China in the 1990s," in O. Bouin, F. Coricelli, and F. Lemoine, eds., *Different Paths to a Market Economy: China and European Economies in Transition*, Paris, France: OECD Development Center.

Broadman, H. G. (1995). "China: Tax Policy Toward Foreign Direct Investment," Economic Policy Note, The World Bank (August).

Chen, B., J. K. Dietrich, and Y. Fang, eds. (2000). *Financial Market Reform in China: Progress, Problems, and Prospects*. Boulder, CO: Westview Press.

Chen, J., and B. M. Fleischer (1996). "Regional Income Inequality and Economic Growth in China," Journal of Comparative Economics 22: 141–164.

Dayal-Gulati, A., and A. M. Husain (2002). "Centripetal Forces in China's Economic Takeoff," IMF Staff Papers 49(3): 364–394.

Demurger, S., J. D. Sachs, W. T. Woo, S. Bao, G. Chang, and A. Mellinger (2002). "Geography, Economic Policy, and Regional Development in China," NBER Working Paper 8897, National Bureau of Economic Research, Cambridge, MA.

Feldstein, M. S., and C. Horioka (1980). "Domestic Savings and International Capital Flows," Economic Journal 90(358): 314–329.

Feng, Y., and H. Zhang (2000). "Provincial Distribution of Direct Foreign Investment in China: A Pooled Time-Series Empirical Study," in B. Chen, J. K. Dietrich, and Y. Fang, eds., *Financial Market Reform in China: Progress, Problems, and Prospects*. Boulder, CO: Westview Press: 401–424.

Fisher, R. C. (1996). *State and Local Public Finance*, 2nd edition. Chicago: Irwin.

Hofman, B. (1998). "Fiscal Decline and Quasi-Fiscal Response: China's Fiscal Policy and System 1978–94," in O. Bouin, F. Coricelli, and F. Lemoine, eds., *Different Paths to a Market Economy: China and European Economies in Transition*. Paris, France: OECD Development Center.

Hu, Z. L. (1995). "Social Expenditure Assignments in China: Issues and Responses," in A. Ehtisham, Q. Gao, and V. Tanzi, eds., *Reforming China's Public Finances*, pp. 113–136. Washington, DC: International Monetary Fund.

Jian, T., J. D. Sachs, and A. M. Warner (1996). "Trends in Regional Inequality in China," NBER Working Paper 5412, National Bureau of Economic Research, Cambridge, MA.

Jin, H., Y. Qian, and B. Weingast (1999). "Regional Decentralization and Fiscal Incentives: Federalism Chinese Style," mimeo, Stanford University, March.

Kaiser, S., D. A. Kirby, and Y. Fan (1996). "Foreign Direct Investment in China: An Examination of the Literature," Asia Pacific Business Review 2(3): 44–65.

Kanbur, R., and X. Zhang (1999). "Which Regional Inequality? The Evolution of Rural-Urban and Inland-Coastal Inequality in China from 1983 to 1995," Journal of Comparative Economics 27: 686–701.

Lee, J. (1995). "Regional Income Inequality Variations in China," Journal of Economic Development 20(2): 99–118.

Li, S., and Lian, P. (1999). "Decentralization and Coordination: China's Credible Commitment to Preserve the Market under Authoritarianism," China Economic Review 10: 161–190.

Lou, J. (1997). "Constraints in Reforming the Transfer System in China," in A. Ehtisham, ed., *Financing Decentralized Expenditures: An International Comparison of Grants*, pp. 349–360. Brookfield, MA: Edward Elgar.

Martinez-Vazquez, J., and C. Wong (2003). "Two Large Experiments in Fiscal Decentralization Compared: China and Russia." International Studies Program Working Paper 03–13, Andrew Young School of Policy Studies, Georgia State University.

McLure, C. E., Jr. (1998). "The Revenue Assignment Problem: Ends, Means, and Constraints," Journal of Public Budgeting, Accounting & Financial Management 9(4): 652–683.

Montinola, G., Y. Qian, and B. R. Weingast (1995). "Federalism, Chinese Style: The Political Basis for Economic Success in China," World Politics 48(1): 50–81.

Naughton, B. (1996). "China's Emergence and Prospect as a Trading Nation," Brookings Papers in Economic Activity 2: 273–343.

Naughton, B. (2000). "Provincial Economic Growth in China: Causes and Consequences of Regional Differentiation," in M.-F. Renard, ed., *China and Its Regions, Economic Growth and Reform in Chinese Provinces*. Cheltenham, UK: Edward Elgar.

OECD (2002). Foreign Direct Investment in China: Challenges and Prospect for Regional Development, Paris.

Qian, Y., and B. R. Weingast (1996). "China's Transition to Markets: Market-Preserving Federalism, Chinese Style," Journal of Policy Reform 1: 149–185.

Qian, Y., and B. R. Weingast (1997). "Federalism as a Commitment to Preserving Market Incentives," Journal of Economic Perspectives 11(4): 83–92.

Qiao, B., J. Martinez-Vazquez, and Y. Xu (2002). "The Tradeoff between Equity and Growth in China's Fiscal Federalism," International Studies Program Working Paper 02–16, Andrew Young School of Policy Studies, Georgia State University.

Shi, L. (2001). "Efficiency and Redistribution in China's Revenue-Sharing System," in J.-J. Dethier, ed., *Governance and Development in China, India and Russia*. Boston: Kluwer.

State Statistical Bureau (1998). China Development Report, Beijing.

Sun, H., and Chai, J. (1998). "Direct Foreign Investment and Inter-Regional Disparity in China," International Journal of Social Economics, v. 25 (2-3-4): 429–447.

Sun, H., and F. B. Tipton (1998). "A Comparative Analysis of the Characteristics of Direct Foreign Investment in China, 1979–1995," The Journal of Developmental Areas' (Vol. 32(2)): 159–186.

Sun, Q., W. Tong, and Q. Yu (2002). "Determinants of Foreign Direct Investment across China," Journal of International Money and Finance 21: 79–113.

The Economist (2002). "A Dragon Out of Puff: A Survey of China," 363(8277): 54.

Wang, S. (1997). "China's 1994 Fiscal Reform: An Initial Assessment." Asian Survey, 37(9): 801–818 (September).

Wei, S.-J., and Y. Wu (2001). "Globalization and Inequality: Evidence from Within China," NBER Working Paper 8611, National Bureau of Economic Research, Cambridge, MA.

Wei, S.-J., and Y. Wu (2002). "Globalization and Inequality without Differences in Data Definition, Legal System and Other Institutions," mimeo.

Wei, Y., X. Liu, D. Parker, and K. Vaidya (1999). "The Regional Distribution of Foreign Direct Investment in China," Regional Studies 33(9): 857–867.

Wong, C. (1998). "Fiscal Dualism in China: Gradualist Reform and the Growth of Off-Budget Finance," in D. J. S. Brean, ed., *Taxation in Modern China*. pp. 187–208. New York and London: Routledge.

Wong, C., C. Heady, and W. T. Woo (1995). *Fiscal Management and Economic Reform in the People's Republic of China*. Hong Kong: Oxford University Press.

Woo, W. T. (1998). "Financial Intermediation in China," in O. Bouin, F. Coricelli, and F. Lemoine, eds., *Different Paths to a Market Economy: China and European Economies in Transition*. Paris, France: OECD Development Center.

World Bank (2002). China: National Development and Subnational Finance: A Review of Provincial Expenditures, Washington DC.

Yao, S., and L. Zhu (1998). "Understanding Income Inequality in China: A Multi-Angle Perspective," Economics of Planning 31(2–3): 133–150.

Zhai, F., and S. Li (2000). "The Impact of WYO Accession on Income Disparity in China," in M.-F. Renard, ed., *China and Its Regions, Economic Growth and Reform in Chinese Provinces* pp. 121–146. Cheltenham, UK: Edward Elgar.

Zhang, J., and Y. Zhao (2002). "Economic Returns to Schooling in Urban China, 1988–1999," working paper, Chinese University of Hong Kong and Beijing University.

Zhang, L.-Y. (1994). "Location-Specific Advantages and Manufacturing Direct Foreign Investment in South China," World Development 22: 45–53.

Zhang, T., and H.-F. Zou (1998). "Fiscal Decentralization, Public Spending, and Economic Growth in China," Journal of Public Economics 67(2): 221–240.

Zhang, X., S. Fan, L. Zhang, and J. Huang (2002). "Local Governance and Public Goods Provision in Rural China," mimeo, International Food Policy Research Institute.

Zhang, Z., and J. Martinez-Vazquez (2002). "The System of Equalization Transfers in China," International Studies Program Working Paper 03–13, Andrew Young School of Policy Studies, Georgia State University.

Zhao, R. (1998). "Capital Mobility and Regional Integration in China," mimeo, International Monetary Fund.

APPENDIX: TAX EFFORT DURING THE 1990s

Tax effort in China appeared to lag behind that in other countries during the 1990s. Using data for the 1990s (the latest years available) from Government Finance Statistics (GFS), we calculated the ratio of tax to GDP (T/Y) for 110 industrialized, developing, and transition countries. Following the standard tax effort literature, we estimated

$$T/Y = 1.95 + 0.11(Y/P) - 0.07(A/Y) + 0.16(F) - 0.17(PG)\,\bar{R}^2 = 0.61$$
$$\quad\;(2.97)\;\;(2.24)\qquad\quad(-0.99)\qquad\quad(2.55)\qquad(-5.00)$$

where

$$Y/P = \text{per capita GDP, in U.S. dollars,}$$
$$A/Y = \text{agricultural sector share of GDP,}$$
$$F = \text{imports plus exports as a share of GDP,}$$

and

$$PG = \text{population growth rate.}$$

Variables are expressed in logarithms and t-values are shown in parentheses.

The income and openness variables are significant and have the expected signs. For this period, China has an "expected" tax ratio of 17%, but according to GFS, an actual tax ratio of 12.5%. By the end of the decade, China's tax ratio had risen to about 15% and it was close to 19 % at the end of 2003. The analysis of tax effort in China is subject to the important caveat that a considerable share of funds in the public sector has been for decades channeled to extrabudget financing (Wong 1998). The government has made a sustained effort in recent years to convert and bring into the regular budget accounts many of the extrabudgetary funds (World Bank, 2002). At this time, there is no information on how much of the increase in measured tax effort comes from genuine tax effort or from the new accounting of previous extrabudgetary funds.

SEVEN

Indian Federalism, Economic Reform, and Globalization*

Nirvikar Singh and T. N. Srinivasan

India is a Union of States based on the framework of cooperative federalism. Within the cooperative framework, there is also a requirement to develop competitive strengths for the States so that they can excel at the national level and the global level. Competitiveness helps in ensuring economic and managerial efficiency and to be creative to meet new challenges. These are essential to survive and prosper in a fast changing world of today. In addition, in order to strengthen democratic processes and institution, we should all truly strive for substantive decentralization.

From the speech by Dr. A. P. J. Abdul Kalam on his assumption of office as President of India New Delhi, 25 July 2002

I. INTRODUCTION

In this chapter we examine the interaction between globalization and India's federal system, in the context of the country's past decade of economic reform. In doing so, we recognize that the national government has subnational governments below it and that all these layers of government simultaneously interact with foreign governments and corporations in a global economy. These multiple interactions have become

* Parts of this chapter draw on joint work of Nirvikar Singh with M. Govinda Rao. We are grateful to Shankar Acharya, Amaresh Bagchi, Pranab Bardhan, Francine Frankel, Devesh Kapur, Rakesh Mohan, Urjit Patel, M. Govinda Rao, Jessica Seddon Wallack, Tapas Sen, D. K. Srivastava, and seminar participants at SCID (Stanford), ISEC (Bangalore), and ICRIER (New Delhi) for helpful comments and suggestions; Jahangir Aziz, Laveesh Bhandari, Paul Cashin, Saumitra Chaudhuri, Aarti Khare, M. R. Nair, M. Govinda Rao, Y. V. Reddy, Ratna Sahay, and Christopher Towe for help with data; and SCID at Stanford University for financial support. We alone are responsible for the views expressed here and for any errors or omissions.

more important as reform in India has opened up the economy to foreign trade and investment, They have also reduced certain constraints on subnational governments. Globalization provides challenges as well as opportunities to federal systems such as India's. This chapter seeks to elucidate these and to draw implications for policy and institutional reform.[1]

In economic terms, globalization can be taken as the increased international mobility of goods, capital, labor, and knowledge. A cornerstone of Indian economic reform has been the opening up of its markets to flows of goods and factors of production thus integrating its economy more closely with the global economy.[2] Section II reviews the process of economic reform in India and the outcomes in terms of growth and other economic performance indicators. Within the context of opening up the economy, we can conceptualize reforms as falling into two groups, the first involving redrawing of state–market boundaries and the second concerned with reconfiguring governmental institutions themselves, at several levels of the federation. The first group includes financial sector reforms, assignment of regulatory powers, infrastructure development, and privatization. The second group includes tax reforms, reform of center–state fiscal transfer mechanisms, and decentralization.

Section III provides an overview of India's institutions of federalism. We summarize the legislative system, which is the essence of the federal structure (because it institutionalizes constituents' expression of subnational authority), as well as federal aspects of various branches of government, including the judiciary, bureaucracy, and regional aspects of India's political parties. We then describe the constitutional assignment of powers to different levels of the federation, including tax and expenditure assignments. We summarize the intergovernmental transfer system, in terms of both its initial conception and its subsequent evolution. Finally, we discuss the formal and informal institutions of intergovernmental relations, such as the National Development Council and the Inter-State Council.

Section IV examines the interaction of globalization and India's federal system by looking at national versus subnational reforms. For example, greater openness has increased competition for Indian manufacturing, but both federal- and state-level controls on product markets substantially

---

[1] For examples of recent interest in the intersection of federalism, globalization, and economic policy see Sáez (2002), which is specifically on India, but includes some comparisons to China, and the journal symposium introduced by Watts (2001), which covers a wide range of countries and political and economic issues.

[2] See, for example, Srinivasan and Tendulkar (2002).

hinder the achievement of competitiveness, despite the removal of many industrial-licensing controls. We examine the extent to which state and central policies may need to respond, based on the constitutional assignments of authority. For example, agricultural policy reforms will require a joint approach. We examine the impact of labor market restrictions and government ownership and look at the possible role of the center and states in policy reforms. Finally, we touch on infrastructure issues, such as the extreme problems of the state-owned power sector, and the important federal dimensions that make reform more difficult there. In discussing the financial sector, we highlight the problems caused for the financial sector as a whole by state and central fiscal deficits. We trace this problem to the continued importance of the central government in controlling the financial sector, including the effective "parking" of fiscal deficits in the banking sector. We examine the changes in policy with respect to foreign direct investment (FDI) and the implications of the new ability of state governments to directly seek FDI. We discuss the possibility that privatization of the financial sector can act as a disciplining device on governments at all levels and the possible role of capital account liberalization in achieving rapid, effective privatization of the financial sector.

In Section V we turn to issues of intergovernmental relations in the context of reform. Thus we view the reform process as encompassing the federal system, rather than just interacting with it. We review the ongoing process of strengthening local governments, as well as past and proposed reforms in the intergovernmental transfer and tax systems. We examine the role of the tax system in promoting or hindering the emergence of a unified internal market for goods and services in India and study the potential for reform of tax assignments, tax rates, and tax enforcement. We argue for harder subnational budget constraints as a feature of a reformed federal transfer system. To some degree, reforms in federal governance hold the key to opening the door to further reform elsewhere, by reducing the fiscal burden placed on the private sector by government deficits. We acknowledge the political economy aspects of reform of governance, and we discuss possibilities for politically acceptable packages of fiscal reforms, such as combinations of changes in tax assignment that would be acceptable to the center as well as the state governments.

We also examine issues of growing regional inequality in the context of an economy with fewer barriers to the movement of capital. We relate this to possible implications for regional policy, tax assignments, the intergovernmental transfer system, and the need to harden subnational budget constraints. Section VI offers a summary and conclusion, where we tie in our discussion of real and financial sector reforms and reforms of federal governance with globalization as a process that provides both pressures for change and instruments to achieve positive change.

II. OVERVIEW OF INDIA'S ECONOMY AND RECENT REFORM

India is a large and poor developing country. After independence in 1947, it pursued economic policies that gave the government a primary role in promoting economic development. Although the country's size dictated some kind of federal structure, the arrangements that were adopted in the Constitution (ratified in 1950) and their subsequent evolution gave the central government a dominant position vis-à-vis the constituent units of the nation (states and territories). India's leaders aspired toward an indigenous version of Soviet-influenced socialism, with government as benevolent guardian, leavened with a smattering of Gandhian influences in favor of smallness, self-sufficiency, and rural traditions. The ruling Congress Party adopted a resolution in 1955 that to achieve a "socialistic pattern of society" would be India's objective. This was later incorporated into the Constitution through an amendment in 1976.

Through the 1970s, India's economic growth was reasonable, averaging 3.75% per year, but this was not rapid enough to significantly diminish the number of poor people, nor to deal comfortably with the strains associated with governing a country with substantial ethnic, linguistic, and religious diversity along with economic inequalities. Nevertheless, India was able to preserve both its unity and the political system of parliamentary democracy adopted in its early years. However, this political stability was accompanied by the evolution of an economic system riddled with increasing rigidities, inefficiencies, and corruption, the so-called license-quota-permit raj. This system was accompanied by political and economic centralization, with Soviet-style development planning, but with looser implementation, largely determined at the national level. Some states, such as West Bengal and Kerala, did pursue more independent policies, but these were limited by centrally determined constraints. However, no state government seriously challenged the "socialist" approach to economic management. Meanwhile, with some state-level exceptions (e.g., West Bengal and Kerala), there was relatively little progress in potentially socialist policies such as land reform or universal primary education.

In the 1980s, partly through fresh ideological influences, and partly through the observation of faster growth in many East Asian economies, India's economic policymakers at the national level began to attempt some changes in the details of – if not yet the overall approach to – the role of government in the country's economic development, introducing some liberalization in the trade regime, loosening domestic industrial controls, and promoting investment in modern technologies for areas such as telecommunications. Although this reform process was restricted to the center, it coincided with some weakening of central political control by the end of the decade. Growth accelerated to 5.8% during 1980–1990, but this came at the cost of macroeconomic imbalances. Fiscal and current account deficits worsened from the end of the 1980s, with the effects of heavy borrowing at high interest rates compounded by factors such as the collapse of the Soviet Union (a major trading partner at the time), the invasion of Kuwait, and reversals in capital and remittance inflows from abroad.

In 1991 India faced a severe macroeconomic crisis, and this circumstance became the occasion for a substantial advance in the pace and nature of economic reforms that were being attempted. In particular, the major steps taken were further trade liberalization, in the form of reductions in tariffs and conversion of quantitative restrictions to tariffs, and a sweeping away of a large segment of restrictions on domestic industrial investment. These two changes in the early 1990s have come to symbolize or encapsulate the term "economic reform" in India. These microeconomic reforms were accompanied by efforts to reduce the central government fiscal deficit.

Note that the collapse of the Soviet Union in 1991 and the stellar growth performance of China after its opening to the world economy and initiation of market-oriented reforms in the 1980s were two very significant developments that forced systemic reform in India in the 1990s, as compared to a temporary liberalization (soon reversed) in an earlier balance of payments crisis in 1966. The more thoroughgoing nature of the 1990s reform also opened up space for action by state governments, as we discuss in the following.

The move to reduce the role of government in directly controlling the working of markets had additional implications. It was recognized that sectors such as finance and telecommunications required a new set of regulatory structures suitable for an environment in which bureaucrats were no longer making discretionary judgments on a case-by-case basis. This need was strengthened by the direct and indirect impacts of technological change in such sectors. Furthermore, it was recognized that removing industrial investment controls could not by itself solve India's problem of slow growth; this action needed to be complemented by restructuring the

Table 7.1. *Central and State Fiscal Deficits (% of GDP)*

	Center	States	Total[i]
1990–1991	6.6	3.3	9.4
1991–1992	4.7	2.7	7.0
1992–1993	4.8	2.6	7.0
1993–1994	6.4	2.3	8.3
1994–1995	4.7	2.8	7.1
1995–1996	4.2	2.6	6.5
1996–1997	4.1	2.7	6.4
1997–1998	4.8	2.9	7.3
1998–1999	5.1	4.2	9.0
1999–2000	5.4	4.6	9.6
2000–2001	5.7	4.3	9.8
2001–2002	6.1	4.2	9.9
2002–2003	5.9	4.7	10.1
2003–2004	4.6	5.1	9.4
2004–2005[i]	4.4	n.a.	n.a.

[i] The combined deficit indicators net out the inter-governmental transactions between the center and states and do not equal the sum of the deficits of the center and the states.
[ii] Budget estimate.
Sources: RBI Annual Reports (RBI, 2001, 2002, 2003), Finance Minister's Budget Speech 2004.

working of the labor market and by improving the economy's physical and institutional infrastructure. Achieving the first of these objectives has been hampered by understandable interest-group pressures; the second goal has been constrained by the high level of the government's fiscal deficit, which, after an initial decline, through some fiscal consolidation, has climbed even beyond the 1991-crisis mark.

The high fiscal deficit is largely traceable to subsidies to interest groups, as well as the nature of the interaction between the central and state governments. Table 7.1 summarizes the trends in central and state fiscal deficits over the 1990s.[3] It shows that much of the deterioration in the fiscal deficit has occurred at the state government level. Both the center and the states were severely affected by the large pay increases granted to central government employees in 1997–1998, followed by

[3] For more detailed discussions of these trends, see Acharya (2002), Rao (2002), Srinivasan (2002), and Singh and Srinivasan (2004).

similar increases at the state level the following year.[4] One can also point a finger at relative political instability at the center, beginning in 1996, with government by disparate coalitions becoming the norm. This trend has continued through the election and change of government in 2004. Although "fiscal responsibility" legislation passed in 2003 set firm deficit reduction targets, governments at the center and the states continue to promise subsidies and transfer payments that hinder expenditure control.[5]

Despite the internal political roadblocks to accomplishing comprehensive economic reforms, India was able to achieve a slight acceleration of growth in the 1990s as compared to the previous decade. However, growth statistics indicate that there was a deceleration in the latter half of the 1990s, even before the current global recession took hold. Tables 7.2 and 7.3 provide a summary of the size and structure of India's economy and changes over time as well as economic performance along a wide range of dimensions over the past two decades. One of the striking features of growth in the past decade has been the anemic performance of Indian industry and the associated lack of a shift from agriculture to industry in the share of GDP. In contrast, services have done well, partly as a result of the boom in software exports and, more recently, in information-technology-enabled services such as call centers. These aspects of services, and remittances from nonresident Indians, have contributed to India's reasonably good export performance and to its avoidance of further balance of payments difficulties.

From the perspective of trying to capture the benefits of participating more fully in the global economy, reform, though triggered by a short-run crisis, must also be viewed in the context of long-run globalizing trends. Globalization may bring down prices of some goods, lead to more efficient allocations of factors, and allow relatively capital-scarce countries such as India to gain greater access to foreign capital and technology for enhancing economic growth. This is the standard way in which openness supports private economic activity (and potentially also public activity, especially if the government produces private goods). From the perspective of the government, however, there may be new challenges in a world of factor

---

[4] This is an example of interest group pressures at work: The pay award was larger than that recommended by the technical advisory body, the Fifth Pay Commission, and was not accompanied by the reduction in staffing that the Commission also recommended. See Acharya (2002) and Srinivasan (2002) for further discussion.

[5] For example, see Singh and Srinivasan (2004) for a general discussion, and Srinivasan (2004) for an overview of the latest government's Common Minimum Programme.

Table 7.2. *Gross Domestic Product and Its Sectoral Share*

At 1993–1994 Prices	GDP (At Factor Cost in Rupees)	Sectoral share in GDP[i] (%)		
		Agriculture & Allied	Industry	Services
1950–1951	141557	55.4	16.1	28.5
1960–1961	207704	50.9	20.0	29.1
1970–1971	298580	44.5	23.6	31.9
1980–1981	404246	38.1	25.9	36.0
1990–1991	694925	30.9	30.0	39.1
1991–1992	705149	30.0	29.4	40.6
1992–1993	737018	30.2	29.1	40.7
1993–1994	781345	33.6	23.7	42.7
1994–1995	835864	33.0	24.2	42.8
1995–1996	896990	30.7	25.3	44.0
1996–1997	964390	31.0	25.2	43.8
1997–1998	1012816	29.2	25.3	45.5
1998–1999	1081834	29.2	24.7	46.1
1999–2000	1148369	27.4	24.3	48.3
2000–2001	1198592	26.2	24.9	48.9
2001–2002	1267833	26.4	24.4	49.2
2002–2003	1318321	24.4	24.9	50.7
2003–2004	1426701	24.8	24.0	51.2

[i] Figures up to 1992–1993 relate to prior to revision of GDP.
Sources: http://meadev.nic.in/economy/gdp.htm and http://mospi.nic.in/t1_1996_2003q2.htm.

and goods mobility. The ability of the government to tax is affected, since mobile factors can escape the incidence of taxes that initially are placed on them. Furthermore, regulatory policies can be subject to similar problems in the face of factor mobility, as in fears of races to the bottom in setting regulatory standards.

The reforms of the 1990s gave state governments more freedom to make policies independently, and this has extended the impacts of openness and globalization to the subnational level.[6] In particular, whereas only the national government can determine import duties, state governments now can affect the incentives of foreign capital to enter their jurisdictions. From the perspective of an Indian state, capital from another

---

[6] The responses of the states were varied, as were the results. Bajpai and Sachs (1999) provide a detailed survey and scorecard of the efforts and outcomes for fifteen major states, arguing that the enthusiastic reformers have done better in terms of human development as well as narrow economic well-being. They treat the states as independent actors (within constraints imposed by the center), whereas in this chapter we emphasize the interactions and overlaps of national and subnational reforms.

Table 7.3. *Major Economic Indicators – Annual Growth Rates (%)*

Year	Gross National Product[i]	Gross Domestic Product[i]	Agricultural Production Index	Food Grains Production	Industrial Production Index	Electricity Generation	Wholesale Price Index	Consumer Price Index	Money Supply (M3)	Imports[i]	Exports[i]
1981–1982	5.8	6.0	5.6	2.9	9.3	9.9	–	12.3	12	-4.4	2.6
1982–1983	2.7	3.1	-3.8	-2.9	3.2	7	4.9	8.8	16.6	-2.6	4.6
1983–1984	7.5	7.7	13.7	17.7	6.7	7.6	7.5	12.1	18.2	3.5	3.8
1984–1985	4.2	4.3	-1.2	-4.5	8.6	12.1	6.5	6.3	19	-5.9	4.5
1985–1986	4.5	4.5	2.5	3.4	8.7	8.4	4.4	6.8	16	11.5	-9.9
1986–1987	4.1	4.3	-3.7	-4.7	9.1	9.8	5.8	8.7	18.6	-2.1	9.4
1987–1988	3.6	3.8	-0.8	-2.1	7.3	8.8	8.2	8.8	16	9.1	24.1
1988–1989	10.1	10.5	21.4	21	8.7	10.2	7.5	9.4	17.8	13.6	15.6
1989–1990	6.7	6.7	2.1	0.6	8.6	11.2	7.4	6.1	19.4	8.8	18.9
1990–1991	5.5	5.6	3.8	3.2	8.2	7.8	10.3	11.6	15.1	13.5	9.2
1991–1992	1.1	1.3	-2.0	-4.5	0.6	9.1	13.7	13.5	19.3	-19.4	-1.5
1992–1993	5.1	5.1	4.1	6.6	2.3	5	10.1	9.6	15.7	12.7	3.8
1993–1994	5.9	5.9	3.8	2.7	6.0	7.3	8.4	7.5	18.4	6.5	20.0
1994–1995	7.2	7.3	4.9	3.8	8.4	8.1	12.5	10.1	22.3	22.9	18.4
1995–1996	7.5	7.3	-2.7	-5.8	12.8	8.6	8.1	10.2	13.7	28.0	20.9
1996–1997	8.2	7.8	9.1	10.5	5.6	4.3	4.6	9.4	15.9	6.5	5.3
1997–1998	4.8	4.8	-5.4	-3.5	6.6	6.6	4.4	6.8	17.3	6.1	4.5
1998–1999	6.4	6.5	7.6	6.1	4.1	6.5	5.9	13.1	19.4	2.2	-5.1
1999–2000	6.2	6.1	-0.5	2.7	6.7	6.9	3.3	3.4	13.9	17.2	10.8
2000–2001	3.9	4.0	-6.3	-6.6	5.0	4.5	7.0	3.8	15.0	1.7	21.0
2001–2002	6.1	5.8	7.6	8.6	2.7	4.4	1.6	5.2	14.1	1.7	-1.6
2002–2003	3.7	4.0	-15.6	-18.4	5.7	3.2	6.1	4.1	12.7	19.4	20.3
2003–2004	8.1	8.1	–	–	6.9	–	4.5	3.7	16.6	22.8	17.1

[i] Revised (at 1993–1994 prices).

Sources: http://meadev.nic.in/economy/mei.htm, http://www.nic.in/stat/stat.act.t1.htm, Reserve Bank of India,
http://indiabudget.nic.in/es2001-02/chapt2002/tab12.pdf, http://indiabudget.nic.in/es2001-02/chapt2002/tab16.pdf,
http://indiabudget.nic.in/es2003-04/tables.htm.

country or from another state can be viewed through the same lens, and it must be treated equally in typical policy environments. The final impacts of the entry of capital on a subnational government will therefore depend also on the internal mobility of capital and labor. Hence, in a federal system, attention must be paid to internal mobility of goods and factors, in addition to external liberalization. Subnational tax and regulatory policies can assume greater importance in a scenario of economic reform under globalization. A further consideration is that the fiscal health of the states that results from their policies is likely to impinge on the entire nation's credit rating in world capital markets.[7] We shall explore these aspects of India's subnational economic reforms in Sections IV and V.

Another federal aspect of India's reform is that the decade of the 1990s has seen an increase in regional inequality in some dimensions. Although inequalities may have widened within states as well (for example, the coastal and urban areas of Maharashtra and Gujarat versus their interior rural regions), the main focus has been and will be on widening disparities across the states themselves. This is natural, given the size and political importance of the states, and the fact that the states are the direct and indirect channels for significant financial transfers from the central government. We also consider whether aspects of economic reform, larger global economic forces, and state-level initial conditions and policy responses are increasing regional inequalities within the country, and whether the mechanisms that exist within India's federal structures for managing regional inequalities are adequate.

To conclude this section we return to the national-level overview. Underlying the aggregate performance statistics in Tables 7.2 and 7.3, we have a story of incomplete economic reforms, with sectors such as agriculture still shackled by an inefficient public procurement and distribution system and severe input market distortions, industry hampered by small-scale reservations and inefficient financing, a financial sector still dominated by direct and indirect public control of investible resources, and labor market rigidities that hamper the entire organized (as opposed to informal) segment of the economy. Liberalization of trade and foreign investment – the "globalization" aspect of India's reforms – has helped in some areas, but has not been sufficient, neither to promote widespread competitiveness nor to overcome or rectify the poor state of India's

---

[7] The mechanism by which this occurs can be indirect, through contingent liabilities arising from explicit central counter guarantees for state guarantees to foreign corporations, or direct, through the observation of larger deficits for the center and states combined.

Figure 7.1. India: states and union territories.

infrastructure. Thus the economic reform agenda in India remains lengthy as well as complicated.

III. INDIA'S FEDERAL STRUCTURES

III.1. Political and Administrative Structures

We preface a discussion of the institutions and mechanisms that govern fiscal federal arrangements in India, particularly center–state transfers and loans, with an overview of India's broader federal structure. India is a constitutional democracy, composed of twenty-eight states and seven "Union Territories" (see Figure 7.1). Of the seven, two Union Territories (Delhi and Pondicherry) have their own elected legislatures, whereas the rest are governed directly by appointees of the center. All the states have elected legislatures, with chief ministers in the executive role. Each state also has a governor, nominally appointed by the president, but effectively an agent of the prime minister. The governor normally has only a minor political role at the state level. However, governors have, in the past, used special constitutional provisions (notably Article 356) to dismiss elected legislatures, though this practice has been reined in more recently. The Constitution also assigns certain statutory powers to the states. The exact nature of this assignment, and how it has played out in practice, determine the extent of centralization within the federation.[8]

In addition, since many of the Indian states are quite large in terms of population (with the largest dozen being comparable in population to larger European countries), devolution of powers to the states without any further decentralization below that level may still represent a relatively centralized federation. In practice, devolution of economic and political power to both the states and to local government bodies has arguably been weak compared to other federal systems, since both constitutional assignments and the subsequent exercise of legislative powers have tended to be in the direction of greater centralization. Centralization has also been reflected in bureaucratic and judicial institutions and their interactions with the legislative and executive branches of government, as we elaborate later.

The primary expression of statutory constitutional authority in India comes through directly elected parliamentary-style governments at the national and state level, as well as nascent directly elected government bodies at various local levels.[9] In legislatures at each level, there is the usual playing out of bargaining among individuals, factions, and parties, as analyzed theoretically by authors such as Baron and Ferejohn (1989) and Inman and Rubinfeld (1997). Regional and personal factions have always been important in Indian politics, but the main spoils have typically been control of various ministries, rather than provisions attached to specific pieces of legislation. There have been some ideological factors at work in Indian politics (various shades of socialism, for example), but these are often dominated by material interests.

To the extent that the essence of federalism is based on representative democratic politics at the subnational level, the role of political parties in

---

[8] There are various special provisions (e.g., affecting scope of governance and local property ownership) with respect to the northeastern hill states, and even more so for Jammu and Kashmir (Article 370), though the latter's constitutional autonomy has been reduced over time. This reduction represents a relatively easy amendment procedure, which has tended to increase centralization; examples of this tendency are offered later in this section.

[9] These are all single-constituency first-past-the-post elections, but with some seats reserved for disadvantaged groups, such as scheduled castes (erstwhile "untouchables") at each level.

the interactions between central- and state-level politics is a crucial aspect of federal structures. To illustrate, consider the extreme case where government powers are notionally decentralized, with all residuary powers assigned to the state level, but the national and all state governments are controlled by a single, rigidly hierarchical political party. Here the outcome will effectively be the same as in a centralized, unitary system, since decisions are made at the top of the political hierarchy. For example, during the Nehru era, the prime minister's personal authority and prestige were combined with almost complete legislative control of the center and the states by the Congress Party led by Nehru. In such circumstances, center–state relations were often played out within the ranks of the Congress Party.

Over time, Indian political parties have embodied varying degrees of centralization, including the regional political bosses of the earlier Congress Party,[10] the tightly controlled personalized approach characteristic of the later Congress Party under Indira Gandhi, the more institutionalized hierarchy of the Bharatiya Janata Party (BJP), when it was the main ruling party, and the emergence of explicit regional parties, which have often been partners in ruling coalitions in the last few years.

Certainly, in the past decade, regional parties throughout the country have become significant as a political force. Overall, however, we argue that the institutional expression of federal or centralized structures within political parties has not been a major independent factor in shaping India's federal system, because other forms of central control – administrative, legal, and fiscal – have mattered more.[11] As an example of central control, Article 356 of the Constitution has been used quite liberally to replace or suspend elected state governments that were deemed unsatisfactory by the central government.[12]

---

[10] Following Manor (1995), we may characterize the Congress Party structure itself as federal in nature at this time. In some respects, however, Nehru's personal authority after independence allowed him to dominate decision making, as we have already noted. The preindependence Congress Party was actually more decentralized, with provincial units playing a significant role, and provincial leaders being powerful in their own right, with prominent positions in the formal party hierarchy.

[11] There are many nuances that this conclusion glosses over. See Rao and Singh (2001) for a more detailed discussion.

[12] The use of Article 356 appeared often to violate the spirit of the provision, which was designed for situations of government breakdown. It was in invoking Article 356 that state governors became direct agents of the prime minister. Often, removal of a state government was followed by lengthy direct rule by the central government. Interestingly, the central government has retreated substantially from this approach in the past few years, helped by a stand taken by the president at the time.

More recently, following a provision in Article 263 of the Constitution, and recommendations of the Administrative Reforms Commission in 1969 and the Sarkaria Commission on Center–State Relations in 1988, the Inter-State Council (ISC) was created in 1990. The ISC has since become a forum where some political and economic issues of joint concern can be collectively discussed and possibly resolved. The ISC includes the prime minister, state chief ministers, and several central cabinet ministers as members. Although the ISC is merely advisory and has been viewed as weak – especially since central governing coalitions give regional parties more direct say in policy (Majeed, 2002) – it has formalized collective discussion and approval of several important matters impinging on India's federal arrangements, including tax sharing and interstate water disputes.[13] An older, similar body is the National Development Council (NDC), but it is narrower in scope. The NDC serves as a forum for bargaining over five-year-plan allocations. It is chaired by the Prime Minister, and its members include selected central Cabinet Ministers, Chief Ministers of the states, and members of the Planning Commission.[14]

The next level of governance that embodies aspects of federal structures is the bureaucracy. Just as elected politicians ideally act as agents of their constituents, bureaucrats in turn act as the agents of elected officials. Bureaucrats, as career employees, are partly insulated from political whims and pressures, but ultimately in a democracy they must be subordinate to elected representatives. Therefore a unitary, hierarchical bureaucracy cannot by itself negate a federal political structure in the same way that a powerful, centralized, national political party might. However, a

---

[13] Sáez (2002) provides a detailed history of the conception and creation of the ISC, as well as an assessment of its working to date (Chapter 4). In his conclusion, he characterizes the ISC as "a disappointment" and "far from being effective" (p. 216). Although he is right in pointing out the many weaknesses and failures of the ISC, particularly with respect to changing Article 356, or enabling implementation of its many recommendations, we have noted instances of its usefulness in developing agreement on specific institutional reforms that have federalist dimensions. Kapur (2001) provides other examples as well. To understand precisely where the ISC plays a positive role, note that it has not succeeded in implementing its own independent agenda, but it is able to facilitate intergovernmental agreement on issues brought to the table by the center. In Section V, we discuss the potential for expanding such a role, in contrast to Sáez's view of the ISC as "emblematic of a broader failure of inter-governmental institutions in India" (p. 216).

[14] The NDC was set up, at the suggestion of the Planning Commission, by a cabinet resolution to serve as the highest reviewing and advisory body for planning. Its terms of reference cover the formulation of long-term guidelines for the national plans, and all matters of social economic policy. At each stage of five-year-plan preparation (at both central and state levels) the NDC weighs in with its advice and it formally approves the plans before they are presented for discussion, debate, and eventual approval by the parliament and state legislatures. See Reddy (1979) for further description.

centralized bureaucracy can act as the agent of such a political party, against the requirements of a federal system. There have been elements of such action in the workings of Indian bureaucracy at the subnational level, serving the interests of the central government over those of state or local governments.

The Indian bureaucracy is provided constitutional recognition. The central and state-level tiers of the "public services" are given shape through the provisions of Part XIV of the Constitution. Since each political layer of government requires its own administrative apparatus, any bureaucracy in a federation will have a federal character. In particular, state governments must be able to appoint and dismiss bureaucrats to implement state-level policies.[15] This is certainly the case in India, where there is a central bureaucracy as well as an independent bureaucracy in each state.

The key component of the bureaucracy is the Indian Administrative Service (IAS). IAS members are chosen by a centralized process, and they are trained together. However, they are then assigned to particular states and become, technically as well as in most practical matters, members of a state-level bureaucratic hierarchy as well. Although an IAS member's entire early career is spent within the home state, and senior appointments at the state level carry considerable power and prestige, the greatest attraction lies with appointments within the central government. The structure of the IAS was designed as a compromise between, on the one hand, the desire to have an effective apparatus at the state level, where most of the tasks of day-to-day administration, development, and law and order were assigned by the Constitution, and, on the other hand, the fear of promoting regional loyalties over national ones (with the further fear of national disintegration). However, this compromise has been somewhat problematic for the working of federalism, since conflicts arise between state and central politicians (the latter acting through IAS members assigned to the central government) in directing state-level IAS bureaucrats.

At the national and state levels, the judiciary constitutes a distinct branch of government, though the legislative branch influences appointments. At the local level, IAS members are vested with some judicial authority. In judging whether the law was broken and who broke the law, the judiciary acts as a specialized agent of elected officials who frame laws.

---

[15] In practice, dismissal is almost impossible, something that is true for the entire organized sector in India. However, state governments use (and misuse) the power to transfer bureaucrats to assert political control over the bureaucracy.

The higher levels of the judiciary also act as judges of the laws themselves, within the context of the overarching legal and constitutional framework.

The Supreme Court stands at the top of the Indian judicial hierarchy. Its powers include broad original and appellate jurisdiction and the right to pass on the constitutionality of laws passed by Parliament. In practice, there has been conflict between the Supreme Court and the legislature/executive over the scope of these powers, and their boundaries remain subject to bargaining, though one can generalize that the Court has been overshadowed by the central legislative/executive branchs.[16] The President, in consultation with the Prime Minister, appoints justices of the Court.

At the state level, below the Supreme Court, are the high courts. Each high court's justices are appointed by the president, in consultation with the Chief Justice of the Supreme Court and the state's governor. Paralleling the situation at the center, the state's Chief Minister is in a position to influence the Governor's advice. High courts also have both original and appellate jurisdiction. In addition, they superintend the work of all courts within the state, including district courts, as well as various courts subordinate to the district courts. These subordinate courts are specialized, with smaller civil matters being separated from criminal cases, for example. Criminal cases are dealt with in magistrates' courts, where IAS members serve.

The formal judiciary, therefore, is a well-defined hierarchy, with a relatively clear assignment of tasks. This assignment and hierarchy are overly centralized and not enough matters are disposed of at lower level courts. This reflects a lack of resources devoted to lower level courts (though the resource problem exists at all levels), as well as a centralized assignment of scope of jurisdictions. The problem is compounded by the nature of the appeals process, and by the failure of higher level courts to control appeals.[17] Also, judges below the state level are typically not appointed by local government officials, representing a significant departure from a federal system below the state level.

---

[16] In early constitutional decisions, the Court placed fairly narrow limits on the power of the legislature to amend the Constitution, and in specific instances, it has allowed the center to extend its powers over the states quite liberally (see Footnotes 8, 12, 18, and 20). The executive, particularly under Indira Gandhi, has also tried to control judicial appointments to its advantage. Many of the broader issues of federal institutions are being considered by the current Constitutional Review Commission of India.

[17] "Public interest petitions" to the higher courts, while democracy enhancing in spirit, have also sometimes been used for obstructionist purposes to benefit particular interest groups.

The inefficiencies of the judicial system in India reflect not only inadequate decentralization within the judiciary itself but also inadequate delegation of powers by the legislative/executive branch. In particular, the expansion of state intervention in the economy that occurred in the first three decades after independence, with the central government encroaching on the states' assignments, took place effectively outside judicial review.[18] Inadequate judicial power is a constitutional problem, because this delegation is absent in some of the particulars of the Constitution. A weaker central legislature in the 1990s appears to be allowing the Supreme Court to play a more effective checking role. However, it does not solve the resource allocation problems that must be corrected for the smoother working of day-to-day judicial functions.[19]

Finally, the police have a special role, involving both the bureaucracy and the judicial system. Ideally, the police are impartial investigators and monitors, preventing violations of law where possible and complementing the judiciary in enforcement. However, the police are also organized as a bureaucracy under the control of politicians – like other branches of administration, but unlike the judiciary, with its notional independence. The actual functioning of the police in India has become subject to politicization and the encroachment of the central government into law and order, constitutionally a state subject.[20] India has a variety of central and state police forces, with the Indian Police Service (IPS), the superior officer cadre, being organized on similar dual lines to the IAS. This puts its members on a different footing than members of state police forces, who are recruited directly by state governments, even though IPS officers are assigned to particular states.[21]

---

[18] Furthermore, the 42nd Amendment in 1976, during the emergency declared by Prime Minister Indira Gandhi, moved the "Administration of justice; constitution and organization of all courts, except the Supreme Court and the High Courts" from the State list to the Concurrent list.

[19] The pressure for correction might come from competition among subnational jurisdictions pursuing commercial motives. As states and localities try to attract investment and commercial activity, they may come under pressure to provide supportive judicial systems. This argument applies more to contract enforcement, or property rights enforcement more broadly, than to the criminal justice system. In this respect, the lack of training of India's lawyers and judges in even rudimentary economics has sometimes led to judicial decisions with substantial negative impacts on the economy, as in judicial interpretations of labor laws.

[20] Item 2A in the Union list, inserted by the 42nd Amendment, gives the center power to deploy "any other force subject to the control of the Union." This need not always be a negative: For example, state governments may fail to protect minority rights, as in the case of Gujarat in 2002; however, there the central government also failed to act.

[21] For example, recently the chief minister of Tamil, Nadu, J. Jayalalitha, came into conflict with the center over the posting of IPS officers in her state.

To conclude this description, we note that the existence of different dimensions of governance implies that a federal political system cannot exist simply through a constitutional assignment of responsibilities to different layers of government. Each level of government in a federal system must have the authority not only to raise revenues but also to carry out decisions made at that level. In India, the IAS, the IPS, and the judiciary are all perhaps more centralized than they need to be, given the current federal political system. Whereas independent India began with a relatively circumscribed federal model, independent political competition at the state government level has thrived in recent years. This decentralization has not been fully matched in the other dimensions of government, but it may need to be for a more effective federal system to operate. The growing relative importance of regional parties, coupled with the tendency for regional concentration of "national" parties such as the BJP and the Congress Party, appears to be leading to some change in this direction.[22]

III.2. Assignments and Transfers

Assignments of authority include important nonfiscal dimensions, as we have briefly discussed in the context of politics, administration, and law. However, control over how public resources are raised and spent represents a crucial aspect of any federal system. We describe the tax and expenditure assignments that form the basis of India's fiscal federal institutions, and we consider the system of center–state transfers resulting from and complementing the assignment of fiscal authority in India. We also consider the nature of intergovernmental loans and their importance as implicit transfers.

The Indian Constitution, in its Seventh Schedule, assigns the powers and functions of the center and the states. The Schedule specifies the exclusive powers of the center in the Union list and exclusive powers of the states in the State list; those falling under the joint jurisdiction are placed in the Concurrent list. All residual powers are assigned to the center. The nature of the assignments is fairly typical of federal nations and broadly fits with economist's theoretical rationale.[23] The functions of the central

---

[22] A separate issue from the degree of decentralization in federal administrative structures is that of corruption. Although it can be argued that decentralization increases the inefficiency created by corruption, which is pervasive at all levels, this is not a logically necessary consequence. See Singh (2004) for a discussion of these issues.

[23] Economic theories of government are based on the idea that public (nonrival and nonexclusive) goods are not well provided by the market mechanism. This does not in

government are those required to maintain macroeconomic stability and international trade and relations and those having implications for more than one state. The major subjects assigned to the states comprise public order, public health, agriculture, irrigation, land rights, fisheries and industries, and minor minerals. The states also assume a significant role for subjects in the Concurrent list such as education and transportation, social security, and social insurance.

The assignment of tax powers in India is based on a principle of separation; that is, tax categories are exclusively assigned either to the center or to the states. Most broad-based (in principle though not in practice) taxes have been assigned to the center, including taxes on income and wealth from nonagricultural sources, corporation tax, taxes on production (excluding those on alcoholic liquors), and customs duty. A long list of taxes is assigned to the states. However, only the tax on the sale and purchase of goods has been significant for state revenues. This narrow effective tax base is largely a result of political economy factors that have eroded or prevented the use of taxes on agricultural land or incomes by state governments. The fact that the center has also been assigned all residual powers implies that taxes not mentioned in any of the lists automatically fall into its domain.

The tax assignment system has some notable anomalies. The separation of income tax powers between the center and states based on whether the source of income is agricultural or nonagricultural has opened up avenues for both avoidance and evasion of the personal income tax. Second, even though in a legal sense taxes on production (central

itself justify a federal governance structure. However, if governments are not perfectly informed and intrinsically benevolent, subnational governments may be better able to judge the desired levels of local public goods and, potentially, can be given more specific electoral incentives to do so than national governments. The assignment of expenditure responsibilities then follows, taking account of economies of scale, access to resources, and externalities or spillovers. With respect to revenue authority, tax assignments are what matter as a first approximation (neglecting intergenerational issues), since the interest on borrowing must also come out of taxes. Allocational efficiency is the usual starting point here. For example, mobility across jurisdictions makes it harder for subnational jurisdictions to raise revenue from taxes than for the central government. Of course for internationally mobile factors, even national jurisdictions face problems in collecting taxes. Also, mobility depends on the relative benefits provided through public expenditures, so that jurisdictions can counter mobility by providing appropriate benefits at the margin to those who are taxed. Finally, tax coordination by subnational jurisdictions can be an effective alternative to central assignment (see Section V). If efficiency implies that more taxes should be collected by the center, there will be a mismatch between revenues and expenditures for subnational jurisdictions. The result of the differing determinants of optimal assignments of expenditure and tax authorities can be a "vertical fiscal imbalance," where subnational governments rely on the center for revenue transfers.

manufacturing excises) and sale (state sales taxes) are separate, they tax the same base, causing overlapping and leaving less tax room to the latter. Finally, the states are allowed to levy taxes on the sale and purchase of goods (entry 54 in the State list) but not services. This, besides providing avenues for tax evasion and avoidance, has also posed problems in designing and implementing a comprehensive value added tax (VAT), as discussed further in Section V.

The realized outcome of the Indian assignments of tax and expenditure authority, their particular history of implementation, and the response of different levels of government and tax payers to the assignment has been a substantial vertical fiscal imbalance. In 1998–1999, the states on average raised about 35% of total revenues, but they incurred about 57% of total expenditures.[24] Transfers from the center made up the balance. Perverse fiscal incentives for the states in this system have, in fact, increased the imbalance. Moreover, the states' ability to finance their current expenditures from their own sources of revenues has tended to decline over time, from 69% in 1955–1956 to about 55% in the 1990s. In terms of total expenditure, the states were even more dependent on the center, with only 44% of their overall spending being covered by own revenue in 1998–1999.

The Constitution recognized that its assignment of tax powers and expenditure functions would create imbalances between expenditure "needs" and abilities to raise revenue. The imbalances could be both vertical, among different levels of government, and horizontal, among different units within a subcentral level. Therefore, the Constitution provided for the sharing of the proceeds of certain centrally levied taxes (e.g., noncorporate income tax, Article 270, and Union excise duty, Article 272) with the states, as well as grants to the states from the Consolidated Fund of India. Recent constitutional changes in this scheme have simplified this sharing arrangement, and these are discussed in Section V.[25] The shares of the center and the states and their allocation among different states, are determined by the Finance Commission, which is also a constitutional creation and is appointed by the President of India every five years (or earlier if needed). In addition to tax devolution, the Finance Commission is also required to recommend grants to the states in need of assistance under Article 275.

---

[24] See Rao and Singh (2002, Table 7.1). Figures for subsequent years are quite similar.

[25] Seignorage revenue of the central government is not recognized in the Constitution and is not shared with the states.

So far, twelve Finance Commissions have made recommendations and, barring a few exceptions, these have been accepted by the central government. However, the methodology and processes of these Commissions have been criticized. There are two main criticisms: (i) The scope of the Finance Commissions through the presidential terms of reference has been too restricted; and (ii) The design of their transfer schemes has reduced state government incentives for fiscal discipline (through "gap-filling" transfers), while doing relatively little to reduce interstate inequities. Note that larger government deficits at the subnational level and, to some extent, increases in interstate inequalities in the past decade are related to the functioning of India's intergovernmental transfer system. We shall return to these issues in Section V.

Whereas the Finance Commission decides on tax shares and makes grants, a separate body, the Planning Commission, makes grants and loans (in the ratio 30:70 for the major states) for implementing development plans. Historically, as development planning gained emphasis, the Planning Commission became a major dispenser of such funds to the states. As there is no specific provision in the Constitution for such plan transfers, the central government channeled them under the miscellaneous, and ostensibly limited, provisions of Article 282.[26] Before 1969, plan transfers were project-based. Since then, the distribution has been done on the basis of a consensus formula decided by the NDC.[27]

The Planning Commission works out five-year-plan investments for each sector of the economy and each state, using social accounting matrices and a rather mechanistic growth model. With this as background, the states work out their respective annual plans for each year, based on estimated resource availability, which potentially includes the balance from current revenue (including Finance Commission transfers), contributions of public enterprises, additional resource mobilization, plan grants and loans, market borrowings, and other miscellaneous capital receipts. At this stage, a certain amount of bargaining for resources goes on through

---

[26] The Planning Commission was established by a cabinet resolution in March 1950, within three months of the coming into force of the Constitution on January 26, 1950. The constitutionality of its transfers has, in fact, been questioned by legal scholars, but its political support has remained firm, given India's long emphasis on government-led development. Coordination of the Finance and Planning Commissions' decisions was later sought by appointing a member of the Planning Commission to serve on the Finance Commission, but the impact of this step has been somewhat limited.

[27] The "Gadgil formula" is named after the deputy chairman of the Commission in 1969. This example illustrates the role of the NDC as an important arbiter of the overall plans and their transfers to the states.

the NDC and in state-by-state discussions to determine plan loans and grants. At the end of this process, the Planning Commission approves the state plans.

Finally, various ministries give grants to their counterparts in the states for specified projects; these are either wholly funded by the center (central sector projects) or require the states to share a proportion of the cost (centrally sponsored schemes). The ostensible rationale for these programs is financing activities with a high degree of interstate spillovers or that are merit goods (e.g., poverty alleviation and family planning), but they are often driven by pork-barrel objectives.[28] These projects are supposed to be monitored by the Planning Commission and coordinated with the overall state plans.

There are over 100 such schemes, and several attempts in the past to consolidate them into broad sectoral programs have not been successful. These programs have provided the central government with an instrument to actively influence states' spending, replacing the pre-1969 plan transfers in this role. The proliferation of schemes may also have increased the size and control of the bureaucracy. Although the NDC recently appointed an investigative committee, which recommended scaling down and consolidating centrally sponsored schemes, implementation of this was weak.

In addition to explicit transfers, intergovernmental loans, to the extent that they are subsidized, also constitute transfers to subnational governments. Ideally, borrowing should be to finance investment, but the state governments have increasingly used borrowing to meet current expenditure needs (approaching 50% in 1998–1999). State governments can only borrow from the market with central government approval if they are indebted to the center, and this constraint is binding for all the states. Central loans now constitute about 60% of the states' indebtedness, with another 22% being market borrowing, and the remainder made up of pension funds, shares of rural small savings, and required holdings of state government bonds by commercial banks (Rao and Singh, 2002; Srinivasan, 2002). Although these captive sources of finance are limited, the states have been able to soften their budget constraints further by off-budget borrowing or nonpayment by their public sector enterprises (PSEs). For example, the State Electricity Boards (SEBs) have been tardy in paying the National Thermal Power Corporation, a central PSE (Srinivasan, 2002).

---

[28] For example, programs can be for very specific local projects and can have conditionalities such as employment requirements.

There are other sources of softness in state government budget constraints. The central government guarantees loans made to state government PSEs by external agencies. The center has also in the past forgiven loans made to state governments, presumably to gain political advantage. Even in the case of attempts to impose conditions on state borrowing that would encourage fiscal reforms, the center has been unable to harden budget constraints. In particular, in 1999–2000, eleven states signed memoranda of understanding (MOUs) with the center, promising fiscal reforms in exchange for ways and means advances (essentially, overdrafts) on tax devolution and grants due to them. In some cases, however, the center has had to convert these advances into three-year loans. The Reserve Bank reports stopping payments to three states (Reserve Bank, 2001), but the political difficulty of not bailing out states that are both poor and populous is obvious.[29] In Section V, we will connect up these problems with implicit as well as explicit transfers, in the context of economic reform efforts, fiscal deficits, and global pressures.

IV. NATIONAL VERSUS SUBNATIONAL REFORMS

IV.1. Manufacturing

Increased competition for Indian manufacturing has been one result of greater openness since 1991. Ahluwalia (2002b) notes that Indian firms have upgraded technology and expanded to more efficient scales of production over the past decade. Among larger firms, there have been substantial changes in relative size, indicating a dynamism that was absent before the reforms. Despite these positive signs, India's manufacturing growth has been modest, and manufacturing exports have also not taken off. Many authors have noted the fact that India's rates of protection are still relatively high, contributing to a high cost of production. Continued federal and state level controls on product markets substantially hinder the growth of this sector. Rigid labor laws and poor infrastructure are other contributing factors to low productivity and high costs, as are rigidities such as small-scale industry reservations.[30]

---

[29] These kinds of political considerations also constrain the center to make plan loans at the same interest rate to all states, removing that marginal incentive device as well. In this context, the ISC may have a greater role to play in constructing a broader bargain with respect to reform, as we discuss in Section V.

[30] Significant progress on this front has been made very recently; see Mohan (2002a).

Many of the problems of Indian industry can be traced to laws at the national level, but it is becoming clear that state-level reforms are also needed. For example, a study by McKinsey & Company (McKinsey Global Institute, 2001) suggests that, starting from a base of 5.5% GDP growth for India, reforms at the state level can add 2 percentage points to growth, almost as much as their estimate of the potential contribution of further reforms by the central government (2.6 percentage points). The McKinsey report identifies the top three roadblocks to higher growth as product market barriers, land market barriers, and government owner-ship. In the case of land markets in particular, state- or local-level con-trols, on land use, including protected tenancies, rent controls, and zoning restrictions, are quite significant.[31]

The situation is complicated by the fact that state laws may piggyback, or be enabled by, central-level legislation. Reform therefore requires a coordinated approach, since the center is often not in a position to nullify state legislation directly. In the case of labor laws, the main legislation is at the national level, in the form of the Industrial Disputes Act of 1947, the Industrial Employment Act of 1946, and the Contract Labour (Abolition and Regulation) Act of 1970. The national laws require firms with more than 100 workers to get the permission of state governments for closing plants or laying-off workers. This permission is rarely given. However, state governments also have the right to restrict contract labor, and variations in their use of this power are significant. Another key source of variation among states is the way that worker safety laws are enforced, with government inspectors in some states using these laws as a significant vehicle of rent extraction.[32]

Dollar, Iarossi, and Mengistae (2002) have examined the quantitative impact of state-level variations in policy on manufacturing productivity. Using a survey of 1,000 manufacturing establishments across ten Indian states, they find that states that are poor performers and are identified by survey respondents as having a "poor investment climate" have total

---

[31] For example, Chennai has less restrictive land use controls than Delhi or Mumbai, and it has seen a faster growth of more efficient modern food retailing (McKinsey, 2001, p. 8). Note that inefficient and lengthy judicial proceedings (Section III) compound the problems created by these and other laws. A caveat is that the McKinsey methodology is somewhat vague, and its downgrading of infrastructure as a constraint may not be accurate. Dollar et al. (2002) (see further in the chapter) emphasize infrastructure.

[32] Forbes (2002, Table 4.2) details eleven kinds of mostly state and local inspection (factory conditions, taxation, etc.) According to him, eight of these have not changed in character since 1991.

factor productivity (TFP) that is 26% lower than that of the high-performing states. About a tenth of this gap is found to be due to a higher regulatory burden (specifically, labor market regulations) in the worse states. The advantage of such quantification, of course, is that it enables a basis for policy recommendations with respect to subnational reforms.

IV.2. Agriculture

Opening the economy, reducing protection of industry, and exchange rate depreciation have all helped India's agricultural sector by moving relative prices in its favor and making exports more competitive. The growth performance of agricultural exports, as measured by the increase in share of world exports, has been somewhat better than that of manufacturing (Ahluwalia, 2002b). Nevertheless, there are significant areas where coordinated reforms by the center and the states can improve performance. Severe distortions of both input and output prices have distorted cropping patterns and hindered diversification into higher value-added, non-food-grain crops. Some of the price distortions (fertilizers and outputs) are the responsibility of the center, whereas others (water and electricity) result from state governments' subsidies. Restrictions on FDI and domestic distortions have also hindered development of agroprocessing industries.

At the same time that subsidies are removed, farmers need to be freed from a range of outdated laws and institutions. Some of these laws go back in spirit to World War II–era scarcities. The Essential Commodities Act empowers state governments to restrict the movement of agricultural products across state and even district boundaries and to limit the stocks that food traders can hold. Various state-level Agricultural Produce Marketing Acts force food traders to buy produce only in regulated markets, making direct contractual relationships difficult, and sometimes reducing the bargaining power of farmers.[33] These restrictions are compounded by an inefficient central government food procurement and distribution system (Srinivasan, 2002). Ahluwalia (2002b) suggests that, in such cases, the center needs to not only repeal its own restrictive laws but also put limits on the laws that states can pass. From a federalist perspective, however, this may require explicit bargaining between the center and the states,

---

[33] Even in the richest agricultural surplus state of Punjab, intermediaries in both the input and output markets often have monopolistic positions created by government regulations. Nirvikar Singh was told, by a state government official, of at least one case where pesticide distributors successfully lobbied the state government to prevent direct contracting of farmers with manufacturers at steep discounts.

since the latter have considerable constitutional authority with respect to agriculture.[34]

Finally, the fall in investment in agricultural infrastructure is well known. It appears to have begun in the 1980s, before the current reforms (Gulati and Bathla, 2001). Certain kinds of infrastructure relate to production and require public investment, which has been choked off by the fiscal problems of the state governments. Other infrastructure can support more efficient marketing of agricultural produce. Some (airports, roads, etc.) may require public investment, but other attracting investment may simply require removal of a range of outdated and often contradictory legal restrictions on agricultural trade within the country. A symptom of the problems of Indian agriculture is that partial liberalization has, in some cases, made imports of minimally processed foods, such as packaged juices from middle-income Asian countries, cheaper than domestic production.

IV.3. Services

The rapid growth of India's service sector, reflected in its increasing share of GDP (see Table 7.1) has certainly been supported by the growth of the information technology (IT) sector, particularly in software. The IT sector directly and indirectly demonstrates several possible benefits of reform. Whereas the sector clearly benefited from the availability of the right human capital, and from favorable tax policies, one of the key supporting factors was simply the absence of crippling regulations. Since software did not come under many of the restrictive laws that have strangled Indian manufacturing, new firms were able to operate much more flexibly than they might have otherwise. India's new outward orientation also helped, and software exports grew from US$100 million in 1990–1991 to US$6 billion in 2000–2001 (NASSCOM, 2002a). This growth was a significant factor in India's avoidance of further balance of payments problems and, by the late 1990s, probably contributed one percentage point to GDP growth. The IT sector also benefited from, as well as spurred, reforms in the telecommunications sector that included substantial liberalization and modernization of the regulatory framework.[35]

---

[34] The states' constitutional authority extends to all agriculture, including agricultural education and research, water (supplies, irrigation and canals, drainage and embankments, and storage), land tenures and transfers of agricultural land, land improvement and agricultural loans, and fisheries.

[35] See Singh (2002) for further discussion of the role of IT in India's economic development.

From a federalist perspective, the IT sector has helped to build a political constituency for reform at the state level, though events in 2004 suggest that this constituency is not broad enough to guarantee electoral success. States such as Karnataka and Andhra Pradesh have explicitly competed for investment in IT, through policies to develop physical and educational infrastructure. Other states, such as Punjab, have also tried to catch up in this area. However, the IT industry remains regionally concentrated.[36]

Whether this contributes to regional inequalities depends on the degree of labor mobility, both geographic and occupational, and access to the education system: Such mobility in India, which has been historically low, appears to have increased in recent years, particularly for technical professionals. To the extent that much of the recent growth is coming in IT-enabled services, which require more and less technically skilled labor for jobs ranging from software development to answering phone calls, the benefits can accrue to a broader group. These may difuse some of the regional concentration issues.

IV.4. Privatization, Infrastructure Development, and Regulation

Government production of private goods, its provision of public infrastructure, and its regulation of industry all have important implications for the performance of the Indian economy. The low productivity and poor return on capital of PSEs in India have been well documented (e.g., McKinsey Global Institute, 2001; Kapur and Ramamurthi, 2002). With national and state governments owning enterprises in a broad cross section of industries, the scope of potential privatization is quite sweeping. The political difficulty of this task was behind the absence of any meaningful privatization in the first decade of economic reform, and though this situation improved with the creation of a Ministry of Disinvestment and appointment of an active minister, the change in national government in 2004 reversed these developments.

The large implicit subsidies for those employed in public sector enterprises are an important aspect of the resistance to privatization, and one can guess that patronage and rent-seeking opportunities have contributed to the lack of political enthusiasm from government ministries. Also, in the case of state-level public enterprises such as the SEBs, there are additional twin problems of huge deficits and the need for coordinated reform

---

[36] For example, 80% of India's IT-enabled services companies are located in only six metropolitan areas (NASSCOM, 2002b).

of the power sector (see the following discussion). The previous central government created the post of a Minister of State for Disinvestment, and in this position Arun Shourie drew up a list of twenty-seven central PSEs to be disinvested as soon as practical. These include Air India, VSNL, Hindustan Copper Ltd., India Tourism Development Corporation, State Trading Corporation, and Indian Petrochemicals Corporation Ltd. However, opposition within the government to disinvestment of the large oil companies, Bharat Petroleum and Hindustan Petroleum, led to a postponement of their privatization, as well as that of other central government oil, gas, and power companies, and the whole effort has stalled with the change in government.

Although the SEBs are directly owned by the state governments, center–state relations have also impinged on privatization when central PSEs (constituting the bulk of the assets of the public sector) in particular state jurisdictions have been privatized or proposed for privatization. Because privatization has been so limited, there are few examples, but the initial case served as a test. The first significant privatization that occurred was of the Bharat Aluminium Company (BALCO). The company's labor unions opposed the privatization and went on strike. The government of the new state of Chhattisgarh (carved out of Madhya Pradesh) took an aggressive stance against the disinvestment. Although some substantive issues of the fairness of the bidding and the sale of tribal land were involved, the case raised the potential of states obstructing privatization when the center had finally got it rolling.

The stance of the Chief Minister may be understood in terms of responsiveness to a local interest group and as an attempt to bargain for transfer payments from the center. The Supreme Court, however, finally upheld the sale of the company and dismissed actions by the state government against the new private sector owners. Kapur and Ramamurthi (2002) have discussed the court judgment in detail, concluding that it represents a significant precedent for preventing the use of legal maneuvers such as "public interest legislation" to obstruct privatization. The Chief Minister of Chhattisgarh subsequently actively sought further investment from the buyer of BALCO.

Turning to infrastructure, we note that the term can include various physical, social, and economic indicators, but attention is usually focused on public and quasipublic goods such as electric power, irrigation, roads and railways, telecommunications, and ports. In many of these cases, the poor quality of the available infrastructure acts as a constraint on growth (Dollar et al., 2002). Variations in infrastructure across states also

Table 7.4. *Relative Infrastructure Development Indices,*
for Fourteen Major States

	1980–1981	1991–1992	1996–1997
Bihar	83.5	81.7	77.8
Rajasthan	74.4	82.6	83.9
Uttar Pradesh	97.7	102.3	103.8
Orissa	81.5	95.0	98.9
Madhya Pradesh	62.1	71.5	74.1
Andhra Pradesh	98.1	96.8	93.1
Tamil Nadu	158.6	145.9	138.9
Kerala	158.1	158.0	155.4
Karnataka	94.8	96.5	94.3
West Bengal	110.6	92.1	90.8
Gujarat	123.0	122.9	121.8
Haryana	145.0	143.0	137.2
Maharashtra	120.1	109.6	111.3
Punjab	207.3	193.4	185.6
All India	**100**	**100**	**100**

Source: Ahluwalia (2002a), citing data produced by the Center for Monitoring the Indian Economy.

explain a quarter of the difference in high-performing and low-performing states, in the sample analyzed by Dollar et al. Various aggregate measures of infrastructure are possible. Table 7.4 reproduces data on one such index, produced by the Centre for Monitoring the Indian Economy (CMIE) from Ahluwalia (2002a, Table 7.8). The fourteen major states listed are ordered according to their per capita gross state domestic product (GSDP) in the initial year, from poorest to richest. The data show considerable variation across states but also a remarkable amount of stability over the period, with simple correlations between any two years all being over 0.96, and the coefficient of variation showing a slight decline, from 0.35 in 1980–1981 to 0.29 in 1996–1997.[37]

Infrastructure areas such as telecommunications and power have seen some privatization of PSEs, as well as entry by private firms. These developments require new regulatory structures to set and enforce the "rules of the game." These structures have been slow to develop in forms that break away from old-style bureaucratic control structures. In

---

[37] These calculations do not weight the indices by population, but weighting is unlikely to change the conclusion of stability.

telecommunications, the creation of a new regulatory institution, the Telecoms Regulatory Authority of India (TRAI) has been essentially at the national level, with the central government shaping its evolution. The TRAI has had problems in creating and implementing a new regulatory framework that does not involve ex ante case-by-case discretion (Dossani, 2002a). However, telecommunications reform has progressed substantially, driven in part by the enormous success of the IT sector, and the pressure brought by this sector in emphasizing the need for efficient and inexpensive telecommunications to keep it internationally competitive. Any political handicap caused by the concentration of IT success in just a few states has been mitigated by the desire of other states to emulate successful ones and the realization that an efficient telecommunications sector is necessary in this quest. However, the heterogeneity among states has influenced the formulation of the center's telecommunications policy, particularly in imposing conditions such as the division of the country into "circles" for the purpose of licensing private entrants.

In the case of electric power, however, the federal issues with respect to regulation are more salient, and these have inhibited progress.[38] Electric power is a concurrent responsibility of the center and the states. Each state has had an SEB that is vertically integrated with respect to generation, transmission, and distribution and is part of the state government. Various political compulsions and inefficiencies have led to large losses by the SEBs, and they have been a major contributor to the states' fiscal deficits.[39] Furthermore, power generation has lagged seriously behind targets, and availability of reliable electric power has become a serious bottleneck for growth.

Given this situation, the power sector received early attention in the economic reform process, with attempts to attract private participation, set forth in a 1991 policy document. Over the next decade, Rs. 373 billion in FDI in the power sector was approved, making up 14% of total approvals, but actual investment has lagged, with several well-publicized disputes and withdrawals by foreign companies, the Enron case being only the most prominent of these (Mukherjee, 2002). The need to dismantle the vertical integration of the power sector, the simultaneous involvement of the central and state governments, the lack of understanding of the

---

[38] See, for example, Dossani and Crow (2001), Dossani (2002b), and Sáez (2002, Chapter 6).

[39] The problem of SEB losses is worse than budget figures indicate. In 2000–2001, the losses of the SEBs were over Rs. 260 billion, of which only Rs. 60 billion was accounted for in the state budgets by way of explicit subsidies to the SEBs.

technical details of power contracting by some of those on the Indian side, and the role of various interest groups all had an effect in delaying or even derailing power sector reform.

One of the biggest hurdles has been the effective bankruptcy of the SEBs, leading to foreign investors in generation demanding guarantees from the state governments, as owners of the SEBs, for payments for electricity sales to the SEBs. Since the state governments themselves were in financial stress, they further asked for a counter guarantee from the central government for payment in case the state government failed to fulfill its guarantee. Enron received such a guarantee and counter guarantee; it had to invoke it in 2001, while being overtaken by larger problems of the parent company. Other foreign companies that had planned to invest in generation all pulled out because satisfactory payment arrangements could not be made.

In 1997, the central and state governments tried again to coordinate reform, with a Common Minimum National Action Plan for Power (CMNAP). The CMNAP recommended corporatization of the SEBs, though within a public ownership framework, and the creation of independent regulatory commissions at the central and state levels. The CMNAP also recommended some specific regulatory approaches and private entry in the distribution component of the sector. Andhra Pradesh, Haryana, and Orissa had already set up their own State Electricity Regulatory Commissions (SERCs), but other states moved only after the center passed legislation in 1998 to set up its Central ERC and to enable the states to create their own SERCs. State governments proceeded to do this in 1999, and some also moved forward with corporatization and some unbundling of generation, transmission, and distribution. The delay in creating effective independent regulatory bodies, however, has meant that reform has proceeded in a somewhat chaotic manner. The regulatory commissions have been unable to establish the rules of the game, both because they have been preempted by earlier ad hoc decisions and because they have not had much time to establish their own rules of operation. However, independent regulation and private sector participation appear to be the only way out of the political quicksand.

IV.5. Financial Sector Reform

Much of financial sector reform has focused on making India's capital markets more efficient. Institutional improvements, such as electronic trading and settlement, and guidelines for corporate governance have begun to take hold. Although securities market reforms have had the highest profile, some steps have also been taken in reforming debt markets and in the banking sector. Notably, a market for government debt has been established, and the central government now borrows at rates that are more market determined. In banking, there has been some reduction in interest rate controls and statutory requirements to invest in government securities, strengthening of prudential norms and regulatory oversight, and adoption of policies enabling increased competition from private (domestic and foreign) banks.

Financial markets require some regulation, both by market participants and the government, and the development of modern financial regulatory institutions in India is still taking place.[40] Many issues of financial sector reform are purely national in scope. However, the nature of the financial system overall involves financial repression (essentially, price and quantity controls in the financial sector), which in turn has had implications for central and state fiscal deficits. We explore this connection between financial sector reform and federalism. We also address the question of how much India's capital markets should be opened up. Although trade barriers have been reduced, and current account convertibility has been introduced, capital account convertibility remains a topic of policy debate. We examine this debate in the context of India's federal finances.

We noted in Section III that fiscal deficits at the state level have increased despite the central government's apparent formal authority to strictly control state borrowing. We identified two possible causes of this phenomenon. First, the central government has increasingly used discretionary loans, often with interest subsidies or even *ex post* conversion of loans to grants, as a component of political influence.[41] Second, the states have used PSEs and other off-budget devices to run even larger deficits in practice.[42] For both the center and the states, the ultimate enabler of both these trends has been the nature of India's financial system.

Severe financial repression, along with direct ownership and control of much of the financial system, has permitted the central government to

---

[40] The Securities Exchange Board of India (SEBI), though it has had some missteps in trying to prevent market manipulation, represents a great improvement over the previous situation.

[41] This statement is based on casual empiricism, but it is consistent with the political effects found in formal quantitative analyses of explicit transfers (Rao and Singh, 2001).

[42] See also Lahiri (1999), Rao (2000b), and Mohan (2001).

Table 7.5. *Commercial Bank Deposits and Priority Credit*[i]

	1969	1990	1993	1996	1997	1998	1999	2000	2001	2002	2003
Deposits of Scheduled Commercial Banks as % of National Income[ii]	15.5	48.6	50.4	46.3	46.4	49.6	50.3	53.5	58.9	60.7	66.0
Share of Priority Sector Advances in Total	14.0	40.7	34.4	32.8	34.8	34.6	35.3	35.4	35.5	34.8	35.1

[i] 1969 data are for June, other years use March data.
[ii] At current prices.
Source: RBI statistical tables, http://www.rbi.org.in/sec7/54001.pdf.

"park" central and state deficits in the financial system without having to print money and cause politically dangerous inflation. Public sector mutual funds, such as the Unit Trust of India (UTI), and financial intermediaries, such as the Industrial Development Bank of India (IDBI), have suffered from a combination of lack of bottom-line objectives and accountability. Though the central government is rectifying these problems in individual cases, these issues pervade the financial sector.[43] One simple indicator of government financial control is the large percentage of credit allocation by commercial banks that goes to "priority sectors." As Table 7.5 shows, this ratio has not fallen appreciably since reform began and remains much higher than in 1969, when the banks were nationalized.[44]

The cost of financial repression and deficit parking has been continued inefficient capital allocation and lower growth than might otherwise be attainable. A broad reform of the financial sector is required, but

[43] After two earlier bailouts, the government announced that UTI investors must bear all capital risks, but only after a third, costlier bailout announced in August 2002. It has also announced that the IDBI will be corporatized. In each case, the measures may not go far enough. Bhattacharya and Patel (2002) have made a strong case that incomplete reforms do nothing to deal with the moral hazard problems of India's financial intermediation sector. If anything, the problems may have increased in recent years. However, unlike the case of Argentina, India's state governments cannot directly borrow from banks that they own, because nationalized banks are central government owned, though there are small cooperative banks effectively controlled by state governments.

[44] Shankar Acharya has pointed out to us that this observation must be qualified by noting that the definition of "priority sector" has expanded somewhat over time.

the constraints imposed by the web of government-controlled financial institutions and their bad loans to the public sector pose a severe hurdle. If thorough financial sector reform is held back because it threatens the public sector house of cards, there may be a case for the government tying its hands through greater external liberalization of capital markets. Even without such liberalization, both the public sector and private financial sector in India are vulnerable to downgrading by international ratings agencies such as Moody's and Standard & Poor's, making India susceptible to the kinds of severe financial crisis that have affected other countries.[45] However, whether capital account liberalization can be a mechanism for financial sector and fiscal discipline probably depends on continued improvements in regulatory oversight.[46]

In suggesting greater exposure to global markets as a disciplining device for the Indian public and private finances, we are not neglecting other policy avenues. For example, the Eleventh Finance Commission, given a much broader charge than previous commissions, recommended a slew of measures to promote fiscal discipline: an overall ceiling of 37.5% of gross receipts of the center for all transfers to the states; hard budget constraints for all levels of government with respect to wages and salaries; greater autonomy along with hard budget constraints for public sector enterprises; more explicit controls on debt levels for state governments; and improvements in budgeting, auditing, and control.[47] It is not at all clear, however, that "greater autonomy along with hard budget constraints for public sector enterprises" will work in the absence of greater competitive discipline. Furthermore, by not working, it will continue to undermine any limits on states' debt levels. In addition to external

---

[45] For example Standard & Poor's lowered its long-term local currency rating to BBB− from BBB and revised its outlook on local and foreign currency to negative in August 2001, citing "the continued deterioration of the government's financial profile, with persistently high fiscal deficits resulting in a rising burden of public debt." On September 19, 2002, it further downgraded India to BB+, citing similar reasons (www.standardandpoors.com/RatingsActions/RatingsNews/Sovereigns/index.html). Although ratings are notoriously imperfect, having failed to predict, for example, the 1997 financial crisis in South Korea and Thailand, they do influence foreign investors.

[46] As Pranab Bardhan has emphasized to us, and as significant instances of accounting fraud continue to emerge in the United States, the private sector also is subject to moral hazard in the absence of effective oversight.

[47] Institutional mechanisms to detail and implement such recommendations include an Expenditure Reforms Commission, which has issued a series of reports, and a Fiscal Responsibility and Budget Management Act, which has been passed, followed by a task force report detailing implementation. Several states have also passed similar laws, though their enforceability remains to be seen.

competition, internal competition in the financial sector is also necessary, and here privatization of public sector assets must be considered.[48]

Financial sector privatization, which requires central action, can affect the nature of the demand for credit by reducing politically motivated subsidies, and by reducing overall interest rates through a reduction in government crowding out of private borrowing. The other side of the equation concerns the supply of credit. Deficit parking has been abetted by the existence and operation of public sector financial institutions. The need for privatization applies to these as well. Where does this leave the different levels of government with respect to financing the urgent needs for public infrastructure? One might argue against privatization of the financial sector if the past approach of public subsidies and directed lending had been successful in efficiently and effectively building such infrastructure: In fact, it has failed badly. In any case, fiscal incentives can be used to direct lending, without public ownership, potentially increasing transparency and efficiency.

In the context of federalism, not only can privatization in the financial sector have direct impacts on efficiency and growth, but it can also support the goal of allowing explicit center–state transfers to meet their own objectives – particularly that of enhancing horizontal equity – more effectively, by limiting implicit transfers. With respect to transfers for capital purposes, whereas central and state governments will always have the option of making conditional grants and project loans to lower level governments, the practical limitations on monitoring and incentive provision for such transfers (including the ultimate fungibility of transferred funds) suggest the greater use of unconditional block grants, with marginal capital funds coming through market borrowing.[49] We take this up further in Section V.

---

[48] Note that the center – state issue with respect to the working of the financial sector has not been just one of levels of credit but also of credit allocation across states. Hence, our discussion of fiscal deficits also relates to concerns about political economy influences and growing interstate disparities. In fact, the problem grew after the nationalization of commercial banks in 1969, which concentrated economic power in the hands of the center. With insurance and many other financial institutions already under central control, the central government became a virtual monopolist in the financial sector.

[49] Obviously, the smaller the government, the less will be the feasibility of significant reliance on the market. However, as we have emphasized earlier, many of the Indian states are comparable to countries in terms of population size and fiscal domain. The possibility of market borrowing raises issues of institutional reform to allow indebted state governments to seek funds in the capital market without permission from higher level governments, as well as the need for a credit rating agency to rate state governments. Credit rating in India is in its infancy but is developing rapidly (for example, see www.icraindia.com).

IV.6. Foreign Direct Investment

Privatization, foreign capital flows, and infrastructure development all intersect in the realm of foreign direct investment. An important part of the Indian economic reform agenda has been to attract greater levels of FDI, especially that which will bring in new technology and improve infrastructure. There remain restrictions on sectors where FDI is allowed (e.g., retailing and wholesale trading) and limits on FDI in other sectors (e.g., telecommunications, banking, insurance, and civil aviation), and the government approval process can still be time consuming.[50] Nevertheless, cumulative FDI approvals have crossed US$20 billion for the past decade though actual investment is quite a bit lower. A major policy shift allowed state governments to directly seek FDI, rather than having the central government be the only channel. As a result, state governments have actively competed for FDI, though with results that have varied dramatically across states.[51] In that respect, FDI has more transparent regional impacts than foreign portfolio investment, which was allowed from 1993 onward. In terms of magnitude, portfolio investment has been quite significant, on the order of US$20 billion since liberalization.

In September 2002, the committee on FDI headed by N. K. Singh recommended raising FDI limits in some sectors, opening up others to FDI, removing some exit barriers, improving targeting of potential investors, and facilitating approvals. The last would come about through several administrative and legal changes that would provide a more integrated approval process at both the central and state levels. In particular, the committee recommended that individual states also streamline and integrate their approval processes, covering environmental clearances, industrial relations, and worker health. Some of these recommendations, however, were confined to Special Economic Zones. It is arguable whether the precise relaxations of limits proposed are optimal or likely to be effective (Roy, 2002; Jha, 2002), and the potential impacts in the absence of further domestic financial sector reform may be a cause for concern (Jha, 2002). As in the case of disinvestment, political opposition has surfaced,

---

[50] There are two FDI approval routes. Automatic approval through the central bank, for certain categories, is supposed to take only two weeks. The bulk of FDI approvals, however, come through the Foreign Investment Promotion Board (FIPB), which is discretionary, and takes several weeks more at a minimum. Sáez (2002) also characterizes approval processes as "still cumbersome" (p. 226).

[51] In some cases, state governments have been less than enthusiastic, whereas in others they have faced their own obstacles. Sáez (2002) discusses some of these problems in the context of FDI in the power sector.

Table 7.6. *FDI Approvals from August 1991 to July 2001 for Fourteen Major States*

	FDI Approvals (Rs. Million)	1991 Population (Millions)	FDI per Capita (Rs.)
Bihar[i]	8833.43	86.374	102.27
Rajasthan	25916.69	44.006	588.94
Uttar Pradesh[i]	43304.25	139.112	311.29
Orissa	82289.14	31.660	2599.15
Madhya Pradesh[i]	97709.14	66.181	1476.39
Andhra Pradesh	124701.31	66.508	1874.98
Tamil Nadu	222804.00	55.859	3988.69
Kerala	14360.83	29.098	493.53
Karnataka	208156.32	44.977	4628.06
West Bengal	84234.59	68.078	1237.32
Gujarat	168555.48	41.310	4080.26
Haryana	31947.46	16.464	1940.44
Maharashtra	456286.23	78.937	5780.38
Punjab	19519.22	20.282	962.39
14 States	**1588618.09**	**788.846**	**2013.85**

[i] Figures for Bihar, Madhya Pradesh, and Uttar Pradesh include FDI approvals for Jharkand, Chhattisgarh, and Uttaranchal, respectively.
Sources: FDI – Secretariat for Industrial Assistance Newsletter, August 2001; population – http://www.censusindia.net/data.html

and even consideration of the report by the cabinet – let alone implementation – has stalled. Despite these roadblocks, the overall direction of the proposals represents a significant conceptual step with respect to facilitating FDI, and they continue to be on the table with the new national government.

Statewise data for total FDI approvals for the "reform decade" 1991–2001 are presented in Table 7.6. Using the 1991 population figures from the census of India, we also calculate per capita approvals. The simple correlation of the per capita FDI approvals with the infrastructure index for any of the three years in Table 7.5 is very low (less than 0.1). To some extent, this reflects the unreliability of FDI approvals as an indicator of actual investment, but more importantly, this is a consequence of the particular infrastructure index used, in which, for example, a state such as Karnataka is measured as having very low infrastructure development, despite its concentration of workers with high levels of technical skills. Most significantly, the coefficient of variation for the per capita FDI approvals (using population-weighted measures of mean and standard deviation) is 0.93, which is much higher than the corresponding measure for the infrastructure index. Thus it appears that FDI is drawn to a few favored locations, with a concentration even more than would be dictated by broad infrastructure measures. At least one important determinant of the intended destinations of FDI has been the success of India's IT sector, which was discussed previously.

To the extent that variations in FDI across states are influenced by specific policy initiatives and narrowly focused government investments in infrastructure, such as might be the case in Karnataka, there is scope for state governments to compete more effectively for FDI that might have a longer term impact on infrastructure. For example, Punjab, with the highest index of infrastructure, lags substantially in FDI, but it might conceivably correct this with policy adjustments. In general, the result of economic reform has been to remove central efforts to direct the location of FDI, as well as to relax restrictions on its nature and amount. The regional concentration of FDI is less of a concern if labor mobility is sufficient to ensure that workers can go where new jobs are created, and if public resources are channeled in ways that allow basic social infrastructure such as urban sanitation to complement private sector investments in aspects of infrastructure such as telecommunications, where the private returns to be captured are potentially higher. In Section V, we return to the impacts and implications of the regional concentration of FDI in India.

V. INTERGOVERNMENTAL RELATIONS

V.1. Center–State Transfers

We outlined some of the problems with the current transfer system in the previous two sections. What are possible reforms that can be made in the transfer system? One example of the process of reform comes from the case of tax-sharing arrangements. The Constitution specified certain categories of centrally collected taxes that were to be shared with the states, according to criteria to be determined by the Finance Commission. In particular, personal income taxes were a major component of tax transfers from the center to the states, which received 87.5% of such tax revenues. In contrast, income tax surcharges were kept entirely by the center. Academic commentators suggested that there were obvious incentive problems with such arrangements, and the Tenth Finance Commission recommended alternative arrangements whereby a proportion of overall central tax revenues would be devolved to the states. This required bargaining and agreement among the center and the states, as well as a constitutional amendment, but this has all been accomplished.[52]

Tax sharing between the center and the states reflects one dimension of the bargaining that must take place among a federation's constituents. Presumably, the initial effect of the change will be to leave the overall shares of the center and the states in aggregate near their previous values, avoiding the problem of creating clear initial losers from the reform. Principles of this sort might be used to tackle a harder problem, that of revising the formulae used to divide the states' share of tax revenue among them. These formulae are quite complex, without embodying any clearly defined objective, either of interstate (horizontal) equity or of provision of incentives for fiscal prudence.

Given that there are other transfer mechanisms as well, and that those will be used with discretion, there is a case for the Finance Commission overhauling its formulae completely to achieve greater simplicity. Such an overhaul can, in theory, be designed to respect the present status quo to a great extent but it can also be designed deal more directly with horizontal inequities in fiscal capacity (appropriately defined to avoid soft budget constraints). This is preferable to ad hoc grants for poorer states, made at the margin. In this respect, one welcome change related to tax sharing is recommended in the Eleventh Finance Commission report. This is the reversal of the earlier practice of keeping a portion of shareable tax revenues from union excise duties exclusively for allocation among states according to the amount of their estimated post-tax-devolution deficits, which amounted to converting part of the tax share into "gap-filling" grants, lacking both in transparency and incentives for fiscal prudence. Stopping that practice is a small step toward hardening the states' budget constraints.

The case for reform of transfer formulae also applies to those Planning Commission transfers that are calculated on the basis of the 1969 Gadgil formula. The past scope of Finance Commissions has been much narrower than what the Constitution of India implies for their role.[53] Moving away from this restriction, one welcome innovation in the Eleventh Finance Commission's terms of reference was the consideration of the overall

---

[52] See Rao and Singh (2001) for further detail on the new arrangements and on their initial implementation by the Eleventh Finance Commission.

[53] According to Article 280, the Finance Commission's duties include recommendations with regard to "grants-in-aid of the revenues of the States out of the Consolidated Fund of India," which appears to include Planning Commission grants made under Article 282.

fiscal position of India's federal system. The Commission recommended a reassessment of plan transfer formulae, with this task to be brought within the scope of the Finance Commission.[54] It also noted the severe muddle with respect to Planning Commission transfers, with economically meaningless distinctions between plan and nonplan categories of expenditure. It recommended reform of the financing of the plans so that plan revenue expenditure is financed from available revenue receipts after meeting nonplan expenditure, with borrowing used only for investments. Finally, a recommendation for rolling multiyear budgeting could presumably be a step away from the less flexible plan cycle.[55]

These proposed reforms would not solve problems of increasing interstate inequalities (see later in this section). However, they would make the formal transfer system clearer and simpler and make it easier to understand its objectives and its impacts. Removing a significant portion of center–state transfers outside the political economy arena, clearly targeting them toward horizontal equity objectives, and doing so in a manner that does not create perverse incentives for recipients, is feasible and desirable in itself.

Of course, there are many other influences on the fiscal positions of the states. Rao, Shand, and Kalirajan (1999) have noted the important impacts on state domestic products (SDP) of implicit transfers and of private sector investment flows: The causality is two-way, with both these tending to favor the better-off states. They also point out the unknown regional effects of direct central government expenditures. In Section III, we discussed the problems created by soft budget constraints in the dimension of loans made to the states through the Planning Commission and other avenues. Just tackling tax sharing and related transfers will still leave these problems open. The Eleventh Finance Commission's recommendation of an overall transfer ceiling of 37.5% does not seem to deal with loans and implicit transfers.

One might, in fact, question whether the Planning Commission is appropriate in an economy where liberalization has taken hold. Where there is a justification for national level coordination because of externalities that cross state borders (as in the case of roads or power, for example), different central ministries and/or state governments can negotiate

---

[54] The broader issue of the proper role of the Planning Commission is addressed later in the chapter.

[55] Singh and Vasishtha (2004) find that levels of plan transfers vary substantially across plans.

and cooperate directly. Where there is no such justification, formulaic transfers, determined by the Finance Commission so as not to distort states' fiscal incentives, seem sufficient. The Planning Commission would be largely redundant in such an institutional framework. Srinivasan (2002) has suggested replacing it with two institutions analogous to the World Bank (IBRD) and the International Development Authority (IDA), making "hard" and "soft" loans, respectively, to richer and poorer states. Although this would clarify the objectives of such "transfers," as targeted for capital spending (something that has become lost in the current working of the Planning Commission), it would still be subject to monitoring and commitment problems that would leave budget constraints soft. A more radical alternative would be to allow all states to use market borrowing, with only poorer states receiving grants for capital spending. As discussed in Section IV, this will require further reform, including privatization, of the financial sector. Issues of credible commitment to a "no-bailout" policy would remain, but private lending through the market may still be more transparent and efficient than lending from central government tax receipts.

Two other areas of ongoing reform also bear on the transfer system, either by changing the environment within which it works or through direct interactions. The assignment of tax authority is obviously important in influencing the starting point from which intergovernmental transfers are made. Second, the explicit strengthening of local governments, with formal transfer systems being introduced for state–local transfers, must impact center–state fiscal relations. We consider these issues next.

V.2. Tax Reform

There are several ways in which the tax system impinges on overall reform and the performance of the economy. Taxes create allocative distortions, and these have sometimes been particularly severe in the Indian case, often raising costs for industry to uncompetitive levels. Tax revenue is clearly a critical source of financing for overcoming infrastructure bottlenecks and providing minimum standards of public services. Globalization and opening up the economy have two direct impacts. First, to the extent that aggregate tariff revenue falls as tariff rates are lowered, they increase the importance of other sources of tax revenue. Second, the mobility of national and subnational tax bases increases, making it more difficult to tap these sources. These forces mean that high effective tax rates on narrow and mobile bases, aside from the inefficiencies they create, are also now more difficult to sustain. However, as we discuss in the following, remedying this situation requires coordinated reforms, certainly at the central and state levels, and possibly at the international level, in the structure of tax treaties between countries.

Some elements of tax reform in the past two decades[56] are well known: a reduction in tariff rates, reductions in direct tax rates coupled with attempts to broaden the tax base, and a gradual movement from excise duties and sales taxes to VAT at both the central and state levels, the last being to avoid cascading and very high and variable effective rates of indirect taxation. Comparing 1990–1991 with 1999–2000, we see the impact of some of these changes: an increase in the direct-tax-to-GDP ratio from 2.16% to 3.24%, accompanied by an increase in the number of filers from 6.1 to 17.8 million; this has been more than offset by a decrease in the central indirect-tax-to-GDP ratio from 8.84% to 6.23%, driven by reductions in the percentages of central excise duties as well as customs duties.[57] State sales taxes and excise duties have also shown a proportionate decline, so that the overall tax-to-GDP ratio has declined by almost two percentage points in the 1990s (Rao, 2000a). Although the overall decline merely reverses an increase that took place in the 1980s, the fact that it has occurred at higher GDP levels raises questions about long-term implications. Some of the lack of buoyancy in tax revenues may be due to the recent slowdown of manufacturing. However, there are also dimensions of tax reform that have yet to be tackled.

Three areas yet to be fully integrated into the tax base are agriculture, small-scale industry, and services. Agricultural taxation, in the form of the land tax (assigned to the states), has withered away. Small-scale units for protected by the policy of reserving some activities for smaller firms only are either exempt from paying excise duties or pay lower rates than other firms in the same sectors. This cuts out an important part of the tax base, provides an avenue for tax evasion, makes administration more complex, and provides a further incentive for small-scale units to remain small (Mohan, 2002a). To the extent that small-scale reservations can be removed, this problem will be reduced, but since these tax breaks were introduced relatively recently (in 1986), they might be delinked from the politically more difficult (but desirable) removal of reservations. Finally, the problem created by the failure of the Constitution to explicitly

---

[56] Many reforms started with the report of the Tax Reform Committee of 1991, but some began earlier. Mohan (2002b) lists some of the most significant tax reforms in India.

[57] These figures are from Singh and Modi (2001, Tables I, III, and IV).

include "services" within the scope of states' sales tax authority has been recognized for some time and is in need of correction.

The Tax Reform Committee had also recommended minimizing exemptions and concessions, simplification of laws and procedures, development of modern, computerized information systems, and improvements in administration and enforcement (Rao, 2000a). Das-Gupta and Mookherjee (1998, Chapter 6) detailed the problems with Indian tax administration, in terms of the incentives of both those paying taxes and those enforcing them. However, several years later, Singh and Modi (2001), focusing on central tax collection, still noted, "The tax enforcement effort has left much to be desired ... from the view point of a decline in total tax collected as a percentage of collectible tax, the pendency of assessment work and the dilatory process of the Appeal redressal mechanism." Thus it is clear that much remains to be done in this respect. The benefits of improvements in this area are likely to be large, not only because of the direct benefits of improvements in central information systems and institutions of enforcement but also because these can provide a model for states to improve their tax administration as well.

A reform that directly affects India's federal system lies in indirect taxes, which, as we have noted, have not increased proportionately with GDP in the past decade. As Rao (2000a) puts it, "The most important challenge in restructuring the tax system in the country is to evolve a coordinated consumption tax system." Rao provides some detailed recommendations on the current assignments of indirect taxes, with respect to issues such as rates, interstate sales taxes, and tax administration for a dual VAT coordinated between the center and the states. Rao also notes the problem created by the failure of the Constitution to explicitly include "services" within the scope of states' sales tax authority. This problem has been recognized for some time, but it has increased in importance as the structure of GDP has shifted from commodity production to services; fixing this was also recommended by the Eleventh Finance Commission.

Moving taxation of services from the Union list, where it implicitly lies through the center's residual powers over taxes not explicitly specified in the Constitution, to the Concurrent list will require a constitutional amendment. Such an amendment must be proposed by the central government, but it will benefit the states. Rao incorporates political economy considerations by suggesting that an amendment be tied to persuading the states to reduce and eventually eliminate taxation of interstate sales, thus removing some of the internal barriers that have plagued the development of a true national market within India.[58] This will also smooth the implementation of a destination-based VAT for the states. Note that such reforms can also reduce tax exporting by the richer states (Rao and Singh, 1998; Rao, Shand, and Kalirajan, 1999).

Taxation of services illustrates a broader issue addressed by the Eleventh Finance Commission, which recommended in general giving the states more power to tax, to reduce the vertical fiscal imbalance. This approach takes some pressure off the fiscal transfer system, allowing states that can obtain political support to more flexibly tax their own constituents to deliver benefits to them. Another possible example of such a tax reassignment would be to allow states to piggyback on central income taxes. This, too, would require a constitutional amendment. With tax sharing no longer applied to specific tax "handles," but to tax revenues in total, this change would give states more flexibility at the margin, where they properly should have it. Note that states are already assigned the right to tax agricultural income, though their use of this tax is minimal. This separation has no economic justification and merely promotes tax evasion. Piggybacking, along with a removal of the distinction between nonagricultural and agricultural income (possibly with provisions to mitigate the effects of risks in agriculture), would represent a major improvement in tax assignments. Whether the political economy logic can work for this case of tied reforms, as suggested here for the case of services, is worth considering.

To summarize our discussion, we see that much remains to be done in terms of tax reform. Some measures can be initiated by the center acting alone, but many others require agreement or coordination between the center and the states. These include possible reassignments of tax authority, as well as changes in tax administration. Recognizing the play of differing interests may help in devising reform packages that balance potential

---

[58] Although the fundamental problem in India is the absence of an interstate commerce clause such as that in the U.S. Constitution, there is still room for bargained solutions that will reduce internal trade barriers. For example, the recent replacement of local transit taxes (*octroi*) with state entry taxes in some states has shifted the problem up one level, reducing the number of entities that have to be involved in the negotiation. Earlier, in 1975, the central government entered into an agreement with the states to abolish sales taxes on textiles, sugar, and tobacco, replacing them with an additional central excise duty, the entire proceeds of which were assigned to the states. Interestingly, this bargaining perspective of federalism, which we have emphasized heavily in this chapter, finds an echo in the following statement of the recent task force on implementation of the FRBM Act (Government of India, 2004): "The Task Force proposes a 'grand bargain' whereby States will have the power to tax all services concurrently with the Centre" (p. 6).

losses against gains and thereby increase the probability of acceptance. Rationalizing India's tax system at all levels of government has become more important because of the opening up of the economy to foreign competition. Therefore continued tax reform should be a priority. How to implement this across different levels of the government will be considered after we discuss decentralization.

V.3. Decentralization

The political motivations and history of local government reform in India have been quite different from those that led to the economic reforms of the 1990s. Nevertheless, there is a complementarity between the two sets of reforms that benefits from their temporal coincidence. After a long history of debate on decentralization, a central government committee recommended that local bodies should be given constitutional status. Two separate amendment bills were introduced, covering *panchayats* (village governments) and municipalities, respectively, passed by Parliament in 1992, ratified by more than half the state assemblies, and brought into force as the 73rd and 74th Amendments to the Constitution in 1993. These amendments required individual states to pass appropriate legislation, since local government remained a state subject under the Constitution, and they have done so.[59]

Until the recent legislative changes, the ability to exercise local suffrage was very limited. The amendments require direct elections to local bodies to be held every five years. If a local government is dissolved prematurely by the state, elections must be held within six months, something that was not required earlier. Rao and Singh (2000, 2001) have characterized this aspect of local government reform as replacing "hierarchy" with "voice"[60] as the primary accountability mechanism, and they have explained this as a positive step based on the ability to provide more targeted incentives to government decision makers, based on the narrower locus on which their performance can be judged. Of course, this is subject to the caveat of transparency and effective monitoring being achievable. Local government reform has also changed the nature of tax and expenditure assignments to these governments, instituting a system of formal state–local transfers modeled on that of the central Finance

---

[59] See Rao and Singh (2000, 2001) for more details. See also Mathur (1999) for an assessment of urban governments and reform.

[60] See Hirschman (1970) for the introduction and discussion of this terminology.

Commission. Accepting that there are some serious issues with the new assignments, including problems of local capacity and efficiency, both with respect to revenues and expenditures, we focus here on the new transfer system.

Although it has been argued that formal transfers from the center and states to local governments could accentuate fiscal deficit problems, an explicit, rule-governed system can instead make existing problems more transparent, as a first step toward mitigating them. Local government finances, particularly for urban bodies, had steadily worsened over the period before local government reform, under a system of hierarchical control and monitoring by state governments. This is not to imply that the State Finance Commissions (SFCs) represent an immediate improvement. Almost all SFCs have given their initial reports, and the Eleventh Finance Commission summed them up as follows: "Many SFC reports have not... provided a clear idea of the powers, authority and responsibilities actually entrusted to the local bodies. Many of these reports also do not clearly indicate the principles formulated for sharing or assignment of State taxes, duties, tolls, fees and the grants-in-aid" (Paragraph 8.11b).

However, this situation is somewhat better than the previous one of ad hoc and discretionary transfers and control of local bodies by state governments: Local government reform has added welcome transparency to existing problems, as well as greater certainty to transfers.

The Eleventh Finance Commission was, rightly, reluctant to provide the states with grants requested by them to supplement their own transfers to local governments, noting that the amendments do not justify this softening of the states' budget constraints. The Commission's main recommendations with respect to local government related to assignment and incentive issues for various sources of tax revenue. Land and profession taxes were identified as two possible sources of revenue. The recommendation of surcharges on state taxes earmarked for local government is similar to the piggybacking we proposed for the states on central taxes. It would be useful to allow local governments to determine their own rates, perhaps subject to a state-imposed minimum level. These recommendations are straightforward – the problems arise in defining details and assuring implementation. This point also applies to the Commission's discussion of property taxes, replacements for *octroi*, and local user charges.

The analysis of Rao and Singh (2000) suggests that incentive efficiency with respect to government expenditure must be the starting point for revenue enhancement efforts. The Commission was right to suggest a quicker transfer of expenditure responsibilities to local governments: They are unlikely to do worse than state governments have so far done, in the provision of basic civic amenities. Grants to the lowest tier of local government recommended by the Commission may help to jumpstart the process of making local governments effective providers, if they can break out of their historical low-level equilibrium of revenue collection and service provision.

The Commission also recommended grants for improved accounting, auditing, and database building for local governments. These measures, if implemented effectively, can have a substantial positive impact on capacity, transparency, and accountability in the delivery of local government services such as primary education and basic health care. The report also discussed some of the potential conflicts between the existing institutional apparatus of central and centrally sponsored schemes and the role envisaged for local governments[61] and detailed problems that are arising from states' reluctance to devolve authority to their subordinate governments. One example of the latter problem is the failure of state governments to implement their own SFCs' reports. In the case of the central Finance Commission, the bargaining power of the states and the role of precedent have worked to ensure the implementation of most recommendations. In the case of the states, local governments may need outside help, for example from the courts, to pressure reluctant state governments.

Primary education and basic health and nutrition represent important aspects of any country's development, and it is widely accepted that India's performance on these fronts has been mediocre or worse (e.g., Dreze and Sen, 1995). Global comparisons and the process of globalization have the effects this relative failure and its negative consequences in terms of low productivity as well as direct welfare losses. In this respect, greater responsibility of state and local governments in ensuring adequate levels of education, health, and nutrition as a result of the aforementioned reform processes may have positive impacts by increasing the efficiency with which scarce public resources are raised, transferred, and spent. As we discuss later in this section, some of the poorer states have been able

---

[61] Currently, central discretionary transfers, which are meant to be implemented at the district or block level, swamp local government capacity for action and for their own revenue raising (Rajaraman, 2001). Replacing these with conditional or unconditional grants from the states (with the ultimate source possibly being unconditional grants from the center) will allow more effective functioning of local governments. This ties in with our earlier discussion of reform of the center–state transfer system.

to overcome resource constraints to achieve quantifiable improvements in this area of "human development."

V.4. Intergovernmental Institutions

Local government reform has complicated intergovernmental relations in India, by allowing the center to bypass state governments to some extent, such as by making direct transfers to local governments. In fact, it has been argued that this was the political motivation for such reform. In general, the economic reform process has changed the nature of center–state interactions, and this has been compounded by coalition rule at the center. Issues of fiscal deficits, tax reform, policies toward FDI, infrastructure development, and regulation all require some coordination between the center and the states. In this context, institutions such as the ISC may actually have a greater role to play than earlier.

Although states that are pivotal, and hence politically powerful, in a coalition government at the center may be able to directly extract concessions from the central government (as the government of Andhra Pradesh[62] appears to have done in some cases in the previous national government), this does not make the ISC redundant. The potential role of the ISC is precisely to provide an alternative to such ad hoc bargaining. Furthermore, bargaining over durable changes in rules governing the federation is quite different from bargaining over specific instances. For example, the ISC was an important forum for gaining acceptance of the change in tax sharing recommended by the Tenth Finance Commission.[63] More recently, it has also been a place where an important change in the rules governing interstate water disputes has been approved by the states (Richards and Singh, 2002). Clearly, tax reform, changes in the way that states borrow, policies toward FDI, and regulation of sectors such as power are all areas where the ISC can provide a less public, more focused forum for bargaining over issues that jointly affect the center and the states than is possible in either house of Parliament.

The role of the ISC may also be expanded if the current process of planning is reformed, as we have argued earlier in this section. The NDC

---

[62] It is important to note that the Telegu Desam Party of Andhra Pradesh also controlled the state government at that time. In other cases (the Dravida Munnetra Kazhagam of Tamil Nadu and Trinamool Congress of West Bengal) the regional party in the ruling coalition may not have been in a position to represent its state's interests as forcefully or directly.

[63] See also Kapur (2001) for additional examples.

now serves as the bargaining forum for plan transfers and loans, and we have suggested that these might be replaced by a dual system of block grants and market-based loans. This change would make the NDC redundant. Instead, the ISC may be the place for evolving a new institutional framework, one that encompasses bargaining over general rules, not specific instances. In this respect, our perspective is an extension of Riker's instrumental view of federalism, as "a constitutional bargain among politicians," with the motives being "military and diplomatic defense or aggression" (Riker, 1975, pp. 113–114). Our extensions to this concept are to include bargaining not just in constitution making but also in evolution of subsequent governance, and not just for territorial protection or gain but also over splitting the economic pie.

We can summarize the main message of this section as follows. A further devolution of expenditure assignments, as is being implemented in the ongoing local government reform, makes sense from an efficiency perspective, because it allows better-targeted incentives for government decision makers. This must be accompanied by devolution of tax assignments to keep vertical fiscal imbalances from overwhelming such incentives. Since vertical fiscal imbalances will still arise, we argue for a simpler transfer system that does not distort marginal incentives. Although there is still room for transfers and loans that are earmarked for capital expenditure, we argue that here, too, marginal incentives are crucial, and that providing these through the market may be the only efficient avenue in practice. This argument is based on the recognition that political influences will distort choices in the absence of such discipline, no matter how legal restraints are structured. Decentralization and privatization may seem to exacerbate problems of interstate inequality, but they also enable higher level governments to focus more clearly and directly on redistribution as an objective wherever it is deemed necessary. The transition to a new set of rules requires bargaining over change, and we have suggested the ISC as a formal institution within which this might occur.

V.5. Regional Inequalities[64]

To the extent that globalization and economic liberalization may increase inequality across the constituent units of India's federation, they could

---

[64] See Rao and Singh (2001) for more details on previous studies, including those not covered here.

Table 7.7. *Convergence Studies for India's States*

Study	Period	No. of States	Main Results
Cashin and Sahay (1996)	1961–1991	20	Slow absolute and conditional convergence. Weak impact of internal migration.
Nagaraj, Varoudakis, and Véganzonès (1998)	1970–1994	17	Absolute divergence; conditional convergence. Share of agriculture, infrastructure, political, and institutional factors (state fixed effects) matter.
Rao, Shand, and Kalirajan (RSK, 1999)	1965–1995	14	Absolute and conditional divergence, faster in early 1990s. Private investment matters.
Aiyar (2001)	1971–1996	19	Conditional convergence; infrastructure, private investment, and nonmeasured institutional factors matter.
Ahluwalia (2002a)	1981–1999	14	Gini coefficient of per capita SDP (weighted by population) increased from late 1980s, through 1990s. Convergence not allowed for, but private investment matters for growth.

exacerbate political tensions and, in the extreme, threaten the country's unity. Various secessionist movements have certainly existed throughout India's postcolonial history. Hence, we examine the evidence on increasing regional inequality, discuss possible causes and the likely political effects of any such increases, and consider policy responses in the context of an environment of continued globalization. In particular, we examine whether there might be conflicts between the objective of moderating regional inequalities and those of promoting market efficiency and hardening budget constraints. In doing so, we discuss some of the political and economic factors that necessarily shape a federal bargain.

Many studies have examined the issue of regional inequalities in India, whether they are increasing, and how changes are affected by initial conditions such as the level of infrastructure development. These studies are partly motivated by the fears of some that, as India integrates into the global economy, enclaves that successfully pursue this integration will grow rapidly, leaving the rest of the economy behind. These studies typically use the framework of growth theory to examine absolute or conditional convergence.[65] A small subset of these studies is summarized in Table 7.7.

Here, we extend earlier studies by examining whether flows of capital to different states affect regional inequalities for the 1990s.[66] We proxy interstate movements of domestic capital with bank credit–deposit ratios for the fourteen major states. Trends over the past two decades are summarized in Table 7.8. The average credit–deposit ratio shows a slight decline from 1980 to 1995 and is thereafter about the same in 2001. The (unweighted) standard deviation creeps up from the initial year to 1995 and increases further in 2001. Although the increase is not great, the sharp decline in the credit–deposit ratio for the states of Bihar and Uttar Pradesh is striking. Also, the correlation between the ratio and per capita SDP jumps dramatically from 1995 to 2001, after a much smaller increase in the earlier period (1980 to 1995), even when the coefficient of variation of per capita SDP for these states does not increase.

Table 7.9 presents results for some simple convergence regressions, focusing on three different financial variables: FDI approvals per capita over the decade 1991–2001, 1990 per capita bank credit (a proxy for private investment), and 1990 credit–deposit ratios. The results are quite striking. First, the evidence for convergence or divergence is inconclusive, since the coefficient of base-year SDP is never significantly different from one.[67] Second, any one of the financial variables taken individually is estimated to have a significant impact on growth of SDP. When two or more financial variables are included, there is evidence of multicollinearity, but

---

[65] Thus, one can identify three possible scenarios: absolute convergence, where different entities are moving toward the same steady state, conditional convergence, where they are converging to (possibly very) different steady states, and divergence, where there is no evidence of convergence. The last case is inconsistent with neoclassical growth models, but it conceivably fits some endogenous growth models. Note that conditional convergence is quite consistent with increasing disparities across entities. Variables such as literacy, health, and physical infrastructure, as well as the economic policies followed, may be the conditioning variables. Although the evidence for any type of convergence across disparate countries is quite weak, one might expect greater possibilities for convergence across similar regions or constituent units of a federation than across countries.

[66] Migration data, when available, can allow one to also look at interstate flows of labor. However, such data may underestimate migration (Srivastava, 1998).

[67] This is true whether one uses a one-sided or two-sided test.

Table 7.8. *Credit–Deposit Ratios by State*

	1980	1995	2001
Bihar[i]	0.41	0.33	0.24
Rajasthan	**0.68**	0.46	0.48
Uttar Pradesh[i]	0.42	0.35	0.28
Orissa	0.59	0.54	0.41
Madhya Pradesh[i]	0.56	0.53	0.47
Andhra Pradesh	**0.74**	**0.76**	**0.63**
Tamil Nadu	**0.94**	**0.91**	**0.91**
Kerala	**0.68**	0.45	0.43
Karnataka	**0.75**	**0.68**	**0.59**
West Bengal	0.60	0.54	0.44
Gujarat	0.58	0.47	0.49
Haryana	**0.72**	0.47	0.42
Maharashtra	**0.79**	**0.70**	**0.85**
Punjab	0.43	0.41	0.41
Average	0.65	0.58	0.57
Std. Deviation	0.15	0.16	0.18
Coeff. of Var.	0.22	0.27	0.32
Coeff. of Var. (SDP)	0.32	0.40	0.36
Corr.[n] with per Capita SDP	0.11	0.18	0.59

[i] Figures for Bihar, Madhya Pradesh, and Uttar Pradesh in 2001 include Jharkand, Chhattisgarh, and Uttaranchal, respectively. SDP and population figures used to calculate correlations were for closest available years.

Sources: RBI Bulletins, National Accounts Statistics, and Indian Census.

otherwise the results are robust. These results are consistent with a story where domestic and foreign capital are complements, and taken together with our earlier discussion of credit–deposit ratios and of FDI approvals, the evidence is suggestive of mobile domestic and foreign capital driving growth. From an efficiency point of view, this is probably a good thing, but the equity consequences bear some consideration. We assess the evidence and discuss possible policy implications.

First, it is important to note that some of the evidence for divergence among India's states appears in the 1980s, before the recent reforms. The 1980s saw an appreciable increase in India's growth rate compared to earlier periods. Hence, the 1990s reforms cannot be the sole cause in increased regional inequality. Measures such as the Gini coefficient do

Table 7.9. *Growth Regressions*[i]

Variable	(1)	(2)	(3)	(4)	(5)	(6)	(7)
Constant	−0.86	−0.02	−0.70	−1.16	0.13	0.84	1.18
	(−0.94)	(−0.02)	(−0.76)	(−1.65)	(0.11)	(0.79)	(1.12)
1990–1991 ln SDP per Capita	**1.14**	**1.02**	**1.08**	**1.14**	**0.96**	**0.90**	**0.85**
	(9.75)	(9.79)	(9.71)	(12.71)	(6.41)	(6.21)	(5.95)
FDI Approvals p. c. 1991–2001		**5.4×10^{-5}**	2.4×10^{-5}		6.3×10^{-6}	3.3×10^{-5}	
		(2.76)	(0.81)		(0.19)	(1.25)	
Credit–Deposit Ratio (1990)			0.35	**0.52**	0.33		
			(1.34)	(3.10)	(1.26)		
Credit per Capita (1990)					8.9×10^{-5}	9.7×10^{-5}	**16.6×10^{-5}**
					(1.12)	(1.19)	(2.71)

[i] Dependent variable is log of 1998–1999 per capita SDP; t statistics are in parentheses.

353

Table 7.10. *State-Level Human Development Indices*

	1981		1991		2001	
	Value	Rank	Value	Rank	Value	Rank
Andhra Pradesh	0.298	9	0.377	9	0.416	10
Bihar	0.237	14	0.308	14	0.367	14
Gujarat	0.360	4	0.431	6	0.479	6
Haryana	0.360	5	0.443	5	0.509	5
Karnataka	0.346	6	0.412	7	0.478	7
Kerala	0.500	1	0.591	1	0.638	1
Madhya Pradesh	0.245	13	0.328	12	0.394	12
Maharashtra	0.363	3	0.452	4	0.523	4
Orissa	0.267	10	0.345	11	0.404	11
Punjab	0.411	2	0.475	2	0.537	2
Rajasthan	0.256	11	0.347	10	0.424	9
Tamil Nadu	0.343	7	0.466	3	0.531	3
Uttar Pradesh	0.255	12	0.314	13	0.388	13
West Bengal	0.305	8	0.404	8	0.472	8
All India	0.302		0.381		0.472	
Unweighted Average	0.325		0.407		0.469	
Standard Deviation	0.071		0.075		0.072	
Coefficient of Variation	0.219		0.185		0.155	

Sources: Planning Commission (2002).

suggest that interstate inequality has increased particularly in the 1990s, but the evidence from our growth regressions is not conclusive.[68]

Second, the studies typically use SDP to measure outcomes. Thus, remittances by internal migrants (e.g., Biharis working as agricultural laborers in Punjab) and external ones (Keralites working in health care in the Middle East) are being missed by the analysis. Internal as well as international remittances, once included, might change the picture. Although we do not have statewise income data, other outcome measures can be used. Table 7.10 shows the Human Development Indices (HDIs) for the fourteen major states, at decade intervals for three years, 1981, 1991, and 2001. The HDI includes literacy, infant mortality, access to safe water, and durably constructed housing, as well as formal education, poverty ratios, and per capita expenditure. Coupled with a rise in HDI over the two decades has been a relatively constant standard deviation

---

[68] However, estimated Gini coefficients for personal income distribution do not show any increase from 1990 to 2000.

of the distribution across states, resulting in a substantial fall in the coefficient of variation (CV). The CV for the HDI is also lower than the CV for SDP, though this could be an artifact of the scales used for components of the HDI. These data suggest that other factors (e.g., remittances or government expenditures) do mitigate some of the apparent regional inequalities in India.

Despite the qualifications we have discussed, commonly held perceptions of growing inequality or unfairness may be enough to require policy attention. Previous secessionist movements and other regional political tensions have been driven by a complex mix of ethnic, linguistic, and economic factors, but economic policies have often been part of the political response.[69] At the same time, the central government's fiscal situation does not allow for money to be thrown at such problems. We have argued here for reforms in the intergovernmental transfer system that might allow better targeting of transfers to deal with states that may be left behind by liberalization, through grants or soft loans for infrastructure investment, restricted to poorer states. Transfers may be more effective if they are based on simpler formulas and objectives, without the center trying to impose direct controls. However, Ahluwalia (2002a) argues for imposing more effective conditionalities on transfers to improve the use of transferred funds by the states. This could work against reduction in interstate inequalities. Furthermore, this recommendation assumes that the center is able to effectively monitor such conditionalities, something that has not been true in the past.

In general, even formulaic transfers can be subject to political influence effects (Rao and Singh, 2000), as part of the ongoing federal bargaining process. Also, equalizing transfers may be offset by other (implicit) transfers that favor better-off states.[70] Furthermore, the impact of intergovernmental transfers may be to distort the fiscal incentives of recipients in ways that hurt short-run efficiency and long-run growth, as is argued

---

[69] This point also applies if one allows for internal migration. Although migration may help to support convergence, in a heterogeneous country such as India, it may bring its own set of problems. If effective equalizing fiscal transfers can reduce interregional migration pressures or slow down the process, they may have a positive role in preserving interethnic or other intergroup peace. Srivastava (1998), based on microsurveys, suggests that temporary employment opportunities drive a substantial amount of migration in India, beyond what is reflected in national statistics.

[70] Rao, Shand, and Kalirajan (1999) argue that explicit center–state transfers have had moderate impacts on interstate inequalities and that these effects have been outweighed by implicit transfers through subsidized (public and private) lending and through interstate tax exportation.

Table 7.11. Revenues and Expenditures[i] of the States, 2000–2001

Major States	Per Capita GSDP (Rs)	Per Capita Own Revenue (Rs)	Own Revenue as % of GSDP	Per Capita Current Expenditure (Rs)	Percentage of Own Revenue to Current Expenditure
High-Income States	**22461**	**2931.6**	**13.1**	**4386.6**	**66.8**
Gujarat	18685	2684.6	13.2	5167.6	52.0
Goa	44613	14310.3	15.8	11904.8	120.2
Haryana	21551	3209.7	12.1	4107.9	78.1
Maharashtra	22604	2741.3	11.1	3852.6	71.2
Punjab	23254	3333.2	10.2	4712.7	70.7
Middle-Income States	**17635**	**1868.8**	**10.6**	**3400.4**	**55.0**
Andhra Pradesh	14878	1930.2	10.7	3320.2	58.1
Karnataka	16654	2148.1	11.3	3580.9	60.0
Kerala	17709	2295.8	10.2	3689.4	62.2
Tamil Nadu	18623	2342.5	11.3	3594.3	65.2
West Bengal	14874	1091.0	5.5	3092.7	35.3
Low-Income States	**9013**	**846.8**	**9.4**	**2243.4**	**37.7**
Bihar	4813	338.2	8.9	1515.5	22.3
Chhattisgarh	10405	1264.0	4.9	2455.2	51.5
Jharkhand	9223	1128.0	9.0	2229.4	50.6
Madhya Pradesh	11626	1061.9	11.5	2695.5	39.4
Orissa	8733	900.5	9.3	2785.3	32.3

Rajasthan	13046	1297.2	10.4	2864.2	45.3
Uttaranchal	NA[ii]	1295.5	NA[ii]	4912.7	26.4
Uttar Pradesh	9323	791.2	8.1	2135.6	37.0
Special Category States	**12339**	**1155.9**	**9.4**	**5715.4**	**20.2**
Arunachal Pradesh	13352	1067.8	5.3	9992.3	10.7
Assam	9720	798.7	7.2	3317.0	24.1
Himachal Pradesh	17786	1660.5	7.8	7420.6	22.4
Jammu & Kashmir	12373	1150.4	7.9	6080.0	18.9
Manipur	12721	406.0	3.1	6032.3	6.7
Meghalaya	12063	1066.8	6.3	5878.4	18.1
Mizoram	14909	679.0	3.8	12845.6	5.3
Nagaland	12594	506.8	3.7	7291.0	7.0
Sikkim	14751	5998.1	15.9	12200.6	49.2
Tripura	13195	729.6	4.8	5838.9	12.5
All States	**14359**	**1570.1**	**10.9**	**3191.1**	**49.2**

i Revenues and expenditures are net of lotteries.
ii NA, not available.

GSDP – Gross State Domestic Product

Sources: Finances of State Governments, 2001–2002, Reserve Bank of India, Public Finance Statistics, Ministry of Finance, Government of India. From Rao and Singh (2005, Table 4.2).

in the literature on "market-preserving federalism" (see, e.g., Weingast, 1993). One need not take an extreme position on this to agree with the view that limiting the size and scope of intergovernmental transfers can increase efficiency, while also arguing that targeting transfers to poorer regions or states is politically desirable.

In the context of equity objectives, it is important to be clear about the connection between reforming the intergovernmental transfer system and interstate inequalities in income. Reforms cannot cancel out increases in interstate income inequalities. However, they can make the formal transfer system clearer and simpler, which should make it easier to define its proper objective as one of enabling state governments to potentially provide minimal levels of public services. Table 7.11 (adapted from Table 7.4 of Rao and Singh, 2002) indicates the relative magnitudes of state government revenues and expenditures (and hence center–state transfers[71]) compared to SDPs. For the fourteen major states (excluding Goa), own revenue ranges from about 5% to 12% of GSDP and ranges from about 30% to 70% of current expenditure. Center–state transfers cannot equalize posttransfer per capita incomes, but they can substantially reduce inequalities in public service provision. The imperative is to do this in a manner that does not adversely affect incentives for raising own revenue. It is also important to note that some of the problems cannot be identified at the state level. States such as Maharashtra and Karnataka have high-income urbanized regions as well as much poorer rural regions within their boundaries. In such cases, the creation of stronger local governments and more formal mechanisms for transfers to them may help, as we have argued here.

Finally, intergovernmental transfers can only do so much, and greater decentralization of tax assignments is an important complementary policy, as we have suggested earlier. In particular, such decentralization of taxes can make it easier to harden budget constraints in the long run by clarifying accountability, even if bailouts are not completely precluded. This perspective is also in the spirit of market-preserving federalism or of Breton's (1996) view of competitive federalism. At the same time, we recognize that higher level governments will always exercise discretion where they can, a position forcefully taken by Riker (1975). In this respect, we are sympathetic to the view expressed by Frankel (2002) that avenues for the exercise of political discretion are necessary in the case of

---

[71] The difference between revenues and expenditures is made up of transfers and net fiscal deficits.

intergovernmental transfers. Nevertheless, one can strive to improve efficiency through institutional changes that promote effective monitoring and evaluation, including more market-based mechanisms for financing capital spending.

VI. CONCLUSION

Our chapter has sought to examine the interaction of India's federal system and its ongoing economic reforms in the context of globalization. In our analysis, we have explicitly recognized that the national government has subnational governments below it and that all these layers of government simultaneously interact with foreign governments and corporations in a global economy. We have examined real and financial sector reforms, including assignments of regulatory powers, infrastructure reform and development, and privatization. Despite the incomplete nature of financial reform, we have presented some evidence in Section V that liberalization is making a difference, with foreign and domestic capital together driving growth, and leading to some of the differential growth across states that has been observed in the past decade. However, we have also noted the problems created by government fiscal deficits and government control of the financial sector, with subnational fiscal deficits burgeoning in ways that have been difficult to control directly, given the existing federal institutions, and financial sector control allowing politically difficult solutions to be postponed.

Motivated by concerns over fiscal deficits, regional inequalities, and inefficient expenditures at all levels of government, we also considered reforms that directly affect intergovernmental relations. These included taxes, intergovernmental transfer mechanisms, local government reforms, and institutions of intergovernmental bargaining and cooperation. Reforms in federal governance may be the key to opening the door to further reform elsewhere, by reducing the fiscal burden placed on the private sector by government deficits. We have acknowledged the political economy aspects of federal governance, where many reforms require the support of important constituents of the federation; and we have discussed possibilities for politically acceptable packages of fiscal reforms, such as combinations of changes in tax assignment that would protect different revenue bases and therefore be acceptable to the center as well as the state governments.

The benefit of an approach that explicitly takes account of India's federal institutions is that we have been able to identify some areas in which the states may be able to achieve positive reforms acting independently (such as land use and workplace inspections) and other areas where coordination between the central and the state governments in designing and implementing reform policies may be more appropriate (such as agricultural trade, taxation, and electric power). Furthermore, we have highlighted the challenges of greater openness to the world economy in a federal system, including erosion of national and subnational tax bases, greater difficulties in maintaining fiscal balances, and the possibility of growing regional disparities as capital flows more freely to federal constituents with superior infrastructure and more attractive returns. The fiscal consequences of openness require urgent attention to the financial position of the government in particular, as well as of the financial sector as a whole. Political perceptions of regional inequalities require more efficient mechanisms for managing internal inequities. Together, they suggest the avenues of further reform that we have outlined in the chapter, including financial sector privatization and an overhaul of the entire intergovernmental transfer system to achieve greater simplicity, transparency, and incentive efficiency.

Bibliography

Acharya, S. (2002). *India's Macroeconomic Management in the Nineties*. New Delhi: Indian Council of Research in International Economic Relations.

Ahluwalia, M. S. (2002a). "State Level Performance under Economic Reforms in India," in A. Krueger, ed., *Economic Policy Reforms and the Indian Economy*. pp. 91–128. Chicago: University of Chicago Press.

Ahluwalia, M. S. (2002b). "Economic Reforms in India Since 1991: Has Gradualism Worked?," Journal of Economic Perspectives, 16(3): 67–88.

Aiyar, S. (2001). "Growth Theory and Convergence across Indian States: A Panel Study," Chapter 8 in T. Callen, P. Reynolds, and C. Towe, eds., *India at the Crossroads: Sustaining Growth and Reducing Poverty* pp. 143–169. Fund Washington, D.C.: International Monetary.

Bajpai, N., and J. Sachs (1999). "The Progress of Policy Reform and Variations in Performance at the Sub-National Level in India," Development Discussion Paper No. 730, Harvard Institute for International Development, November.

Baron, D., and J. Ferejohn (1989). "Bargaining in Legislatures," American Political Science Review 83: 1181–1206.

Bhattacharya, S., and U. Patel (2002). "Financial Intermediation in India: A Case of Aggravated Moral Hazard," paper presented at 3rd Annual Stanford Conference on Indian Economic Reform.

Breton, A. (1996). *Competitive Governments: An Economic Theory of Politics and Public Finance*. New York: Cambridge University Press.

Cashin, P., and R. Sahay (1996). "Internal Migration, Center-State Grants, and Economic Growth in the States of India," International Monetary Fund Staff Papers 43 (1): 123–171.

Das-Gupta, A., and D. Mookherjee (1998). *Incentives and Institutional Reforms in Tax Enforcement: An Analysis of Developing Country Experience*. Delhi: Oxford University Press.

Dollar, D., G. Iarossi, and T. Mengistae (2002). "Investment Climate and Economic Performance: Some Firm Level Evidence from India", paper presented at 3rd Annual Stanford Conference on Indian Economic Reform.

Dossani, R. (2002a). Telecommunications Reform in India, Asia/Pacific Research Center, Stanford University, June.

Dossani, R. (2002b). India's Power Sector Reforms, Asia/Pacific Research Center, Stanford University, June.

Dossani, R., and R. T. Crow (2001). "Restructuring the Electric Power Sector in India: Alternative Institutional Structures and Mechanisms," Working Paper, Asia/Pacific Research Center, Stanford University.

Dreze, J., and A. Sen (1995). *India: Economic Development and Social Opportunity*. Delhi: Oxford University Press.

Forbes, N. (2002). "Doing Business in India: What Has Liberalization Changed?," in A. Krueger, ed., *Economic Policy Reforms and the Indian Economy*. Chicago: University of Chicago Press.

Frankel, F. (2002). Discussant's Comments, Workshop on Federalism in a Globalized Environment, CREDPR, Stanford University, June 6–7.

Government of India (2004). Report of the Task Force on Implementation of the Fiscal Responsibility and Budget Management Act, 2003, Ministry of Finance, July.

Gulati, A., and S. Bathla (2001). "Capital Formation in Indian Agriculture: Revisiting the Debate," Economic and Political Weekly 36: 20.

Hirschman, A. O. (1970). *Exit, Voice, and Loyalty; Responses to Decline in Firms, Organizations, and States*. Cambridge, MA: Harvard University Press.

Inman, R., and D. Rubinfeld (1997). "The Political Economy of Federalism," in D. Mueller, ed., *Perspectives on Public Choice: A Handbook*. Cambridge, UK: Cambridge University Press.

Jha, P. S. (2002). "Counsel of Despair," The Hindu, September 12, 2002, http://www.hinduonnet.com/thehindu/2002/09/12/stories/2002091202511800.htm.

Kapur, D. (2001). "India's Institutions and Economic Performance," paper presented at conference on Public Institutions in India: Performance and Design, Harvard University, February.

Kapur, D., and R. Ramamurthi (2002). "Privatization in India: The Imperatives and Consequences of Gradualism," paper presented at 3rd Annual Stanford Conference on Indian Economic Reform.

Lahiri, A. K. (1999). "Practising Sub-National Public Finance in India," paper presented at the First Meeting of the Global Network Conference, Session on Decentralization, Governance and Public Goods in Large Economies, Bonn, Germany, December. New Delhi: NIPFP.

Majeed, A. (2002). Untitled paper presented at Roundtable on Mechanisms of Intergovernmental Relations in India, Institute of Social Sciences, New Delhi, April 22.

Mauor, J. (1995). "Political Sustainability of Economic Reform," in Cassen, R., and U. Joshi, eds. *India: The Future of Economic Reforms* pp. 339–363. New Delhi: Oxford University Press.

Mathur, O. P. (1999). "Decentralization in India: A Report Card," Working Paper, National Institute of Public Finance and Policy, New Delhi, March.

McKinsey Global Institute (2001). India: The Growth Imperative, September.

Mohan, R. (2001). "Achieving Higher Economic Growth: The Fiscal Deterrent," paper presented at 2nd Annual Stanford Conference on Indian Economic Reform, June.

Mohan, R. (2002a). "Small Scale Industry Reservations," in A. Krueger, ed., *Economic Policy Reforms and the Indian Economy*. Chicago: University of Chicago Press.

Mohan, R. (2002b). Discussant's Comments, Workshop on Federalism in a Globalized Environment, CREDPR, Stanford University, June 6–7.

Mukherjee, A. (2002). "Foreign Firms Pulling Out of Power Projects," The Hindu, July 8, www.hinduonnet.com/stories/2002070802271300.htm.

Nagaraj, R., A. Varoudakis, and M.-A. Véganzonès (1998). "Long-Run Growth Trends and Convergence across Indian States," OECD Technical Paper No. 131.

NASSCOM (National Association of Software and Service Companies) (2002a). Software Export, www.nasscom.org/it industry/sw export.asp.

NASSCOM (National Association of Software and Service Companies) (2002b). FY02: Software and Service Industry Performance, July 18, www.nasscom.org/download/ FYo2-results.pdf.

Planning Commission (2002). National Human Development Report. New Delhi: Government of India.

Rajaraman, I. (2001). "Growth-Accelerating Fiscal Devolution to the Third Tier", paper presented at NIPFP-DFID-World Bank Conference on India: Fiscal Policies to Accelerate Economic Growth, New Delhi, May.

Rao, M. G. (2000a). "Tax Reform in India: Achievements and Challenges," Asia-Pacific Development Journal 7(2): 59–74.

Rao, M. G. (2000b). "Fiscal Decentralization in Indian Federalism," processed, Bangalore: Institute for Social and Economic Change.

Rao, M. G. (2002). "State Level Fiscal Reforms in India," paper presented at Cornell University, Conference on Indian Economic Reform, April 19–20.

Rao, M. G., and N. Singh (1998). "Fiscal Overlapping, Concurrency and Competition in Indian Federalism," Working Paper 30b, Center for Research on Economic Development and Policy Reform, Stanford University.

Rao, M. G., and N. Singh (2003). "The Political Economy of Center-State Fiscal Transfers in India," in J. McLaren, ed., *Institutional Elements of Tax Design and Reform* pp. 220–247. Washington, D.C.: World Bank.

Rao, M. G., and N. Singh (2001). "Federalism in India: Political Economy and Reform," paper presented at the conference, "India: Ten Years of Economic

Reform," at the William Davidson Institute, University of Michigan, September 2001.

Rao, M. G., and N. Singh (2002). "Fiscal Transfers in a Developing Country: The Case of India," paper presented at University of Birmingham conference on comparative federalism.

Rao, M. G., and N. Singh (2005). *The Political Economy of Indian Federalism*. New Delhi: Oxford University Press.

Rao, M. G., R. Shand, and K. P. Kalirajan (1999). "Convergence of Incomes across Indian States: A Divergent View," Economic and Political Weekly, March 27– April 2.

Reddy, Y. V. (1979). *Multilevel Planning in India*. New Delhi: Vikas.

Reserve Bank of India (2001). *Annual Report 2000–2001*. Bombay: Reserve Bank.

Richards, A., and N. Singh (2002). "Inter State Water Disputes in India: Institutions and Policies," in International Journal of Water Resources Development 18(4): 611–625.

Riker, W. (1975). "Federalism," in F. I. Greenstein and N. W. Polsby, eds., *Handbook of Political Science, Vol. 5*: 72–93. Reading, MA: Addison-Wesley.

Roy, A. (2002). "Facilitating FDI," The Hindu, September 30, 2002, http://www.hinduonnet.com/thehindu/2002/09/30/stories/2002093000020200.htm.

Sáez, L. (2002). *Federalism without a Centre: The Impact of Political and Economic Reform on India's Federal System*. New Delhi: Sage Publications.

Singh, N. (2002). "Information Technology and India's Economic Development," in K. Basu, ed., *India's Emerging Economy: Performance and Prospects in the 1990s and Beyond* 223–262. Cambridge, MA: MIT Press.

Singh, N. (2004). "Some Economic Consequences of India's Institutions of Governance: A Conceptual Framework," India Review 3(2): 114–146.

Singh, N., and T. N. Srinivasan (2004). "Fiscal Policy in India: Lessons and Priorities," paper presented at NIPFP-IMF Conference on Fiscal Policy in India, New Delhi, January.

Singh, N., and G. Vasishtha (2004). "Some Patterns in Center-State Fiscal Transfers in India: An Illustrative Analysis," UCSC working paper.

Singh, N. K., and A. Modi (2001). "Direct Tax Reform in India," paper presented at 2nd Annual Stanford Conference on Indian Economic Reform, June.

Srinivasan, T. N. (2002). "India's Fiscal Situation: Is a Crisis Ahead?," in A. Krueger, ed., *Economic Policy Reforms and the Indian Economy*. Chicago: University of Chicago Press.

Srinivasan, T. N., and S. D. Tendulkar (2002). *Reintegrating India with the World Economy*. Washington, DC: Institute for International Economics.

Srivastava, R. (1998). "Migration and the Labour Market in India," The Indian Journal of Labour Economics 41: 583–616.

Watts, R. (2001). "Introduction: Federalism in an Era of Globalisation," International Social Science Journal 53: 9–12.

Weingast, B. (1993). "Constitutions as Governance Structures," Journal of Institutional and Theoretical Economics 149: 233–261.

EIGHT

Mexico's Decentralization at a Crossroads

Alberto Diaz-Cayeros, José Antonio González, and Fernando Rojas

> Democratization, decentralization, and development. These three sequential forces have swept the world over the last decade and have redrawn the maps of politics, power, and prosperity.
>
> Giugale and Webb (2000)

I. INTRODUCTION

The implicit assumption in this recent World Bank book on Mexico is that democratization leads to decentralization and that the latter leads to development. In all fairness, the publication and the Bank have been careful to point out that not all decentralization is good for development. This chapter argues that, in practice, not all democracies have equally auspicious forces driving the decentralization process.

Decentralization can, but does not necessarily, improve accountability, equity, and government performance. From the citizen's point of view, the specific benefits that decentralization can bring about depend on the way they are represented politically as well as the kinds of institutions that form and implement government policy. Moreover, the costs and benefits of decentralization depend largely on the entry points and intermediate goals for the transition from the centralized state to a decentralized public sector. There is no standard path toward decentralization; and countries also rarely plan their path toward a final version of the decentralized state – the process is more often the result of internally inconsistent accumulated reforms adopted over time in response to changes in the political balance.

This chapter is centered on two interconnected developments that account for the main challenges for Mexico's decentralization today. First, basic political incentives have been at odds with decentralization efforts during the first two phases of decentralization – roughly from the early 1980s to the mid-1990s. Although the mood of the country during the past five or so years is gradually leading to a realignment of political goals with decentralization policy aims, the cumulative effect of more than twenty years of reform creates a formidable barrier to streamlining the process of decentralization. Second, the specific features of democratic institutions and processes in Mexico have become important stumbling blocks, rather than promoters, of an efficient and equitable decentralization process.

The central problem of fiscal federalism in Mexico today is that subnational governments lack clear jurisdiction over most policy areas resulting in a lack of accountability for policy choices. The federal government holds crucial pieces of the process and key mechanisms to hold any level of government accountable for policy failures are imperfect. If something goes wrong, subnational governments usually blame the federal government, and in many cases the federal government steps in to correct the problem. State governments thus have few incentives to carry out their mandates.

The issue in Mexico today is not whether there should be more or less decentralization – more or less revenues (or sources of revenues) given to subnational governments to alleviate vertical or regional imbalances[1] – but rather how to create better incentives for the uses of the political and economic resources currently granted to different levels of government. Much attention has been focused, for example, on the fact that the vertical fiscal imbalance is high, but we would argue that the lack of institutional arrangements for a well-designed transfer system (or redistribution of revenues sources for that matter) is a larger impediment to effective public policy. If political institutions remain as they are, greater decentralization will likely reduce accountability and increase regional tensions by widening the gap between who pays taxes and how, where, and by whom budgets are spent. Decentralization and fiscal federalism reform, like all other democratic political institutions in Mexico, need to be adapted to a new environment of multiparty competition and shifting fiscal power, so that actors, both in the center and in the regions, have the right incentives to carry out their tasks.

---

[1] See Giugale and Webb (2000).

Like many other countries, Mexico has not followed a planned path toward decentralization. Pragmatic decisions over time have led to frequent course adjustments. When analyzed ex post, four turns can be clearly identified as the main phases of the Mexican process of decentralization during the past twenty years. Each phase has been characterized by the use of a particular set of technical instruments that were basically adequate for reaching the specific goals of Mexico's decentralization at each point in time. Each one of the four phases of Mexico's decentralization has broadly followed changes in the broad political context at each point in time. When necessary, governments have sacrificed technical purity in adjusting decentralization goals and tools to political pressures that appear to be of overall concern at a given time. It has only been recently, during the last two phases of Mexico's pursuit of decentralization, that sound fiscal and management guidelines such as elimination of discretionary transfers or enhanced accountability have coincided with government styles and political agendas. Besides the broad political context, increasing technical refinement in the design of the decentralization framework has also been stimulated by governments' own evaluation of the process of decentralization as well as lessons learned from countries going through similar waves of decentralization. Still, political barriers often demand enactment of policies or instruments – as in the case of the reform of social investment funds – that go in the opposite direction from sound decentralization policies.

Since the goals of and approaches to decentralization as well as selected technical instruments were ordinarily conditioned by the political context, it is no surprise that instruments often missed the proposed decentralization target. However, it is the cumulative effect of the four phases of decentralization reform – more than the particular set of measures and instruments adopted at each phase in time – that makes the current decentralization framework inconsistent and hard to reform on a piecemeal basis. As many decentralization experts have indicated in the past, the Mexican system is confusing and sends many inconsistent messages to decentralization stakeholders. The best the country can do in these circumstances seems to be to first build consensus toward a Mexican model of federalism and decentralization and then enact an overhaul of fiscal federalism and the overall distribution of revenues and responsibilities among levels of government.

The existing literature exploring the subtleties of fiscal federalism in Mexico has been thorough, but it has generally missed a critical political economy issue: Mexico's current political scenario does not allow for a

comprehensive reform of fiscal federalism. The existing political institutions of the Mexican federal arrangement produce a very strong status
quo bias, particularly in the current context of multiparty competition.
Multiple veto players[2] must be made better off to allow for any change
in the current system, so that prospects for reform depend on the possibility of constructing a large enough political coalition. Given that the
coalition must agree on a redistribution not only of political power but
also of economic resources, such a coalition is unlikely to form in the
current political climate. In fact, our analysis suggests that in addition
to there being a status quo bias, the few incremental changes that have
been possible point in the direction of decreasing accountability, exacerbating the problems of the Mexican federal pact. In a more realistic
scenario, Mexico's decentralization reform has to follow an incremental
path, focusing on the gradual alignment of incentives. This chapter discusses ongoing marginal reforms and suggests ways in which they can be
strengthened.

The chapter is organized as follows. Section II provides an overview
of Mexico's political economy, including a discussion of the relationship
globalization, decentralization, and democratization. It provides some
background on the institutional features of Mexico's federalism that have
generated a political impasse in the budgetary processes, hindering the
reform of the system of intergovernmental transfers and preventing a
significant overhaul of Mexico's fiscal federalism. Section III then discusses four key reform moments of the process of decentralization. Mexico's decentralization began by depriving states of own revenue sources,
thereby widening the gap in the benefit principle between who taxes and
who receives the benefits of public action, and weakening government
responsiveness and accountability. Second, the process of deconcentration in education, health, and water provision has yet to reap its benefits.
Third, we argue that the growth of broadly defined earmarked fiscal transfers during the past few years is a result of the process of discussion and
approval of the federal budget. Since the Partido Revolucionario Institucional (PRI) lost its majority in the Chamber of Deputies in 1997, approval
of the federal budget has been made contingent on the provision of ever
larger transfers to states and municipalities. The last part of Section III
outlines current federal attempts to reestablish hard budget constraints,
a clear division of responsibilities, and accountability via subnational

---

[2] On veto players see Tsebelis (1995).

borrowing regulations and intergovernment performance agreements. Section IV briefly concludes the chapter.

II. POLITICAL AND REGULATORY FRAMEWORK: THE BACKDROP FOR FISCAL FEDERALISM

Mexico is organized as a federal republic with thirty-one states and a Federal District located in Mexico City. The 1917 Constitution clearly establishes a democracy with separation of powers, along lines similar to the United States. However, the specific organization of Mexican legislatures and institutions regulating its state–central government relations are dramatically different. The differences were critical for the design of decentralization, because of the effects they had on political accountability and representation. This section describes the political institutions and their role in the decentralization process. Given the inherited political institutions, it is unlikely that a major decentralization reform will be approved by the legislature. Instead, only marginal reforms can be expected in the future, based on broad state coalitions.

II.1. State Representation in National Politics through Two Legislative Chambers

Within a bicameral system, the Chamber of Deputies is elected every three years, with no immediate reelection, through a mixed system of single member districts (SMD) and proportional representation (PR).[3] The same ballot is cast to vote for both the SMD candidate and the PR party list. Such an organization of the legislature tends to increase the number of political parties represented, given the relatively high mean district magnitude, and mitigate the particularistic (or personal) incentives of legislatures, in favor of a greater partisan discipline. Since immediate reelection is prohibited however, legislators have an incentive to focus on passing legislation that will benefit the jurisdiction where their future career objectives can be obtained: usually the state congress, a municipal presidency, the Senate, or the governorship of their state. Though incentives to reward local interests are tempered by party control over placement on the PR lists, legislators elected through party lists (who usually

---

[3] Two-hundred of the 500-member body are made up by these compensatory seats in five multistate districts. For discussions of the Mexican political arrangement see Diaz-Cayeros and Magaloni (2001) and Cornelius and Craig (1995).

Box 8.1. *The Fiscal Pact*

The Mexican Constitution allows for overlapping authority among federal, state, and municipal governments. Whereas Article 73 establishes some taxes that are exclusively under federal jurisdiction (which include, among others, natural resources, most excises, and taxes on the financial sector), Article 31 in the Constitution establishes the obligation of all Mexicans to pay taxes without making any distinction among federal, state, or municipal levels of government.

Hence, tax assignment is not the product of constitutional provisions; rather, it is a consequence of a secondary law, the Law of Fiscal Coordination (Ley de Coordinación Fiscal – LCF), which establishes the revenue-sharing system and since 1998 incorporates most of the decentralized federal expenditure transfers to states and municipalities. States belong to the revenue-sharing agreement through their voluntary "adhesion" to the system. The LCF is what prevents state governments from creating their own sales or income taxes, because the creation of those taxes would be considered a violation of the revenue-sharing agreement. The LCF establishes a clear provision for what would happen if a state decided to exit the revenue-sharing agreement: All the federal taxes would remain in place, and the revenue-sharing allocation to the rest of the states would be calculated as though the exiting state still remained in the system, hence making the federal government the residual claimant of that revenue.

The LCF establishes clear formulas for the allocation of revenue sharing to both states and municipalities, but the states also have their own formulas for allocating funds among their municipal governments. The LCF also establishes formulas for the allocation of expenditure transfers (called aportaciones), although their behavior, particularly in the case of education funds, is driven more by historical inertia in the distribution of funds than by the use of explicit quantitative indicators.

---

occupy some of the important leadership positions in the legislature) are often concerned about advancing local careers in their states.

This legislative career behavior is quite different from the one that used to prevail when the PRI was a hegemonic party, virtually uncontested in its nominations for any public office. During the heyday of PRI hegemony, the legislature would rubberstamp any bill submitted by the president (who was also the leader of their party) because the president controlled all the nominations to future elective posts as well as appointments to the federal bureaucracy. With the onset of democratization, starting in the 1980s, but clearly evident after 1997, legislators from all parties in the lower house are torn between incentives to remain loyal to partisan mandates (to secure a future position among those controlled by the party leadership) or to follow localist careers aligned with the governors and the local parties in their states.

Willis, Garmand, and Haggard (1999, 2001) have established that there is a direct link between a push toward greater decentralization and the local nomination of elective posts in party systems in Latin America. In their argument, decentralization is more prevalent when nominations are controlled by local party organizations because politicians' fates depend on citizen demands at the local level. The Mexican case is ambiguous in this context, because deputies are not responsive to either partisan or local incentives, but to a mixture given by the mixed electoral system, the nonreelection clause, and the fused ballot for both PR and SMD races. Moreover, the internal organization of the lower chamber favors strong party leadership through committee assignments.

Perhaps the most important effect of the electoral system in the lower house of the legislature is that it promotes the fragmentation of the body, with the representation of at least three effective political parties. This fragmentation has been observed at least since 1988, although it was not until 1997 that its political implications became obvious: The president's party does not control the majority in the Chamber of Deputies. The political science literature has stressed that this is the Achilles' heel of presidential systems of government as compared to parliamentarism, because divided governments can make the cooperation between the president and the legislature problematic. More importantly, a combination of presidentialism and multipartyism is likely to be destabilizing, given the difficulty for reaching compromises and cooperation between a fragmented legislature and a president with a smaller group of party allies.[4]

In contrast to the U.S. Senate, which is quite symmetric in terms of its power relative to the lower chamber, and where the representation of states is equal, the Mexican Senate is weak and the representation of states is diluted by partisan considerations. The Mexican Senate has less formal powers than the lower chamber because it has no authority over the federal budget. Four members per district are elected concurrently

---

[4] The literature on this debate is enormous, but a good summary can be found in Linz (1990). The link between multipartyism and parliamentarism as a difficult combination can be found in Mainwaring (1993).

with the presidential election every six years through a mixed system.[5] Voters cast only one ballot for party lists of two senators. The party with the most votes receives two Senate seats (the full slate wins), a third Senate seat is filled by the first candidate on the list proposed by the party with the second highest vote count; and the last senator comes from an at-large national PR party list. This means that half of the senators are responsive to partisan influences, in terms of their placement in the PR lists or at the top of the state lists (and hence they are eligible for the minority seat, even when losing). The Mexican Senate, meant to be the sphere of representation of state interests, is a also weak institution compared with the lower chamber because of its lack of budgetary authority. The Senate reflects state interests poorly, since half of its members owe their seats more to the party (which either placed them at the top of the binomial formula, or put them in a high place in the PR party list) than to state constituencies.

In the time of PRI hegemony a Senate seat was an attractive post mostly because it was the springboard for politicians to seek nominations to their state governorships. (Around a third of the governors in the 1935–1988 period came directly from a Senate seat.) In that sense, the Senate represented state interests through the political ambition of its members in the era of PRI hegemony. However, after democratization the greater partisan makeup of the body, resulting from the mixed system gradually introduced since 1988, together with the fact that the Senate has no influence on how the federal budget is allocated to the states, means that senators do not constitute the "natural" defenders of state interests in the federal pact.

The peculiar combination of (and sometimes conflict between) local and partisan incentives for politicians in the lower and upper chambers in Mexico suggests that deputies might paradoxically be more likely to serve state interests than senators. This is because SMD deputies can use alliances with state governors, mayors, or local political groups to strengthen their chances of election in a way that Senators cannot. To the extent that deputies can use their role in the budgetary approval process as a bargaining chip in the distributive struggles between governors and the federal government, they can align their interests more readily with those of their home states than can most senators.

The complications among government branches are hence most evident in budgetary politics. The executive is procedurally strong in the formulation of the budget, since the Ministry of Finance (Secretaria de

---

[5] This is a relatively high district magnitude for an upper chamber in a federal system.

Hacienda y Credito Publico – SHCP) is dominant in that process, but it is weak in implementation. The allocation of veto powers and voting powers to the executive and two legislatures creates a system where there are strong incentives to increase expenditures in the budgetary approval stage. The ability to reduce expenditure once approved, in case there are revenue shortfalls, has until now been granted to the Ministry of Finance. But there is no reason for deputies to remain passive in this process in the future, as they become, in the years to come, more knowledgeable about the budget process and as their staffers become more professionalized. The amount of discretion available to the SHCP to reallocate expenditure among budget categories will become increasingly diminished, as congressional oversight, which in the hegemonic PRI era was practically nonexistent, becomes stronger.

Partisan factions and state delegations have few incentives within the current system to support the presidential budget, since it is unclear whether the president can veto an amendment-laden version passed by the lower house. The Senate cannot vote on the expenditure budget, but the Constitution establishes that presidential veto powers operate only when a bill is voted by both chambers. Because the Senate is not involved in the budget bill, a strict interpretation of the Constitution implies that the president cannot veto the budget approved by the lower chamber. In practice, the question of whether the president can veto a budget is hotly debated and presidents have not vetoed budgets since the 1920s.[6] However, regardless of how a constitutional controversy over a budget veto would be settled by the Supreme Court, if the threat of a veto is ever used, the uncertainty surrounding this institutional feature seriously diminishes the bargaining power of the president vis-à-vis the legislature.

Moreover, the lack of an established reversion point that allows for the president to use some budget (such as the previous year's or the proposed bill) in case the Chamber of Deputies cannot agree on one by December 31 gives additional leverage to deputies who can hold back their support for the budget. Legislators' main incentive is thus to push for amendments that might increase the share of local government transfers in the federal budget.

These budgetary funds are tied, however, according to the LCF, to the revenue estimated by the federal government (Recaudación Federal Participable – RFP). Changes to the formulas and allocation criteria related to fiscal federalism need to be approved by both the Chamber

---

[6] See Weldon (1996).

of Deputies and the Senate, which makes it difficult to change the budget legislation once enacted. When the budgetary process increases funds transferred to the states, it is difficult for decreases to be made later if the increased funds are incorporated in the LCF.

II.2. Subnational Politics

The directly elected governors, the counterpart to the national executive, have become key players in the decentralization process. They are elected according to a staggered electoral calendar, so that only a handful of them are elected concurrently with the president and the federal legislature. It is not until the fifth year in the (six-year) presidential term that the majority of the governors have been elected during the current presidential term. This staggered election setup implies that governors do not ride federal or presidential coattails, so their electoral claim to representation is independent from that of the federal government.[7] The president's influence on subnational policy is thus constrained by the governors he or she inherited. In the past, PRI presidents controlled governors through political channels. As more governors are not affiliated with the party of the sitting president (and this is likely to continue to be a feature in Mexico's political landscape in the future) cooperation between executives in Mexico will require federal concessions.

The institutional power of governors differs across states. Some can freely appoint and dismiss their cabinets and propose legislation, whereas others are quite constrained by their unicameral legislatures and local judiciaries. Except for the informal influence they can exert on their state deputies or senators, governors have no arena in which they can debate the issues of federalism. Finance ministers from the states, together with representatives from the federal finance ministry, the SHCP, can discuss fiscal federalism every year in the Reunion Annual de Funcionarios Fiscales, but their decisions have no political weight. The Confederacion Nacional de Gobernadores (CONAGO), organized in 2001 by the twenty-three governors from parties other than the Partido Acción Nacional (PAN) (to which president Fox belongs), is a becoming an increasingly powerful organization. All states now belong to the Conago Governors meet roughly once a month to debate national politics. In most cases, the meetings concentrate on fiscal federalism issues.

---

[7] This is a key difference with respect to Argentina, Brazil, or other federal systems, in which national and local elections are usually concurrent.

The municipal level of government has played a key role in Mexican federalism, notwithstanding that municipalities are not, strictly speaking, partners in the federal pact. There is no specific mechanism for the representation of municipal interests within the state-level institutional structure, except to the extent that they belong to local congressional districts. However, municipal interests are primarily protected by the federal constitution. In contrast to other federal regimes, state legislatures do not determine the main characteristics and attributes of local governments. Provisions in the federal constitution determine the composition of municipal councils, the functional areas where municipalities have exclusive jurisdiction, and the transfer of federal and state financial resources. State legislatures can decide the characteristics of the property tax, which is the main source of revenue for municipalities, and can determine the allocation of some, but not all, of the federally mandated transfers across their municipalities.

In short, the political institutions in Mexico have generated a complex set of veto players with varying political incentives. The mixed system in the legislature generates a fragmented lower chamber, where no party is likely to control the majority and multiparty coalitions must be formed to pass legislation. Career advancement motivations lead deputies to cater to either partisan or state interests – districts are neglected. The Senate represents party, rather than state interests, and thus there is no natural forum for the debate over federalism. The budgetary process involves a weak president, necessitating oversized coalitions held together by side payments to gain budgetary approval. States, as represented in the Senate, have no decision power in the expenditure budget approval, but they may block changes to the status quo in the fiscal federalism arrangement. Governors have little counterweight to their power over subnational matters, but they lack institutional forms to coordinate as a united front vis-à-vis the federal government. Municipalities have incentives to press, through their copartisans in the federal legislatures, for greater devolution. They have no incentive to align their positions with their state governments and legislatures.

III. THE FOUR MOMENTS OF MEXICO'S DECENTRALIZATION

Mexico is currently undergoing a slow, uncertain transition in the decentralization process. The overwhelming majority of the literature agrees that democratization in the country has created a demand for decentralization and that the latter is leading (or will lead) to more equitable and efficient public spending. Comparing with other Latin American countries, there is a sense that Mexico is set on an inevitable path to greater decentralization. Subnational governments are spending ever-increasing shares of total public expenditures and appear to be managing more and more responsibilities in specific functional sectors.

To understand the current decentralization framework it is necessary to look at the recent evolution of decentralization in Mexico. A thorough historical recount of the relationship between states and the federal government is a long one and well beyond the scope of this paper.[8] We propose, instead, to highlight four key moments and policy reforms placed one on top of each other giving rise to the framework that exists today:

1. the overhaul of the sales tax and the introduction of the National Value Added Tax (VAT, or the IVA as it is known in Mexico) through the Sistema Nacional de Coordinación Fiscal in 1980;
2. the National Agreement to Modernize Basic Education in 1992 as a response to pressure from democratically elected governors;
3. the undoing of another key reform that occurred in the late 1980s (the transformation of the social investment programs and funds that were first established as part of the macroeconomic stabilization and structural reform program of the late 1980s and early 1990s); and
4. efforts to deal with today's mosaic of different measures taken on top of each other, which create confusion in almost every aspect of decentralization.

III.1. A Transfer Led Decentralization

The first key reform that shaped the modern decentralization framework was the overhaul of the sales tax and the introduction of the VAT through the Sistema Nacional de Coordinación Fiscal (SNCF, often referred to as Pacto Fiscal) in 1980. The states joined voluntarily, giving up their share of revenues on the sales tax and eliminating some remaining state excise taxes in exchange for a share (initially 13%, gradually increased to 20%) of unconditional revenue transfers (participaciones) from the VAT, the federal income tax, and some oil fees in the middle of a massive oil boom. This centralized most indirect taxes while guaranteeing unconditional, almost automatic, resources to the states. Over time, the derivation component

[8] See Careaga and Weingast (2003) and Courchene, Diaz-Cayeros, and Webb 2000 for good historical summaries of fiscal relations from the early 1920s to 1980.

of revenue from the sales taxes was changed to a more equalizing formula, which was only marginally tied to fiscal effort. The impact of the reform of 1980 on the potential for decentralization reform in Mexico is still felt today.[9]

The remarkable aspect of this reform is that there was no accompanying transfer of responsibilities to go with the increased funding. The original idea was that states would receive the same amount of resources as before, but the actual amount of participaciones increased drastically without any corresponding revenue responsibilities or precise expenditure requirements laid out. States began programs that in many cases duplicated federal programs without any clear division of responsibilities. The role of unconditional revenue-sharing transfers, coupled with other transfers that came later, made Mexico's decentralization primarily expenditure based.

After states abdicated their capacity to tax sales in 1980, the main sources of state revenues became the payroll taxes and automobile registration fees (ISAN and tenencia). Payroll taxes produce almost half of the states' own tax revenues (45.6%, but the share increases to 63% if one excludes the Federal District), but own revenues account for only 9.2% of total revenues of state governments owing to the dominance of revenue sharing.

Automobile registration and user fees are formally federal taxes, but they are directly and completely assigned to the states. Compliance with these taxes appears to be improving over the past few years. States are both learning from and competing with one another, facilitating tax compliance to taxpayers (through better billing, bank payments, etc.) and gradually linking services to tax revenues.

Other taxes have been proposed for the state level with the well-known and explored advantages and disadvantages. These include individual

---

[9] Many Latin American countries preferred general revenue-sharing arrangements similar to those adopted by the Mexican Fiscal Pact of the 1980s. This was, for instance, the case with Brazil, Colombia, and Venezuela during the late 1980s. However, none of those countries deprived so drastically the intermediate level of government of their own tax bases. On the contrary, the Brazilian Constitution of 1988, the Colombian tax reform of 1983 and the Venezuelan Decentralization Law of 1988 each expanded the regional tax base. It must also be admitted that some Latin American countries initially pursued sector decentralization in a similar vein to the way Mexico did in the 1990s. This was, for instance, the case with Brazil's return to democracy in the late 1980s and the Colombian first phase of decentralization reform of 1986–1987. However, Colombia soon changed course toward a more gradual, negotiated transfer of sector responsibilities under the Constitution of 1991 and law reform of 1993. Venezuela enacted a negotiated approach to sector decentralization since the country first enacted decentralization in 1988.

income taxes, excise taxes on alcoholic beverages and tobacco products, corporate income tax, retail sales tax, and a compensating VAT. Implementation of any of these does not appear likely in the near future. The main concern is that different state taxation regimes could affect the allocation of production and could hinder interstate trade.

Municipal governments also depend on federal funds. The main source of own municipal revenues is the real estate property tax, comprising 13% of total net revenue and 74.2% of municipal own revenues. Except for Mexico City, the collection of property tax is low. Municipal governments have not updated cadastres effectively or frequently.

It is useful to remember that the creation of a highly centralized system, characterized by weak subnational taxing powers and high fiscal and political dependency, was only possible because of the political dependence of governors, municipal presidents, local and federal deputies, and senators on a hierarchical system of career advancement created by the hegemonic PRI. The party centrally controlled the nominations that allowed for career advancement, while protecting its members from the challenges of democratic competition. The president, as the leader of the party, used his power and resources in the federal sphere to subdue local autonomy. Centripetal forces in the regions were not eliminated, though, leading to the continuous resurfacing of decentralization demands that accompanied the process of democratization since the early 1990s.

Not collecting taxes is an enviable position for subnational governments that share a culture of political patronage based upon pyramidal relations with centralized governments or political parties. Those governments would prefer to spend without collecting taxes since such governments are not interested in receiving the credit of good expenditure management. In single-party systems, revenue is often collected without asking citizens what their money should be spent for. Given the difficulty of eliciting cooperation and compliance, authoritarian systems often rely on rents from natural resources such as oil and minerals to support their activities. In multiparty competitive systems, the fiscal challenge for a government is to find a balance between the taxes that are raised and the public goods that are provided according to citizen's demands. Such a balance can only be reached through transparent fiscal systems that are perceived as fair. The budgetary battles of each year are the expression of the political compromises reached by those seeking to keep such balance.

In the Mexican federal arrangement, however, state and municipal governments often spend by sending funds to those citizens who have the most capacity to press for them, rather than according to a political balance of revenue collected and goods and services provided. The federal budgetary battles have become, in recent years, an expression of the lack of accountability of local governments. In each budgetary round since the PRI lost its absolute majority in 1997, transfer funds have been increased and new ones have been created to obtain legislative support for the presidential bill.

Public expenditures have been decentralized quickly in Mexico, whereas subnational tax revenues have hardly increased. Mexico's level of subnational expenditure in 1996 was still significantly below Brazil's and Argentina's. Thus, although the federal fiscal pact of 1980 represented an important move in the direction of fiscal decentralization, Mexico is still a relatively centralized country as measured by the share of subnational treasury disbursements in the country's total public expenditure. Subnational taxes are well below other Latin American federations, such as Argentina and Brazil. This imbalance presents a potential problem in and of itself because states are so dependent on the central government for transfers and because the potential increases in collection efficiency at the state and local level for some taxes have not been realized. Brazil, for instance, authorizes states to charge the VAT. Colombia, not even a federal state, authorizes its subnational units (departments) to charge more excises than Mexican states.

As a result of a dismally low subnational tax effort, it is not surprising that states are dependent on federal transfers. Table 8.1 shows the high dependency of state and municipal governments on transfers. The states are ranked according to their degree of poverty.[10] Only the Federal District has a sizable share of self-generating revenue – though it still accounts for less than half of total revenues.

Every federal system is characterized by regional transfers that bridge the inevitable gap between substantial subnational responsibilities and subnational taxation. Indeed, no subnational jurisdiction with substantial responsibilities is able to fully finance its own activities. However, the crucial question on the grounds of accountability is whether, at the margin, new expenditure projects are financed by new taxes or expansions of the tax base that are locally borne. That is, the benefits of fiscal federalism are possible when the benefit principle holds at the margin. In Mexico, the federal fiscal pact (SNCF) that started in 1980 established a hard-to-reverse trend of further weakening the benefit connection between taxes and expenditures. Local governments have grown used to a system of

[10] The index is the Foster–Greer–Thorbecke index with a poverty line set at twice the minimum wage.

Table 8.1. *Transfers, Own Revenue, and Fiscal Dependence in 1999*

	State Funds			Municipal Funds		
	Transfers	Own Revenue	Dependence	Transfers	Own Revenue	Dependence
Chiapas	2555	298	89.6%	676	19	97.3%
Oaxaca	2245	79	96.6%	703	30	95.9%
Zacatecas	2544	145	94.6%	696	65	91.4%
Guerrero	2538	190	93.0%	736	69	91.4%
Puebla	1732	206	89.4%	559	0	99.9%
San Luis Potosí	2260	192	92.2%	607	51	92.2%
Hidalgo	2398	173	93.3%	657	68	90.7%
Yucatán	2230	297	88.3%	702	45	94.0%
Veracruz	2077	146	93.4%	567	49	92.1%
Tabasco	4292	303	93.4%	1073	38	96.5%
Campeche	3915	579	87.1%	907	79	92.0%
Durango	2712	215	92.7%	624	74	89.3%
Michoacán	2041	186	91.6%	545	61	89.9%
Tlaxcala	2654	171	93.9%	726	28	96.3%
Guanajuato	1739	300	85.3%	504	95	84.2%
Querétaro	2517	262	90.6%	660	151	81.4%
Nayarit	2971	246	92.4%	712	56	92.8%
Quintana Roo	2952	469	86.3%	664	301	68.8%
Tamaulipas	2526	405	86.2%	523	88	85.6%
Jalisco	1854	381	83.0%	466	176	72.6%
México	1771	193	90.2%	453	141	76.3%
Morelos	2255	346	86.7%	592	37	94.1%
Aguascalientes	2702	232	92.1%	701	148	82.6%
Chihuahua	2128	437	83.0%	498	196	71.7%
Coahuila	2454	434	85.0%	501	119	80.8%
Sinaloa	2255	299	88.3%	505	141	78.2%
Nuevo León	2132	703	75.2%	501	213	70.2%
Colima	3376	246	93.2%	803	95	89.4%
Baja California Sur	4318	178	96.0%	773	376	67.3%
Sonora	2611	459	85.1%	533	163	76.6%
Baja California	2509	458	84.6%	477	228	67.6%
Distrito Federal	3339	2451	57.7%			

Source: Calculated from data by Courchene and Diaz-Cayeros (2000).

revenue sharing that does not reward collection effort, and where the blame for high taxes, or the lack of financial resources to fulfill citizen demands, can always be attributed to the federal level of government.

There are currently two main types of federal transfers: unconditional revenue sharing (participaciones) and conditional transfers

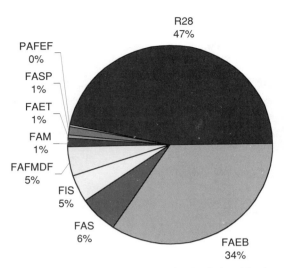

Figure 8.1. Composition of transfer funds in the federal budget of 2002.

(aportaciones). The system of unconditional transfers (participaciones) began in the 1970s but took its recent form in the early 1980s when the sales tax was transformed to the current VAT. Participaciones (Item or Ramo 28 in the budget) represent 47% of all transfers (Figure 8.1). The transfer amount is equal to 20% of the federal income tax, the VAT, and oil fees; in other words, participaciones come from the most important sources of revenue. In terms of the distribution of these funds across states, the LCF establishes that 45.17% is allocated on a per capita basis, 45.17% is allocated on a historical mostly constant, basis (with a very small component to reward fiscal effort), and 9.66% is allocated in a way that compensates the other two criteria. Diaz-Cayeros (1995) demonstrated a gradual convergence across states in the per capita distribution of these funds. Most of these funds are allocated through the Fondo General de Participaciones and the funds have unrestricted use.

Conditional transfers or aportaciones (including those for the Federal District in Ramo 25) amounted to about 53% of total transfers to subnational governments in 2002. The so-called Ramo 33 aportaciones have become a complex amalgam of eight transfer programs. Nevertheless, one could group them into two broad types of expenditures. Most of Ramo 33 is made up of funds for tasks that were originally carried out by the federal government. The most important are education and health expenditures represented by FAEB (for education) and FAS for health. The second is made up of funds whose original intent was to provide matching grants to finance public works, education, and public safety, among other programs.

The obvious way to reduce subnational governments' fiscal dependence on federal transfers is to increase subnational taxation. Indeed, international experience suggests a variety of creative ways to increase subnational taxation, including intergovernment tax-sharing agreements. Although several ways to increase subnational taxation have been proposed in recent years, the truth is that increasing subnational own tax revenues in Mexico has become politically difficult. In fact, what is going on is exactly the opposite: There is a natural race to the bottom in subnational taxes. This will continue to be the case as long as citizens cannot observe a difference in the quality of public service delivery with increases in taxes.

III.2. Deconcentration, Partial Decentralization, and Confusing Responsibilities as a Result of Democratization at the Subnational Level

In 1989 the northern state of Baja California elected the first opposition governor since the PRI was founded in 1929. Soon an increasing number of states and municipalities opted for governments of different party affiliations than that of the federal government. States and municipalities increasingly developed fiscal policies and development agendas of their own.

By 1992 the federal government announced that it was ready to transfer responsibilities, beginning with the social sector (specifically, education responsibilities) to the country's thirty-two federal entities. In the agreement, the federal government attempted to transfer both the education responsibility and the corresponding share of the federal expenditure budget to the states. In practice, the 1992 reform of education was more deconcentration than decentralization, since most of the education transfers, including the detailed payroll, were fully earmarked. Deconcentration of education was precedent-setting for other sectors: A similar model was followed in health; and the federal government retained jurisdiction over water as a national resource (though the distribution of water was primarily municipal). This reform, coupled with the reform that centralized the collection of the VAT in exchange for unconditional transfers, placed key public sector activities – health, education, and water – in jeopardy because of the lack of accountability for the ultimate delivery of the service. Boxes 8.2 and 8.3 describe policy changes in education and water.

Box 8.2. *Education Decentralization*

Education in Mexico is a classic case of deconcentration rather than decentralization. The process of decentralization began in 1992 during the Salinas administration, when the Education Ministry (Secretaría de Educación Pública – SEP) signed the National Agreement to Modernize Basic Education. The agreement was signed by the national teachers' union and the federal and state governments.

It appeared to be a solid start in the decentralization of the educational system. However, the federal government remains in charge of setting standards, developing curricula, running teaching programs, training teachers, producing textbooks, and monitoring and evaluating subnational performance. The federal government finances most infrastructure in the sector, though the states have some say on the way these funds are spent.

The crucial shortcoming is that the federal government effectively continues to operate the schools. The tasks of constructing and operating the schools and paying the teachers, along with the corresponding funds that were previously under federal jurisdiction, have been delegated to the states, but the funds are fully earmarked and most decisions are made by SEP in Mexico City. In effect, the states only distribute the checks and execute the plans with earmarked funds already provided by SEP. Even the teachers' detailed payroll is specified in the transfer of funds. States do have some leeway to hire and fire teachers and negotiations for wage increases are made at the state level, but the state sections of the federal teacher's union do not feel committed by those agreements and the actual incremental wage bill is bargained by the national union in Mexico City.

Therefore, most meaningful decisions are still made at the federal level. The municipalities have little or no role in the process, although these entities are closest to the actual delivery of service. The decision to exclude municipalities, which had been the primary providers of education until the 1930s, was probably made because of the great heterogeneity in the administrative capacity of local governments.

The changes have introduced confusion between preexisting state school systems and the federal system, which need to be reconciled. The extent of state systems varies dramatically across states, which raises an additional issue of horizontal imbalance in the transfer of education funds. Deconcentration of payroll and other operations has created administrative inefficiencies without offsetting gains in allocation efficiencies that should come with decentralization.

Box 8.3. *Water Sector Decentralization*[i]

At first glance, progress in the decentralization of water and sanitation services has been significant. The process of water decentralization began in 1991 when the National Water Program transferred responsibilities from the federal government to the municipalities. Of 135 cities with populations of over 50,000, 118 have autonomous water utilities. Municipal governments set water tariffs for a third of them, the state congress sets them for the rest. However, this does not mean that water utilities are well managed. In fact, water utilities are often an important source of municipal governments' income and therefore the administration is subject to municipal politics. Coverage, leakage, quality, and efficiency all vary tremendously.

More importantly for this study, decentralized provision of water and sanitation is also plagued with confusion and uncertainty. However, the way confusion prevails over clear division of responsibilities in water and sanitation is different from the ambiguity in social sector decentralization. In the case of water, the federal level is clearly responsible for collecting, transporting, and selling "block water" (big volumes of water). As a general rule, the federal government sells water to the states and the states sell water to municipalities and other local providers. The source of the problem is not the formal division of responsibility but the lack of enforcement of the price for water. The federal National Commission of Water (Comisión Nacional de Agua – CNA) does not enforce water payments, thereby leading states to do likewise. In turn, local providers feel little incentive to effectively apply water charges to final users. Poor cost recovery practices lead to substantial subsidies at all levels of government. Since perverse incentives are transmitted from the top down, no level of government is effectively accountable for under-financing – and eventually underprovision or exhaustion of sources – of water.

---

[i] Much of this material is covered in Giugale and Webb (2000). Mexico City is an especially complex case where even the national legislature has some say in the administration of the water utility.

Notwithstanding decentralization efforts, in Mexico there are few if any responsibilities that are fully and exclusively assigned to states or municipalities. Distribution of responsibilities according to the law is confusing by itself (see Table 8.2) and, in practice, the division of labor among levels

Table 8.2. *Mexico's Responsibility Assignment*

Expenditure Function	Federal Government	State Governments	Municipal Governments
Defense	100%		
Police	Federal and border corps; federal transfers to state and municipal policy	Special policy (concurrent with federal); state public order and safety	Local policy corps
Foreign Affairs	100%		
Labor Policies	100%		
Monetary and Financial Policies	100%		
Foreign Trade and Diplomatic Relations	100%		
Mail and Telecommunications	Along with private providers		
Transportation	Most railroads, ports, and airports have been privatized	Some airports	Local public transportation
Roads	Federal highway construction and maintenance (C&M); rural road financing	State feeder roads (C&M); maintenance of secondary feeder roads; implementation of rural road development	Local streets
Environmental Standards	National standards; biosphere reserves; national monuments and parks	States can adopt their own standards, complying with the federal ones; state parks	Land use permits; local parks; solid waste
Education (Massive Deconcentration)	Policies, programs, and norms; evaluation and audits of subnational performance; financing through transfers	Operation, administration, and implementation of mandates and programs; maintenance (concurrent);	Minimal role; school maintenance and some construction

	(Ramo 33); labor relations, wage-setting, and most training; federal technical institutes and universities		construction of technical schools and some universities
Health	Policies and norms through the social security institute; financing through transfers in Ramo 33; most capital structure decisions; evaluation and audit of subnational performance; labor relations and wage determination; secondary and tertiary hospitals	Primary care for rural population and urban poor; some financing; administration of programs and self-evaluation; epidemiology and preventive care; reproductive health	
Water and Sanitation		Water supply and sewage (concurrent)	Garbage collection; water supply and sewage; some water systems have been privatized but municipalities retain debt liability

Source: Giugale and Webb 2000 and authors' information.

of government is even more complicated. In practice, responsibilities cannot be easily identified or verified. Therefore it is easy for different levels of government to pass the blame to each other.

The movement toward decentralization faced four major constraints that ended up reducing decentralization to a confusing mix of deconcentration and partial decentralization. It can be said that the decentralization movement of the early 1990s imprinted the wrong signals in Mexico's decentralization – and those signals are still present today. What the country has done in the second half of the 1990s and the first years of this millennium can be read as a series of patchy reforms to attempt to reverse the problems created by the extreme centralism of the federal fiscal pact initiated in 1980 and the processes of decentralization of health, education, and social infrastructure now contained in the federal fiscal pact (LCF).

The four major constraints faced by the decentralization movement of the early 1990s were the following:

- The federal fiscal pact of the early 1980s debilitated the states' taxing powers while transferring resources the states had already committed to a wide range of activities, including health and education expenditures that either duplicated or were parallel to those of the federal level.
- There was considerable political resistance to effectively empowering subnational governments. Transfer of resources and responsibilities were generally perceived as further weakening the monopoly power of the PRI government.
- Trade unions were not prepared to accept fragmentation of their power under a one-party state to negotiate collective bargaining agreements on a subnational scale or otherwise debilitate their power-sharing position. Unions were also not prepared to accept fiscally weaker managers.
- Civil society did not mobilize in favor of decentralization. Service users had no basis to expect states would perform better – in terms of coverage, quality, or expenditure efficiency – than the federal level.

In the end, Mexico adopted a social sector decentralization scheme that conveys perverse incentives to all stakeholders. From the revenue point of view, the main concern of the federal level was to equate fiscal transfers with health or education payroll. Although states are technically contractors of teachers and doctors, federal rules and collective bargaining agreements between unions and the federation still prevail. Production functions for health and education were kept highly rigid, thereby limiting any efficiency-enhancing adoptations to local circumstance. Parents, teachers, or social security users can hardly establish any connection between paying taxes and state health or education services. As time has passed since the decentralization agreement of 1992, states have kept demanding additional resources to ensure payment of wage increases. Other factor inputs – such as medical or education supplies, equipment, or physical facilities – have received little attention. In fact, many states still leave education sector management to trade union leaders. Supply-side focus in management deters attention to educational demand, performance, and monitoring of teacher quality.

From the point of view of expenditure responsibilities, the federal level has not been able to do away with human resource management or micromonitoring earmarked transfers for payroll or supplies. In the case of education, most states keep parallel, separate (federal, state) teacher administrations. In the case of health, different degrees of dual (federal, state) systems – created or consolidated through ad hoc measures – offer different service quality and coverage to the same population. This confusing division of responsibilities weakens accountability and government responsiveness and deters potential local or regional ownership.

Essentially, the country still waits for the benefits of decentralized administration of social services. Although politicians continue to claim credit for the country's growing share of social expenditures at the regional or local levels, the truth is that there is little or no connection between decentralization and higher coverage or quality of service. Nor can it be said that current subnational expenditures in health or education are more efficient than previously centralized expenditures. Moreover, it would be hard for a state or local government to claim political credit for better management or enhanced performance. Citizens are generally apathetic to who is administering the service. The federal level – although still responsible for social policy – finds it difficult to monitor or stimulate subnational governments. States find that accepting responsibility for social services not only leads to cumbersome administration but elevates their fiscal and political dependency. It is small wonder that some states (Oaxaca in the south or Aguascalientes in the center of the country) have already offered to return responsibility for social services to the federal government. States now have to administer responsibilities whose costs and production functions are largely determined at the federal level.

III.3. The Third Phase: The Politics of Transformation of Social Investment Funds

The third phase of Mexico's decentralization, although primarily related to the expenditure to finance investment projects at the local level, is linked to the international processes of globalization. To understand the transformation of the social investment funds into decentralized expenditure transfers in the late 1990s, one has to go back to the origin of these funds. In the aftermath of the debt crisis Mexico shifted its development strategy, seeking to reap the benefits of open international markets. Though tentative at first, trade liberalization was accelerated in the late 1980s as part of the strategy for controlling inflation. The successful 1987 stabilization gave the country the first sound footing for growth since the debt crisis. When the Carlos Salinas administration came into office in 1988, Mexico was already a relatively open economy to international trade, although serious questions remained as to the commitment of the government to retaining an open-trade regime. The reformist administration embarked on an ambitious program of reforms, including restructuring the foreign debt, privatization, deregulation, and an overhaul of the budgeting system. Although initially the administration sought to diversify commercial ties with Europe, it became clear that the fate of the country was closely linked to that of the United States when the Berlin Wall fell. The negotiation of NAFTA, the North American Free Trade Agreement, soon followed.

The Mexican economy became thoroughly integrated with the world economy. Its geographic proximity to the United States, coupled with the ambitious reform program, has turned the country into the largest exporter and importer in Latin America, accounting for almost half of the region's foreign trade. Trade has diversified dramatically: Oil is no longer the most important determinant of Mexico's external sector performance, although it still constitutes the most important source of public revenue.

As part of the macroeconomic stabilization and economic reform process, Mexico and most of Latin America experimented with some form of a social investment fund. To alleviate poverty and maintain social cohesion, central governments created social investment funds that bypassed the regular government structure and made exceptions to ordinary disbursement and control procedures, channeling large amounts of funds directly into "social infrastructure investments" that would benefit the poor. In the case of Mexico, bypassing ordinary procedures only became a problem in the context of democratization. Special funds were targeted to poor communities, and the national government kept influence and control over the funds' menu of eligible expenditures and individual allocation decisions. Much of the federal government's social spending in myriad programs and ministries were consolidated into a high-profile poverty-relief program, Programa Nacional de Solidaridad, under a single ministry, the Secretaría de Desarrollo Social. The creation of Pronasol, as the program was known in Mexico, left a mark for the future evolution of fiscal federalism.

Pronasol was meant to mitigate the negative effects of liberalization and economic reform among the poor. As a social investment fund, it included an important element of social participation, which won the program wide acclaim in international policy circles. Projects were selected based on local committees' petitions for funds. These groups provided some of the inputs in the project (such as labor); state and municipal governments had to match federal funds for approved projects. One apparently unintended consequence of the program was municipal empowerment, as the program increasingly transferred funds directly to municipalities, enabling them to decide by themselves the projects they would fund for social infrastructure at the local level. The Social Development Fund that evolved from Pronasol became the most important source of funds public good provision at the local level in Mexico. It was fully decentralized in 1997, with funds allocated according to a formula composed of municipal-level poverty indicators.

The Salinas administration ended in 1994, the year that NAFTA came into effect. It was a turbulent political year – the world took notice of the plight of Mexico's indigenous peasants with the Chiapas rebellion, and the PRI's presidential candidate as well as one of its top officials were murdered.[11] By the end of the year, the economy was showing weaknesses: An exchange rate misalignment, a creeping banking crisis, and outright policy blunders by the incoming administration led to a currency crisis in December of that year.

The recovery from this crisis in 1995 was far from even across Mexican regions.[12] Unbalanced growth generated tensions among the already very

---

[11] The PRI nevertheless carried the election, the cleanest elections in Mexican history to that date.

[12] Though Salinas left office in political disgrace, it should be recognized that the speed with which the country was able to rebound after a deep recession in 1995 was, to a large extent, the consequence of the transformation of Mexican industry and its trade orientation achieved during his administration's previous years.

unequal Mexican states, which sought to redress some of their fiscal difficulties with help from the federal government. The political fallout of the crisis was the victory of opposition parties in state elections and most of the important municipal races between 1995 and 1997. By the midterm federal elections of 1997 it was obvious that federalism and decentralization had become central issues in the political landscape. In that election, the PRI lost control of the lower chamber for the first time in its history. The Zedillo government embraced federalism, democratization, and decentralization as central goals.

By the late 1990s, there was an increasing consensus that there was too much discretion in too large a share of the federal spending targeted to subnational governments, particularly, in the expenditure decisions of the poverty relief program Pronasol. Multiparty competition and the pressure for clearer decentralization rules moved Congress to transform the Pronasol funds into earmarked, formula-based discretionary transfers. The Zedillo administration began to transform these funds into formula-based transfers to states and municipalities, while initiating an ambitious household-targeted poverty program, PROGRESA.

The complete transformation of these funds into incentive-compatible conditional transfers has become difficult to accomplish because aportaciones quickly developed their own stakeholders. The new structure of the funds, although much improved, has not prevented or eliminated discretionary government decisions. These funds have been at odds with a more incentive-compatible decentralization on at least two counts. First, social investment funds became a way to distort congressionally approved compensation formulas and horizontal equalization goals. Second, funds frequently financed responsibilities that were being transferred to subnational governments, thereby debilitating subnational fiscal responsibility and intergovernment accountability.

The federal government began moving in the direction of achieving greater transparency in the allocation of resources to subnational governments in the mid-1990s, before the PRI had lost its majority in the Chamber of Deputies. In 1996 the bulk of resources from budget item 26 were transformed into a formula-based, poverty-targeted transfer with the creation of the Fondo de Desarrollo Social Municipal (FDSM). Still, owing to a peculiar compromise whereby each state was assured 1% of the funds regardless of its poverty levels, 3% of the funds remained allocated on a basis other than poverty. Moreover, distribution of the FDSM resources from states to municipalities followed a different formula in which population was heavily weighted. This contrasted with the distribution of the federal transfer to the states, which was calculated on a poverty-based formula that could have been readily extended to and applied at the municipal level.[13] Those "adjustments" to the sophisticated poverty formula utilized for most of the transfer from the federation to the states can only be understood as concessions granted to state governments and legislators with local agendas to get the budget approved. In any case, the process of transformation of social investment funds became more aggressive since the introduction of the FDSM, in the 1997 budget, as primarily a formula-based, poverty-targeted transfer.

The 1998 budget gathered previously dispersed earmarked transfers and special funds under Ramo 33. Grants for education, health, social infrastructure, and other preexisting federal transfers were then incorporated into the fiscal law. Although the transfers governed by Ramo 33 are commonly thought of as formula driven, the fact is that distribution of the largest transfers – those for health and education – obey more the supply-driven historical distribution of social expenditures in the federal budget than an explicit territorial compensation or demand-based subsidy formula.

An overlooked aspect of that budgetary process was the creation of a new fund, the Fondo para el Fortalecimiento de los Municipios y el Distrito Federal (Fortamun) and its incorporation into the LCF. Fortamun was created to elicit support from the opposition parties for the approval of the budget. A smaller fund was originally considered in the presidential bill as part of the strategy by the Finance Ministry to help states in their debt overhang. According to the original executive bill submitted to Congress, the new fund was not going to be allocated by the SHCP according to debt conditions in each state, but on the basis of equal per capita terms. After legislative discussions, the size of Fortamun was tied to the evolution of federal revenues, and its permanence was guaranteed by its inclusion in the LCF, and, although the law states that it should preferably be allocated for purposes of debt reduction, it can be allocated in practice to a wide range of purposes, as selected by each individual state.

Table 8.3 shows the legislature-made modifications that were consonant with the logic of the argument. The per capita allocation of funds to strengthen municipalities and the Federal District was increased by almost 25%. The adjustment to various funds was not related to the dynamics of federal revenues. The adjustment in health and infrastructure, for

---

[13] For the best discussion and analysis of this process, see Mogollón (2002).

Table 8.3. *Modifications of Selected Decentralized Budgetary Items, 1998*

	Approved Budget (millions of pesos)	Proposed Bill (millions of pesos)	Difference
Participaciones	112,403.0	113,438.6	−0.9%
Fondo de Aportaciones para la Educación Básica y Norma	67,512.6	67,512.6	0
Fondo de Aportaciones para los Servicios de Salud	10,546.2	10,808.9	−2.4%
Fondo para la Infraestructura Social Municipal	9,142.3	9,262.6	−1.3%
Fondo de Aportaciones para el Fortalecimiento de los Municipios y del Distrito Federal	6,732.1	5,400	24.7%

instance, went beyond the change in the shared tax revenues. Whereas the calculation of participaciones depends strictly on the dynamics of federal revenues (since their formula refers to the shared taxes), the calculation of the aportaciones is primarily a function of year-to-year political negotiations among the executive, the legislature, and the states and the Federal District at the time of budget discussions. The aportaciones have become the wild card to introduce additional transfers that are not formula based.[14]

The 1999 budget also increased transfers to the states through a new fund, the Public Safety Fund. Although that fund was meant to be formula based, the criteria used for the allocation among states did not become clear until years later. However, to generate an increase for the Fortamun, Congress eliminated the participation of the Federal District in Fortamun. This strategy was similar to that used in the past by the federal government, which has used the Federal District as the federal entity that can bear adjustments that benefit all states without generating political turmoil.

The 2000 budget presents additional evidence of discretional increases of resource to the states to get the budget approved. The adjustments in the revenue side, as can be seen from the participaciones row in Table 8.4,

---

[14] The 1998 budget contained an additional concession to the states, which was a provision that ISAN, which is part of revenue sharing, would be fully administered by the states.

Table 8.4. *Modifications of Selected Decentralized Budgetary Items, 2000*

	Proposed Bill (millions of pesos)	Approved Budget (millions of pesos)	Difference
Participaciones	161,712.8	160,883.3	0.5%
Fondo de Aportaciones para la Educación Básica y Normal	118,404	118,198.7	0.2%
Fondo de Aportaciones para los Servicios de Salud	20,022.7	20,262.1	−1.2%
Fondo para la Infraestructura Social Estatal	1,937.9	1,927.9	0.5%
Fondo para la Infraestructura Social Municipal	14,051.7	13978.7	0.5%
Fondo de Aportaciones para el Fortalecimiento de los Municipios	15,030.3	14,952.1	0.5%
Fondo de Aportaciones Múltiples	5,206.2	5,179.2	0.5%
Fondo de Aportaciones para la Seguridad Pública de los Estados y del Distrito Federal	5,170.0	5,170.0	0.0%

increased funds available by half a percentage point. This same adjustment is observed in the funds for social infrastructure and Fort-amun, which, by legal mandate, have to keep strict correspondence with federal revenues. However, education funds were not adjusted in that proportion, whereas health took a disproportionate adjustment.[15] The funds for public safety, now firmly embedded in the structure of aportaciones, were kept at the presidential requested level. Hence, the 2000 budget confirmed the 1999 precedent as to how fiscal transfers could be adjusted to please subnational governments (and corresponding political interests) in the years the states are prepared to negotiate rather than take the federal government hostage during the budgetary battle.

The 2001 budget was discussed in the midst of cautious behavior on the part of legislators, since most politicians were eager, even if the PRI

---

[15] The figures for education include the Federal District, which in the presidential bill was still under a different budgetary item.

lost the election, to prevent a crisis like the one that occurred at the end of 1994. The budget witnessed the creation of a fund to strengthen states, a concession that was quickly adopted by the federal government, notwithstanding that the rationale for that fund was unconvincing.

In 2002, the state-strengthening fund was retained even though the original executive proposal intended to phase this fund out. In the distribution of Fondo de Infraestructura Social (FIS) among states, a major advance was the elimination of the provision that 1% of that fund be distributed to each state, regardless of poverty indicators. However, the most influential factor in determining the actual allocations for the aportaciones in the 2002 budget was the expectation of additional revenue stemming from the tax reform, which eventually became a revenue shortfall. Congress believed that additional revenue would allow it to fund a large state-strengthening fund as well as substantial increases in FIS and Fortamun (see Table 8.5). As the first months of the year progressed, however, the executive had to correct the budget in line with the slow evolution of revenue collection. In the end, it became necessary to downsize the aportaciones to maintain the fiscal deficit targets. Nonetheless, aportaciones were a critical factor for the approval of the budget negotiations during that year.

The discussion of the recent evolution of the aportaciones reflects how the transformation from largely discretionary fund management to transparent, formula-based transfers has followed two contradictory forces, each one of them trying to give final shape to the Ramo 33 transfers. On the one hand, the administration seeks to transform an increasing share of those funds into transparent formula-driven transfers; on the other, year after year there appears to be a need to "invent" another fund that can be assigned to states or municipalities following loosely defined criteria – regardless of their poverty conditions or infrastructure needs – to garner enough support to get the budget approved.

The foregoing discussion indicates that the current balance of political forces (including traditional political culture) appears to prevent the full transformation of the various social investment funds transferred to states and municipalities into incentive-compatible instruments that reward effort. Opposing political forces working within the federal legislature have partially transformed (yet prevented full transformation of) the funds that finance social infrastructure in states and municipalities – inherited from the macroeconomic stabilization period – into budgetary items subject to allocation and disbursement rules capable of guaranteeing effectiveness, efficiency, accountability, evaluation, and control. The

Table 8.5. *Modifications of Selected Decentralized Budgetary Items, 2002*

	Approved Budget (millions of pesos)	Proposed Bill (millions of pesos)	Difference
Fondo de Aportaciones para la Educación Básica y Normal	150,142.0	146,182.0	2.7%
Fondo de Aportaciones para los Servicios de Salud	26,758.9	25,758.8	3.9%
Fondo para la Infraestructura Social	21,783.9	19,729.5	10.4%
Fondo de Aportaciones para el Fortalecimiento de los Municipios y el Distrito Federal	22,326.7	20,221.2	10.4%
Fondo de Aportaciones Múltiples	7,092.8	6,423.9	10.4%
Fondo de Aportaciones para la Educación Tecnológica	2,862.2	2,822.8	1.4%
Fondo de Aportaciones para la Seguridad Pública	3,000.0	3,000.0	0.0%
Programa de Aportaciones para el Fortalecimiento de las Entidades Federativas	14,700.0	0.0	100.0%
Participaciones	219,192.9	207,087.6	5.8%

reason behind the apparent schizophrenic behavior of the Congress is that it is in the legislators' interest as members of Congress to negotiate unconditional resources to their states on an individual basis rather than seek to establish rules that would allocate resources based on fiscal effort or expenditure efficiency. Since the legislature has the power to hold the central government hostage during budget negotiations and approval, the central government uses those funds to "buy" the votes of different members of Congress. The problem is compounded because, without the possibility of reelection, the partisan coalitions that have passed the budget in that last five years have little concern for their constituent jurisdictions.

It is true that the transformation of social investment funds took place with surprising speed and smoothness in the case of Mexico. Other Latin American countries (including Bolivia, Colombia, the Dominican Republic, Ecuador, Peru, and most Central American countries) have been forced to either postpone or entirely forget the transformation of the funds by the funds' own built-in interest and apparent delivery capacity.

However, resistance to substituting decentralization and transparency for centralized patronage has not withered away in the case of Mexico. Year after year, at the time of budget negotiations within and between the executive and the legislature, there appears and reappears the claim for new, broadly defined funds that further complicates to the already weak picture of subnational accountability and control.

The implication of this discussion is that "economic solutions" to the transformation of FIS and other social funds will not work in the medium or long term until the political forces (including political incentives) underlying current legislative decisions are properly dealt with. This is easier said than done. Each country has an idiosyncratic budget process with legislatures that have different incentives. In Mexico, the links among the budget process, the social investment funds, and the incentives of the legislature have been largely missed by studies on decentralization.

IV. THE FOURTH PHASE: MONITORING, CONTROL, AND EVALUATION

At the beginning of this millennium, Mexico's decentralization is incomplete at best. Relations between the federal level and subnational governments are plagued by substantial vertical imbalances, confusing division of responsibilities, and lack of clear accountability, monitor, and control mechanisms. From the point of view of distribution of revenues, the fiscal pact that began in 1980 and is still going on – though reformed several times – severely limits tax capacity and cripples potential tax effort at the state level. Sector decentralization initiated in the early 1990s lacks a well-defined incentive framework for subnational efficiency in key sectors such as education, health, water, or roads. Formula-driven transfers that are broadly targeted to earmarked purposes, and elimination of most federal discretionary transfers in 1998–2000, although steps in the right direction, fell short of effectively transforming broadly defined transfers or enhancing subnational accountability and responsiveness. In sum, Mexico is still far from having a decentralization framework that meets the most essential basic conditions for decentralization to improve governance, including vertical balances, clear division of responsibilities and accountability, and intergovernment coordination for efficiency in service delivery.

A major overhaul of the fiscal federalism arrangement appears unlikely. Aware of some of the problems with decentralization, the country has for some time entertained the idea of a comprehensive overhaul of fiscal federalism. However, political and technical difficulties have deterred any sustained effort to this effect. The technical obstacles to introducing a sound distribution of revenue sources, transfers, and responsibilities are formidable. There is only limited tradition of accounting, budgeting, and reporting standards at subnational levels. Besides, the country does not appear to be politically prepared for either a comprehensive or an overnight reform of the country's fiscal federalism. Before pushing further with the design, enactment, and implementation of a sophisticated federalist model tailor-made to Mexico, the country needs to continue getting rid of the centralizing tendencies rooted in the political and fiscal dependency mechanisms that remain in operation.

The problem with the proposed comprehensive reform is twofold. First, the political mood of the country does not seem prone to such a major political consensus, and second, current management capacity at each level of government does not appear to match the necessary requirements of a new intergovernment system in terms of roles and responsibilities, enhanced autonomy, and efficient coordination among levels of government. Since no political consensus on comprehensive decentralization reform would be feasible unless levels of government and intergovernment relations are ready to implement it, the rest of this section will deal with the second set of obstacles to streamlining decentralization reform in Mexico.

The governors of the Mexican states have become the key players in the drama of the reform of the Mexican fiscal pact. With the creation of CONAGO in 2001, governors have successfully created an institution that allows them to present a unified front to the federal government. The Conago has addressed in its joint declarations various policy issues ranging from macroeconomic stability to social policy and budgetary issues, but fiscal federalism has been their central concern from the start. The second meeting of Conago in 2002 proposed devoluting a fraction of the VAT rate to the states, making some bases of the income tax exclusively controlled by the states, and gradually increasing unconditional revenue sharing transfers. But the most important achievement of the Conago was convincing the federal government to convene in February 5, 2004, a National Fiscal Convention (the Convención Nacional Hacendaria), in charge of redesigning the federal fiscal pact.

Among legislators in the Chamber of Deputies, a survey at the end of 2003 suggested that almost two-thirds of the representatives thought that the reform of fiscal federalism was the most important topic on their agenda. A third believed that federalism will be strengthened if more resources are transferred to subnational governments, whereas two-thirds thought that the devolution of tax authority was necessary for advances in federalism. Hence, there seems to be some agreement among legislators in that the improvement of the fiscal pact requires a redrawing of fiscal authority. Eighty percent of the legislators agree on decreasing the VAT and allowing states to keep a 2% surcharge. However, they disagree most dramatically on expanding the base of that tax to include foodstuffs and medicines. Deputies of the governing PAN agree with that proposal, but PRI deputies disagree. The partisan division shows up also in the issue of tax devolution: 83% of the PAN legislators want greater tax authority to SNGs. In the PRI the support is lukewarm: Only 52% see this as the way to strengthen federalism.[16]

The Mexican Congress is characterized by a high degree of party discipline, given the incentives provided by centralized closed-list nomination procedures, multimember districts, and no reelection (60% of the seats are SMDs, but the incentives for personal vote are seriously reduced by the no reelection rule). It is not very likely that partisan groups in Congress will be fragmented in their decisions concerning fiscal federalism.

As discussed by Diaz-Cayeros (2004), if partisan groups voted with perfect party discipline, the smallest winning coalition that could pass a reform on fiscal federalism would be formed by the governing PAN and the left-wing Partido de la Revolución Democrática (PRD). Such coalition is very unlikely to form. There is a long-standing ideological rift between those parties, which has prevented them from agreeing on most policy issues in the past. Striking a balance between devolution to SNGs (which the PAN supports) and redistribution to the poorest states from the federal level (which the PRD supports) would probably be an insurmountable problem. Moreover, the PRI controls the Senate, so it constitutes a veto player for any legislative reform. Moreover, one should take into account that the former hegemonic party also controls most of the governorships, and state executives increasingly exert more influence over their federal deputies.

A coalition between PRI and PRD, although oversized, would have greater chances of passing a legislative change in both chambers. However, Diaz-Cayeros (2004) shows that such a coalition would include state legislative delegations with starkly contrasting interests in the area of fiscal federalism. The PRI legislative group includes both some of the poorest and most transfer-dependent states in the south and some

---

[16] *Reforma*, November 18, 2003.

Box 8.4. *Recent Developments*

The federation and some of the states have been actively pursuing expenditure coordination schemes that combine federal resources with federal transfers to subnational governments since 2000. Matching grants programs (commonly known as pari passus) have been expanded, particularly for poverty alleviation purposes through subsidized programs in the areas of agriculture, nutrition, health, and employment creation. The previous Zedillo administration initiated the FORTEM program, geared to capacity building at subnational levels via a combination of conditioned loans and subsidies. The Zedillo administration also experimented with intergovernment performance agreements for health and the environment.

The Fox administration has supported innovative ways to funnel transfers to guarantee intergovernmental payments for water. It has also further expanded the search for a more balanced package of fiscal transfers that gives more weight to transparency, monitoring, evaluation, and controls and less weight to transfers that are either freely disposable or hard to evaluate in terms of allocation or production efficiency. A few examples of the Fox administration's move in this direction are the following: (i) current delegation and or transfer of agriculture responsibilities (including human resource management) through intergovernment negotiated agreements, as in the case of the federal–Coahuila agreement; (ii) ongoing reform efforts to strengthen budget result indicators for subsidized programs jointly administered by the federation, the states, and municipalities; (iii) a matching grants program for water, electricity, and rural roads targeted to isolated indigenous communities and coordinated by the Ministry of Social Development (SEDESOL); and (iv) the extension by the Ministry of the Comptroller and Administrative Development (SECODAM) of transparency and anticorruption tools and standards to subnational governments via intergovernment performance agreements.

of the most advanced, industrial, and fiscally autonomous states in the north.

A third possibility in coalition formation for the passing of a reform to fiscal federalism in Mexico would be a partial PAN and PRI coalition of states that are not fiscally dependent, in which party discipline would be broken. In such a scenario blocs of state party delegations from eleven rich, large states would have to create a system that reinforces derivation principles and assures that more resources remain where they are generated. Such a scenario would probably generate important tensions for the PRI, which has generally been in favor of redistribution favoring the poorer states.

In any of these scenarios, what becomes clear is that the transformation of the recommendations emerging from the Convención Nacional Hacendaria into actual legislation through Congress will be an arduous process.

IV.1. A Piecemeal Incremental Approach to Reform

Mexico appears to be entering still one more phase of the federalism – decentralization process since the beginning of the present decade. The Fox administration appears convinced that Mexico should not keep expanding fiscal transfers while no level of government is clearly accountable for service delivery. More than merely implementing additional fiscal transfers or decentralization of new responsibilities – as frequently demanded by state governments or opposition parties – the federal government is struggling to reorganize the patchy, often inconsistent, structure the country has built for over two decades. Effective implementation of this fragmented decentralization framework appears to be more realistic than immediately adding still one more layer to the pile of distribution of revenues and responsibilities. At this point in time in the evolution of Mexico's decentralization, ensuring decentralization meets the basic principles of clear accountability and efficiency enhancement appears to be more important than pursuing the politically and fiscally uncertain path of fiscal federalism reforms. Although the strategy has not been explicitly formulated, Mexico seems to be pursuing two mutually reinforcing purposes: (i) fiscal discipline and hard budget constraints at state and local level and (ii) transparency, monitoring, and control of decentralized spending.

The Fox administration is struggling to enforce the new market-oriented framework for subnational borrowing inherited from the Zedillo administration to effectively enforce fiscal discipline and a hard budget constraint at the subnational levels. In this case, the country appears to have selected a powerful instrument capable of reaching the intended objective. Indeed, during 2000–2001 Mexico pioneered a market-oriented reform that minimizes (federal) moral hazard, stimulates market enforcement of fiscal sustainability and provides transparency and disclosure mechanisms. The 2000–2001 reform eliminates the participation of the federal government in guaranteeing subnational debt. The risk is now borne by creditors, who are required to make proportionate capital provisions according to the indebtedness capacity of the borrowing subnational entity. Indebtedness capacity is measured by independent credit rating agencies. The interest rate will be related to the borrower's and/or the loan risk. Rather than the federal government, subnational governments will provide guarantees of their own.

International experience has demonstrated time and again that market-oriented subnational borrowing regulatory frameworks similar to the one recently adopted by Mexico require a strong political will. When subnational governments find that accessing capital markets is more demanding than in the past, they tend to put the pressure back on the federal government to relax development banks' prudential regulations. Although the new system is still too young to predict the likely reactions of the federal government to growing subnational pressures, available evidence indicates that the government is firmly behind the new regulatory framework – even at the cost of feeding additional political opposition from overindebted subnational governments. This is not an insignificant political cost at a time when all factions appear to be at odds over a number of fiscal and nonfiscal issues.

For transparency and control, the preferred instrument of the new phase appears to be performance-driven (conditional) transfers that pursue strategies and results identified by subnational governments within a wide menu of sector options.[17] Given that radical redistribution of tax revenue sources may have to wait for some years to come, and that some key sector responsibilities (such as water, education, or health) have been partially transferred, the federal government's best chance to achieve decentralization efficiency and accountability is to resort to intergovernment fiscal transfers and borrowing regulations to create incentives for states to meet the required minimum standards as well as provide fiscally sustainable service delivery. In particular, the Fox administration is using two instruments – conditional grants and credit lines – as incentives for intergovernment agreements (convenios) by which subnational governments effectively assume result-oriented responsibilities tied to additional

---

[17] Enhanced transparency and accountability is also being pursued at the federal level. The National Plan for Transparency and Anti-Corruption as well as myriad individual financial restructuring, process simplification, and information technology strategies are being planned or implemented throughout the federal level. In fact, the National Plan for Transparency and Anti-Corruption is also being extended to subnational governments via intergovernment performance agreements.

resources. Subnational governments have to meet those conditions either as a prerequisite for receiving a grant or a loan (eligibility criteria) or during execution of grants or loans. The federal government is now trying to balance revenues and responsibilities by emphasizing results-conditioned transfers. This is an evolution from the general revenue-sharing agreements of the early 1980s, the confusing deconcentration and decentralization sector transfers of the early 1990s, or the – largely uncontrolled – formula-driven transfers of the late 1990s.

The current phase can be seen as imposing stricter federal government controls and, in that regard, reinforcing a pyramidal, center-based public sector. However, it is more appropriate to interpret this phase as an inevitable step toward capacity building for efficient service delivery at subnational levels and enhanced intergovernment coordination. Mexico cannot keep adding fiscal transfers to subnational governments – as is frequently demanded on primarily ideological grounds – unless citizens perceive substantial progress in subnational fiscal responsibility, clear division of responsibilities, and sector performance and results.

The priority presently given to the purpose of strengthening mechanisms for checks and balances can hardly be challenged from a technical point of view. It appears to be the only way to guarantee Mexico's original intention of elevating expenditure efficiency via sector decentralization. It is also a way to prevent disillusion and frustration that may eventually generate the kinds of recentralization forces currently seen in other Latin American countries.

The problem with the current approach, however, lies in the primary tool selected for enhanced transparency and accountability. Negotiated transfers that incorporate specific performance-, output-, or investment-related benchmarks are the main tools, but it is unclear how performance will be measured. In theory, government financial agencies (e.g., development banks such as Banobras) should play a critical role in promoting, signing, monitoring, and enforcing contracts with interested states or municipalities. This "incomplete contract approach" (as those performance and result-oriented contracts are known in the fiscal decentralization literature) might help move Mexico into the realm of disbursement based on compliance with the agreed benchmarks. However, federal financial agencies do not appear to be equipped to effectively play their new role. Furthermore, it is hard to think of any other federal agency that has the necessary information and leverage power to adequately identify appropriate benchmarks or performance or result indicators for each individual contract. The absence of the necessary information will probably weaken the credibility of federal agencies as capable monitoring and enforcing agencies. Moreover, intergovernmental performance agreements – even when smoothly developed – are politically sensitive in and of themselves.

An additional problem with the current choice of instruments for transparency enhancement is that those instruments attempt to solve two different decentralization objectives that can hardly be combined into one single set of tools. One is the challenge of setting the minimum fiscal and institutional standards that subnational governments must meet to ensure efficiency and accountability in service delivery. The other is the challenge of reaching sector-specific performance and/or results. Relying on a single set of instruments (intergovernment performance contracts) to achieve the two purposes is difficult. International experience tells us that whenever those two targets have been intended with one single shot, the result is either weak monitoring and enforcement or a heavy burden of conditions that weakens subnational governments' incentives to sign those complex incomplete contracts.

Fiscal transfers and borrowing requirements are being used by the federal government to achieve three objectives: (i) common minimum accounting, budgeting, and reporting standards, (ii) sound subnational fiscal and financial management, and (iii) more clearly defined sector responsibilities. However, the tools being used by the federal government have limited leverage. There is a problem with the size of the incentive tools the federal government is currently managing for intergovernment performance agreements. Because the two biggest types of fiscal transfers – the participaciones and the aportaciones – are not being conditioned on enhanced subnational performance, additional conditionality is being introduced through ad hoc intergovernment arrangements regarding matching grant or subsidized (pari passu) programs and special credit lines managed by federal development banks. Up to now, the federal government has not yet added accountability and performance requirements at the time of annual budget negotiations regarding the potentially powerful earmarked aportaciones.

Minimum standards and performance conditionality are being required in ways that add a heavy burden to and weaken the incentive effect of lending and grants instruments. Were Mexico to insist on adding a heavy load of requirements on relatively weak instruments, the country may learn the hard way that Latin American countries that have tried to combine both minimum standards and sector conditionality (performance or results) have failed to reach either goal. For instance, Colombia had problems with its recent "certification process": the political and fiscal pressure to bypass or somehow accept less-than-minimum eligibility requirements proved to be too much for federal ministries to resist when deciding to transfer resources or performance-required loans.

In sum, Mexico's current quest for transparency, efficiency, and accountability in decentralized service provision is unlikely to lead to completion of the most basic decentralization prerequisites or streamlining decentralization. The instruments being used are too weak or inadequate to reinvigorate decentralization and federalism reform.

V. CONCLUSIONS

Mexico's decentralization process is in a deep transition. The current decentralization framework can best be understood in terms of four reforms placed on top of each other in the past twenty to twenty-five years: (i) the centralization of taxing powers in exchange for unconditional revenues with the introduction of the VAT tax in 1980; (ii) the deconcentration of key sectors in the early 1990s, the most important of which were education, health, and water; (iii) the creation of social investment funds in the late 1980s and their subsequent transformation into formula-driven transfers in the late 1990s; and (iv) the current administration's attempt to deal with the current framework and decentralization pressures through two instruments that appear to be too weak to address all the objectives.

These key reforms create a confusing picture of responsibilities with no clear responsibilities at any level of government for key public services. In addition, there are deep imbalances in revenue and expenditures at the subnational level. The gaps are alleviated through transfers that are not providing the best incentives for efficient tax collection, expenditures, or service provisions.

The conclusions of this chapter are not too optimistic. Given today's political and technical constraints in Mexico, the question is how can Mexico reinforce decentralization and minimize the risks of future fiscal federalism reform by creating incentives to move toward more comprehensive reform of fiscal federalism? It appears that the increased democratization in Mexico is not the most auspicious atmosphere for improving the fiscal relations framework. The chapter argues that the current political institutions are unlikely to pass a far-reaching reform of the decentralization framework that would place Mexico on a path to a more efficient and equitable fiscal federalisms framework. The best route appears to be incremental changes that at least point in the right direction and are solid steps toward improved efficiency and equity of revenue collection and expenditures at the subnational level as well as incentive-compatible transfers from the federal government. The problem appears to be that the instruments currently being used are too weak to achieve substantial progress. The Convención Nacional Hacendaria provided a forum to develop a clear view of what is the best decentralization framework for Mexico but it will be important to have the right instruments to continue to make progress while at the same time reassess the path chosen.

Bibliography

Careaga, M., and B. Weingast (2003). "Fiscal Federalism, Good Governance, and Economic Growth in Mexico," in D. Rodnk, ed. In *Search of Prosperity: Analytic Narratives on Economic Growth*. Princeton, NJ: Princeton University Press: pp. 399–438.

Courchene, T., Diaz-Cayeros, A., and S. Webb (2000). "Historical Forces: Geographic and Political," in Giugale and Webb, eds. *Achievements and Challenges of Fiscal Decentralization Lessons from Mexico*. Washington, DC: World Bank: pp. 123–138.

Courchene, T., and Diaz-Cayeros, A. (2000). "Transfers and the Nature of the Mexican Federation" in M. Giugale and S. Webb, eds., *Achievements and Challenges of Fiscal Decentralization Lessons from Mexico*. Washington, DC: World Bank: pp. 200–236.

Craig, A., and W. Cornelius (1995). "Houses Divided. Parties and Political Reform in Mexico," in S. Mainwaring and T. Scully, eds., *Building Democratic Institutions. Party Systems in Latin America*. Stanford: Stanford University Press: pp. 249–297.

Diario Oficial de la Federacion (1998). Presupuesto de Egresos de la Federacion para el Ejercicio Fiscal de 1998.

Diario Oficial de la Federacion (1999). Presupuesto de Egresos de la Federacion para el Ejercicio Fiscal de 1999.

Diario Oficial de la Federacion (2000). Presupuesto de Egresos de la Federacion para el Ejercicio Fiscal de 2000.

Diario Oficial de la Federacion (2001). Presupuesto de Egresos de la Federacion para el Ejercicio Fiscal de 2001.

Diario Oficial de la Federacion (2002). Presupuesto de Egresos de la Federacion para el Ejercicio Fiscal de 2002.

Diaz-Cayeros A. (1995). "*Economic Development and Regional Inequality: Toward A New Federal Pact in Mexico*. Mexico City: Miguel Angel Porria.

Diaz-Cayeros, A. (2004). "Coaliciones Legislativas y Federalismo Fiscal," Política y Gobierno XI(2): 231–262.

Díaz-Cayeros, A., and B. Magaloni (2001). "Party Dominance and the Logic of Electoral Design in Mexico's Transition to Democracy," Journal of Theoretical Politics 13(3): 271–294.

Díaz-Cayeros, A., R. Gamboa, and F. Hernández Trillo (2002). "Fiscal Descentralization in Mexico: The Bailout Problem," Working Paper, Interamerican Development Bank.

Giugale, M., and S. Webb, eds. (2000). *Achievements and Challenges of Fiscal Decentralization. Lessons from Mexico*. Washington, DC: World Bank.

Hernandez Chavez, A. (1998). La politica Economica de Mexico en el Congreso de la Union (1982–1997) Mexico City: Fondo de Cultura Económica.

Levy, S. (1998). "Análisis Metodológico de la Distribución de los Recursos en el Ramo 33," in Comisión de Desarrollo Social Instrumentos de Distribución de los Recursos del Ramo 33. México City: Cámara de Diputados.

Linz, J. (1990). "The Perils of Presidentialism," Journal of Democracy 1: 51–69.

Mainwaring, S. (1993). "Presidentialism, Multipartism, and Democracy: The Difficult Combination," Comparative Political Studies 26(2): 198–228.

Mogollón, O. (2002). "De la Discreción a las Fórmulas: Mecanismos de Distribución de Recursos Descentralizados para Alivio a la Pobreza," M.A. thesis, ITAM.

Scott Andretta, J. (2002). "La otra cara de la reforma fiscal: la equidad del gasto publico," CIDE

Secretaria de Hacienda y Credito Publico (1998). Proyecto de Dictamen del Presupuesto de Egresos de la Federacion para el Ejercicio Fiscal de 1998.

Secretaria de Hacienda y Credito Publico (2000). Exposicion de Motivos del Proyecto de Presupuesto de Egresos de la Federacion para el Ejercicio Fiscal de 2000.

Secretaria de Hacienda y Credito Publico (2002). Proyecto de Dictamen del Presupuesto de Egresos de la Federacion para el Ejercicio Fiscal de 2002.

Tsebelis, G. (1995). "Decision Making in Political Systems: Veto Players in Presidentialism, Parliamentarism, Multicameralism and Multipartyism," British Journal of Political Science 25 289–325.

Ugalde, L. C. (2000). *The Mexican Congress: Old Player, New Power*. Washington, DC: CSIS Press.

Weldon, J. (1996). "The Mexican Congress and the Presidency 1917–1940," paper presented at the Annual Meeting of the American Political Science Association, San Francisco, August.

Willis, E., C. Garman, and S. Haggard, Stephan (1999). "The Politics of Decentralization in Latin America," Latin American Research Review 34(1): 7–56.

Willis, E., C. Garman, and S. Haggard (2001). "Fiscal Decentralization: A Political Theory with Latin American Cases." World Politics 53(2): 205–26.

NINE

Transfer Dependence and Regional Disparities in Nigerian Federalism

Tamar Asadurian, Emmanuel Nnadozie, and Leonard Wantchekon[1]

I. INTRODUCTION

The entire history of Nigeria has been characterized by conflict among regions, social classes, and ethno-religious groups over resource allocation. Exploitation of oil deposits in the East and Midwest in the 1960s has only added to the intensity of the conflict: There have been over fifty ethno-religious conflicts and numerous other types of conflict since 1960. Regional disparities are widely perceived as one of the causes of continuing ethnic tensions in Nigeria. According to Post and Vickers (1973, p. 58), the most important grievance of various regions since the early 1950s has been that their wealth was being used to subsidize poorer regions.

Nigeria's recent history has also been characterized by extremely centralized political and economic power. Of the country's forty-three years of independence (obtained from Britain in 1960), twenty-eight have been under military rule. The country was nominally a federation at this point, but local leaders were appointed by the central government. Local elections have come with the recent transition to democracy, but the center still dominates via its control over resources and the allocation of the transfers that make up a large portion of their budgets.

This chapter focuses on how Nigerian fiscal federalism, especially the characteristics of the country's system for transfers to state and local governments, has affected and been affected by these regional disparities and tradition of centralization. Overall, we argue that Nigeria is not fiscally

[1] We thank T. N. Srinivasan, Jessica Seddon Wallack, and conference participants at Stanford University for comments.

federalist but, rather, a de facto centralized distributive state. We analyze the effects of the system on local public goods provision and, ultimately, on interregional disparities. We argue that central government transfers can lead to underprovision of local public goods and a decrease in social welfare. The concurrence of the oil boom and fiscal centralization bred a transfer-dependent system lacking appropriate accountability and proper incentive structures. Disparities among states have persisted, though the incidence of poverty overall has converged with the decline of the South's performance.

The early literature on spatial economic development posits that regional disparities, in terms of income, education, and health services, tend to diminish over time owing to market forces (Kuznets, 1955; Hirschman, 1958; Williamson, 1965). With increased factor mobility, physical capital tends to move from more affluent to less affluent regions and human capital from less affluent to more affluent regions. It is also argued that the process is facilitated by political decentralization. Tanzi (1995) argues that decentralization is particularly attractive in heterogeneous societies and regionally divided countries. This analysis echoes the Weingast (1995) analysis of market-preserving federalism, which also considers local fiscal power to be growth enhancing.

However, in practice, decentralization seems to be consistent with persistent regional disparities in Nigeria. The country is not alone; persistent inequalities in Brazil and Russia, for example, have led several authors to question the validity of the positive effect of decentralization on economic performance and hence on interregional equity (Wibbels, 2000; Treisman, 2001; Rodden, 2001; Bardhan, 2002).

The divide between classical theory and practice is similarly apparent with respect to provision of public goods. Oates' (1972) decentralization theorem states that welfare will be maximized when each local jurisdiction provides public goods (except those with externalities or economies of scale). Tiebout's (1956) consideration of mobility strengthens the case for decentralization: Citizens "vote with their feet" and select the best-suited community for them.

Nigeria, however, appears to be a better example for critics of these theories. Tiebout's expected gains from federalism, for example, are conditional upon the subnational governments' ability to form their own policies and effectively compete for constituencies. Potential efficiency gains, therefore, hinge on true local autonomy and vertical accountability. States in Nigeria, however, have weak fiscal autonomy and are dependent on the federal government for revenue that is largely funded by rents rather than taxes. Subnational governments have only recently been elected, and it remains to be seen whether this will create a strong incentive to use what little autonomy they have well. National-level accountability is limited, as the oil-rich central government does not rely on the citizens for tax compliance and has resources with which to strategically buy support.[2]

The process of resource allocation has also been highly arbitrary and politicized. The few nominal rules governing resource allocation are generally ignored.[3] As a result, states that are politically pivotal are likely to receive more federal transfers than those that are not, leading, in Nigeria's case, to substantial redistribution away from oil-producing states. The lack of subnational electoral accountability led to federal transfers being misappropriated by state and local elites, which ultimately resulted in underprovision of public goods. Therefore, the double effect of transfer and resource dependence precluded accountability, which even in a democratic context has been recognized in the literature as a main prerequisite for economic gains.

In the following sections, we will show how the discovery and subsequent dependence on oil combined with military rule hindered autonomous and accountable institutional structures and instead bred a discretionary, transfer-dependent system that has had adverse effects on interregional disparities as well as intrastate income inequality.

II. BACKGROUND TO NIGERIA AND THE NIGERIAN ECONOMY

An oil-exporting developing country, Nigeria has had an embattled history characterized by economic crises, political instability, ethno-religious conflict, and a major war during 1967–1970. Nigeria is the most populous country in Africa with a population of 126 million people and an annual population growth rate of 2.4% in 2000 (World Bank, 2002). The country is made up of over 250 ethnic groups, living in an area approximately of 924,000 square kilometers (356,664 square miles), slightly larger than twice the size of California.

Exploration for oil in Nigeria began in 1908, but the establishment of the first oil well in 1951 marked the beginning of the country's overwhelming dependence on oil. The early 1970s saw a rise in oil exploration and development in Nigeria. Whereas the percentage of oil revenue to total revenue comprised a modest 26% in 1970, this figure quickly grew to 82%

---

[2] Wantchekon (2002) presents a formal model of how resource wealth feeds state autonomy.
[3] See Odedokun (1990) and Yekini (1992).

in 1974. The ascendancy of oil as the major source of revenue persisted throughout the following two decades. The percentages of oil revenue of total revenue for the years 1993, 1994, 1995, and 1996 were 84%, 79%, 53%, and 51%, respectively.[4] When world oil prices rose sharply in the 1970s, Nigeria's GNP per capita also rose tenfold (from US$110 in 1969 to US$1,110 in 1982). By 2000, however, the GNP per capita had fallen back to US$260, though petroleum production continues to provide 25% of Nigeria's GDP, over 90% of foreign exchange receipts, and 70% of budgetary revenues. Nigeria currently produces roughly 2.2 million barrels of oil per day.

Nigeria also has vast reserves of natural gas, which are only beginning to be exploited. In other sectors, agriculture offers employment for 43% of the labor force and accounts for 28.5% of GDP in 2000 (World Bank, 2002). Ninety percent of the sector's output comes from the crop sector, which is largely based on small-scale farming. The service sector, dominated by wholesale and retail trade, accounts for 28% of GDP and manufacturing accounts for less than 5% of GDP in 2000 (World Bank, 2002).

Despite the rich resource base, the country remains poor. Growth in the Nigerian economy, especially in the postboom period, has been low and volatile (see Figure 9.1, Panel 1). The average annual growth rate (based on World Bank data) was 3.4% from 1970 to 1980 and 1.4% from 1981 to 1990. From 1991 to 2000, the Nigerian economy grew by an average of only 2.7%. Given the high population growth rate of 2.4%, this economic growth rate was insufficient to have an appreciable effect on Nigerians' standard of living. The country has also experienced periods of hyperinflation, especially in the 1970s and 1990s. Inflation has decreased somewhat, but it is still not at satisfactory levels and the price level has shown a high degree of instability over the years (see Figure 9.1, Panel 2). Overall, as the panels in Figure 9.1 show, Nigeria's macroeconomic conditions are poor.

Of particular interest is Panel 6 of Figure 9.1, which shows Nigeria's crushing debt burden. Nigeria has a considerable external debt burden and the balance of payment is extremely volatile. In 1976, Nigeria owed a mere US$1.3 billion to external creditors. By 1980, its external debt had reached US$8.9 billion. Between 1980 and 1990, Nigeria's external debt nearly quadrupled from US$8.9 billion in 1980 to US$33.4 billion in 1990. Nigeria's external debt rose to a high of US$34 billion in 1995 (about 140% of GDP). Nigeria's high external debt burden places a serious constraint

---

[4] These data are from the Central Bank of Nigeria (Vol. 7, No. 2, 1997).

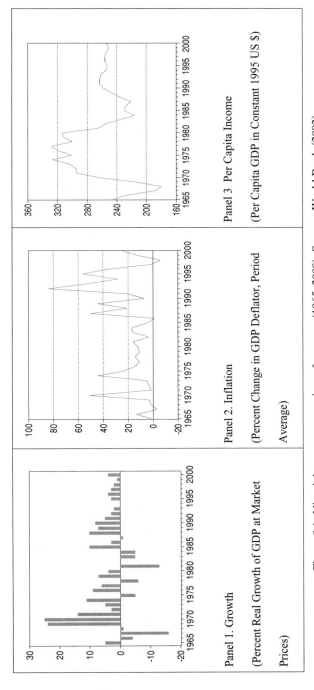

Figure 9.1. Nigeria's macroeconomic performance (1965–2000). *Source:* World Bank (2002).

Panel 1. Growth

(Percent Real Growth of GDP at Market Prices)

Panel 2. Inflation

(Percent Change in GDP Deflator, Period Average)

Panel 3 Per Capita Income

(Per Capita GDP in Constant 1995 US $)

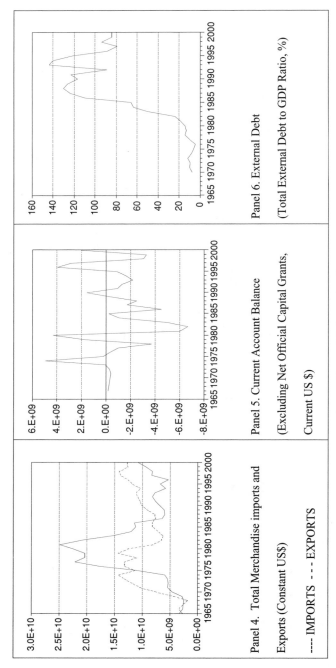

Panel 4. Total Merchandise imports and

Exports (Constant US$)

---- IMPORTS - - - EXPORTS

Panel 5. Current Account Balance

(Excluding Net Official Capital Grants,

Current US $)

Panel 6. External Debt

(Total External Debt to GDP Ratio, %)

Figure 9.1 (*continued*)

on development because debt repayments absorb resources that could be channeled into domestic investment and development efforts.

Three major features characterize Nigeria's international trade: a history of high volatility in the trade volume (see Figure 9.1, Panel 4); lack of commodity diversification, with primary products being (by far) the dominant export commodity; and export market concentration. The country's balance of payments situation reflects this anomaly, as the current account fluctuations reflect (Figure 9.1, Panel 5).

Data from United Nations Development Program's (UNDP) *Human Development Report* (2003) show the stark reality of Nigeria's economic and human development crises. Nigeria ranks 148 of the 174 countries in the Human Development Index, which measures the overall achievements in a country based on the three basic dimensions of human development – longevity, knowledge, and a decent standard of living.[5] According to UNDP (2003) a significant proportion of Nigerians live in conditions of extreme poverty, with over 70% of the population living on less than US$1 a day.[6] The adult literacy rate is 63.9%.

Despite Nigeria's low level of human development, it has made great improvements in the past thirty years. For example, life expectancy at birth in 1960 was fifty-eight years and in 1995 it was sixty-nine years. Although this number is still low compared with many developed countries, it indicates that improvements have been made in the standard of living. Furthermore, primary and secondary school enrollment has increased greatly. In 1970, primary school enrollment was only 37% but by 1995 it had increased to 89%. Moreover, the percentage of people receiving secondary education has increased sevenfold. Only 4% of secondary-school-age children attended school in 1970 but by 1995, 30% of secondary-school-age children were receiving education. As we show in the rest of the chapter, however, these numbers have worsened since the 1990s and are characterized by significant interregional disparities.

II.1. Economic Policy and Reforms

The Nigerian state has been characterized by rent-seeking and predation, in contrast to the East Asian and Japanese models of the activist

---

[5] The rankings are determined by a country's life expectancy, educational attainment (adult literacy combined with primary, secondary, and tertiary enrollment), and adjusted income as measured by the UNDP in 2003.

[6] This is the population below an income poverty line of US$1 a day (1993 Purchasing Power Parity US$) during 1983–2000 (UNDP, 2002).

developmental state and the intermediate cases typified by Brazil and India.[7] As Evans (1992, p. 8) has noted, the state structure that exists in Nigeria is subject to important limitations, such as lack of Weberian bureaucracy, and lack of capacity to pursue collective goals in a predictable, coherent way and any interest in doing so. Growth in state capacity tends to be slower than economic expansion and therefore does not automatically expand when tasks increase. Thus, economic policy failure accompanies low state capacity.

Macroeconomic policy has often failed in Nigeria for a variety of reasons, mostly because of a lack of reform to eliminate policy imbalances and biases of the past. Other reasons include lack of implementation of reforms when they are introduced; poor design, sequencing, and implementation of policies; and policy insufficiency. Macroeconomic policymaking began, albeit implicitly, during the colonial period in the form of the 1946–1955 Ten-Year Plan of Development and Welfare for Nigeria. This plan marked the origins of economic planning and an import-substitution policy in Nigeria. On this plan, Okigbo (1989, p. 32) wrote the following:

The real criticism of the Ten-Year Plan is not that there were no overall macroeconomic targets to use as reference; rather, it is that there was no set of explicit statements as to how the goals proposed in the Plan should be achieved. The Plan document did not indicate what policies should be used to ensure that the proposals were fully carried out, that the local Nigerian revenues would be raised to meet local financial commitments, and that foreign loans would be serviced.

After independence, Nigerian leaders maintained the colonial monoproduct economy and national development through development planning. They did not transform the economy to adapt it to domestic realities, perhaps because of the daunting development challenges they faced and lack of human and capital resources. In the 1960s, Nigeria continued agricultural export-led growth along the lines of the colonial predecessors. However, having realized the abnormalities of the colonial economic system, Nigeria attempted to industrialize. But industrialization failed in the midst of inadequate infrastructure, lack of skilled labor, shortage of spare parts, and lack of comparative advantage in capital-intensive industries. Nigeria remained basically an agricultural economy. The rural–urban

---

[7] For instance, see Evans (1992) for an analysis of the different views of the state as elaborated by Marx, Durkheim, Polanyi, Weber, and Gerschenkron and how this analysis culminates in illustrating the issue of rent-seeking, predation, and absolutism in Nigeria's federalism.

gap intensified because of the maintenance of colonial urban-biased policies.

Postindependence Nigerian economic policy can be divided into three periods: a boom from 1973 to 1981, a shock from 1981 to 1986, and an adjustment from 1986 to 2000 (Bevan et al., 1992). The boom, or more appropriately the boom in petroleum prices, created a significant amount of windfall revenue. The federal government became the main distributor of the oil windfall. The initial response to the first boom was to reinforce foreign reserves, which was the proper policy, but as Bevan et al. (1992) show, this was followed by massive investment in public sector megaprojects. The oil boom supported the previous trajectory of import-substitution industrialization. Nigeria increased imports (see Figure 9.1, Panel 4), government spending, and money supply. The unmeasured policies of the federal government generated Dutch disease, leading to deagriculturalization through the spending and resource movement effects.[8] The tremendous increase in oil revenue coupled with fiscal and monetary expansion and real exchange-rate appreciation generated a spending effect on expanding nontradable sectors (food production, import-competing industries, building and construction, general government, and services) and a resource movement effect from the contracting sectors (export agriculture, non-import-competing manufacturing, public utilities, and nonoil natural resources) to the expanding sectors. From 1970 onward, the percentage of nonoil exports and manufactured goods never climbed above the 1988 figure of 8.8% (see Table 9.1). The dominance of oil stifled the growth of nonoil industries.

The Nigerian government demonstrated an urban bias in its allocation of national development resources during this period. It neglected and indeed abandoned the agricultural sector, which fell into decline during the mid-1970s, when the oil boom began. This decline mostly affected the export subsector. Rural–urban and agricultural–nonagricultural gaps widened. Nonetheless, although there were significant macroeconomic distortions, the impact of Dutch disease was not uniform across the states depending on the nature of the state economy, its location, and whether it has an important economic center as Lagos. There was a short-lived boom in the nontradable agricultural and nonagricultural sectors but the boom

---

[8] The term *Dutch disease* refers to the deindustrialization of a nation's economy when discovery and exploitation of a valuable natural resource leads to an increase in the value of the currency (thus handicapping exports) and crowds out other firms of economic activity.

Table 9.1. *Nigeria's Dependence on Oil Exports, 1970–1998* [i]

	Percentage Oil Exports	Percentage Nonoil Exports	Manufactured Products
1970–1974	100	0	0
1975–1979	100	0	0
1980	100	0	0
1984	97.3	2.7	0
1985	97.2	2.8	0
1986	93.8	6.2	0
1987	93.0	7.0	0
1988	91.2	8.8	0
1989	94.7	5.1	0.2
1990	97.3	2.5	0.2
1991	96.5	3.1	0.4
1992	98.1	1.7	0.2
1993	97.8	2.1	0.1
1994	97.7	2.2	0.1
1995	97.8	1.9	0.3
1996	98.2	1.6	0.1
1997	97.7	2.0	0.2
1998	95.4	4.5	0.1

[i] Central Bank of Nigeria, Statistical Bulletin.

was undoubtedly softened or liquidated by inflationary pressure, policy distortions, urban-biased policies, and excessively liberal import policies of the government.

Although petroleum increased Nigeria's financial resources and balanced foreign trade in its favor, the tremendous financial capital generated social and economic disorders. Over time, successive governments saw the accumulation and quick evaporation of foreign reserves. The year 1981 saw a deterioration and progressive decline of the terms of trade, which had previously been rising from the 1960s. Also, the index of export unit value declined from 1981 and did not recover until 1990. The real effective exchange rate index was 329 in 1979; by 1985 it had more than doubled to reach an all time high of 689. Many of these distortions and economic instabilities were policy induced (see Figures 9.2 and 9.3).[9]

The shock occurred when oil prices collapsed. Faced with severe problems of declining oil revenues and financial and economic crisis, in 1985, under General Ibrahim Babangida, Nigeria introduced IMF-style reforms

[9] These figures were obtained from World Bank (2002).

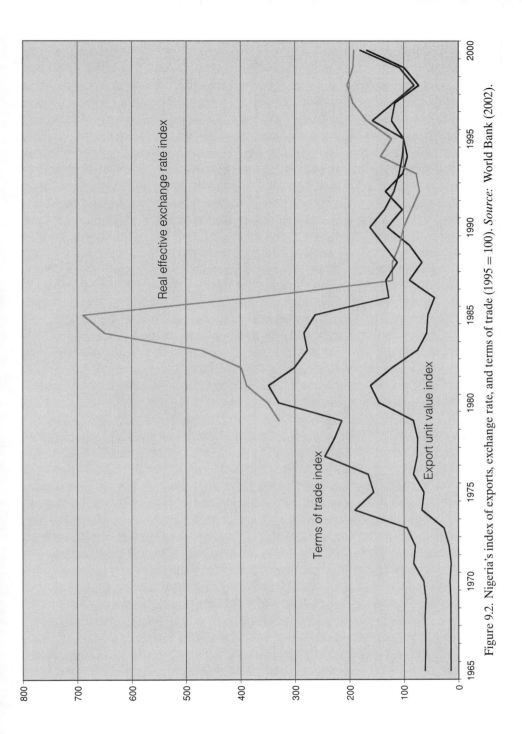

Figure 9.2. Nigeria's index of exports, exchange rate, and terms of trade (1995 = 100). *Source:* World Bank (2002).

417

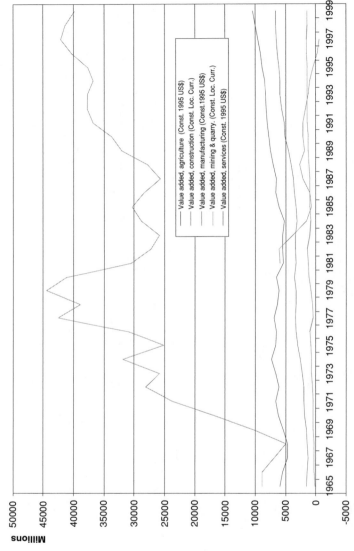

Figure 9.3. Value added by various sectors of the Nigerian economy, 1965–2000. *Source:* World Bank (2002).

418

to stabilize the economy. When Babangida took office, Nigeria had a significant level of debt – 66% of GDP in 1985 (an elevenfold increase from 1975) – forcing it to adopt IMF policies and eventually invite the IMF in. The 1980s saw minimal industrialization, more poverty, worsening economic conditions, and debt-driven austerity measures.

In the last phase (from 1986 onward), according to Nnadozie (1995), structural adjustment punished the poor and created distributive conflicts that resulted from the unequal sharing of the social costs of the adjustment. Toward the late 1980s and early 1990s the impact of distributive conflicts on adjustment efforts became apparent. With the exception of 1990 when the inflation rate was 7%, between 1986 and 1996, the inflation rate remained above 20%, attaining a galloping 84% in 1992 and 56% in 1995.

II.2. Federalism and Economic Policymaking

Macroeconomic policy during the colonial period was rudimentary, but the establishment of federal ministries involved in planning and policies marked the beginning of overlapping roles, causing duplication, institutional ambiguities, and proliferation of public institutions (Idachaba, 1989). Federalization led to inefficient bureaucracy and red tape, as macroeconomic policy became corrupted by political and personal considerations, often to the detriment of the economy.

The overlapping jurisdictions did not, however, limit arbitrary policy changes or increase accountability in policymaking. Given the extreme centralization in the Nigerian federation, policy changed as regimes changed in Nigeria, resulting in a stop-and-go reform program. In fact, much of the uniqueness of Nigerian's macroeconomic policy misadventure "is explained by the succession of governments" (Bevan et al., 1992). Frequent changes in development strategy became rampant in the 1970s and 1980s. Agricultural policy was a case in point as Nnadozie (1995, pp. 131–132) illustrates in the following passage:

The Nigerian policy evolved from a discriminatory policy in favor of export agriculture from the colonial period up to 1970, to having no coherent agricultural policy in the 1970s, to a reverse discriminatory policy in favor of food production in the 1980s, and finally to a second reverse discriminatory policy in favor of export agriculture in the late 1980s and 1990s.

At the same time that the country was undertaking import-substitution industrialization, it embarked on a massive food import scheme in response to the policy-induced hyperinflation in the 1980s. The federal government got directly involved in agricultural production and between 1976 and 1983 Nigeria moved successively through three agricultural development programs – the National Accelerated Food Production Program (NAFPP), Operation Feed the Nation (OFN), and the Green Revolution – as each administration abandoned its predecessor's program and introduced a new one.

Political business cycles became part of the Nigerian economy. Similarly, the military administration during the first boom in 1974 embarked on import-substitution industrialization through public sector megaprojects. This administration was followed by a civilian administration that oversaw the second boom. "An initial accumulation of reserves in 1979 and 1980 quickly evaporated as a result of increased spending, while public and publicly guaranteed indebtedness (outstanding and disbursed) more than tripled (to over US$12 billion in 1983). The civilian regime was thus able to spend its way to victory in the 1983 elections; it was, however overthrown in a military coup soon after" (Bevan et al., 1992, p. 2).

The centralization that characterized Nigeria's federal structure created problems of accountability, resulting in bad macroeconomic policy for several reasons. The structure was so far removed from its grass roots that accountability and control was impossible. The multiple institutions with overlapping roles resulted in confusion over policy responsibilities in addition to contradictions in the overall strategy. In the same vein, it became difficult for the center, which was bureaucratically weak and ill-equipped, to address the economic interests of the highly divergent society, nor could it accommodate interregional, rural–urban, and intersectoral differences.

The main role of subnational voices in macroeconomic policy was thus limited to the implicit threat of a coup. Although a military dictatorship is not accountable to and therefore not subject to removal by the voters, it can be overthrown by a coup. To succeed, coups need an atmosphere of society-wide resentment of and dissatisfaction with the existing order.

These conditions were present in 1985, when Babangida and his cohorts overthrew the Buhari military regime (who had overthrown Shagari's civilian administration in 1983). The new government gave the existing economic disaster that the country was facing as its main reason for the coup, and it received widespread popular support. Consequently, the Babangida regime understood that the survival of its own dictatorship depended on its ability to tackle Nigeria's economic crises and the country's crushing debt burden or at least to appear to do so. It is against this backdrop that Nigeria adopted IMF-type economic reforms initially without the IMF since the public roundly rejected the idea in the open debate that the president had organized.

III. OVERVIEW OF NIGERIA'S FEDERALISM AND INTERGOVERNMENTAL TRANSFERS

III.1. Political Structure

The Nigerian federation has changed significantly in time and in space since the colonial period. One way in which successive Nigerian governments have struggled to solve the country's extreme diversity and intractable ethno-religious problem has been to create more states (from the original three regions in 1946 to thirty-six states in 2001) to satisfy the yearning for ethnically homogenous political units and, in some way, to minimize interethnic conflicts.

Historically, there were three regions in Nigeria in 1946: one in the North and two in the South. In 1963 a third region, Midwest, was created in the South. During each of these periods, the South always had more subnational and subregional divisions (states, provinces, and divisions) than the North. However, in 1967, General Yakubu Gowan created six states in the North and six states in the South. Then, in 1976, under General Murtala Mohammed, the tide turned in favor of the North, marking the beginning of northern hegemony and political domination in Nigeria's federalism. In that year, for the first time in Nigerian history, the North had a superiority of ten states and 152 local governments compared to the South's nine states and 148 local government areas.

Thereafter, the country saw a progressively increasing number of states and local governments in favor of the North, culminating in General Abacha's 1996 Decree 36, which provided for the creation of twenty states and 414 local governments in the North (including the federal capital territory) and seventeen states and 355 local governments in the South. This arrangement, along with the federal capital territory, was later adopted in Nigeria's 1999 Constitution as the structure of the Federal Republic of Nigeria. The increasing interregional disparity in Nigeria's federal structure, engineered by the disproportionate northern political domination, underscored the country's allocative distortions.

It is difficult, however, to view this process as the development of a truly federal state. The establishment of subnational governments was accompanied neither by well-defined governmental jurisdictions nor by subnational governmental autonomy. In some sense, the proliferation of states was a response to centralizing tendencies. The centralization of authority that began in 1966 during the Ironsi regime resulted in the federal takeover of national development. Centralization of the commodity marketing boards, the major source of subnational governments' revenue, came later, in 1976. Consolidation and centralization of revenue collection led to the loss of fiscal autonomy by the subnational governments. Together with the system of revenue allocation based on the principle of equality, these changes increased the demand for the creation of states since forming a state became a means for various groups to access oil revenues. In addition to the huge costs associated with a new state, however, the creation of more states has increased competition for resources at the center, exacerbated transfer dependence, and rendered some states virtually financially unviable.

The current federal system is set out in General Abubakar's 1999 Constitution, which formed the foundation for the Obasanjo administration. It states, "Nigeria shall be a Federation consisting of states and Federal Capital Territory" (FCT) with three branches of government: the executive, judiciary, and legislature (Constitution of Nigeria (1999). The House of Assembly (or National Assembly) consists of a Senate and a House of Representatives and has, under the 1999 Constitution, the legislative power of the state of the federation. The Constitution also recognizes thirty-six states and 768 local government areas, with each state having an executive branch led by the governor and a House of Assembly.

These institutional checks and balances at the federal and state levels do not extend to the local levels. In fact, the structure of the relationship between the bureaucracy, judiciary, and legislature or functional branches of government is designed to provide accountability, although this has not often been the case. This structure is absent in the local government areas (LGAs), where each of Nigeria's 768 LGAs recognized in the Constitution is headed by an elected chairperson who serves with elected councilors.

III.2. Revenues

III.2.a. Overview. Nigeria's revenue system and intergovernmental transfer system have been characterized by centralization, instability, and transfer dependence. One revealing indicator of the degree of Nigeria's fiscal centralization is the types of taxes within different levels of governments' jurisdictions and the corresponding rights to revenue from each type of tax. Table 9.2 reflects the fiscal regulations outlined in Nigeria's

Table 9.2. *Nigerian Major Tax Jurisdiction and Right to Revenue, 1999*[i]

Types of Tax	Jurisdiction		Right to Revenue
	Law	Administration and Collection	
1. Import duties	Federal	Federal	Federation Account
2. Exercise duties	Federal	Federal	Federation Account
3. Export duties	Federal	Federal	Federation Account
4. Mining rents and royalties	Federal	Federal	Federation Account
5. Petroleum profit tax	Federal	Federal	Federation Account
6. Company income tax	Federal	Federal	Federation Account
7. Capital gains tax	Federal	Federal	State
8. Personal income tax	Federal		State
9. Personal income tax: armed forces, external affairs, nonresident, residents of the f.c.t and Nigerian police	Federal	Federal	Federal
10. Licensing fees on television and wireless radio	Federal	Local	Local
11. Stamp duties	Federal	Federal/State	Local
12. Capital transfer tax (CTT)	Federal	State	State
13. Value added tax	Federal	Federal	Federal/State/Local
14. Pools betting and other betting taxes	State	State	State
15. Motor vehicle and drivers license	State	State	State
16. Entertainment tax	State	State	State
17. Land registration and survey fees	State	State	State
18. property taxes and survey fees	State	Local	Local
19. Market and trading license and fees	State	Local	Local

[i] *Source:* Nigeria Constitution 1999.

1999 Constitution. Of the nineteen types of taxes listed in the table, the federal government has jurisdiction and rights over several important sources of revenue such as import duties, excise taxes, mining rents, and petroleum profit taxes. In contrast, the types of taxes that fall to the state and local levels are ones that are relatively harder to collect (e.g., market and trading licenses and fees). Olomola (1999, p. 484) provides data on Nigeria's tax system for 1990, almost a decade earlier, which also indicates that the federal government had power over the significant sources

Table 9.3. *Distribution of Revenue (%) to the*
Federal, State, and Local Government, 1997

Oil revenue	71.5	–	–
Independent revenue	1.4	28.5	8.11
Value added tax	5.8	14.7	24.33
Custom and excise	10.8	–	–
State allocation	–	–	2.22
Company tax	4.5	–	–
Grant and others	5.9	3.75	–
Federation account	–	53.25	64.9
Stabilization fund receipts	–	0.47	–

of tax revenue in the country. Thus, based on tax jurisdiction and right to revenue, power is concentrated at the federal level.

The economy at the federal level is heavily dependent on oil revenue. From Table 9.3's 1997 figures, we see that the federal level receives all oil revenue, which in turn comprises over 70% of total federal revenue on the average. Oil as a percentage of total revenue has consistently been above 50% (with a high of 86% in 1992).

As a result of the concentration of revenue rights and jurisdiction at the national level, subnational governments have become dependent on national transfers for their expenditures. State and local governments received an average of 53.25% and 64.9%, respectively, of their revenue from the federal account. The less economically developed North has typically been the most dependent on transfers (Table 9.3).

One consequence of state dependence on federal government revenue transfers is that "the execution of local projects followed a declining trend" (Olomola, 1999, pp. 486–487). Transfer dependence comes at a high price to the states because it significantly reduces their autonomy and ability to execute local projects and pay salaries. The central government uses allocations to control state government behavior and to punish errant states by withholding their allocation, thereby making it difficult for the states to pay salaries to state employees. Between 1993 and 1996, several projects at the state level experienced delays in the release of statutory allocations, leading to nonpayment or late payment of workers' salaries in some states (Olomola, 1999).[10]

---

[10] There are also instances of shortfalls in expected revenue (defined as the expected share to be transferred to states relative to the actual amount received). The difference between the two figures, for example in 1996, resulted in a 65.2% shortfall (Olomola, 1999, p. 488).

Table 9.4, adapted from the UNDP's Human Development Report for Nigeria (1997), establishes the dependence of the state on federal government transfers. For the years 1990–1993, internally generated revenue (IGR) per state is reported. To determine the degree of dependence, we use the total recurrent expenditure (TRE). The dependency ratio (DR) is then calculated as $1 - (IGR/TRE)$; the higher the value of DR, the more transfer dependent is the state. For 1990, average dependence was 80.98%. The South-East (oil-producing) region had the lowest ratio at 69.63%, whereas the North-East exhibited the highest dependency at 89.63%. This trend continued in 1991. Whereas average dependency for the year was slightly lower at 79.13%, the South-East had the lowest dependency (68.81%), and the North-East stayed at the high end (91.33%). The following year, the country average again decreased slightly (77.11%), whereas regional averages seemed to slightly converge: The lowest dependency ratio was maintained by the South-East (68.99%), whereas the North-West was at the other end of the continuum at 85.17%.

An important thing to note is that the difference between the highest and lowest DRs decreased from 20 percentage points in 1990 to 16 by 1992. In 1993, the South-West's DR was the lowest at 74.3%, whereas the North-East's was the highest at 94.7%. Although the difference between the two figures (North-East's and South-West's) moved back up to 20 percentage points, it is worthwhile to note the increased dependence of the South-East (about 8 percentage points in four years), the decreased dependence of the South-West (about 8 percentage points in four years), and the constant dependence of the country overall.

Table 9.4 reveals a few overall trends. In general, Nigerian states maintain a high-dependence on federal government allocations for their recurrent expenditure, as the average DR for the four years was 80% and all regions' dependence has been on the rise with the exception of the South-West. This dependence increased slightly for the South-East and simultaneously decreased for the South-West.[11]

Further, Akpan (1999) uses an indicator similar to the UNDP indicator to calculate state government dependency ratios. He estimates dependence as the ratio of internal (state) revenue to recurrent expenditure, which captures state capacity to cover its costs. The data indicate that such high-dependency states as Yobe and Niger can cover only 5.4%

---

[11] The apparent reduction of state dependence, as sometimes suggested by dependency measures, reflects an increasing share of states in VAT revenues and should, therefore, not be mistaken for any increased state power or responsibility (Olomola, 1999, p. 485).

Table 9.4. Internally Generated Revenue (IGR; million naira) and Dependency Ratio (DR; %) by State[i]

	South-East			South-West			North-West			North-East	
	IGR	DR		IGR	DR		IGR	DR		IGR	DR
1990											
Akwa-Ibom	45.0	91.9	Kwara	73.3	83.4	Kaduna	95.5	86.9	Adamawa	41.9	90.3
Anambra	186.6	55.8	Ogun	78.0	74.0	Kano	130.8	94.4	Bauchi	48.5	94.3
Benue	163.9	96.9	Ondo	120.2	75.4	Katsina	65.0	56.0	Borno	34.8	93.7
Cross-River	33.2	92.2	Oyo	49.6	93.5	Niger	11.5	97.5	Plateau	171.0	80.2
Delta	81.9	24.5				Sokoto	119.9	80.5			
Edo	81.9	24.5									
Imo	241.3	86.8									
Rivers	88.6	84.4									
Average 1990 (80.98)		69.63			81.58			83.06			89.63
1991											
Abia	107.0	89.4	Kogi	3.4	97.2	Jigawa	9.1	93.0	Adamawa	146.3	94.1
Akwa-Ibom	63.9	91.9	Kwara	105.3	81.5	Kaduna	109.9	71.5	Bauchi	69.4	93.2
Anambra	45.8	57.7	Ogun	239.3	-4.8	Kano	201.3	93.6	Borno	92.7	86.4
Benue	40.0	91.1	Ondo	80.1	84.2	Katsina	72.4	50.4	Plateau	123.7	80.4
Cross-River	51.6	92.1	Osun	18.1	85.0	Kebbi	1.4	99.1	Taraba	4.5	94.7
Delta	25.9	52.9	Oyo	50.8	91.2	Niger	24.1	96.3	Yobe	0.4	99.2
Edo	27.5	75.2				Sokoto	136.1	84.2			
Enugu	34.4	-41									
Imo	230.7	81.2									
Rivers	148.8	97.6									
Average 1991 (79.13)		68.81			72.38			84.01			91.33

426

1992

State			State			State			State		
Abia	135.0	82.1	Kogi	32.3	92.3	Jigawa	23.9	93.0	Adamawa	60.0	89.2
Akwa-Ibom	101.9	79.7	Kwara	104.4	81.1	Kaduna	323.1	67.5	Bauchi	69.5	93.0
Anambra	138.0	83.4	Ogun	92.3	84.9	Kano	136.9	84.6	Borno	164.9	75.0
Benue	27.9	96.3	Ondo	72.3	90.9	Katsina	50.6	91.6	Plateau	123.8	73.2
Cross-River	61.2	90.2	Osun	82.4	83.8	Kebbi	107.4	77.4	Taraba	178.2	50.3
Delta	324.1	54.3	Oyo	442.7	15.7	Niger	21.4	95.5	Yobe	23.6	96.2
Edo	84.7	84.3				Sokoto	108.0	86.6			
Enugu	87.0	0.3									
Imo	139.4	84.9									
Rivers	551.9	34.4									
Average 1992 (77.11)	77.53	68.99	Average		74.78	Average		85.17	Average		79.48

1993

State			State			State			State		
Abia	173.2	78.0	Kogi	34.1	50.8	Jigawa	69.8	79.1	Adamawa	69.6	94.4
Akwa-Ibom	132.8	85.5	Kwara	83.6	81.6	Kaduna	198.7	85.0	Bauchi	84.7	92.0
Anambra	218.2	73.9	Ogun	98.4	86.0	Kano	188.4	82.5	Borno	51.0	93.6
Benue	103.7	90.2	Ondo	87.9	76.9	Katsina	119.3	84.4	Plateau	55.0	95.8
Cross-River	151.4	76.8	Osun	118.1	79.4	Kebbi	147.9	79.2	Taraba	30.0	95.5
Delta	510.6	54.2	Oyo	221.7	71.1	Niger	21.6	95.0	Yobe	22.0	96.9
Edo	106.6	90.2				Sokoto	62.2	86.3			
Enugu	123.1	86.0									
Imo	124.0	83.8									
Rivers	617.7	56.7									
Average 1993 (82.76)		77.53	Average		74.3	Average		84.5	Average		94.7

i Adapted from Nigeria 1996 Human Development Report. Negative dependency ratio means that there is more than enough to pay for recurrent expenditures. Dependency ratio is calculated as 1 − (IGR/TRE). The average dependency ratio for all states through 1990–1993 (calculated by taking the yearly averages) was 80%. The average dependency ratios for each state through 1990–1993 were South-East: 71.24, South-West: 75.76, North-West: 84.19, and North-East: 88.79.

and 6.5%, respectively, of their current expenditure from their internal revenue (Akpan, 1999). According to Akpan, the ratios of the southern states of Lagos, Rivers, Delta, and the northern state Kaduna on the one hand, and the northern states of Yobe, Niger, Jigawa, and Kogi on the other, are the best and worst performing states, respectively. "Using internal revenue generation capability and other ratios, states in the southern part of the country are relatively more self-reliant than their northern counterparts" (Akpan, 1999, p. 83). Further data on the proportion of each state's budget that is represented by transfers from the central government corroborates the trends revealed through the UNDP measure and data on state transfer dependence.[12]

III.2.b. Discussion. The type of revenue assignment across levels of governments discussed so far (Table 9.2), including the centralization of oil revenue, may not be inconsistent with generally accepted principles in fiscal federalism. Concern over the volatility of oil revenue suggests that it would be better managed by the central government (Ahmad and Mottu, 2002). Centralization is also seen as an equalizing mechanism if resources are not evenly distributed geographically. However, only in an "unconstrained world" would centralization of oil revenue be most appropriate (Ahmad and Mottu, 2002).

Several problems – unchecked power, bad governance, and weak accountability – arise with centralization of oil revenue in the Nigerian context. In Mexico, for example, the central government has rights to most oil revenues and shares a portion with subnational governments. However, revenue sharing has been neither contentious nor fiscally destabilizing (lately) because a relatively transparent formula is applied and because the share of the revenue to subnational levels does not represent a large part of their overall revenue (Ahmad and Mottu, 2002, pp. 17–19). As already discussed, the situation differs in Nigeria and the trend continues: In 1999, 75% of Nigerian state revenue was composed of revenue from the federal government, much of it comprising oil. Oil revenue accounted for almost 33% of public sector revenue in Mexico over 1997–2000, in contrast to an 82% share of oil revenue in total general government revenue in 2000 for Nigeria. Oil accounted for 40% of Nigeria's GDP over this time period, whereas Mexico's share between 1997 and

---

[12] In particular, Akpan (1999) measures dependency as statutory allocation as a percentage of total revenue for each state and statutory allocation as a fraction of the total expenditure. The tables from Akpan are available on request.

2000 was 5.3% of GDP (Ahmad and Mottu, 2002, pp. 17–19). Nigeria's state governments are highly dependent on revenue sharing, revenue mostly comprises oil, and rules are contentious because they are based on derivation and distribution. The benefits of centralization of oil wealth in Nigeria, then, are highly limited by political economy concerns.

Centralization of oil wealth has led to accumulated power at the federal level and corruption and poor institutional quality at all levels of the government. It is well established in the literature linking natural resource abundance and bad governance that in the presence of nondemocratic regimes, which were rampant in postindependence Nigeria, dependence on natural resources leads to worsening of governance (see, for instance, Wantchekon, 2002). In authoritarian or weakly democratic countries, assigning almost entirely the primary revenue base to the federal level leaves the power of the center further unchecked and enables more discretionary behavior. An alternative arrangement that would share tax bases (essentially more decentralization instead of revenue sharing) between federal and local levels would provide for a more even and efficient distribution of power between levels of government.

Moreover, in Nigeria, formula-based revenue sharing, where the center distributes funds to lower levels, intensifies the problems of dependence on oil price volatility and procyclicality in fiscal management. Revenue sharing does not allow for proper (countercyclical) fiscal management in the context of almost full transfer and oil dependence because states receive and spend according to changes in oil revenue with responsibilities in expenditure remaining stable (Ahmad and Mottu, 2002, p. 10). For example, the high price of oil 2000–2001 "led to a large increase in the distribution of financial resources to subnational governments, particularly to oil-producing states, without the assignment of new expenditure responsibilities."[13]

The lack of conditions imposed on these large intergovernmental transfers has adversely affected incentives to provide an equitable distribution of public goods. Revenue allocation is not based on clear assignment of spending responsibilities or minimum public services provision. Although allocations have been used as political tools to leverage the federal power and control over state behavior, these were not conditionalities designed to attain desirable economic objectives, fiscal discipline, or accountability. Indeed, the fact that a state receives transfers for financing most of its expenditure does not automatically imply that such expenditures would

---

[13] See Ahmad and Mottu (2002, p. 18).

necessarily be unproductive, but lack of democratic oversight allowed states in Nigeria to use their transferred resources in whatever way suited the elites' interest. The corruption and waste that characterize the state transfers arose because of the military governors who ruled the states for many years were not subject to voter control or sanctions from the central government.[14]

In summary, the two main problems in Nigerian fiscal federalism are centralization of oil revenue at the federal level and absence of conditionality at the subnational level. Therefore, at least partial rights to revenue to state governments combined with requirements for public service provision would help constrain both central and state governments.

III.3. Revenue Allocation

In the history of Nigeria, fiscal federalism and revenue allocation have been contentious insofar as they have been heavily politicized and inherently inequitable. In contemporary Nigeria, oil has taken center stage as the main determinant of the politics and patterns of revenue allocation. Along with this oil dominance came federal government dominance and control of national revenue as well as a progressive neglect of the regions from which oil revenues emerge. Hence, Nigeria's revenue allocation history has been characterized by five prominent features: (1) the primacy of revenue from natural resources, especially oil, as the main determinant of the politics and patterns of allocation; (2) federal domination and control of national revenue; (3) the neglect of regions from which revenues emerge; (4) the continuous reduction of allocations by the federal government to states coupled with a progressive shifting of federal responsibilities to the states; (5) the intensification of appropriative struggles as the inherently inequitable and highly politicized arrangements have proven to be a constant source of tension and conflict.

To provide a brief background, we need to consider some history. From the creation of the three Nigerian regions – East, West, and North – in 1946, the lines of revenue allocation battles were drawn. Subsequent government actions and constitutional stipulations have either exacerbated

---

[14] Because of the Constitution's vagueness and local councilors' lack of power, many LGA chairpersons exercised personal control over LGA revenue allocations from the federal government. The capture of LGA budget by autocratic LGA chairpersons led to widespread incidences of corruption and paying off supportive councilmen in 2001–2002, which was widely reported in the Nigerian news media. The state legislatures were forced to intervene, investigate, reprimand, and even suspend some LGA chairpersons.

the problems or had no impact at all. From 1946 onward, many principles have been developed and used to determine revenue-sharing formulas and fiscal federalism. They range from the principle of derivation to that of even development and from the principle of need to that of national unity.

Further, although the system already operates de facto as a centralized state, the Constitution has been changed to legalize central domination of revenue collection and allocation. One of the key characteristics of at least six of Nigeria's nine constitutions is the excessive centralization of economic power at the federal level. Even the modest level of political decentralization is not accompanied by economic decentralization and fiscal autonomy; rather, we see, especially in the 1999 Constitution, a dominant federal government that redistributes oil revenues to the states and local governments.

The 1999 Constitution provides, in Chapter VI, for the establishment of a Revenue Mobilization, Allocation, and Fiscal Commission by the president. The question of oil revenue and fiscal federalism is addressed in Subsection C162(2). According to the Constitution, the president sets up the Revenue Mobilization, Allocation, and Fiscal Commission and recommends an allocation formula. The Commission acts mainly in an advisory capacity, and the National Assembly determines the allocation to various states. The states then allocate money to the local governments following the National Assembly's prescription.

State revenue allocation is disaggregated into four regions (North, East, West, and Midwest). From 1977 to 1995, the North's share is consistently the highest, ranging between 45% to 54% (Table 9.5).

A correlation analysis based on 1996 data (Table 9.6) shows that the strongest relationship to state statutory allocation is found to be land mass, population density, number of local governments, and population. Therefore, allocations are not derivation based as suggested by the low correlation between internal revenue and state statutory allocation.[15]

Hence, centralization of wealth and the dependence of subnational units on federal transfers are major features of the Nigerian economy.

---

[15] Using data for 1998, Ahmad and Singh (2003) find a low correlation between per capita income and transfers as well as between the number of hospital beds and transfers, indicating that transfers do not have a strong relationship with need. Additionally, they do not find a distinct pattern of redistribution among regions; instead the data suggest that differences in transfers per capita are greater within states than within regions. This needs to be studied more carefully and is in line with our finding of a convergence in transfer dependence.

Table 9.5. *Statutory Revenue Allocation (%) to the Former Four Regions, 1977–1996* [i]

Region	1977	1978	1979	1980	1981	1982	1983	1984	1985	1986	1987	1988	1989	1992	1993	1994	1995
North	47.03	47.4	48.1	45.8	46.1	48.4	48.4	48.4	46.5	49.2	49	49.1	49	49.9	54	53.4	49.6
East	24.25	25.7	24.7	26.7	27	23.7	23.7	23.6	21.1	23.1	23.6	24.3	24.4	23.2	21.7	20.7	24.2
West	17.6	18.1	18.4	17.6	17.7	18.9	19	19	17.6	19.2	18.9	18.5	18.5	18.8	14.7	16	15.5
Midwest	11.12	8.87	8.83	10	8.9	7	6.9	6.9	5.9	6.4	6.5	6.3	6.4	4.79	5.58	5.88	7.05

[i] CBN annual reports and statement of accounts.

432

Table 9.6. *Correlation of the Determinants of Federal Government Statutory Allocation to States and Local Governments* [i]

Determinants	Spearman's Rank Correlation Coefficient for States	Spearman's Rank Correlation Coefficient for Local Governments
Population	0.4793	0.1998
No. of local governments	0.4090	0.5403
Internal revenue	0.2833	0.3739
Ethnicity	0.0564	0.1052
Oil producing (endowment)	0.0129	0.0517
Land mass	0.4589	0.4517
Population density	0.5109	0.2862
State statutory allocation	–	0.4275

[i] *Source:* CBN 1996 Statistical Bulletin and CBN 1996–1997 Annual Report and Statement of Account.

Further, data point to a low correlation between transfers and derivation. Indeed, there may be need for oil revenue transfer to ensure the viability of some non-oil-producing states. However, derivation rights to the oil-producing states are stressed here because substantial redistribution away from the oil-producing region is evidence of the politicized process. Therefore, although maintaining some form of equalizing transfer (with oversight) would be necessary to correct for revenue disparities, a more decentralized system would balance the power of the central government.

As far as allocation goes, the Constitution states "that the principle of derivation shall be constantly reflected in any approved formula as being not less than 13% of the revenue accruing to the Federation Account directly from any natural resources."[16] The problem is that even if there appears to be some flexibility in establishing the appropriate derivation-based allocation ratios, the fact that the oil-producing states have a significant minority in the National Assembly (since the non-oil-producing North dominates) makes it impossible for any significant change to be made to the allocation formula. More importantly, like the previous constitutions, the 1999 Constitution places the control of oil revenues squarely in the hands of the federal government. It decides how to allocate these revenues to Nigerians. Considering the suboptimal outcomes of federal

---

[16] The Supreme Court, in 2002, ruled that the 13% derivation rule applied only to onshore production (Ahmad and Singh, 2003).

government management of Nigeria's oil wealth, it is doubtful that this is the most efficient resource allocation system for Nigeria. Before turning to the development implications of such phenomena, we first examine more closely the evolution of the revenue allocation formula.

III.4. Evolution and Transformation of Nigeria's Revenue Allocation Formula

Okigbo (1965) identified two phases in the evolution of public finance in Nigeria: one from 1900 to 1945 and a second phase beginning in 1945. The two phases correspond to major spatial and political reorganizations in Nigeria. In his words, "The evolution of the current pattern of fiscal structure and relationships in Nigeria is a reflection of its constitutional history" (Okigbo, 1955, p. 4). Okigbo's second phase, 1945 and beyond, marks the beginning of the battle between derivation and need as a basis for the determination of the revenue allocation formula for the Nigerian federal government and the states. Okigbo shows that the Native Authority Acts of 1904 and 1906 defined the tax collection system and revenue-sharing formula between the British Administration and native authorities. Further, he describes the Amalgamation of Northern and Southern Nigeria in 1914 as "the first major landmark in the evolution of Nigerian fiscal relationships" (Okigbo, 1955, p. 7). The Amalgamation itself, in Okigbo's view, was financially motivated to reduce the dependency of the North on Britain by supporting it with the more financially viable South. We note that the North–South power paradox and the South's subsidization of the North are indeed historical – a legacy of British colonialism.

Table 9.7 disaggregates the evolution of Nigeria's federalism into twelve periods, delineating the different fiscal commissions that have been appointed to recommend principles of revenue allocation. From the table we can see that in the preindependence period of 1947–1948, the accepted principles for revenue allocation by the Sir Sydney Philipson and S. O. Adebo Commission were on the basis of derivation and even progress. The movement to quasifederalism followed with the Hicks–Phillipson Commission, which allocated based on derivation, need, and national interest. The third disaggregation (1954–1958) was a federal system under the Sir Louis Chick Commission based on derivation and fiscal independence, followed by the Raisam Commission in 1959–1960. "Up to 1958 ... derivation was the most important principle for revenue sharing ... At that time, oil had not gained a central place in the Nigerian economy. The main sources of revenue and engine of growth for the Nigerian economy were agricultural export crops" (Okoh and

Table 9.7. *Evolution and Transformation of Nigeria's Federal Character*[i]

Year/Political System	Fiscal Commissioner	Recommendation	Accepted Principle
1947/48 Unitary system	Sir Sydney Philipson and S.O Adebo		a. Derivation b. Even progress
1952/53 Quasi-federal system	Prof. J. R. Hicks and Sir Sydney Phillipson		a. Derivation b. Need c. National interest
1954/58 Federal system (3 regions, later Cameroon became a separate region)	Sir Louis Chick		a. Derivation b. Fiscal independence
1959/60 Federal system (4 regions)	Sir J. Raisman and Prof. R. C. Tress		a. Derivation b. National unity c. Fiscal independence
1964/67 Federal system (4 regions Cameroon inclusive & Midwest)	Mr. H. Binn	a. Regional financial comparability b. Continuity of service c. Minimum responsibilities	a. Derivation b. Fiscal independence c. National Interest East 30%, North 42%, Midwest 8%, West 20%
1968 Federal system	Chief O. Dina	a. Minimum national standard of basic needs b. Population c. Tax effort d. Financial prudence e. Fiscal adequacy f. Balanced development g. Independent revenue h. Derivation i. National interest	a. Equality of states 50% b. Population 50% c. Derivation
1975/76	Federal Military Governmment (F.M.G.)		a. Equality b. Population c. Derivation
1977	Prof. A. O Aboyade	a. Equality of access to dev. opportunities (25%) b. National minimum std. for national integration (22%) c. Absorptive capacity (AC) (20%) d. Independent revenue and minimum tax effort (18%)	a. Equality of access to dev. opportunities (25%) b. National minimum std. for national integration (22%) c. Absorptive capacity (20%) d. Independent revenue and minimum tax effort (18%)
1977	Prof. A. O Aboyade	e. Fiscal efficiency (15%): federal 57%, state joint (AC) 30%, local government, 10%, special grant A/c 3%	e. Fiscal efficiency (15%): federal 60%, state joint A/c 30%, local government 10%

(continued)

Table 9.7 (*continued*)

Year/Political System	Fiscal Commissioner	Recommendation	Accepted Principle
1979	Dr. Pius Okigbo		Declared Ultra Vires by the Supreme Court
1981	Federal Government Revenue Acts 1981/82		Federal 53%, state 35%, local government 10%, a. Sharing of states allocation b. Minimum responsibility c. Equality of states d. Population e. Social development f. Internal revenue effort g. Derivation h. Ecology
1988/89	Gen. Danjuma	Vertical allocation: federal government 47%, state government 30%, local government 15%, special funds 8%, Special funds fct 1%, stabilization 0.5%, savings 2%, derivation 2%, OMPADEC 1.5%, Dev. of nonoil 0.5%, gen. ecology 0.5% Horizontal allocation: equality of states: 40%, population, 30%, social dev. factor, 10%, land mass & terrain–int. rev. effort 20%	Vertical allocation: federal government 50%, state government 30%, local government 15%, special funds 5%, Special funds fct 1%, stabilization 0.5%, savings%, derivation 1%, OMPADEC 1.5%, dev. of nonoil %, gen. ecology 1% Horizontal allocation: equality of states 40%, population 30%, social dev. factor 10%, land mass & terrain–int. rev. effort 20%
12. 1999	Federal Military Governmment		Federal government 48.5%, state government 24%, local government 20%, FCt 1% gen ecology 2%, stabilization 0.5%, derivation (MR) 1%, OMPADEC 3%

i Adapted from Agiobenebo (1999, pp. 45–47).

Egbon, 1999, p. 409). Nigeria maintained these principles throughout the 1960s.

By the end of the 1960s, oil production in the South-East had become the major source of export earnings and revenue and, consequently, the South-East had become increasingly dependent on its oil production. As a result, economic power was concentrated in the South. However, Northern political dominance led to (Northern) military rule over the periods of 1966–1979 and 1984–1999. Thus from the beginning of the 1970s, revenue allocation formulas shifted from derivation and moved toward redistributing oil earnings away from the South-East oil region: "The beginning of indigenization legislation (Decree No. 13, 1970) ushered in new principles: population, equality of states, and the decline of the importance of derivation as oil revenue became more significant . . . other principles gained ascendancy . . . relinquishing derivation to the background" (Okoh and Egbon, 1999, p. 409). After 1970, there have been incessant changes in the revenue allocation formula. The vertical allocation has generally favored the federal government and horizontal allocation (among states) has focused on equality of states and population and, hence, less on derivation (as we discussed in the preceding section).

The early impetus for the strong central power that shapes today's revenue allocation was when, in trying to prevent the disintegration of Nigeria after the civil war, the federal government led by General Gowon arrogated overwhelming powers. As oil began to play a more prominent role in the Nigerian economy, at the wake of the civil war, it provided an additional impetus for increased centralization by an already centralized state.

Given the strategic importance of oil, "beginning in 1958, the development of the oil industry and the state grew pari passu."[17] Federal control of oil revenues came as part of progressive overall federalization and centralization that occurred in Nigeria following independence. This progressive strengthening of the federal government emanated from three sources. First, in filling the investment and development gaps left by the colonial authority, the state began to play an important economic and political role in Nigeria immediately after independence. This role increased concomitantly with the power of the central government as it provided national infrastructure and capital investment, which the private sector – severely underdeveloped under colonialism – could not provide.

Second, the immediate postindependence Nigerian economy was decentralized with the regions playing a more prominent role than the

---

[17] See Nnadozie (1995, p. 22).

national government. But increasing regionalization was fraught with divisiveness, which ultimately led to the political crisis of 1964–1965, resulting in the call for change in favor of a stronger central government. Therefore, when General Aguiyi Ironsi (the first Nigerian military ruler) took power following the abortive coup of 1966, his stated goal was, among other things, to preserve national unity and to eradicate regionalism, ethnocentrism, and corruption (Osaghae, 1998). The military takeover of government at the beginning of the civil war in 1966 was the first step toward centralization. A 1968 decree established a revenue allocation formula that gave the federal government 75% of oil revenues, with the states and local governments receiving 22% and 3%, respectively. In 1977, an attempt to change the formula failed.

Hence, centralization of power in Nigeria came about as a response to the economic needs and political crises of the mid- to late 1960s that characterized the existing regional arrangement. The federal government had been considerably strengthened and consolidated over the years in response to political problems. When oil became an important national resource, the federal government extended its control over it and then, by becoming the eleventh member of OPEC in 1971 and wresting control of oil revenue from multinational oil firms, it totally exerted its control of oil.

The 1979 Constitution, established by the military, consolidated the federal oversight that has continued up to the present time. This development had major ramifications for public finance and fiscal federalism in Nigeria. In 1981, the Nigerian Supreme Court judgment attributed 58.5% to the federal government (plus 2.5% for the federal capital territory), 31.5% to the states, and 10% to local governments.[18]

We see again that the federal government controlled a significantly large proportion of the national revenue, since only 31.5% was allocated to the state governments, but there seemed to be recognition that the oil-producing areas deserved some share of the revenue that was generated from their land. Five percent of the allocation to state governments was to be retained for oil-producing states. Nnadozie states,

The formula that the law sought to replace and which found itself once more operative, gave 75% to the federal government, 22% to states and 3% to local governments. This revenue-sharing formula permitted the federal government to

---

[18] Note that according to the Federal Government Revenue Act 1981/82 (see Table 9.7) the implemented allocation differed.

expand the share of the petroleum rent subjected to its direct management. In reality, the share of the federal receipts transferred to the states diminished.[19]

Since 1999, the prevailing formula provides the federal government with 56% of revenue (broken down by an allocation of 48.5% plus the remainder after allocations of 24% to state governments and 20% to local governments). Accordingly, the federal government still receives the largest share of federally collected revenue and state fiscal autonomy has not been enhanced. In the words of Olomola, "It is clear from the foregoing that the issue of revenue allocation in the country has been characterized [by] changing criteria, controversies and conflicts. The authoritarian role of the federal government (especially military regimes) in establishing fiscal jurisdiction continues unabated" (Olomola, 1999, p. 490). However, centralization did not resolve the problem it was meant to address for the transfer system was not equitable, nor did it bring about national development.

Despite a recent trend suggesting a potential convergence in transfers, as we show in the next section, this arrangement has disproportionately favored the North as the highest transfer recipient of revenue generated in the South-East. According to Okoh and Egbon (1999, p. 406) and echoing our earlier analysis, the statutory allocation of oil revenue predominantly goes to the non-oil-producing states. In fact, an average of only 13% of oil revenues, since the 1990s, has been appropriated to states that produce oil.[20]

Although data on intrastate inequality are scarce, there are data on regional economic and welfare indicators, to which we now turn. The North, the recipient of most central government transfers, persists in being underdeveloped relative to the South. We also see that the South's rising dependence of late is coupled with its declining performance as revealed by poverty indices.

---

[19] See Nnadozie (1995, p. 22).

[20] Although we argue that this politicized system of transfer dependence that led to significant transfers to the North has undermined the development of the country, the literature offers rival interpretations. According to the Azam (1995, 2001), transfers from the oil-rich South to the relatively economically poor but militarily and politically powerful North have been good for growth because they have diverted further conflict that the North could have credibly inflicted. In the absence of transfers to the politically powerful North, conflict and instability may have erupted, which would have been bad for growth (e.g., the civil war after the East sought autonomy). However, according to the alternative view of McGuire and Olson (1996) and Adam and O'Connell (1999), transfers to the North have had an adverse effect on growth since Northern interests are overrepresented. (These remarks benefited from comments by Steve O'Connell.)

V. TRANSFERS AND INTERREGIONAL DISPARITIES

Nigeria's history is filled with extreme diversity and severe interregional disparities. The interregional disparities are aptly exemplified by Nigeria's extremely divergent human development outcomes. The UNDP (1997, p. 4) Nigeria Report describes the disparity as follows:

Regional disparities in Nigeria are among the worst in the world. A ranking of the Nigerian states by HDI puts, for example, the Edo and Delta States (formerly Bendel State) on top with an HDI of 0.666 while Borno has an HDI of 0.156. Were Edo and Delta States constituted into a separate sovereign country, their 'nation' would rank 90th in the world – relatively high among the medium-level human development countries while Borno as a separate polity would rank lower than any country in the world.... Wide regional disparity is Nigeria's Achilles heel – the primary source of its perennial conflicts, political instability and social unrest.

What we would like to establish in this section is twofold. First, these regional disparities, between North and South, as displayed by human development indicators, have persisted. Second, indicators suggest that there has been an increase in overall poverty incidence and a narrowing interregional gap in poverty owing to the South's declining performance. The South's declining performance occurs alongside its increased dependency (as seen in previous sections). Likewise, increased overall transfer dependence occurred alongside increased incidence of poverty throughout the country. We begin with a look at disparity between the North and the South by examining the human development index (HDI) for Nigerian states in 1993.[21]

In calculating Nigeria's HDI, the UNDP uses three components: life expectancy at birth, educational attainment index, and real GDP per capita (PPP\$).[22] We see in Table 9.8 (the table for 1993 HDI), broken down by regions, that the South-East has the highest ranking (0.42) whereas the South-West, North-West, and North-East have the respective levels of 0.18, 0.15, and 0.13. Note that each region has a ranking

---

[21] Note that the HDI figures indicated in the previous quote are taken from the UNDP Human Development Report of 1994, whereas the HDI table we provide here is for 1993 levels.

[22] HDI is based on a country's position in relation to a final target expressed as a value between 0 and 1. Countries with an HDI below 0.5 are considered to have a low level of human development, those between 0.5 and 0.8 a medium level, and those above 0.8 a high level (UNDP Nigeria Report, 1996, p. 3).

Table 9.8. Human Development Index (HDI) and Real Per Capita GDP (PPP$) for Nigeria, 1993[i]

South-East			South-West			North-West			North-East		
State	HDI	Per Capita GDP	State	HDI	Per Capita GDP	State	HDI	Per Capita GDP	State	HDI	Per Capita GDP
Anambra	0.174	860.1	Kwara	0.183	1020.1	Kaduna	0.101	876.4	Bauchi	0.127	762.2
Bendel	0.631	5003.3	Ogun	0.126	619.3	Kano	0.161	692.6	Borno	0.042	957.8
Benue	0.188	809.5	Ondo	0.212	422.9	Niger	0.191	1262.0	Gongola	0.214	665.1
Cross-River	0.513	2626.0	Oyo	0.210	678.1	Sokoto	0.128	1246.2	Plateau	0.149	1224.1
Imo	0.466	1341.1									
Rivers	0.539	4860.7		0.18	685.1		0.15	1019.3		0.13	902.3
Average	0.42	2583.45									

[i] Source: UNDP Nigeria Report (1996).

under 0.5, which the UNDP classifies as a low level of development. The two highest levels are in the South.[23]

Disparities are also evident from data on population per doctor per state, which is reported for 1991 in Table 9.9. A considerable dichotomy is indicated between the North and the South. Whereas, as Table 9.9 shows, there are approximately 8,000 people per doctor for both Southern regions, the North-West suffers the most with over 67,000 people per doctor, and the North-East fares slightly better at about 38,000 people per doctor.

Aka's (2000, p. 181) data on states' relative shares in domestic energy consumption for the years 1976–1981 show that the lowest shares all appeared in the North. More current data from UNDP corroborates the ongoing trend of North versus South disparity in terms of energy data. For the years 1993–1994 (shown in Table 9.10), the percentage of population having access to electricity shows a stark difference between regions. In the North-Western and North-Eastern states an average of 18.54% and 17.13%, respectively, of the population had access. The shares of the South-East and South-West were significantly higher at 34.22% and 54.75%. Note that these disparities are apparent despite the exclusion of Lagos from the South-West to avoid an upward bias.

Turning to the indicators of educational outcome, we see that regional disparities are further corroborated in terms of educational attainment, adult literacy rates, mean years of schooling, gross enrollment in tertiary institutions, or female enrollment rates. Aka (2000, p. 170) provides data on primary enrollment by state for the years 1975–1976, 1976–1977, 1977–1978, 1978–1979, and 1979–1980. For the sake of brevity, we discuss the

---

[23] According to the UNDP (1996, p. 28), high HDI results from high per capita income "complemented by a correspondingly high educational attainment, high adult literacy and an above the average life expectancy at birth" From Table 9.8 we learn that "Niger, Kwara, Plateau and Sokoto states with their relatively high real per capita income rank lower than states like Oyo, Ondo and Gongola which although have low per capita income enjoy higher expectation of life at birth." The disparity between high HDI and per capita income suggests two things. First, per capita income conceals a great deal of inequality since it might be suppressing true disparity levels. Second, the implication is that there is high inequality within states, suggesting that transfers are not used efficiently. As such, Soludo's (2001) finding of convergence of income per capita in Nigerian states might be obscure. To avoid this bias, we will consider components of HDI and other indicators separately to reveal a more telling description of development levels (see Table 9.10). Note that we do find convergence (among poverty incidence) in Nigeria; however, this is due to declining performance overall, especially of the South, and is quite different from Soludo's findings.

Table 9.9. *Population per Doctor per State, 1991 (Excluding Lagos)*[i]

South-East		South-West		North-West		North-East	
Abia	7949	Kogi	16343	Jigawa	235827	Adamawa	23087
Akwa-Ibom	12039	Kwara	3849	Kaduna	9406	Bauchi	33034
Anambra	8872	Ogun	7958	Kano	21177	Borno	10956
Benue	11933	Ondo	11292	Katsina	114069	Plateau	4513
Cross-River	8111	Osun	5440	Kebbi	46869	Taraba	54837
Delta	7450	Oyo	3189	Niger	20182	Yobe	100820
Edo	3085			Sokoto	24676		
Enugu	3532						
Imo	5168						
Rivers	10215						
Average	7,835.4		8,011.83		67,458		37,874.5

[i] *Source:* UNDP Nigeria Report 1996.

first and last group of years. In 1975–1976 Imo, Bendel, Anambra, Cross River, and Oyo, all located in the South (east and west regions), had the highest enrollment rates. In the same group of years, the Northern states of Niger, Plateau, and Sokoto had the lowest rates. The years 1979–1980 provide a similar picture as three out of five states with the highest primary enrollment were in the South-East and South-West, whereas the Northern states again had the lowest numbers. The same pattern also existed, as the highest primary school enrollment was in South-Western Osun

Table 9.10. *Percentage of Population Having Access to Electricity*[i]
(Excluding Abuja (FCT) and Lagos), 1993–1994

South-East		South-West		North-West		North-East	
Abia	43.06	Kogi	32.29	Jigawa	6.62	Adamawa	18.59
Akwa-Ibom	13.28	Kwara	60.03	Kaduna	39.66	Bauchi	17.82
Anambra	57.64	Ogun	62.51	Kano	29.19	Borno	19.14
Benue	13.20	Ondo	52.68	Katsina	9.89	Plateau	29.73
Cross-River	24.65	Osun	58.78	Kebbi	7.11	Taraba	5.11
Delta	48.54	Oyo	62.22	Niger	30.39	Yobe	12.36
Edo	60.05			Sokoto	6.90		
Enugu	28.29						
Imo	24.72						
Rivers	28.77						
Average	34.22		54.75		18.54		17.13

[i] *Source:* UNDP Nigeria Report (1996).

Table 9.11. *Top Ten States in Enrollment at Different Levels of Education*[i]

Primary Enrollment (1997)	Secondary Enrollment (1997)	Federal Colleges of Education by States of Origin		Admission to Universities by State	
		Male	Female	Male (1998)	Female (1998)
Kano	Lagos	Bauchi	Enugu	Imo	Imo
Adamawa	Oyo	Kogi	Oyo	Delta	Anambra
Benue	Delta	Ondo	Ogun	Anambra	Delta
Oyo	Imo	Anambra	Ondo	Lagos	Abia
Borno	Ondo	Delta	Kogi	Ogun	Lagos
Akwa-Ibom	Osun	Oyo	Anambra	Abia	Ogun
Kaduna	Ogun	Ogun	Rivers	Edo	Rivers
Lagos	Rivers	Abia	Imo	Rivers	Edo
Osun	Benue	Enugu	Abia	Osun	Enugu
Plateau	Akwa ibom	Imo	Cross-River	Ondo	Akwa-Ibom

[i] Compiled from Annual Abstract of Statistics, Nigeria.

(97.2%), South-Eastern Imo (96.7%), South-Eastern Anambra (95.9%), and South-Eastern Edo (95.5%). Again, the lowest enrollments are all Northern states: Yobe, Sokoto, and Bauchi. For secondary education, the highest enrollment is in South-Eastern Delta with 95.8%, followed by South-Western Ondo with 95.4%, South-Eastern Edo with 94.6%, and South-Eastern Imo with 94%. The lowest enrollments once again are Northern Yobe (14.5%) and Sokoto (19.3%).

Table 9.11 shows education data for 1997 and 1998. The table lists the top ten states in enrollment at different levels of education and reveals that the northern regions fare poorly in nearly all measures. When we move beyond the primary enrollment indicator and look at secondary enrollment, there is not a single Northern state on the list (Northern states are highlighted). College and university indicators, broken down by sex, also indicate that the North lags behind in education levels.

The educational index of the HDI is devised by the adult literacy rate and the combined primary, secondary, and tertiary enrollment ratio. It is clear from UNDP data shown in Table 9.12 that the South-East and the South-West, with indexes of 38.05 and 29.82, rank far higher than the North-West and North-East at 10.35 and 19.33. Adult literacy, naturally, as a component of the educational index, mirrors this disparity: The South-East enjoys an adult literacy rate of 55% and the South-West has 43%, whereas the North-West falls 40 percentage points behind the South East

Table 9.12. *Educational Attainment in 1993 (%)*[i]

South-East		South-West		North-West		North-East	
Anambra	29.70	Kwara	27.67	Kaduna	21.04	Bauchi	27.21
Bendel	45.07	Ogun	28.80	Kano	08.31	Borno	06.85
Benue	18.64	Ondo	34.83	Niger	11.01	Gongola	18.05
Cross-River	47.36	Oyo	27.97	Sokoto	01.04	Plateau	25.19
Imo	51.67						
Rivers	35.88						
Average	38.05		29.82		10.35		19.33

[i] *Source:* UNDP Nigeria Report (1996).

at 15%.[24] The North-East fares relatively better at 28% adult literacy. Likewise, mean years of school, the second component of the education index, follows the same pattern. The Southern regions have an average of over three years of mean schooling; whereas the Northern regions lag far behind at under one year for the North-West and under two years for the North-East.

The UNDP also reports regional data on gender educational attainment. Female enrollment in tertiary institutions is significantly higher in the Southern regions, where it is above 20%; the percentage of females in the North-West is a shocking 3% and the North-East slightly higher at 5%. There is less disparity in female primary and secondary school enrollment as shown in Table 9.13. Nevertheless, the Northern regions fall behind in both indicators.

Hence, the North unambiguously lags behind the South in terms of overall human development (as exemplified by the HDI), access to electricity, and education. Thus far, we have established this gap in development, which may be associated with the North's relative higher dependence on statutory allocations from the federal government, and its low internal revenue generation. Additionally, we saw evidence suggesting the South's dependence ratio has been slowly converging to the North's, yielding a fairly homogenous dependence throughout the country, relative to the past. Moreover, alongside the convergence among dependency, data from the National Bureau of Statistics (NBS) between 1980 and 1995 show a convergence among poverty levels owing to the South's declining performance, which is now what we turn to.

[24] Tables for adult literacy and mean years of schooling are not reproduced here.

Table 9.13. *Percentage of Females Enrolled in Primary and Secondary Schools in 1994* [i] *(Excluding Abuja (FCT) and Lagos)*

South-East		South-West		North-West		North-East	
Primary Enrollment							
Abia	50.36	Kogi	46.26	Jigawa	33.23	Adamawa	41.14
Akwa-Ibom	50.39	Kwara	46.81	Kaduna	41.73	Bauchi	38.75
Anambra	50.36	Ogun	49.99	Kano	36.29	Borno	41.15
Benue	42.66	Ondo	49.99	Katsina	30.50	Plateau	43.59
Cross-River	49.02	Osun	50.31	Kebbi	30.79	Taraba	36.32
Delta	60.39	Oyo	50.33	Niger	38.22	Yobe	35.20
Edo	52.15			Sokoto	26.02		
Enugu	48.15						
Imo	48.9						
Rivers	50.33						
Average	50.27		48.95		33.83		39.36
Secondary Enrollment							
Abia	46.72	Kogi	42.85	Jigawa	28.12	Adamawa	33.59
Akwa-Ibom	51.02	Kwara	44.16	Kaduna	44.53	Bauchi	34.95
Anambra	51.02	Ogun	47.74	Kano	24.91	Borno	38.74
Benue	32.24	Ondo	46.60	Katsina	27.36	Plateau	38.44
Cross-River	46.62	Osun	48.52	Kebbi	27.10	Taraba	28.08
Delta	41.12	Oyo	51.68	Niger	36.96	Yobe	29.79
Edo	51.85			Sokoto	11.99		
Enugu	56.15						
Imo	51.85						
Rivers	55.25						
Average	48.38		46.93		28.71		33.93

[i] *Source:* UNDP Nigeria Report (1996).

V.1. Convergence in the Incidence of Poverty

Table 9.14 presents data on the incidence of poverty in various Nigerian regions from 1980 to 1996. In 1980, the South-East's average poverty incidence was 14.67% with the South-West having a slightly higher incidence at 21.5%. The North, in contrast, had higher levels at 35.4% for the North-West and 38.83% for the North-East. Five years later, all regions had significantly elevated figures: The South-East's percentage, for example, jumped to 42.07% (see Table 9.14). Overall poverty incidence moved up about 21 percentage points in the five-year period from 1980 to 1985 (from 27.6 to 49.33). It is worthwhile to note that the average of the South (east and west combined) in 1980 was 17.4% and in 1985 was 42.33%.

Table 9.14. Poverty Incidence (%), 1980–1996[i] (Excluding Abuja (FCT) and Lagos)

South-East		South-West		North-West		North-East	
1980							
Anambra/Enugu	12.8	Kwara/Kogi	33.3	Kaduna/Katsina	44.7	Adamawa/Taraba	33.4
Benue	23.6	Ogun	20	Kano/Jigawa	37.5	Bauchi	46
CrsRvr/AkwaIbom	10.2	Ondo	24.9	Niger	34	Borno/Yobe	26.4
Edo/Delta	19.8	Oyo/Osun	7.8	Sokoto/Kebbi	25.4	Plateau	49.5
Imo/Abia	14.4						
Rivers	7.2						
Average	14.67	Average	21.5	Average	35.4	Average	38.83
1980 Average	27.6						
1985							
Anambra/Enugu	37.7	Kwara/Kogi	39.3	Kaduna/Katsina	58.5	Adamawa/Taraba	47.2
Benue	42.9	Ogun	56	Kano/Jigawa	54	Bauchi	68.9
CrsRvr/AkwaIbom	41.9	Ondo	47.3	Niger	61.4	Borno/Yobe	50.1
Edo/Delta	52.4	Oyo/Osun	28.3	Sokoto/Kebbi	45.8	Plateau	64.2
Imo/Abia	33.1						
Rivers	44.4						
Average	42.07	Average	42.73	Average	54.93	Average	57.6
1985 Average	49.33						

(continued)

Table 9.14 (*continued*)

South-East		South-West		North-West		North-East	
1992							
Anambra/Enugu	32.3	Kwara/Kogi	60.8	Kaduna/Katsina	32	Adamawa/Taraba	44.1
Benue	40.8	Ogun	36.3	Kano/Jigawa	38.7	Bauchi	68.8
CrsRvr/AkwaIbom	45.5	Ondo	46.6	Niger	29.9	Borno/Yobe	49.7
Edo/Delta	33.9	Oyo/Osun	40.7	Sokoto/Kebbi	37.9	Plateau	50.2
Imo/Abia	49.9						
Rivers	43.4						
Average	40.97	Average	46.1		34.625		53.2
1992 Average	43.72						
1996							
Anambra/Enugu	51	Kwara/Kogi	75.5	Kaduna/Katsina	67.7	Adamawa/Taraba	65.5
Benue	64.2	Ogun	69.9	Kano/Jigawa	71	Bauchi	83.5
CrsRvr/AkwaIbom	66.9	Ondo	71.6	Niger	52.9	Borno/Yobe	66.9
Edo/Delta	56.1	Oyo/Osun	58.7	Sokoto/Kebbi	83.6	Plateau	62.7
Imo/Abia	56.2						
Rivers	44.3						
Average	56.45	Average	68.93		68.8		69.65
1996 Average	65.96						

[i] *Source:* NCS 80, 85, 92, 96.

The 1980 average for the North (east and west) moved from 37.11% to 56.26%. Thus, both North and South saw an increase in poverty incidence but the South's jump was higher (25 versus 19 percentage points). From 1985 to 1992, the country average declined to some extent, especially owing to the improvement of the North-West. We see from Table 9.13 that, by 1996, the country was enduring an overall poverty incidence of approximately 66%. Recall that the country average over a decade earlier was 27.8%. The significant change occurred in the combined South's average of 17.4% in 1980 increasing to 61.44% in 1996. The North too suffered from higher rates as its combined average moved from 37.11% in 1980 to 69.23% in 1996. However, the South's declining performance is much starker. Therefore, across time, all states (and thus regions) have experienced a higher incidence of poverty, leading to a "convergence" in the level of development. For example, we see that in 1996 the South-West, North-West, and North-East have very similar ratios and that the South-East trails behind only slightly.

UNDP data on social indicators for 1995, which reported on the zones of North-East, North-West, Middle-Belt, East, South-West, and South, support the convergence hypothesis. Despite the difference in the way the states were grouped, the figures show similarity among regions. For example, for all regions presented in Table 9.15, the ratio of poor households to total households ranged from 62.4% in the South-West to 74.9% in the North-East. Likewise, the reported prevalence of stunted growth are homogenous relative to the disparities we discussed earlier.

VI. POLICY RESPONSES

A number of reforms have been enacted in Nigeria to solve some of the problems arising from regional disparities.[25]

The Nigerian government established the "Federal Character" program designed to address the underrepresentation of individuals from certain ethnicities or regions in governmental positions and public service. In principle, the Federal Character program constitutionalized a quota and preferential system, designed to address the perceived ethnic imbalances left over from the colonial era. In reality, the results have been anything but encouraging. It has damaged the notion of quality and excellence in public life and created a new group of disadvantaged and

---

[25] This section (especially the portion on reforms) was written with the assistance of Ruth Uwaifo.

Table 9.15. Selected Social Indicators by Zones (%) 1995[i]

Zones	Poor Households	Stunting	Wasting	Underweight	Households with Unsatisfactory Refuse Disposal Methods	Households Using Stream Water
North-East	74.9	53.4	13.8	30.9	90.6	18.7
North-West	71.0	51.4	9.7	26.3	94.0	16.0
Middle-Belt	68.7	–	–	–	89.7	38.5
East	70.0	51.3	9.2	23.8	86.5	47.5
South-West	62.4	49.1	11.6	31.7	77.2	25.6
South	73.4	–	–	–	92.4	47.8
Nigeria	72.0	52.3	10.9	28.3	88.5	31.7

[i] Source: UNDP Nigeria Report (1996).

disgruntled people within the country. In fact, one can argue that it may have negatively affected institutional and service quality.

More recently, seventeen states engaged in legal actions against the federal government, demanding that the current revenue-sharing formula be amended. In response to state demands, in 1999, the Niger Delta Development Commission was established to address the grievances of the oil-producing areas. However, there has been a renewed insurgency and pattern of violence in 2004. For instance, the rebel group "Niger Delta People's Volunteer Force" threatened to resume armed struggle on October 1, 2004, targeting oil company employees. It advised foreign embassies to pull their nationals out of the oil region (Associated Press, 9-28-2004). An agreement for a cease-fire has been reached between the armed group and the Nigerian government. The government claimed to have provided a framework for a continuing dialogue for the rehabilitation of the region (CNN, 10-1-2004).

Important steps are being taken to reform public administration to increase accountability and control corruption. An Independent Corrupt Practices and Other Related Offenses Commission was established in 2000 by the National Assembly. The commission has the power to investigate allegations of corruption against public officials and bring charges against them if necessary. The commission can inspect and seize assets of the suspects and can even appoint independent councils to investigate allegations against governors, the chief justice, and even the president (Salisu, 2001). Although it is too early to evaluate the effectiveness of these reforms, one can note that corruption still runs rampant, especially among the political elite, as exemplified by the allegations and counterallegations of corruption that centered around the attempt to impeach President Obasanjo in 2002. But given the nature of the Nigerian economy, only long-term political changes coupled with a diversification of the economy can help restore some degree of efficiency and interregional equity. Any discussion of the existing constitutional framework and reform in Nigeria must include, among other issues, whether or not the federal government should continue to control and distribute oil wealth as well as the optimum fiscal federalism. The appropriate revenueallocation formula would likely aid economic progress.

We acknowledge that a more decentralized oil revenue system would change neither the fact that revenue is still rent income instead of a stable tax revenue nor that non-oil-producing states would still need revenue transfers. However, as we mentioned earlier, a more decentralized revenue assignment coupled with requirements for minimal public service delivery would help devolve power away from center and increase accountability mechanisms locally.

VII. CONCLUSION

There is a growing empirical literature suggesting the existence of a positive and robust correlation between natural resource wealth and authoritarian governments.[26] It is argued that an abundance of natural resource rents causes an increased competition for control of the state, which is linked to high levels of violent political conflicts and the use of resource rents by the ruling party to maintain their hold on political power.

The rentier authoritarianism hypothesis is particularly valid in the context of Nigeria. The evidence suggests that Nigerian governments became increasingly centralized and authoritarian as the country became more dependent on oil revenues. This evolution was greatly facilitated by Decree No. 13 of 1970, which reduced mining rents and royalties to oil-producing states, Decree No. 9 of 1975, which transferred all mining rents and royalties from the states of origin to the federal government, and by the 1989 Constitution amendment that provided a greater discretionary power to the federal government in the process of revenue allocation.[27]

The results presented in this chapter complement earlier analysis on rentier states by documenting the way in which centralization and politicization of the process of revenue allocation generated financially dependent states and persistent regional disparities. Although total national revenue has increased significantly over time, poverty has soared and interregional poverty gaps have narrowed to the detriment of the resource-rich states. The results indicate that fiscal federalism is incompatible with authoritarianism and that major democratic and institutional reforms are necessary to generate a growth-enhancing and equitable federal system.

Bibliography

Adam, C. S., and S. A. O'Connell (1999). "Aid, Taxation, and Development in Sub-Saharan Africa," *Economics and Politics* 11 (3): 225–254.

---

[26] See Wantchekon (2002) for a review.

[27] The amandment states that "the federal government may make grants to a state or a local government to supplement the revenue of that state or local government in such a sum and subject to such terms and conditions as may be prescribed by the National Assembly" (Section 162 (1); from Yekini, 1992, p. 49).

Agiobenebo, T. (1999). "Assignment, Criteria and the Fiscal Constitution: An Excursion into a Theory of Rational Fiscal Federalism," in Aigbokan, B, ed. *Fiscal Federalism and Nigeria's Economic Development: Selected Papers from the 1999 Annual Conference of the Nigerian Economic Society* pp. 25–51. Ibadan, Nigeria: The Nigerian Economic Society.

Ahmad, E., and E. Mottu (2002). "Oil-Revenue Assignments: Country Experiences and Issues," IMF Working Paper No. 02/203.

Ahmad, E., and R. Singh (2003). "Political Economy of Oil-Revenue Sharing in a Developing Country: Illustrations from Nigeria," IMF Working Paper No. 03/16.

Aka, Ebenezer O. (2000). *Regional Disparities in Nigeria's Development: Lessons and Challenges for the 21st Century*. Lanham, MD: University Press of America.

Akpan, G. E. (1999). "Fiscal Potentials and Dependence in Nigeria," in Aigbokan, B, ed. *Fiscal Federalism and Nigeria's Economic Development* pp. 73–100. Ibadan, Nigeria: The Nigerian Economic Society.

Azam, J.-P. (1995). "How to Pay for the Peace? A Theoretical Framework with Reference to African Countries," Public Choice 83: 173–184.

Azam, J.-P. (2001). "The Redistributive State and Conflict in Africa," Journal and Peace Research 38(4): 429–444.

Bardhan, P. (2002). "Decentralization of Governance and Development," Journal of Economic Perspectives 16(4): 185–205.

Bevan D., P. Collier, and J. W. Gunning (1992). Nigeria: Policy Responses to Shocks, 1970–1990, An International Center for Economic Growth Publication. San Francisco: ICS Press. Constitution of Nigeria (1999).

Evans, P. (1992). "The State as Problem and Solution: Predatum, Embedded Autonomy, and Structural Change," in S. Haggard and R. Kaufman, eds., *The Politics of Economic Adjustment: International Constraints, Distributive Conflicts, and the State* p. 8. Princeton: Princeton University Press: pp. 139–181.

Hirschman, A. O. (1958). *The Strategy of Economic Development*, New Haven: Yale University Press.

Idachaba, F. S. (1989). "State-Federal Relations in Nigerian Agriculture," MADIA Discussion Paper 8. Washington DC: The World Bank.

Kuznets, S. (1955). "Economic Growth and Income Inequality," American Economic Review 45(1): 1–28.

McGuire, M. C., and M. Olson Jr. (1996). "The Economics of Autocracy and Majority Rule: The Invisible Hand and the Use of Force," Journal of Economic Literature 34(1): 72–96.

Government of Nigeria, Federal Office of Statistics. National Consumer Survey (NCS), various years.

Nnadozie, E. (1995). *Oil and Socioeconomic Crisis in Nigeria: A Regional Perspective to the Nigerian Disease and the Rural Sector*. Lewiston: Mellen University Press.

Nnadozie, E. (2002). "Are Growth and Development Constitutional Issues in Nigeria?," Paper presented at the Centre for the Study of African Economies, University of Oxford Conference 2002, "Understanding Poverty and Growth in Sub-Saharan Africa," St. Catherine's College, 18–19 March 2002.

Nwuke, K. O. (2001). "Managing Multi-Ethnicity: Lessons from Nigeria," paper presented at the Institute on Race and Social Division, Boston University.

Oates, W. (1972). *Fiscal Federalism*. New York: Harcourt Brace Jovanovich.

Odedokun, M. O. (1990). "Flow-of-Funds as a Tool for Analysing Budgetary Behaviour of Nigerian State Governments: Evidence from the Civilian Era," *World Development* 18(5): 743–752.

Okigbo, P. N. C. (1965). *Nigerian Public Finance*, African Studies Series, No. 15. Evanston, IL: Northwestern University Press.

Okigbo, P. N. C. (1989). National Development Planning in Nigeria 1900–92, London: Currey.

Okoh, R. N., and P. C. Egbon (1999). "Fiscal Federalism and Revenue Allocation: The Poverty of the Niger Delta," in *Fiscal Federalism and Nigeria's Economic Development*. Ibadan, Nigeria: The Nigerian Economic Society: 405–419.

Olomola, A. S. (1999). "Restructuring Nigeria's Fiscal System: Rationale, Strategies and Policies," in *Fiscal Federalism and Nigeria's Economic Development*. Ibadan, Nigeria: The Nigerian Economic Society: 477–499.

Osaghae, E. E. (1998). *Crippled Giant: Nigeria since Independence*. Bloomington and Indianapolis: Indiana University Press.

Post, K., and M. Vickers (1973). *Structure and Conflict in Nigeria 1960–65*. Madison, WI: University of Wisconsin Press.

Rodden, J. (2001). "Creating a More Perfect Union: Electoral Incentives and the Reform of Federal Systems." MIT, mimeo.

Salisu, M. (2001). "Incentive Structure, Civil Service Efficiency and the Hidden Economy in Nigeria," Discussion Paper No 2001/86, United Nations University.

Soludo, C. C. (2001). "Growth Models and Regional Divergence: Implications for Public Policy in Nigeria," Department of Economics, University of Nigeria, Nsukka.

Tanzi, V. (1995). "Fiscal Federalism and Decentralization: A Review of Some Efficiency and Macroeconomic Aspects," in Bruuo, M., and B. Pleskovic, eds. *Annual World Bank Conference on Development Economics* 1995: 295–316.

Tiebout, C. (1956). "A Pure Theory of Local Expenditures," Journal of Political Economy 64: 416–424.

UNDP (1995). Human Development Report 1994. New York: United Nations.

UNDP (1997). Human Development Report, Nigeria 1996. United Nations Development Programme, Lagos, Nigeria.

UNDP (2002). Human Development Report 2002, available at www.UNDP.org.

UNDP (2003). Human Development Report 2003, available at www.UNDP.org.

Wantchekon, L. (2002). "Why Do Resource Abundant Countries Have Authoritarian Governments?," Journal of African Finance and Economic Development 5(2): 17–56.

Weingast, B. (1995). "The Economic Role of Political Institutions: Market-Preserving Federalism and Economic Development," Journal of Law, Economics, and Organizations 11: 1–31.

Wibbels, E. (2000). "Federalism and the Politics of Macroeconomic Policy and Performance," American Journal of Political Science 44(4): 687–702.

Williamson, J. G. (1965). "Regional Inequality and the Process of National Development," Economic Development and Cultural Change 13: 3–45.

World Bank (2002). *World Bank Africa Database*, Washington DC: The World Bank.

Yeniki, S. (1992). *The Politics of Revenue Allocation in Nigeria.* Lagos: Batnam Press.

Selected Government Publications

Central Bank of Nigeria, Statistical Bulletins (1990).
Central Bank of Nigeria, Statistical Bulletins (1995).
Central Bank of Nigeria, Statistical Bulletins (1998).
Central Bank of Nigeria, Statement of Account and Annual Report (1989).
Central Bank of Nigeria, Statement of Account and Annual Report (1999).
Central Bank of Nigeria, Bullion Publication, Multiple articles (January/March 2000).
Central Bank of Nigeria, The Changing Structure of the Nigerian Economy and Implications for Development.
Central Bank of Nigeria, Economic and Financial Reviews (multiple editions).
Central bank of Nigeria, Briefs (1988).
Data bank, Lagos Online resources.

TEN

Conclusions and Lessons for Further Study

Jessica S. Wallack and T. N. Srinivasan

I. INTRODUCTION

What does the division of responsibilities and powers across levels of government – federalism – look like? How did it get to be this way? And how does federalism interact with the economic and political contexts, particularly growing integration with the international economy and ongoing economic reforms?

The chapters of this book seek to answer these three questions for a diverse array of countries. Argentina, Australia, Canada, China, Brazil, India, Mexico, and Nigeria span the full range of economic, political, and social contexts in which federalism currently exists. Nevertheless, there are some striking commonalities in their experiences with federalism.

This concluding chapter compares and contrasts three aspects of the countries' experiences with federalism. First, we discuss the division of expenditure and redistribution responsibilities, as well as taxation powers. The countries had a common tendency toward de facto (though not always de jure) centralization of control over expenditures. There were varying degrees of clarity in the assignment of responsibilities; in many cases, central and subnational government functions were interdependent so that subnational autonomy was limited. Taxation also tends to be fairly centralized in the countries we studied in this project, with subnational governments varying in the extent to which they exploit the tax bases assigned to them. The allocation of tax revenues, in particular whether all taxes were shared or only specific taxes were shared between national and subnational governments, appeared to influence all levels of governments' choice of taxes.

Public sector enterprises also complicated the picture in some countries. Subnational enterprises' profits and liabilities are effectively additional revenues and expenditures that are interchangeable with the resources assigned in the division of expenditure and taxation responsibilities or the intergovernmental grants system. The chapters on China and India in particular illustrate the additional fiscal complications that national and subnational public sector enterprises create.

Redistributive goals and mechanisms vary more across countries, though political pressure to allocate funds was common even in those countries where redistribution criteria left little room for discretion.

Second, we highlight some of the common political dynamics that have shaped federalism in the project countries. We use the example of changes in the division of taxing powers to illustrate how similar bargains between the central government and the subnational governments evolve in different contexts. Nearly every country in our study has moved toward a system in which the central government controls most of the revenue base, in return for various promises of grants to the subnational government. This common trend has evolved differently – and encountered varying resistance from subnational governments – across countries. The dynamics of redistribution and sharing of expenditure responsibilities vary more across subsets of countries.

The third and fourth sections move on to the interaction of federalism with its context of global integration and ongoing economic reforms. The authors' discussions of their countries' experiences with globalization strike several common themes. Many are worried about globalization's effect on income differentials across subnational regions. Foreign direct investment and exporting industries have tended to be regionally concentrated within India, China, Mexico, and Brazil, for example. Governments' capacity to redistribute (which is never very extensive, according to the evidence presented in these chapters) has also been reduced by global competitive pressures that limit the extent of taxation possible.[1]

Overall, the countries' experiences point to the conclusion that government redistribution of income will not be sufficient to offset the inequalities emerging because some parts of the country are initially better placed to take advantage of opportunities opened up by globalization, whereas

---

[1] Rezende and Afonso's chapter on Brazil, in particular, argues that economic reforms, including privatization, in Brazil have also contributed to growing inequalities because private owners do not pursue the same social goals as governments. The smaller government presence in the economy limits the extent to which policymakers can influence the distribution of income.

others are not. Policies to address underlying infrastructure and governance differences that handicap some subnational regions' effort to attract investment or build up exporting industries would have more effect. The effect of infrastructure and regulatory differences on variation in state growth rates in India, in particular, supports this conjecture.[2]

Most of the chapters also include some discussion of subnational borrowing and the efficacy of various market-based and rules-based regimes for restraining subnational debt.[3] Market-based regimes, in which subnational borrowing is limited only by investors' willingness to finance debt, appear to be more sustainable but also difficult to implement. The central government has to be able to commit credibly not to bail out subnational governments, and nonmarket avenues for subnational borrowing (such as state-owned banks) have to be limited. The country chapters raise some questions about what constitutes a "credible" commitment that would lead investors to evaluate the subnational government in the absence of federal guarantees. Both Australian and Argentine central governments have bailed out subnational governments, for example, but only the latter is seen as having failed to provide a credible commitment. Global integration can, in principle, enhance credibility if national governments bind themselves by the rules of international trade agreements or accept conditionalities attached to IMF and World Bank loans, but we did not see clear evidence for this pattern emerge in the countries studied here.

Rules-based regimes are easier to put into place, but the rules require constant revision. Subnational governments seem particularly adept at circumventing most central government imposed rules to restrict borrowing. Madden's Australia chapter provides an illustrative account of the central government's efforts to cap subnational borrowing with rules before moving to market oversight.

Federalism's impact on economic reforms has varied across countries. Most authors see the need for negotiations between central and lower level governments as an impediment to reform, though the source and strength of subnational bargaining power varies widely across countries. The main generalization that can be drawn is that center–state diplomacy, or direct meetings between policymakers in the two levels of government,

---

[2] Singh and Srinivasan's chapter reviews work on this topic.

[3] Subnational indebtedness can obviously build up in a closed as well as open economy. We include it in our discussion of the interaction of globalization and federalism because integration with international markets increases both the scope for borrowing and the potential macroeconomic consequences of subnational indebtedness.

appears to be more effective than leaving negotiations to be carried out within national legislatures full of subnational representatives.

II. DIVISION OF RESPONSIBILITIES AND POWERS ACROSS LEVELS OF GOVERNMENT

The detailed country case studies were particularly useful in fleshing out the reality behind summary indicators of the division of responsibilities and powers across levels of government. Central and subnational expenditure responsibilities are frequently intertwined, so subnational governments have less autonomy than raw spending figures would indicate. Taxing powers are typically more centralized in practice, and in terms of the percent of revenues collected at each level of government, than the constitutional regime requires. The formulas for grants and transfers vary widely across countries and most authors noted that the actual practice for distribution of funds differed from stated goals.

II.1. Expenditure Responsibilities: De Jure Devolution and De Facto Limits

Table 10.1 outlines fiscal arrangements, the heart of the division of resources and responsibility in federal systems.[4] Expenditure powers, at least nominally, are relatively decentralized compared to revenue-raising responsibilities. The general recommendations of the principle of subsidiarity seem to have been followed in most of the countries studied in this volume. China's expenditure assignment is one exception: Much of the social safety net, for example, is a subnational responsibility. Health and education expenditures are the responsibility of the lowest level, county and township governments, despite the spillovers across regions.[5]

These figures and formal assignment of responsibility, however, present a misleading view of actual subnational policy autonomy. The expenditure

---

[4] The Government Financial Statistics data (collected by the International Monetary Fund) presented in Table 10.1 are widely used as measures of the extent of decentralization, though the assignment of expenditure responsibility is a very imperfect indicator of the assignment of actual policy authority. We view them as providing a rough comparison of resource flows handled by subnational governments, not as a measure of relative decentralization.

[5] Canada's constitution also assigns the "local" matters of education and health policy to subnational governments, but the federal government uses its spending power to influence these policy areas. The national government's extensive funding of health and education dates back to the middle of the twentieth century.

Table 10.1. *Fiscal Structure (ca. 2000)*

Country	SNG[i] Tax: % Total Revenues (net of sharing)	% Own Revenues in Expenditures[ii]	SNG Expenditures: % Total Expenditure (including disbursement of earmarked funds)	SNG Deficit as % of Total Deficit	# Number of States[iii]
Argentina	40.26	44 (2000)	42.15	81.78	24
Australia	23.18	50.6% (2000)	45.61	SNG deficit: A$2 billion; center surplus: A$16 billion	8
Brazil	43.30[iv]	74.6	33.61	21.61	27
Canada	41.55	91.5 (2000)	51.47	SNG deficit: C$8 billion; center surplus: C$14 billion	13
China	54.95	53.76 (2000)[v]	56.45	SNG surplus: 12.6 billion yuan; center deficit: 240 billion yuan	28
India	37.35	44 (1998)	47.04	45.75	35
Mexico	18.17	9.2 (2000)	30.41	SNG surplus: 6.2 billion pesos; center deficit: 69 billion pesos	32
Nigeria	n/a[vi]	17.34 (1994)	n/a[vi]		

[i] SNG: Subnational governments.

[ii] From country chapters, various tables. Applies to highest tier of subnational government unless otherwise specified.

[iii] "States" is here taken to mean the highest level of subnational government and includes 'federal districts' and autonomous territories where applicable.

[iv] 'This figure includes municipalities' taxes as well as state government taxes.

[v] This number may overstate the degree of control that subnational governments have over expenditures, as their discretion over the officially labeled "own revenues" is often quite limited.

[vi] n/a: data are not avalable.

Source: IMF Government Financial Statistics.

figures do not differentiate between expenditures that are mandated by the central government and financed by earmarked transfers and those that the subnational governments can actually allocate as they see fit. They also do not include expenditures on government employees or transfers to make up losses of state-owned enterprises. The subsidies to state-owned electricity-generating companies in India, for example, have only recently begun to be stated explicitly in state government budgets.

Moreover, nominal divisions of responsibility rarely entail clean divisions of sovereignty over policy. The central government often retains control over hiring standards and pay scales for the workers who implement the subnational policies. Funding for capital expenditures frequently comes from central government grants with varying criteria.

Expenditure restrictions are the most common form of complications in the division of responsibilities. Asadurian, Nnadozie, and Wantchekon's chapter takes the most extreme view in arguing that Nigeria is a de facto centralized distributive state because local governments are almost completely dependent on central government for money, but other chapters contain similar accounts of constraints on subnational governments' nominal expenditure authority.

China appears to be quite decentralized, with about 70% of government budgetary expenditures being made at the subnational level, but Bahl and Martinez-Vazquez note that there is a "significant command-control" element that includes binding expenditure laws and numerous expenditure mandates. Civil servants' wages, for example, are centrally mandated. Subnational governments have avoided some of these restrictions by maintaining off-budget accounts, but 1994 reforms made revenue collections more transparent and thus limited subnational governments' ability to circumvent restrictions. There is also no law that spells out the exact division of responsibilities among the five tiers of government.

Diaz-Cayeros, González, and Rojas argue that most of Mexico's subnational expenditures can be seen as "deconcentrated" expenditures rather than decentralized. Their description of Mexico's decentralized education system demonstrates the need to pay attention to the entire picture of control over expenditures to assess the amount of local policy input. In this case, the states are formally charged with constructing and operating schools and with paying the teachers, but these responsibilities are funded by explicitly earmarked transfers from the central government. The local authorities essentially distribute checks carrying out decisions made in the central Ministry of Education. Their account of decentralization of health care in Mexico is a second example. There are several subsystems: a highly centralized federal Social Security Institute (SSI), which covers most of the formally employed people in the country, and a Ministry of Health system, which oversees health care for the poor. The SSI has decentralized internally and has more regional offices, but subnational governments still have little say in health care provision. The Ministry of Health program is formally decentralized but is funded by transfers to state governments that are earmarked on the basis of national decisions.

The discussions of the assignment of responsibilities are less detailed in the chapters on Brazil and Argentina, but we can still see evidence of how transfer arrangements can affect the de facto division of powers. Many of Brazilian states' social expenditures are financed by transfers negotiated in ad hoc agreements ("convenios") subject to sizeable and unpredictable annual revisions, thus complicating the states' longer term planning. The Constitution provides for concurrent responsibilities, but further details have not yet been passed into law.[6]

In Argentina, decentralization leaves more room for local control, but poorer provinces have less autonomy as they rely on special compensatory federal programs to supplement the main unconditional transfers. Tommasi also cites evidence that people are not sure which level of government – federal or provincial – is responsible for education. The teachers' unions, which prefer to negotiate collective contracts with the federal government, picketed the National Congress to demand a wage increase. Although technically education is a provincial policy, it is de facto controlled by the central government.

Canadian and Australian subnational governments are constitutionally very powerful, but they have been constrained by the national government's "spending power." The nineteenth-century federal constitution intended to create a strong central government in Canada but, paradoxically, resulted in unusually independent provinces two centuries later. As mentioned previously, the "local matters" such as education, health, and social services left to lower levels of government became a more important component of government activities.[7] The central government, nevertheless, limited this independence with conditional grants listing acceptable expenditures in the 1950s–1970s. The strength of central "spending

---

[6] The unpredictability of revenue transfers also indicates the extent of risk sharing across the central and state government. Whereas the Brazilian chapter illustrate the damaging consequences of having subnational governments bear most of the risk and face volatile transfers, the consequences of the Argentine central government's guaranteed levels of transfers in the 1999 and 2000 fiscal pacts illustrate the danger of moving too far in the opposite direction.

[7] Two constitutional amendments were required to create federal unemployment insurance programs (in 1940) and pensions (in 1951), though provinces remain the dominant spenders in health care and education.

power" over provinces has declined over the past decades, however, as the conditional grants changed to block grants in 1977. The current Health and Social Transfers are no longer linked to expenditures in health care or social services.

Australia's states have a similar position: They have sole jurisdiction over law and order, education, health, social and community services, and infrastructure. The negotiations between central and state officials over the size and use of Specific Purpose Payments, however, "carry clear costs of complex and confusing organizational arrangements" according to Bird and Vaillancourt.

The chapter on India highlights a form of complication of the division of expenditure responsibilities that is less common. The recent trend in India (in contrast to China) has been to give states greater control over local policies, but assignment of "responsibility" for policies is complicated by overlapping administrations. National-level bureaucracies, operating parallel to local bureaucracies, impact local policy. Although each level of government has its own bureaucracy, most decision-making positions at all levels are staffed by members of the national Indian Administrative Service (IAS). IAS members are nationally recruited through competitive examinations and trained at a national academy. On completion of training, however, each recruit is formally assigned to a state and he or she belongs to that state's "cadre" from then on. Officers belonging to a state cadre can be deputed to the central government and appointed to positions of prestige. In principle they are to return to their home state once their tour of duty at the center is completed. This career path creates a possible conflict of interest, particularly when states' and central governments' orders may be incompatible. Similarly, the police force has both national- and state-level cadres, with the national police officers having greater influence than their local counterparts even within the states. The judicial branch, in theory independent of all politicians, is the most centralized of all. The president appoints members of the state-level high courts, though in consultation with state chief ministers. The fact that many local policies are implemented and enforced by officials with national allegiances makes it hard to identify the specific impact of local politicians separately from the influence of the national government and its appendages.

II.2. Centralized Revenue Control

The degree of central control over revenues, when coupled with grants and transfers systems (discussed in the following) that do not always reward tax effort or good policies, has weakened subnational governments' incentives for efficient fiscal policy. Centralized taxation is a common pattern in these countries (Tables 10.1 and 10.2). The revenue figures in Table 10.1 are imperfect measures of the degree of subnational control over revenue sources. On the one hand, they overstate subnational revenues for most countries studied in this book, as they are recorded after revenue transfers from the central government to states have taken place.[8] The states' own revenue collections, as evidenced by the relatively limited tax bases and instruments under their jurisdiction, are universally lower than these figures. On the other hand, the basic figures in Table 10.1 and list of taxes in Table 10.2 also do not include subnational revenues from subnationally owned government enterprises, a potentially significant source of revenues for China in particular. Bahl and Martinez-Vazquez's's chapter describes the "backdoor federalism" created through Chinese subnational governments' negotiations to secure revenues from regionally owned enterprises.

Subnational governments in Brazil (states and municipalities), for example, collected 31% of total revenues but were allocated 40.7% of disposable tax revenues in 2001.[9] Within these totals, however, the states (the first tier of subnational governments) collected a higher proportion of revenues than they spent, whereas the municipalities were heavily dependent on transfers. The predictability of and conditions attached to the proportion of subnational revenues from shared centrally collected taxes vary from country to country.

Most of the authors note high vertical fiscal imbalances in their country, providing varying measures of its severity. Provinces in Argentina received 56% of total resources from the common pool of national taxes. Twelve of Brazil's twenty-seven states have own revenues of less than 50% of their budgets. Moreover, the authors argue that Mexico, Brazil, and Argentina seem to be trending toward greater expenditure decentralization with greater central control over revenue collection. Revenue raising in Canada has varied over the years: The federal government collected 18% of revenues in 1933, but 82% after World War II. Indian states raised 35% of total revenues, but they accounted for about 57% of total expenditures. Indian states relied on transfers from the center for 56% of overall spending in 1998–1999. The Nigerian government has full control

---

[8] The percentage of subnational expenditures funded by own resources (direct and indirect taxes) would be a preferable measure, but this is not widely available.
[9] See Government of Brazil (2001).

Table 10.2. *Taxes*

Country	Central Government	Subnational Governments	Lower Tiers
Argentina	Income, sales, excise, fuel, social security, trade	Goods and services, wealth tax	Goods and services, wealth tax
Australia	Personal and corporate income, payroll, financial and capital transactions, trade, excise; also goods and services tax distributed to states	Motor vehicles, property, payroll, gambling, insurance, and debit taxes; prior to 1997: franchise fees on alcohol, gas, tobacco	Taxes on property (municipal rates)
Brazil	Social security, personal and corporate income, trade, financial operations, general sales tax collected on value added basis, VAT applied at manufacture level	ICMS tax (Tax on the Circulation of Goods, Interstate and Intercity Transportation and Communication Services, Even When the Operation Is Initiated Abroad, a VAT-type tax), motor vehicle tax	Service tax, property tax, urban real estate tax
Canada	Constitution allows any tax; in practice use income and sales tax	Constitution allows any tax except trade; in practice use income and sales tax	Property tax
China	Collects most taxes (1994 reforms introduced local tax administration); all but trade and excise tax shared with subnational governments	Individual income tax (central gov. can set rates, provincial government retains part of collections and has administrative responsibility)	Some land use taxes, entertainment levy
India	Income, wealth from nonagricultural sources, corporate & production taxes, customs taxes	Sales tax (nominally agricultural land and income, but not used); SNGs are moving away from sales to a common VAT; share land and commercial crops taxes with local governments	20 exclusive taxes including terminal taxes, levies on goods entering area, property and building taxes, oil, food, timber, fishery and produce taxes, and profession and labor taxes; small overall tax revenues[i]
Mexico	VAT, income	Payroll taxes, auto registration, user fees	Property tax
Nigeria	Oil revenues, import duties, excise, mining	Market and trading license	

[i] From Rao and Singh (2000).

over oil revenues, the largest single source of revenue in the country. Similarly, Australia has one of the higher vertical fiscal imbalances among developed country federations. China's subnational governments have almost no formal revenue-raising powers and, after the reforms of 1994, little de factor revenue authority.[10]

II.3. Redistribution: Central Prerogative

Much of the explicit redistribution in the countries is carried out by national governments, as most countries have such centralized revenue collection that it would be difficult for local governments to find the levers with which to redistribute extensively. Brazilian states' autonomy to set the rates for different items covered by the ICMS tax (Tax on the Circulation of Goods, Interstate and Intercity Transportation and Communication Services, Even When the Operation Is Initiated Abroad) and Canada's practice of allowing provinces to set their own rates and vary the progressiveness of their tax schedules are the few examples of subnational redistribution policy.[11] Subnational social expenditures on education, health, and other social services, such as China's subnational welfare programs, also have an important redistributive component.

The countries vary in the explicitness of their redistribution goals as well as the match between the stated goals and the instruments used. The higher income countries tend toward equalizing per capita revenues across subnational units, whereas other countries' stated goals are mixed and difficult to discern from redistribution programs.

Canada's federal–provincial transfers are focused on the goal of equalizing per capita revenues across provinces more than specifically addressing equalization of services provided. Similarly, Australia's grants system is based on the principle of horizontal fiscal equalization and is aimed at providing states with an equal capacity in service provision. The grants are calculated on the basis of the states' revenue-raising capacity as well as the cost of services in each area. Within this framework, however, several specific purpose grants are aimed at influencing service quality.

Other countries have less clearly stated allocative goals. Nigeria's are perhaps the least transparent and have evolved substantially over the past few decades from being based on derivation to even development

---

[10] The sole exception is that local governments may set the rate of the land use tax within a given range and can choose whether or not to levy the entertainment tax.

[11] Canadian states' flexibility in setting their own tax structure increased in 2000 with the change to provincial taxes on income rather than surcharges on the federal income tax.

to poverty and national unity. Table 9.7 in to Asadurian et al. identifies no less than twelve distinct periods with varying allocation criteria. A comparison of pairwise rank correlations between grants allocation and various state characteristics (Asadurian et al., Table 9.7) suggests that land mass, population density, number of local governments, and population have the strongest explanatory power.

The goals for each segment of India's transfers are clearly stated, but the overall resource allocation is more opaque. The Finance Commission's grant allocation is based on efforts to equalize fiscal capacity, as in Australia and Canada.[12] The Planning Commission's grants and loans are distributed to states to fill resource gaps in financing their five-year development plans. Sector grants for more than a hundred so-called centrally sponsored schemes are nominally meant to finance activities with interstate spillovers, but these are in practice often used for pork-barrel projects. Mexico's grant system also involves myriad conflicting components aimed at addressing different policy goals. The formula seeks to not only promote equality across states in per capita terms, but also respect the historical allocation resources and to reward differential tax collection and economic activity, as well as compensate states receiving little in resources on the previous grounds." (Diaz-Cayeros et al., this volume, Section III.1)

Shared taxes in Brazil are allocated according to states' populations, whereas federal transfers for specific social policies are negotiated on an ad hoc basis. Recent measures have introduced legal criteria that take into account the size of the population and the nature of services provided for allocating money to finance health care.

China's revenues are returned to provinces largely on the basis of origin of collections, doing little to address the gap between the interior provinces and the comparatively rich and developed coastal states. Bahl and Martinez-Vazquez argue that this "counterequalizing" feature of revenue sharing is unlikely to change as the coastal provinces are also more politically powerful than the interior.

The available information on allocation of transfers within states suggests that these are less transparent and more varied than the interstate transfers. Nigerian state governors and local elites, for example, are said to have captured most of the transfers from the center so that the transfer

---

[12] Until recently, Finance Commission allocations included "gap-filling" grants to make up for expenditure overruns. This had been a source of soft budget constraints for the subnational governments.

flows have increased intrastate inequalities. This misuse of resources is particularly marked in this resource-rich country, where the revenues raised do not come from taxes. In theory, states are supposed to redistribute to local government areas according to the National Assembly's orders, but this does not appear to be the case.

Indian states' transfers to lower levels of government were until recently ad hoc, as the third tier of government was not universally recognized. Transfers are now allocated according to the recommendations of State Finance Commissions, but the implementation of these commissions' reports is rarely checked and funds are not always disbursed as promised. The new government elected in June 2004 has proposed making grants directly to the local governments, bypassing the first tier of subnational governments, the states. Not surprisingly, many state governments have voiced strong opposition on the grounds that this violates federal principles in the Constitution.

The allocation of funds from the central government to municipalities in Brazil is perhaps the most explicit among the arrangements described in the chapters. Central government transfers to states' capital cities are distributed on the basis of population and the inverse of the states' per capita incomes. Population is the sole criteria for other municipalities, but the formula is not linear – the transfers increase at a diminishing rate as population increases. Nevertheless, Rezende and Afonso note that anomalies in the within-state distribution of federal transfers sometimes benefit well-off people living in poor regions.

Grant allocation mechanisms typically allow some room for political influence. The politically independent Australian Commonwealth Grants Commission (CGC) determines the distribution of the shared tax revenue and other general-purpose transfers that make up 60% of transfers to states, but specific purpose grants are distributed through the relevant ministries and determined by negotiations between state and central government officials in the particular policy areas.[13] Madden notes that even Australia's horizontal fiscal equalization system, a highly technical grants allocation arrangement administered by the CGC, is subject to political pressures. States seek to influence the assessment of revenue and expenditure disabilities by arguing about how various parts of their budgets are categorized. Brazil's transfers are a similar mix of shared tax revenues (though allocated on the basis of state coefficients fixed in a 1989

---

[13] Although the CGC is officially only an advisory body, its recommendations are generally accepted by the government.

law rather than annually updated fiscal capacity equalization criteria as in Australia) and sector grants negotiated through ad hoc agreements. Canada also has part of its transfers allocated by formula and a variety of sector-specific transfer programs.

Argentina and Brazil, countries where smaller states are overrepresented (in terms of having a lower population-to-representative ratio) in legislative bodies that control grants, allocations tend to be biased against large provinces and in favor of smaller regions. In Brazil, the overrepresented poorer and less populated regions have budgets per capita of one and a half times the more densely populated states. Tommasi also notes that the costs of reforms in Argentina, as measured by transitional unemployment, were unequally distributed. Mexico and Canada, in contrast, countries where small states are overrepresented in the relatively less powerful upper house only, do not show as strong a pattern of redistribution from large to small states.[14] In Nigeria, transfers overwhelmingly favor the militarily and politically powerful North over the oil-rich South despite a constitutional commitment to distribute revenues at least partly on the basis of derivation, non-oil-producing states received almost twice as much transfer per capita as the oil-producing states.

The grant-making procedure's degree of insulation from subnational representatives also matters for ensuring that resources are used to further development goals rather than political ambitions. It is not simply a matter of designing grants that create the right incentives for their subnational recipients; the procedure must also ensure that those subnational users cannot manipulate the arrangements for allocation.

III. POLITICAL DYNAMICS

The chapters' descriptions of the evolution of federal arrangements suggest that these difficulties in creating the federal structure envisioned in classical analysis are at least in part based on policymakers' self-interested behavior. The patterns of devolution themselves suggest a political expediency more than a plan to improve welfare. Overall, the country studies imply that an assumption of self-interested politicians involved in multilevel contest for reelection and riches is a better picture of reality than the collection of benevolent social planners in economic federalism analysis.

---

[14] It is important to note, however, that these analyses do not control for all possible economic reasons for such transfers.

The evolution of several countries' taxation and revenue-sharing systems provides an example of politically motivated changes in federalism.

III.1. Opportunism and Federal Evolution: Taxation

III.1.a. How Did Taxation Get So Centralized? Although the observed gap between subnational governments' revenue and expenditure could be due in part to their undercollection of the taxes they have jurisdiction over, the fact that the central government has either negotiated or been constitutionally assigned the most lucrative tax bases undoubtedly contributes. Parts of some countries' high Vertical fiscal imbalance stems from constitutional assignment of revenue-raising powers; in others agreements between central and state governments have modified the assignment of tax powers to cede more powers to the central government. The latter appears to be mostly for political expediency, though efficiency of collection sometimes plays a role (such as in Canada). The central government gains a way to influence lower level governments by redistribution, more control over one side of fiscal policy, etc., whereas the lower level governments obtain funding with less administrative effort.

The cases of Argentina, Mexico, Canada, and Australia are illustrative of the political trend toward centralized tax collection. "Fiscal pacts" have eroded Argentine provinces' constitutional rights to tax. Similarly, subnational governments in Mexico exchanged revenue-raising power for a larger share of grants from the central government in a series of tax agreements. Diaz-Cayeros et al. argue, for example, that the creation of a highly centralized revenue-raising system and limited devolution of expenditure powers was only possible because of the political dependence of governors and other subnational politicians on the party leaders in the central government. Canadian provinces first agreed to cede all rights (again, allowed in the constitution) to impose income taxes to the central government in return for fixed annual payments as part of a war finance agreement in the 1940s. Most provinces (except Ontario and Quebec) extended these agreements for the next two decades until the 1970s when the pendulum began to shift back toward local control over taxes.

Australian states have also participated in these revenues-for-tax powers arrangements, though not without periodically challenging the federal tax dominance. Australian states have been requesting greater revenue-raising powers since the 1950s. States brought a challenge to the central government's effectively exclusive right to impose income taxes to the High Court in the 1950s, raised political awareness of the fiscal imbalance again in 1969–1970, and formed a working party requesting more tax devolution in the 1980s.[15] The central government has, for the most part, been able to appease these demands with larger financial grants and most recently the agreement to distribute 100% of the new Goods and Services Tax (GST) revenue to the states.

In other cases, subnational governments have simply not exercised their taxing powers to maintain or attract support from key groups in society. States in India, for example, cater to agriculture in their revenue raising. They have the exclusive right to tax land assets and income from agriculture but most states have let the land tax that existed at the time of independence in the late 1940s wither away over subsequent years and have not imposed any tax on agricultural incomes.

III.1.b. Which Taxes Are Imposed? Governments at all levels appear to choose tax bases to maximize revenues while minimizing tax collection effort. Each level of government tends to focus, not on the taxes most efficient in raising revenue, but on the taxes whose revenues they can keep. For central governments, this can mean focusing on collecting taxes that do not have to be shared with subnational governments. Subnational governments often use inefficient but easy to collect taxes such as turnover taxes or trade taxes to raise revenues. The authors find that many subnational governments focus on lobbying the central government for more transfers instead of improving their own ability to collect from the few tax bases they do have rights to.

Tommasi argues that Argentina's high social security and financial transactions taxes are an indirect result of the tax-sharing agreement that allows these taxes, unlike most others, to be kept by the central government. Similarly, federal authorities in Brazil focused on improving tax collections via the earmarked "social contributions," from which variable amounts are shared with the states according to ad hoc agreements – as fiscal policy tightened in the late 1980s and the central government bailed out states in the mid and late 1990s. There was less effort to improve traditional tax collections, as more than half of these automatically had to be shared with the states. The national government has also revived turnover taxes as part of its efforts to find nonshared taxes to provide revenue to

---

[15] The High Court of Australia did determine that states had the right to impose their own income tax, but the Commonwealth retained effective control as it could still use its power to attach conditions to grants to block states from imposing their own income taxes.

meet debt payments and primary surplus targets. India and Argentina are the only countries in this study that have explicitly addressed these kinds of incentive problems, albeit in different ways. The Indian Constitution was amended in 2000 to have a proportion of overall central tax revenues be distributed rather than proportions of certain taxes only. The Argentine constitution was amended in 1994 to specify that all new federal taxes would be shared, thereby limiting the federal government's incentive to develop new non-shared tax bases, but not affecting their incentives to expend more tax effort on the existing non-shared bases than shared tax bases.

Subnational governments, like national governments, have relied heavily on the taxes that do not have to be shared. Madden, for example, reports that Australian states have employed inefficient taxes to increase own-revenue as a result of being effectively excluded from imposing income taxes and sales taxes. Mexican states obtain almost half of their own tax revenues from a payroll tax, despite the fact that this tax does not necessarily draw from the same base of people that receive services when people live in one state and work in another.[16] Argentina's subnational governments use a turnover tax to obtain more than 50% of provincial own revenues. These taxes distort industrial structure, as they tax each step that is carried out by a different company, thus creating strong incentives for vertical integration. China's subnational governments augmented their official share of locally collected taxes by hiding funds in extrabudgetary accounts and giving local businesses tax breaks at the central government's expense before the tax reforms of 1994 limited this process. Chinese provinces have also acted to restrict capital mobility, as companies' retained profits are part of local government revenues.

Authorities are also more likely to rely more heavily on easy-to-collect taxes even if they are highly distortionary. Mexico's municipalities, for example, are discussing the use of a levy on public industry to supplement the more difficult to collect property taxes.[17] India's subnational governments have the rights to agricultural land and income taxes, but they have not relied on these as much as the less politically difficult sales taxes. China's tax structure, where all taxes are centrally collected and reassigned on a derivation basis, has created an incentive for states to

---

[16] The origin-based tax is likely to distort industries' location decisions as well because it is levied at different rates, but this cannot be expected to be a state government's concern.

[17] Local business taxes are widely used, despite economists' criticism of such arrangements. Bird (2003)'s reexamination of the potential benefits of business taxation is an exception.

boost their share in national collections in the easiest ways possible. This can be seen most clearly in states' efforts to impose unofficial protectionist measures to increase their share in the proceeds from collections-based value-added tax.

Policy choices, such as whether revenue sharing takes the form of a small percentage of total taxes or a larger percentage of a few national taxes, which may seem irrelevant in classical analysis with benevolent social planners, are very relevant in this context. India's switch to sharing a percentage of total taxes with subnational governments has been recent, but we would expect the mix of taxes used on this country to become more efficient when politicians are no longer working to maximize the nonshared revenues.

III.2. Redistribution: Politics and Plunder

The design of most of the countries' redistribution systems shows the strong influence of political deal making. The degree of central control over collecting and distributing the larger part of national revenues makes it a focal point for subnational governments' efforts to secure more resources. In addition to the previously discussed negotiations over formulas for sharing specific taxes, there is continual debate about the allocation rules for general redistribution from central revenues. States' efforts to increase their share in national revenues range from attempts to manipulate existing criteria to campaigns to alter the rules themselves.

State lobbying efforts to extract transfers generally have a range of potential central government targets, as multiple bodies oversee redistribution and at least some of them are not rules based or the rules can be changed by simple majority vote in the legislature.[18] As discussed previously, the typical arrangement is one body that oversees general grants or allocation of shared tax revenue and several ministries involved in sector-specific grants. In India, for example, there are relatively firm constitutionally mandated allocations of shared revenues and grants overseen by the Finance Commission, but there are also allocations through the Planning Commission in support of the state five-year plans and grants administered through central government ministries to finance various sector-specific projects. Although most transfers are allocated by formula

---

[18] Nigeria is an exception, as all transfers are determined by the National Assembly with recommendations from the presidentially appointed Revenue Mobilization, Allocation, and Fiscal Commission.

in Mexico, agreements between the president and legislature can (and frequently do) create new funds and a large portion of sector-specific aid is disbursed through social spending programs accountable to the executive branch. Redistribution in Argentina has followed a similar evolution of proliferating funds approved by the legislature.

III.3. Stops and Starts: Change in Allocation of Responsibilities

The countries studies in this volume got stuck in inefficient arrangements for three reasons. In some cases, policy changes with clear economic rationales never happen because no interested group pushes for them. In others, the federal arrangement creates incentives for active preservation of less-than-optimal divisions of responsibilities. Policy arrangements meant to solve problems in implementing federalism can also shield levels of government from pressure to come to a longer term solution.

The separate regulatory oversight of Canada's subnational stock exchanges, for example, may create barriers for the internal market, but there has not been substantial pressure to move toward a more unified national securities administration.[19] The economic basis for centralization is clear: Differences in security requirements complicate placement of stocks in more than one market and thus disrupt internal investment flows. The variation in requirements also limits potential economies of scale in preparing accounting statements. The political push for centralization, however, has been weak. The dominance of the Toronto Stock Exchange and the option to place securities on the U.S.'s New York Stock Exchange appear to have dulled investors' demands for a national security regulator and possibly limited the efficiency cost of having multiple regulatory regimes, provinces have also been hesitant to give up one of their powers. The issue has also been cast as a matter of maintaining the provinces' constitutional powers over property rights in the face of central government encroachment. Individual states have been loath to agree to a national body for fear of weakening their provincial capital markets.[20]

---

[19] The federal government has recently renewed the push for a Canadian SEC, with the creation of a "wise person committee" to study the issue. As of 2004, the Canadian Securities Administrators, a council of territorial securities regulators, had committed to greater harmonization of territorial rules.

[20] India's stock exchange, however, has been moving in an opposite direction – from local broker-dominated exchanges to a national exchange and a national regulatory commission.

Other examples can be found where further decentralization might make economic sense, but national and subnational interest groups defend the status quo. Education in Mexico, for example, is de facto controlled by the central Ministry of Education. One major factor in preserving this system is that the teachers' unions in various states prefer to negotiate collective contracts with the federal government and so oppose moves toward decentralization.

Centralized tax administration is an example of the third set of circumstances in which inefficient federal arrangements become entrenched. Subnational governments' inability to collect taxes has often been cited as a reason for centralization, but this appears to be a self-fulfilling claim because central collection and guaranteed distribution removes subnational governments' incentives to improve their tax administrations. Tommasi, for example, argues that the lack of incentives for raising local taxes or assisting the national government in tax compliance is an important factor in the fact that Argentina's tax compliance at both provincial and national levels is low by international standards. Diaz-Cayeros et al. write that Mexicans' compliance with automobile registration and user fees increased after responsibility for these taxes was fully assigned to the states. Continued central government limits on subnational expenditure responsibilities also lessen the pressures to allocate resources efficiently. Subnational governments can only be held responsible for service provision to the extent that they can make decisions about how to spend money, as well as how to implement the chosen policy.

III.4. Pressures for Change: Accountability to Above and Below

The conventional analysis has traditionally seen citizen pressure as the guiding force for subnational leaders' decisions. Accountability to local interests, however, relies on an informed, active citizenry with the means and motivation to punish leaders. Elections are a necessary but not sufficient condition, particularly where electoral corruption and interest group bribery is commonplace and the incentives to vote are weak or nonexistent. Most of the countries included in this research project have elected subnational governments for most of the subnational units. Nigeria's subnational governors were appointed by the central military government until recently, but other countries have at least a few decades history of subnational elections.

Even ignoring the formidable and inherent collective action problem, it is not clear, however, whether citizens have the incentive to reward or punish via these elections. The motivation to push leaders toward more efficient (low-cost) provision of public goods is lacking where there is a tenuous connection between taxes and services provided. Part of Tiebout's (1956) elaboration of the gains for decentralization is that benefits should be decided on and paid for by residents of the area benefiting from them. The high vertical fiscal imbalances discussed here mean that this match between taxes and expenditures is rarely made.[21] The majority of revenue for state spending in Mexico, for example, comes from federally distributed shares of national taxes. There is only a faint connection between taxes citizens pay and services local governments provide, leading citizens to (sensibly) push for larger expenditures rather than more efficient use of resources.

The match between taxes and expenditure does not seem to be present in Argentina, either. Tommasi provides a diagram of revenues–expenditure matching that highlights the labyrinthine nature of the process and the arbitrary linkages between specific taxes and economically unrelated spending purposes. In Nigeria, where states' revenues have little to do with taxes paid, Asadurian et al. cite evidence that states' use of federal transfers tilts toward consumption, rather than capital expenditures, in election years. Singh and Srinivasan's chapter on India advocates greater decentralization of taxing power (or even a provision that allowed states to piggyback on central income taxes) so that states would have to obtain political support (presumably via good service provision) to tax their constituents.

Lack of transparency is also an impediment to creating lines of accountability to constituents. Citizen oversight has markedly increased in the few cases where government actions and their impacts have been more explicitly and publicly described. Brazilian states' response to the increased public scrutiny after the Fiscal Responsibility Law has been encouraging. The law combines strict limits on debt and transfers from the center with requirements to publish government accounts in an effort to encourage more active citizen oversight. Rezende and Afonso cite several cases of improved fiscal management in states that had previously been known for poor fiscal management. Similarly, Australian states' fiscal management has improved after their accounts as well as market credit ratings were better publicized.

---

[21] The average Vertical fiscal imbalances reported here are the static outcomes of state and federal governments' expenditure choices. Incentives for expenditure, however, depend on how the marginal dollar of expenditure is financed.

When there is little pressure from the bottom for performance, financial pressures from the top could in theory provide a substitute. The residual central government influence, however, does not appear to have created incentives for subnational efficiency.

In several cases, the federal government simply does not impose any cost restrictions on subnational governments. The Mexican federal government, for example, sells water to the states but does not always force the states to pay. The states then sell it to municipalities, where they do not enforce the price, leaving municipalities with little incentive to recover the costs from local users. Similarly, transfers for health care in Canada before 1997 were considered "50 cent dollars" as the government provided open-ended grants to cover half of various medical costs. China's subnational pension funds are a third example. Regional "pay-as-you-go" pension funds have been reporting a much faster growth of liabilities than contributions, and problems are likely to worsen as the population ages. The central government, however, has obviated any incentives for reform by making contributions to these systems.

In other cases, governments attempt to use grants to affect states' incentives, but these are either ineffective or create further distortions. The Fox administration in Mexico is attempting to use conditional grants and credit lines as incentives to prod subnational governments into signing agreements that promise results in exchange for further resources, but these efforts appear marginal. The two biggest types of fiscal transfers – unconditional participaciones and earmarked aportaciones – are not conditional upon subnational performance (other than meeting minimum standards in the health sector). The performance-conditional grants, matching funds, and special credit lines are only a small part of transfers to the state and thus unlikely to influence their behavior much.

"Fiscal Pacts" in Argentina have been an attempt to impose some policy discipline on provincial governments, but the provincial governments usually do not hold up their end of the bargain. Australia's sector-specific grants involve nontrivial conditionalities on their use, but it has been argued that the actual incentive effect is small because funds from other unconditional grants are fungible. India's intergovernmental transfer system includes grants for centrally sponsored schemes that have been used by central government ministries to influence various part of subnational governments' spending, but it is unclear how effective these conditionalities have been, as the central government is not always able to effectively monitor them. In addition to the fact that funds are fungible, monitoring a subset of state governments' spending activities is not enough to ensure that their total spending is appropriately allocated.

IV. GLOBALIZATION AND FEDERALISM

The main finding on how globalization has affected federalism in the countries is that integration with the world economy tends to magnify the consequences of any preexisting distortions created by federal arrangements. It can also, however, create strong incentives for economically beneficial reform at all levels of government. The uneven distribution of foreign direct investment, for example, tends to exacerbate preexisting inequalities if there is no internal migration. The competition to attract resources can take the form of competing tax concessions and exceptions to regulation (the so-called race to the bottom) if subnational governments either do not have the policy autonomy or the capacity to compete by improving infrastructure or human capital. The increased pool of resources allows subnational governments to build up nationally destabilizing debts where subsidized credit, implicit bailout guarantees, and captive state-owned banks shield them from the costs of their borrowing. Global market attention to creditworthiness, however, can also discipline fiscal management more effectively than explicit rules. The main policy challenge for federalism in a global economy is to channel the competition into pressures for reform rather than races to the bottom.

IV.1. Distributional Concerns

Globalization creates new unevenly distributed windfalls that turn the spotlight on the country's redistributive abilities. In the absence of migration, the distribution of this windfall tends to exacerbate, at least in the short run, if not necessarily in the long run, preexisting inequalities in infrastructure and human capital as investment flows to areas of the country that already have some advantages. Redistribution by fiat – taxing one place and spending elsewhere – has so far been no match for market allocation of resources. The policy implication we can extract is that countries should focus less on explicit redistribution and more on creating conditions for all citizens to have equal access to market opportunities.

There is substantial underlying variation in resource bases across most of the subnational units in the countries. Argentina, for example, has fertile agricultural land in the pampas and concentrated oil reserves in the south. Nigeria's southern states have large oil deposits, whereas the north does not. China's western states are essentially landlocked deserts; the coastal regions are more temperate, have more rain and fertile soil, and access to trading routes. The patterns of settlement that have evolved have added to these resource inequities. Cities are also not evenly distributed across subnational units, creating disparities in local tax bases and costs of service provision. Recent theories of economic geography suggest that agglomeration economies make cities engines of growth so that this uneven distribution is another source of some of the disparities in growth across regions within some countries.[22] Brazil's more industrialized southeast has long dominated the economies of the northeastern states. Canada's provinces are slightly less varied, though there are still important disparities in income: GDP per capita in Alberta, for example, is almost twice as high as that in Newfoundland.

Globalization has added to these initial sources of inequalities in development. Some countries react to global competition by cutting social expenditures or by limiting the role of the state in the economy. Crises, generally sparked in part by international factors or by countries' own adjustment to shocks to external terms of trade, interest rates, and capital flows, also have a short-term regressive effect on income distribution. Rezende and Afonso, for example, argue that the recent increase in interstate inequality in Brazil is the result of increased pressures of globalization and macroeconomic stabilization that resulted in lower social expenditures, particularly on infrastructure. They also argue that the extensive privatization program has decreased the federal government's ability to address disparities across states.

The primary channel between globalization and inequality, however, is that some states are able to take advantage of foreign markets and investment more readily than others. States in northern Mexico, southern and coastal Brazil, southern and western India, and coastal China, for example, have grown faster than their counterparts in other regions. Regional disparities have grown in Australia, with South Australian and Tasmanian regions losing per capita income even as other regions profited during the economic liberalization over the first half of the 1990s. This creates new tensions in the competition for resource distribution. Disparities in China's provincial incomes have increased as some have been opened to foreign direct investment and others remained restricted.[23] Bahl and Martinez-Vazquez attribute a substantial part of the current disparities

---

[22] See, for example, Fujita, Krugman, and Venables (1999).

[23] The authors cite several studies that find conditional convergence in provincial GDP, but differences in these steady-state levels of GDP are strongly influenced by the importance of foreign direct investment in the provinces.

between China's regions to Deng Xiaoping's regionally specific market reforms. Regions that were first opened to foreign investment and private enterprise in the 1980s are now far richer than those that remained closed and dominated by state-owned enterprises.

Migration would, in theory, limit the growth in interstate per capita income differentials because people would move to take advantage of the new jobs created. Subnational migration is limited, however, by linguistic and ethnic differences (Nigeria, India, and Canada) and laws (China). The segmentation of China's markets is perhaps the most extreme. Capital allocation within states is politically determined. The *hokou* system of registration punishes households for migrating by denying health, education, and other benefits if they move out of the region in which they are initially registered. The central government has granted investors only selective access to regional markets.[24] The central government's tax policies, combined with the dominance of state-owned enterprises in the economy also discouraged capital mobility: Retained profits were considered part of local government revenues, thus giving the regional governments a strong incentive to discourage movement to other regions.

Changes in inequality are also linked to differences in subnational policies that affect the state's competitiveness in the global economy. Singh and Srinivasan's chapter cites studies showing that Indian states with higher regulatory burdens have significantly lower total factor productivity than others. The authors also cite several studies on growth across Indian states that find a significant effect of interstate policy differences on the extent of (conditional) convergence. Infrastructure quality appears to be one of the most robust of these policy factors. Rezende and Afonso also argue that Brazilian states' tax breaks and promises of access to central government transfers have been important for attracting resources.

IV.2. Redistribution: What Works in a Global Economy?

Most of the authors express doubts about their countries' ability to use transfers (described in Table 10.3) to affect the inequalities across states or offset changes resulting from globalization. Madden cites a study showing little, if any, effect of the grants system on reducing Australian income

---

[24] The authors note that there has been some loosening of controls on labor movement, with an increase in both rural-to-urban migration within regions as well as some movement across provinces.

Table 10.3. *Transfers*

Country	Unconditional	Conditional
Argentina	"Coparticipación" tax-sharing agreement is dominant transfer; also "Fund for Regional Disequilibria"	Earmarked transfers for capital spending
Australia	~60% on the basis of horizontal equalization, accounting for revenue-raising capacity and cost of services	Specific-purpose payments ~40%
Brazil	"Constitutional Funds," tax sharing; also, regional development fund for North, Northeast, Center-West; constitutional fund to compensate for the exemption of exports from the ICMS	Population-based transfers for basic health care and ad hoc agreements for other social services
Canada	Equalization of fiscal capacity, takes into account provincial tax capacity; health and social transfers are per capita grants nominally related to expenditures on health and on postsecondary education and social services but not conditional on spending in these areas	Program-specific transfers for agricultural income support, social housing, language, etc.
China	Tax sharing of most taxes, including 25% of VAT, on a derivation basis (~50% of total transfers)	Ad hoc conditional grants and subsidies (~50%)
India	Tax sharing, allocations recommended by Finance Commission	Planning Commission determines grants and loans for development plans, sector grants from ministries
Mexico	~50%, allocated on basis of population, past allocation, and compensation for poverty	~50% in 8 funds, most importantly for education and health; Fortamun fund designed to strengthen municipalities has the least strict conditionality, as it should be used "primarily for public safety, debt service, or any other use."
Nigeria	Distribution of tax revenue correlated with land mass, population density, number of local governments, population; little relationship to source of revenue or statutory allocations	Ad hoc withholding of grants

inequality as measured by the Gini index. He notes that the system is also unlikely to offset the effects of structural adjustment after greater integration with the world economy, as the redistribution takes place at a different geographic level than the adjustment. The Brazilian government's efforts to reduce interstate inequalities are said to have been somewhat successful in reducing income disparities until the mid-1980s, but this convergence slowed and recently reversed.

Some improvement in interregional disparities is seen in only two countries. Nigeria's redistribution of resource wealth from the oil-rich states to others has been effective in bringing about a perverse kind of convergence as the southern states' standard of living and income levels have fallen while poverty indicators in Northern states have remained steady. Significant interregional disparities in health and education indicators remain. Singh and Srinivasan find that government expenditures do appear to have mitigated some regional inequalities in India, though the overall functioning of the system is far from perfect.

Regardless of the sources of the inter- and intraregional inequalities present prior to the intensification of globalization – which make some regions simply better prepared than others to take advantage of it – the longer term effect of globalization depends on policies that enable resources to move within and across subnational boundaries. Transfers to explicitly address disparities in infrastructure, regulation, and market conditions that affect the states' ability to attract growth-enhancing investment and individuals' ease of migration across states would help, but countries in this study have not focused on these policies. Few central governments have imposed strict conditionalities to ensure state spending on infrastructure or regulatory reforms to ease cross-border transactions. Australia's extensive microeconomic reforms, which reduced regulatory barriers across states, are an exception. The explicitly stated goals for distributing resources have been either to equalize fiscal capacity without directing states' actual use of funds or to ensure that access to basic social services is comparable across regions.

IV.3. Competition for Resources

Exposure to the international economy can also create perverse policy incentives for subnational leaders if their options for differentiating their states from the rest are limited. States with few fiscal powers make concessions in any way that they can. Rezende and Afonso argue that Brazilian states' competition for foreign resources can only be efficiency enhancing – in the sense of motivating subnational officials to provide a better economic environment – if subnational governments have more leeway over resource allocation than Brazilian states do. The current situation, in contrast, is one in which the states compete with fiscal incentives and promises of political support for access to federal funds. Madden cites a similar argument about the inefficiencies in Australian states' use of the few revenue instruments they have to compete for investment. India's subnational taxes illustrate the latter point: Each state's taxes, although small in terms of overall revenue raised, affect decisions to produce or sell across state lines. Chinese provinces' preferential tax treatments for investors became a significant drain on tax collections in the early 1990s, leading the central government to restrict these tax powers and close many of the hundreds of "special economic zones" that provinces had created.

Varying experiences with subnational privatizations illustrate the difficulty, however, of predicting the effects that states' interaction with international markets can have on the nation's ability to compete for resources. We might expect that allowing states to interact with international markets would be a strong force for increased rates of privatization. Offering state-owned enterprises to foreign as well as domestic purchasers generally raises the sale price and attracts foreign direct investment. More often, however, we see states' policies hampering efforts to privatize state and nationally owned enterprises. The Indian government's efforts to attract investment in the electricity sector, for example, are limited by the electricity generators being required to sell exclusively to bankrupt state-owned monopolies.

IV.4. Globalization, Overborrowing, and Macroeconomic Stability

All of the countries in our sample had some sort of buildup of subnational debt. Argentina's national and subnational governments borrowed extensively both at home and abroad over the past two decades, contributing to several balance-of-payments crises. Restrictions on borrowing have tightened somewhat with reforms in the 1990s, but debts still rose and provinces began to issue large amounts of domestic bonds as the country entered into the 2001 crisis. Australian state governments contributed their part to their countries' financial difficulties in the late 1980s.[25] The state development corporations were the main culprits, as they became

---

[25] Australia's subnational debt did, however, decrease in the 1990s.

involved in risky investments that created contingent liabilities outside the purview of the central government's debt restrictions.

Brazilian states joined the federal government in heavy domestic and international borrowing before access to external credit was cut off after all levels of government defaulted in the early 1980s. Brazilian states' domestic debts, however, reached their apex in the mid-1990s (comprising 17% of GDP in 1996, including arrears and guarantees for state projects) as the high interest rates necessitated by the monetary stabilization strategy increased the impact of the debt burden. China's official records show a small overall budget deficit, but there is substantial evidence that state-owned banks have covered operating deficits of state-owned enterprises, generating an off-budget deficit. State-owned banks have also been forced to engage in "policy lending" to finance state expenditure overruns. Nonperforming loans, a direct consequence of directed lending policies, form a significant share of state-owned banks' loan portfolios, creating an additional contingent liability for subnational governments.

India's states have made substantial contributions to that country's continued high deficits. State and central government deficits as a percentage of GDP have overtaken the central government deficit as of 2003–2004: Deficits were 5.1% of GDP and 4.6%, respectively. The states borrow heavily from the central government (with central loans now about 60% of states' indebtedness), most likely anticipating some likelihood of debt forgiveness as the central government has done so in the past. States have also loosened budget constraints by avoiding payments for their purchases from centrally owned public sector enterprises. Mexico's subnational deficit was only about 10% of the total public debt in 1997, but these numbers obscure several federal bailouts as well as the impact of substantial "extraordinary" transfers from the central government.

Canada and Nigeria, in contrast, seem to have avoided excessive subnational government deficits, although the latter country's overall debt burden was considered "crushing." The Nigerian case is surprising, as foreign borrowing with federal guarantees was authorized from 1977 to the early 1990s and states were also authorized to issue securities to financial institutions.[26] It is likely that some form of market discipline prevented indebtedness because the federal guarantee was unlikely to be more credible than state guarantees.

---

[26] See Mered (1997).

IV.5. What Has Caused the Debt Buildup?

As with inequality, the roots of the public debt buildup are largely domestic. Subnational governments' dependence on the central government for financing a large portion of their expenditures plays some role. Expenditure planning cannot react quickly enough to sudden policy changes, thus creating deficits to be financed. Bird and Vaillancourt argue, for example, that Canadian provinces had trouble shedding their debt loads in part because of cuts in national transfers. Similarly, Australian states' debt increased with sharp cuts in central grants in the 1980s. China's lower levels of governments have a similar problem in planning budgets: Expenditure plans are made or mandated before revenues from ad hoc conditional grants and unstable revenue-sharing systems are decided.

The second reason behind the larger deficits in the developing countries is that subnational governments rationally expect a bailout in case of default: Some are simply too politically important to be allowed to go bankrupt. They are thus not internalizing the costs of the debts they incur.

The third factor behind the debt buildup concerns the supply side: Several subnational governments in our sample controlled state-owned banks and/or owned enterprises that could borrow on their behalf. In some cases this "borrowing" was simply lack of payment of bills. Restricting subnational governments' access to nonmarket sources of credit has been an integral (and difficult) part of reforms. Argentina and Brazil privatized many of their subnational banks or removed their political dependence on subnational policies. The Indian government has begun to restrict the supply of credit obtained through state-owned enterprises by deducting what state-owned enterprises owe nationally owned companies from the states' transfers.

IV.6. Restricting Borrowing: What Works?

These excessive deficit burdens can lead to higher inflation and interest rates, while the accumulation of public debt potentially crowds out private investment. Subnational borrowing cannot simply be banned, however, as it is more efficient and intergenerationally equitable for subnational governments to borrow to finance lumpy capital expenditures, for example, than fund them through immediate increases in taxes. The policy consensus is that subnational governments should be made to feel hard budget constraints, but the details of creating these incentives are less

Table 10.4. *Borrowing*

Country	External Borrowing Allowed?	Domestic Borrowing Allowed?
Argentina	Yes, with central gov. approval	Yes, with central gov. approval
Australia	Yes	Yes
Brazil	Yes, with central gov. approval	Yes, with central gov. approval
Canada	Yes	Yes
China	No	No
India	No	Yes, with central gov. approval if any debt outstanding; central bank manages borrowing for all states
Mexico	No	Yes
Nigeria	No (yes, with central gov. guarantee until 1995)	Yes

clear and are only beginning to emerge from careful review of country case studies.[27]

The countries have addressed the subnational debt buildup with varying degrees of success. Marketbased regimes, where limits on borrowing stem from investors' (un-)willingness to lend, tend to be more successful at limiting subnational debt if there is strong central government commitment not to bail out lower level debtors.[28] Rules-based regimes have been a second-best option for restricting subnational borrowing (particularly international borrowing) when this commitment cannot be made. Mexico, Argentina, and Canada have market-based regimes, whereas Brazil and India have reacted to debt crises by creating more stringent rules regulating subnational borrowing. Australia has used both methods over the past decades, but currently it has a market-based regime. Table 10.4 summarizes provisions for subnational domestic and foreign borrowing.

Rules-based approaches involving central government oversight of borrowing require a credible threat to punish subnational governments if they fail to maintain fiscal discipline as well as constant vigilance and policy adjustment to close loopholes.[29] Brazil's debt regime, the most

[27] See Rodden, Eskeland, and Litvack (2002).
[28] Neither the chapters nor the literature on fiscal federalism provide much insight into how to make such a credible commitment, but they do describe several cases where the commitment (and credibility) was broken.
[29] Threats (such as economic sanctions imposed on a country by the rest of the world) often lead to undesirable outcomes. The threatened government taking actions to avoid or adjust to the punishment might choose actions that are at the expense of future growth (e.g., cutting public investment) or at the expense of the poor (e.g., cuts in spending on education and health).

successful rule-based system in our sample, incorporates market discipline coupled with more restrictions on borrowing and more comprehensive attention to the states' fiscal practices.[30] The federal government can sequester shares in federal revenues or void favorable refinancing of earlier debt if states attempt to evade repayment. These provisions have been tested and enforced when the governor of Minas Gerais attempted to default in 1999, but the debt was repaid with funds retained by the federal government. As further insurance that the high levels of indebtedness would not return, Brazil also implemented a Fiscal Responsibility Law in May 2000 applicable to all levels of governments. In addition to restrictions on deficit levels and expenditure increases, the law emphasizes transparency so that monitoring by the market and citizens is encouraged. Punishment for noncompliance includes personal punishments for officials as well as more standard administrative penalties. Rezende and Afonso present preliminary evidence that the law has encouraged fiscal responsibility, but they caution that it may be too soon to draw firm conclusions.

Argentina provides a more typical example where rules limiting subnational borrowing are ineffective. The rules are incomplete: Despite the restrictions the currency board placed on central bank creation of money, provinces circumvented this restriction on the currency supply by issuing their own bonds, effectively substituting for currency. Provinces agreed to ask their legislatures to sanction balanced budgets in the Fiscal Pact of 1992, but there has been no compliance on this front. Perhaps the most successful part of the new regime is the restriction (similar to Brazil's) that provinces collateralize their debt with their transfers from the central government, but even this provision has been weakened as tax-sharing payments have dropped.

The Indian government's formal authority to control state borrowing has also not prevented an increase in states' deficits. Singh and Srinivasan argue that this deterioration has been in part due to the central government's use of discretionary loans in addition to the states' use of public sector enterprises and other off-budget devices to evade borrowing restrictions. As in Argentina, eleven Indian states signed memoranda of understanding with the central government in 1999–2000 that promised

---

[30] The federal government took advantage of the heavily indebted states' requests for a bailout to demand a variety of public sector reforms (including most notably privatization and adoption of new fiscal practices) in exchange for refinancing loans in 1995. Most state-owned banks, a key source of funds for states attempting to circumvent restrictions on other access to loans, were privatized at this point. Only seven financial institutions are still in state governments' hands.

fiscal reforms in exchange for advances on tax devolutions and grants. The fiscal reforms do not appear to have been forthcoming and the central government has had to stop payment in some cases.

Market oversight appears better than rules-based systems at restricting subnational borrowing when the investors are well-informed and motivated to gather information and the governments have a long history of resisting bailout pleas. Canadian provinces have free access to both national and international capital markets, for example, and provinces have been relatively disciplined. The varying role of the Australian Loan Council demonstrates some of the pitfalls of rules-based regimes and the potential gains from relying on market discipline. The Loan Council, composed of the heads of the central and subnational governments, used a rules-based approach to regulate subnational borrowing until 1984. States' indebtedness increased over this period as they found ways to avoid having to obtain the council's approval.[31] There were efforts to close the loopholes when the system was changed to global limits on borrowing in 1984, but these rules could still be evaded by borrowing through state-owned businesses. Subnational debt only began to decline with the switch to a market-based system in 1992. The main debt-restricting power of this system appears to come from the mandatory publication of actual and estimated budgets. Scrutiny by the market and the public forces states to seek good credit ratings actively rather than just loopholes.

Australia does not seem to be alone in learning this lesson: Several other countries have moved from rules (with varying comprehensiveness and enforcement) to market-based debt restrictions. Mexico recently changed the rules for subnational borrowing to increase market, rather than central government, scrutiny of borrowing. Subnational governments must now provide loan guarantees of their own and their creditworthiness is rated by independent rating agencies. The approach appears to have been relatively successful in altering incentives.

Market oversight can, however, fail when there is either a perceived lack of political commitment or access to investors who do not have incentives to monitor their debtors. Argentina's borrowing framework has moved toward market discipline by eliminating politically induced loans from provincial banks, but, in contrast to Mexico, it has not demonstrated the political will to avoid bailouts.[32] The federal government lost credibility in its threat not to bail out provincial governments when it effectively

---

[31] In 1984, only 25% of states' borrowing (compared to 95% in the beginning of that decade) was approved by the Loan Council.

[32] The Ministry of the Economy must technically review the issues of provincial bonds, but Tommasi reports that this oversight has not been particularly restrictive.

bailed out the province of Buenos Aires after its governor had gone on a preelection spending spree. The agreement between the province and the national government established a nominal debt ceiling and a primary spending cut in exchange for federal promises of financial support. The financial support came, with the Central Bank giving a $65 million rediscount to the Provincial Bank of Buenos Aires in November 2001, but the debt ceiling and primary spending cut did not materialize.

V. FEDERALISM AND ECONOMIC REFORM

Most of the authors illustrate the impediments to reforms in a federal polity, as states interested in the distributional consequences of trade liberalization, privatization, tax reform, and so on, behave like organized interest groups in national-level politics. Subnational governments also frequently control policies that can either enhance or frustrate the intended effects of national-level reforms. Intergovernmental cooperation, which requires effort on both sides, is needed to bring about synergy between responses at state and national levels.

The creation of subnational units with any kind of independent jurisdiction changes the political economy environment by creating more actors who must approve policies. Subnational influence on national politics is by no means exclusively a feature of federal systems; but it tends to be strengthened where regional divisions are institutionalized. States can also serve as vehicles for national representation of particular ethnic groups in national politics. The proliferation of states in Nigeria and the demand for creation of new states in India, for example, suggest that the institutional status as a state has some value in achieving national political benefits.

Shared resources and policy responsibilities affect a country's degree of flexibility in everyday economic policy as well as structural changes. Section V.2 discusses several illustrative examples of the interaction between federalism and fiscal policy and privatization.

V.1. Managing the State–Center Relationship

Bargaining over reforms takes place in three main arenas: through national political institutions, via political parties, and in forums for central–regional "diplomacy." Cooperation among levels of government in carrying out broad national reforms is affected by political circumstances as much as the design of federal institutions. Overall, arrangements for central–state "diplomacy" appear to be the most effective way to reach agreement.

Conflicts between regional and national interests tend to play out as
negotiations between executive branches (or ruling coalitions) and legislatures in both federal and unitary democracies, but federalism appears
to increase the intensity of these struggles by strengthening politicians'
incentives to represent subnational interests. Mexico's legislators in the
House of Representatives, for example, can be elected for only one term
and are thus frequently very concerned with defending state interests to
facilitate their move from national legislative office to a state governorship or other local office. Diaz-Cayeros et al. argue that the proliferation
of transfer funds is due in large part to this conflict, as the funds are needed
to buy regional support for any reforms. Rezende and Afonso's chapter
notes a similar influence of Brazilian states on national policies, though
they do not speculate about its causes.

Center–state conflicts have been particularly damaging in Argentina.
Subnational governments and elections in Argentina create a need for
local party bosses, who in turn control nomination for national legislators. As a consequence, major national reforms – such as an overhaul
of the national social security system – could only be carried out after
provinces were guaranteed concessions. Former President Menem was
able to amend the constitution to allow himself another term in office
only after agreeing to an earlier amendment spearheaded by a group
of provinces to ensure their control over the allocation of national tax
revenues. Argentina's strong subnational representation in national politics also forced large fiscal concessions to the states that ultimately contributed to the 2001 crisis. The tax-sharing law and a series of Fiscal Pacts
made more and more concessions to the states, decreasing the national
government's fiscal flexibility. As noted earlier, the 1999 Fiscal Pact committed the central government to transfer a fixed amount to the provinces,
independent of the revenues collected, which ended up bankrupting the
central government in the recession that followed.

The legislatures in Canada and Australia, however, are not as strong
advocates of states' interests. One possible factor in Canada is that the
House of Commons is elected by majority vote, which tends to create
some bias toward serving local constituents. The Australian case is more
puzzling, as the local party leaders' control over Senate nominations is
similar to that in Argentina.[33] Although regional conflicts do arise in the

---

[33] One possibility is that Australian parties are more hierarchically structured so that local
party leaders have less power than do their counterparts in Argentina.

Indian parliament, Singh and Srinivasan write that the main fault lines are between parties or sector-specific ministries' interests.

Regional and national interests also interact through the party structure. Mexico's intergovernmental relations, for example, were very cooperative until the dominant Partido Revolucionario Institucional (PRI) began to lose its political monopoly in the 1990s. The election of some non-PRI leaders at subnational levels led to increased demands for more subnational control over social sector programs. Intergovernmental relations have changed dramatically and the central government now has to create new transfer funds each year to gain support to pass a budget.[34] Working in the other direction, states in India occasionally exert a strong influence on national politics via their link to parties in the coalition government at the center. Canada's central and subnational parties have an unusual degree of separation: Federal and provincial parties operate separately, even in cases where they share the same name. Party ties in Canada also do not smooth center–state conflicts. Bird and Vaillancourt note that even leaders belonging to parties with the same names take different policy stances at federal and provincial levels, there is also variance in policy stance across provinces.

Party ties affecting the relationship between the president and governors can also be a key component of center–state relations. The national executive rarely (with the exception of India) has formal institutional control over subnational executives, but it can often gain political control from coattail electoral effects.[35] Presidents can often gain some loyalty from governors whom they helped to elect. This is the case in Argentina and Brazil, whereas Mexico's governors, in contrast, are elected according to a staggered electoral calendar so that the president cannot gain the support of a majority of governments with electoral help until the fifth year of a six-year term.

There are also cases where national and subnational politicians negotiate directly. The Australian government has utilized this mechanism effectively by moving over the past decade from periodic ad hoc Special

---

[34] The disintegration of these informal party ties also affected cooperation in federalism outside the political arena: The sharing of jurisdictions – where one level of government controlled capital spending and the other set essential workers' wages, for example – functioned more or less adequately when there were officials from the same party at all levels of government, but such sharing has become more problematic with multiparty competition.

[35] This formal power is used sparingly and executives can only be removed for a limited period of time.

Premiers' Conferences on specific issues to annual meetings of the Council of Australian Governments. Madden writes that this growth of intergovernmental committees has eased center–state frictions and contributed greatly to the passage of microeconomic reforms in the 1980s. In other countries, these kinds of direct negotiations have been helpful in containing secessionist pressures. Much of the wrangling between secessionist Quebec and the Canadian federal government has taken place in ad hoc First Ministers' Conference.

Among the developing countries in this study, India has made the most extensive use of these kinds of direct negotiation. India created the Inter-State Council (ISC) in 1990 to provide a forum in which the prime minister, state chief ministers, and some cabinet officials can discuss political and economic issues. This advisory body cannot make policy, but it appears to have played an important role in formalizing collective discussions, particularly tax-sharing arrangements. Singh and Srinivasan recommend a greater role for the ISC as an alternative to ad hoc bargaining over the basic rules for intergovernmental relations. India also has the National Development Council, a narrower body where the prime minister, central government cabinet members, state chief ministers, and members of the Planning Commission bargain over five-year-plan allocations.

The National Confederation of Governors (CONAGO) has become more important in Mexico as political party ties between governors and presidents have declined. It meets roughly once a year to debate national politics, generally concentrating on fiscal federalism. The group's proposals carry no official weight, but they do shape legislative discussion. Diaz Cayeros et al. attribute the recent formation of a National Fiscal Convention to redesign the federal fiscal pact to CONAGO's "convincing." State finance ministers and representatives from the federal Finance Ministry also meet annually.

Fundamental disagreements about the federal structure (debates, for example, over jurisdictions) tend to appear in the court system. One possible reason for this is that if the federal structure is written into the constitution, changes can be difficult to move through the legislature because there is generally a supermajority requirement for doing so. Courts can "reinterpret" parts of the constitution and make smaller changes more easily. The Australian High Court, for example, aided the federal government in carrying out reforms (such as environmental legislation) in policy areas that had previously been under the states' oversight when it ruled that the Commonwealth could override state governments through its external affairs powers. High Court decisions have also narrowed the state governments' tax bases.

The Nigerian High Court has been involved in disputes between the states and central government over revenue allocation. Seventeen Nigerian states recently sued the central government to demand changes in the revenue allocation formula, thus prompting the establishment of the Niger Delta Development Commission. When the question of jurisdiction over unemployment insurance first came up in Canada, a judicial ruling interpreted this new policy area as part of the provinces' jurisdiction. A Supreme Court ruling also assigned cable television to the federal government. The Canadian central and provincial governments' long-running negotiations over constitutional reforms are an interesting exception: They have taken place in meetings between central and subnational premiers.

V.2. Federalism and Fiscal Reforms

The central government's ability to control subnational spending depends on its ability to enforce restrictions on grants or alter their amounts, changes that can be difficult if subnational approval (especially by supermajorities in the legislature) is needed. Revenue shares, once promised, are difficult to rescind when changes require approval by a legislature made of representatives from subnational regions. The effect of raising taxes is dulled by the fact that some proportion of these is automatically channeled back to subnational governments. Political constraints on changing amount of revenues ceded to subnational governments and controlling their use make these a far greater source of fiscal leakage than is apparent from simply looking at taxation and expenditure assignments.

The extent of the rigidity varies with the political design of the revenue-sharing agreements. The central government's fiscal power is highest when revenue shares can be altered without subnational approval or when subnational use of these revenue shares is controlled, but this is rarely the case. It is more common for changes in the revenue shares to require subnational approval and thus exact some other concessions from the central government. Once the revenues have been disbursed, central governments have little ability to prevent subnational governments from spending them.

Nigeria stands at one extreme of the spectrum. The central government has nearly complete control over how revenues are disbursed. Even constitutional promises to states – such as the provision in the 1999 constitution that at least 13% of the revenue from national resources would be returned to those states producing it – carry little weight. China's tax sharing appears to be similar. Although all taxes except excise duties and trade taxes are shared with provinces (about 44% overall), the central government has at least the formal political power to change these assignments at will.

Among the countries where national and subnational governments interact on more equal footing, those that have implemented institutions for direct bargaining between state and national executive branches appear to have had the most flexibility in transfers. Australia, for example, was able to cut the share of revenues to subnational governments during fiscal tightening in the 1980s. These cuts were part of a reform package that was largely negotiated in meetings of regional and national premiers. These intergovernmental bodies were also instrumental in negotiating the 2000–2001 tax reforms that affected subnational governments' revenue shares. Similarly, India's ISC is said to have been an "important forum" for gaining acceptance of the changes in tax sharing recommended by the central government Finance Commission. It is, however, unclear why this kind of diplomacy appears to resolve disputes more efficiently than other forms of center–state interactions, but the pattern in the countries studied here may warrant further investigation.

Brazil and Mexico, countries with high institutional barriers to changing revenue allocation formulas, appear more constrained by transfer commitments. Brazil's fiscal adjustment was hampered by the revenue promises made to the state in the 1988 Constitution and subsequent agreements. The share of central tax revenues actually at the central government's disposal declined from about 66% at the beginning of the 1980s to about 54% in the mid-1990s.[36] A new wave of centralization pushed the central government's disposable tax revenues to 58.4% of total revenues as of 1999. Nevertheless, with all of the restrictions on federal funds and promises to the subnational governments, the federal government had relatively little room to reallocate expenditures more efficiently to meet budget targets. Mexico's fiscal system leads to a similar predicament. Legislation dealing with the sharing of revenues in the federal fiscal pact must be voted on by both houses of Congress, a higher barrier to hurdle than the more typical requirement of a vote in the lower house only. Diaz-Cayeros et al. emphasize the difficulty of any change in the level of transfers to subnational governments.

---

[36] See Ter-Minassian (1997).

Argentina presents the most extreme example, because the rigidity of revenue assignments has increased over time and culminated in crisis. Provinces negotiated bilateral agreements with the central government during 1985–1988. Each province could threaten to not support national policy initiatives if funds were too low, but no province by itself had the power to prevent policy from being made. These bilateral agreements were replaced by legally defined shares in 1988–1992, a collective effort that led to a historic high in the provinces' share of revenues. It was possible but difficult to change these promises. The central government was able to reduce the amount going to the provinces by 15% for 1992–1993 to reform social security, but only after binding itself even more tightly by setting a guaranteed floor for transfers and creating several new discretionary funds. The rules for distributing revenues were written into the Constitution in 1994 along with restrictions that further changes could occur only with explicit provincial approval. At this point, Argentina could not raise taxes without having to cede nearly half the revenues to the provinces that then spent it. The culminating event, however, was the 2000 Fiscal Pact between center and provincial governments in which fixed revenue amounts, rather than shares, were committed to the subnational governments. The federal government expected to gain revenues from new taxes, while keeping its obligations to subnational units the same. Instead, a recession hit and revenues dropped, whereas the obligations to transfer to subnational governments remained fixed.

V.3. Joint Reforms: Privatization

Countries' experiences with privatization illustrate a second type of federal impact on economic reforms: the need to coordinate policies when the reforms take place in shared jurisdictions.

The fact that privatization in most countries must be a joint effort has slowed the sale of state-owned assets in several of the countries in this volume. Brazil's comprehensive privatization program, which has included sales by both federal and subnational governments, is the relatively successful case. The federal government successfully forced privatization as part of reforms in exchange for subnational debt refinancing and also assisted in coordinating privatization via the National Council for Privatization. The 1990s privatization program has earned a total of US$103 billion for ninety-seven federal privatizations and thirty-six state privatizations. Nevertheless, states' lack of coordination in electricity regulation has slowed implementation.

Privatization has been a politically difficult enterprise in India, not the least because of state government support for their constituents' opposition to national privatization plans.[37] The state of Chattisgarh, for example, supported labor unions opposed to privatization by the central government of the Bharat Aluminum Company. The state actually sued the new private owners, but these disputes were settled in favor of the owners in a Supreme Court case. India's states (and central government) continue to exert control on product markets, checking the effect of openness to international markets on firm efficiency. Singh and Srinivasan emphasize that it will be necessary for both states and central government to remove product controls. As in Brazil, moving toward a comprehensive electricity regulatory framework will be a joint effort at coordination among the existing national Electricity Regulatory Commission (ERC) and the state ERCs (SERCs). The State Electricity Boards (SEBs), vertically integrated producers and distributors of energy, have been running at a large loss for years and have not been producing sufficient energy to meet growing demand. The financial condition of the SEBs has hindered privatization, as investors demand guarantees of payment as long as they have to sell to a monopoly SEB that has not always made its payments.

One clear lesson is that the details of center and state cooperation in regulation is as, if not more, important for performance than the actual privatization. Confusion over the states' and central governments' regulatory framework slowed electricity privatization in Brazil, for example. Despite the existence of a federal regulatory framework, regulation in practice varied across states because relations between federal and state regulators were not clearly delineated in the federal framework and thus were open to interpretation. India has also worked to privatize electricity generation, but it has had little success in either improving the reliability or efficiency of electricity supply or retaining the few foreign investors it has attracted because central and state governments have not worked out a clear, credible regulatory framework. States' regulatory institutions also varied; some states had single-purpose regulators, whereas others put all regulation in their jurisdiction together. Australia's substantially publicly owned electricity sector, however, provides more dependable,

---

[37] The newly elected government in 2004 has announced that it will not privatize public enterprises that are making profits in a competitive environment. Privatization is seen as a last resort, after exhausting other possibilities, even for enterprises that operate at a loss.

competitively priced electricity under the National Competition policy agreement between the center and the states.

How well have the three motivating questions been answered? How general are these lessons?

Some of our findings confirm those in earlier studies. Few would be surprised that politicians at all levels of government seek to maximize their own level of government's resources and jurisdictions rather than their citizens' welfare, for example. The evolution of taxation responsibilities via political negotiation and the costs of side payments to enact reforms echo much of the recent empirical literature on federalism. Most would accept the finding that the most important contributions (or detractions) of federal states to economic development come from the way they interact with market forces, and especially the international economy. That states in Brazil, China, and other countries compete for foreign direct investment and that redistributive efforts pale in comparison to the uneven changes in income that come about from different exposure to international markets (as in China) or differing ability to attract investment and benefit from trade (as in Brazil or India) are familiar stories.

The country studies in this book illustrate several points to motivate further research. First, globalization matters. Exposure to international goods and capital markets affects the geographical distribution of resources and the potential for incurring unsustainable debt obligations. Foreign investment is a new prize to be won either by competing through policies such as tax and regulatory concessions or through the creation of efficient and affordable infrastructure. The former strategy is not generally welfare maximizing, whereas the latter is likely to have welfare benefits over and above those from foreign investment.

Second, the economic outcomes of international integration depend on the interaction of global markets and federal institutions. Foreign direct investment will have uneven benefits as long as infrastructure differences persist. Regionally unbalanced growth will contribute to growing interpersonal inequality as long as migration is restricted. Competition for resources will take the form of tax breaks as long as subnational governments do not have the autonomy to differentiate themselves in other ways. Global investors will continue to feed overborrowing subnational governments as long as they perceive that the national government is willing and able to bail out lower levels. All of these policies – attention to

infrastructure, maintenance of internal markets, clear subnational jurisdictions, and incentives to internalize the costs of borrowing – are included
as goals in the conventional analysis, but they become considerably more
consequential when considering federations in a global environment.

Perhaps most importantly, each chapter in this book also tells a story
of constant change, both in the federal structure and its politico-economic
environment. As examples in previous sections (such as reaction to rules-
based borrowing restrictions and tax regimes) demonstrate, the federal
structure itself also fluctuates over time. The various levels of government
are rarely content to work within the system as is. There are constant
pressures for change that affect the way federalism functions at any given
time. Federal arrangements are incomplete contracts that, at best, aim at
self-enforcing efficient interactions with and across levels of government.
At worst, federal states fall into opportunistic cycles that no single actor
or feasible coalition has the incentive to break.

Bibliography

Bird, R. (2003). "A New Look at Local Business Taxes," Tax Notes International
    19 (May): 695–711.
Fujita, M. P. Krugman, and A. Venables (1999). *The Spatial Economy: Cities,
    Regions, and International Trade*. Cambridge, MA: MIT Press.
Government of Brazil (2001). Tax Revenue in Brazil. Federal Revenue
    Secretariat. Available online at http://www.receita.fazenda.gov.br/Principal/
    Ingles/SistemaTributarioBR/BrazilianTaxSystem/transfers.htm.
Mered, M. (1997). "Nigeria," in T. Ter-Minassian, ed., *Fiscal Federalism in Theory
    and Practice*. Washington, DC: International Monetary Fund. Pp. 593–614.
Rodden, J., G. Eskeland, and J. Litvack, eds. (2002). *Fiscal Decentralization and
    the Challenge of Soft Budget Constraints*. Cambridge, MA: MIT Press.
Ter-Minassian, T. (1997). "Brazil," in T. Ter-Minassian, ed., *Fiscal Federal-
    ism in Theory and Practice*. Washington, DC: International Monetary Fund.
    Pp. 438–456.
Tiebout, C. (1956). "A Pure Theory of Local Expenditures," Journal of Political
    Economy, 64: 416–424.

Index